# Economic Growth in the 1990s

*Learning from a Decade of Reform*

# Economic
# Growth
## in the 1990s
### Learning from a
### Decade of Reform

**THE WORLD BANK**
Washington, D.C.

9688415.
KSG- PED 130

ISBN-13: 978-8-213-60434-5
ISBN-10: 0-8213-6043-4
e-ISBN: 0-8213-6044-2

**Library of Congress Cataloging-in-Publication Data**

Economic growth in the 1990s : learning from a decade of reform.
    p. cm.
  This report was prepared by a team led by Roberto Zagha, under the general direction of Gobind Nankani.
  Includes bibliographical references and index.
  ISBN 0-8213-6043-4 (pbk.)
    1. Developing countries—Economic policy. 2. Economic stabilization—Developing countries. 3. Privatization—Developing countries. 4. Developing countries—Politics and government. I. Zagha, Roberto. II. Nankani, Gobind T., 1949– III. World Bank.

HC59.7.E295 2005
338.9'009172'4—dc22

2005043405

# Contents

## Tables

## Figures

## Boxes

# Foreword

> When you get right down to business, there aren't too many poli-
> cies that we can say with certainty deeply and positively affect growth.
> —Arnold Harberger, July 2003
> (*IMF Survey*, 216)

> Therefore, the real lesson for the architects of growth strategies is
> to take economics more seriously.
> —Dani Rodrik, September 2003
> (*Growth Strategies*, 30)

AT THE START OF THE 1990s, economists thought the road ahead was clear. What for many countries had been the "lost decade" of the 1980s made it evident that government interference in the economy—through price controls, foreign exchange rationing, distorted trade regimes, repressed financial markets, and state ownership of commercial enterprises—wasted resources and impeded growth. Hence, the logic went, rolling back the state would lead developing countries to sustained growth.

Much of this vision was reflected in the "Washington Consensus." Articulated by John Williamson in 1990, the Consensus was meant to synthesize the reforms that most economists in the World Bank, the International Monetary Fund, the U.S. Treasury, and some of Washington's think tanks believed were needed to rescue Latin American countries from cycles of high inflation and low growth.

When the Consensus was formulated, the current of opinion was already shifting toward a smaller role for governments more generally. Privatization and deregulation were taking hold in the United Kingdom, in the United States, and in Eastern Europe and the former Soviet Union. Williamson had emphasized that the Consensus was to be applied judiciously, not mechanistically, but it quickly took on a life of its own, becoming the expression of what economists both inside and outside Washington thought developing countries needed for growth and development. This thinking guided much of the advice by the World Bank and was reflected in the conditionality associated with adjustment loans. Some of its key aspects were reflected in the World Bank's *1991 World Development Report*, although that report stressed the importance of achieving the right balance between government and market, rather than choosing between them, and was generally more nuanced on the impact of specific reforms. The Washington Consensus was not the only point of view among economists. But it was the dominant view, making it difficult for others to be heard, and it provided the framework for many of the reforms implemented during the 1990s by a wide spectrum of countries around the world.

The results of these reforms were unexpected. They exceeded the most optimistic forecasts in some cases and fell well short of expectations in others. Although implemented in a manner that departed from conventional wisdom—in terms of speed and design of reform, large presence of the state and, until very recently, high levels of import protection—domestic liberalization and outward orientation were associated with spectacular growth, poverty reduction, and social progress in East and South Asia. At the same time, booms and busts continued in Latin America and extended to East Asia and other regions as well. For most countries emerging from the former Soviet Union, the 1990s will be remembered as a costly and traumatic decade. Sharp declines were followed by a prolonged and as yet incomplete recovery, with results varying from relative success in the Czech Republic, Hungary, and Poland to costly transitions in most other countries. Africa did not see the take-off that was expected at the beginning of the decade, although many countries showed signs of recovery in the late 1990s. Costly financial crises rocked Mexico (1994), East Asia (1997), Brazil (1998), the Russian Federation (1998), Turkey (2000), and Argentina (2002). Some countries managed to sustain rapid growth with just modest reforms, and others could not grow even after implementing a wide range of reforms.

Interpreting the reasons for this wide variation is the central task of this report. A common interpretation has been that countries that grow have reformed enough, and countries that have not achieved sustained growth have not reformed enough. But for many economists and, perhaps more important, the policy makers they advise, this interpretation is not entirely satisfactory. Unquestionably, macroeconomic stability, domestic liberalization, and openness lie at the heart of any sustained growth process. But the options for achieving these goals vary widely. Which options should be chosen depends on initial conditions, the quality of existing institutions, the history of policies, political economy factors, the external environment, and last but not least,

the art of economic policy making. The range of options puts the onus on economic analysis to guide policy making effectively. In dealing with growth processes, economists have no formula. They have broad principles and tools—in the same way that principles and tools can be used to build an airplane. If those are not appropriately put to use, the airplane may not fly, or may not weather storms well. The manner and sequence in which economic principles and tools are used will determine whether specific growth country strategies will succeed or not.

This volume is part of a three-pronged exercise the World Bank undertook to learn from the experience of the 1990s from three perspectives: (1) analytical (this book); (2) policy (13 policy makers who were at the forefront of policy implementation in the 1990s drew lessons from their experience during a one-year cycle of lectures at the Bank); and (3) operational (13 former Bank country directors drew lessons from their work at the Bank in a series of papers, to be published separately). From all three perspectives, growth was at the center of the discussion. An institution whose primary business is finance and advice for poverty reduction needs to understand what causes growth and what sustains it. Poverty declines rapidly where growth is rapid and sustained. Poverty stagnates where growth is tepid. A few exceptions notwithstanding, the unambiguous impact of rapid growth on poverty reduction was confirmed again in the 1990s. However, growth is difficult to predict because it implies social transformation: a break with past trends, behaviors, and institutions that reflect deep forces in societies and how they organize themselves.

The findings of the analysis confirm and build on the conclusions of an earlier World Bank report, *The East Asian Miracle* (1993), which reviewed experiences of highly successful East Asian economies. They confirm the importance for growth of macro-stability, of market forces governing the allocation of resources, and openness. But they also emphasize that these general principles translate into diverse policy and institutional paths, implying that economic policies and policy advice must be country-specific and institution-sensitive if they are to be effective.

The central message of this volume is then that there is no unique universal set of rules. Sustained growth depends on key functions that need to be fulfilled overtime: accumulation of physical and human capital, efficiency in the allocation of resources, adoption of technology, and the sharing of the benefits of growth. Which of these functions is the most critical at any given point in time, and hence which policies will need to introduced, which institutions will need to be created for these functions to be fulfilled, and in which sequence, varies depending on initial conditions and the legacy of history. Thus we need to get away from formulae and the search for elusive "best practices," and rely on deeper economic analysis to identify the binding constraints on growth. The choice of specific policy and institutional reforms should flow from these growth diagnostics. This much more targeted approach requires recognizing country specificities, and calls for more economic, institutional, and social analysis and rigor rather than a formulaic approach to policy making.

The messages in this book were well received during the extensive consultations that we held during its preparation. While there is a sense of discomfort associated with the ending of a conviction, there was a strong sense that the findings of the report spoke to the experience of the 1990s and helped its understanding. There was also appreciation and recognition that the complexity and diversity of growth experiences are not amenable to simplistic policy prescriptions. They require more refined and rigorous economic analysis. There was general acceptance for the realization of the multiple ways in which policies and institutions can fulfill the functions of growth. At the same time there was concern that these degrees of freedom could be misused by policy makers and interpreted as "anything goes." It was recognized, however, that rigid formulas were not

an appropriate response to this challenge, and that while economic policy advice should be cognizant of the strengths and weaknesses of institutions and downside risks, it should not be influenced by mistrust. In September 2004, 16 well-known economists gathered in Barcelona and issued a new consensus that reflects their views on growth and development.[1] The Barcelona Consensus echoes much of the findings of the World Bank's work, which in turn reflects recent academic research by several of the signatories.

We expect this change in thinking to influence operational decision making in the World Bank and aid agencies in general. In the Bank in the last few years, these perspectives have been translated into new analytical and operational instruments such as poverty and social impact analysis and country-driven poverty reduction strategies, which seek to bring analytical rigor and empirical accuracy to the evaluation of policy reforms, and country specificity into growth strategies. To mainstream this approach to the formulation of growth strategies needs persistent efforts and willingness to experiment. The new perspectives also have implications for behavior—in particular the need for more humility. And, last but not least, they highlight the need for a better understanding of noneconomic factors—history, culture, and politics—in economic growth processes. The operational implications of these perspectives will be explored separately.

*Gobind Nankani*
Former Vice President and Head of Network
Poverty Reduction and Economic Management
now Vice President for Africa
World Bank

Washington, D.C.
March 2005

---

1. Olivier Blanchard, Guillermo Calvo, Daniel Cohen, Stanley Fischer, Jeffrey Frankel, Jordi Galí, Ricardo Hausmann, Paul Krugman, Deepak Nayyar, José Antonio Ocampo, Dani Rodrik, Jeffrey D. Sachs, Joseph E. Stiglitz, Andrés Velasco, Jaime Ventura, and John Williamson. The Barcelona Consensus is online at http://www.barcelona2004.org/eng/eventos/dialogos/docs/agenda_eng.pdf

# Acknowledgments

THIS REPORT WAS PREPARED BY a team led by Roberto Zagha, under the general direction of Gobind Nankani when he was vice president of the World Bank Poverty Reduction and Economic Management Network (PREM). Current PREM vice president Danny Leipziger's support and encouragement made it possible to complete this volume. The team consisted of J. Edgardo Campos (chapter 9), James Hanson (chapter 7), Ann Harrison (chapter 5), Philip Keefer (chapter 10), Ioannis Kessides (chapter 6), Sarwar Lateef (chapter 9), Peter Montiel (chapter 4), Lant Pritchett (chapters 2 and 8 and country notes), S. Ramachandran (chapters 6 and 7 and country notes), Luis Servén (chapter 4), Oleksiy Shvets (chapter 3 and country notes), Helena Tang (chapter 5), and Roberto Zagha (chapter 1 and country notes). Major contributions were also made by Ihsan Ajwad, Takako Ikezuki, Richard Messick, and Shilpa Pradhan.

Peer reviewers were Rui Coutinho, Ricardo Hausmann, Ravi Kanbur, and Devesh Kapur. The report was discussed during the World Bank's Poverty Reduction and Economic Management Week and benefited from comments by Robert Buckley, Jeffrey Hammer, Carlos Felipe Jaramillo, Deepak Mishra, Peter Moll, and Dina Umali-Deininger. It also benefited from comments from several World Bank chief economists, in particular Shanta Devarajan, Alan Gelb, Homi Kharas, Michael Klein, Mustapha Nabli, Guillermo Perry, and Guy Pfeffermann. Uri Dadush, Bernard Hoekman, Richard Newfarmer, and Alan Winters commented on trade and other selected aspects of the report. Isher Ahluwalia, Danny Leipziger, Edwin Lim, Carlos Antonio Luque, Samir Radwan, Arvind Virmani, John Williamson, and Adrian Wood provided valuable suggestions and advice at different stages of the report. Joelle Chassard commented extensively on key parts of the report. Patricia Clarke Annez's and Indermit Gill's ideas and suggestions throughout the different phases of preparation were invaluable. Comments from Theodore Ahlers, Emmanuel Akpa, Mahmood Ayub, Milan Brahmbhatt, Jean-Jacques Dethier, Shahrokh Fardoust, Farrukh Iqbal, Kathie Krumm, Pradeep Mitra, and Sudhir Shetty are gratefully acknowledged. François Bourguignon's interest in this work, as well as his ideas, comments, and suggestions were particularly insightful and useful, and helped articulate the main messages of the report.

Montek Ahluwalia, Masood Ahmed, Eliana Cardoso, Sudhir Chittale, Michele de Nevers, Ian Goldin, Frannie Leautier, and Nicholas Stern provided valuable suggestions at the start of the exercise. The report also benefited from discussions on earlier drafts in Washington at USAID, in Delhi at the Indian Council for Research on International Economic Relations, in Geneva at the International Labour Organization, at the DAC senior economist meeting in Stockholm, at the Economic Research Forum in Cairo, at a seminar in the Department of Economics of the Universidade de São Paulo, and workshops in Dar-Es-Salaam and Kampala. As part of the consultation and discussion process, comments from the public on the draft volume were gathered through the World Bank's external Web site. Muriel Darlington ably handled the management and logistical aspects of the report. The report design, editing, and production were coordinated by the World Bank's Office of the Publisher under the supervision of Stephen McGroarty with crucial support from Mark Ingebretsen, Nancy Lammers, and Santiago Pombo-Bejarano. Todd Pugatch dealt with a wide range of substantive and logistical issues. Alfred Friendly and Rachel Weaving were responsible for editing.

# Chapter 1

# Overview

ECONOMIC GROWTH IS A RECENT event in the history of humanity. During most of 4 million years of evolution, people made limited economic progress and their material well-being changed very little. In the last few centuries, however, goods and services started to be produced at increasingly lower cost in hours of effort. The hours of work needed to produce basic goods such as water or heat at the dawn of civilization were several hundred times those needed today (DeLong 2000). Similar increases in productivity have been achieved for an expanding range of goods and services. Most of this progress has taken place in the last two centuries, during which technological progress has been exceptionally rapid, and economic growth unprecedented (figure 1.1).

It is only in the last 50 years that mainstream economics has focused on the determinants of Adam Smith's "natural progress of opulence" and on how growth could be accelerated. Many questions about growth still lack satisfactory answers. Yet few issues are more important for the world's future than the ability of developing countries to raise both productivity and the rate at which they accumulate capital.

This overview chapter first briefly reviews our understanding of growth before turning, in section 2, to the facts and controversies of growth and policy reforms in the 1990s. Section 3 draws the broad lessons coming out of the growth experience of the 1990s, and section 4 offers lessons specific to key policy and institutional

reforms. Section 5 sketches operational implications. Subsequent chapters set out the facts about growth in more detail, and then examine the main areas in which economic and institutional reforms concentrated during the 1990s—macroeconomic stabilization, trade, financial sector, privatization and deregulation, modernization of the public sector, and political reforms. The chapters aim to draw lessons from gaps between expectations and outcomes. Most chapters are also followed by a Country Note that expands on issues insufficiently dealt with in that chapter, or that considers country-level perspectives.

---

FIGURE 1.1

**Worldwide Growth in Real GDP per Capita, 1000–Present**

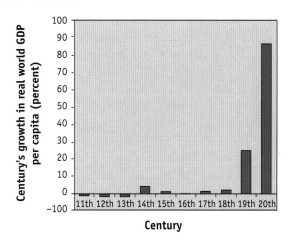

*Source:* DeLong 2000.

---

# 1. Understanding Economic Growth

Absent definitive theories, views on growth have been shaped by facts and changed by experience. Until the 1970s, the growth strategies of developing countries focused on accelerating the rate of capital accumulation and technological adoption. Import substitution, state-owned enterprises, controls over the financial sector, central planning, and a variety of price controls and state interventions in the economy were some of the policies that governments used to take the "commanding heights" of the economy and guide resource allocation to areas thought to be most conducive to long-term growth. Confidence in governments was born from their (partial) success in addressing the Great Depression, in expanding production during World War II, and reconstructing Europe and Japan. Economists and policy makers saw that market forces disrupted growth and that governments were able to restore it, and to expand capacity efficiently. The generation of economists that followed, however, familiar with experiences of developing countries in the 1970s and 1980s, saw the waste of enormous resources in ill-conceived government initiatives, the costs of poor macroeconomic management, and the ease with which well-intentioned public policies could be diverted to serve narrow political or economic interests. Understandably, this later generation of economists and policy makers came to believe that the cost of government failures was considerably larger than the cost of market failures, that government interventions interfered with development, and that containing the role of the public sector in the economy, reducing its use of resources, and limiting its discretion were essential for economic growth.

## New Growth Theory

This shift in views was supported by a new strand of academic research that started in the second half of the 1980s and gathered impetus during the 1990s, when there was a resurgence of academic and empirical work on growth.

Up to then, thinking about growth had been dominated by the Solow model, the basic model with which we still think about economic growth, in which growth is a function of the accumulation of capital, accumulation of labor, and productivity growth. This model leaves out much of what needs explaining. In particular, it views long-run growth as entirely determined by exogenous factors, independent from structural characteristics of the economy such as openness, scale, and saving rate, and, most important, from the policies influencing such variables. Also, while left unexplained in the model, productivity growth drives the empirical story. Solow himself estimated that technological change explained more than half of per capita output growth in the first half of the 1900s in the United States. Calculations by the World Bank indicate that it explained one-third of the increase in per capita income in East Asia up to the early 1990s (World Bank 1993). Other exercises reach similar conclusions on the large role of productivity gains in growth experiences.

At first the New Growth Theory seemed to hold the promise of linking policies to growth performance. It appeared at a time when evidence was accumulating—from the growth experience of the 1970s and 1980s—suggesting that the accumulation of capital was not a panacea, and that misguided policies were costly for growth. The new evidence provided the conceptual foundation for aggregate cross-country regressions, which throughout the 1990s sought to capture the effect of policies on long-term growth (Barro 1991; Temple 1999) and provided the strongest intellectual foundation for the view that better policies would deliver faster growth.

A number of empirical problems became evident, however, related to the crude manner in which policy variables enter the cross-country regressions; the fact that differences in the institutions underlying policy design and policy implementation are not captured; the lack of robustness to changes in time periods and specifications; the crudeness of the assumption that the same model explaining growth in the Republic of Korea or Brazil could be used for

Bolivia or Rwanda; and the poor predictive power of policies as indicators of performance.

If, as suggested by the growth regressions, policies matter for growth, policy improvements should lead to higher growth. Both in the 1980s and 1990s, policies improved relative to other decades, but growth performance remained well below that of the 1960s and 1970s (Easterly 2001). More recently, empirical research has argued that when a measure of "institutional quality" is included in cross-country regressions, the explanatory power of other variables, including all measures of "policies," becomes negligible (Acemoglu, Johnson, and Robinson 2001; Rodrik, Subramanian, and Trebbi 2002; Easterly and Levine 2003; and IMF 2003e). This suggests that "good" institutions matter more for growth than "good" policies—that "institutions rule."

In hindsight, the breakthroughs expected from the New Growth Theory have not materialized. Nonetheless, in the process, greater clarity was reached on the facts about growth, analysts paid

greater attention to the role of institutions, and studies brought the issue of inequality—both within and between countries—increasingly to the fore.

## Growth in Developing Countries: Divergence, Variability, and Unpredictability

Research during the 1990s was able to extend the availability of data over long periods. This made it clear that growth was not a linear process, and that it did not conform to the theoretical prediction that per capita income in developing countries would eventually converge with that of industrialized countries. In fact, there has been "divergence big time" in the evolution of per capita incomes (Pritchett 1997), both between industrialized and developing countries and among developing countries themselves. This is the case whether the period being considered is the last 40 years (figure 1.2) or the last 10 (figure 1.3).

FIGURE 1.2

**Economic Growth in Perspective, 1960–2002**

(GDP per capita)

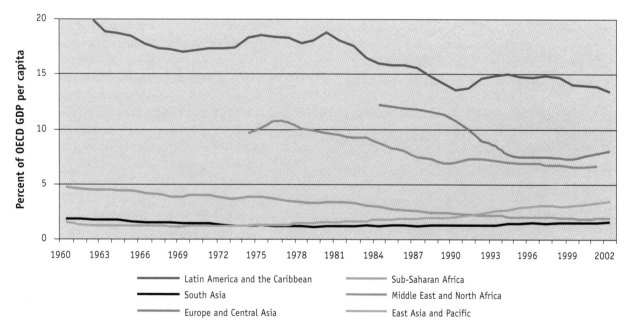

*Source: WDI 2003.*

*Note:* Regions' GDP per capita is shown as a percentage of the OECD GDP per capita (total regional GDP over total population).

As a result, worldwide inequality has changed from being the result almost exclusively of differences among people *within* countries to being the result primarily of differences *across* countries (figure 1.4).

The consideration of growth over longer periods also highlights the *variability* of growth in developing countries. The experience of Latin America since the 1980s, the collapse of growth in Africa in the last two decades, and the economic collapse of Eastern Europe after several decades of sustained growth stand in sharp contrast to the stability of growth among industrialized countries, which have grown at roughly a constant rate (except for the interruption of World War II and recovery years) for more than 100 years. It also contrasts with the experience of East Asian countries. What is remarkable about East Asia is not that it experienced a crisis in 1997, but that it experienced so few crises over the preceding decades. By and large, developing countries have one year of negative per capita growth roughly once every three years. In East Asia, the average is half that rate. Korea has only had only three years of negative per capita growth since 1961.[1]

FIGURE 1.4

**Fraction of World Inequality Accounted for by Differences across Countries**

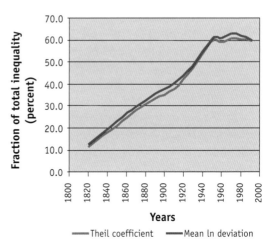

*Source:* Bourguignon and Morrison 2002.

The variability of growth helps to explain why growth in the developing world is so difficult to predict. Instances of economists (including, for example, 1977 Nobel Laureate James Meade on Mauritius) making highly inaccurate predictions have become part of the economic folklore. Many of the economic successes of today—Bangladesh, Indonesia, Korea, or Mauritius—were considered "basket cases" in the 1960s, when Africa's growth prospects were seen as superior to those of overpopulated Asia—a view captured in *Asian Drama* (Myrdal 1972). In the later 1990s, just before the second most dramatic economic crisis in its history, Argentina was seen as a model for developing countries and believed to have found the path to sustained growth. At a more technical level, World Bank growth projections, as well as growth projections by other forecasters, tend to be systematically overoptimistic (a point that was highlighted in the World Bank's *World Development Report 1991*).

While a rare occurrence thus far, sustained growth has improved the lives of millions. Countries where sustained growth has taken place (mostly in South and East Asia, including Bangladesh, China, Indonesia, India, and Viet-

FIGURE 1.3

**Regional Perspectives on Growth in the 1990s**

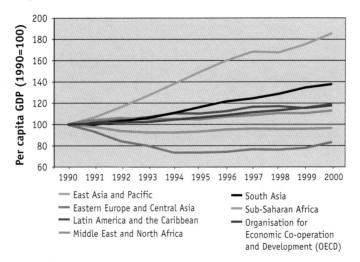

*Source:* WDI 2003.

nam) account for a large proportion of world population. Out of 117 countries with populations of more than half a million people, only 18 have been able to sustain growth rates exceeding industrialized countries' growth and hence narrow their per capita income gap with those countries.[2]

## Institutions

Defined as the rules and norms constraining human behavior (North 1990), institutions include the informal rules and norms that govern personal and social behavior and the formal rules and norms governing economic, social, and political life. Institutions enable societies to organize themselves and function in an orderly manner by solving problems central to life in society, particularly agency problems, containment of predation by individuals or the state, and collective decision making. Societies' performance depends on how effectively their institutions resolve these problems.

The importance of institutions for economic prosperity is not a novelty learned from the 1990s. From different perspectives, Adam Smith, Karl Marx, and Max Weber highlighted the role of institutions in the development of a market economy and formation of a capitalist society. Economists dealing with development in the 1950s and 1960s were aware that the development challenges faced by a plantation economy differed from those faced by a society where economic and political power were not concentrated (Rostow 1952, 1960; Adelman and Morris 1965). Latin American economists of the Structuralist school saw in the legacy of colonialism, embedded in institutions serving the interests of a small, landed elite, the source for economic performance inferior to that of the United States or Canada (Furtado 1963). This imbalance formed a part of the justification for an activist state: inflation helped to mobilize resources from the wealthy elite who resisted more efficient forms of taxation; states sponsored investments in manufacturing, particularly in capital-intensive industries, because old economic interests resisted change and were unwilling to take on risks inherent in new industrial activities; price controls did not have serious economic consequences because the concentration of wealth precluded the redeployment of resources in response to changes in demand (Seers 1962).

While there are some *functions* that institutions need to perform in any society, the *form* through which institutions can perform these functions can vary considerably (Virmani 2004). Most of the empirical work on the importance of institutions leaves open the question of how to improve institutional performance. Merely adopting some other country's laws and formal regulations is no guarantee of achieving the same institutional performance. Recently, accession to the World Trade Organization and integration into regional supranational entities such as the European Union and the New Economic Partnership for Africa have strengthened incentives for institutional improvements. East Asian countries have long realized the importance of institutional change and innovation, and the 1997 crisis made this realization all the more acute, creating renewed impetus to modernize institutions, including political institutions. But for most developing countries, improving the quality of their institutions remains a challenge.

## Fairness, Growth, and Institutions

Another important strain of ideas in the 1990s came from the resurgence of interest in inequality as an apparent influence on growth and institutional performance. A recent body of literature suggests several channels through which inequality affects economic growth. Fairer societies offer their citizens more public goods, more social support, and more social capital. Hence they are more capable of sharing the costs and benefits of improving economic policies, and in turn facilitating consensus building and decision making (Deaton 2003a). Fairness also facilitates agreement on the provision of public goods that have strong beneficial side effects on society, such as health services, water supply, or waste disposal. Other channels through which inequality affects growth are market structures and microeconomic incentives. A better distribution of wealth reduces credit constraints, and broader availability of credit is found to have a significant and positive effect on growth rates. If individuals are limited in their borrowing capacity, reallocating capital toward the poorest will increase aggregate productivity.

Even if one concludes that greater equality influences growth positively, there is still considerable ignorance about the means through which greater equality can be achieved. Governments have long sought, with varied degrees of success, to redistribute income through land redistribution, employment programs, subsidies, and promotion of broad access to credit, infrastructure, health, and education. The large, underresearched area for further study includes questions related to the impact of public spending on equity, both in a static sense (incidence of public spending) and a dynamic sense (changes in individuals' earnings potential).

Recent literature has emphasized the important links between the distribution of assets in a society and the institutions that emerge. Knowledge is still rudimentary about how institutions emerge and are established in a society, but economic research in the 1990s has provided some insights. First, economic incentives influence what type of institutions emerge and when. The enforcement of property rights to land, for example, will depend on the benefits of enforcement relative to its costs, which for each owner depends on the extent to which other owners enforce their property rights. In an extractive economy, for example, if landowners in general do not enforce their property rights, it is uneconomical for one landowner to enforce his: workers will find it attractive to exploit land and appropriate the rents for themselves. Only when this coordination problem is resolved will economic incentives be sufficient for enforcement of property rights (Hoff and Stiglitz 2001). Second, concentrated economic and political interests influence institutions. This can be seen from experiences with land distribution in Latin America, and also from the United States in the early 1900s, when the government decided to regulate matters hitherto left to private parties and the courts; the reason for the shift was a perception that judges and the courts, having been corrupted by powerful

economic interests, were unable to render fair and equitable judgments. *World Development Report 2001* provides other examples of how economic incentives affect the emergence of institutions that sustain the functioning of markets, and the different coordination or risk-reducing problems that they are meant to resolve.

## 2. Facts and Controversies of the 1990s

At the beginning of the 1990s, most economists working on development and many policy makers shared the conviction that more efficient use of resources would lead to growth. This was believed to require, first, macroeconomic prudence, domestic liberalization, and outward orientation, which in turn required freeing market incentives and opening the economy. Hence fiscal deficit reduction, realignment of exchange rates to eliminate black market premia, lifting controls on prices, deregulation of interest rates and liberalization of the financial sector, and reduction of tariffs and other restrictions on imports all became central to the policy reform programs implemented in the 1990s.

Second, conventional wisdom held that to achieve greater efficiency required a reduction in the role of the state. There was evidence that the state discretion that was inherent in growth strategies based on infant industry, import substitution policies, and the growth of public enterprises had been misused more often than anticipated, had often been captured by narrow interest groups, and served as the source of endemic corruption. Addressing this problem required reducing state discretion, downsizing governments, and encouraging a much greater role for the private sector. Hence privatization, deregulation, elimination of quantitative restrictions and of licensing requirements, and dismantling agricultural marketing boards and other forms of state monopoly all became central to reform programs. Seeing the need to strengthen the organizational effectiveness of the state, and the efficiency with which the state used public resources, reformers rationalized government functions and undertook civil service, legal, and budget reforms. Democratic processes were expected to provide checks and balances and further incentives to this process.

Third, it was believed, reforms had to be rapid. Earlier, some of the first authors to argue in favor of abandoning the *dirigiste* framework of early development economics (notably Little, Scitovsky, and Scott 1970; McKinnon 1973) had argued explicitly in favor of a gradualist reform strategy (in respect to trade and the financial sector, respectively).[3] But in the course of the 1980s the economics profession began to be influenced by the enthusiasm of leading politicians for "the magic of the market." Arguments in favor of "big bang" and "shock treatment" became prominent. By the time that the transition to a market economy got under way in the former socialist economies, "a belief in gradualism had almost become tantamount to a confession of a lack of reforming virility" (Williamson and Zagha 2002).

## A Decade of Significant Change

The 1990s provided ample opportunity for these views to be implemented. The Russian Federation, Eastern Europe, and Central Asia embraced capitalism and a new generation of leaders made it a priority to rebuild their economies on the basis of capitalist principles, markets, and privatized firms. Regarding the speed of reform, while there were divergences, the balance of opinions supported rapid rather than gradual reform. China, the largest developing economy continued the reforms it had begun in 1978 with further liberalization of the domestic economy, and increased openness. After its crisis in 1991, India, the second-largest developing economy, speeded up liberalization started in the 1980s. President Collor of Brazil announced a radical program of economic reform aimed at reducing hyperinflation and reversing several decades of state-led import-substituting industrialization. In Argentina, President Menem set the country on a course of eliminating hyperinflation through a currency board as well as ambitious market reforms, which saw the privatization of state-owned businesses and liberalization and opening

of the economy. In Bolivia, reforms by Paz Estensoro that had brought hyperinflation to a halt in the mid-1980s were continued in the 1990s, regardless of the parties in government. In Africa, the devaluation of the African Financial Community (CFA) franc increased competitiveness and many other reforms were implemented throughout the region. In Tanzania, President Mkapa started an ambitious program of reforms. In South Africa, the transition to a multiracial democracy was followed by steps toward liberalizing the economy.

Leaders such as Rawlings of Ghana and Museveni of Uganda strengthened fiscal fundamentals, achieved macroeconomic stability, liberalized the economy, and reduced the role of the state. Privatization, retrenchment of the public sector, and liberalization of trade were the focus of economic policy changes in countries as diverse as the Central African Republic, Ghana, and Tanzania. Reforms in the Middle East and North Africa were less ambitious but were nonetheless significant in the Arab Republic of Egypt, Jordan, Morocco, and Tunisia. On the political front, democracy spread in former communist countries and Africa, and was consolidated in Latin America. These and other changes gave rise to expectations that the 1990s would accelerate growth and social progress in the developing world.

### Rapid Growth, Take-offs, and Social Progress

India and China, together accounting for 40 percent of the developing world's population, grew fast in the 1990s for a second decade in a row, as did many other countries in South and East Asia, including Bangladesh, Sri Lanka, and Vietnam. Chile continued to grow in Latin America, Tunisia in North Africa, and Botswana and Mauritius in Africa. New high performers appeared and annual gross domestic product (GDP) growth for the decade was rapid in an array of countries: Mozambique (7.8), Uganda (6.8), Dominican Republic (6.0), Tunisia (5.0), and Poland (4.5). Countries affected by the crisis in East Asia made an unexpectedly rapid recovery.

Notwithstanding unevenness across regions, the incidence of poverty continued to decline throughout the 1990s—more rapidly in East Asia than in South Asia and more rapidly in South Asia than in Latin America. In Africa, however, the incidence of poverty increased slightly. Growth was the main force behind virtually all cases of significant reductions of poverty, including in China and India. But particularly in Latin America, there were instances such as Brazil and Bolivia where social indicators improved without significant growth.

Alongside these positive developments, however, there were several negative surprises.

### "Transition Recession" in the Former Soviet Union and Eastern Europe

The transition from a communist, centrally planned economy to a capitalist one was expected to be difficult. But the depth of the output collapse was not widely predicted. The length of the transition—in which many countries in 2003, more than a decade later, remain far below their previous levels of output—was not widely forecast. Nor was the variability among countries in the depth and duration of the output collapse. Though recoveries have started to emerge—in the Czech Republic, Hungary, and Poland, for example—it will take years, and in some cases, decades, for most former Soviet countries to regain their per capita income levels prevailing at the beginning of the transition.

### Continued Stagnation in Sub-Saharan Africa

The failure of growth in Africa—either of powerful and rapid growth in a single large country or in a substantial number of smaller ones—was a surprise. Despite good policy reforms, debt relief, continued high levels of official assistance, promising developments in governance, and a relatively supportive external climate, no take-off has ensued. While some positive developments occurred in the later 1990s, such as in Mozambique, Tanzania, and Uganda, and still persist at the time of writing, it is too early to conclude that Africa has turned the corner.

### Financial Crises

Financial crises in the 1990s were less predictable than in the 1970s and 1980s. Macroeconomists,

bank restructuring experts, and emerging-market private traders rolled from crisis to crisis: from Mexico during 1994–95, to Korea, Malaysia, Thailand, Indonesia during 1997–98, Russia in 1998, Brazil in 1998, and Turkey in 2001 to the latest and perhaps most worrisome of all, in Argentina during 2001–02. The evolution of spreads in the months preceding the financial crises suggests that few were anticipated.

### Delay in Recovering Growth, Particularly in Latin America

It was hoped that the "lost decade" of the 1980s would be reclaimed in the 1990s. Macroeconomic stabilization, fiscal austerity, trade liberalization, and privatization were expected to lead to rapid growth. Although growth was the fastest in two decades until 1998, its collapse thereafter following the reversal in capital flows created the general perception that the growth payoffs have been smaller than expected.

### Argentina: The Collapse of the Hard Peg

Argentina was the most successful example of a trend in the 1990s to create macroeconomic stability by legal and institutional changes intended to reduce the scope and latitude of government's discretion. Exchange-rate arrangements that set a fixed rate for *peso* convertibility were not only incorporated into law but also made especially difficult to alter, and changes were made in the operation of the central bank to make these limitations a reality. As part of a package of reforms, this convertibility plan eliminated Argentina's hyperinflation and, for a period, it restored economic growth.

Once Argentina achieved stability with growth, there was considerable discussion—particularly after the devaluation of Brazil's *real* in January 1999—as to whether the country should abandon its rigid exchange rate system. Views diverged among economists. Looking back, the former Governor of Argentina's Central Bank described the abandonment as a marriage to be broken when it was going well (Mario Blejer, World Bank 2005b). For fear that markets could overreact, Argentina's authorities maintained the system. When the plan collapsed, the result was politically and economically costly by design. Thus the damage was not a surprise. But the demise of the convertibility plan itself was a surprise, for two reasons. First, its initial successes had suggested longevity was possible; it had reduced rapid inflation and initiated a boom in the early 1990s, and it had weathered the "Tequila" after-shocks of the Mexican crisis reasonably well. Second, while the end of convertibility was costly by design, its actual cost exceeded the most pessimistic forecast.

## Interpreting the Results

From a growth perspective, the net result of the contrasting experiences of the 1990s is that developing countries as a group grew faster than in the 1980s. In East and South Asia this reduced the income gap with industrialized countries, but in other regions, the gap increased. In Latin America, there were clear gains up to 1998, reversed in the late 1990s and early 2000s (figures 1.2 and 1.3).

Analyzing policy reforms of the 1990s, several studies (Loayza, Fajnzylber, and Calderón 2002; Lora 2001a; Easterly 2001) find that countries that improved their policies—strengthening macroeconomic management, opening up their economies, liberalizing their financial sectors—grew faster in the 1990s. However, they also find a large unexplained negative effect associated with both the 1990s and the preceding decade. Together with analysis of individual country experiences and overoptimistic forecasts by international financial organizations and private entities, these studies give an empirical base to perceptions that the economic policy reforms of the 1990s yielded results below expectations.

It has been suggested that lower growth in OECD (Organisation for Economic Co-operation and Development) countries might have depressed developing countries' growth in the 1990s (Easterly 2002). In reality, the 1990s was favorable for developing countries, even if not every country found ways to benefit. Exports from developing countries as a group grew much faster than in previous decades. Real interest rates were lower. Debt obligations claimed fewer resources, and foreign direct investment and financial flows to developing countries were much larger. If commodity prices affected developing countries adversely, the damage was not dramatic and should have been offset by the increasing share of manufacturing exports—except in a small group of least developed and Sub-Saharan African countries that remained highly dependent on agricultural exports.

All in all, while external factors played a role, explanations of performance must be sought primarily in developing countries' domestic policies.

Good performance has been associated with domestic and external liberalization; Chile, India, China, and other countries in East Asia are all more open than in previous decades and have moved toward greater reliance on market forces. But many aspects of these countries' policies are still far from compliant with conventional wisdom. For example, India has registered fiscal deficits several times higher than Brazil's or Argentina's, with lower inflation and lower interest rates. While this fiscal trend is clearly unsustainable in the long run, and measures have been taken to correct it, it is clear that there is more to macroeconomic stability than a superficial reading of the size of the fiscal deficit. China has built extremely large contingent liabilities related to unfunded pensions and nonperforming loans in the banking system. While, again, this is not a sustainable situation, it suggests that economies do not operate in mechanical ways, and that dynamism in one sector can offset the cost of inefficiency in others. Similarly, India's and China's industries, though increasingly competitive in export markets, remain protected and state enterprises still play a large (though declining) role in these economies.

The mismatch between predictions and results, and the successes of China, India, and Vietnam where there were substantial deviations from the full package of reforms, suggest several possible explanations. First, sufficient time may not have yet elapsed for results to emerge in all countries. Over time, market-oriented reforms may ultimately yield the results expected. Growth rates in African and other developing countries have rebounded since 1997; Argentina is experiencing its second year of rapid growth after the collapse of 2001–02; and growth rates in Eastern Europe have increased. Second, perhaps the reforms implemented in the 1990s were not sufficiently ambitious. Insufficient fiscal adjustment in Latin America, very partial privatization in Africa, and insufficient openness to international trade in the Middle East and Northern Africa may explain performance below expectations in these regions. A third possible explanation is that there were incoherencies in the implementation of policies. Argentina introduced a rigid exchange rate without the fiscal and financial conditions needed to sustain it. Fiscal adjustments in some African countries were achieved at the cost of reducing productive public spending. Open capital accounts encouraged pro-cyclical flows. Correction of these incoherencies may enable growth to resume.

Perhaps most important, while reforms in the 1990s focused on increasing the role of markets and decreasing the role of the state, they tended to neglect the role of institutions. Francisco Gil Diaz, Mexico's Minister of Finance (as quoted in Krueger 2004), recently suggested that

> The policies that have been undertaken are not even a pale imitation of what market economics ought to be, if we understand market economics as the necessary institutional framework for a sound economy to operate and flourish. What has been implemented throughout our continent is a grotesque caricature of market economics.

State enterprises were privatized without much attention to the operation of the markets in which they would function. Financial liberalization swelled the resources, foreign and domestic, that ineffective intermediaries channeled to state enterprises and related borrowers, contributing to the massive crises. In some cases, lack of competitive political forces and such institutions as a free press allowed those who were politically well connected to take advantage of privatizations and to take control of nat-

ural resources while enabling corruption to flourish.

These explanations are not mutually exclusive; one or more may apply to specific country circumstances. The experience also holds some deeper lessons. For example, while at one level Argentina's experience teaches that fixed exchange regimes require a very demanding set of conditions, a deeper lesson is that rigid rules are no substitute for credibility, and that government's discretion needs to be checked, not replaced with rules. Another deeper lesson is that the reforms of the 1990s did not focus on the binding constraints. For example, they reduced fiscal deficits when perhaps the binding constraints were lack of public capital and aggregate demand. Or they reduced tariffs on imports when perhaps the binding constraint was the workings of the financial sector. Or they focused on correcting government failures, when the binding constraints were market failures.

## 3. Lessons from the 1990s

### *Promote Growth, Not Just Efficiency*

Reforms need to go beyond the generation of efficiency gains to promote growth. The policy focus of reforms in the 1990s enabled better use of existing capacity but did not provide sufficient incentives for expanding that capacity. While this emphasis on efficiency was warranted at a time of extremely large distortions and waste, it also explains the frequent instances of stabilization without growth or liberalization without growth. The experience highlights the importance of the investment climate, and of providing predictable conditions for investors and other economic agents.

It also highlights that growth entails more than the efficient use of resources. Growth entails structural transformation, diversification of production, change, risk taking by producers, correction of both government and market failures, and changes in policies and institutions. It is also a process of social transformation: people will change activities and live in different places. Social relations will change, and the informal networks of rural life will be lost as other more formal networks and organizations are established. Entrepreneurs will invest in new machinery to produce new products and adopt new organizational forms. Farmers will adopt new farming methods and change their product mix. The economy will produce and demand different goods and services. These changes take place over time, alongside changes in institutions that render them possible. Any growth strategy needs to include actions, on both the policy and the institutional front, that address and support this process of change.

Better policies can bring efficiency gains, and may increase incentives for investment, but without amounting to a growth strategy. They will not necessarily induce the behavior by private investors and the public sector that is needed to put an economy on a sustained growth path. For this, faster accumulation of physical and human capital by both the private and the public sector is essential, as are gains in productivity.

This may explain why the growth impact of the reforms of the 1990s was smaller than expected. The incentives needed to expand productive capacity ("expanding the frontier" in economists' parlance) differ from those that are needed to use existing capacity better ("movements toward the frontier"). What matters for growth is less the degree to which policies approximate the ideal than "the extent to which a given development strategy is able to mobilize the creative forces of society and achieve ever-higher levels of productivity" (Alejandro Foxley, in World Bank 2005b). And, in Albert Hirschman's words (1958):

> Development depends not so much on finding optimal combinations for given resources and factors of production as on calling forth and enlisting for development purposes resources and abilities that are hidden, scattered, or badly utilized.

In retrospect, it is clear that in the 1990s we often mistook efficiency gains for growth. The "one size fits all" policy reform approach to economic growth and the belief in "best practices"

exaggerated the gains from improved resource allocation and their dynamic repercussions, and proved to be both theoretically incomplete and contradicted by the evidence. Expectations that gains in growth would be won entirely through policy improvements were unrealistic. Means were often mistaken for goals—that is, improvements in policies were mistaken for growth strategies, as if improvements in policies were an end in themselves. Going forward, the pursuit of policy reforms for reform's sake should be replaced by a more comprehensive understanding of the forces underlying growth. Removing obstacles that make growth impossible may not be enough: growth-oriented action, for example, on technological catch-up, or encouragement of risk taking for faster accumulation, may be needed.

## Common Principles and Diverse Ways to Implement Them

Another mistake often made in the 1990s has been the translation of general policy principles into a unique set of actions. The principles of the *1991 World Development Report*, "macroeconomic stability; domestic liberalization, and openness," have been interpreted narrowly to mean "minimize fiscal deficits, minimize inflation, minimize tariffs, maximize privatization, maximize liberalization of finance," with the assumption that the more of these changes the better, at all times and in all places—overlooking the fact that these expedients are just *some* of the ways in which these principles can be implemented.

There are many ways of achieving macroeconomic stability, openness, and domestic liberalization. As seen above, for example, the goal of achieving macroeconomic stability does not imply a need to minimize fiscal deficits at all times. A lower fiscal deficit achieved today through off-budget contingent liabilities, or through cutting back public investments and thus reducing long-run growth and the future tax base, may mean a higher fiscal deficit in the future. A lower fiscal deficit does not even guarantee greater macro stability if it is based on external borrowing in which interest rates are reduced at the cost of greater vulnerability to exchange rate fluctuations, or if it is based on building off-budget liabilities through the banking system, which eventually translate into an increase in public debt—as Latin American countries and Turkey found to their cost in the 1980s and 1990s. Similarly, trade integration can be achieved through various means that offset the effect of tariffs and reduce the implicit tax on exports. Duty rebate schemes, subsidized credit to exporters, and other forms of export promotion, export processing zones, infrastructure, and transport corridors have all helped China, India, Korea, and Mauritius to integrate into the world economy while keeping their tariffs relatively high in the initial phases of integration and reducing them gradually over time. Thailand's and Indonesia's foreign domestic investment regimes had few restrictions, whereas those of Korea and India had many until very recently—but both Korea and India found alternative instruments to access and adopt modern technologies. Financial intermediation can be increased by relaxing entry restrictions in the banking system, or by improving the workings of the legal system, particularly those parts that deal with the repossession of collateral.

To sum up, "getting the policies right" mistakes means for ends. Clearly not everything can be right at once, and not everything needs to be "right" for growth to take place—as witnessed in examples from Bangladesh, China, India, Indonesia, and many other countries.

## Common Functions and Diverse Ways to Achieve Them

To sustain growth requires key functions to be fulfilled, but there is no unique combination of policies and institutions for fulfilling them. The successful growth experiences in eight East Asian economies, reported in the World Bank's *East Asian Miracle* (World Bank 1993), resulted from diverse policy and institutional paths, but common functions were fulfilled along these paths.[4] This perspective has several implications.

First, different policies can yield the same result, and the same policy can yield different results, depending on country institutional contexts and underlying growth strategies. This nonformulaic result holds not only for the eight East Asian economies featured in the 1993 study, but also for a larger set of countries 10 years later. Countries with remarkably different policy and institutional frameworks—Bangladesh, Botswana, Chile, China, Egypt, India, Lao PDR, Mauritius, Sri Lanka, Tunisia, and Vietnam—have all sustained growth in per capita income at rates above the U.S. long-term growth rate of close to 2 percent a year.

Second, common to all successes is that four functions have been fulfilled: rapid accumulation of capital, efficient resource allocation, technological progress, and sharing of the benefits of growth. Rates of progress in these four functions have not always been uniform, but successful countries have achieved a balance among them over time, and disruptions have ensued when the balance was not achieved. While there can be substitution temporarily, the balance will need to be reestablished at some point.

For example, Korea's policies in the 1960s and 1970s sought to encourage risk taking by the private sector. Import protection and priority lending contributed to higher levels of capital accumulation, at the cost of efficient allocation, which became a more important priority in the 1980s. The Soviet Union, well into the 1960s, grew rapidly on the basis of sacrificing consumption, accumulating capital, and maintaining a relatively equitable income distribution. But its considerable progress in science and technology was not effectively deployed in production and, more important, resource allocation was enormously wasteful. Eventually, the costs of this inefficiency and the political reforms of the late 1980s combined to bring growth to collapse. In India, a "big push" in capital formation in the decades following independence was complemented in the 1980s—when evidence of misallocation and low productivity growth began to emerge—by policies that gradually freed market forces and increased efficiency in resource allocation (Virmani 2004), thus ensuring not only the sustainability of growth but also its acceleration.

Factoring these four functions into analyses of growth makes it easier to understand why both policies and institutions play a role. For example, capital accumulation by the public sector requires sound tax policies and administration, sustainable macro policies, and a bureaucracy that is capable of formulating and managing public expenditure programs effectively and of choosing programs with high returns. Accumulation by the private sector requires at least reasonably secure private property rights, stable expectations about the future, a stable macroeconomy, and access to finance. One country might strengthen private investment by, say, improving expectations, whereas another country could achieve the same result by, say, reforming the financial sector.[5] Similarly, efficiency in allocation requires not only reasonably sound policies—such as competitive exchange rates and an open trade regime—but also institutions that can enforce contracts and enable markets to function (World Bank, *World Development Report 2001*). Technological catch-up requires not only investment and trade policies that enable a country to attract foreign direct investment (FDI) and import equipment, but also institutions that, depending on the country's development stage, promote adaptive research or a patent regime. Indeed, in some instances, it is institutions and political realities that define the set of feasible policies, as testified by Russia's former Minister of Finance Yegor Gaidar (World Bank 2005b):

> If I were the tsar of Russia, I would have done everything differently . . . But if I were deputy prime minister and finance minister, in a government without a parliamentary majority and under many pressures, I would have done more or less what we did.

Different policies can have the same effect, and the same policy can have different effects, depending on the context. In large economies, with access to foreign technology and equipment, competition and economies of scale lessen the efficiency cost of trade restrictions and markedly widen the scope for successful inward-oriented industrialization. Brazil, China, and India were able to develop manufacturing, many segments of which became internationally competitive, whereas in small countries such as Jamaica and Uruguay, or Sri

Lanka in the 1960s and 1970s, the market was too small; the benefits of inward-looking industrialization were negligible and did not justify its costs. Sri Lanka became successful only after it began to liberalize imports in late 1977 and follow export-oriented policies. Thus, the same inward-industrialization policy produced different outcomes because country characteristics differed.

Conversely, a given policy can yield different results because of institutional variation. In Japan during the Meiji industrialization and, more recently, in Korea, public institutions were able to resist pressures from narrow interest groups. Public enterprises were run efficiently, and state ownership built capacity in sectors that the private sector had not entered because of perceived high risks. The same policy in Bolivia, however, where public enterprises were run for the benefit of narrow interest groups, did not play a strategic role in the industrialization process, and most of the enterprises were liquidated when Bolivia had to stabilize its economy in the 1980s. In the case of India, it has been shown that in the presence of poor institutions, liberalization can lead to less growth than expected (Virmani 2004).

Like that of policies, the effect of institutions depends on the context. Security of ownership rights has been achieved in different ways and to different extents in different country contexts. In Soeharto's Indonesia, securing returns depended on connections with the ruling elite. In contemporary China, the definition and enforcement of property rights depend on party and local government support—and only recently have initiatives been taken in this direction. And in India, success depends on the functioning of a judiciary modeled after western legal systems.

Sharing the benefits of growth has been important in all sustained growth experiences, and particularly in countries with authoritarian forms of government, where it has helped to legitimize regimes that often were neither fully representative nor democratic. Various policies have been used to promote the sharing of the benefits of growth. They include land reform and redistribution of other assets; public expenditures on infrastructure (the 8-7 program in China); social spending (Tunisia); policies to increase opportunities to economically underprivileged groups (affirmative actions for *bumiputra* in Malaysia); and poverty-targeted programs (food stamps in Sri Lanka or employment programs in India and Bangladesh).

To sum up, diversity in the form of successful growth experiences should be no surprise. Each successful country was successful in its own way.

## Government Discretion Needs to Be Managed and Checked, Not Replaced by Rules

Because developing countries' societies resolve agency, predation, and collective decision-making problems less effectively than do those of industrialized countries, much of the reform effort in the 1990s sought to introduce policies that would limit the discretion of national authorities in growth strategies and minimize demands on institutions. Privatization, financial liberalization, and removal of quantitative restrictions on imports are examples of policy reforms meant not only to improve incentives for more efficient allocation but also to reduce the need for government discretion. Dollarization, fiscal rules, and integration in larger economic unions are examples of institutional reforms meant to replace government discretion by rigid rules; they are consistent with the sense that, on balance, the costs of failures outweigh the benefits of discretion in the workings of an activist, developmental state.

However, government discretion cannot be dispensed with altogether, so it is important to find ways in which it can be exerted effectively. What was learned in the 1990s is not only that sound policies do not necessarily engender the institutions of a modern economy—that institutions are not entirely endogenous—but also that institutions can prevent the adoption of growth-oriented policies or offset their impact. Experience showed how much institutions matter, and how hard it is to work around their absence or to improve their quality. Above all, the experience showed that government discretion cannot be bypassed. It is needed for a wide range of activities that are essential for sustaining growth, ranging from regulating utilities and supervising

banks to providing infrastructure and social services. Improving institutions that support the implementation of policies, and strengthening checks on the use of discretion, are more promising guiding principles than seeking to eliminate government discretion.

Much of the complexity encountered in the realm of economic institutions is also found in the institutions governing political life. The formal institutions of democracy, for example, do not necessarily ensure appropriate checks on discretion, nor are those checks always absent in authoritarian regimes. Mechanisms and levels of accountability can take very different forms, rarely amenable to the simplicity of formal political institutions. Much of the growth success of East Asian countries can be attributed to these countries' ability to allow discretion by different government agencies, alongside checks on this discretion that made them accountable. The forms of these checks varied: an authoritarian development-oriented political leader in some cases (Soeharto's Indonesia, Korea in the first decades of its take-off), the checks and balances inherent in complex one-party systems (China), or the normal checks and balances of a democratic regime (India, Sri Lanka).

## Prudent Macroeconomic Management Is at the Heart of Successful Growth Strategies

Avoidance of busts usually requires avoidance of booms. The costs of the crises of the 1990s in terms of forgone growth, social distress, and public debt highlight once again the importance of prudent macroeconomic management. They also stress the importance of avoiding macroeconomic vulnerabilities, and the risks associated with indiscriminate opening of the capital account. Last but not least, they stress the importance of responding quickly to downturns. One difference between successful and less successful growth experiences is the frequency of downturns: virtually nonexistent for China, Korea, or Malaysia, but numerous for Argentina, Brazil, and Turkey.

In addition to dealing with crises effectively, it is also important to reduce financial fragilities and hence vulnerability to shocks. The financial crises of the 1990s differed from the many that preceded them because of their cost and their suddenness, and they were much harder to predict. The risks of financial integration had been underestimated and its gains overestimated. In the 1990s in emerging market economies, the opening of the capital account to financial inflows triggered large surges that lowered the costs of sovereign and private borrowing and helped reduce inflation. For those reasons, governments (with exceptions such as those of Chile, India, Korea in the early and mid-1990s, and Malaysia) encouraged these inflows. Of the 10 economies that received the largest inflows, however, 7 suffered severe crises that took the form of large output declines, higher incidence of poverty, and large exchange rate devaluations. The three exceptions were China, India, and Hong Kong (China).

Each crisis was preceded by a large surge in inflows that either led to appreciation of the real exchange rate and increased current account deficits or, as in some East Asian countries, created an external debt maturity profile excessively biased toward the short term, and exposed unhedged commercial banks to currency and maturity risks. In current account crises—many of which arose in the context of stabilization programs anchored on a nominal exchange rate—the sequence of events followed a remarkably similar pattern: a surge in capital inflows put pressure on the exchange rate to appreciate; the current account deficit of the balance of payments increased; private-sector and government debt exposures fed resistance to letting the exchange rate adjust; governments sought to sustain the rate by drawing down reserves, but the policy lacked credibility, or reserves were insufficient to sustain it; a large devaluation followed; and the tightening effect of the devaluation was amplified by the consequences of currency mismatches for the balance sheets of banks or those of their borrowers and of firms. In Indonesia and Korea, for example, where current account deficits were relatively small, the trigger was the need for a large debt rollover at a time when investors were retreating from emerging markets and when risk perceptions were on the rise. This was accentuated, in Indonesia, by the uncertainty of the political transition.

The booms and busts of the 1990s are reminiscent of some of the crises of the 1980s. They teach several important lessons. First, as with most liquidity surges, busts inevitably follow booms: avoiding the bust requires avoiding the boom and strengthening the fundamentals. Countries such as Chile, India, or Malaysia that managed inflows, including through the imposition of restrictions, were able to weather the crises much better than countries that took no such precautions. Can a boom be distinguished from a favorable lasting trend, ex ante? In most cases the distinguishing factors are the volume of the surge, the pressure it puts on the exchange rate, and its impact on bank credit. Second, the crises of the 1990s highlight the extent to which banks can amplify the consequences of a crisis, and the risks associated with currency mismatches, including mismatches on the borrowers' balance sheets. Third, sovereign borrowing in foreign currencies is risky. While sovereign borrowing should, in theory, help a country to access external resources on better terms, in practice it has encouraged governments and private firms to take excessive risks.

## Move Away from Formulaic Policy Making and Focus on the Binding Constraint(s)

A vital lesson for policy formulation and policy advice is the need to be cognizant of the shadow prices of constraints, and to address whatever is the *binding constraint* on growth, in the right manner and in the right sequence. This requires recognizing country specificities, and more economic analysis and rigor, than does a formulaic approach to policy making. Policy makers face the practical problem that no scientific method permits ex ante identification of the most important constraint(s) binding growth in specific country circumstances, and hence the specific measures that are needed to address it (them). During the 1980s and 1990s, China's approach was to "cross the stream by groping for the stones." Constraints were identified and dealt with as the growth process unfolded, through experimentation and trial and error (chapters by Lim and Huang, in World Bank 2005a).

Which policy should be introduced, and when, varies considerably from case to case depending on initial conditions and institutional endowments. For example, one can generally assume that where hyperinflation is raging, or public debt demands high real interest rates—as it does in Argentina, Brazil, Jamaica, and Turkey, for example— macroeconomic stabilization is the first priority. Where trade restrictions are extreme and hinder utilization of existing capacity, as in many countries of the Middle East and North Africa, reducing them will be essential. Where there is uncertainty regarding the future course of economic policies, as in Bolivia, Democratic Republic of Congo, and Nigeria, financial sector liberalization will do little to channel resources to private investment. Where property rights are poorly defined and enforced, and regulation prevents the movement of domestic resources across sectors, as is still the case in some Central Asian and some African countries, trade liberalization will be of little effect.

Experimentation and learning is hence an important part of the growth process. The *East Asia Miracle* study highlighted that behind the miracle was the East Asian countries' willingness to experiment, and ability to learn from, not to persist in, their mistakes. This approach helped them identify, at any point in time, the constraint that most severely limited growth, and the right sequence of policies needed in each situation. There may be situations in which a country needs to address many constraints at once, as during the transition of Eastern European countries. These situations are rare, however. In most cases, countries can deal with constraints sequentially, a few at a time. Success in addressing one or a set of constraints makes it easier to deal with the others, and may help establish virtuous circles.

## 4. Lessons from Policy and Institutional Reform Experiences in the 1990s

The economic policy reforms of the 1990s focused on improving efficiency in the allocation

of resources through macroeconomic stabilization, liberalization of trade and the financial sector, privatization, and deregulation. Deregulation and reduction in the role of government were expected to improve the governance of the public sector through improvements in incentives for performance, more transparency, and fewer opportunities for rent seeking. Institutional reforms focused on improving collective decision making and solving agency problems through democratization, decentralization, and public sector reforms aimed at enhancing the efficiency, transparency, and accountability of government activities. From 60 countries choosing their leaders through competitive elections in 1989, the number rose to 100 by 2000. Delegation to subnational levels of government of political, administrative, and financial powers has taken place not only in federated states such as India, Brazil, and Russia but also in smaller states and centralized states such as Bolivia and the Czech Republic. Deregulation and privatization have been trends virtually everywhere, even though the intensity of the reforms has varied significantly from region to region.

What have we learned from a decade of reforms in these areas?

## *Macro Stability Needs to Be Achieved in a Manner That Is Sustainable and Pro-Growth*

The rise in real interest rates in the late 1970s and early 1980s, combined with a variety of commodity price shocks, had rendered unsustainable the fiscal stances, debt levels, and exchange rate regimes of most countries in Latin America, East and South Asia, Africa, and the Middle East. Performance differed sharply between countries that rapidly adjusted to these shocks (Korea and East Asian countries in general) and those that did not (Brazil, Nigeria, and many other countries in Latin America and Africa).

As a result, the Structuralist view that inflation and macro instability were inevitable companions of structural transformation and growth was replaced in the 1990s by the strong belief that macroeconomic stability was needed for growth.

The 1990s indeed saw considerable progress in this area: fiscal deficits declined in most countries, exchange rates were adjusted to reflect market realities, black markets for foreign exchange disappeared, and inflation declined virtually everywhere. However, while macroeconomic policies as conventionally measured improved in a majority of countries, the growth benefits failed to materialize. In addition, financial crises were numerous, with severe adverse effects on economic growth and poverty.

The openness of the capital account was a key source of fragility that, combined with unsound policies in the financial sector (such as currency mismatches on banks' or final borrowers' balance sheets in the absence of hedging instruments) and appreciation of the real exchange rate, helps to explain many of the crises of the 1990s. Countries such as India have avoided appreciation of the real exchange rate, and made the opening of the capital account a medium-term goal, to be realized contingent on strengthened economic performance (including fiscal adjustment), export diversification, and achievement of a sound banking system. Chile and Malaysia, among others, did not hesitate to tax capital inflows when excessive liquidity threatened to destabilize the economy, and they maintained the competitiveness of the real exchange rate. These countries fared much better than those that opened themselves to external liquidity surges. Notwithstanding the theoretical arguments in favor of capital account openness, the evidence on growth is inconclusive and volatility clearly increased. A major lesson of the decade is that restrictions should be placed not so much on outflows as on inflows. Obviously, differentiating an unsustainable boom from a positive sustainable trend can be difficult, but standard indicators of vulnerability such as indebtedness, evolution of the real exchange rate, and current account deficits have proven to be reliable, if imprecise, tools.

Macroeconomic stabilization programs often suffered from other design flaws, which created serious macroeconomic fragilities. While primary deficits did decline over the 1990s, public debt increased in most countries, whether because of the bank recapitalization costs of financial crises (as in Indonesia, Turkey), or because of the cost of contingent liabilities being shifted to the public sector (pensions in Argentina), or because of high real interest rates on the public debt (as in Brazil and Jamaica). Other design flaws help explain why the search for macro-stability may in some cases have actually been inimical to growth. A preoccupation with reducing inflation led some countries to adopt exchange rate regimes that ultimately proved destabilizing—price stabilization was achieved at the cost of appreciating exchange rates. Fiscal adjustment was often based on highly distortionary taxes (for example, on external trade or on domestic financial transactions); or on cuts in spending on productive infrastructure or human capital that proved detrimental to sustained growth; or on borrowing abroad where interest rates were lower but currency exposure increased risks. Hence a single-minded pursuit of macro-stability sometimes came at the cost of public spending that might have both increased growth and made stability more durable.

There are two lessons to draw from this experience. First, even with macroeconomic stability, macroeconomic vulnerabilities induced by policy flaws can be serious, and these can have tremendous costs. However, indicators of *sustainable* macro-stability are less self-evident than common indicators of fiscal and external stance suggest. The inability of financial markets (as measured by country risk premia) to predict most of the financial crises of the 1990s provides further evidence that unambiguous indicators of risk are difficult to find.

Second, the institutions underlying macroeconomic outcomes and stability matter as much as stability itself. There is ample evidence that budgetary processes influence fiscal outcomes and that countercyclical fiscal policy rules strengthen macroeconomic stability. Centralized budget processes lead to better balanced fiscal outcomes over time, and countercyclical fiscal policies shorten cycles and narrow their amplitude. Few governments find it politically appealing to run fiscal surpluses during good times, however. Transparent fiscal rules, with stipulated penalties for noncompliance, may be effective in some contexts. In others, the creation of institutions such as oil stabilization funds may be needed to save windfalls. One promising example is Chile's Structural Surplus rule, which establishes fiscal policy targets adjusted for the variation in growth over the cycle. Other proposals, yet to be adopted, have focused on creating an independent fiscal policy council, modeled along lines similar to an independent central bank, that would set annual deficit limits. Another institutional dimension of fiscal policy is transparency. Uncertainty about the state of the fiscal accounts probably played a large role in generating the volatility of the risk premiums that developing-country borrowers faced during the 1990s. There is also evidence that more transparent budgetary processes brought down deficits and debt.

For monetary policy, institutional arrangements are equally important to ensure that low and stable rates of inflation are achieved and maintained, and that they last. However, there are no magic institutional shortcuts to monetary credibility, which has to be earned through anti-inflationary performance. The institution of an independent central bank—with a commitment to price stability that takes the form of a publicly announced inflation target—has succeeded among emerging market economies during the past decade (Brazil, Chile, Colombia, Korea, Mexico, Peru, South Africa, and Thailand). This institutional arrangement has the important advantages of flexibility (since the central bank is not constrained in *how* it attains its inflation target) and commitment (since the central bank's prestige is publicly put on the line).

## Trade Openness, a Key Element of Successful Growth Strategies, Can Be Achieved in Many Ways

During the 1980s, the performance of countries that responded to shocks by increasing their outward orientation (East Asian countries) contrasted sharply with that of countries that did not (Latin America, Africa, most countries of the Middle East and North Africa). Most policy makers concluded that openness mattered for growth and, as a result, during the 1990s, most

developing countries significantly reduced tariffs on imports and dismantled other forms of trade restrictions. As in the case of macroeconomic reforms, however, the results varied and, in general, fell short of expectations. Whereas openness helped efficiency and growth in many cases (East and South Asian countries, Botswana, Chile, Mauritius, Tunisia), it failed to do so in many others. Several lessons emerge.

First, openness to trade has been a central element of successful growth strategies. Although the paths taken toward greater integration with the world economy were far from uniform during the 1990s, the most successful developing countries reduced barriers to international trade and foreign investment during the decade.

Second, trade is an opportunity, not a guarantee. Trade reforms in some countries yielded few gains in terms of export expansion or increased economic growth, while creating social and economic adjustment costs. Liberalization of trade in Argentina in the 1980s and 1990s, and in Chile in the early 1980s, for example, was accompanied by an appreciation of the real exchange rate that reduced the competitiveness of domestic industries, and incentives to exports—with adverse consequences for the balance of payments and the real economy. In some countries of Eastern Europe in the 1990s, trade was liberalized while property rights were not well defined, and the institutional base for a market economy was not well developed. These, and other institutional issues preventing the free movement of resources, often meant that trade reforms did not expand economic opportunities but restricted them instead (Bolaky and Freund 2004). Such experiences do not imply that less trade reform would have been desirable, but that trade reform must be done sensibly, as part of an effective growth strategy.

Third, countries that have successfully opened their economies have done so following a striking variety of policy approaches. They have opened up different sectors at different speeds (for example, Bangladesh and India). Some, such as China and Mauritius, have achieved partial liberalization through the establishment of export processing zones, and some have combined unilateral trade reforms with participation in regional trade agreements (Mexico and countries in Central and Eastern Europe that have now joined the European Union). These differences, and differences in the range of complementary policies adopted, make it difficult to pin down the statistical relationship between trade integration and growth. The academic debates on whether openness to trade causes higher growth are riddled with problems of measurement, reverse causation (faster-growing countries tend to open their markets more quickly), and omitted variable bias (countries that successfully lower tariffs and increase growth also adopt other complementary policies).

Fourth, the distributive effects of trade liberalization are diverse, and not always pro-poor. Trade reforms were expected to be pro-poor because in most societies the relatively wealthy and urban classes have been more successful at using protection for their own benefit. The expectation was that trade reform would increase the incomes of the unskilled. Yet evidence from the 1990s on the relationship between trade reforms and poverty is to date mostly indirect. Even where trade policy has reduced poverty, there are still distributive issues. An important policy lesson is that countries need to help the affected workers move out of shrinking (import-competing) sectors into expanding (exporting) sectors.

Fifth, the preservation and expansion of the world trade system hinges on its ability to strike a better balance between the interests of industrialized and developing nations. Though more supportive of development than at the beginning of the 1990s, the world trade system is still biased against the poor. Notwithstanding a decade of significant expansion of international trade, global markets are most hostile to the products the world's poor produce—agricultural products, textiles, and labor-intensive manufactures—and problems of escalating tariffs, tariff peaks, and quota arrangements systematically deny the poor market access and skew incentives against adding value in poor countries. These problems are embedded in the remaining structure of protection in both industrial countries and developing countries (the latter owing to their own antiex-

port biases and also to higher barriers to trade in developing-country markets), and they can be addressed through collective actions. Those actions are best achieved through the Doha Round and the World Trade Organization (WTO). Although there is a role for nonreciprocal preferences and for reciprocal regional approaches, such preferential arrangements are economically arbitrary; they come at a cost to excluded countries and are not the best way to generate the right incentives for investment.

## Design Privatization and Deregulation with Regard to Institutional Strengths and Weaknesses

Privatization and deregulation have a potentially large efficiency impact and can benefit the population at large, including the poor. But there is a need to keep expectations realistic as to what they can achieve, to establish the institutions that are key to success, and to design privatization strategies taking into account institutional strengths and weaknesses.

Privatization and deregulation were key areas of reform in the 1990s. Commercial public enterprises, development banks, and other forms of public interventions in the economy, even when meant to address market failures, had become discredited because in many instances they had failed to work well in practice. State activist policies using discretion, combined with weak accountability in public sector organizations and weak political accountability of states to citizens, were producing costs that were just too high. The end of communism, and the deregulation revolution in the United States and the United Kingdom, added further impetus for the wave of privatization that swept across the industrialized and developing world in the 1990s.

The results varied. In most countries, privatization brought unambiguous gains in terms of more efficient use of resources, more investment, and enhanced welfare for consumers. At the same time, however, privatization itself failed to bring about all the gains for investment and growth that were expected of it. It is also clear that too much was expected from privatization, particularly in some areas of infrastructure, but also in terms of the governance improvements it would bring. In cases where the overall package of reform failed to bring about the expected growth, even the efficiency gains of privatization were put in question—a problem that is particularly serious in Latin America and Africa, where it has in some cases derailed the privatization process.

In addition, the process of privatization has often been less than fully transparent and competitive, and this has left sequels that in some cases can be costly to repair—particularly where privatization has led to concentration of economic power, as it has in many parts of Africa and Eastern Europe.

Privatization is not just about finding "better owners" than the government but about changing governance to separate the commercial from the political. As is now widely accepted, government ownership of a commercial firm makes this separation difficult. But privatization does not automatically ensure this separation. The well-publicized difficulties of doing business in countries such as Russia show that a government can use a wide range of laws to influence a firm's decisions without ownership. Separating the commercial from the political requires institutions that define and limit government powers. Notwithstanding the claims of some privatization advocates, institutions to support a well-functioning market economy will not spring up quickly in response to demand. The lack of effective institutions permits predation through several avenues, not just the government: in extractive industries, for example, the mining or petroleum firm and the government are beholden to each other, and either could act or collude at public expense. Vested interests could act through either the public or private sector, and poor shareholder oversight over a firm, as well as poor public oversight over governments, permits misappropriation.

Turning to utilities, the second major area of privatization during the 1990s, there are three main lessons. First, expectations of private investment in infrastructure have been overly optimistic—because (1) underpricing continued to be a problem that governments did not fully

address, (2) the risks of infrastructure investment were not appreciated, and (3) governments could not credibly commit to a policy and regulatory regime. At the beginning of the 1990s, the private sector was expected to enter virtually all areas of infrastructure, including roads, but experience has since shown that the risks involved in infrastructure investment are often too large to be taken up by the private sector.

Second, if privatization is overstated as a means of severing the link between economics and politics, regulation as a means of restoring the link is underappreciated. The clearer the separation between economics and politics, the better it is for each: commerce will be more efficient and politics less corrupt. But the more complex the regulatory issue, the more likely are mistakes, and the less likely that bad regulation (and capture of the regulators by vested interests) will be detected. Even if detected, the poorer the institutions, the less likely it is that bad regulation will be corrected.

Third, the reform experiences of network utilities clearly show that there is no universally appropriate reform model, and that privatization is not necessary or indispensable for every country. Every restructuring and privatization program needs to explicitly consider the specific features of each sector (its economic attributes and technology) as well as the country's institutional, social, and political characteristics. Important lessons in this respect are as follows:

- Regulatory reform should promote competition, not control; competition is the most effective regulator.

- Getting the economics right is key. Understanding the source of benefits helps in structuring the reform. A pricing policy that does not allow adequate revenue cannot improve the situation even if a utility is privatized or an independent regulator is established. For example, as of 2000, in almost all Commonwealth of Independent States (CIS) countries, household electricity prices covered less than 50 percent and industrial prices were less than 70 percent of the long-run marginal costs of supply.

• Institutions differ, and hence regulatory agencies cannot be easily transplanted. Countries differ greatly in their economic structures and in their institutions—the whole chain that includes courts (where appeals are made), legislatures (where laws are passed), the press (which informs the electorate), an engaged public (which demands more from governments), and academia (which trains regulators and encourages studies of problems). These institutional differences across countries determine why what is sound regulation in one country is ineffectual in another. They are analogous to the differences in performance of state-owned firms: they are disappointing in some countries (India, Mexico) but not in others (Sweden or France).

Pensions are an area in which the private sector's contribution has most clearly fallen short of expectations. Eastern European countries with almost universal pension coverage trimmed the benefits of their defined benefit schemes, out of fiscal necessity. Many Latin American countries sought to phase out their defined benefit schemes and replace them with mandatory coverage by private providers through defined contribution schemes. Few of these schemes have lived up to their billing: despite favorable demography their coverage remains low because of the small size of the private formal labor market; their administrative costs have been high, partly because insurance costs are included and partly because of start-up costs, and they remain dependent on government finances because there are few securities besides government paper to invest in. There was really no way to isolate these countries' social security and pension schemes from their governments without allowing them a greater range of investment in external markets.

## The Impact of Financial Liberalization on Growth Depends on Underlying Institutions and on Macroeconomic Management

Over the 1980s and 1990s, as part of the general shift to a more market-oriented economy, the approach to finance shifted away from holding down interest rates, limiting competition, and relying on governments to allocate credit and toward more market-based, internationally open systems. Financial liberalization reflected the reaction to the costs, corruption, and inefficiencies of financial repression; the demands of government and the public for more financial resources and services; and the pressures from greater trade, travel, and migration, and better telecommunications.

Contrary to expectations, financial liberalization did not add much to growth, and it appears to have augmented the number of crises. As expected, deposits and capital inflows rose sharply as a result of liberalization. But, other than in a few East Asian and South Asian countries, capital markets did not provide resources for new firms. Numbers of stock market listings declined, even in the newly created markets in the transition countries that were sometimes used for privatizations. Also, although relevant time-series data on access are weak, and contrary to expectations, it appears that access to financial services did not improve substantially after liberalization.

The explanation for these disappointing outcomes lies largely in weak institutions, concentrated economic and political power, and macroeconomic shocks. The implicit and explicit guarantees that were extended to depositors and investors weakened the market discipline that might have limited the activities of weak lenders. By the end of the 1990s, much of the deposit growth had been absorbed by central bank debt and government deficits. The state banks, which remained important during the 1990s, and financial industrial conglomerates used their increased deposits to expand lending to state enterprises, well-connected borrowers, and other parts of financial-industrial conglomerates. Regulation and supervision were weak, reflecting not just technical problems but also political pressures for leniency. Eventually the poor quality of lending was exposed in crises, as were the weaknesses of the bank privatizations in the context of the weak institutional environment and the exclusion, in many cases, of international banks.

The lack of improved credit access reflected not only the preemptive borrowing by the public sector and central banks but also weak informational and legal frameworks. Lack of information on borrowers hindered lenders and gave borrowers no incentive to maintain a good credit record. Weak legal and judicial frameworks (designed to protect borrowers and often responsive to economic and political elites) reduced the incentives to service debts; they made it difficult for new borrowers to gain access to finance by pledging collateral effectively and made it difficult for lenders to execute collateral.

The 1990s reinforced the old lesson that successful financial liberalization depends on macroeconomic management. No banking system, however sound in principle, can withstand a serious macroeconomic crisis. Dealing with a banking crisis is quite complex, involving highly political issues of liquidity support to banks (which can easily contribute to capital flight and devaluation), bank closure, and handling of explicit and implicit guarantees to depositors; experience in the 1990s suggests that it is difficult to avoid socializing the losses and a fall in output. Further, open capital accounts and volatile international capital flows place a large premium on sound macroeconomic management. Internationally, few attempts have been made to reduce the volatility of capital inflows (reducing volatility depends on limiting the upside, not just trying to stop outflows when a crisis develops). Chile's implicit taxes on short-term inflows appear to have had success in extending maturities, reducing inflows, and limiting volatility against small shocks, albeit at the cost of reducing credit availability to the private sector (Edwards 1999; Forbes 2003). Part of India's success in avoiding a 1997 crisis stemmed from its limits on banks' (and firms') offshore borrowing, even as it allowed inflows into the stock market and eased direct foreign investment. Indonesia's limits on state banks' external borrowing did reduce their growth, but excessive inflows to private banks and corporations were a major factor in the 1997 crisis. Except for Chile's taxes on short-term flows and some attempts to hold down interest rates, countries have made few attempts to remove the

incentives to banks for increasing their offshore borrowings. All attempts at limiting excessive inflows depend on political will to restrict them during a boom. In practice, countries often have eased restrictions on capital inflows to prolong a boom with negative consequences when the flows necessarily slowed.

Improvements are being made in regulation and supervision in an attempt to limit financial crises, but experience in the industrial countries, where political and economic power is more diffuse than in developing countries, suggests that this will not be easy. In the United States, for example, financial economists have raised concerns about some U.S. banks being too big to fail. Also in the United States, political forces and regulatory forbearance are often cited as contributory factors in the savings and loan crisis. In many developing countries a few large banks, often state-owned, dominate the system. Bankers and major borrowers are often one and the same. Limits on connected lending are a problem because the industrial-financial groups are also the main entrepreneurs in many countries, even large ones. If problems of loan quality develop, the political strength of the economic and political elite will likely lead to regulatory forbearance in loan classification and provisioning standards. These kinds of problems suggest that attempts to improve the regulatory and supervisory framework need to include a substantial effort to improve market discipline, through better information on the banks and credible limits on deposit guarantees. Increased entry of well-known foreign banks, which have a reputation to protect, can also improve the functioning of the system.

Thus, in finance, the 1990s may best be regarded as a transition period. The high expectations for liberalization were met only in resource mobilization. Resource allocation, which makes a key contribution to development, did not generally improve. However, much of the debris of the old financial system was removed by the crises, albeit by government recapitalization bonds that now represent much of the system's assets.

As the connecting link between savers and investors, the contribution of finance to growth depends not only on macroeconomic stability and reasonable interest rates, but also on the quality of financial intermediaries and information and of the legal and regulatory framework. Improving the contribution of finance to development will depend not only on market-based finance but also on sound institutions, appropriate incentives for lenders, further improvements in informational and legal frameworks, and, ultimately, on a more competitive political system that is able to reduce the power of political-economic elites and their ability to tap the financial system.

## *Pragmatic, Incremental Approaches to Public Sector Governance Are More Effective*

Economic performance depends partly on governance, which in turn is shaped by underlying institutions, defined broadly as the "rules of the game" that shape the behavior of organizations and individuals in a society (North 1990, 3).[6] A crisis of governance of varying intensity pervades much of the developing world, with the poor paying the heaviest price for it.

Public sector reforms in the 1990s sought to change the structure of organs of the state, and incentives within them, in the hope of improving government efficiency and responsiveness. From mega-reforms such as decentralization to less sweeping reforms in budget or personnel management, the aim was to find a balance between the discretion of politicians and bureaucrats over policy making and policy implementation and their accountability for decisions and actions. The fall of authoritarian regimes and the consequent spread of democratic processes constrained the previously wide discretion of many governments. Decentralization sought to further limit central government discretion while granting local governments more managerial autonomy. Legal, judicial, and legislative reforms were initiated to establish institutional checks on executive power. Public management reforms sought to give public managers more flexibility in decision making while demanding greater accountability from them for their decisions. Perhaps partly because of the immense difficulty of addressing problems in political institutions,

many countries and donors in the 1990s focused largely on reforming legal and judicial systems— a channel of political accountability that seemed more amenable to technocratic solutions, often using models directly transplanted from industrialized countries.

Most of the reforms had little effect on behavior. The ills that they sought to treat—non-meritocratic civil services, weak financial controls, opaque or incoherent budget processes—are deeply rooted in local political and institutional arrangements that favor the status quo.

The decade was not all discouraging, however. Homegrown initiatives gave hope for improving government performance. In some instances, civil society engagement and participation and innovative applications of information technology led to improvements in transparency and accountability in public decision making and consequently to some increase in government responsiveness, efficiency, and effectiveness. The challenge is scaling up these initiatives, given political constraints and historical inertia.

The designs of governance reform strategies in the 1990s typically fell into two broad types: "big bang" or ad hoc incrementalism. Big bang approaches proved to be largely inconsistent with capacity constraints and political realities. Their main results were major changes in formal rules: new or amended constitutions, new legislation, ostensibly independent courts and audit institutions, and so forth. Meanwhile, the informal rules shaping the incentives that face politicians, bureaucrats, and citizens remained in place.

Ad hoc incrementalism has also been problematic. Many of the ad hoc reforms were symbolic, intended to preserve the old informal rules while pretending to reform. Some represented well-motivated attempts of individual or small groups of reformers who, for lack of support, were undermined by jealousy, intrigue, or fatigue. More important, they tended to be unrelated to a more coherent reform strategy and thus over time many lost their steam.

An important general lesson is that technocratic responses to the governance crisis work only in very auspicious settings—where there is com-

mitted leadership, a broad-based coalition in support of reform, and sufficient capacity to carry the
reform process forward. Clearly, these conditions
exist in only a few developing countries, and rarely
in those that most need governance reform.

State building is a complex process that
requires time, leadership, and social capital. Governance reforms have to find a delicate balance
consistent with the country's politics, history, and
culture. What may be needed are highly focused,
pragmatic interventions that may be termed
"strategic incrementalism." These interventions
are opportunistic because they exploit the willingness to reform, but they are grounded in political realities and consistent with the capacity
constraints of the country concerned.

## Politics: Checks and Balances Are Central to Accountability and Results, but There Is No Single Way to Achieve Them

Institutions resolve a number of problems in
society, of which two are particularly important:
collective decision-making processes and principal-agent problems.[7] Not all preferences can be
represented in collective decision making, and
principal-agent problems can be reduced but
never resolved.

Both theory and evidence suggest that the
formal rules of democracy do not ensure efficient, accountable, and credible government, and
conversely that nonelected governments are not
incapable of responding to citizens or of acting
accountably. Though the number of elected governments grew significantly in the 1990s, the
decade produced no clear evidence that elected
governments perform better in delivering policies benefiting average citizens than do nonelected ones. The experience did confirm,
however, that relative to the situation in richer
democracies, private investors in most developing-country democracies receive less enforcement of their contractual and property rights,
and average citizens are not as well treated by the
state as special interests.

By the close of the 1990s, we had begun to
understand the complicated interaction of formal political institutions with informal rules and

norms. Elected governments are most likely to
make policies at the expense of the majority and
in favor of narrow segments of the population
when citizens are badly informed about what
government does, when political competitors
cannot make credible promises to voters, and
when society is polarized. Evidence shows that
uninformed or polarized citizens and noncredible politicians undermine the connection
between voters and politicians in democracies.
Long-run economic growth and the provision of
public goods are significantly higher in democracies with more credible politicians, better
informed citizens, and less social polarization.
Nondemocracies vary substantially as well: those
that have internal checks on the exercise of discretion by the executive seem to perform better,
in terms of both growth and public policy performance, than others. The lesson here is that
governments of all kinds, elected or not, are most
credible and most likely to respect property
rights when they face checks and balances on
their decision making.

Another lesson of the 1990s is that policies
fail when citizens cannot hold politicians
accountable for poor performance and when
governments cannot make credible commitments. Credible, sustainable reform depends on
the checks and balances provided through political institutions. In democracies, checks and balances and elections prevent arbitrary policy
reversals by governments. But they are not the
only means to hold governments accountable:
broad-based political parties can in some circumstances substitute for democratic checks and balances in one-party states.

## 5. Operational Implications

The complete operational implications of this
study still need to be fully developed. Some preliminary ideas are outlined below.

### For Analysis

On the analytical front, the first implication is the
need to redress the balance between analysis of

*policy instruments* and analysis of *strategies*—under-standing strategies as coherent sets of actions that are intended to initiate and sustain growth. Over the years, in institutions such as the World Bank, the focus of research gradually has shifted away from country-specific growth experiences to focus increasingly on policies—trade, finance, macro, privatization to name a few—with secondary importance given to country contexts.[8] At the same time, outside the World Bank there has been increasing emphasis on individual country experiences (for example, Rodrik 2003b, and the research programs sponsored by the Global Development Network).

The second implication is the need to recognize country specificities in country economic analysis, acknowledging that policies are conceived and implemented within a specific institutional, social, and historic context. Recent economic and sector work at the World Bank already seeks to achieve a better balance between country specificities and the lessons from country experiences, but more is needed fully to recognize that country-specific market structures and institutions have a strong influence on policy outcomes. In particular, this recognition calls for harder and more rigorous economic, institutional, and social analysis.

Third, analytical work needs to change its orientation, away from seeking to assess how far policies diverge from optimality, to seeking to assess what policy and institutional conditions—for capital accumulation, shared growth, productivity growth, and risk taking in a country-specific context—are needed to set the growth process in motion.

## For Strategy

There is a need to rethink the focus of growth strategies and of development assistance. Up to now, that focus has been on the nation state with the implicit assumptions that (1) development outcomes within the boundaries of a nation state are homogeneous, and (2) all developing countries' per capita incomes could and should converge with those of industrialized countries. There is now greater evidence and

acknowledgment that these two assumptions do not always hold. Convergence is much less a force now than anticipated a decade or more ago. Within countries such as Brazil, China, and India, income differences across regions are as large as income differences across countries, and even in relatively small Bolivia, income differences between the lowlands and the highlands are large. This recognition implies a need to pay much greater attention to the forces driving agglomeration and migration, both within and across countries.

## For Research

On the research front, two issues in particular warrant further examination. The first relates to development agencies' role in aid-dependent countries. The agencies' large role in financing the budget has forced them to be involved in budget processes, weakening national decision making and rendering the concept of "ownership elusive in practice" (Kwesi Botchwey, World Bank 2005a), particularly in aid-dependent Africa. Clearly, forms of engagement developed for project finance do not apply to budget finance. There may be a need to explore new approaches to the transfer of resources to these countries, rooted in public finance, such as those typically used in federated nations that have chosen rule-based, arms-length systems of transfers.

Second, the unit of analysis for economic and social development has traditionally been the nation state, reflecting the assumptions (outlined above) that nations are homogeneous and that all nations would be able to catch up to the income levels of industrialized countries. There is a rich research agenda on these assumptions that needs to be articulated. All nations may not succeed in reaching industrialized countries' income levels within a reasonable time frame—partly because institutions can take such a long time to develop, but also because the economics of agglomeration and poles of development do not necessarily follow national boundaries. Research in this area may yield important implications for the role of nations and migration, and also for the optimal degree of discretion regarding national policies.

## For Operations

On the operational front, the recognition that not everything needs to be right for growth to succeed, and that partial success may sometimes be a more pragmatic goal than optimal policies, has obvious consequences for the type and extent of conditionality associated with development lending. Again in this case, more rigorous economic analysis should help to distinguish what are binding constraints, and thus to inform decisions. The record suggests that forecasts need to be realistic and mindful of the forces driving growth.

## For Behavior

On the behavioral front, if solutions must be found in specific-country contexts, rather than applied from blueprints, those who advise or finance developing countries will need more humility in their approaches, implying more openness on the range of solutions possible, more empathy with the country's perspectives, and more inquisitiveness in assessing the costs and benefits of different possible solutions.

## Notes

1. See Country Note C, "Poverty and Inequality: What Have We Learned from the 1990s?"
2. Countries successful at "converging" include most South Asian countries (Bangladesh, Bhutan, India, Nepal, Sri Lanka); many East Asian countries (China, Indonesia, the Republic of Korea, Lao PDR, Malaysia, Thailand, Vietnam); and Botswana, Chile, the Arab Republic of Egypt, Lesotho, Mauritius, and Tunisia. See Country Note B, "Lessons from Countries That Have Sustained Their Growth."

3. This point of view was reinforced by the fiasco of the collapse of the Southern Cone stabilization programs of the late 1970s, in which strong currency appreciations combined with rapid reductions in tariffs to create an adverse shock to industry, ultimately derailing the stabilization programs. Most analysts soon blamed the collapse on excessive speed, leading to faulty sequencing of the reform program: they argued that capital accounts had been liberalized too soon, without waiting until fiscal probity had been established and both trade and the domestic financial system had been successfully liberalized.
4. This study reviewed the growth experience of eight economies: China, Hong Kong (China), Indonesia, Japan, Korea, Malaysia, Taiwan, Thailand, and Singapore. The report highlighted the variations in policy and institutional environments under which these economies reached unprecedented rates of growth. It emphasized that, with few exceptions, the state in the economies studied had taken an activist role to stimulate risk taking in both the private and the public sector. It concluded that while highly successful in East Asia, the institutions needed for replicating this activist role may not be present in other contexts.
5. It has been argued, for example, that the increase in India's growth rate in the early 1980s was less the result of the reforms introduced at that time than of the private sector's changing expectations regarding the future—where the government was credible in ensuring reduced expropriation risks and a more welcoming environment (Rodrik and Subramanian 2004).
6. Public sector governance refers to how the state acquires and exercises the authority to provide and manage public goods and services. Corruption, which refers to the use of public office for private gain, is the mirror image of governance: bad governance invariably leads to corruption; but corruption can likewise perpetrate bad governance.
7. The principal delegates the implementation of a task to an agent but must monitor the agent efficiently to ensure that the task is accomplished.
8. A recent World Bank research project focusing on individual country experiences is *Aid and Reform in Africa* (World Bank 2001c).

*Part 1*

# Facts of the 1990s

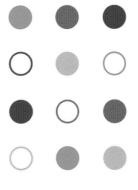

*Chapter 2*

# Grist and the Mill for the Lessons of the 1990s

THE ECONOMIC CHANGES OF THE 1990s conformed to no theories. In this chapter we review the lessons that can be drawn from the economic events of the decade, and also the new ideas, theories, and issues that were born of those events and of efforts to order and understand them. To be sure, facts and ideas so clearly affect one another that it is difficult to separate them cleanly: what constitutes the relevant "facts" is determined by ideas, while new ideas are often the result of attempts to grapple with the facts. Nevertheless, distinctions are helpful to organize the discussion, so section 1 reviews the facts about developing countries' economic performance that form grist for the mill of lessons, and section 2 discusses the ideas that came on to the development agenda in the 1990s.

## 1. Events of the 1990s: Disappointments and Pleasant Surprises

Perhaps the most important experiences of the 1990s are those that defied not just forecasts but conditional forecasts. Lessons, pleasant and unpleasant alike, emerge from unexpected occurrences.[1]

Assessing whether outcomes are surprising requires a model that implicitly or explicitly links causes with outcomes. Thoughtful people continually update their working mental models in response to events,[2] and this continuous learning makes the empirical sources of lessons very difficult to isolate in retrospect. Hence this chapter attempts to measure the events of the 1990s against the conventional wisdom of the mainstream of development economists. To pin down that elusive concept we choose the specific expression of the *zeitgeist* as the World Bank's 1991 *World Development Report* (*WDR 1991*). So, had someone known in 1990 the direction and magnitude of the changes in politics, policy, and institutional reform, and known how the global economic environment unfolded in the 1990s, and had they used roughly the same model of market-friendly development as the *WDR 1991*, which of the economic outcomes of the 1990s would they *not* have predicted?

On this basis, the 1990s produced five disappointments and three pleasant surprises. The five disappointments are:

- The length, depth, and variance across countries of the output loss in the transition from planned to market economies in the former Soviet Union (FSU) and Eastern European countries.

- The severity and intensity of the international and domestic financial crises that rolled through East Asia.

- Argentina's financial and economic implosion after the collapse of its currency convertibility regime.

- The weakness of the response of growth to reform, especially in Latin America, and the unpopularity of many of the reforms.

- The continued stagnation in Sub-Saharan Africa, the paucity of success cases there, and the apparent wilting of optimism around the "African Renaissance."

The three pleasant surprises are:

- Bright spots of sustained rapid growth, especially in China, India, and Vietnam, throughout the decade (box 2.1).

- The strong progress in noneconomic indicators of well-being in spite of low growth in some cases.

- The resilience of the world economy to stresses.

## Five Disappointments

### 1. Output Losses during the Transition in the FSU and Eastern Europe

Everyone knew that the transition from a communist, centrally planned economy to a capitalist

---

**BOX 2.1**
**Per Capita Growth in the 1990s: Forecast and Actual**

The figure below compares actual per capita gross domestic product (GDP) growth in the 1990s with the forecasts either offered in the *WDR 1991* or made in the early 1990s. The forecasts correctly predicted the rough direction—that Africa would grow slowly and East Asia fast—but made mistakes in exactly the regions one would expect. Growth was overestimated for Sub-Saharan Africa, Latin America and the Caribbean, Eastern Europe (excluding the former Soviet Union), and Eastern Europe and Central Asia (including the former Soviet Union), and underestimated for India (and South Asia) and China (and East Asia). The Middle East and North Africa, a region about which *WDR 1991* said little, grew at almost exactly the pace forecast.

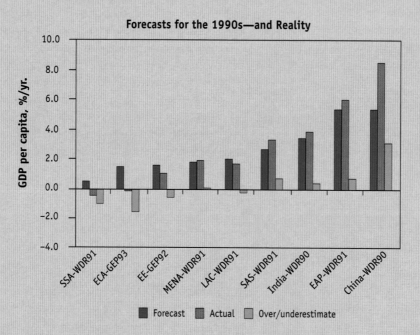

**Forecasts for the 1990s—and Reality**

■ Forecast   ■ Actual   ■ Over/underestimate

*Note:* SSA: Sub-Saharan Africa; ECA: Eastern Europe and Central Asia; EE: Eastern Europe (excluding Russian Federation); MENA: Middle East and North Africa; LAC: Latin America and Caribbean; SAS: South Asia; EAP: East Asia and Pacific.

economy of one type or another would be neither smooth nor easy. Anticipation that adjustment costs would cause output to fall and then to rise led to the expectation of some "transformational recession" (Kornai 2000c), but the depth and duration of the recession were hard to forecast.

In fact, the depth of the contraction in transition countries is striking. At the trough, their GDP per capita (unweighted) was a mere 42 percent of its pretransition peak (figure 2.1). The contractions in individual countries ranged from 20 percent in some countries to about the average in the Russian Federation and to more than 60 percent in Ukraine.[3]

Data through 2002 show that for most of the FSU/Eastern European countries, the transition has lasted more than a decade, and that for many it will last much longer.[4] While some countries (for example, Poland, Hungary) now have output greater than their pretransition levels, *on average* the Eastern European/FSU countries are only at 84 percent of their pretransition output. For example, even if Ukraine managed to grow steadily at 5 percent a year, starting in 2002, it would take until 2017 to regain its previous peak—implying a transformational recession of more than a quarter of a century at best.

A few historical and contemporary reference points provide useful perspective to the fall in output and the length of the transition:

- In OECD-country recessions, the typical peak-to-trough fall in GDP since 1950 has been only 2.3 percent.

- In Indonesia, the worst-hit of the countries that were affected by the 1997 Asian crisis, GDP per capita fell by 17 percent, and regained its previous level four years after the onset of the crisis.

- In the United States during the Great Depression, output per capita fell by 31 percent, and recovered to its precrisis level in 10 years.

- While the data are obviously somewhat uncertain, the output fall from pre–World War II peak (1938) to postwar trough was 51 percent in (West) Germany and 45 percent in Japan; both of these countries regained their

FIGURE 2.1

**Depth and Duration of the Transformational Recession: Eastern European and Former Soviet Union Countries**

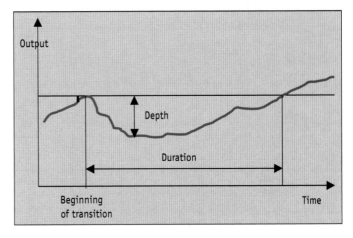

*Source:* Author's own elaboration (for illustration purposes only).

1938 level of output by 1953—eight years after the end of the conflict.

Not even the most pessimistic observers in 1990 foresaw that the *typical* transition recession would be substantially larger than the Great Depression in the United States and that the time taken to recover would be more than twice as long as for the defeated countries after World War II.

A further surprise is the enormous variation in the depth and length of the transition across countries. A substantial part of this variation can be attributed to the speed and depth of policy reform (see, for example, World Bank 2002c) or suitability for capitalism. Almost no one is surprised that the transitional recession was shallow and short in the Czech Republic, Hungary, or Poland, all of which had the advantages of a more European heritage—and hence were eligible for early discussion of accession to the European Union—and being "good reformers." More surprising is an apparent U-shaped relationship between countries' proximity to Europe and the depth and duration of the transition (Mukand and Rodrik 2002). Conditions were much worse in Georgia and Ukraine than in more distant parts of the former Soviet Union such as Uzbekistan, Kyrgyz Republic, and Turkmenistan (figure 2.2).

FIGURE 2.2

## Depth of the Recession, Ratio of Current to Pretransition Output, and Relationship with Distance from Brussels

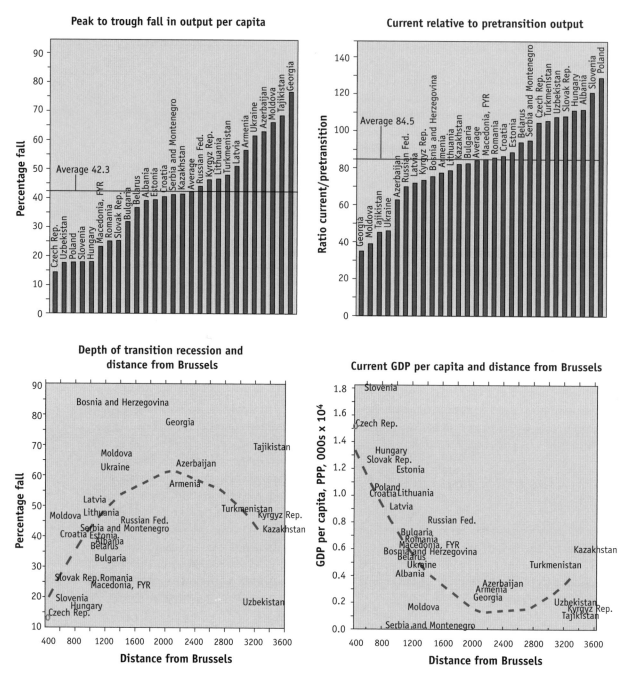

*Source:* Mukand and Rodrik 2002; EBRD 2003.

## 2. East Asian Financial Crisis

The 1990s saw a string of financial crises in which the exchange rate, banking system, and internal and external debt interacted in ways that sharply depressed output—with adverse effects on wages, poverty, jobs, and living standards—and caused large losses in the banking system. Macroeconomists, bank restructuring experts, and the emerging-market private traders rolled from crisis to crisis—notably in Mexico during 1994–95; the Republic of Korea, Thailand, and Indonesia during 1997–98; Russia and Brazil in 1998; and Turkey in 2000—to the most recent and perhaps most worrisome of all, Argentina during 2001–02.

It is worthwhile to discard any presumption that all of these crises teach the same lesson, or that they necessarily teach new ones. There are two reasons why.

First, that there *were* financial crises in the 1990s cannot count as a surprise. Every decade of the 20th century has seen a financial crisis in at least some major countries. Crises have been more common in the period of floating exchange rates (since the early 1970s) than previously (Eichengreen 2002). But the boom-and-bust cycle of exuberant capital inflows followed by sharp curtailments of lending was a continuing, not a new, phenomenon in the 1990s.

Second, some of the crises of the 1990s reinforce old lessons. The links between financial crises and banking sector crises reinforced lessons from the 1980s, in which a number of financial crises in Latin America led to large banking losses (Caprio and Honohan 2001); the 1990s' financial crises required large shares of GDP to reestablish sound banks. Turkey's crisis, as does that in the Southern Cone in the 1980s, teaches the dangers of exchange-rate-based stabilization programs with inflation inertia and open capital accounts. Arguably, the Russian crisis teaches the old lesson that if one loses control of the fiscal situation, sooner or later the economy will spiral out of control. And, except for its speed and intensity, the Mexican crisis of 1994 was not fundamentally surprising.

By contrast, however, the crisis in East Asia *was* a surprise. Even by June 1997 no one had predicted it. One way of illustrating its wholly unexpected magnitude, and the speed with which it came on, is to compare the nominal interest-rate differentials, between borrowing in local currency and in U.S. dollars, with the realized depreciations (figure 2.3).

Even as late as June 1997, the interest rate differential was less than 10 percentage points. Yet between June and December 1997 the currencies of all three countries depreciated by more than 80 percent. To be sure, uncovered interest parity often fails as a predictor of exchange rates. But the magnitude of the difference and the fact that private sector actors were making huge, unhedged transactions at these interest rate differentials emphasize that the world's financial markets, and not just complacent government bureaucracies or hidebound multilateral institutions or academics, were caught unawares.

The crisis in East Asian countries was surprising because it did not share the characteristics of many previous exchange rate crises: slow growth or declining output, large and growing public sector fiscal imbalances, large public sector

---

FIGURE 2.3

**Interest Rate Differentials Did Not Predict the Magnitude of the Impending Devaluation of Three East Asian Currencies**

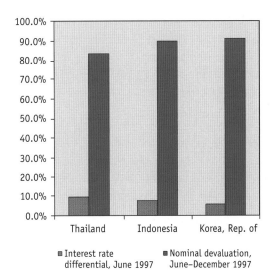

■ Interest rate differential, June 1997    ■ Nominal devaluation, June–December 1997

*Source:* Staff calculation from *World Development Indicators 2003* and *International Financial Statistics 2003.*

indebtedness, or obvious substantial and persistent overvaluation of the currency. Even with the benefit of hindsight, economists had a hard time creating empirical models that predicted it (Radelet and Sachs 1998) and even observers who argue that the crisis was driven by "fundamentals" concede that its timing and intensity were not anticipated.

### 3. Collapse of the Convertibility Regime in Argentina

Economically, the decade known as the 1990s could be said to end with the Argentina crisis of 2001. This crisis deserves special mention as a surprise because Argentina had provided the clearest and, for the better part of the 1990s, most successful example of a trend to reinforce macroeconomic stability by reducing the discretion of the government through legal and institutional changes. The exchange rate arrangements that made the *peso* convertible at a fixed rate were made part of the legal environment (and a part that was especially difficult to alter) and changes were made in the operation of the central bank to make the convertibility immutable. As part of a package of reforms, the convertibility plan was enormously successful at eliminating Argentina's hyperinflation and, for a period, in restoring economic growth.

It is no surprise that the demise of the convertibility plan was messy politically (the president resigned before the end of his term), or economically, since the demise had been made very costly by design. What is surprising is the demise itself. First, the plan's initial successes had suggested that longevity was possible. The plan succeeded in reducing rapid inflation and initiating a boom in the early 1990s, and it weathered the "Tequila" aftershocks of the Mexican crisis reasonably well. Second, the plan was popular domestically and praised internationally during nearly all of the 1990s, and everyone knew that ending it would be costly.[5]

### 4. Lack of Rapid Growth, Particularly in Latin America

Hopes were high that the so-called lost decade of the 1980s in Latin America would be followed by the "found decade" of the 1990s. Surely the substantial and painful first-generation economic reforms—macroeconomic stabilization, fiscal austerity, trade liberalization, privatization—would pay off with rapid growth and poverty reduction. Today, the general perception is that the growth payoff has been smaller than expected (figure 2.4).

An index of economic reform (Lora 2001a) suggests that during the 1990s the economic climate improved substantially for nearly every country in the region. Not only did the region-wide mean improve, but the variance among countries declined as well (figure 2.5). This index suggests that policies were better in nearly *every* country in Latin America in 1999 than they were in Chile in 1985.

Growth in GDP per capita did not reflect these improvements in policy. In the early 1990s it appeared that the policy changes were finally paying off, but by 1995 the Mexican crisis had a dampening effect on the region. Then when another recovery seemed to be in the making, the international financial crises and their repercussions pushed per capita growth rates to about zero, where they have fluctuated since 1998.

Loayza, Fajnzylber, and Calderón (2002) assess with depth and care the extent to which

FIGURE 2.4

**Growth Was Much Slower in the 1980s and 1990s than Predicted by Empirical Models That Linked Growth to Policy Reform**

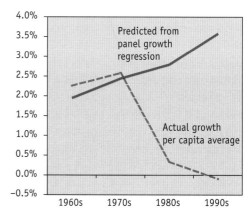

*Source*: Easterly 2002.

FIGURE 2.5

**Although Nearly Every Country in Latin America and the Caribbean Has Pursued Economic Reform, Growth Has Been Slow**

Distribution of reform index for 16 Latin America and Caribbean countries
(box plots showing mean, 10th, 25th, 75th, and 90th percentiles)

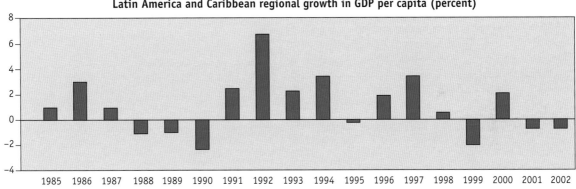

Latin America and Caribbean regional growth in GDP per capita (percent)

*Source:* Lora (2001a) for data on reform; *WDI 2003* for growth.

the growth outcomes in Latin America are a surprise. The authors do regressions that relate growth to transitional convergence and cyclical reversion, structural policies and institutions, stabilization policies, and external conditions. They find that the growth rate changes between any two decades can be attributed to changes in policy outcomes across the two periods, but that the effect is very small.

As shown in column 2 of table 2.1, the authors find that the coefficients on all of the classes of variables (excepting the institutional indicators) have the expected signs and statistical significance. Their analysis suggests, for instance, that because of the increase in secondary enrollment rates between the 1980s and 1990s, growth should have increased by 0.7 percent per year.[6]

All other variables are similarly calculated.

The results thus raise two striking points. First, they do not measure up to expectations about the effectiveness of policy reform. For instance, for Brazil they suggest that the impact of all structural and stabilization policies (except for education) was to slow the country's growth rate during the 1990s by 0.34 percent per year. Most Brazilian policy makers, if not most Brazilians, would probably be surprised to learn that the policy environment in the 1990s was (net of education) less conducive to economic growth than in the 1980s.[7] This unexpected result may partly reflect the fact that actual growth coefficients are in some sense smaller than popularly conceived, or than were reported in "selling" policy reform; after all, the link between policy

TABLE 2.1

# Growth Regressions and "Policy" Impacts, with Two Country Examples

| | | | Contributions to growth (% per year) of the various growth correlates—calculated as the difference across the two decades in the variable times the regression coefficient | | | |
|---|---|---|---|---|---|---|
| | Estimates (coeff., | | Brazil | | Bolivia | |
| Category | Variable | t-stat.) | 1990s vs.1980s | 1990s vs. 1970s | 1990s vs. 1980s | 1990s vs. 1970s |
| Cyclical and convergence | Initial GDP per capita | −.018 (3.80) | 0.03 | −0.68 | 0.11 | 0.13 |
| | Cyclical recovery | −.227 (8.52) | 0.89 | −0.31 | −0.02 | −0.58 |
| | Growth rate of TOT | .072 (4.98) | 0.27 | 0.24 | −0.12 | 0.04 |
| Structural and "institutions" | Log "policies" (secondary enrollment) | .017 (6.7) | 0.7 | 1.21 | 0.11 | 0.47 |
| | Log (private domestic credit/GDP) | .0066 (4.28) | 0.13 | 0.07 | 0.81 | 0.87 |
| | Log (SATI/GDP) | .0096 (3.14) | 0.41 | 0.37 | 0.33 | 0.28 |
| | Log (government consumption/GDP) | −.015 (3.18) | −0.72 | −0.91 | −0.26 | −0.28 |
| | Log (main telephone lines per capita) | .0071 (2.71) | 0.36 | 0.87 | 0.36 | 0.39 |
| | PC ICRG indicators | −.0012 (.68) | | | — | |
| Stabilization "policies" | Log (100+inflation rate) | −.0048 (1.89) | 0.14 | −0.51 | 0.88 | 0.04 |
| | Std. dev. output gap | −.277 (3.76) | 0.14 | 0.24 | 0.08 | −0.06 |
| | RER overvaluation | −.0061 (3.90) | −0.13 | −0.02 | 0.17 | 0.19 |
| | Systemic banking crisis | −.029 (7.42) | −0.67 | −0.96 | 0.58 | 0 |
| Unexplained period effects | | | −0.48 | −1.72 | −0.48 | −1.72 |
| | | | Contribution to shifts in growth | | | |
| Structural policies | | | .88 | 1.61 | 1.35 | 1.73 |
| Stabilization policies | | | −0.52 | −1.25 | 1.71 | 0.17 |
| Total policies | | | 0.36 | 0.36 | 3.06 | 1.9 |
| Total policies less education | | | −0.34 | −0.85 | 2.95 | 1.43 |
| Projected *change* in growth | | | 1 | −2.12 | 2.54 | −0.23 |
| Actual *change* in growth rate | | | 1.49 | −4.68 | 3.48 | −0.14 |
| Actual growth 1990s | | | 1.07 | 1.07 | 1.53 | 1.53 |
| Actual growth 1980s (col. 3, 5)/1970s (col. 4, 6) | | | −0.42 | 5.75 | −1.95 | 1.67 |

*Source*: Loayza, Fajnzylber, and Calderón 2002, tables II.2, D3, D4.

*Note*: TOT stands for terms of trade; SATI stands for structurally adjusted trade intensity, and measures openness to trade; PC stands for principal component, which extracts the most salient features of the various governance indicators measured by the ICRG, the International Country Risk Guide (www.icrgonline.co); RER stands for real exchange rate.

actions and policy outcomes and growth was often not explicitly quantified. The regression implies that reducing inflation from one standard deviation above the mean to the mean—that is, a reduction in inflation of 60 percentage points, from 80 percent per year to 20 percent per year—would lead growth to increase by 0.2 percent per year (barely a tenth of a cross-national standard deviation in growth rates).[8] Certainly, no one has ever advocated a stabilization package on the basis of a 0.2 percent per year gain in long-run growth.

Second, this careful econometric analysis of growth emphasizes that slower growth in the 1990s remains a mystery. The growth regressions include "unexplained" period variables that allow growth to be lower, all else being equal. The estimated impact of the period variable for the 1990s versus that for the 1970s is 1.72 percent per year; thus a country with exactly the same policies in the 1990s as in the 1970s would grow 1.72 percent per year more slowly in the 1990s than in the 1970s. The implications can be seen from column 6 of table 2.1, for Bolivia: while policies predict Bolivia's growth to be 1.9 percent per year *faster* in the 1990s than in the 1970s, the net predicted growth in the 1990s is actually *slower* by 0.23 percent per year, because the positive impacts of policy are offset by the period effect of 1.72 percent per year (and negative cyclical reversion impacts). Bolivians may well ask, "Wait a second. We did all these stabilization and structural policy changes and grew at 1.53 percent per year in the 1990s, whereas in the bad old 1970s we grew at 1.67 percent per year—*¿qué pasa?*" The answer this empirical analysis gives is that without policy reform, Bolivia's economy would have contracted—because of a large, unexplained reduction in growth in the 1990s that is common to all countries. This hardly provides a satisfactory resolution to the question of slower growth.

## 5. Continued Stagnation in Sub-Saharan Africa

The failure to create real engines of growth in Sub-Saharan Africa must count as a disappointment, if not a surprise.[9] Despite declared good intentions, a historic process of debt relief, continued unprecedented levels of official assistance, pressure for policy reform, promising developments in governance, and a not terribly unfavorable external climate, no widespread and definitive take-off has occurred. Living standards and real incomes have declined precipitously in many countries. No country has achieved sustained growth sufficient to transform its economy and pull its neighbors along. A particular disappointment has been the failure of South Africa and Nigeria—the two largest economies and potential growth engines for their respective regions—to develop into economic powerhouses.

## Four Pleasant Surprises

The more positive developments of the 1990s also hold lessons.

### 1. Sustained Rapid Growth in China, India, Vietnam, and Several Other Countries

The adoption of market-oriented and globalizing reforms paid off in extraordinarily rapid growth and rapid poverty reduction in the 1990s in formerly socialist and planned economies of Asia, including India and China, which together account for 40 percent of the developing world's population (figures 2.6 and 2.7).

The methodological details of the measurement of poverty generate substantial disagreement,[10] but there is no question that China, India, and Vietnam have drastically reduced destitution (consumption-expenditure poverty based on the dollar-a-day standard) and poverty (measured using national standards). Headcount poverty at the international standard of roughly US\$1 per day has been halved in a single decade. In Vietnam, 30 percent of the population has moved out of absolute poverty (defined using a national standard) since 1993—a historic accomplishment.

The successes of these three countries during the 1990s are particularly important because they preclude any facile reaction to the experiences of the former Soviet and Eastern European countries and Latin America. If one believes that market-friendly and globalizing policies will increase

FIGURE 2.6

## Accelerating Growth in China, India, and Vietnam

### Evolution of GDP per capita, India, 1950–2000

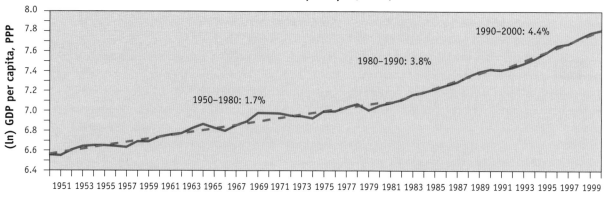

1950–1980: 1.7%

1980–1990: 3.8%

1990–2000: 4.4%

### Evolution of GDP per capita, China, 1952–2000

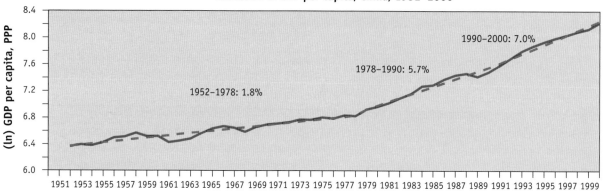

1952–1978: 1.8%

1978–1990: 5.7%

1990–2000: 7.0%

### Evolution of GDP per capita, Vietnam, 1976–1999

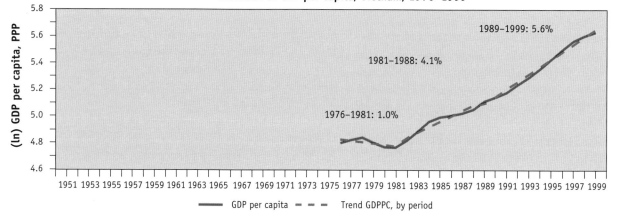

1976–1981: 1.0%

1981–1988: 4.1%

1989–1999: 5.6%

———— GDP per capita    – – – Trend GDPPC, by period

*Note:* PPP stands for purchasing power parity; GDPPC stands for GDP per capita.

*Source:* Author's calculations from Aten, Heston, and Summers (2001).

FIGURE 2.7

**Poverty Reduction Was Rapid in India, China, and Vietnam in the 1990s**

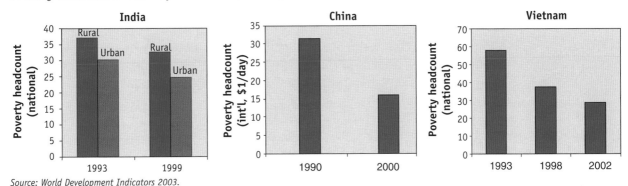

*Source: World Development Indicators 2003.*

*Note:* The 1993 data are from the 50th round of the National Sample Survey; the 1999 data are from the 55th round.

growth, then perhaps the three Asian countries represent the expected rule and the others represent the exception. There is much to be said for this view, but there are three senses in which the Asian countries may not match the conventional wisdom.

First, the reforms these countries undertook in the 1990s were pursued in a gradual, piecemeal, and, many would argue, heterodox fashion. China dramatically reduced the fraction of production supplied by state-owned enterprises, but much less by privatizing existing assets than by allowing the entry of new firms. Especially in the early stages, the new firms were not private enterprises in the usual sense but township and village enterprises. And though India undertook trade reform, it did so in a very gradual way: though its average tariffs fell dramatically, it retained some of the highest tariffs in the world.

Second, while they were near the top of the charts on growth performance, these countries were far from perfect in their policies and institutions during the 1990s. Table 2.2 ranks the three countries on four indicators of the quality of governance that are often thought to be important for growth. On all four indicators these countries ranked either near the middle of the range of countries or in the bottom half. For example, while China ranked 3rd in the world in growth, it was only 63rd in the world in control of corruption (by these measures).

Third, after growth in all three countries accelerated in the 1980s, it slowed down in the late 1980s and many observers thought that the growth spurt had had its day. But it then took off again, even more rapidly, in the 1990s (see figure 2.6 above).

Despite the vagaries of the world economy, several other countries experienced take-offs and realized substantial and sustained economic growth in the 1990s. New performers included Chile, with annual GDP growth of 6.4 percent; the Dominican Republic (6.0); Poland (4.5); Bangladesh (4.9); Sri Lanka (5.1); and Uganda (6.8).

## 2. Improvements in Social Indicators despite Economic Stagnation and/or Crisis

Social indicators—particularly basic education and child health—have continued to improve,

TABLE 2.2

**Despite Their Rapid Growth, China, Vietnam, and India Rank Low on Many Measures of Institutional Quality**

| Country | Government effectiveness | Rule of law | Control of corruption | Regulatory quality | Growth |
|---|---|---|---|---|---|
| China | 58 | 103 | 63 | 94 | 3 |
| Vietnam | 80 | 107 | 105 | 135 | 4 |
| India | 79 | 73 | 86 | 101 | 14 |
| Out of: | 180 | 164 | 151 | 180 | 136 |

*Source: Kaufmann, Kraay, and Mastruzzi 2003.*

often in spite of a lack of substantial progress in economic output and in spite of stagnant or falling wages.

Particularly in a number of Latin American countries, enrollment and grade attainment rates improved significantly in the 1990s. Brazil took just 10 years to raise the enrollment rate of the poorest 20 percent of children from 75 to 94 percent (figure 2.8). This progress was the result of a thoroughgoing educational reform that changed the flow of fiscal funds and responsibilities among the center, states, and municipalities. The surprise is that the reform was implemented successfully in a difficult economic environment.

In many instances, negative social impacts of crises were avoided. During Indonesia's deep and dramatic economic crisis, enrollment in both primary and secondary school fell only modestly in the first year and then quickly regained or exceeded precrisis peaks. A recent study tracking the same households over time found that enrollment rates for children aged 7–15 were higher in 2000 than in 1997, before the crisis—and substantially higher for the poor (Strauss et al. 2004). The crisis was accompanied by aggressive efforts

to mitigate the impacts with social safety net programs in education, health, nutrition, and employment (Suryahadi, Sumarto, and Pritchett 2003). The relatively small impact on key social indicators of even a large economic crisis is a pleasant surprise—as many observers had doubted that such mitigating responses were politically or administratively feasible or could be of any economic consequence.

## 3. Resilience of the World Economic Environment

> The biggest misjudgment that I can remember making . . . was the sense of profound pessimism about Russian economic reform that I had in the fall of 1998, and . . . if you had said that by 2003, they would be issuing Eurobonds at 300 basis points spreads, I would have thought that it was absolute madness.
>
> —Lawrence Summers, "Speaking from Experience," lecture at the World Bank, February 2, 2004

While the volatility of capital flows in international capital markets made policy management difficult and imposed large costs, the international economy in the 1990s proved robust to a number of negative shocks (see chapter 3).

First, the overall global economy allowed for reasonably stable growth in exports from developing countries. This was despite the large risks of a major recession in the OECD (had the cycles of the major economic powers coincided), enormous swings in exchange rates, and large problems in Japan. In the 1990s the annual income growth of the high-income countries was 6.8 percent—faster than in either the 1970s or 1980s.

Second, capital flows were resilient. While the volatility of financial flows is a major risk and source of vulnerability, quick recovery of flows in the aftermath of a crisis can smooth the transition path.

Third, in many instances, recoveries from crisis were quite rapid. One of the most frequently mentioned features of globalization is the speed with which money and information can rocket

FIGURE 2.8

**Enrollment Rates of Children Aged 7–14 in Brazil Rose Substantially for All Income Groups—But Most Dramatically for the Poorest**
(percentage)

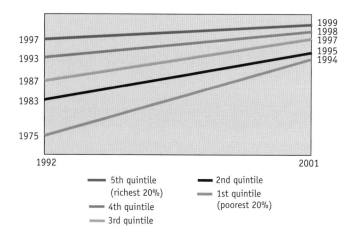

5th quintile (richest 20%)      2nd quintile
4th quintile                     1st quintile (poorest 20%)
3rd quintile

*Source:* "Education in Brazil, 1995–2002." Presentation by Paulo Renato de Souza, former Minister of Education of Brazil.

around the globe.[11] An examination of the speed of output recovery shows that the cost of financial crisis to the trend growth of output ranged from a minor hiccup (as in Korea) to a long-term deceleration (as in Indonesia). As the impressions of policy makers such as Lawrence Summers illustrate, the quick recovery of economic activity (and lowering of spreads) in Russia counts as a pleasant surprise indeed.

## 2. A Mill for the Lessons of the 1990s

During the 1990s three interrelated strands of research provided lessons about economic policy. They focused on:

- The theory and empirics of economic growth;

- The role of institutions; and

- The issue of inequality within and across countries.

All three contributed to, deepened, and in some instances changed the ideas emerging from the 1991 *World Development Report*.

### Growth Theory, Resurgent, Meets Facts about Development

The 1990s saw the resurgence of economic growth theory. To take stock in a few pages of a theoretical and empirical literature that spans thousands of individual papers, the following discussion groups the lessons into four categories:

- New, stylized facts about the growth process in developing countries;

- The new growth theory itself;

- Findings that emerge from the growth-regression literature; and

- Problems with the empirical growth-regression literature.

### New, Stylized Facts of the Growth Process

The resurgence of interest in economic growth, combined with increasingly reliable data on GDP

in comparable purchasing power units both over time (created by Angus Maddison [2002]) and across countries (from the World Bank and the Penn World Tables project on price comparisons) augmented the attention paid to the basic facts of the growth process. In the 1990s the research emphasized four characteristics of that process.

*Growth fact 1:* Among the economically most advanced countries, growth has been steady and nearly equal across countries for more than 100 years (except during World War II and subsequent recovery) (figure 2.9). The average annual growth of GDP per capita in these 16 countries was almost exactly the same during 1890–1910 (at 1.5 percent) as it was during 1970–90 (at 1.8 percent). Except for a boom, with growth averaging more than 3 percent during 1950–70, the growth rate has been very stable. And, except during and just after World War II, growth rates have varied little among the leading countries, with the fastest-growing countries (90th percentile) usually growing only 1–1.5 percent a year faster than the slowest (10th percentile).

*Growth fact 2:* Over the long historical sweep, the steady growth of the industrialized countries has led to widening gaps between them and the

FIGURE 2.9

## Stable Growth in Industrialized Countries

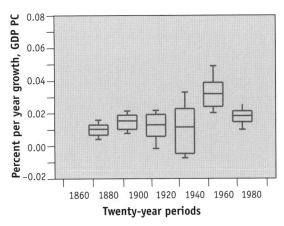

### Distribution of growth rates across OECD by period

*Note:* The figure is a box-plot diagram of the growth rates of GDP per capita of 16 industrialized countries for 20-year periods.

*Source:* Author's calculations based on data from Maddison (1995).

poorer countries (Pritchett 1997). Looking at income inequality among all individuals in the world, figure 2.10 from Bourguignon and Morrison (2002) shows the fraction of the world distribution of income that is due to differences across countries versus the fraction that is due to differences within countries. At the onset of modern economic growth, in the 1820s, only about 10 percent of the inequality was due to differences in average incomes across countries. But between then and roughly 1950, this proportion grew steadily, so that today more than 60 percent of the income inequality in the world is attributable to differences in incomes across countries. Thus in 1820 one's position within the income distribution of one's own country was much the most important factor, but by 1960 the country one lived in was the most important.

*Growth fact 3:* Growth rates differ enormously among the developing countries. Table 2.3 shows the differences in the growth rate of GDP per capita between the rapid and slow-growing countries during periods of 10 years, 20 years, and for 1960–2000—a period for which data exist for nearly all countries. In any given period the difference between the countries in the 10th percentile and in the 90th percentile of the distribution of growth rate is enormous: 6.5 per-

centage points for decades, more than 5.5 percentage points for 20-year periods, and 4.5 percentage points for the 40-year period. Simultaneously, some countries are booming, some are growing slowly, some are caught in stagnation or a poverty trap, and some are experiencing sharp declines.

Large and sustained differences in growth rates lead to large differences in material well-being. If a country with a per capita income of US$1,000 (at purchasing power parity) were to accelerate its growth by 5.7 percent a year—raising its position from the 10th to the 90th percentile in the country growth ranking—then, after a 20-year period, its per capita income would be triple what it would have been otherwise. According to every indicator of material well-being—from child mortality to consumption of electricity—countries at triple the level of income are *qualitatively* different places to live (table 2.4).

*Growth fact 4:* Enormous changes in growth rates occur in nearly every developing country. Three facts emerging from research suggest that countries sustain episodes of growth and make transitions from one growth episode to another.

FIGURE 2.10

**Fraction of World Income Inequality Explained by Differences across Countries**

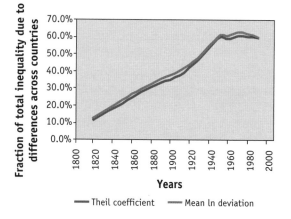

*Source:* Bourguignon and Morrison 2002.

TABLE 2.3

**Growth Rates Differ Enormously across Countries over Periods from One Decade to Forty Years**

| Period | Difference in growth rates in percent per year | |
|---|---|---|
| | Range from 10th to 90th percentile | Two standard deviations |
| 1960s | 6.03 | 4.61 |
| 1970s | 6.96 | 5.55 |
| 1980s | 6.81 | 5.06 |
| 1990s | 6.07 | 5.76 |
| **Average for decades** | **6.47** | **5.25** |
| 1960–80 | 5.41 | 4.07 |
| 1970–90 | 6.23 | 4.64 |
| 1980–2000 | 5.59 | 4.34 |
| **Average for two decades** | **5.74** | **4.35** |
| 1960–2000 | 4.52 | 3.83 |

*Source:* Author's calculations from Aten, Heston, and Summers (2001).

TABLE 2.4

## A Growth Rate of 5.7 Percent per Year Higher for 20 Years Would Roughly Triple a Country's per Capita Income

| Country | GDP per capita, $ purchasing power parity | Under-5 child mortality rate | Primary school completion | Poverty ($1/day) | Access to improved water | Electricity usage (kWh/capita) |
|---|---|---|---|---|---|---|
| **Countries about $1,000** | | | | | | |
| Benin | 1,020 | 158 | 39 | | 50 | 43 |
| Eritrea | 950 | 111 | 35 | | 7 | |
| Nepal | 1,350 | 91 | 65 | 37.7 | 44 | 39 |
| **Countries about $3,000** | | | | | | |
| Indonesia | 2,990 | 45 | 91 | 15.2 | 62 | 329 |
| Ecuador | 3,130 | 30 | 96 | 20.2 | 70 | 611 |
| Sri Lanka | 3,390 | 19 | 100 | 6.6 | 46 | 227 |
| **Countries about $9,000** | | | | | | |
| Chile | 9,180 | 12 | 99 | 4.2 | 85 | 2,011 |
| Malaysia | 8,280 | 8 | — | | 89 | 2,352 |

*Source: WDI 2003.*

The three facts are a lack of persistence of growth rates over time (Easterly et al. 1993); a large deceleration of growth in the 1980s (Ben-David and Papell 1994); and large changes in countries' growth rates, often around specific episodes of acceleration or deceleration (Hausmann, Pritchett, and Rodrik 2004). While it had long been emphasized that growth was volatile over the business cycle of three to five years, growth rates have now been found highly volatile over the medium run (10 to 20 years). Unlike most industrial countries, which grow at a remarkably steady pace, growth in most developing countries involves booms, busts, and periods of stagnation alongside periods of rapid growth (figure 2.11) Very few developing countries have been able to sustain growth for longer than two decades.[12] The accelerations and decelerations in growth rates from one period to another are often as large as the differences across countries. Therefore research has focused not only on average growth rates over arbitrary periods (5, 10, 20 years) but also on the initiation of periods of decline and of acceleration. Among the many episodes of rapid growth, some end in busts, some revert to slow growth, and some continue (table 2.5).

For example, Mauritius is an African country that has achieved rapid growth (Subramanian and Roy 2001), but growth in Mauritius has been far from steady. Using the method outlined in Hausmann, Pritchett, and Rodrik (2004) for dating growth episodes, it is shown that Mauritius has had two episodes in which growth accelerated, beginning in 1971 and again in 1983, with growth petering out after the first but continuing after the second (figure 2.12).

The existence of growth episodes, often around identifiable periods of reform or deliberate policy action, pointedly raises the question of whether something beyond laissez-faire is feasible and desirable to kick-start growth.

## New Growth Theory

Because it postulated a relationship between policies and growth, the new growth theory initially seemed very promising for development economists. In hindsight, however, its contributions to development economics have been few.

Romer and many others succeeded in creating models in which incentives for purposive behavior in innovation were compatible with equilibrium steady states—that is, in which technological progress was endogenous to growth. A recent excellent review by Jones (2004) points out, however, that the "first generation" new-growth models had two serious empirical defects.

FIGURE 2.11

# There Is Some, but Weak, Correlation of Growth Rates across Decades

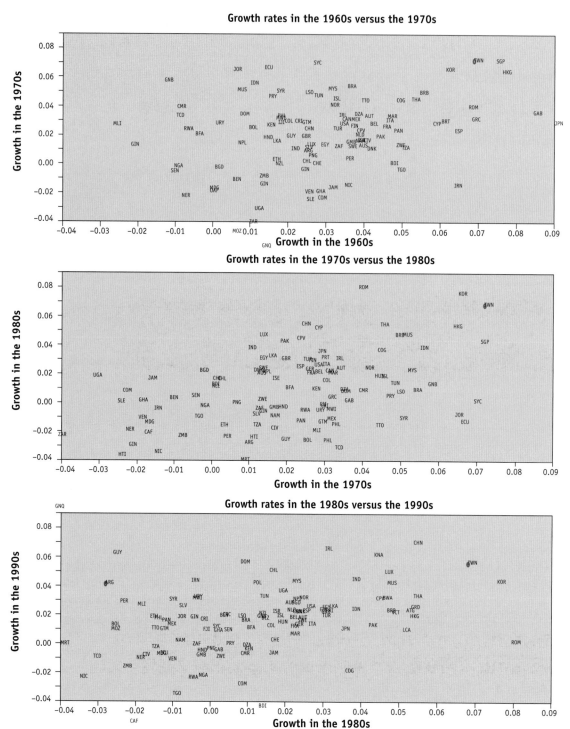

TABLE 2.5
## Episodes of Rapid Growth Set in Context
Countries with an episode of rapid growth and year of the initiation of the episode, listed according to growth rates 7 years before the initiation of rapid growth and 10 years after.

| Growth rate after episode[a] (percent) | Growth rate before episode[b] (percent) Negative before (< 0) | Slow before (≥ 0–2) | | Above average before (≥ 2) | |
|---|---|---|---|---|---|
| Negative < 0 (after) | Ghana (1965) Gambia (1969) Jordan (1973) Nigeria (1967) Chad (1973) | Ecuador (1970) Mali (1972) Malawi (1970) Rwanda (1975) Trinidad and Tobago (1975) | | Congo, Rep. of (1978) Algeria (1975) Indonesia (1987) Panama (1975) Romania (1979) Syria (1974) | |
| Slow ≥ 0–2 (after) | Dominican Republic (1969) Pakistan (1962) Uganda (1977) | Argentina (1963) Australia (1961) Great Britain (1982) Nicaragua (1960) Uruguay (1974) | Zimbabwe (1964) Colombia (1967) Lesetho (1971) New Zealand (1957) | Brazil (1967) Israel (1967) Paraguay (1974) Thailand (1986) | |
| Above average ≥ 2 (after) | Chile (1986) Cameroon (1972) Egypt (1976) Indonesia (1967) Morocco (1958) Mauritius (1971) Thailand (1957) | Canada (1962) Peru (1959) Portugal (1985) Syria (1969) United States (1961) Sri Lanka (1979) China (1978) Congo, Rep. of (1969) Denmark (1957) | Spain (1984) India (1982) Ireland (1958) Ireland (1985) Korea (1962) Mauritius (1983) Nigeria (1957) Pakistan (1979) Panama (1959) | Belgium (59) Botswana (69) Spain (59) Finland (67) Japan (58) Malaysia (70) | Tunisia (68) Taiwan (61) Finland (58) Israel (57) Korea (84) Singapore (69) |

*Source*: Hausmann, Pritchett, and Rodrik 2004.

*Note*: An episode of rapid growth is a seven-year period in which growth accelerates by at least 2 percent per year over the previous trend, to a rate that is 3.5 percent per year or faster.
a. Growth rate in the 10 years from 7 years after the initiation of the growth episode (t+7 to t+17) (with at least 7 years of data—no episodes after 1986)
b. Growth rate in the seven years before the initiation of the episode of rapid growth (t, –?7)

First, nearly all these models have scale effects that predict that larger economies will grow faster, but (as is clear from figure 2.9 above) the long-run growth of the industrial countries has been very steady, and it is difficult to make this prediction match the data.[13] If there are scale effects, either they are very small or they are off-set by many other factors working to reduce growth.

Second, since the new growth literature was primarily about the steady-state growth of the richer industrial countries, it focused on the very long run and on incentives for expanding the technological frontier. It is not particularly useful for most developing countries, whose primary interest is in short-to-medium-term growth and technological catch-up. In particular, only a tiny fraction of the observed variation in growth rates over medium to long periods can possibly be explained by differences in the steady-state growth rates of the technological frontier (Bernard and Jensen 1999). Essentially, the steady-state growth of the technological frontier cannot be less than zero for theoretical reasons (the economy would

FIGURE 2.12

## Growth Episodes in Mauritius, 1950–2000

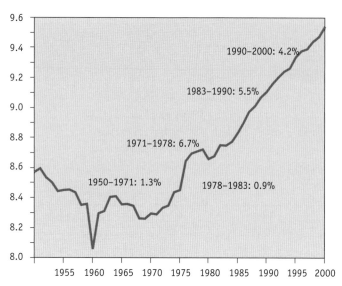

*Source:* Hausmann, Pritchett, and Rodrik 2004.

the policy, institutional, and structural correlates of growth, sometimes examining causal channels.

*Decompositions into proximate determinants of growth.* A substantial amount of empirical research examined the extent to which growth was explained by the measured accumulation of observable factors of production (principally physical capital, labor, and human capital/schooling) versus a residual (Senhadji 2000; Bosworth and Collins 1996, 2003; World Bank 1993; and many others). This literature found that:

- While measured factors, particularly physical capital, are strongly correlated with growth, they explain at most half of the cross-country variance in growth (Easterly and Levine 2003).

- While for many reasons one would have expected faster growth in the developing countries, the growth rate of the residual is puzzlingly low in most of them: negative in many and less than the OECD rate in nearly all (Bosworth and Collins 1996, 2003).

- A large debate about the residual in East Asia concluded that there was no particularly East Asian pattern.[15]

The main point to be learned from this literature is that the empirical findings of growth accounting do not have any particular policy implications. The findings did not resolve the question of causality or of the determinants of accumulation. First, the proportion of growth that can be attributed to increases in capital, rather than in productivity, depends on the way one counts the correlated components (Klenow and Rodriguez-Clare 1997). If one attributes to capital all of the increase of growth accounting, then capital accounts for much of growth. By contrast, if one attributes to capital only the component of growth that is due to changes in the capital/output ratio (capital deepening), and attributes the remainder of capital stock growth to increases in productivity, then productivity shifts appear to drive much more of growth.

Second, naming the residual from growth accounting something such as total factor productivity (TFP) has its dangers. Equating the residual

disappear), and it cannot be more than about 1 percent a year (since empirically this is about as high as any long-run estimate of total factor productivity growth in leading countries). This limitation implies that if a country were, by some means, to accomplish a shift from the lowest to the highest steady-state growth of the technological frontier, its growth would accelerate by only about 1 percentage point a year. Since even at the 40-year horizon, the 10th/90th percentile range of growth rates is 4.5 percentage points a year,[14] differences in the steady-state growth of productivity cannot account for much of the observed variability of growth rates across countries even over a period as long as 40 years.

## Empirical Findings from the Growth-Decomposition and Growth-Regression Literature

One of the principal, if unintended, benefits of the new growth theory for development is that it legitimated empirical work into the determinants of economic growth. Indeed, it unleashed a veritable flood of such studies. One branch of the literature decomposed growth into its proximate determinants, and a different branch examined with TFP (and particularly then equating TFP with some notion of technological progress) implies that the measurement is correct in every other respect. A good deal of research has emphasized how vulnerable the TFP calculation is to a variety of methodological problems. The functional form and the share assigned to capital affect the results a great deal. And the use of cumulated investments as a proxy for capital, particularly public capital, has no firm theoretical foundation and can create large difficulties in deciding whether to attribute a lack of growth to "low productivity with a large amount of factors" or "low efficacy of investment in creating factors" (Pritchett 2000).

*"Growth" regressions and the correlates of growth.* An enormous literature[16] relies on linear regressions of growth on explanatory factors X and the lagged level of income. Here the explanatory factors included in "X"[17] can be characterized as:

- "Policy outcome" or "policy" variables such as inflation, trade shares, or exchange rate overvaluation;

- "Institutional" variables such as the rule of law, governance indicators, or corruption; and

- "Structural" variables such as geographic location.

To summarize the lessons from this literature without getting bogged down in detail, one needs to take a "syndrome" rather than a "symptom" approach to understanding the correlates of growth.[18] The growth regression literature has identified five syndromes that lead to low growth: that is, five phenomena for which the overall weight of the evidence suggests an important relationship, even if it cannot be identified precisely (table 2.6).

In a sense, growth regression results have been unfairly criticized for a lack of robustness when they are able to indicate "syndromes" but not "symptoms." An example is persistent exchange rate overvaluation, a common and particularly well- documented syndrome of the 1970s. A country that pegged its exchange rate but had domestic inflation in excess of international levels saw its real exchange rate become overvalued. In such a situation its export growth might slow,

a current account imbalance might emerge, reserves might be low, the country might restrict imports in order to cope with the shortage of foreign exchange, a black-market premium might develop, and/or the country might pursue ambitious import substitution behind protective barriers to save foreign exchange. The same syndrome and set of symptoms could be set in motion if relative prices fail to respond to a fall in the terms of trade. In the 1990s examples of this syndrome often ended with a large recession (after a period of slow growth) and/or a crisis followed by a substantial devaluation and a stabilization program. If all of these symptoms (slow export growth, import barriers, black-market premium, exchange rate instability, and so forth) were caused by the same underlying syndrome, the data and regressions would not be able to distinguish which particular symptom "caused" the slow growth.[19]

## Problems with the Empirical Growth-Regression Literature

This is not the place to review the myriad methodological problems of the cross-national growth-regression literature.[20] But from a policy point of view, it is useful to point out three main problems.

First, growth regressions cannot predict turning points. The basic problem is that most indicators of policies, institutions, and structure are much more stable than indicators of growth performance (Easterly 2003a). This leads to two further problems. First, it is very difficult to distinguish causality since, unlike characteristics such as the rule of law or effectiveness of the bureaucracy, growth episodes often have discrete starting dates. Second, a finding that over a period of, say, 30 years the rule of law is on average associated with higher growth does not give much guidance as to how to initiate and sustain an episode of growth.

Second, in spite of the name, growth regressions are really not about growth but about the *level* of output. One of the puzzles of the growth literature is that even though in a mechanical sense a growth regression explains growth, nearly all of the functional forms used are simply

TABLE 2.6

## "Syndromes and Symptoms" Summary of the Empirical Growth-Regression Literature

| Low growth syndrome | Description of the syndrome | Symptoms | Generalizations that cannot be made based on robust evidence |
|---|---|---|---|
| Governance and institutions | Governments that are not developmental (for example, predatory states, weak states, "captured" states, elite-dominated states) Uncertain property rights | High corruption, ineffective bureaucracy, low rule of law, high risk of expropriation, high transaction costs, political instability Insufficient private investment property rights | Democracy is good (or bad) for growth Authoritarian governments/ dictatorships are good (or bad) for growth Need for formal western-style definition and enforcement of |
| Macroeconomic | Inability to maintain a reliable and stable means of payment internally and externally | High and variable inflation/money supply growth/exchange rate depreciation, high fiscal deficits, persistent episodes of exchange-rate overvaluation, periodic financial crisis, debt-service problems | Reducing inflation will increase growth Reducing a fiscal deficit will increase growth |
| External policies | Policies that inhibit the ability of goods, ideas, and finance from abroad to contribute to increasing productivity | Low growth of imports/exports, disincentives to existing and new export products, persistent exchange rate overvaluation, "irrationally" distorting trade measures | Free trade will raise growth |
| Financial sector | Financial sectors that cannot provide credit to private sector investors | Low monetary depth, high penetration of central/state-owned banks, legal systems that do not facilitate contract enforcement | Immediate financial liberalization is necessary for growth |
| Bad luck | Geographic location or natural endowment that creates pressures inimical to development | Landlocked, continent indicators, susceptibility to disease conditions, point-source resource dependence | |

*Source:* Author's own elaboration.

dynamic variants of a model in which *levels* of policy or institutional variables affect *levels* of economic output.[21]

Third, their specification of policies is incorrect.[22] Recent empirical research has found that, when a measure of institutional quality is included in cross-country regressions, the explanatory power of other variables, including all measures of policies, becomes negligible (Acemoglu, Johnson, and Robinson 2001; Rodrik, Subramanian, and Trebbi 2002; Easterly and Levine 2003; IMF 2003f). This reasoning suggests that good institutions matter more for growth than do good policies. From a syndrome viewpoint, it is easy to see that this is not an assertion that "policies don't matter"—of course they do. Rather the question is whether good

policies can be sustained and implemented in the absence of adequate public sector organizations and institutions.

## Institutions

Well before the 1990s, Adam Smith and Max Weber from their different perspectives highlighted the role of institutions in the development of a market economy and the formation of a capitalist society. In the 1950s and 1960s, economists writing about development were aware that the challenge faced by a plantation economy, or a dual economy, differed from that faced by a society with no concentration of economic and political power (Rostow 1952, 1960; Adelman and Morris 1965). And Latin American economists of the Structuralist school saw in the legacy of colonialism, embedded in institutions serving the interests of a small landed elite, the source of economic performance inferior to that of the United States or Canada (Prado 1972; Furtado 1963). In turn, their perception formed part of the justification for an activist state: inflation helped to mobilize resources from the wealthy elite who resisted more efficient forms of taxation; the state sponsored investments in manufacturing, particularly in capital-intensive industries, because old economic interests resisted change and the risks inherent in new industrial activities; and price controls did not have serious economic consequences because the concentration of wealth precluded the redeployment of resources in response to changes in demand (Seers 1962).

In Rosenstein-Rodan's words, the challenge of development has long been how to make sure that "nature makes a jump" (Rosenstein-Rodan 1984; see also Meier and Seers 1984). Some countries have radically transformed and modernized institutions through revolutionary and authoritarian means (as in Russia in the 1920s, Turkey in the 1930s, and China in the 1950s) or through large-scale nationalization (as in Bolivia and Madagascar in the 1960s, and former Zaire and Sri Lanka in the 1970s). In others, the state has taken on a developmental role—as in Korea, Brazil, Turkey, and India in the 1950s, 1960s, and 1970s—acting as entrepreneur on a large scale and also introducing the incentives needed for import-substituting industrialization.

Import substitution policies, command and control, central planning, "big push," a coordinating role for the state, balanced growth, linkages, all have a strong economic rationale, which was persuasively put forward in the early development literature (Rosenstein-Rodan 1943; Hirschman 1958; Gerschenkron 1962; Rostow 1962).[23] These big ideas found a particularly receptive environment in the 1950s and 1960s. But though the interventions generally succeeded in igniting growth, they failed to sustain it—a failure that has discredited strategies based on active inducements to industrialization.

This is where "institutions" come into play. For example, the notion of development banks did not become discredited because of some ideological shift that made development banking intrinsically taboo, or some theorist's discovery that in principle activist policies could not improve on laissez-faire. Development banks became discredited because in many instances they did not work in practice: activist policies using discretion, combined with public sector organizations and institutions with weak accountability (including that of states to citizens), produced costs that were just too high.

Thus the lesson of the 1990s is not *that* institutions matter, but rather:

- *How much* they matter;

- How difficult it is to work around their absence or to make transitions in institutions; and

- How difficult it is to improve institutional quality.

In the 1990s it was hoped that the strength of policies could overcome the weaknesses of institutions, and that policies capable of generating economic prosperity would ultimately generate incentives for establishing effective institutions. In response to the costs and perceived inefficacy of interventions where institutions were weak, much of the reform effort of the decade sought to limit governmental discretion in decision making. On balance, the risks of failure were deemed larger than the benefits of allowing discretion to an activist developmental state, and this led to an emphasis on rules that reduced discretion: for example, dollarization, fiscal rules, or integration in larger economic unions. However, as discussed below in chapters 8 and 9, it is virtually impossible to eliminate the discretion exercised by the nation state. A better way forward is to look for institutions to control the exercise of discretion rather than for policies or rules to eliminate discretion, which have proved to have a risky downside.

## Improving Institutional Quality

In any society, institutions need to perform certain core functions: ensuring the security of people and property, establishing mechanisms for collective decision making, and organizing a state capable of carrying out key government functions. An important realization of the 1990s was that the design of institutions for these core functions can take a broad range of forms. Most of the empirical work on the importance of institutions has focused on the link between institutional performance and economic performance, and almost none examines the link between institutional *design* and performance. Yet it is now broadly acknowledged that merely adopting some other country's laws and formal regulations is no guarantee of producing the same institutional performance, and that different arrangements can lead to equally successful outcomes.

For example, China's arrangements for securing property rights differ from India's, yet both countries offer relative security to investors. In Soeharto's Indonesia, by contrast, the enforcement of one's property rights depended on one's closeness to the ruling elite. Similarly, financial systems in the United States and the European Union have different institutional foundations, but both perform at comparable levels of efficiency. As another example, different democracies perform very differently, showing that the formal institutions of democracy are insufficient to ensure a government's accountability and credibility. While in some countries these institutions have delivered satisfactory outcomes, in others they have not (see chapter 10 below). Within countries, institutions do not function homogeneously: De Soto (forthcoming) has shown that within a country the enforcement of property rights varies across income and social groups, with the least security for the least privileged, and he has documented the ensuing adverse consequences for investment incentives and for incomes.

## Fairness and Growth

Another important strain of ideas in the 1990s was a resurgence of interest in inequality and equity. This important concern has many dimensions, but we focus here on the impact of inequality on economic growth and on the interrelationship between inequality and institutions.[24]

Inequality can affect economic growth through several channels. "Equal societies have more social cohesion, more solidarity, and less stress; they offer their citizens more public goods, more social support, and more social capital" (Deaton 2003a), and hence are more capable of sharing the costs and benefits of improving economic policies—which facilitates forming consensus and decision making. More equality also facilitates agreement on the provision of public goods, such as health, water supply, and waste disposal, that have strong externalities.[25]

Aghion, Caroli, and Garcia Penalosa (1999) explain the positive impact of equality on growth by reference to market structures and microeconomic incentives. They find that a better distribution of wealth reduces credit constraints, and that greater availability of credit has a significant positive effect on growth. If individuals have limited borrowing capacity, reallocating capital toward the poorest will increase aggregate productivity. They also find that better distribution of wealth will reduce instability at the individual level and hence at the aggregate level, and consequently will mitigate the impact of instability on aggregate growth.

While there is clear evidence that greater equality augments growth, there is much ignorance on how greater equality can be achieved. A large agenda for deeper research exists on how to achieve greater equality, including investigating the impact of public spending on equity, in both a static (incidence of public spending) and a dynamic sense (changes in individuals' earnings potential).

## Inequality and Institutions—A Two-Way Street

Recent literature has emphasized the important links between the distribution of assets in a society and the institutions that emerge. Knowledge about how institutions emerge and are established is still rudimentary, but economic research in the 1990s has provided some insights.

First, economic incentives influence what type of institutions emerge and when. For example, the enforcement of property rights to land will depend on the benefits of enforcement relative to the costs—a ratio that depends on the extent to which other landowners enforce their property rights. In an extractive economy, if all landowners enforce their property rights, the alternatives for laborers decline, and so do their wages, and as a result, rents on land increase. If landowners in general do not enforce their property rights, it is uneconomical for one of them to enforce his or hers: the alternatives for laborers, and hence their wages, will be greater because they can exploit land where property rights are not enforced. Only when this coordination problem is resolved do economic incentives become sufficient for enforcement of property rights (Hoff and Stiglitz 2001).[26]

Second, the concentration of economic and political power influences the breadth of access to economic and social opportunities. In 1800, Argentina's per capita income was equivalent to that of the United States, whereas Brazil's, Chile's, Mexico's, and Peru's were only 40–50 percent of that of the United States. Two centuries later, Argentina's per capita income is one-fifth that of the United States, and Brazil's, Mexico's, and Peru's are one-fifth or less, whereas Chile's has remained about the same. The reason for this divergence in economic performance is that the United States, where access to economic, social, and political opportunities was much broader, was able to create a much greater flow of economic opportunities.[27] Because population densities were much lower in the United States, there were fewer incentives to establish predatory institutions oriented toward extracting rents

---

**BOX 2.2**

**How Money and Power Can Influence Patterns of Institutional Development**

Societies' choice of institutions depends on a variety of contextual variables, including history as embedded in existing institutions, the distribution of economic and political power, and the type of problems these institutions seek to solve. Glaeser and Shleifer (2003) show how money and power subverted the workings of justice in the United States in the late 1800s and early 1990s, leading to the creation of regulatory agencies to handle matters previously resolved by courts.

Before 1900 numerous commercial and other disputes in the United States were resolved through private litigation: "Courts ruled on such matters as corporate liability in industrial accidents, on anti-competitive practices such as railroads' rebates, on safety of foods and medicines, and even on the constitutionality of income tax." Private litigation was the principal way to deal with the socially harmful acts that had been accelerated by the industrial revolution: "Trains were also wild beasts; they roared through the countryside, killing livestock, setting fire to houses and crops, smashing wagons at grade crossings, mangling passengers and freight. Boilers

exploded; trains hurtled off tracks; bridges collapsed; locomotives collided in a grinding scream of steel. Railway law and tort law grew up, then, together. In a sense, the two were the same" (Friedman 1985, quoted in Glaeser and Shleifer 2003).

Traditional theories of regulation—justifying regulation on the grounds of market failures—fail to explain this evolution. Glaeser and Shleifer show that a fundamental change made it more efficient for American society to increase its reliance on regulations: "Commercialization and industrialization of the economy in the second half of the 19th century created firms with vast resources. As the scale of enterprise increased, the damage from industrial accidents rose proportionately, as did the incentives to avoid paying damages. The cost of influencing justice, however, did not rise as fast. As a consequence, individuals and small companies were unlikely to prevail against "robber barons . . . . Woodrow Wilson repeatedly complained about the failure of the courts to stand up to large corporations because, he said, 'The laws of this country do not prevent the strong from crushing the weak.'"

*Source*: Glaeser and Shleifer 2003.

for the benefit of a small elite. Except in the United States and Canada, growth in former European colonies has been influenced by the concentration of economic and political power, which has restricted access to economic and social opportunities, created less secure property rights, and influenced the course of development for several centuries.

Some recent illustrations of how inequality influences institutions and economic growth come from India and the United States. In India, in the state of West Bengal, tenancy reform in the late 1970s increased the share of output that tenants could retain, and strengthened tenancy rights; a sharp increase in yields ensued (Banerjee et al. 2001; Banerjee, Gertler, and Ghatak 2002; Hoff 2003). Another instance of concentrated economic and political interests influencing institutions comes from the United States in the early 1900s, when the government decided to regulate matters hitherto left to private parties and the courts. The reason for this shift was a perception that judges and the courts had been so corrupted by powerful economic interests as to be unable to render fair judgments (box 2.2).

## Notes

1. Not all unexpected occurrences teach lessons, however. An analogy with earthquakes might help. Earthquakes cannot be predicted; the lessons learned from one are not about better prediction. But the physical and economic damage from an earthquake can be predicted based on its magnitude, location, and the design and construction of the affected structures. These damage prediction models can be updated in response to events—particularly when they fail badly, in predicting either too much or too little damage.
2. Accused of changing his views, Keynes responded with a famous quip: "When the facts change, I change my mind—what do you do, sir?" (Moggridge 1976, 163–64).
3. While these data on GDP per capita are widely accepted, they are controversial. Many analysts argue that mismeasurement of the value of pretransition output and the undercounting of the new informal sector mean that the fall in output has been less severe than it appears (see, for example, Shleifer and Treisman 2004). Everyone, however, agrees that the recession in most countries was deep, long, and hard.

Particularly when taking into account the substantial increases in inequality during the transition, it seems that the median household is potentially even worse off than the evolution of the mean incomes suggests.

4. See Country Note E, "Eastern Europe's Transition: Building Institutions."
5. The "precommitments" in the Argentine case were as credible and were fought for as creditably as one could wish. No one could argue that Argentines should have been asked to suffer more to defend the convertibility plan—and fail.
6. However, the regression estimated impact (0.017) times the change on ln (secondary enrollment) (0.41—this is in natural logs so it is roughly a percentage increase) is that $0.7=(0.017)\times(0.41)\times100$.
7. The general impression (Birdsall 2002) and most indicators of policy change (Lora 2001a) suggest widespread and substantial policy reform in Latin America in general, and in Brazil in particular.
8. That is, mean of Log(100+inflation rate)=4.79, standard deviation is 0.4047. The growth impact of a reduction of one standard deviation is $-0.0048\times0.4047=0.0019$, which corresponds to a reduction from 80 percent to 20 percent inflation.
9. There was hope that with the passing of the first generation of political leaders, their successors could effect a transformation. For instance, President Clinton in 1998 met with five heads of state (Afwerki, Kabila, Kagame, Museveni, and Zenawi) and proclaimed a "new Africa Renaissance sweeping the continent." Unfortunately, only two months after Clinton's hopeful declaration all five leaders were at war—mostly with one another.
10. For example, there is an enormous literature on the measurement of poverty in India, with a large number of estimates of poverty rates. The controversy stems from two major sources: (1) the discrepancy between the rate of growth of personal consumption expenditures in the national accounts and that of reported expenditures in household surveys; and (2) changes in the method of the surveys between the 50th and 55th rounds of India's National Sample Survey (NSS). Here we use the estimates of Deaton (2003c), which are based on the NSS, and use a plausible technique to adjust for the changes in the recall period between the rounds.
11. One of the less frequently mentioned is the fickleness that this induced in the opinions bandied about in financial and international institutions. In 1996 the East Asian model was perhaps misunderstood but it was unquestionably sought after; in early 1998 the financial crisis threatening the entire region was cited as proof that the whole East Asian model was misguided and that the economies needed fundamental reform if they were to recover from crisis. By 2000, as Korea sailed out of the crisis, that type of talk ended as abruptly as it had started.

12. See Country Note B, "Lessons from Countries That Have Sustained Their Growth."

13. Individual national economies and the world economy are *enormously* larger today than 100 years ago. Take the best possible case, in which the relevant "market size" is just the national economy. The U.S. economy in 1990 was 55 times larger than in 1870, but the growth of per capita GDP was 2.6 percent during 1870–80 and 1.8 percent during 1980–90. Of course, the relevant variable in the models is "market size." This can be defined to include trade with the rest of the world, so that Market Size=Domestic Economy+$\lambda$*(Rest of World) so that $\lambda$=1 implies all countries face the same market size. But this makes the empirical point about the problem of historically nonaccelerating growth in the leading countries even stronger because (1) with reduced transport costs and lower trade barriers $\lambda$ has increased, and (2) the rest of the world has grown, so that the true market size growth for the United States could be much higher than the 55-fold increase in the U.S. domestic economy.

14. The two standard deviation range is 3.8 percentage points a year (table 2.3).

15. Some countries had rapid growth of the residual while others had growth, when correctly measured, at about the OECD level or less.

16. This gained momentum with Barro (1991) and has been reviewed many times, perhaps most notably by Temple (1999).

17. Over and above the proximate determinants of investment in physical or human capital, which may or may not be included depending on how individual authors want to examine channels of causation.

18. A syndrome is an underlying disease process that manifests itself in related symptoms. A doctor might be interested in which of a particular set of symptoms (nausea, fever, pains) best predicts an underlying syndrome or differentially diagnoses one syndrome versus another. She might be interested in the underlying biological causes behind certain syndromes but be equally interested in the impact of a syndrome on the health of the patient, no matter what its etiology.

19. In the absence of some well-developed notion of a syndrome, it is not good practice to criticize the robustness of a variable because its significance level is changed by the addition of another variable. Nor is deciding what are the robust correlates of growth by simply throwing all available variables into a mechanical procedure (Sala-i-Martin 2003). Suppose, for instance, that one syndrome had only 1 measure

(symptom) while another had 10 empirical measures that were sufficiently highly correlated that multicollinearity caused their individual t-statistics to fall below some threshold level when included jointly. Then growth regressions with one symptom of each syndrome would give roughly the right answer, while mechanical "horse races" to assess robustness would give the wrong answer.

20. See reviews by Temple (1999) and Pritchett (2000).

21. Just as in the Solow model, the growth impact of policy reform is a transitional effect in moving from one level of income to another. Chapter 8 addresses the question of whether the impacts of policy reforms as estimated from aggregate (growth) models are consistent with those from microeconomic studies of gains from reform.

22. Also in chapter 7, this volume returns in depth to a second empirical problem: there are many economic models that do not predict a linear relationship between measures of policy outcomes or a summary statistic of policy actions.

23. The arguments made by the early authors have since been formalized in a number of theoretical papers (Murphy, Shleifer, and Vishny 1989; Hoff and Stiglitz 2001; Rodrik 2001a) that identify the market failures that these interventions addressed and clarify theoretically the economic intuition on which they were based.

24. Focused on economic policy, this study does not address concerns about the inequities in diseases such as AIDS or malaria, nor about access to social services such as education, nor about gender equity, nor about specific social injustices. These may be at least as important as the present topic.

25. See Country Note C, "Poverty and Inequality: What Have We Learned from the 1990s?"

26. *WDR 2001* provides other examples of how economic incentives affect the emergence of institutions that sustain the functioning of markets and the different coordination or risk-reducing problems they are meant to resolve.

27. Whereas at most 2 percent of the population voted in Argentina, Brazil, or Chile at the end of the 1800s, more than 10 percent voted in the United States, where the participation rate in voting also increased much faster. Three-fourths of the U.S. population owned land, whereas less than a fifth did so in Argentina, and far fewer did in Brazil. Access to education was similarly better distributed in the United States.

# Economic Growth from the *Very* Long-Term Perspective of History

To economists, the reasons for countries' growth performance lie in the incentives created by policies and institutions. Typically, economists examine questions such as the following: Does taxation discourage savings and investment? Are a country's public institutions capable of enforcing property rights and delivering public goods? Does the trade regime facilitate integration in the global economy? Does the private sector have sufficient confidence in the future direction of policies? Are fiscal policies consistent with the long-run solvency of the public sector? Underlying these questions is the goal of ascertaining whether the country has enough incentives to use existing resources and to accumulate capital—factors that ultimately determine growth performance.

On the other hand, since the early writings of Montesquieu, Karl Marx, and Max Weber, social scientists and economic historians have sought to uncover the deep underlying reasons for the wealth and poverty of nations. From their perspective, economic growth is deeply rooted in a country's history and structural conditions, which shape societies' choices and ultimately the policies and institutions they adopt. In this context, they seek to address questions such as the following: Was there something special about Western Europe that made it the birthplace of the Industrial Revolution, notwithstanding the earlier and superior scientific and technological achievements of China and the Arab world, and Asia's superior agricultural productivity? Something that was absent elsewhere, in the Americas, Africa, or Asia? Why did India's economy stagnate for so long, despite its enormous natural wealth and human skills that until the 1700s were superior to Europe's? Analyzing long-run growth implies analyzing complex historical and political processes. Scholars have proposed numerous hypotheses to uncover the "deep" exogenous forces at work. Three of these forces have received the most attention in economic research: geography, openness to foreign trade, and institutions.

Since Montesquieu, authors have periodically considered geography as a "deep," truly exogenous factor explaining economic performance. There are many channels through which physical geography affects growth: a country's geography shapes its natural-resource endowments (oil, minerals, diamonds) and public health environment (disease burden), and limits or enhances agricultural productivity (quality of soils, amount of rainfall). A striking one-third of the world's gross domestic product (GDP) is produced in the temperate ecological zones within 100 km of the world's navigable waterways; these zones amount to only 4 percent of the world's landmass. Almost none of the industrialized countries are in the tropics or subtropics, or landlocked (Gallup, Sachs, and Mellinger 1999).

In an authoritative study on the long-run geographic determinants of development, social ecologist Jared Diamond (1997) argues that Eurasia had large geographical advantages over the Americas and Africa, and that these lie at the heart of current income disparities. He argues that since plant and animal species spread most effectively within ecological zones, the east-west orientation of the Eurasian landmass made it easier to diffuse early human technologies across the continent. As a result, Eurasia enjoyed a larger diversity of plant and animal species, and thus easier domestication of useful species, than did societies in America and Africa—continents that are oriented north-south. High-productivity agriculture led to large, dense, stratified societies, with subsequent advances in technology (weaponry, oceangoing ships) and political organization.

Another important causal factor widely studied in economic history is international trade, and hence access to sea-based trade and proximity to export markets. Economists since Adam Smith's *An Inquiry into the Nature and Causes of the Wealth of Nations* have argued that foreign trade helps economic growth because it encourages the division of labor and specialization, the locomotives of human development throughout history. Numerous empirical studies have shown that openness and growth proceed "hand-in-hand" (Balassa 1978; Sachs and Warner 1995; Ben-David 1993; Krueger 1997; Frankel and Rose 1996). Historically, two remarkable examples of early industrialization are the island nations of Britain and Japan, one being the cradle of the industrial revolution, and the other the only successful industrialization in Asia until the second half of the 20th century.

Finally, recent analyses of long-term economic growth emphasize the crucial role played by institutions, that is, the formal and informal rules and norms that govern personal and social behavior; including the socioeconomic arrangements that constrain predation by the state and individuals (North 1990). Institutions were a central focus of attention for the Latin American Structuralist school in the 1950s and 1960s; but today they are seen by some as the most significant factor in long-term development. Recent econometric and case studies have shown that even when controlling for historical endogeneity, institutions remain "deep" causal factors, while openness and geography operates at best through them (Acemoglu, Johnson, and Robinson 2001; Rodrik 2003b; Rodrik, Subramanian, and Trebbi 2002).

Of course, hypotheses explaining economic growth are difficult to verify empirically. Countries are not amenable to controlled experiments, and, in reality, complex relationships are at work among geography, institutions, and trade. Each factor can potentially reveal valuable insights about the true causes of countries' development successes and failures. For instance, Western Europe benefited both from the geographical advantages of east-west continental orientation discussed by Diamond (1997) and from being predominantly a coastal region in the temperate ecozone (Gallup, Sachs, and Mellinger 1999). All of this made land scarce and valuable (Herbst 2000). Additionally, rugged mountainous relief effectively separated Western Europe into a system of "competing jurisdictions of decentralized power," constantly warring with one another, none being able to completely defeat and control the others (Landes 1998). These factors raised returns to innovation, discovery, and adoption of new warfare techniques, which later gave Europeans first-mover advantage over other parts of the world.

Another perspective on the "European economic miracle" (Jones 1981) emphasizes the key role of risk, uncertainty, and predation in the formation of European socioeconomic and political institutions, issues that have long been familiar to economists. Two fundamental forces were at work. First, the distribution of income in Europe was unusually equal relative to, for instance, Asia. "Late Manchu China with a population of some 400 million supported a two percent of the population elite which consumed in the late 1800 one fourth of the national product. Whereas a relatively large share of the population of Europe had risen above subsistence level before the Industrial Revolution, the vast majority of the population in China, Northern India, Mesopotamia and Egypt hovered slightly above or below the threshold of survival." Smaller inequalities allowed for a social environment able to keep in check predation by both individuals as well as organized groups, including the state. "Europe alone managed the politically remarkable feat of curtailing arbitrary power, thus reducing risk and uncertainty, encouraging more productive investment, and promoting growth." Second, in Europe's natural environment, adverse shocks (in the form of floods, earthquakes, epidemics) were less common than in, for example, China or India and contributed to reducing the uncertainty associated with investment decisions, thereby increasing the incentives for individuals and firms to invest and take risks (Jones 1981).

Economic development is deeply embedded in countries' history and structural conditions, and understanding these is essential for the design of effective growth strategies. The rest of this report highlights the widely differing strategies adopted by successful countries, and that the art of formulating effective growth strategies lies in careful consideration of country-specific factors, opportunities, and constraints.

*Chapter 3*

# Something Special about the 1990s?

DEVELOPING COUNTRIES' growth in the 1990s was higher than in the 1980s but lower than expected. Per capita income in the median developing country continued to grow more slowly than that in the median Organisation for Economic Co-operation and Development (OECD) country, and except in East and South Asia the growth of developing countries as a group continued to trail that of OECD (figure 3.1). This encouraged perceptions that the reforms of the 1990s had a disappointing payoff for growth.

Was developing countries' growth really disappointing during the decade? If so, could it be that an adverse external environment held them back? What about these countries' own policies? Did policies improve over the decade as much as commonly believed? Section 1 of this chapter reviews measures of growth performance over the 1990s, and section 2 examines global economic trends, finding that the external environment was not unfavorable for growth. Section 3 analyzes the extent of economic reforms during the decade, showing that they were extensive and significant.

## 1. Developing Countries' Growth during the 1990s

While per capita income in the median developing country has grown more slowly than that in

FIGURE 3.1

**Growth in Developed and Developing Countries, 1963–99**

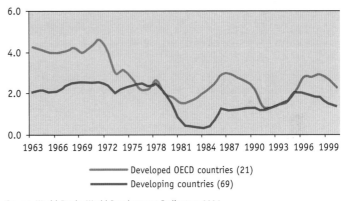

*Source*: World Bank, *World Development Indicators 2004*.

*Note*: Median of GDP per capita growth rates, five-year moving averages; 69 developing countries and 21 OECD countries for which complete series exist for 1961–2002. The Republic of Korea is included in the group of developing countries.

the median OECD country, the per capita income of the average citizen in the developing world has grown at least as fast as that of his or her counterpart in OECD countries (table 3.1).

This difference highlights the several possible ways in which developing countries' growth performance can be measured, and that the appropriate gauge to use depends on the purpose. One measure is the weighted average of per capita income growth, where the weights are developing countries' population or gross domestic product (GDP). This approach provides an indicator of aggregate performance but does not cap-

TABLE 3.1
## Growth in Developed and Developing Countries, 1960s–1990s

|  | 1960s | 1970s | 1980s | 1990s | 1990–2002 |
|---|---|---|---|---|---|
| Median GDP per capita growth |  |  |  |  |  |
| Developing countries (69) | 2.0 | 1.8 | −0.5 | 1.3 | 1.0 |
| Developing countries (78) | ... | 1.9 | −0.3 | 1.0 | 1.0 |
| Developing countries (93) | ... | ... | −0.2 | 1.0 | 0.9 |
| Developing countries (116) | ... | ... | ... | 0.6 | 0.8 |
| Developed OECD countries (21) | 3.8 | 2.7 | 2.0 | 1.9 | 1.8 |
| Import demand growth |  |  |  |  |  |
| High income | ... | 3.4 | 6.3 | 7.1 | 6.0 |
| Developing countries | 15.2 | 4.7 | 1.8 | 7.9 | 7.2 |
| GDP per capita growth |  |  |  |  |  |
| High-income countries | 4.2 | 2.6 | 2.5 | 1.8 | 1.7 |
| Developing countries | 3.6 | 2.9 | 0.7 | 1.8 | 1.8 |
| GDP growth |  |  |  |  |  |
| High-income countries | 5.4 | 3.8 | 3.1 | 2.5 | 2.3 |
| Developing countries | 5.8 | 5.1 | 2.6 | 3.5 | 3.4 |

Source: World Bank, World Development Indicators 2004.

Note: Average cumulative GDP per capita growth rates for the decade (for example, 1990s are 1991–2000 growth rates). Except for the median, all statistics refer to the sum of GDPs for the relevant group of countries, divided by the total population of that group.

ture variations across developing countries. For example, if China grows fast but Malawi does not, the aggregate measure will largely reflect China's performance simply because of China's size. Even if many smaller countries parallel Malawi's level of accomplishment, the weighted average will still not capture their growth performance.

An alternative, the unweighted average, corrects for this deficiency by treating each country as an observation, but it introduces another bias in that it may give an undue weight to outliers. For example, the discovery of oil in Equatorial Guinea enabled that country to grow at rates about 15 percent a year in the 1990s. Because of Equatorial Guinea's high growth rate, measuring Africa's performance through an unweighted average would give the impression that the continent grew faster than it did. Bosnia and Herzegovina is another example. Following the war, its per capita GDP grew by 80 percent. This observation alone would skew the estimate of the average for *all* developing countries upward by 0.5 percent. The higher the variance, the less representative the arithmetic average will be.

In the discussion in this chapter, the growth performance of a group of countries is measured using median statistics, a standard consistent with the focus of this report on policies and on country performance—for which the country is the most suitable unit of analysis.

Using the median as a summary statistic is not without its own problems, however. First, if the number of small countries is sufficiently large, the median will represent their performance. But it is not always proper to give the same weight in the analysis to China as to Uruguay, to India as to Estonia, and gauging developing countries' growth with medians might bias results in the "many small countries" picture just as using aggregate data biases them in the "China-India" direction. Thus in the analysis that follows we report aggregate data and medians together whenever possible.

A second problem with using medians as a summary statistic is that they can easily be regionally biased. Comparing developing countries' growth across decades using means requires us to follow a fixed sample of countries that have a complete GDP per capita series for the period in question. But out of the 69 countries that meet this criterion from the 1960s on, nearly three-fourths are from only two regions: Latin America and the Caribbean (21) and Sub-Saharan Africa (28). Extending the sample of countries and, of necessity, limiting the timeframe to the later decades, we find a smaller pick-up in the median country growth rate over the 1990s. The magnitude of the apparent growth contraction in the 1980s also shrinks depending on the number of countries included in the sample. Extending the 1990s to include 2001 and 2002 reduces median per capita growth significantly from 1.3 percent to 1 percent for the sample of 69 countries (mostly as a reflection of Latin America's performance), and reduces it marginally for the larger samples (table 3.1).

As noted above, estimating growth on the basis of the performance of developing countries as a group, where the per capita GDP is the aggregate GDP for all developing countries divided by the total population, shows a much higher per capita growth of 1.8 percent a year in the 1990s. This figure reflects the above-average growth performance of China and India, two countries whose combined GDP increased during the 1990s from one-seventh of all developing countries' GDP to one-fourth. (China's GDP

alone grew from 9 to 17 percent.) If one excludes China's contribution of 1.1 percent (13 percent of all developing countries' GDP in 1995, growing at 9 percent over the 1990s) the developing countries' growth rate drops to 0.7 percent. If one excludes India (7 percent, growing at 3.6 percent) it drops further to 0.6 percent. Because of the size of these two economies, and ignoring that the concept applies to economies, not to people, it has even been argued that these trends demonstrated absolute convergence (Fischer 2003).

A regional perspective on growth during the 1990s suggests that the change in performance during the decade is the result of changes in performance in three regions: the Middle East and North Africa and Latin America and the Caribbean, where performance improved, and Eastern Europe and Central Asia, where performance deteriorated (table 3.2).

## 2. Global Economic Trends in the 1990s

During the decade a tremendous increase took place in global integration in goods, services, and investment flows (table 3.3).

TABLE 3.2

## Developing Countries' Growth, 1990s: Regional Perspectives
(growth of GDP per capita for median country in each region)

|  | 1960s | 1970s | 1980s | 1990s |
|---|---|---|---|---|
| Sub-Saharan Africa (28†–41) | 1.4 | 0.6† – 0.9 | −1.0† – −0.9 | −0.4† – −0.2 |
| South Asia (5†–6) | 1.7 | 0.7 | 3.1† – 3.3 | 3.0† – 3.1 |
| Middle East and North Africa (6†–12) | 2.4 | 3.6 | −0.2 – 0.7† | 0.5† – 1.0 |
| Latin America and the Caribbean (21†) | 1.8 | 2.6 | −0.7 | 1.8 |
| Europe and Central Asia (1†–24) | 6.2‡ | 4.3 | 1.5 | −1.8 – 1.0† |
| East Asia and Pacific (8†–12) | 2.1 | 5.5 | 1.6† – 2.6 | 2.9 |

*Source:* World Bank, *World Development Indicators 2004.*

*Note:* This table gives a regional perspective on developing countries' growth. As indicated in the text, median estimates depend crucially on the choice of countries. † denotes the estimate for the group of countries with complete GDP per capita data over four decades, 1960–2002. For example, for 1970 Sub-Saharan Africa, 0.6 percent is the median growth for the group of countries with complete GDP series over these four decades. If one includes in this group the countries for which GDP data are available starting in 1970 through the 1990s, the growth rate rises to 0.9 percent. Figures in parentheses represent the number of countries with complete GDP per capita series starting in 1960 "†" as well as the number of countries for which data are available for the 1990s. For example, ‡ in Europe and Central Asia indicates that only one country (Turkey) has a complete GDP per capita series that starts in the 1960s, but 24 countries have data available for the 1990s.

TABLE 3.3
## Global Integration, 1980–2000

| | Exports and imports of goods and services as a share of GDP (in current US$) | | | FDI flows as a share of GDP (in percent) | | |
|---|---|---|---|---|---|---|
| | 1980–85 avg. | 1990 | 2000 | 1980 | 1990 | 2000 |
| Developing countries | 41.0 | 39.2 | 55.3 | 0.3 | 0.8 | 2.6 |
| Developed countries | 40.7 | 39.1 | 46.4 | 0.6 | 1.0 | 5.1 |

*Sources:* Trade and FDI (foreign direct investment) flow figures from IMF *Balance of Payments Statistics;* GDP from the World Bank's *World Development Indicators.*

*Note:* A nominal measure is used here because of the difficulty in obtaining price deflators for services trade. Regardless of whether a real or a nominal measure is used, there was still a large increase in trade integration on the "goods" side in the 1990s. The analysis in the rest of this chapter regarding goods trade uses "real" measures, with nominal values deflated by the relevant price indexes.

Notwithstanding this improvement in integration, some empirical studies suggest that negative external shocks reduced developing countries' growth in the 1990s below their potential, offsetting the positive impact of economic reforms.

Analyzing policy reforms in developing countries, Loayza, Fajnzylber, and Calderón (2002) and Easterly (2001) find that countries that reformed their policies—improving macroeconomic management, opening the economy, liberalizing the financial sector, and so on—grew faster in the 1990s than countries that did not take such steps. At the same time, both of these studies find that an unexplained negative shock affected all countries not only in the 1990s but also in the 1980s. In their studies, dummy variables for the 1980s and 1990s are large and statistically significant, implying that, other things held equal, developing countries grew nearly two percentage points more slowly in the 1980s and 1990s than in the 1960s or the 1970s.

Both of these studies have come under criticism. Loayza, Fajnzylber, and Calderón's study has been criticized because it uses outcome variables, such as a country's ratio of trade to GDP, or financial depth or inflation rates, to represent the extent of economic reforms, and thus is unable to attribute changes in economic growth to actual changes in policies, or to claim that Latin America's reforms added significantly to that region's economic growth (Rodrik 2003a).

Ignoring these specification problems, if period dummies truly capture the external environment over a period of time, the Loayza and Easterly studies provide an intuitively appealing explanation as to why the reforms of the 1990s did not generate the results expected: surely the reason must be a negative external shock.

Easterly (2001) finds that the slowdown in economic growth of developing countries' OECD trading partners provides a potential explanation for the decade shift dummies:

> In contrast, the effect of OECD trading partner growth on LDCs' home country growth is huge (if anything, implausibly large) . . . one less percentage point of OECD trading partner growth is associated with 2.1 less percentage points of home country growth.

Comparing the two 20-year periods 1960–70 and 1980–90, Easterly highlights that growth in high-income and developing countries moved closely together (figure 3.2), and that growth slowdowns in industrialized countries over the 1970s and 1980s mirrored and preceded those in developing countries during the "lost decade" of the 1980s. But when he examines the 1990s separately, he finds that the relationship between developed and developing countries growth is not that strong.

There is little doubt that that the 1980s—the "lost" decade—had its share of negative shocks, including declines in primary commodity prices, a collapse in oil prices, a sharp hike in U.S. interest rates, debt crises, a sudden stop in capital flows

FIGURE 3.2

## Growth Slowdowns in Developed and Developing Countries

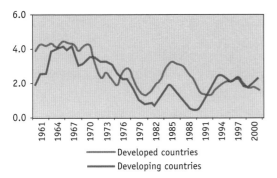

— Developed countries
— Developing countries

*Source*: World Bank, *World Development Indicators 2004*.

*Note*: GDP per capita growth rates (weighted averages), 1961–2002.

TABLE 3.4

## Unprecedented Growth of World Trade, 1990s
(average annual cumulative growth rates, percent)

|  | 1960s | 1970s | 1980s | 1990s |
|---|---|---|---|---|
| World GDP growth | 5.5 | 3.7 | 3.0 | 2.6 |
| World trade growth | 7.9 | 5.7 | 4.9 | 6.6 |
| Developing countries |  |  |  |  |
| Export growth | 6.1 | 5.2 | 5.2 | 7.4 |
| Import growth | 6.4 | 7.7 | 1.6 | 5.3 |
| High-income countries |  |  |  |  |
| Export growth | 8.3 | 6.3 | 5.0 | 6.6 |
| Import growth | 8.7 | 4.9 | 5.3 | 6.8 |

*Source*: World Bank, *Global Economic Prospects*.

*Note*: Imports and exports are of goods and nonfactor services.

to developing countries, and a collapse in import demand from developing countries.

But it is harder to tell the same story about the 1990s. Certainly the financial shocks of the decade—notably in Asia, the Russian Federation, and Turkey—may suggest that the external environment was inimical to developing countries' growth. But trade and capital flows, which are two major channels whereby economic performance in industrialized countries affects developing countries, were both expanding dramatically during the 1990s. Analyzing indicator-by-indicator the variables underlying the external environment suggests indeed that the 1990s was not unfavorable to developing countries' growth.

## *Unprecedented Expansion of International Trade*

World trade boomed in the 1990s. The overall volume of trade grew 2.5 times faster than world GDP, compared to the average of 1.5 times over the period since World War II. Import demand expanded at an accelerating pace in industrialized countries and also recovered in developing countries (table 3.4).

The merchandise export growth of developing countries quadrupled in the 1990s, rising to

an annual rate of 8.5 percent from less than 2 percent in the 1980s.

## Increased Integration through Trade

Taking export shares in GDP as a measure of globalization shows that developing countries are now more integrated with the world economy than are high-income countries (figure 3.3). Between 1990 and 2000, developing countries' export revenues doubled as a share of GDP, rising from 12.5 to almost 25 percent.

The exports-to-GDP ratio for the median developing country rose during the 1990s from 24 to 27 percent (figure 3.4).

The exports-to-GDP ratio alone is not a sufficient measure of trade integration, because changes in relative prices will alter it even if there are no changes in real flows. But given that the median developing country sustained a stable real exchange rate over the 1990s (figure 3.5), the rising ratio does suggest increasing integration into world trade over the decade.

Services trade rose during the decade, though goods trade integration dominated the globalization scene (table 3.5).

## Diversification into Higher-Value Products

The composition of developing countries' exports shifted dramatically from agricultural and resource exports into manufactures, which now constitute nearly 80 percent of exports from all

FIGURE 3.3

**Export Shares of GDP, 1980–2002**

(percent)

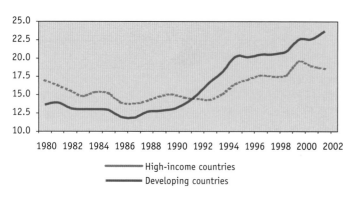

Source: World Bank, *Global Economic Prospects 2003*.

FIGURE 3.5

**More Competitive Real Exchange Rates**

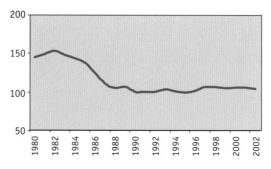

Source: World Bank, *World Development Indicators 2004*.

Note: Median real effective exchange rate index. Sample of 52 developing countries, 1995 = 100.

FIGURE 3.4

**Faster Integration into World Trade during the 1990s**

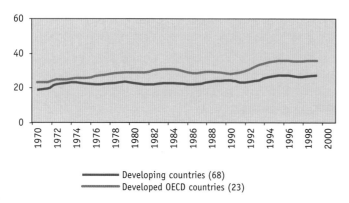

Source: World Bank, *World Development Indicators 2004*.

Note: Median exports of goods and services as a percentage of GDP; 68 developing and 23 OECD countries, 1970–2000. Balancing the sample of developing countries over different decades—that is, including all countries for which data are available—does not significantly alter these results.

income group of 1980 also raised the share of manufactures in their exports, but somewhat less rapidly, to nearly 70 percent.[1]

## Not All Developing Countries Benefited

The rising tide of exports did not lift all boats, however. Forty-three countries achieved no increase, on average, in their merchandise exports between 1980 and 2000 (World Bank 2003b), and their share in world exports declined. A group of least-developed and Sub-Saharan countries remained highly dependent on primary commodity trade, and often on just one or two commodities. Many in this group were plagued by civil conflict and engaged in politically motivated trade embargoes. Both of these factors were often complicated by inept governance.

## International Terms of Trade: No Clear Trend

Developing countries suffered no large terms-of-trade shocks during the decade (figure 3.8).

Although primary commodity prices had declined in the 1980s relative to those of manufactures, they were stable over the 1990s, fluctuating without a clear trend (figure 3.9). Analyzing the impact of commodity-price cycles during the 1990s, a number of studies have concluded that overall these cycles were more effectively managed than in previous decades and should not have adversely affected the prospects for

developing countries (figure 3.6 and table 3.6). Many countries successfully diversified into medium- and high-technology products.

Countries whose incomes were low in 1980 managed to raise their exports of manufactures from roughly 20 percent of their total exports to more than 80 percent (figure 3.7). As a result, many grew quickly and entered the ranks of today's middle-income countries. The middle-

TABLE 3.5

## Exports and Imports of Goods and Services as Shares of GDP, 1980–2000
(current US$)

| Export and import shares of GDP | Developed countries | | | Developing countries | | |
|---|---|---|---|---|---|---|
| | 1980 | 1990 | 2000 | 1980 | 1990 | 2000 |
| Goods | 34.2 | 31.0 | 36.8 | 37.1 | 31.6 | 45.9 |
| Services | 7.7 | 8.1 | 9.6 | 7.9 | 7.6 | 9.4 |
| Goods and services | 41.8 | 39.2 | 46.4 | 45.1 | 39.2 | 55.3 |

*Sources*: Trade figures from IMF *Balance of Payments Statistics*; GDP from the World Bank's *World Development Indicators*.

developing countries' growth (World Bank, *Global Economic Prospects 2001*). Even for non-oil-exporting Sub-Saharan countries, changes in real incomes were generally small and the policy environment was much better than in the previous decades.

Oil prices were generally lower in the 1990s than in the 1970s and 1980s, and since most developing countries are oil importers rather than oil producers, this drop has meant a generally favorable trend (figure 3.10).

### Expansion of International Capital Flows

The largest increase in integration in the 1990s was in investment flows. Globally, FDI as a share of GDP more than quadrupled between 1990 and 2000.

After reaching a nadir in the late 1980s, capital flows to developing countries expanded rapidly during the 1990s (figures 3.11 and 3.12). Capital flows to all regions were unambiguously stronger on average than in the 1970s and in the 1980s.

Private capital flows boomed, rising from 1 percent of developing countries' GDP in the 1980s to more than 4 percent in the 1990s, and displacing official flows as the principal source of finance. Official flows declined slightly, to less than half a percent of developing-country GDP by the end of the decade.

A combination of pull factors (liberalization of capital accounts and domestic financial markets) along with a range of push factors (regulatory changes in mature market economies) resulted in an explosion of international invest-

FIGURE 3.6

## Developing Countries Diversified into Manufactures, 1960s–1990s

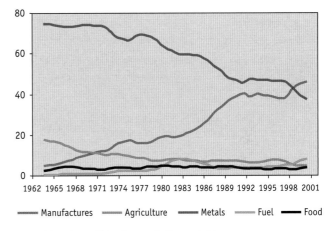

*Source*: World Bank, *World Development Indicators 2004*.

*Note*: Median merchandise export shares, three-year moving average; 60 developing countries with complete data, 1962–2002. For some countries a few missing observations were filled in by simple linear interpolation. Technically, because the median could be a different country in each year, the sum of the shares is generally smaller than 100. Thus, they have been renormalized.

ment in all countries, mature and developing. A growing consensus holds that push factors explain much of the acceleration. Servén, Albuquerque, and Loayza (2003) find that global factors became progressively more important in FDI flows over the 1990s, and by the end of the decade could explain (in a statistical sense) nearly half of these flows. The flood of credit was facilitated by advances in financial technology, such as vehicles for risk pooling (mutual funds), the development of new financial instruments (derivatives and securitization), and a decline in

TABLE 3.6

## Diversification Took Place before the 1990s

| | Manufactured export shares | | | |
| Regions (number of countries in sample) | 1970 | 1980 | 1990 | 2000 |
|---|---|---|---|---|
| Sub-Saharan Africa (24) | 7.0 | 8.1 | 18.5 | 15.9 |
| South Asia (5) | — | 53.2 | 76.1 | 77.3 |
| Middle East and North Africa (12) | 9.6 | 13.2 | 26.9 | 26.5 |
| Latin America and the Caribbean (21) | 15.4 | 25.8 | 36.1 | 46.6 |
| Europe and Central Asia (4) | — | 60.7 | 64.3 | 79.2 |
| East Asia and Pacific (6) | — | 3.5 | 39.2 | 58.2 |

*Source*: World Bank, *World Development Indicators 2004*.

*Note*: Median share of manufactures in overall merchandise exports; sample of 72 developing countries. Numbers of sample countries are shown in parentheses. For some countries, a few missing observations were filled in by simple linear interpolation. Average for given and two preceding years used—for instance, "1970" is an average of 1968–70 export shares.
—. Not available.

FIGURE 3.7

## Developing Countries' Exports of Manufactures, 1981–2001

*Source*: World Bank, *Global Economic Prospects 2004*.

FIGURE 3.8

## No Large Terms-of-Trade Shocks for Developing Countries, 1990s

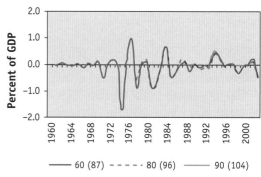

*Source*: World Bank, *World Development Indicators 2004*.

*Note*: Median terms-of-trade shocks as a percentage of GDP, 1970–2000. Numbers of developing countries in the sample in parentheses.

nominal and real interest rates. The London interbank offered rate (LIBOR, both nominal and real) was much lower in the 1990s (figure 3.13), and one result was an energetic search for yield.

Conditions in developing and emerging market countries clearly influenced the geographical destination of capital flows. Growth in many developing countries accelerated in the 1990s; many had completed external debt restructur-

FIGURE 3.9

**Decline in Nonenergy Commodity Prices**

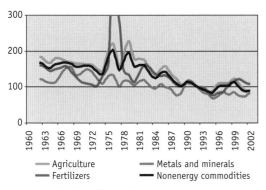

Source: World Bank staff calculations.

Note: Constant dollar indexes deflated by manufactures unit value (MUV) index with 1990=100, 1960–2003.

FIGURE 3.10

**Oil Prices Were Lower in the 1990s than in the 1970s and 1980s**

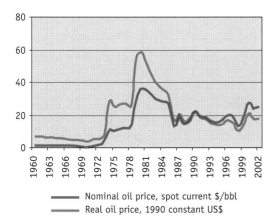

Source: Economist Intelligence Unit.

FIGURE 3.11

**Capital Flows to Developing Countries Expanded in the 1990s**

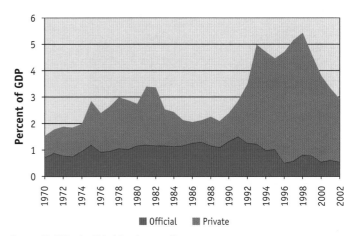

Source: World Bank, *Global Development Finance 2004*.

Note: Aggregate net resource flows to developing countries as a percentage of GDP.

ings, successfully stabilized their economies, embarked on substantial liberalization of their financial sectors, and, as discussed in section 3 below on policy reforms, had undertaken significant privatization.

Underlying the expansion in capital flows to developing countries were two important shifts in the structure of these flows: first, from bank lending to bonds and portfolio financing and, second, a shift from debt to equity. Up to the time of the Brady plan in 1989, the developing coun-

tries' main creditors were not bondholders but commercial banks. In the 1970s and 1980s, as commercial banks recycled oil surpluses from oil producers to other developing countries' banks, banks accounted for about 90 percent of developing countries' public external debt to private creditors. Developing countries' debt expanded at double-digit annual rates in the 1970s. The debt crises of the 1980s slowed the growth of bank financing, and by the end of the 1980s, the banks' share had declined to nearly 30 percent. The Brady plan restored market confidence in international lending to developing countries, and debt flows increased again in the 1990s. Successful macro-stabilization in many emerging economies, the opening of their capital markets, and technological innovation contributed to the rapid growth of bond finance (see figure 3.12, right side).

In the shift from debt to equity, FDI played an important role, as nonfinancial corporations increased their exposure to developing countries. Developing countries accounted for about 30 percent of global FDI flows—a share that remained stable over the decade. While North-South FDI flows declined, South-South FDI increased substantially over the 1990s, from less

FIGURE 3.12

## Capital Flows Were Driven by a Surge in FDI and Portfolio Equity Flows

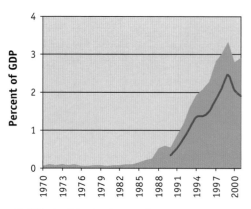
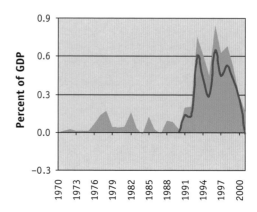

*Source*: World Bank, *Global Development Finance 2004*.

*Left:* Net FDI flows to developing economies as a percentage of GDP. Solid line is the flows to the top 10 recipients (in descending order): China, Brazil, Mexico, Argentina, Poland, Chile, Malaysia, Thailand, Czech Republic, and R. B. de Venezuela.

*Right:* Portfolio flows to developing economies as a percentage of GDP. Solid line is the flows to the top 10 recipients (in descending order): Argentina, Mexico, Brazil, Turkey, Russian Federation, Philippines, India, China, Colombia, and Malaysia.

FIGURE 3.13

## Nominal and Real Interest Rate, 1980–2002
(London interbank offer rate)

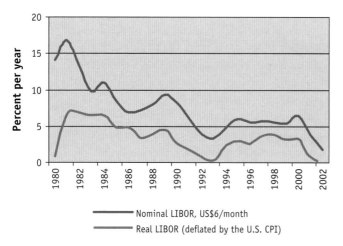

Nominal LIBOR, US$6/month
Real LIBOR (deflated by the U.S. CPI)

*Source:* Bloomberg.

than 10 percent of the total at the beginning of the decade to nearly 40 percent at the end.

Empirical studies suggest that FDI flows to developing countries were largely *horizontal* in the past, as when multiplant firms chose to replicate roughly the same activities in many countries to serve the local markets in those countries.

Such investment choices were usually motivated by trade costs, such as for transport and tariffs, though in the 1990s they were also related to the privatization of utilities and the entry of foreign banks (Shatz and Venables 2000).

What distinguished the 1990s was the rapid growth in international *vertical* FDI, that is, investment by firms that break up the production of final goods geographically into discrete stages, typically choosing the location for each stage on the basis of factor abundance. Along with technological progress and policy reforms that liberalized trade and finance, this investment led to the creation of global production networks that locate each stage of production in the country where it can be accomplished at the least cost. In developing countries as a group, parts and components exports (a proxy for participation in global networks) grew faster during the 1990s than in the 1980s, and much faster than in industrial countries (figure 3.14). As a result, developing countries' share of global parts and components exports increased from a mere 7 percent in the early 1990s to 21 percent in 2000.

The possibilities for participating in international trade expanded during the 1990s as the global division of labor changed and more resources were shifted into labor-intensive activities, in which developing countries have a comparative advantage (World Bank 2002b).[2] At the same time, however, global production networks were concentrated in just a few countries: the top five emerging-market exporters of parts and components (China, Mexico, Korea, Malaysia, and Thailand) accounted for 78 percent of the total.

Such concentration on just a few large developing countries was the defining feature of private capital flows over the 1990s. At the end of the decade, the top 10 recipients of FDI received more than 70 percent of all net inflows, and for the top 10 portfolio equity recipients, the proportion was even higher. While it is true that the largest recipients are also the largest emerging economies, the amounts of financing that they attracted accounted for a large share of their GDP and exports (World Bank 2002b).

For the median developing country, by contrast, portfolio capital flows were effectively zero throughout the 1970–90 period. Further, the spreads at which economies borrowed were high during the decade, reflecting creditors' focus on risk, not just returns. Moreover, many countries experienced sudden stops—abrupt and extremely disruptive reversals in the flow of capital—and quite a few were struck by financial crises.

Should one then conclude that the external financial environment for developing countries in the 1990s was largely negative? The answer is no.

First, the supply of funds available to the developing countries was far greater in the 1990s than in any previous decade. Figure 3.15 suggests that capital flows to the median country at least did not decline, and those to a few large economies rose sharply.

Second, significant deregulation and liberalization, as well as financial innovations, greatly expanded the choice of investment vehicles. Third, the group of investors was growing, to include banks, nonfinancial institutions, mutual and pension funds, and individual investors. Fourth, considerable progress was made over the decade in improving the transparency, data sharing, and circulation of information between investors and emerging markets. By the end of the 1990s, many more countries were rated (a

FIGURE 3.14

**Developing Countries' Parts and Components Exports Grew Faster in the 1990s**
(percent per year)

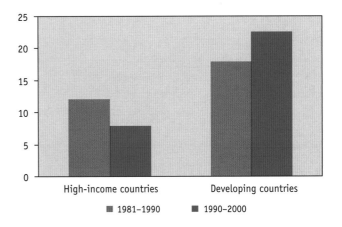

*Sources*: UN Comtrade and World Bank.

prerequisite for borrowing internationally), even after adjusting for the emergence of former Soviet Union republics as new sovereign borrowers. The result of such diversity of investors and instruments, as well as much better understanding of emerging markets as an "investment class," was that international capital flows became a much more resilient and viable form of development financing. This coming of age could be seen at the end of the 1990s: when debt flows dried up, equity flows remained significant—unlike in the 1980s, when the drying-up of bank lending led to a protracted debt crisis.

Fifth, though the spreads at which economies borrowed were high during the decade, reflecting creditors' concern with risk, they cannot be compared with those of previous decades; as noted above, bond financing emerged only in the early 1990s after the completion of Brady restructuring.

Sixth, the financial and banking crises that rocked the 1990s were not a new phenomenon (see chapter 2 and Kindleberger 1984, 2000), and their severity was largely a reflection of the underlying fragility of the economies affected (Reinhart and Kaminsky 1999), rather than of adversity in the international environment.

FIGURE 3.15

**Capital Flows to a "Median" Developing Country as a Percentage of GDP, 1970–2002**

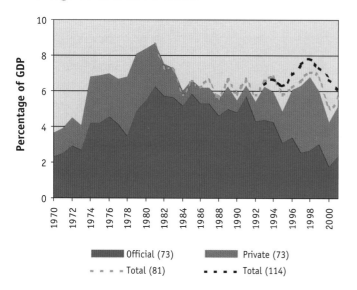

Official (73)        Private (73)
- - - Total (81)     ▪ ▪ ▪ Total (114)

Source: World Bank, *Global Development Finance 2003.*

FIGURE 3.16

**Developing Countries Paid Less Interest On External Debt in the 1990s**

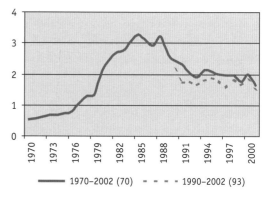

—— 1970–2002 (70)   - - - - 1990–2002 (93)

Source: World Bank, *Global Development Finance 2004.*

Note: Median interest payments on the external debt as a percentage of gross national income; sample sizes in parentheses.

Seventh, developing countries' interest payments on external debt were lower in the 1990s (figure 3.16). Throughout the decade, heavily indebted poor countries continued to receive an unprecedented amount of debt relief. The Highly Indebted Poor Countries' debt relief initiative of the International Monetary Fund (IMF), the World Bank, and other multilateral and bilateral creditors had committed US$40 billion for debt relief to 26 countries by the end of the decade. Moreover, large positive net transfers from the International Development Association (IDA) and bilateral concessional sources offset negative net transfers for the International Bank for Reconstruction and Development (IBRD), IMF, and private sources—in effect becoming another form of debt relief by replacing concessional debt with nonconcessional lending containing a large grant element.

*Conclusion: No Unusual Adversities in the External Environment*

From this brief review of the features that are most commonly thought to represent the exter-

nal environment, it is difficult to conclude that adverse external conditions explain why developing countries' growth was below expectations in the 1990s. International trade expanded rapidly and so did capital flows to developing countries in the 1990s. The context was one of relatively stable terms of trade, reasonably low oil prices, and lower interest payments on developing country debt.

True, the averages mask vast divergences in experiences and growth outcomes: some countries indeed suffered from real exchange rate appreciation; some were adversely affected by a decline in their terms of trade; while for others the prospects of growth were frustrated by the continued import protection in developed countries; and so on. Yet overall it is still difficult to argue for negative shocks in the external environment that could account for the negative common shocks postulated in Loayza, Fajnzylber, and Calderón (2002) and Easterly (2001).

Econometrically, lower OECD growth explains away the negative dummies for the 1990s, as in Easterly (2002).[3] Yet the channels through which OECD countries influenced developing countries' performance are unclear. Easterly himself indicates that

The OECD slowdown *may have* caused the LDC slowdown . . . However, I am not able to demonstrate a clear mechanism by which these external shocks translated into lower growth for the developing world. A variable that interacts OECD growth with the share of OECD trade in the economy is insignificant, for example [emphasis added].

It is always possible to find *some* adverse external shock affecting *some* countries. But econometric testing is always a joint hypothesis test of the economic theory and the empirical model. Unable to determine precisely what aspects of the external environment produced such an adverse shock, or what are the exact channels through which slower OECD growth affected developing countries' performance, Easterly (2001) suggests a possibility that the type of growth regressions used in the empirical analysis might be misspecified, given that stationary economic growth is regressed on nonstationary, upward-trending, indicators of policy performance:

> Alternatively, I have shown that the significance of the 1980s and 1990s decade dummies in regressions omitting OECD growth reflects *in part mis-specification rather than shocks* [emphasis added].

In short, it is difficult to conclude that adverse external conditions explain why growth was below expectations in developing countries over the 1990s, and Easterly's suggestion that the dummies result from econometric misspecification needs to be taken seriously.

## 3. Policy Reforms in the 1990s

Developing countries made significant policy changes during the 1990s.

The reform agenda of the 1990s ranged from financial deregulation and privatization to upgrading labor codes and mounting anticorruption campaigns, but the most impressive results during the decade came from opening up, or further opening up, economies to international trade and capital flows. Tariffs were cut, the coverage of nontariff barriers shrank, black mar-

ket premiums disappeared, and real exchange rates became more competitive.

### Trade Liberalization

On balance, developing countries made convincing progress in opening their economies to international competition. Since the mid-1980s, they have nearly halved their average tariff rates from 28 percent (1980–85) to 15 percent (1995–2000). (See figure 3.17.)

Further, all of the developing regions have at least halved the incidence of nontariff barriers (table 3.7), and in most countries tariff-rate dispersion has declined significantly.

Progress has varied by regions, countries, and policy instruments. Countries in South Asia, Latin America, and East Asia achieved the most impressive gains in opening their economies, but there was little progress in the Middle East and North Africa and only moderate successes in Africa. Over the span of a few years, Latin American countries became more open to international trade and capital than East Asian countries did over decades. South Asia remained the most protectionist region with the highest tariff rates, even after a decade of reforms involving the deepest tariff cuts and a sharp reduction in tariff dispersion (table 3.8). Africa's moderate reduction of tariffs masks drastic reforms in a number of individual countries. Kenya reduced its import tariffs from 41 percent in the late 1980s to 14 percent in 1999. Guinea did the same, from 76.4 percent to 10.8 percent. In some Middle Eastern and North African countries, the signing of trade agreements with the European Union in the late 1990s eventually started a gradual process of opening up (World Bank 2003j).

### Financial Sector Liberalization

The liberalization of finance has been at least as impressive as that of trade (figure 3.18). The main goal of financial reform was to grant greater operating freedom to market intermediaries and at the same time to strengthen prudential regulation and oversight. As a result, at the end of the decade only South Asia's financial systems remained "partly repressed" according to the

FIGURE 3.17

**Reduction in Tariffs in Developing Countries, 1980–2000**

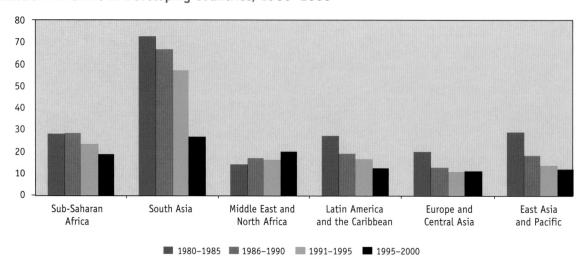

*Sources:* World Trade Organization, World Bank, UNCTAD.

*Note:* Median average tariff in percent, based on unweighted averages for all goods in ad valorem rates, or applied rates, or most-favored-nation rates, whichever data are available for a longer period.

Abiad-Mody measure, and economies in Latin America and Sub-Saharan Africa had moved to "partly liberalized" status.[4] The Abiad-Mody measure is complete only up to 1996, but significant reforms had already been instituted by then.

Although financial reforms were largely implemented in packages, they tended to focus most closely on steps to eliminate interest controls and credit controls, such as directed credit schemes, sectoral credit ceilings, and high reserve

TABLE 3.7

**Reduction in Nontariff Barriers in Developing Countries, 1990s**

| Country | 1989–94 | 1995–98 |
|---|---|---|
| Sub-Saharan Africa (12) | 26.0 | 10.4 |
| South Asia (4) | 57.0 | 58.3 |
| Middle East and North Africa (4) | 43.8 | 16.6 |
| Latin America and the Caribbean (13) | 18.3 | 8.0 |
| East Asia and Pacific (7) | 30.1 | 16.3 |

*Source:* Michalopoulos 1999.

*Note:* Average number of commodities subject to nontariff measures as a percentage of total. Figures in parentheses are the number of countries in each region for which data are available. In the case of South Asia, significant reductions have taken place since.

requirements. Less rapid successes were achieved in privatization and the liberalization of entry barriers such as licensing requirements and limits on the participation of foreign banks.

Although there are exceptions within each region, countries within regions tended to liberalize their financial sectors at roughly the same time and in roughly the same way. Latin American countries carried out drastic and rapid reforms in the late 1980s and early 1990s. By contrast, East Asian countries implemented financial liberalization gradually, starting in the early 1980s, opening up in small policy steps with the whole process stretching over the 1990s. South Asian countries reformed only in the early to mid-1990s. South Africa in 1980 and the Arab Republic of Egypt in 1987 followed a "big bang" approach to financial liberalization, while others including Ghana, Morocco, and Zimbabwe followed a rather gradual approach (Abiad and Mody 2002).

## Liberalization of the International Financial System

Equally significant were the measures taken to lift restrictions on the international movement of cap-

TABLE 3.8
## Tariff Dispersion Decline in the 1990s

| Region | 1990–1994 | 1995–1998 | 1999–2002 |
|---|---|---|---|
| **South Asia** | | | |
| Bangladesh | 114.0 | 14.6 | 13.6 |
| India | 39.4 | 12.7 | 12.4 |
| Sri Lanka | 18.1 | 15.4 | 9.3 |
| **Africa** | | | |
| South Africa | 11.3 | 7.2 | 11.7 |
| Malawi | 15.5 | 11.6 | 10.5 |
| Zimbabwe | 6.4 | 17.8 | 18.6 |
| **East Asia** | | | |
| Philippines | 28.2 | 10.2 | 7.3 |
| Thailand | 25.0 | 8.9 | 14.3 |
| Indonesia | 16.1 | 16.6 | 10.8 |
| China | 29.9 | 13.0 | 10 |
| **Latin America** | | | |
| Argentina | 5.0 | 6.9 | 7.2 |
| Brazil | 17.3 | 7.3 | 12.9 |
| Colombia | 8.3 | 6.2 | 6.2 |
| Mexico | 4.4 | 13.5 | 9.3 |

*Source*: World Bank, *World Development Indicators 1998, 2000, 2003*; WTO Trade Policy Reviews, various issues.

*Note*: Country observations are for one year within the time periods noted above.

FIGURE 3.18
## Financial Sector Liberalization, 1973–96

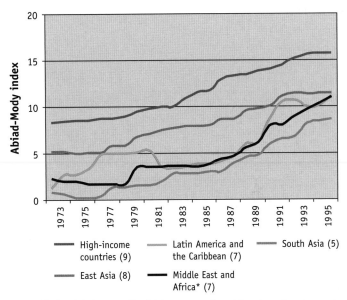

*Source*: Abiad and Mody 2003. The database covers financial sector policy changes in 35 countries over the 24 years from 1973 to 1996.

*Note*: The Middle East and Africa region also includes Turkey. Figures in parentheses are the number of countries in each region for which the index has been calculated. See note 6.

ital. The numbers of countries using multiple exchange rates and requiring compulsory surrender of export receipts declined, and several countries moved slowly to liberalize their current and capital account transactions (table 3.9 and figure 3.19). However, financial crises in the late 1990s, in East Asia in particular, forced policy makers to reevaluate the conventional wisdom that opening the capital account as soon as possible is the right policy to follow (see chapter 3).

### Tax Reforms

Although not as extensive as trade and financial liberalization, tax reforms were a significant area of reform during the 1990s (Lora 2001a; IDB 1997). To increase revenue and to reduce the efficiency cost of taxation, many developing countries lowered their marginal tax rates, simplified and rationalized their tax systems, introduced value added taxes, and strengthened tax collec-

tion. Countries of Central and Eastern Europe and the former Soviet Union designed new tax codes. Liberalization of trade altered tax structures by sharply reducing the share of trade taxes in total tax revenues.

The fiscal reforms were implemented in a much more stable macroeconomic environment than that of the 1980s. Fiscal balances improved in most regions and inflation declined. Real exchange rates that had been overvalued in the 1960s and 1970s were devalued.

## 4. Conclusions

The economic environment of the 1990s has often been seen as unstable, volatile, and unforgiving for economic growth. In reality, however, it was quite favorable for developing countries. During the decade, practically all developing countries embarked on ambitious market-oriented reforms. Since the mid-1980s most of these countries have

TABLE 3.9

## Capital Account Restrictions Were Progressively Dismantled, 1970–97

|  | 1970 | 1980 | 1990 | 1997 |
|---|---|---|---|---|
| Multiple exchange rate practices |  |  |  |  |
| Sub-Saharan Africa (46) | 20 | 19 | 18 | 14 |
| South Asia (7) | 50 | 16 | 14 | 0 |
| Middle East and North Africa (16) | 33 | 33 | 18 | 23 |
| Latin America and the Caribbean (31) | 24 | 39 | 42 | 19 |
| East Asia and Pacific (16) | 11 | 2 | 13 | 3 |
| High-income countries (21) | 17 | 10 | 0 | 0 |
| Current account restrictions |  |  |  |  |
| Sub-Saharan Africa (46) | 88 | 73 | 73 | 82 |
| South Asia (7) | 100 | 79 | 86 | 86 |
| Middle East and North Africa (16) | 70 | 43 | 52 | 47 |
| Latin America and the Caribbean (31) | 48 | 44 | 58 | 48 |
| East Asia and Pacific (16) | 45 | 28 | 31 | 62 |
| High-income countries (21) | 38 | 26 | 20 | 10 |
| Capital account restrictions |  |  |  |  |
| Sub-Saharan Africa (46) | 97 | 95 | 97 | 85 |
| South Asia (7) | 100 | 84 | 86 | 86 |
| Middle East and North Africa (16) | 70 | 50 | 52 | 47 |
| Latin America and the Caribbean (31) | 66 | 71 | 84 | 53 |
| East Asia and Pacific (16) | 79 | 64 | 63 | 68 |
| High-income countries (21) | 85 | 70 | 52 | 0 |
| Surrender of export proceeds |  |  |  |  |
| Sub-Saharan Africa (46) | 97 | 95 | 96 | 77 |
| South Asia (7) | 100 | 100 | 100 | 57 |
| Middle East and North Africa (16) | 68 | 50 | 52 | 38 |
| Latin America and the Caribbean (31) | 79 | 85 | 97 | 50 |
| East Asia and Pacific (16) | 93 | 82 | 63 | 56 |
| High-income countries (21) | 68 | 55 | 40 | 0 |

*Source*: International Monetary Fund.

*Note*: The data show percentage of the countries imposing restrictions according to IMF methodology. Years are three-year averages, except for 1997, which is the 1996–97 average. Figures in parentheses are the number of countries in each region for which the index has been calculated.

succeeded in reducing tariffs, liberalizing their financial sectors, privatizing their public enterprises, and reducing their deficits. Driven by exports of manufactures, world trade grew much faster in the 1990s than in any previous decade. Aggregate financial flows recovered rapidly in the 1990s after reaching a nadir in the late 1980s, and an average developing country experienced no significant decline in capital inflows. For the median country, capital flows regained their average level of the 1970s in 1997, with portfolio and FDI flows growing particularly fast. Real interest rates, high in the 1980s, came down in the 1990s, and so did oil prices. Large numbers of poor countries received unprecedented amounts of debt relief. By most common indicators of macroinstability, the 1990s were less volatile than previous decades. On the macroeconomic front, inflation declined, real exchange rates significantly depreciated, and black market premiums disappeared. From any perspective, the positive changes witnessed during the decade were quite remarkable and created a reasonable expectation of higher growth.

## FIGURE 3.19

### Effects of Liberalizing the Financial Sector, Developing Countries

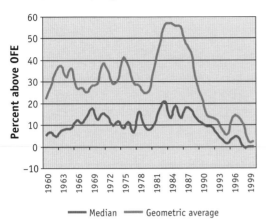

Median — Geometric average

*Sources*: Levine and Renelt 1995; World Currency Yearbook; Wood 1988; World Bank, *Global Development Finance* and *World Development Indicators*.

*Note*: Median black market premium and its geometric average, 1960–2000; 103 developing countries.
OFE official exchange rate.

# Notes

1. Notwithstanding the rising U.S. growth rate in the 1990s, high-income countries as a group grew more slowly than in previous decades first and foremost because of the slowdown in Japan, which accounts for 20 percent of industrialized countries' GDP. Japan grew at just 1.4 percent in the 1990s, far below its historic average of 6.3 percent over the previous two decades. The United States (32 percent of industrialized countries' GDP) grew only slightly faster during the roaring 1990s than in the 1980s: 3.3. versus 3.2 percent annually.

2. These changes were not just due to declines in the prices of agricultural and resource commodities relative to manufactures—the strong shift in the composition of exports shows up even when price changes are removed. Further, it was not just due to a few large, high-growth exporters such as China and India. Excluding China and India, the share of manufactures in developing-country exports grew from one-tenth in 1980 to almost two-thirds in 2001. It increased sharply, but not equally, in all regions. The laggards included Sub-Saharan Africa and the Middle East and North Africa, which have yet to reach 30 percent. Many countries, particularly the poorest, remain dependent on exports of agricultural and resource commodities.

3. For instance, only 4 percent of U.S. affiliates' production in the European Union is sold back to the United States, whereas for developing countries the figure is 18 percent and for Mexico it is more than 40 percent (Shatz and Venables 2000).

4. It should be kept in mind that there are questions as to whether participation in global production-sharing actually leads to higher productivity, to faster growth in value added or employment, or to any other positive spillovers.

5. The slowdown in developed countries' growth over the 1990s was a mixed experience—neither universal nor particularly sharp. Three-fourths of the slowdown was a result of the prolonged recession in Japan; the United States grew no more slowly, and the European Union only moderately more slowly.

6. The Abiad-Mody index of financial liberalization is an aggregate of six components of financial sector policy: credit controls, interest rate controls, entry barriers, regulations and securities markets, privatization in the financial sector, and international financial transactions.

## Country Note B

# Lessons from Countries That Have Sustained Their Growth

At the beginning of the 1990s, it was broadly agreed that countries needed "to get their policies right" to achieve growth and overcome what for many, particularly in Latin America and Africa, had been the "lost decade" of the 1980s. Getting "policies right" had a well-defined meaning. On the macro front, it meant reducing fiscal deficits, moving away from foreign exchange rationing and multiple exchange rate systems, lowering inflation, freeing interest rates, and increasing the independence of monetary policies. On the structural front, it meant reducing the scope for state intervention and discretion through privatization and rationalization of government agencies, freeing external trade and replacing restrictive trade regimes by more uniform and lower tariffs, and liberalizing the financial sector. As discussed in several chapters of this report, the extremely varied results that emerged from this experience—some exceeding the most optimistic forecasts and others below expectations—made it evident that the issues were more complex than was thought at the beginning of the decade.

While chapters 4–7 review experience with the implementation of specific policies across countries, this note focuses on the experience of individual countries that have sustained growth during the 1990s. Defining a successful growth experience is itself not straightforward. The first section of this note identifies a list of countries judged "successful" from a growth perspective in the 1990s on the basis of arbitrary yet reasonable criteria.

The second section discusses what can be learned from these country experiences. Growth requires four functions to be fulfilled. As noted in chapter 1, at different points in time one function is more binding on growth than another, and each can be fulfilled in different ways. The successful countries provide illustrations of "functional equivalents" (Rodrik 2002b), showing that function does not define form, that there are several ways of fulfilling the same function, and that income convergence does not imply convergence of policies and institutions. For economists and the policy makers they advise, this is perhaps the central realization of the 1990s. The implication is that there are no best-practice policies that will always yield the same positive result—there is no unique way to succeed. Sustained growth depends less on whether policies conform to some ideal than on whether they identify binding constraints accurately and address them effectively. Successful growth strategies address specific, binding constraints on—for example—faster accumulation of capital or higher productivity growth by experimenting and by adjusting policies and institutional arrangements to changes in economic, institutional, and political conditions. Similar conclusions were first reached in a 1993 study, *The East Asia Miracle* (World Bank 1993) and this note suggests that they can be generalized to a wider set of countries.[1]

## Defining Successful Growth Experiences

The frequency of growth episodes stands in sharp contrast to the few cases in which growth has been sustained over time (chapter 2). In the last 50 years, most countries have experienced at least one, and often more than one, period of several years of growth. But few countries have sustained growth over decades (Easterly et al. 1993; Hausmann, Rodrik, and Pritchett 2004). Sustaining growth for long periods is what enables developing economies to reach the income levels of industrialized economies, as have Hong Kong (China), the Republic of Korea, and Singapore. Therefore, in selecting the successful growth experiences of the 1990s, care must be taken not to include episodes of growth that are not part of a long-term trend, and not to exclude relatively modest growth rates sustained over the long run.

There is no foolproof method. A "successful" growth experience in the 1990s is defined here as one meeting two criteria: catching up with advanced economies over the 1990s, and sustaining this growth over time. The first criterion meant selecting countries with a rate of per capita income growth over the 1990s sufficient to narrow the per capita income gap with the United States: that is, per capita income growth of at least 1.7 percent a year during the 1990s. Out of 117 developing countries with populations of more than half a million, 42 countries grew faster than the United States in the 1990s (table B.1).

Many of these countries, however, were recovering in the 1990s from output collapses in the 1980s stemming from external shocks, macroeconomic crises, civil conflicts, or other adverse circumstances. Thus, to avoid the inclusion of possibly transitory recoveries and to narrow the definition of successes to countries more likely to be on a sustained growth path, the second criterion meant selecting countries with per capita income growth of at least 1 percent a year during the 1980s. This eliminates 24 countries such as El Salvador, the Islamic Republic of Iran, Lebanon, Mozambique, Peru, and Sudan (table B.1). The 1 percent threshold chosen for the 1980s is obviously arbitrary. Applying the same criterion over two decades, that is, choosing countries that narrowed the per capita income gap with the United States both in the 1980s and in the 1990s, would eliminate countries such as Bangladesh and Tunisia, which have given all indications of being on a sustained growth path. And applying the same criterion over the past four decades would be too restrictive, since it would limit the list to only six economies: Botswana, the Arab Republic of Egypt, Korea, Lesotho, Malaysia, and Thailand.

The two criteria yield a list of 18 countries that account for about 60 percent of the world's population and are extremely diverse economically, politically, and historically. The results throw up a number of surprises, including countries such as Egypt or Nepal, known for highly distorted policy environments and governance weaknesses, which have nonetheless succeeded from a growth—and also social development— perspective. The group includes resource-rich (Botswana, Indonesia) and resource-poor economies (Bangladesh, Vietnam); well-established democracies (Botswana, India); recently democratized or democratizing countries (Korea, Bangladesh) as well as one-party states (China, Vietnam, Egypt); and landlocked (Botswana, Lao PDR) and island economies (Mauritius, Sri Lanka) as well as continental economies (China, India). Some of the successful countries have had a relatively recent colonial history (Mauritius, Indonesia), others a quite distant one (Chile), and some have never been colonized (Bhutan, Nepal, Thailand). In some, corruption is pervasive (Indonesia, Bangladesh), and in others it is no longer a significant issue (Korea, Malaysia). The public sector in Chile, notwithstanding its ownership of the copper sector, plays a much smaller role than its counterpart in China or India, and concentrates on formulating appropriate policy and regulatory frameworks and delivering essential social and infrastructure services. Chile has privatized extensively, not only enterprises but also its social security system, whereas Egypt has relied on public investments and state-owned enterprises, which, as is the case in China and Vietnam, account for a large share of the economy. The banking system has been freer and sounder in Malaysia and Mauritius than in Bangladesh, China, or India. Sri Lanka and Chile started to open their economies in the 1970s, whereas China and India started significantly reducing trade barriers only in the 1990s. Macroeconomic prudence has taken on different meanings in different countries. In some countries, it has meant keeping fiscal deficits low. In India it has meant a structure of public debt with long maturities mostly denominated in local currency. India's fis-

TABLE B.1

## Growth Successes in the 1990s

| | 1990 | 1980 | 1980–2002 | GDP per capita in 1980 | Population (millions) |
|---|---|---|---|---|---|
| China | 8.6 | 7.7 | 8.2 | 167 | 1,262 |
| Vietnam* | 5.7 | 1.9* | 4.6* | 185* | 78 |
| Korea, Rep. of** | 5.0 | 7.4 | 6.1 | 4,098 | 47 |
| Lebanon | 4.4 | n.a. | n.a. | n.a. | 4 |
| Chile | 4.3 | 2.1 | 3.3 | 2,665 | 15 |
| Mozambique | 4.3 | –1.4 | 1.6 | 160 | 18 |
| Mauritius | 4.1 | 4.9 | 4.4 | 1,745 | 1 |
| Sudan | 3.9 | –0.1 | 2.1 | 227 | 31 |
| Malaysia | 3.7 | 3.1 | 3.4 | 2,297 | 23 |
| Dominican Rep. | 3.7 | 0.4 | 2.2 | 1327 | 8 |
| Lao PDR* | 3.6 | 1.4* | 2.9* | 284* | 5 |
| India | 3.6 | 3.6 | 3.6 | 228 | 1,016 |
| Thailand | 3.4 | 6.0 | 4.6 | 1,116 | 61 |
| Bhutan | 3.4 | 5.4 | 4.3 | 232 | 1 |
| Uganda* | 3.2 | 0.7* | 2.2* | 236 | 22 |
| Sri Lanka | 3.1 | 3.1 | 3.1 | 455 | 18 |
| Poland | 3.1 | — | — | — | 39 |
| Bangladesh | 3.0 | 1.1 | 2.1 | 249 | 131 |
| Tunisia | 2.9 | 1.1 | 2.1 | 1,641 | 10 |
| Iran, Islamic Rep. of | 2.7 | –0.7 | 1.2 | 1,380 | 64 |
| Botswana | 2.7 | 7.2 | 4.7 | 1,538 | 2 |
| Guyana | 2.7 | –3.0 | 0.1 | 927 | 1 |
| Indonesia | 2.6 | 4.4 | 3.5 | 503 | 206 |
| Cambodia | 2.6 | — | — | — | 12 |
| Panama | 2.6 | –0.7 | 1.1 | 3,042 | 3 |
| Trinidad and Tobago | 2.4 | –1.2 | 0.8 | 4,612 | 1 |
| Costa Rica | 2.4 | –0.5 | 1.1 | 3,097 | 4 |
| Burkina Faso | 2.3 | 0.8 | 1.6 | 181 | 11 |
| Greece | 2.2 | 0.3 | 1.2 | 10,702 | 11 |
| Egypt, Arab Rep. of | 2.1 | 2.9 | 2.5 | 731 | 64 |
| El Salvador | 2.1 | –1.5 | 0.5 | 1,595 | 6 |
| Nepal | 2.1 | 2.4 | 2.2 | 148 | 23 |
| Albania | 2.0 | –0.8 | 0.7 | 910 | 3 |
| Lesotho | 2.0 | 2.4 | 2.2 | 360 | 2 |
| Peru | 2.0 | –3.0 | –0.3 | 2,569 | 26 |
| Benin | 1.9 | –0.5 | 0.8 | 362 | 6 |
| Namibia | 1.9 | –2.4 | –0.1 | 2,469 | 2 |
| Ghana | 1.9 | –1.3 | 0.4 | 394 | 19 |
| Syrian Arab Rep. | 1.9 | –1.1 | 0.5 | 719 | 16 |
| Mali | 1.8 | –1.9 | 0.1 | 305 | 11 |
| Fiji | 1.8 | 0.2 | 1.1 | 2,311 | 1 |
| Ethiopia* | 1.8 | –1.7* | 0.3* | 117* | 64 |

Source: World Bank, *World Development Indicators (WDI) 2003*.

*Note*: Successful countries (shaded in blue) that grew by more than 1.7 percent a year, which was the growth rate of GDP per capita in the 1990–2002 period.

* Indicates that the GDP per capita data series starts later than 1980 (Vietnam in 1984, Lao PDR in 1984, Uganda in 1982, and Ethiopia in 1981). Population in millions as of 2000. GDP per capita is in 1995 U.S. dollars.

** The Republic of Korea has graduated into the ranks of developed countries, but is included in this table because during the 1980s it was still considered part of the developing world.

—. Not available.

cal deficits (10 percent of GDP) have risen while external indebtedness has declined.

What is common among these countries has been their persistent ability to grow over time. In low-income countries, positive shocks often become growth episodes. Examples of such shocks include the adoption of new agricultural technologies, investments in infrastructure, increases in commodity prices, or new industrial investments. The challenge of development is to transform growth episodes into sustained growth. Albeit with different degrees of success, the 18 countries have been able to meet this challenge.

In seeking to learn from the experience of the successful countries, three issues need to be kept in mind. First, one or two decades is not long enough to lift a low-income developing country to the income levels of industrialized economies. China, at its current exceptionally high levels of growth, would still need 35 years to catch up with Korea's current per capita income. Second, growth over one or two decades does not ensure that it will be sustained in the future. Brazil experienced growth for almost a century, followed since the early 1980s by persistent stagnation of its per capita income. Argentina had a similar experience of long periods of growth followed by prolonged stagnation. Third, there are large differences in performance among the 18 countries: China's per capita income grew at 8 percent a year over two decades, whereas Nepal's grew at just over 2 percent.

## *Diversity of Experiences: East Asia Lessons Relearned and Generalized*

Key functions to be fulfilled in sustained growth processes are the accumulation of capital, allocative efficiency, technological progress, and the sharing of the benefits of growth. The discussion below illustrates the different ways in which these functions have been fulfilled.

### Accumulation of Capital

The 18 countries have accumulated capital faster than other economies. At times the difference has been as large as 10 percentage points of GDP

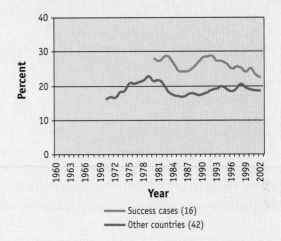

FIGURE B.1
**Investment as a Share of GDP**

———— Success cases (16)
———— Other countries (42)

*Source*: World Bank, *World Development Indicators 2004*.

*Note*: Only 16 success cases (out of 18) are listed owing to incomplete data.

(figure B.1). Why have governments in these countries been able to invest more than the typical country? Why have entrepreneurs in these countries been more willing to take on risks and invest, often in new activities? Typical explanations range from the existence of an entrepreneurial class and institutions ensuring that investors can appropriate their returns, to policies that reduce uncertainty on returns and encourage risk taking through privileged access to credit, imports, or other inputs.

Four features seem to differentiate these 18 countries from less successful developing countries.

*First, growth overrode other social and economic objectives.* Growth was a central objective of policies not only rhetorically but in practice. While each country followed its own specific growth strategy, a common element was a focused determination to adjust policies and institutions pragmatically whenever growth started to falter. Key in this process were the use of unambiguous indicators of performance (such as exports), institutions with some degree of accountability, and exit strategies when results were below expectations. Downturns or adverse shocks have been taken as opportunities for decisive reforms that strengthened economic foundations, rather than as excuses for inaction.

The oil shock of the 1970s, for example, was an opportunity for Korea to open its economy and expand exports (a sustainable longer-term strategy) whereas Brazil responded by raising tariffs and introducing a second phase of import-substitution policies (an approach that had negative growth consequences in the long run) (chapter 5). Both India and Sri Lanka faced balance of payments crises in the later 1980s and early 1990s; India responded with stabilization measures and a comprehensive reform strategy that liberalized and opened its economy, and Sri Lanka adopted a more flexible exchange rate policy, renewed its emphasis on privatization, and introduced further trade reforms. Tunisia's response to debt problems in the 1980s was to shift to a more competitive exchange rate, a gradual opening of the trade regime, and limitations on external borrowing—all of which remained key features of its policies throughout the 1990s. Chile established the credibility of its socially oriented new administration during the democratic transition in the early 1990s by strengthening fiscal policies while expanding social spending. Korea's response to the 1998 financial crisis was to relax restrictions on foreign direct investment and improve corporate and banking governance. Botswana responded with effective stabilization policies to each of the terms-of-trade shocks it suffered, which were generally severe because of the limited diversification of the economy.

Similarly in Indonesia, each of the external shocks the country faced provided a stimulus to strengthen the policy regime. With the fading of the second oil boom in the early 1980s, Indonesia introduced two devaluations and microeconomic reforms that diversified exports and strengthened productivity growth. Even though these reforms did not resolve deep-seated institutional problems related to corruption and cronyism at the top, and to a weak judiciary, they were sufficient to put the country on a growth path that was sustained for nearly two decades. In multiethnic Malaysia, the response to the racial riots of 1969—which could have destabilized the country for decades and reduced growth far below its potential, as hap-

pened in Sri Lanka—was a New Economic Policy aimed at sharing wealth equitably for all Malaysians through growth. In China, when growth faltered in the late 1990s, the government expanded public investment and rationalized the export regime. More recently, the Asian financial crisis provided the opportunity to reform banking and corporate governance in Indonesia, Korea, and Malaysia. In these three countries, the recent economic reforms have been accompanied by political change fostering democracy and accountability at the highest levels of government.

*Second, and partly because growth was such a central objective, the 18 countries show remarkably narrow fluctuations in their growth rates over time.* A record of steady growth is of central importance because it reduces the uncertainty associated with investment decisions. As noted above, developing countries seldom sustain their growth: low average growth typically results from volatile growth rates, rather than absence of episodes of rapid growth. What distinguishes countries such as Botswana, Chile, China, India, Indonesia, Korea, and Malaysia is less that they achieved high levels of growth in some years than the fact that they have systematically avoided episodes of slow growth. By and large, developing countries experience a year of negative per capita growth roughly once every three years, whereas in East Asia, the average is half that rate and in Organisation for Economic Co-operation and Development (OECD) countries one-third that rate (table B.2). Korea has had only three years of negative per capita growth since 1961. Ability to avoid downturns and periods of low growth is what explains East Asia's "miracle" growth relative to other developing countries as well as the 18 countries' above-average performance.

*Third, the ability to reduce the volatility of growth is the result not only of decisive responses to shocks, but also of macroeconomic policies that reduced vulnerabilities and hence the costs of shocks.* The 18 countries have had less recourse to external debt than other developing countries (figure B.2). While access to external capital helps to increase the pool of savings so that an economy can grow faster, it also can be misused and weaken macroeconomic discipline (see Country Note F on financial crises).

TABLE B.2

## Economic Successes: Steady Growth, 1960–2002

| | Years in which growth rate was | | | |
| --- | --- | --- | --- | --- |
| | Negative | Below 1% | Below 2% | Above 2% |
| All developing countries | 14 | 19 | 24 | 18 |
| Sub-Saharan Africa (28) | 18 | 22 | 27 | 15 |
| Botswana | 2 | 3 | 4 | 38 |
| Lesotho | 10 | 15 | 16 | 26 |
| South Asia (5) | 8 | 11 | 17 | 25 |
| Bangladesh | 11 | 15 | 21 | 21 |
| India | 8 | 10 | 14 | 28 |
| Nepal | 10 | 18 | 22 | 20 |
| Sri Lanka | 4 | 6 | 14 | 28 |
| Middle East and North Africa (6) | 15 | 18 | 22 | 21 |
| Egypt, Arab Rep. of | 4 | 10 | 15 | 27 |
| Latin American and the Caribbean (21) | 12 | 19 | 25 | 17 |
| Chile | 7 | 11 | 18 | 24 |
| East Asia and Pacific (7) | 7 | 8 | 10 | 32 |
| China | 5 | 6 | 7 | 35 |
| Indonesia | 7 | 8 | 10 | 32 |
| Malaysia | 5 | 5 | 7 | 35 |
| Thailand | 2 | 2 | 6 | 36 |
| High-income OECD (22) | 5 | 8 | 16 | 27 |
| Korea, Rep. of | 3 | 3 | 4 | 38 |

Source: WDI 2003.

Note: The table shows evidence for the 89 countries for which growth data are available for the four decades since 1961. Regional aggregates are medians. The table is calculated for countries for which complete 1960–2002 GDP per capita series are available. Thus it excludes Bhutan, Lao PDR, Nepal, Tunisia, and Vietnam. The Republic of Korea "graduated" into a high-income category in the early 1990s, and thus is classified here in the high-income OECD group rather than in East Asia and Pacific.

The 18 countries have kept inflation low and stable (table B.3). Above all, their exchange rates have been much less volatile than those of other developing countries (table B.4).

Fourth, the role of activist industrial policies is still controversial but is likely to have been important. It has been well documented that governments of East Asian countries took an activist role in the process of industrialization and that this supported constructive risk taking by both the public and the private sector. Whether East Asia's exceptional growth has taken place because of or in spite of these industrial policies is controversial. Some studies suggest that had policies and institutions converged to "best practice," growth would have been faster, while others conclude that the fact that all the East Asian "miracles," except Hong Kong (China), adopted activist

industrial policies indicates that these policies played an important role in their growth strategies, regardless of the ability to measure such a role (Hoff and Stiglitz 2001).

## Efficiency in Resource Allocation

The 18 successful economies have had, and in some cases continue to have, various degrees of distortions that weaken efficient resource allocation and cause significant economic waste. In Bangladesh, for example, the poor governance of banks was until recently the source of impaired financial intermediation. In India until the second half of the 1990s, trade restrictions were the source of significant economic efficiency losses.

Yet all 18 economies have gradually and persistently improved their policy regimes on a wide range of fronts: macroeconomic manage-

FIGURE B.2

## External Debt as a Share of Gross National Income

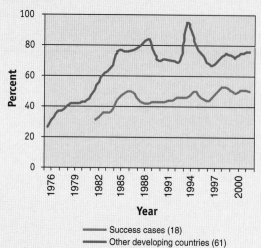

Year

Success cases (18)
Other developing countries (61)

*Source*: World Bank, *World Development Indicators 2004*.

TABLE B.3

## Inflation Volatility

(median of the variance of the inflation rate, consumer prices, per year)

| | |
|---|---|
| Success countries (7), 1961–2002 | 21.1 |
| (10), 1970–2002 | 19.3 |
| (13), 1980–2002 | 17.5 |
| (17), 1990–2002 | 17.5 |
| Other developing countries (35), 1961–2002 | 103.0 |
| (53). 1970–2002 | 89.3 |
| (61), 1981–2002 | 103.0 |
| (74), 1991–2002 | 107.3 |

*Source*: World Bank, *World Development Indicators 2004*; own calculations.

*Note*: Figures in parentheses denote the number of countries in the sample.

ment, external trade, public sector enterprise and utility regulation, and finance. Progress on the policy front is reviewed in chapters 4–7. Of note is the increase in the role of trade in the 18 economies, which points to an increase in their efficiency of resource allocation (figure B.3). The difference between the 18 countries and other developing countries has been widening over time, reaching almost 20 percentage points of GDP toward the end of the 1990s. It is also important to note that

TABLE B.4

## Real Exchange Rate Volatility

(median of the variance of the real effective exchange rate, per year)

| | |
|---|---|
| Success countries (15), 1980–2002 | 44.4 |
| (17), 1988–2002 | 47.5 |
| Other developing countries (66), 1980–2002 | 112.4 |
| (81), 1992–2002 | 117.5 |

*Source*: IMF 2004a.

*Note*: Figures in parentheses denote the number of countries in the sample.

efficiency in allocation is induced not only by sound policies—such as competitive exchange rates and an open trade regime—but also by institutions, for example, that enforce contracts and enable markets to function (World Bank, *World Development Report 2001*, 2005a). In some instances, institutions and political realities help to define the set of feasible policies, as policy makers such as Russia's former Minister of Finance Yegor Gaidar are quick to acknowledge (World Bank 2005b).

## Technological Catch-Up

Productivity growth is a common characteristic of all sustained growth processes. Almost half a century ago, pioneering studies by Abramovitz (1956) and Solow (1956, 1957) found that increases in factors of production accounted for less than a third of U.S. economic growth, and that the bulk of the growth came from working smarter. While factor accumulation is essential, it is no guarantee of success by itself. In most of the Middle East and North Africa, for example, as discussed in Country Note D, capital accumulation has been insufficient to generate rapid growth.

Total factor productivity (TFP) measures the use of better technology and improvements in the quality of labor and capital. Several studies find that TFP explains between half and three-quarters of economic growth, and that differences in TFP account for most of the differences in output growth rates among countries. For example, looking at the growth rates of 74 countries over three decades, the 1998/99 *World Development Report: Knowledge for Development* attributes three-quarters of the differences in growth rates to differences in TFP.

FIGURE B.3

## Integration with the World Economy, 1970–2000

(median of merchandise goods and services trade as a percentage of GDP)

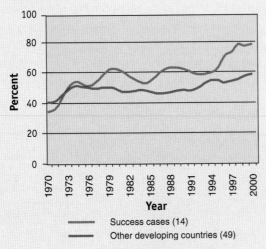

Year

——— Success cases (14)

——— Other developing countries (49)

*Source*: World Bank, *World Development Indicators 2004.*

*Note*: For lack of data, not all the successful countries are included in this figure. However, expanding the sample (by effectively ignoring earlier decades for which no data were available—in the case, for example, of Mauritius and Vietnam) does not alter the results.

Data on productivity are not always reliable and important variables tend to be mismeasured: capital stock aggregates investments of different vintages and hence quality; depreciation adjustments ignore obsolescence; human capital is measured through education inputs, not value, and so forth. And although the old Cambridge capital controversy questioning the meaning of capital in an aggregate production function has been largely forgotten, a recent retrospective concludes that it has not been resolved (Cohen and Harcourt 2003). In China, TFP has accounted for about half of the GDP growth rate in the last two decades, while in the Philippines TFP is negative (Yusuf and Evenett 2002).[2] Productivity has generally grown faster in the 18 successful countries than in the median developing country (table B.5).

Productivity gains result from complex forces in society. Organizational improvements that enable quicker turnaround times for ships in ports may raise productivity as surely as does more nar-

rowly defined technological change. Institutional innovations—such as the creation in the 18th century of public limited liability companies, which enabled greater risk taking by firms; the letter of credit a few centuries earlier; and the introduction of patent protection for innovation—are just as important sources of productivity gains as are breakthroughs in science or technology. For example, while their contribution is difficult to measure, legal reforms in India over the last decade have facilitated the transparency and security of transactions in capital markets, and probably account for a part of the gains in productivity of the last decade. Competition is also important, providing both the incentive and the means to acquire better technologies. Openness is crucial; it does not imply uniform trade tariffs or the absence of protection but it does require access to key inputs at international prices (Harberger 2004, 23). Certain types of production technologies are embedded in imported machinery (or seeds and other inputs). Foreign investment, one manifestation of economic openness, has been important in many of the 18 countries and has often been a major channel for modernizing technology. Foreign direct investment in Malaysia averaged more than 5 percent of GDP for several years, and the percentage is even higher in the most rapidly growing provinces in China. This is not an exhaustive list of the forces behind productivity; others include government and firms spending on research and development (R&D), tertiary education, and additions to human capital or better infrastructure, all of which can improve the functioning of the economy.

The challenge of technological catch-up is about expanding a country's production possibility frontier. This challenge is country-specific because the frontier is defined by technology that includes the organizational and institutional settings in which people and firms operate. Less distorting policies move an economy to its own frontier; but shifts of the frontier itself through technological progress or factor accumulation are the essence of growth processes.

Governments have played a role in technological catch-up in each of the 18 countries, but

TABLE B.5

# Total Factor Productivity Growth of Successful Countries, 1960–2000

| | TFP growth | | | |
|---|---|---|---|---|
| | 1960s | 1970s | 1980s | 1990s |
| China | 0.5 | 0.7 | 4.2 | 5.1 |
| Vietnam* | — | — | — | — |
| Korea, Rep. of** | 2.4 | −0.7 | 2.4 | 0.9 |
| Chile | 0.9 | 0.1 | 0.7 | 2.1 |
| Mauritius | 0.0 | 1.5 | 3.0 | 2.3 |
| Malaysia | 1.0 | 1.1 | 0.3 | 0.9 |
| Lao PDR* | — | — | — | — |
| India | 0.7 | −0.3 | 2.5 | 1.3 |
| Thailand | 1.7 | 0.8 | 2.4 | 0.1 |
| Bhutan | — | — | — | — |
| Sri Lanka | 1.9 | 0.2 | −0.3 | 1.5 |
| Bangladesh | 1.0 | −0.7 | 1.6 | 0.6 |
| Tunisia | 2.2 | 2.0 | −0.2 | 1.1 |
| Botswana | — | — | — | — |
| Indonesia | 1.3 | 1.8 | 0.3 | −0.9 |
| Egypt, Arab Rep. of | 0.2 | 1.5 | 0.0 | 0.9 |
| Nepal | — | — | — | — |
| Lesotho | — | — | — | — |
| Development "successes" (12) | 1.0 | 0.8 | 1.2 | 1.0 |
| Other developing countries (46) | 1.0 | 0.3 | −1.7 | −0.1 |

*Source*: Bosworth and Collins 2003.

* Indicates that the GDP per capita data series starts later than 1980 (Vietnam in 1984, Lao PDR in 1984, Uganda in 1982, and Ethiopia in 1981). Population in millions as of 2000. GDP per capita is in 1995 U.S. dollars.
** The Republic of Korea has graduated into the ranks of developed countries, but is included in this table because during the 1980s it was still considered part of the developing world.
—. Not available.

each in their own way. Korea used bank loans for indirect funding of private firms engaged in modernizing their production methods. Singapore taxed labor to discourage low-skilled jobs. Malaysia funded vocational training, provided tax breaks, and established special economic zones. Many have intervened by imposing local content restrictions. In India, an important contribution of government has been to stimulate the green revolution.

Since economic growth puts a halo on all of a country's policies, it is difficult to discern which incentives have been effective. Further, interventions to improve technology and productivity are hard to evaluate and replicate, and successful initiatives have coexisted with less successful ones. In Brazil, for example, the government correctly identified the potential of computers in the

1970s, and set up a publicly funded research center and protected domestic producers from foreign competition. A large domestic computer industry had developed by the mid-1980s, but Brazilian computers were costlier than the better computers that were available abroad, and the domestic computer industry did not withstand external competition when Brazil liberalized its trade in the 1990s. At the same time, Brazil succeeded in developing commercial airplanes (Embraer), which have won a significant share of the world market. In Indonesia, an attempt to develop an aircraft industry has been more costly than successful: the government spent $400 million on R&D (not just on aviation) and invested some $3 billion in a showcase aircraft factory without success (World Bank, *World Development Report 2005*). By contrast, the garment industry in Bali, Indonesia, was "accidentally" industrialized in the 1980s, after foreign tourists (mainly surfers) saw the commercial potential in Balinese indigenous designs and became marketing intermediaries connecting local producers with foreign retail outlets. This success happened despite the skepticism of the country's then–research and technology minister for Indonesians' becoming "tailors to the world."

## Shared Growth through Opportunities, Public Expenditure, and Distributive Programs

In East Asia, the emphasis on growth led the region's governments to focus on augmenting productive capacity and the efficient delivery of social services, rather than on augmenting consumption among groups that might otherwise be left behind. Since these countries have sought to equalize ex ante opportunities rather than ex post outcomes, efforts to expand opportunities and mechanisms that facilitate upward mobility have played a more important role than distributive programs. Elsewhere, however, direct income transfers or subsidization of specific commodities—as has been common in India, Egypt, Sri Lanka, and Nepal—have played much more important roles.

With few exceptions,[3] ensuring that the benefits of growth reached all segments of the population was part of the growth strategy. To distribute the benefits of growth, governments relied on a different set of policies and programs. In some cases, they redistributed assets and land, while in others they used public expenditures in infrastructure (the 8-7 program in China), social spending (Tunisia), policies to increase opportunities for economically underprivileged groups (affirmative actions for *bumiputra* in Malaysia or scholarships in Bangladesh for girls' secondary education) or poverty-targeted programs (food stamps in Sri Lanka or employment programs in India and Bangladesh). Soeharto's Indonesia developed the concept of "economic democracy," which advocated reliance on the free market for growth. In Malaysia, the New Economic Policy formally articulated a consensus strategy to eliminate the identification of race with economic function. In Chile, distributive programs, and,

since the country's return to democracy, increasing social spending, have been central objectives of policies. In India, reduction of famines and improvement in the living standards of the population have guided policies since Independence. Sri Lanka has maintained a long tradition of inclusion, even though mistargeting and politicization of access to benefits have been serious issues. Egypt and Tunisia have made efforts to raise the consumption levels of low-income groups, for example, through housing programs or subsidies for items of popular consumption.

Growth-oriented strategies for reducing poverty and generating opportunities require access to public services, and all countries have sought to expand public services with different degrees of success. Even in Soeharto's Indonesia, where corruption eroded the effectiveness of some of the country's key institutions, infrastructure and social services were considerably expanded to reach significant segments of the population and played an important role in creating opportunities and distributing the benefits of growth. The expansion of education and health services during the 1970s, as well as the agricultural development policies in the 1960s and 1970s, were both important in this respect. The village grant program (Inpres Desa) is a good example, as well as a case of innovation and adaptation. This program, which started in the 1970s as a top-down grant for centrally prescribed expenditures at the village level, evolved into the village improvement program (VIP), which in turn inspired the Kecamatan Development Program, the largest successful community development program in the world.

Perhaps just as important for rural development as targeted programs, though little recognized as such, has been the maintenance of a competitive exchange rate.

The distributive impact of government programs is difficult to disentangle from the impact of growth. For example, it is well known that returns to education are higher in rapidly growing economies—with the result that investments in education are both capacity enhancing and distributive, and more so at high rates of economic growth. Investments in water and sanita-

FIGURE B.4

## Average Annual Growth of per Capita Income of Different Income Groups, 1980 to Mid/Late 1990s

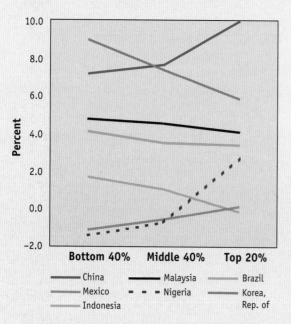

*Sources*: World Bank, *World Development Indicators 2004*; *Global Development Finance* 2004.

tion, and other forms of infrastructure, are capacity enhancing and distributive. What seem to have been important are pragmatic interventions that ensured that the incomes of the bottom 20 or 40 percent of the population grew. In East Asian countries, the incomes of the bottom 40 percent of the population have grown quite rapidly over the last 20 years (figure B.4). Korea is the East Asian country with the highest growth rate of incomes of the bottom 40 percent, even though its average aggregate growth was slower than China's. And even though China itself has seen more rapid growth among the richest 20 percent of its population (the urban middle and upper class), the growth rate of its poorest citizens has still been very rapid, at more than 6 percent a year. By contrast, countries in other regions, as represented by Mexico and Nigeria in figure B.4, have mostly seen below–average growth rates for their poorest 40 percent. Brazil is an exception, but its aggregate growth in this period has been very slow.

This result does not just reflect the initial distribution of income (figure B.5). In 1980, Korea and Nigeria had roughly similar income distri-

FIGURE B.5

## Ratio of Real per Capita Income of Bottom 40 Percent to That of Top 20 Percent, 1980 to Mid/Late 1990s

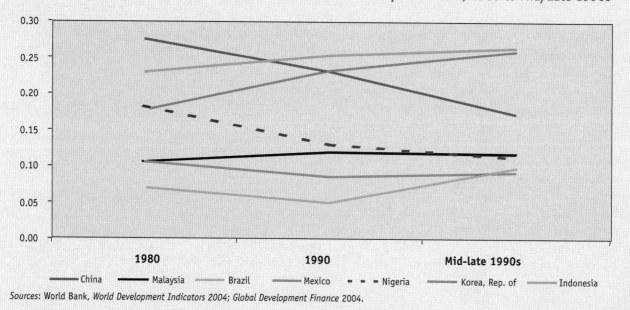

*Sources*: World Bank, *World Development Indicators 2004*; *Global Development Finance* 2004.

TABLE B.6

## Progress on Social Indicators, 1980–2000

| | Under-five mortality rate | | | Secondary school enrollment | | |
|---|---|---|---|---|---|---|
| | 1980 | 1990 | 2000 | 1980 | 1990 | 2000 |
| China | 120 | 49 | 40 | 46 | 49 | 68 |
| Vietnam | 87 | 53 | 30 | 42 | 32 | 67 |
| Korea, Rep. of | 18 | 9 | 5 | 78 | 90 | 94 |
| Chile | 98 | 19 | 12 | 53 | 74 | 86 |
| Malaysia | 63 | 21 | 9 | 48 | 56 | 69 |
| Lao PDR | 218 | 163 | 105 | 21 | 25 | 38 |
| India | 202 | 123 | 94 | 30 | 44 | 49 |
| Thailand | 102 | 40 | 29 | 29 | 30 | 83 |
| Sri Lanka | 100 | 26 | 20 | 55 | 74 | .. |
| Bangladesh | 239 | 144 | 82 | 18 | 19 | 46 |
| Indonesia | 172 | 91 | 48 | 29 | 44 | 57 |
| Egypt, Arab Rep. of | 235 | 104 | 45 | 50 | 76 | 85 |
| Nepal | 234 | 143 | 91 | 21 | 33 | 40 |
| Tunisia | 201 | 52 | 28 | 27 | 45 | 78 |
| Botswana | 142 | 58 | 101 | 19 | 43 | 73 |
| Mauritius | 86 | 25 | 20 | 50 | 53 | 77 |
| Bhutan | 267 | 166 | 100 | .. | .. | .. |
| Lesotho | 190 | 148 | 133 | 18 | 25 | 32 |
| All developing countries | 131 | 103 | 90 | 41 | 47 | 63 |

*Source:* WDI 2003.
.. Not available.

butions as measured by the share of the bottom 40 percent of the population in total income. Yet the relative growth rates of income of the bottom and top strata differed substantially between the two countries. Similarly, Malaysia and Mexico had similar initial income distributions but a different sharing of growth. It appears that the growth strategies themselves produced the different distributional outcomes, and that more equitable outcomes have been more sustainable over time.

Rapid growth was accompanied by wide improvements in social indicators and access to expanding public services. Primary and secondary education expanded massively in Botswana and Indonesia, and health improved vastly in Egypt and Tunisia, as well as in Chile and Malaysia, among other countries (table B.6). While there may be an element of reverse causation—when incomes rise, health and educa-

tion outcomes improve—governments in all the success cases were central to the expansion of social services.

## Notes

1. The experiences of China, the Republic of Korea, Indonesia, and Malaysia were reviewed for the Shanghai Conference on Poverty Reduction (see http://www.worldbank.org/wbi/reducingpoverty/cases-SearchTOC. html), and others as part of the Global Development Network's work on growth (http://www.gdnet/). This country note draws on those sources as well as on World Bank economic and sector work.
2. Harberger (2004) explains how recessions or the absence of Schumpeterian "creative destruction" could produce negative TFP estimates.
3. For example Nepal, where growth has been concentrated in the Kathmandu Valley and has had only a modest impact on poverty.

*Part 2*

# Development
# Controversies
# of the 1990s

# Chapter 4

# Macroeconomic Stability: The More the Better?

MACROECONOMIC POLICIES improved in a majority of developing countries in the 1990s, but the expected growth benefits failed to materialize, at least to the extent that many observers had forecast. In addition, a series of financial crises severely depressed growth and worsened poverty.

What is the relationship between these developments? This chapter argues that both slow growth and multiple crises were symptoms of deficiencies in the design and execution of the pro-growth reform strategies that were adopted in the 1990s with macroeconomic stability as their centerpiece.[1] Section 1 reviews how macroeconomic stability evolved during the 1990s. Section 2 evaluates this experience from the perspective of promoting economic growth, examining how a policy agenda that focused on macroeconomic stability turned out to be associated with a multitude of crises. Section 3 draws lessons, which essentially concern the depth and breadth of the macro reform agenda, the need for attention to macroeconomic vulnerabilities, and the importance of policies outside the macroeconomic sphere.

## 1. Macroeconomic Facts of the 1990s

How did macroeconomic stability evolve over the 1990s? Answering this question requires, first,

a clarification of the meaning of macroeconomic instability and of how to measure it empirically. Conceptually, macroeconomic instability refers to phenomena that make the domestic macroeconomic environment less predictable, and it is of concern because unpredictability hampers resource allocation decisions, investment, and growth.[2] Macroeconomic instability can take the form of *volatility* of key macroeconomic variables or of *unsustainability* in their behavior (which predicts future volatility).

To examine the evolution of macroeconomic stability, we look at the behavior of macroeconomic outcome variables including the growth of real output, the rate of inflation, and the current account deficit. It focuses on the volatility of the growth rate and the levels of inflation and the current account deficit.[3] Changes in the behavior of these endogenous variables can reflect changes in the macroeconomic policy environment as well as exogenous shocks. Thus to distinguish the roles of these two factors we look at the behavior of fiscal, monetary, and exchange rate policy variables as well as at real and financial exogenous shocks to developing countries.

### Stability of Macroeconomic Outcomes

Developing countries have traditionally experienced much greater macroeconomic instability than industrial economies. This problem is widely perceived to have worsened,[4] but in fact the volatility of developing countries' key macroeconomic aggregates declined in the 1990s.[5] For example, the median standard deviation of per capita gross domestic product (GDP) growth fell from 4 percent in the 1970s and 1980s to about 3 percent in the 1990s, although it remained significantly higher than the comparable figure for industrial economies (1.5 percent) (figure 4.1).[6,7] The reduction in GDP volatility was widespread but far from universal: of the 77 developing countries for which complete information is available for 1960–2000, about a third (27 countries) experienced more volatile growth in the 1990s than in the 1980s. In turn, the volatility of private consumption growth also declined relative to the previous decade in low-income developing countries. In middle-income countries, however, consumption volatility remained virtually unchanged at the record highs of the 1980s.[8]

The reduction in the aggregate volatility of GDP growth concealed the increasing role played by extreme instability (figure 4.2). In the 1990s, large negative shocks accounted for close to one-fourth of total growth volatility, against 14 percent in the 1960s and 1970s and 18 percent in the 1980s.[9] And the increasing incidence of growth crises affected not only countries whose growth volatility rose (such as Indonesia, Malaysia, and

the Republic of Korea) but also countries whose growth volatility declined (such as Madagascar, which suffered a large drop in GDP in 1991; Mexico; and Ecuador). There is evidence that this crisis-type volatility is significantly more adverse for growth than normal volatility (Hnatkovska and Loayza 2004).[10]

Inflation rates improved in the 1990s. Among middle-income countries the median annual inflation rate declined from a peak of 16 percent in 1990 to 6 percent in 2000. Among low-income countries, inflation peaked during 1994–95 in the wake of the devaluation of the CFA franc, and then declined (figure 4.3). The incidence of high inflation among developing countries declined sharply after peaking in 1991 (figure 4.4). But over the 1990s as a whole, the number of developing countries experiencing average inflation higher than 50 percent was no smaller than in the 1980s.

Other things being equal, reduced aggregate volatility and lower inflation probably improved the incomes of the poor. The inflation tax tends to fall disproportionately on poorer households,

FIGURE 4.2

**Structure of GDP Growth Volatility, 1961–2000**

(percent, mean of 77 developing countries)

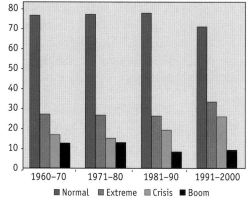

*Source:* Author's own elaboration using data from World Bank, *World Development Indicators,* and Hnatkovska and Loayza 2004.

*Note:* Extreme shocks are defined as those exceeding two standard deviations of output growth over the respective decade. Total volatility = Normal + Extreme; Extreme = Crisis + Boom.

FIGURE 4.1

**GDP Growth Volatility, 1966–2000**

(percent, medians by country income group)

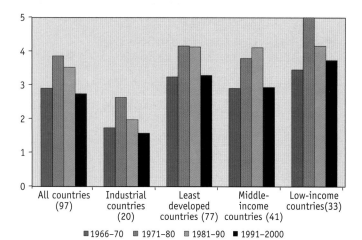

*Sources:* World Bank, *World Development Indicators;* Hnatkovska and Loayza 2004.

FIGURE 4.3

**Inflation Rates, 1991–99**

(GDP deflator, medians by country income group)

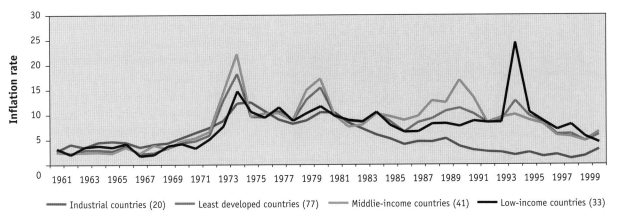

*Source:* World Bank, *World Development Indicators.*

FIGURE 4.4

**High Inflation in Developing Countries, 1961–99**

(relative frequency, percent)

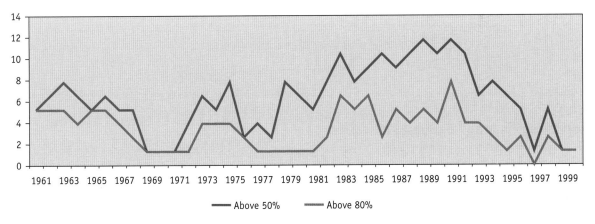

*Source:* World Bank, *World Development Indicators.*

which hold few or no financial assets to shelter them against rising prices, and whose wage earnings typically are not fully indexed to inflation. Through this and other channels, higher aggregate volatility is empirically associated with worsening income distribution.[11]

The median current account deficit among developing countries decreased slightly in the 1990s, although there was a contrast between middle- and low-income countries.[12] In the former,

the median current account deficit/GDP ratio was about one percentage point lower than in the 1970s and 1980s.[13] In the latter, it rose by about half a point in relation to the 1980s to exceed 5 percent of GDP in the 1990s (figure 4.5).

## *Stability of Policies*

Conventional indicators of policy stability also improved over the 1990s. Most notably, the

FIGURE 4.5

## Current Account, 1966–2000

(percentage of GDP, medians by country income group)

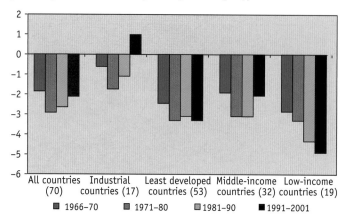

*Sources:* World Bank, *World Development Indicators;* IMF, *BoP4*

*Note:* The countries featured are those for which data are available over the entire period shown.

Since the overall fiscal balance is affected by the trajectory of interest rates on public debt (which is beyond the direct control of the authorities), the primary balance likely offers a more accurate measure of a country's fiscal stance. Its evolution over the 1990s shows clear increases in surpluses, particularly after 1995 (figure 4.7). By the end of the decade, the median developing country held a primary surplus, although a much more modest one than that typical of industrial countries.[14]

It is more difficult to gauge monetary stability, given the diversity of monetary arrangements across developing countries and over time. One rough measure is the resort to seigniorage—that is, money financing of the deficit. Measured by the change in the money base relative to GDP, seigniorage collection rose in the late 1980s and early 1990s, and then declined in middle-income and (more modestly) low-income economies (figure 4.8). The pattern is roughly similar to that of the inflation rate (figure 4.3 above).

The diversity of exchange rate arrangements across countries makes it hard to gauge trends in exchange rate policy for developing countries as a group. One indirect approach looks at

overall fiscal deficit of developing countries shrank from a median value of 6–7 percent of GDP in the early 1980s to 2 percent of GDP in the 1990s, before rebounding to about 3 percent by the end of the decade. The fiscal correction was particularly pronounced among middle-income countries (figure 4.6).

FIGURE 4.6

## Developing Countries' Overall Fiscal Balance

(percentage of GDP, medians by country income group)

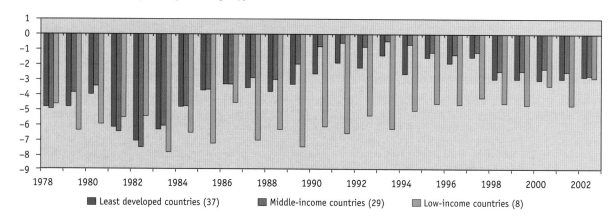

*Sources:* World Bank, *World Development Indicators;* Institute of International Finance.

*Note:* The countries featured are those for which complete data are available from the late 1970s on. The availability of consistent fiscal balance data is very limited, particularly for low-income countries.

FIGURE 4.7

**Primary Fiscal Balance, 1990–2002**

(percentage of GDP, medians by country income group)

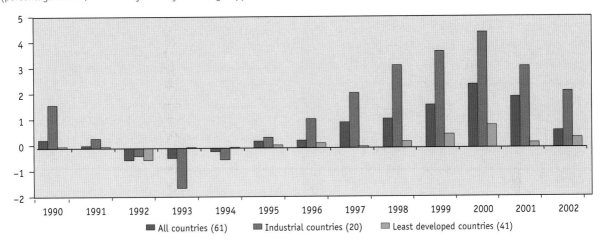

■ All countries (61)   ■ Industrial countries (20)   ■ Least developed countries (41)

*Source:* Fitch Ratings.

*Note:* These data differ in source and coverage from those underlying Figure 4.6. Therefore the two figures are not strictly comparable.

trends in real exchange rates. Real exchange rates depreciated over the 1990s in a majority of developing countries. For the median developing country, the volatility of the real exchange rate (as measured by the standard deviation of the rate of change of the real exchange rate) declined from the record highs of the 1980s, but the decline was limited to middle-income countries, and over the 1990s developing countries as a group exhibited much more volatile real exchange rates than industrial countries (figure 4.9).

The relatively high volatility of real exchange rates partly reflected the high incidence of exchange rate crises (figure 4.10). The incidence of devaluations peaked in 1994, with the devaluation of the CFA franc, and in 1998, with the East Asia and Russian Federation crises. When we look at the decade as a whole, it emerges that exchange rate crises were slightly less frequent in the 1990s than in the 1980s, but much more so than in the 1960s and 1970s.[15]

High real exchange rate volatility and frequent exchange rate collapses suggest that over the 1990s progress in achieving robust nominal exchange rate arrangements was limited.

FIGURE 4.8

**Developing Countries: Seigniorage Revenues, 1966–2000**

(percentage of GDP, medians by country income group)

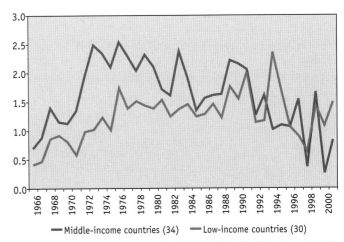

— Middle-income countries (34)   — Low-income countries (30)

*Sources:* IMF, *International Finance Statistics*; World Bank, *World Development Indicators*.

*Note:* The countries featured are those for which data are available over the entire period shown.

## The External Environment

What role did external shocks, real or financial, play in the observed trends in macroeconomic instability?

FIGURE 4.9

## Real Exchange Rate Volatility, 1961–2000

(percent, medians, by income group)

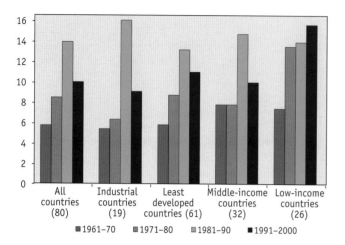

Source: Aten, Heston, and Summers 2001.

Note: Figure shows the standard deviation of the rate of change in the real exchange rate. The countries featured are those for which data are available over the entire period shown.

As to real disturbances, developing countries suffered only modest terms-of-trade shocks in the 1990s (see chapter 3). The volatility of the terms of trade declined in all developing regions, in most cases to levels comparable to those of the 1960s. The only exception was the Middle East and North Africa region, whose terms of trade were still less volatile than in the 1970s and 1980s.

It is more difficult to assess the volatility of the financial environment. The behavior of interest rates in the world's major financial markets captures some of this volatility, but the interest rates paid by developing countries incorporate risk premia that make these rates much more volatile than industrial-country interest rates.[16] Volatility measures based on such risk premia, or indeed on flows of capital to developing countries, are not necessarily good indicators of the volatility of the international financial environment, since they partly depend on events in the borrowing countries themselves.

Figure 4.11 shows the volatility of international net capital flows as measured by their standard deviation. This measure suggests that the external

FIGURE 4.10

## Developing Countries: Exchange Rate Crises, 1963–2001

(relative frequency, percent)

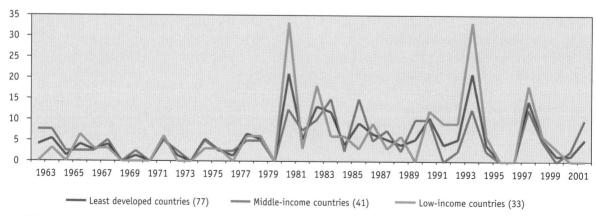

Source: IMF, International Finance Statistics.

Note: For this figure an exchange rate crisis is defined as in Frankel and Rose (1996): a depreciation of the (average) nominal exchange rate that (a) exceeds 25 percent, (b) exceeds the preceding year's rate of nominal depreciation by at least 10 percent, and (c) is at least three years apart from any previous crisis. The countries featured are those for which data are available over the entire period shown.

FIGURE 4.11

**Volatility of Net Capital Flows, 1977–2000**
(percent, medians by country income group)

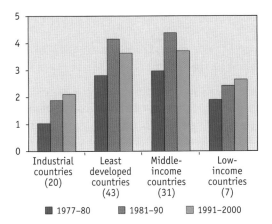

*Source:* IMF, *International Finance Statistics.*

*Note:* Figure shows the standard deviation of net capital flows as a percentage of GDP. Using instead the coefficient of variation leads to qualitatively similar results. The countries featured are those for which data are available over the entire period shown.

FIGURE 4.12

**Developing Countries: Sudden Stops in Net Capital Inflows, 1978–2000**
(relative frequency, percent)

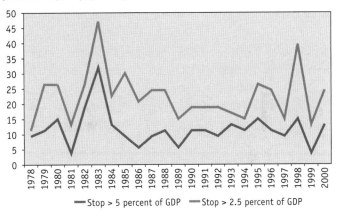

*Source:* IMF, *International Finance Statistics.* Balanced sample includes 53 countries.

*Note:* Data for the first half of the 1970s are too limited to allow a comprehensive analysis. Sudden stops are defined as declines in net capital *inflows* in excess of a given percentage of GDP. Reversals are allowed to take place in adjacent years; using a two-year window leads to similar qualitative conclusions. Note that reversals could have been defined instead in terms of (large) changes in the current account deficit (as done, for example, by Hutchison and Noy 2002). However, when applied to a large cross-country sample such as the one at hand, the latter criterion tends to pick up numerous current account reversals (particularly in low-income countries) owing primarily to terms-of-trade shocks in a context of modest changes in capital flows.

financial environment was modestly less volatile in the 1990s than in the 1980s, but that capital flows to developing countries remained much more volatile than those to industrial countries.

Several observers have pointed out that large capital flow reversals, often termed "sudden stops," can be much more damaging for developing economies than is general capital-flow variability, because such abrupt stoppages force costly and disruptive real adjustments.[17] Sudden stops were not significantly more frequent in the 1990s than in the 1980s (figure 4.12). Their incidence declined in the first half of the 1990s, but then rose again in the second half, peaking about the time of the East Asia and Russia crises.[18]

## 2. Assessing the Experience of the 1990s

The brief review, above, of the macroeconomic facts of the 1990s shows that developing countries achieved notable progress on fiscal consolidation and inflation performance. Better fiscal and nominal stability helped achieve a moderate reduction in output volatility, facilitated by a somewhat more stable external environment.

But the picture was far from rosy. Developing economies remained much less stable than industrial ones. And extreme volatility accounted for a larger share of total volatility than previously. This latter fact accords with evidence suggesting that instances of currency crashes and "sudden stops" in capital inflows did not diminish during the 1990s. The picture is therefore one of dramatic policy improvements in some areas, of more moderate improvements in the stability of macroeconomic outcomes, and of persistent vulnerability to extreme macroeconomic events.

Below we use these findings to interpret the growth performance of developing countries during the 1990s. We first review the analytical links between macroeconomic stability and economic growth and then apply that framework to the experience of the 1990s.

## Links between Stability and Growth

A stable macroeconomic policy environment features a fiscal stance safely consistent with fiscal solvency, a monetary policy stance consistent with a low and stable rate of inflation, and a robust exchange rate regime that avoids both systematic currency misalignment and excessive volatility in the real exchange rate. Policy makers can foster stable macroeconomic outcomes both *directly*—by removing destabilizing policies themselves as sources of shocks—and *indirectly*—by using policies as stabilizing instruments in response to exogenous destabilizing shocks, thus enhancing the stability of key outcome variables. A stable policy framework is not an end in itself: it matters only as a means to secure a more stable overall macroeconomic environment.

Conceptually, the link between policy stability and growth is quite complex. First, the direct contribution that policy stability can make to growth is likely to depend on the institutional setting. What matters is not just whether policies are good today, but the perceived likelihood that they will continue to be so. To have a significant impact on growth, actual gains in macroeconomic stability need to be seen by the private sector as signs of a permanent change in the macroeconomic policy regime. Second, the potential indirect contribution of policy stability to growth—by promoting stable outcomes in the face of external shocks—is likely to depend on how vulnerable the economy is to shocks. Macroeconomic fragility—through which even minor shocks may have large macroeconomic consequences—may make the use of stabilization policies too costly, for fear of potentially adverse effects; here the result is policy paralysis. Or fragility may mean that the instability becomes so severe that no feasible policy adjustments are able to counter it.

These two points suggest that the type of macroeconomic stability likely to be most conducive to economic growth—durable outcomes-based stability—involves much more than just moving fiscal, monetary, and exchange rate policies in stabilizing directions. It requires that policy-based stability be given a solid institutional under-pinning, that sources of macroeconomic fragility be eliminated to the greatest possible extent, and that the authorities actively exploit the scope for stabilization policy created by these two improvements in the macroeconomic environment.

## How Much Macroeconomic Progress Was Made in the 1990s?

As argued above, developing countries achieved significant stability in the traditional macroeconomic policy sense during the late 1980s and early 1990s. These achievements were far from universal, however, and the consequence was that macro instability continued to impede growth in some countries and allowed traditional macro imbalances to generate crises that in many ways resembled those of the 1980s. Neither were the achievements always based on solid institutional foundations to guarantee their permanence, and they frequently did not translate into more effective use of macro policies as stabilization instruments.

A useful framework for discussing these issues is the public sector solvency condition, which requires the present value (PV) of primary surpluses $(T - G)$ and seigniorage revenue $(dM)$ to be at least as large as the government's outstanding stock of net debt $(B)$:

$$PV\ (T - G + dM) \geq B\ (0).$$

Stability requires a monetary and fiscal policy stance consistent with maintaining public sector solvency at low levels of inflation, while leaving some scope for mitigating the impact of real and financial shocks on macroeconomic performance. The former requirement imposes constraints on the size of both the primary deficit $(G - T)$ and its money financing $dM$, while the latter refers to the profiles of monetary and fiscal policy over the business cycle. These requirements apply not only to the present but also to the future, as implied by the present-value term in the expression.[19]

Reassessing developments during the 1990s in the light of the expression above, the following observations emerge:

- Most countries have yet to convey a convincing impression of fiscal solvency.

- Improvement in fiscal balances was often achieved either with stopgap measures that were unlikely to be sustainable or in ways inimical to growth and welfare.

- In many countries, fiscal policy remains destabilizing.

- Lasting nominal stability remains to be credibly established.

- Robust exchange rate arrangements have remained elusive.

- The reform agenda has proved to be incomplete.

We discuss these observations in turn.

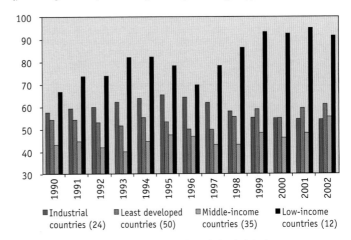

FIGURE 4.13
**Government Debt, 1990–2002**
(percentage of GDP, medians by country income group)

■ Industrial countries (24)   ■ Least developed countries (50)   ■ Middle-income countries (35)   ■ Low-income countries (12)

*Source:* World Bank, *WDI*; IMF, *World Economic Outlook*; Fitch Ratings.

## Most Countries Have Yet to Convey a Convincing Impression of Fiscal Solvency

Fiscal adjustment in the 1990s was often weakened by increases in debt that offset improvements in primary surpluses. Despite the trend toward lower fiscal deficits (figure 4.6 above), the ratio of public debt to GDP remained high in most developing countries (figure 4.13). And an incipient decline in these countries' ratios through 1997 was followed by a rise, so that by 2001–02 the debt ratio of the median developing country exceeded the 1990–91 level.[20] The rising trend appeared to be particularly marked among low-income countries, although data are too limited to draw firm conclusions.[21]

The persistence of high and rising debt over the 1990s reflects several factors.

First, improvements in fiscal performance were not universal. In India, for example, continuing large primary deficits, averaging close to 4 percent of GDP in the late 1990s, were the main factor behind persistent high debt ratios. Fiscal vulnerabilities played a role in the financial crises in Russia in 1998, Ecuador in 1999, and Argentina in 2002.[22] In many cases, the pressure of weak public finances on debt accumulation was revealed by an attempt at rapid disinflation, which implied a drop in deficit

monetization, reflected in the decline in seigniorage revenues (figure 4.8 above). Without an equally rapid correction of the primary deficit, debt issuance was left as the only source of financing. The debt impact of disinflation is confirmed by the statistically significant association between disinflation and subsequent rises in debt ratios over the 1990s.

In a majority of developing countries, however, primary deficits did decline over the 1990s, and other factors accounted for the lion's share of public debt accumulation. Key among these were the costs of banking system bailouts, which in several countries provided the main impetus for the growth in public debt.[23] Some of the banking crises of the 1990s, especially those in East Asia in 1997, had the greatest fiscal impact in history (figure 4.14).[24] Such crises also adversely affected income distribution, through their fiscal impact and other channels involving implicit net transfers from poorer households to financial system participants, in order to rescue and recapitalize the failed banks.[25]

Another factor behind the rise in debt stocks in the late 1990s was large real exchange rate depreciations, undertaken in a context in which the bulk of public debt was denominated in (or

FIGURE 4.14

## Total Fiscal Costs of Systemic Banking Crises as a Percentage of GDP

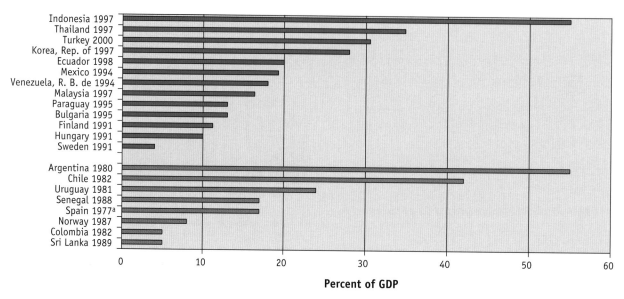

**Percent of GDP**

*Source:* Caprio and Klingebiel 2003.

a. Percentage of GNP.

indexed to) foreign currency. In both Argentina and Uruguay, for example, the collapse of domestic currencies in 2002 more than doubled the debt-to-GDP ratio, from 50 percent to more than 140 percent of GDP in Argentina and from 40 percent to more than 80 percent in Uruguay. Across emerging markets, debt dollarization remained pervasive: the median ratio of foreign currency debt to total public debt rose over the late 1990s to more than 55 percent by 2001 (figure 4.15).

A further reason for the persistence of high debt was the high real interest rates that prevailed in many countries, particularly in the late 1990s. This largely reflected the lack of credibility of stabilization efforts (documented below). Excessive reliance on short-term debt made some countries' overall fiscal outcomes, and thus their rates of public debt accumulation, highly sensitive to changes in domestic interest rates. In some countries, notably Brazil, high real interest rates contributed to a rapid pileup of public debt, further weakening perceptions of solvency and macroeconomic stability.

Thus, as to the solvency constraint introduced above, the bottom line is that, in many countries, increases in the observed value of the primary surplus $T - G$ did not suffice to bring down the burden of public debt.

A strong indication that perceptions of solvency remained shaky in the 1990s is the fact that default risk premia, as measured by sovereign borrowing spreads in international markets, remained highly volatile for most emerging countries (figure 4.16). As noted earlier, the evidence suggests that these premia depend not only on borrowers' existing debt burdens but also on investors' perceptions about the quality of borrowers' policy and institutional frameworks, and medium-term economic growth prospects—a key determinant of public sector solvency (Kraay and Nehru 2003). Thus, the volatility of risk premia likely reflected, among other factors, the markets' shifting perceptions about borrowers' ability to ensure stability and sustain adequate growth.

Perceptions of high default risk are not merely a symptom of perceived vulnerability. They themselves undermine macroeconomic

FIGURE 4.15

## Developing Countries' Foreign Currency Debt, 1997 and 2001

(percentage of general government debt, medians by country income group)

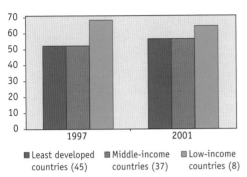

Least developed countries (45)  ■ Middle-income countries (37)  ■ Low-income countries (8)

*Source:* Moody's.

FIGURE 4.16

## Emerging Markets Bond Index Spreads for Latin and Non-Latin Borrowers

(basis points)

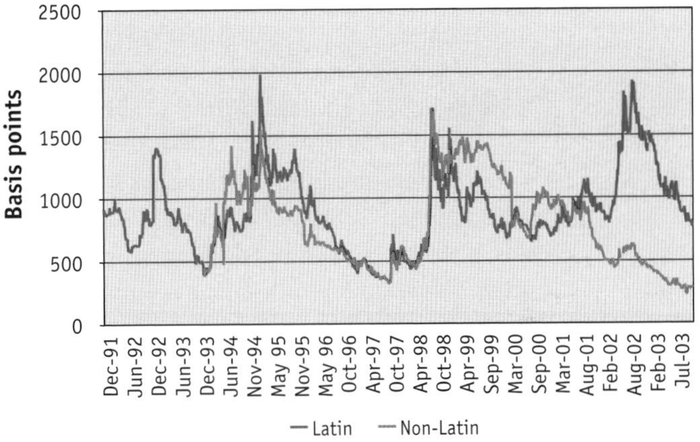

— Latin  — Non-Latin

*Source:* JP Morgan.

stability over business cycles. In particular, they hamper countries' ability to conduct stabilizing policies: when default risk is perceived to be high and highly sensitive to changes in circumstances, a country's attempts to run deficits at times of cyclical contraction may be viewed with suspicion and result in large jumps in risk premia (and thus borrowing costs), in turn discouraging the use of counter-cyclical fiscal policy.[26]

## Often Improvement in Fiscal Balances Was Achieved Either with Stopgap Measures or in Ways Inimical to Growth and Welfare

In numerous instances, fiscal improvements themselves were perceived as purely temporary, either because the measures used to achieve them were clearly transitory or because they directly compromised future growth and welfare. In terms of the solvency constraint above, such adjustments often reduced the current deficit significantly but had little effect (or even an adverse one) on the path of future deficits.

Such temporary fiscal correction was sometimes achieved through fiscal tricks designed to meet short-term targets for deficits or debt without making real progress toward fiscal solvency. A common such device involves changing the timing of expenditures (for example postponing them into subsequent fiscal years or accumulating payments arrears) or revenues (for example,

speeding up the extraction of exhaustible resources or advancing tax collection) without altering their present value, which is the relevant magnitude for solvency. Another popular strategy involves one-time asset sales to finance the retirement of public debt, which in principle implies no change in the government's net worth. Likewise, governments have often resorted to replacing explicit debt with contingent liabilities (for example, granting debt guarantees rather than subsidies to public firms). All these measures improve conventional indicators of cash deficit and gross debt—the two fiscal benchmarks closely watched by investors and international financial institutions—but have no effect on solvency. They represent illusory fiscal adjustment.[27]

In other instances, the appearance of fiscal adjustment may reflect a rise in revenues resulting from a temporary boom in tax bases. This may happen, for example, when a transitory surge in capital inflows boosts consumption in an economy with a value added tax (VAT)-dominated tax system. When the consumption boom ends, a major fiscal gap opens. There is evidence that this mechanism played a significant role in some emerging markets in the 1990s (Talvi 1997).

More generally, many fiscal adjustment episodes have focused more on the quantity than on the quality of adjustment, with very limited attention given to public spending composition and its implications for growth and welfare. Sometimes the result has been adjustment at the cost of social expenditures, leaving critical social needs unmet (IMF 2003a, chapter 6). But reducing spending on health and education may retard growth not just by reducing the accumulation of human capital, but also by undermining political support for sustaining responsible macroeconomic policies. Such measures defeat the ultimate objective of fiscal adjustment—namely, to allow the resumption of sustained growth.[28]

More often than not, productive public expenditures, on items such as human capital formation and infrastructure, have also been compressed in the process of fiscal adjustment. The main reason is that the emphasis on cash deficits and debt discourages projects whose costs are borne upfront but whose returns accrue only over time. Such projects have the same impact on the government's short-term financing needs as does pure consumption or any other spending item, but their impact on solvency is quite different because, unlike consumption, they involve creating assets that yield future tax revenues (either directly or by augmenting output and thence augmenting revenues). The conventional fiscal aggregates—such as the primary or the overall surplus that is closely monitored by international financial institutions and investors—ignore this distinction, and the result is that fiscal adjustment tends to have an anti-investment bias.[29]

To the extent that reduced investment lowers growth and hence future tax bases, such a bias can adversely affect growth and even fiscal solvency itself. Latin America, where reductions in public infrastructure spending supplied the bulk of the fiscal correction achieved by some of the region's major countries in the 1990s, provides a good example of these perverse dynamics.

## In Many Countries, Fiscal Policy Remains Destabilizing

The stabilizing power of fiscal policy depends largely on its ability to mitigate cyclical fluctuations. But in developing countries fiscal policy tends to be pro-cyclical, expanding in booms and contracting in recessions—a pattern that makes it a major source of macroeconomic instability. Take, for example, the cyclical behavior of public consumption. On average in developing countries, a 1 percent increase in GDP growth tends to raise the growth rate of public consumption spending by about 0.5 percentage point. Among industrial countries the corresponding figure is much smaller, at about 0.15 percentage point, and in the G-7 countries the response of public consumption is actually negative.[30]

Among developing countries, fiscal pro-cyclicality peaked in the 1980s and declined somewhat over the 1990s, but it remained much higher than in more advanced countries (figure 4.17). Pro-cyclical fiscal policy played a key role in some of the recent crises, notably in Argentina.[31]

## Lasting Nominal Stability Remains to Be Credibly Established

The preceding points refer to two of the three components of the public sector solvency condition: net debt $B$, and the present value of the primary surplus, PV $(T - G)$. The third component is the present value of seigniorage revenue, PV(d$M$). Developing countries substantially reduced the monetization of their deficits in the 1990s (figure 4.8 above), but in many of them the stability of prices remains vulnerable.

A transitory reduction in d$M$ can be achieved in a variety of ways, but unless durable increases in $(T - G)$ are institutionalized, continuing pressures on the government budget will result in debt accumulation that will in turn create pressures for monetization. In many countries reductions in d$M$ were not accompanied by lasting solutions to fiscal problems. Some countries—notably Argentina, Brazil, Ecuador, Mexico, Russia, and Turkey—reduced inflation rates as the result of exchange rate-based stabilizations. Better price performance allowed them to reduce money growth rates, but the sustainability of this achievement was questionable in all of them. In most, persistent fiscal pressures were accompanied by real exchange rate appreciations and

FIGURE 4.17

## Pro-Cyclicality of Public Consumption, 1980–2000

(rolling 15-year windows, medians by country income group)

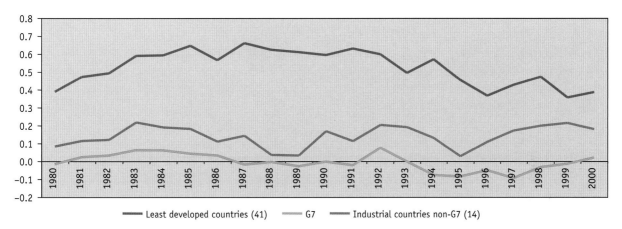

*Source:* Authors' own elaboration using data from World Bank, World Development Indicators.

*Note:* The figure shows the median of country-specific coefficient estimates obtained by regressing the rate of growth of public consumption on the rate of GDP growth (plus a constant).

increases in real interest rates, leading to a pileup of public debt and calling the sustainability of the stabilizations into question. In Argentina and Ecuador, inability to enforce fiscal discipline led to the adoption of hard exchange rate pegs in the hope that these would somehow harden the government budget constraint as well. Their failure to do so shows that such quick fixes do not achieve lasting nominal stability in the absence of an independent commitment to responsible fiscal policies. In Brazil, Mexico, and Turkey, exchange rate–based stabilizations relying on "soft" pegs eventually resulted in currency crises that gave way to short bursts of accelerated inflation. Likewise, the devaluation of the CFA franc largely reflected the failure of the CFA arrangements to enforce fiscal discipline in the face of adverse terms-of-trade shocks (box 4.1).

In the search for nominal stability, some countries in the 1990s placed their reliance on independent central banks with a commitment to price stability. As does a fixed nominal exchange rate, such an arrangement works in principle by committing the central bank to a low value of $dM$, thereby imposing a hard budget constraint on the fiscal authorities and forcing the latter to adjust $(T - G)$ to the requirements of price stabil-

ity. If such an arrangement is to promote lasting price stability, the central bank must be able to resist pressures for monetization arising from the fiscal side. That is, it must achieve true independence from the finance ministry.

The establishment of truly independent and effective central banks has not been a straightforward matter. The creation of independent central banks in República Bolivariana de Venezuela in 1989 and in Mexico in 1993, for example, did not prevent the emergence of the strong political pressures for credit creation that contributed to currency crises in both countries in the first half of the 1990s. Similar pressures were brought to bear on Argentina's central bank in 2001, on the eve of the collapse of the hard peg.

Some observers suggest that a good indicator of de facto central bank independence is the frequency of turnover of the central bank governor.[32] Among middle-income countries, turnover was sharply lower in the 1990s than in the 1980s, and among low-income developing countries it was modestly lower (figure 4.18).

Since the rate of turnover of central bank governors may not be a good indicator of the expected permanence of nominal stability,[33] it may be useful to observe the behavior of the pri-

**BOX 4.1**
## Devaluation of the CFA franc

The 14 West African countries of the CFA franc zone share the CFA franc as their common currency. From 1948 to 1993, the CFA franc was pegged to the French franc, partly to minimize transactions costs in international trade but also to provide a nominal anchor for these economies.

The common currency was reasonably effective in maintaining financial discipline in member countries for an extended period. Until the mid-1980s, these countries enjoyed lower inflation and more sustained economic growth than other Sub-Saharan African countries. But the shortcomings of the hard peg against the French franc became apparent in the mid-1980s when the zone was hit by two external shocks: a sharp deterioration in member countries' terms of trade, arising from a decline in the world prices of their primary export commodities, and a strong appreciation of the French franc against the U.S. dollar. These shocks placed strong pressures on fiscal outcomes, which depended heavily on commodity revenues and trade taxes. Member countries' failure to impose an orderly correction, partly because they could not adjust public sector wages downward, led to sharply higher fiscal and current account deficits, large increases in external debt, and deteriorating growth performance relative to other countries in

Sub-Saharan Africa. The CFA franc became substantially overvalued.

To reverse the worsening economic performance, the currency's first major devaluation was implemented in January 1994, when the official parity was changed from CFAF 50 to CFAF 100 = F 1. The devaluation was accompanied by measures to improve fiscal performance (broadening the tax base and reducing expenditures), as well as structural reforms focused on trade liberalization, increasing flexibility in labor markets, reducing the direct role of government in production, and restructuring financial sectors.

The results of the devaluation were quite positive. Inflation accelerated at first but quickly converged to single-digit levels. Consequently, the real effective depreciation of the CFA franc in 1994 amounted to about 30 percent. Real GDP growth, negative in 1993, averaged 1.3 percent for the zone as a whole in 1994, and accelerated subsequently. Overall fiscal deficits, which had peaked at about 8 percent of GDP in 1993, had fallen to just over 2 percent of GDP by 1996. A substantial increase in saving rates reduced the current account deficit by some 2 percent of GDP between 1993 and 1996. Coupled with capital repatriation and renewed external assistance, this substantially increased the foreign exchange reserves of regional central banks.

*Source*: Clement et al. 1996.

vate sector, to try to infer what the private sector expects about nominal stability.

First, since agents can partly protect themselves against nominal instability by denominating their assets in foreign exchange, one indicator of the confidence that private agents in developing countries may have in the permanence of nominal stability is the incidence of dollarization. Improved confidence in nominal stability should result in a reduced incidence of dollarization.[34] Many developing countries remained heavily dollarized at the end of the 1990s and, as figure

4.19 shows, the median degree of dollarization of bank deposits among low- and middle-income developing countries actually *rose* over the 1990s.[35] The contrast with richer countries is stark: their much lower degree of deposit dollarization showed little change over the same period.

Second, ex post real interest rates tend to be high when actual inflation falls short of expectations and when uncertainty about inflation is high. During the 1990s, real interest rates were declining in industrial countries, but in developing countries they remained high—and indeed

FIGURE 4.18

**Central Bank Independence in Developing Countries, 1975–98**

(annual governor turnover, medians by country income group)

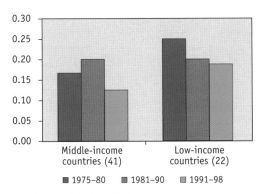

*Source:* Sturm and de Haan 2001.

FIGURE 4.19

**Dollarization of Deposits, 1996 and 2001**

(foreign currency deposits as a percentage of total, medians by country income group)

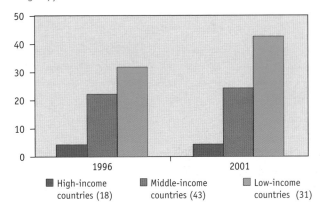

*Source:* IMF, International Financial Statistics.

*Note:* For Austria, Haiti, Israel, Mexico, Macedonia, and Netherlands we take the 1997 data, and for Ghana, Italy, Norway, Tajikistan, and Uganda we take the 2000 data. High corresponds to OECD and non-OECD countries.

were higher at the end of the decade than at the beginning (figure 4.20).

Of course, both dollarization ratios and ex post real interest rates reflect a variety of factors in addition to perceptions of nominal instability, so this evidence is only suggestive.[36] But other indicators point in the same direction. As an extreme example, the currency premium on the Argentine *peso* was positive throughout the 1990s, and it became very large at times of turbulence, in spite of the supposedly irrevocable peg to the dollar that was enshrined in Argentina's Convertibility Law.[37]

## Robust Exchange Rate Arrangements Have Remained Elusive

Progress toward robust exchange rate regimes probably was an early casualty of the search for macroeconomic stability. Many countries adopted exchange rate–based stabilization strategies as a supposedly quick recipe for disinflation, as discussed above. These strategies not only meant adopting single-currency pegs, but also made such pegs very difficult to adjust, since they tied the credibility of the entire stabilization program to the stability of the peg. In effect, defending the peg sometimes became an end in itself, even after the peg had clearly outlived its usefulness. More flexible exchange rate arrangements

have too often been adopted only after currency crises.

The Mexico and East Asia crises, which involved the collapse of a variety of soft pegs, prompted what came to be known as the "two extremes" view of exchange rate regimes. In this view, only irrevocable pegs (including both currency boards and monetary unification or dollarization) and freely floating exchange rates were fit for survival in a world of increasing financial integration, because only these extreme regimes appeared to offer enough transparency to make exchange rate policy easily verifiable and hence credible.[38] There appeared to be an incipient flight away from intermediate regimes,[39] based on the belief that monetary stability required either institutional arrangements that took discretion over money growth rates out of the hands of central banks, or fully independent central banks with reputational stakes in low and stable inflation, as well as the means (legal authority, policy instruments, human-resource capability) to achieve that goal.

The late 1990s showed that neither dollarization nor currency boards offered a speedy shortcut to fiscal orthodoxy and nominal stability.

FIGURE 4.20

## Ex Post Real Interest Rates, 1990–2001

(percent, medians by country income group)

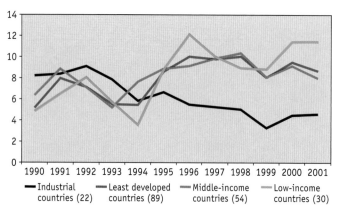

| — Industrial | — Least developed | — Middle-income | — Low-income |
| countries (22) | countries (89) | countries (54) | countries (30) |

*Source:* IMF, International Financial Statistics; World Bank, World Development Indicators.

*Note:* The real interest rate is measured as the (log) difference between the nominal interest rate and the one-period-ahead rate of GDP inflation.

Argentina's experience revealed the threat to stability that was posed by inflexible exchange rates, which made adjustment to real disturbances exceedingly difficult. Earlier in the decade, the fate of the CFA franc had offered the same lesson, though it was less publicized (box 4.1 above).

## The Reform Agenda Has Proved Incomplete

The developing countries' macroeconomic reform agenda of the 1990s was deficient in its very design, in that it left in place—or, worse, created—important sources of fragility.

The first of these sources stemmed from lack of attention to the soundness of the financial sector. While research has shown that an *efficient* domestic financial system is important for growth, the experience of the last decade strongly suggests that a *sound* one is indispensable for macroeconomic stability. The reform agenda of the early 1990s often ignored the central role of the financial system for macro stability—even though this role had been clearly revealed by the Southern Cone crises of the early 1980s. To the standard prescriptions for stability—a solvent fiscal stance, low and stable money growth, and robust exchange rate policies that nevertheless allow adjustment to shocks—it is necessary to add policies that foster a sound financial system.[40]

Few countries achieved a sound domestic financial system in the 1990s. As a result, an important source of macroeconomic fragility was not only left in place but may, indeed, have been magnified in the 1990s. Inadequate attention to financial sector soundness often left the domestic economic environment rife with institutional problems involving moral hazard, rendering both public and private balance sheets highly vulnerable to changes in interest rates and exchange rates. These features posed big obstacles to outcome-based stability in a number of major countries. Ironically, under these circumstances incipient progress along conventional dimensions of macro stability such as disinflation may even have made financial crises *more* likely. For example, the use of the exchange rate as a nominal anchor may have encouraged agents to ignore exchange rate risk and in the case of "hard" pegs such as that of Argentina may have made it more difficult for regulators to induce financial institutions to factor such risk into their portfolio allocations without raising fears that the peg might be abandoned.

Partly because of this gap in the reform agenda, the incidence of systemic banking crises was even higher in the 1990s than in the 1980s (figure 4.21).[41]

A second key source of macroeconomic fragility was increased capital mobility, which made economies vulnerable to sudden shifts in capital flows. The combination of unsound policies in the financial sector and open capital accounts helps explain many characteristics of the crises of the 1990s. Many of these crises involved simultaneous currency and banking collapses. Often banking problems preceded a currency crash, which then fed back into a full-blown financial crisis.[42] Further, many of the crises were not foreshadowed by standard macroeconomic imbalances. Those that were hardest to predict—especially the Mexican and Asian crises—occurred in a setting where the main vulnerabilities concerned financial, rather than macroeconomic, variables and took the form of balance of payments runs similar to traditional bank runs.[43] The deepest of the crises involved serious problems in the financial sector (Mexico,

Asia, Ecuador, and Turkey), in private sector balance sheets (Asia, Argentina), or fiscal insolvency (Ecuador, Argentina). Where none of these problems was present and events took the form of a simple currency crash (as in Brazil), crisis-induced economic contraction was less severe.[44]

## The Growth Payoff

Although many developing countries achieved faster growth in the 1990s than in the 1980s, this achievement was only a modest one, since growth in the 1980s was generally slow. For a majority of countries, growth rates in the 1990s remained well below those of the 1960s and 1970s.[45] Is this growth payoff commensurate with the progress made in macroeconomic stabilization, or is it disappointing? It is important to keep in mind that industrial countries also grew much more slowly in the 1990s than in the 1960s and 1970s. But several other issues also need to be taken into account.

First, as already explained, the growth payoff from macro stability depends on whether stability is perceived as permanent. In many instances progress in stabilization was based on policy changes that were not perceived as durable, or failed to include the reform of underlying institutions. It is these latter reforms that ultimately determine whether policy improvements are sustainable and perceived as such by the private sector. The limited progress made on this front probably undermined the contribution of macro policy improvements—even where they might have been sustained—to raising economic growth. Moreover, a vicious circle may have taken hold in some countries, in that the social consensus that made the policies possible, and was necessary to make them sustainable, faltered in the absence of a fairly prompt growth payoff.

Second, the search for macro stability, narrowly defined, may in some cases have actually been inimical to growth. Preoccupation with reducing inflation quickly induced some countries to adopt exchange rate regimes that ultimately conflicted with the goal of outcomes-based stability. Others pursued macro stability at the expense of growth-enhancing

FIGURE 4.21

**Incidence of Systemic Banking Crises, Developing Countries, 1981–2000**

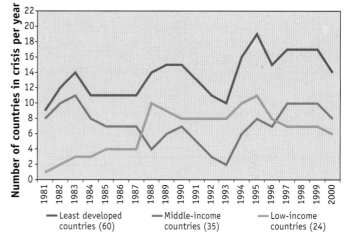

Source: Caprio and Klingebiel 2003.

policies such as adequate provision of public goods, as well as of social investments that might have both increased the growth payoff and made stability more durable.

Seen in this light, some economies may well have been overstabilized. From a microeconomic perspective, the presumed stability gains from further fiscal adjustments may not have justified the costs of forgoing key social and productive expenditures. From a macroeconomic perspective, the narrow focus on stability may have precluded more progress toward counter-cyclical policies. The contrast between the significant fiscal adjustment achieved by most developing countries and the persistence of outcomes-based instability suggests that this factor may have been important.

Third, even in countries that took radical steps toward macroeconomic stabilization, the reform agenda of the 1990s failed to address macroeconomic fragilities. Most notably, inappropriate policies toward the domestic financial sector and the capital account of the balance of payments left many stabilizing economies highly vulnerable to adverse shocks. Extreme macroeconomic volatility actually increased among developing countries during the 1990s, and the adverse impacts of extreme volatility on growth appear to exceed those of normal volatility. Thus, the growth payoff of the macroeconomic policy improvements achieved in the 1990s was limited not only by their weak institutional underpinnings but also by the extreme outcomes-based instability that emerged during the decade, mainly as a result of the fragilities that the reform agenda overlooked.

Fourth, the growth payoff of macroeconomic stability may have been oversold. Macro instability hampers investors' ability and willingness to respond to investment opportunities, understood in the broadest sense of the term, but for macro stability to deliver growth, those opportunities must exist in the first place. Thus while macroeconomic stability may facilitate growth when other forces are driving the growth momentum, it is not enough to drive the growth process itself: growth depends on the policies and institutions that shape opportunities and incentives to engage in growth-enhancing activities. The importance of these complementary factors may not have been sufficiently appreciated early in the 1990s, and gains in macroeconomic stability were often not accompanied by necessary growth-enhancing policies and institutional reforms in other parts of the economy.

In sum, there is little reason to expect a simple, direct association between macro stability and growth. From this perspective, the limited growth payoff that emerged from the gains in macroeconomic stability achieved during the 1990s may not be very surprising.

## 3. Lessons

What lessons can be drawn from the experience of the 1990s? An important lesson is that old verities still hold true: perceived fiscal insolvency, high and unstable inflation, and severely overvalued real exchange rates remain reliable recipes for extreme instability and slow growth. But while in some cases slow growth and frequent crises reflected insufficient policy improvements, the evidence also highlights shortcomings in the reform agenda. Three elements are critical: the institutional framework for monetary and fiscal

policy, the prevention of macroeconomic fragilities, and complementary pro-growth policies. These elements are reviewed below.

### Institutions for Macroeconomic Policy Formulation

The institutional context in which traditional macroeconomic policies are formulated is critical to an adequate resolution of the tradeoff between policy credibility and flexibility. Both credibility and flexibility are required for sustained and sustainable stability that ultimately matters for economic growth. In the fiscal arena, an appropriate institutional setting should ensure transparency; sustainable solvency, possibly through the adoption of fiscal rules; flexibility; and a pro-growth structure of government budgets. With respect to the monetary and exchange rate policies within the purview of the central bank, the most successful institutional innovation to emerge in the 1990s seems to be one featuring an independent central bank with a floating exchange rate regime and a publicly announced inflation target. The following discussion examines these aspects of the institutional framework for the formulation of traditional macroeconomic policies.

### Fiscal Policy

*Budgetary institutions and counter-cyclical fiscal policies.* The critical problem of pro-cyclical fiscal policy persisted through the 1990s. The phenomenon arises because, in the absence of strong budgetary institutions, a "tragedy of the commons" sets in during good times when government revenues are high: political imperatives cause the government to spend all of its resources (even to borrow) in the boom, leaving little margin of solvency from which to finance fiscal deficits when times are bad.

What is required in such situations is to make it politically possible for the government to run fiscal surpluses during good times. This calls for the development of budgetary institutions or the implementation of fiscal rules that force claimants on the government's resources to respect the government's intertemporal budget constraint, thus securing prudent fiscal responses to favorable shocks.

Transparent fiscal rules embodied in the country's constitution or passed into law subject to change only by legislative supermajorities, with stipulated penalties for noncompliance, may be effective in many contexts.[46] In countries where government revenues depend heavily on the prices of primary commodities, institutions such as oil stabilization funds may need to be created to save windfalls. More generally, the key objective is to provide scope for automatic fiscal stabilizers to do their job. One promising example is Chile's Structural Surplus rule, which establishes fiscal policy targets adjusted for the variation in growth over the cycle. An alternative proposal, yet to be implemented, focuses on the creation of an independent fiscal policy council, along lines similar to an independent central bank, to set annual deficit limits.[47] Whatever institutional arrangement is chosen, a basic policy step is to set fiscal deficit targets in cyclically adjusted terms, a practice that could be encouraged by the international financial institutions.

Similar arguments apply to fiscal decentralization. While local provision of public goods has much to recommend it, experience has shown that fiscal decentralization is also vulnerable to a commons problem unless institutional remedies are implemented that impose hard budget constraints on subnational governments. One way to reduce the pro-cyclical bias in decentralized systems is to insulate resource-sharing arrangements from the effects of the cycle.[48]

Another important institutional aspect of fiscal policy is that of transparency. Uncertainty about the state of their fiscal accounts probably strongly influenced the risk premia that developing-country borrowers paid in international capital markets during the 1990s. Enhanced fiscal transparency is an important step in reducing such uncertainty. There is also evidence that more transparent budgetary procedures are associated with lower deficits and debt.[49] The interests of fiscal transparency are well served by a full accounting of the contingent liabilities of the public sector, including those of the central bank, and by explicit recognition of implicit liabilities, including those embedded in public pension systems.

*Fiscal flexibility.* The 1990s showed that fiscal flexibility is as important as fiscal credibility, and that to be effective, fiscal rules need to balance these two objectives. Simple rules are more transparent and hence more easily verifiable, but they need to be flexible enough for fiscal policy to react to a changing economic environment. Overly rigid rules are unlikely to be sustainable or credible, as shown by the recent near-demise of the European Stability Pact owing to its neglect of the role of the macroeconomic cycle.

Another lesson of the 1990s, however, is that it is risky for governments to depart from the path of fiscal rectitude, even when outcomes-based stability would benefit from this step, because markets may interpret it as a sign of fiscal lassitude. The tight fiscal policies adopted by the countries most heavily affected by the Asian financial crisis, immediately after the crisis and while in the grip of severe recessions, exemplify this problem.[50] If such threats to confidence were justified, the importance of improving fiscal institutions is enhanced, since the role of such institutions is precisely to secure the credibility needed for governments to exercise fiscal flexibility without being unjustly punished by financial markets. If the threats to confidence were overstated, however, a key moral of the experience of the 1990s is that it is important not to make a fetish out of fiscal stability as such. The need then is only to achieve enough stability to convince the private sector that there has been a sustainable change in regime. Once this is accomplished, the authorities gain scope to use macroeconomic policy instruments flexibly for stabilization purposes, and should exploit this to achieve outcomes-based stability.

*Sustainable fiscal solvency and the avoidance of fiscal stopgaps.* For a fiscal adjustment to be perceived as durable, it must be based on sustainable policies, and on measures that are likely to enhance growth, on both the expenditure and revenue sides of the government's budget. In short, the *composition* of fiscal adjustment matters. With respect to sustainability, fiscal adjustments should be based on measures that the private sector can expect will increase the *present value* of future primary surpluses. Temporary fiscal stopgaps fall short of this criterion. With respect to growth, some measures such as highly distortionary taxes (for example, on external trade or on domestic financial transactions), or cuts in spending on productive infrastructure or human capital, may raise the present value of the primary surplus at the expense of growth. These policies may even fail to raise the present value of future primary surpluses if their negative effects on economic growth have a sufficiently adverse impact on growth in government revenues (Easterly and Servén 2003).

## Monetary Policy and Exchange Rate Regimes

While the evidence suggests that low and stable rates of inflation are conducive to economic growth, theory suggests that what is most important is convincing the private sector that low and stable inflation is here to stay. In the 1990s this proved hard to do. As does fiscal credibility, price stability requires an appropriate institutional underpinning. One lesson of the decade is that purely monetary arrangements are not enough to ensure the credibility of monetary policy: since not even the most rigid monetary arrangements (a currency board or de jure dollarization) provide a guarantee of hard government budget constraints, fiscal credibility is necessary too. Further, a credible commitment to fiscal solvency is not the same thing as a credible commitment to price stability, since fiscal solvency is in principle compatible with relatively high and fluctuating levels of seigniorage revenue. Thus there is a separate role for monetary institutions that can credibly preclude excessive reliance on seigniorage revenues.

The 1990s showed that monetary credibility has to be earned the hard way, through anti-inflationary performance. In this regard, a successful innovation during the last decade has been the institution of an independent central bank operating a floating exchange rate, and with a commitment to price stability that takes the form of a publicly announced inflation target. Such an arrangement is currently maintained by Brazil, Chile, Colombia, Korea, Mexico, Peru, South

Africa, and Thailand. It has the important advantages of flexibility (since the central bank is not constrained in *how* it attains its inflation target) as well as of commitment (since the central bank's prestige is put publicly on the line). Most important, the adoption of floating exchange rates and inflation targets allows the domestic authorities to establish their anti-inflationary credibility by establishing a track record rather than by attempting to import it through some form of exchange rate peg. The longest running of these arrangements—Chile's—was remarkably successful in maintaining price stability throughout the 1990s, while avoiding severe episodes of real exchange rate volatility. More recent converts to this type of nominal institutional arrangement have also been quite successful thus far.

## *Robustness: The Scope of the Macroeconomic Reform Agenda*

Beyond traditional macroeconomic policies, the proliferation of crises during the 1990s has made it clear that the stability agenda should encompass not just fiscal, monetary, and exchange rate policies, but also policies designed to reduce macroeconomic—especially financial—fragility. These include, in particular, policies directed toward the domestic financial system and toward the management of the country's capital account.

## The Domestic Financial System

The experience of the 1990s once again underlined the importance of an appropriately regulated and supervised domestic financial system to avoid macroeconomic vulnerability arising from the concentration of lending in highly risky activities or the emergence of balance sheet mismatches.

Although the repressed domestic financial sectors that prevailed in many developing countries during previous decades were undoubtedly inimical to economic growth, an important old lesson that was relearned in the 1990s is that necessary reforms in the domestic financial sector are not simply synonymous with liberalization. Removing restrictions on entry, on the setting of interest rates, and on the allocation of the portfolios of financial institutions without simultaneously strengthening the institutional framework in which the financial sector operates creates excessive scope for moral-hazard lending. This leaves financial sector balance sheets vulnerable to insolvency in response even to moderate macroeconomic shocks (see chapter 7).

The key lesson is that, for domestic financial systems that have not already been liberalized, the pace of liberalization should be modulated to reflect the quality of the institutional framework governing the domestic financial sector. As has been widely recognized, the appropriate institutional framework has a number of ingredients: clear and secure property rights, an efficient and impartial legal system to enforce contracts, appropriate legal protection for creditors, well-specified accounting and disclosure standards, a regulatory system that screens entrants while encouraging competition, the imposition of adequate capital requirements and prevention of excessively risky lending, and a supervisory system that can effectively monitor the lending practices of domestic financial institutions. Improving the quality of this framework deserves high priority in the macroeconomic reform agenda.

## The Capital Account

With respect to the capital account, the management of a country's integration into international financial markets remains a controversial part of the institutional agenda. As in the case of the domestic financial sector, enhanced integration with world financial markets promises many benefits, but when the domestic institutional structure is defective the costs—in the form of macro risks—may outweigh those benefits. Increased financial openness makes it easier for investors to punish countries whose macroeconomic policies are perceived to be off-track.[51] Despite the theoretical arguments in favor of opening the capital account, the international evidence is inconclusive on whether this has been conducive to growth.[52] Moreover, the evidence suggests that, contrary to theoretical predictions, it has not helped to reduce macroeconomic (especially consumption) volatility.[53]

The desire to avoid macroeconomic fragility makes a strong case for institutional arrangements regarding the capital account that at least preclude the emergence of maturity mismatches in a country's external balance sheet, since such mismatches can make the country vulnerable to creditor runs analogous to bank runs.[54] The question is *how* to preclude them. Creditors favor short maturities as a means of monitoring borrowers and controlling their behavior precisely when asymmetric information and moral hazard problems are serious. Under these circumstances, therefore, short-maturity borrowing will be substantially less costly to borrowers than long-term borrowing. The problem is, of course, that voluntary short-maturity loans between private parties fail to take into account the social costs associated with the risk of creditor runs.

To tackle this problem, in some East Asian countries, as well as Chile, the public sector has accumulated large foreign exchange reserves to offset liquid liabilities incurred by the private sector. This approach is likely to be very expensive: holding large volumes of low-yielding, short-term assets instead of (illiquid) long-term investments entails serious opportunity costs and even fiscal ones, because the purchase of foreign exchange reserves needs to be sterilized by the sale of typically higher-yielding domestic government liabilities. Meanwhile, the incentives that give rise to short-term borrowing are left in place, and the costs of insuring against creditor runs are ultimately borne by taxpayers.

An alternative route is to discourage the private sector from incurring short-term external liabilities in the first place—by restricting short-term capital inflows—or to make those liabilities effectively less liquid in times of crisis—by restricting short-term capital outflows. Because both of these policies tend to raise the cost of short-term loans, they effectively operate by internalizing the systemic costs associated with the risk of creditor runs.

Can such restrictions be designed to be minimally distortionary with respect to other types of capital flows? And can they be made effective? These questions have attracted considerable attention in recent years. As to restrictions on inflows, the evidence is modestly reassuring. Cross-country and country-specific studies generally conclude that inflow restrictions such as unremunerated reserve requirements (such as the Chilean *encaje*) tend not to affect the overall volume of inflows but to affect their composition, reducing the share of short-term flows in the total.[55] Evidence on the effects of restrictions on outflows is much less conclusive.

On balance, the available evidence suggests that restrictions on short-term capital inflows may have a role to play in the pursuit of outcomes-based macroeconomic stability in developing countries. However, it is important to be aware that such restrictions entail costs to private agents, through their impact on the availability or price of financing.[56]

In addition to maturity mismatches, external borrowing aggravates the problem of currency mismatches, to the extent that foreign lenders are less willing to accept the risk of currency depreciation than are domestic lenders and thus refuse to extend credit in the borrower's currency. The solution here is not to restrict access to external borrowing. In the short run, the solution is to promote the efficient distribution of the exchange rate risk within the domestic economy by ensuring, through regulatory means, that it is appropriately priced and therefore borne by those agents best able to bear it (typically, those holding foreign currency assets, including exporters). In the case of sovereign borrowing, the priority is to ensure that borrowing decisions reflect the existence and potential cost of exchange rate risk. Over the longer term, a larger role in ameliorating the problem of currency mismatches would be assumed by institutional changes that promote credible nominal stability, thus mitigating exchange rate risk. The experience of economies such as South Africa that are starting to be able to borrow externally in their own currencies is consistent with this perspective. The international financial institutions could help advance this process by denominating their lending in local currency, a practice that they are already starting with some emerging markets.

## Complementarities among Pro-Growth Policies

Much of the rest of this volume focuses on the role of pro-growth policies outside the macroeconomic arena. Such policies include, for example, the implementation of an open international trade regime, the adoption of national innovation policies, well-functioning factor markets, and an investor-friendly legal and regulatory environment. In some cases, those policies actually facilitate the adoption of reforms aimed at macroeconomic stability: for example, disinflation or the correction of a real misalignment is easier and less costly to achieve when labor and financial markets are functioning well.

Policies of this type are mutually complementary with policies that focus on creating and preserving macroeconomic stability. An unstable macroeconomic environment tends to undermine the growth benefits of such policies. Still, what we have learned from the 1990s is that macro stability alone is not enough; policies outside the macroeconomic arena are themselves indispensable to harvest the fruits of macroeconomic stability in the form of sustained high rates of economic growth.

## Notes

1. Easterly (2001) also states the view that the multiple crises of the 1990s represent a symptom of, rather than an "explanation" for, the slow growth of the 1990s.
2. In recent years interest has revived, sparked by Ramey and Ramey (1995), in the adverse effects that real and nominal instability can have on economic growth. For a recent evaluation of the growing empirical literature on the subject., see Hnatkovska and Loayza (2004).
3. The level of inflation is strongly associated with its volatility, as well as with the volatility of relative prices. For these reasons, and because high levels of inflation are likely to be viewed as unsustainable, inflation itself is commonly taken as a summary indicator of instability. In turn, the external current account deficit is commonly viewed as a leading indicator of future instability, with excessively large—and thus unsustainable— deficits often predicting a macroeconomic crisis.

4. See IDB (1995); De Ferranti et al. (2000); and Easterly, Islam, and Stiglitz (2001). The popular view that instability is on the rise is documented by Rodrik (2001b).

5. Here the focus is on a sample of 97 countries with populations greater than 500,000, for which there is complete information on real GDP growth over the period 1960–2000. The population lower limit is set to exclude highly volatile island economies. The total sample includes 20 industrial and 77 developing economies, of which three (Israel, Hong Kong [China], and Singapore) are higher-income non-OECD countries.

6. The decline in developing-country volatility over the 1990s is documented also by Rodrik (2001b), De Ferranti et al. (2000), and Hnatkovska and Loayza (2004). The same result holds if volatility is measured by a robust statistic such as the interquartile range instead of the standard deviation.

7. The decline in volatility was statistically significant: formal tests strongly reject the hypothesis that the cross-country distribution of growth volatility did not change between the 1980s and the 1990s, as well as the hypothesis that the changes in volatility across the two decades are centered at zero.

8. The information on private consumption is available only for a slightly smaller country sample. The fact that consumption volatility declined less than income and output volatility in the 1990s is underscored by Kose, Prasad, and Terrones (2003), and has been viewed as a failure of financial openness to provide the consumption-smoothing mechanism predicted by conventional theory.

9. Negative extreme shocks also accounted for a larger fraction of the total volatility of gross national income and consumption in the 1990s than in previous decades. In technical terms, the frequency distribution of growth rates shows heavier left tails in the 1990s. For both GDP and consumption growth, this is confirmed by conventional skewness statistics.

10. There are good reasons why. On the one hand, with a given set of risk management mechanisms, large shocks may be more difficult to absorb than small ones. These threshold effects of volatility have been found to be empirically relevant for investment (Sarkar 2000; Servén 2003). On the other hand, owing to asymmetries built into the economy, negative shocks have qualitatively different consequences than positive ones. A clear example is that of buffer stocks such as bank liquidity or international reserves: large adverse shocks (or a succession of small negative ones) can exhaust them and trigger an adjustment mechanism very different from the one involved for positive disturbances. The same applies to firms' net worth: once it becomes negative, adjustment takes place

through bankruptcies, with the corresponding destruction of productive assets.

11. On the relation between macroeconomic volatility and poverty, see Laursen and Mahajan (2004). Easterly and Fischer (2001) investigate the impact of inflation on the poor.

12. The availability of data on the other indicators presented in the rest of this section is in general much more limited than in the case of growth and inflation. For this reason, the figures below refer to the universe of countries for which information on the variable of interest is available over the entire period shown. That universe varies across different variables, and therefore the conclusions of the analysis have to be taken with some caution.

13. In part, however, this apparent improvement reflects the "sudden stop" of capital inflows to crisis-afflicted emerging-market economies.

14. Other measures of fiscal policy stability also showed an improvement. For example, the volatility of public spending (as measured by the standard deviation of public consumption growth) declined sharply among middle-income countries. Among lower-income economies, however, it showed little change relative to previous decades.

15. In a smaller country sample (whose coverage ends in 1997), Bordo et al. (2001) also find that the frequency of currency crashes declined in the 1990s compared to the preceding 15 years.

16. The fact that weak policies and institutions (or other factors) can result in high default risk even at moderate levels of debt has prompted recommendations for extra-cautious upper bounds on debt ratios for developing economies; see Reinhart, Rogoff, and Savastano (2003). On the other hand, the dependence of spreads on lenders' expectations raises the possibility of self-fulfilling debt crises; see, for example, Cohen and Portes (2003).

17. See Calvo (1998); Calvo and Reinhart (2000); and Mendoza (2001). However, capital flow turnarounds do not necessarily represent exogenous shifts in international investors' sentiment. They reflect in part the effects of developments in the destination economies (resulting from, among other factors, changing domestic policies) as well as in international financial markets affecting the perceived risk and return differentials from investing in different markets.

18. The incidence of capital flow reversals among industrial countries (not shown in figure 4.12 to avoid cluttering the graph) was also fairly high in the 1990s, although admittedly the *level* of capital flows was much higher among them than among developing countries.

19. Indeed, one of the key dilemmas for macroeconomic policy making is how to assure the private sector that

future policies will abide by the requirements of solvency and low inflation, without having to surrender the short-run stabilization capability of monetary and fiscal policy. As discussed later in this section, many of the achievements and disappointments of the 1990s relate to the search for lasting solutions to this dilemma.

20. The same pattern is found in IMF (2003d). Among the 46 low- and middle-income countries in the sample underlying figure 4.13, the debt-to-GDP ratio rose in 24 and fell in 22.

21. These debt-to-GDP ratios do not accurately reflect the debt burdens faced by low-income developing countries relative to the other groups in figure 4.13, since the low-income countries tend to have a larger share of their debt in concessional terms. The focus here, however, is on *changes* in levels of debt over time within each group of countries.

22. For example, the expansionary fiscal stance that Argentina followed during the 1995–97 boom left the authorities virtually no room to adjust to the global real and financial slowdown after the Russian crisis of 1998 and to the real appreciation of the peso under the hard dollar peg; see Perry and Servén (2003). On the Russian case, see Kharas and Pinto (2001). For Ecuador, see Montiel (2002).

23. In some countries, realization of other contingent liabilities, as well as recognition of hidden ones, were also significant sources of debt accumulation. Argentina is a good example; see Mussa (2002).

24. However, Bordo et al. (2001) find that the output cost of banking crises did not rise significantly over the 1990s.

25. See Halac and Schmukler (2003) for a detailed discussion.

26. This is empirically confirmed by Calderón, Duncan, and Schmidt-Hebbel (2003). The scope for independent monetary policy can also be severely limited by the impact of changes in monetary stance on the cost of public debt through the associated changes in the nominal exchange rate and interest rates.

27. The bias is amply documented in both industrial and developing countries; see Easterly (1999). Many industrial countries have engaged in similar practices, particularly in the run-up to the European Monetary Union; see Easterly and Servén (2003).

28. Perhaps the most dramatic example of this problem is the failure of the South African government to address the country's alarming rate of HIV infection more aggressively, an outcome that some critics have blamed on fears of budgetary costs. This situation may not only have undermined the country's long-term growth through a variety of possible channels; it has weakened support for the government's pursuit of macroeconomic stability as well. Similarly, Latin American countries' timidity in addressing poverty

problems, partly driven by fiscal stringency, contributed to the failure of income distribution to improve in the region during the 1990s. Combined with disappointing growth performance, some believe this outcome to have weakened popular support in Latin America for the reform agenda of the past decade.

29. See Buiter (1990, chapter 5); Easterly and Servén (2003); and Blanchard and Giavazzi (2003). A recent review of fiscal adjustment episodes (IMF 2003a) also concludes that in many cases the cuts in public investment were based on overoptimistic private investment forecasts and turned out to be excessive.

30. These estimates are reported in Talvi and Vegh (2000) and Lane (2003). They are broadly consistent with those displayed in figure 4.17. Public consumption, rather than the primary deficit, is used as the measure because public consumption data are available for a much larger sample.

31. The expansionary fiscal stance adopted by the Argentine authorities during the boom of 1995–97 forced them to engage in a self-destructive contraction in the downswing, helping precipitate the macroeconomic collapse of 2001–02. See, for example, Mussa (2002) and Perry and Servén (2003).

32. Most empirical studies conclude that legal central bank independence is not significantly associated with lower inflation across developing countries (Cukierman, Webb, and Neyapti 1992; Campillo and Miron 1997). The likely reason is that there are substantial deviations between the letter of the law and its application. As an exception, however, Cukierman, Miller, and Neyapti (2001) find a significant negative effect of legal central bank independence on inflation in transition economies with a sufficiently high degree of economic liberalization. Gutiérrez (2003) suggests that constitutional sanction of the independence of the central bank, as well as a clear primacy of inflation among its stated objectives, may provide a better measure of its anti-inflationary effectiveness.

33. Long-serving central bank governors may be subservient to finance ministers who place a high premium on the financing of fiscal deficits, and even independent central bank governors need not be firmly committed to price stability. Indeed, the cross-country empirical association between central bank governor turnover and inflation performance is not robust: the relation is negative only when a few high-inflation observations are included in the samples; see de Haan and Koi (2000). This might reflect reverse causality from high inflation to turnover rather than the other way around.

34. Perceptions of nominal instability are not the only factor behind financial dollarization. The degree of *real* dollarization, and the perceived stability of the

real exchange rate, also matter, as do financial system regulations and the availability of other assets sheltering investors from nominal instability (such as instruments indexed to domestic inflation, as in Chile, or short-term interest rates, as in Brazil). For discussion, see de la Torre and Schmukler (2003); Ize and Levy-Yeyati (1998); and IMF (2002b). Thus the interpretation in the text should be taken as suggestive rather than conclusive.

35. On the trends in dollarization, see also IMF (2002b) and Reinhart, Rogoff, and Savastano (2003).

36. For example, the upward drift in interest rates likely reflects also the liberalization of financial systems in many developing countries over the 1990s.

37. Schmukler and Servén (2002).

38. Frankel et al. (2001).

39. A flight out of intermediate regimes was documented by Fischer (2001), for example. But whether it in fact took place has been disputed, particularly because alternative exchange regime classifications tend to provide sharply conflicting verdicts on regime trends. See Masson (2001) and Frankel and Wei (2004) for further discussion.

40. Indeed, in the wake of the crises of the 1990s the IMF has redefined its core competencies to include fiscal, monetary, exchange rate, and *financial sector* policies.

41. The increasing incidence of banking crises is also documented by Bordo et al. (2001).

42. Kaminsky and Reinhart (1999).

43. In accordance with this, the recent analytical literature on crises continues to stress weak fundamentals as a prerequisite for the occurrence of crises, but emphasizes the key role of ingredients such as self-fulfilling expectations and multiple equilibria in triggering them. See Chari and Kehoe (2003) for a recent example. These views assign an increasingly important role to financial system imperfections in full-blown balance of payments crises; see, for example, Krugman (1999).

44. The Russian crisis also turned out not to be very severe, but probably for exogenous reasons (that is, the sharp recovery in world oil prices). More generally, there is evidence that twin crises are usually much more damaging to output than are standard banking-only or currency-only crises; see Bordo et al. (2001).

45. Of course, in the short run the objectives of macro stability and growth may conflict with each other, as stabilization measures often entail an output cost over the near term. But the growth disappointment refers to the performance over the entire 1990s.

46. Perry (2003).

47. See Wyplosz (2002) for details of this proposal.

48. See Sanguinetti and Tommassi (2003) for an analytical appraisal of alternative institutional arrangements. Burki, Perry, and Dillinger (1999a) review the international experience with various institutional arrangements in fiscally decentralized systems.

49. Stein, Talvi, and Gristani (1998); Aalt and Lassen (2003).

50. A recent study by the IMF's Independent Evaluation Unit (IMF 2003b) suggests that the problem is more widespread. The study finds, in particular, that in "capital account crisis" cases what appear in retrospect to have been cyclically appropriate fiscal expansions were not undertaken in part out of fear of adverse effects on market confidence.

51. Countries' misguided attempts to ride the wave of short-term capital have also played a major role in some crisis episodes. In the words of Larry Summers, referring to the role of Mexico's Tesobonos on the eve of the Tequila crisis: " . . . the situation was not one of an innocent country somehow overwhelmed by a flood of capital from the herd of speculators, but rather a situation of countries that, for domestic policy reasons, made very, very active efforts to dine with the devil of speculators—and ended on the menu." In *Leading Policy Makers Speak from Experience* (World Bank 2005b), online at http://info.worldbank.org/etools/bspan/PresentationView.asp?PID=1015&EID=328.

52. The most comprehensive empirical study is that of Edison et al. (2002), who fail to find robust evidence of a significant growth impact. Prasad et al. (2003) argue that there may be "threshold effects": countries with sound policies and institutions are more likely to derive a growth benefit from financial integration.

53. Kose, Prasad, and Terrones (2003).

54. These runs played a key role in the East Asian crisis; see, for example, Rodrik and Velasco (1999). Mismatches may reflect not only an inadequate borrowing strategy but also the reluctance of investors to lend long term in the face of a macrofinancial framework they deem suspect.

55. The reason is that a uniform reserve requirement is more onerous for short-term transactions than for the rest. Montiel and Reinhart (1999) review the cross-country evidence on the effectiveness of inflow restrictions.

56. In the Chilean case, Forbes (2004) argues that these costs were substantial. Johnson and Mitton (2002) find that in Malaysia capital controls served to protect cronyism.

# Poverty and Inequality:
# What Have We Learned from the 1990s?

During the 1990s the number of poor—those living on less than $1 in consumption per day—in developing countries declined from 1.2 billion to 1.1 billion. Globally, the proportion of people in poverty dropped from 28 percent to 21 percent. The global decline masks large variations in regional poverty reduction, which mirror variations in growth performance. Whereas poverty declined rapidly in East and South Asia, it rose in Sub-Saharan Africa and in Eastern Europe and Central Asia. In Latin America and the Caribbean, poverty rates fell marginally in the 1990s, returning to near their 1981 levels. In the Middle East and North Africa, after a significant decline in the 1980s, poverty rates rose slightly in the 1990s (Chen and Ravallion 2004). Even within regions, there are large variations in performance. For example, poverty in the 1990s declined by almost half in Tunisia, increased in Argentina, and declined in Brazil.

How has thinking about poverty evolved in light of experiences, academic research, and country performance in the 1990s?

Up to the 1970s, raising income levels by accelerating growth was seen as the central goal of development policies and the most effective way to reduce large-scale poverty. While inequality was recognized as the important issue in some contexts, such as in Latin America, policies focused on growth, with allowances made for "basic needs": access to water, health, housing, sanitation, and transport. In India, the centrality of growth for reducing poverty had been clear to planners since at least the 1950s and was an explicit objective of successive development plans.[1] In Brazil in the 1960s and early 1970s, the years of the "economic miracle," policies focused

explicitly on "growth first, distribution later," as if the two could be determined independently and sequentially. The neglect of the distributional effects of growth was consistent with the perception that poverty was simply too massive to be reduced without significantly augmenting economic resources. Further, the facts matched the empirical regularities first found by Kuznets (1955): as income rose, inequality first increased and then decreased. This pattern was interpreted by many economists (albeit not Kuznets) as reflecting forces that could not be changed by policies or government interventions.

In the 1970s Robert McNamara's "war on poverty" explicitly focused on the well-being of low-income groups. This was the first time in development policy circles that improvements in the well-being of the poor were singled out as a priority, separate from economic growth and separate from improvements in the welfare of the population at large. This subtle shift began a debate: Is poverty reduction the goal or is it a consequence of economic growth? Can the living standards of the poor improve, and poverty decline, independently of progress on the broader development front? Does distribution of resources to the poor retard growth, or accelerate it instead? These questions stimulated renewed analysis of data on income poverty and inequality.[2] More and better data confirmed Kuznets' intuition that the determinants of inequality were more complex than reflected in Kuznets' law. World Bank research in the 1970s and early 1980s, into policies and government interventions that could change income distribution, focused on cases such as the Republic of Korea's experience of "growth with equity," contrasted with—among others—Brazil's and

Mexico's rapid growth but more concentrated income.

In the 1990s the definition and measurement of poverty, and analysis of individual country poverty reduction experiences, received considerable academic, empirical, and policy attention. Attempts were also made to capture the phenomenology of poverty through a variety of concepts to which social scientists—economists and noneconomists—contributed: social capital, pro-poor growth, empowerment, and voicelessness. Studies carried out in countries such as Brazil, China, and India further improved and refined poverty concepts and analysis, as did poverty assessments by the World Bank and other agencies.[3]

These advances have recently led to the concept of pro-poor growth, which has been defined in various ways—strictly in some cases (for example, as growth that not only raises the incomes of the poor, but does so at a rate faster than per capita gross domestic product [GDP] growth, thus implying simultaneous improvements in income distribution) and less strictly in others (for example, as growth that increases the incomes of the poor regardless of whether the distribution of income improves or worsens). While its policy implications are not yet well defined, the concept of pro-poor growth has elicited strong interest from development aid agencies and from political leaders in developing countries facing pressures stemming from democratization.

Overall, four lessons have emerged from the experiences of the 1990s and from conceptual and empirical work over the decade:

- Sustained growth is vital for poverty reduction.

- Poverty is multidimensional.

- Access to social and infrastructure services is key to the poor: it improves both their opportunities and their welfare.

- Consistent with the broadening of the notion of poverty, there is now more focus on the deeper issue of equity—its meaning, and its possible consequences for growth.

These are discussed next.

## Sustained Growth Is Central to Poverty Reduction

The 1990s reconfirmed earlier beliefs and the messages of the *World Development Report* of 1990 about the centrality of economic growth for generating employment and other income-earning opportunities for the poor. Unlike in industrialized countries, where poverty is often a result of individuals' inability to seize opportunities because of various social pathologies, poverty in developing countries is fundamentally a matter of lack of opportunities. Countries that have sustained rapid growth for long periods have generated opportunities and achieved rapid poverty reduction. And countries with rapid poverty reduction are those that have sustained rapid growth over long periods (notably China, India, and Vietnam). Conversely, countries with large decreases in income have typically seen increases in poverty (as in former socialist economies, and parts of Africa), and countries with increases in poverty have tended to have low or negative growth (as in Latin America).

Appreciating the difference between *growth episodes* and *sustained growth* is of central importance for understanding the relationship between growth and poverty. Growth episodes are quite frequent, and during growth episodes lasting two, three, or more years, poverty outcomes can vary widely. Sustaining growth for several decades is a much rarer accomplishment (see chapter 1 and Country Note B), and yet it is this accomplishment that has enabled developing economies such as Korea, Singapore, or Taiwan, China, to reach the income levels of industrialized countries. The poverty outcomes of sustained growth are much less varied than those resulting from growth episodes. Growth plays a much larger role in poverty reduction during long growth spells than it does during short spells, where changes in measured distribution play a larger role (Kraay 2004).

Translating the goal of pro-poor growth into policies and practical growth strategies remains a tremendous challenge. Short growth episodes can be accompanied by a wide range of distributional outcomes (Ravallion 2003b), and since they have small and often transitory effects on poverty reduction, they provide only limited insights into the impact of sustained growth on poverty or into the types of policies that are appropriate.

One reason for the interest in concepts of pro-poor growth has been the realization that some patterns of growth (such as expansion of labor-intensive agriculture) could have a larger impact on the poor than do others (such as subsidies for capital-intensive industrialization), and even that some groups could lose in situations in which poverty was declining in aggregate (Kanbur 2001).

A second reason is that the palpable impact of targeted programs on poverty has sometimes led to the impression that they could substitute for economic growth. The 1990s saw some successful targeted programs. Mexico's Progresa/Oportunidades, for example, is a large-scale, well-targeted program that makes transfers conditional on investments in human capital; it deservedly receives a great deal of attention, partly because of its well-designed, independent impact evaluation system. India's food distribution system has helped to increase consumption and alleviate the consequences of poverty in some areas of the country, but as an instrument to reduce national poverty it has generally been ineffectual. China's 8-7 program has succeeded in addressing pockets of poverty within a context of rapid growth, expanding opportunities, and rapidly falling nationwide poverty. Elsewhere, some programs have succeeded in alleviating the impacts of crisis (Indonesia), and in improving community-level services, such as Bangladesh's stipend programs to increase girls' enrollment in secondary school. Such programs should be seen as vehicles either for the inclusion of marginalized groups or for improvements in the access of the poor to infrastructure and social services. While they play a very important role, they cannot substitute for growth in achieving rapid and significant reductions in the incidence of poverty. There is no known example of rapid, sustained, and significant reductions in poverty in the absence of sustained economic growth. That is,

while distributive programs are an important component of growth strategies, to ensure the sharing of the benefits of growth, they are no substitute for growth for the purpose of rapid and significant reduction in large-scale poverty.

In recent years, development agencies' focus on the poor, when analyzing poverty or formulating programs for poverty alleviation, has led them to ignore income gains above the poverty line. Yet such gains cannot be ignored socially, empirically, theoretically, or politically. Setting poverty reduction as the only goal of economic growth and economic development ignores the value of income gains above the poverty line, for example, those to the middle class. Since a poverty line is a social convention that a society adopts reflecting its own conditions, we should expect poverty lines to rise with a country's per capita income.[4] It is not reasonable for Vietnam, Brazil, and the United States to have the same poverty line, nor is it reasonable—current growth rates persisting—for Vietnam in 2010 to retain the poverty line it had in 1980. Thus the impact of growth on poverty reduction should be evaluated using both a low and a high poverty line, often using a measure of poverty that is sensitive to the distribution of income below the poverty line as well.

This discussion raises the question of what should be the upper threshold for poverty. Commonly used poverty lines of $1/day at purchasing power parity (PPP), or even PPP$2/day, can only be justified if human well-being is high at such levels of income. Even at the poverty line of $2/day, however, physical indicators of well-being such as education, nutrition, and mortality all indicate severe deprivation. Figure C.1 shows the mortality rate of the richest fifth of the population in several low- and middle-income countries. It shows that the mortality rates of children in the *richest* fifth of families in those countries are much higher than the mortality rates of the *poorest* fifth in rich industrial countries: among the richest fifth of households in countries such as Nepal and Nicaragua, the infant mortality rate is 40 per 1,000, but even among the poorest fifth in Organisation for Economic Co-operation and Development (OECD) countries, the rate is

FIGURE C.1
## Infant Mortality Rates

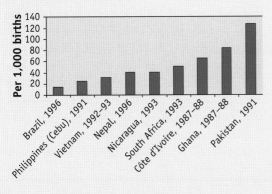

*Source*: Wagstaff 2001.

lower than 10 per 1,000. This suggests that the poverty lines currently in use underestimate the amount of poverty in the world and, possibly, the declines in poverty consistent with achieving the Millennium Development Goals (Pritchett 2003b).

## Poverty is Multidimensional

A key change from *World Development Report 1990* to *World Development Report 2001* was the conceptual expansion of the definition of poverty to include indicators of education and health, risk and vulnerability, and voicelessness and powerlessness. Studies carried out in the 1990s, such as participatory poverty assessments and the *Voices of the Poor* (Narayan et al. 2000), endeavored to capture what poverty means for those who experience it, and rendered it clear that consumption expenditure—the basis for most poverty lines—captures only one aspect of being poor. From this body of work emerged a broader concept of poverty that includes (1) the usual measures of consumption poverty, (2) education and health, (3) risk and vulnerability, and (4) voicelessness and powerlessness. *World Development Report 2001* emphasized the multidimensional nature of the phenomenon of poverty, which has been increasingly emphasized since.

While broadening the definition of poverty is a conceptual step forward, there are no empirical

measures of poverty according to this definition, because some of its dimensions are not amenable to measurement. More research is being done, but there are thus far no well-established empirical relationships regarding broadly defined poverty.

That said, the broadening of our understanding of poverty has led to a search for more encompassing indicators, especially in relation to the following.

*Education and health indicators.* The key role of education and health in well-being and development has been emphasized since economics began. The shift in the 1990s toward a greater recognition of the importance of education and health as development objectives has also led governments to be more realistic and pragmatic in their pursuit of those objectives. These messages are summarized in *WDR 2004* on service delivery.

*Risk and vulnerability.* A key fact that emerged in the 1990s—both from the expanded availability of data that tracked the same households over time (panel data) and from qualitative work such as *Voices of the Poor*—was the role of risk and vulnerability in explaining poverty in developing countries. In industrialized countries, little of the poverty is transient because social safety nets and higher incomes, and hence higher savings, help to smooth consumption. Poverty in rich countries is best understood as an issue of social marginalization resulting from culture and nurture, restraining individuals' ability to seize opportunities. In developing countries, by contrast, most poverty is transient poverty, responding to the flow of opportunities as individuals fall into or out of poverty. Empirical research on the dynamics of poverty, pioneered by Jalan and Ravallion (1998) in China and followed up by many others (for example, Baulch and Hoddinott 2000) has found a high incidence of transitions in and out of measured poverty.[5] In the most extreme case of the volatility of poverty episodes, in Pakistan more than half of households (55 percent) were poor either in 1986 or five years later in 1991—but only 3 percent were poor in both periods (table C.1).

"Poverty" as an empirical phenomenon hence consists of many individuals and households experiencing an episode of poverty and, especially in some countries, surprisingly few "poor people" who are always below the poverty line. This means that many more households are *vulnerable* to an episode of poverty than are actually poor at any point in time. These insights have encouraged attempts to address risks and vulnerabilities as part of an overall social protection strategy, in preference to an exclusive focus on chronic poverty or on the poorest of the poor.

*Voicelessness and powerlessness.* Among the shifts in development thinking that have affected attitudes toward poverty reduction, perhaps the most important has been the move away from the view that *the* solution to all ills is a well-designed program implemented by a well-ordered civil service bureaucracy and centrally funded from public resources (Pritchett and Woolcock 2004). That view tends to make "the poor" a distinct category of people who are the passive recipients of development rather than its active agents. Now, centered around themes such as "community based," "community driven," "bottom up," and "participatory" development; "local governance"; "empowerment"; "social capital"; and "inclusion, cohesion, and accountability," there is recognition that key elements of local development practice in poverty reduction cannot be delivered ready made, but must be homegrown or locally grown (Narayan et al. 2000).

Work on theory and empirical research that could shape the design of relevant programs and practices is just beginning. There are reasons to be cautious because, while some empirical studies show that programs function better with greater local engagement (Isham, Kelly, and Ramaswamy 2002; Galasso and Ravallion 2000), it is far from a foregone conclusion that more "local" decision making necessarily increases "voice" in a useful way (see, for example, Platteau 2004; Bardhan 2002). Much more needs to be known about the design of local decision making that effectively increases voice.

## Access to Services by the Poor: Learning from Experience

Economists tend to view poverty in terms of the consumption of private goods, but other social scientists emphasize the importance of public goods as well. This is because public goods can both improve income-earning opportunities (as in the case of access to roads, markets, water, public transport, education, health, rural employment programs) and directly improve welfare (through access to the same)—thus blurring the distinction between growth-enhancing public policies and distributive policies that are implemented through public services.

A broader understanding of poverty thus highlights the importance of access by the poor to goods and services that are typically publicly provided. Shortfalls in the delivery of such publicly provided goods can lead the poor to perceive that poverty has increased, even though survey data based on the consumption of private goods may suggest the opposite (Kanbur 2002).

Delivery of social and infrastructure services was the central theme of *WDR 2004*, which highlighted that the effective provision of services for the poor cannot be delinked from addressing the root problems of voicelessness and powerlessness. As that report showed, while the provision of public services to the poor and nonpoor alike is a key developmental issue in any developing economy, it is not a straightforward matter, nor is it a matter of resources alone, but one of striking the appropriate incentives for accountability and per-

TABLE C.1

### Surveys Tracking Individuals over Time Show Only a Small Portion of Poverty Is Accounted for by People Who Are Always Poor

|  |  | Percentage of the population that is... (by headcount ACE poverty) | | |
|---|---|---|---|---|
|  |  | Always poor | Sometimes poor | Never poor |
| Zimbabwe | 1992–96 | 10.6 | 59.6 | 29.8 |
| Pakistan | 1986–91 | 3.0 | 55.3 | 41.7 |
| South Africa | 1993–98 | 22.7 | 31.5 | 45.8 |
| Russian Federation | 1992–93 | 12.6 | 30.2 | 57.2 |
| Ethiopia | 1994–97 | 24.8 | 30.1 | 45.1 |
| Côte D'Ivoire | 1987–88 | 25 | 22 | 53 |

*Source:* Adapted from Baulch and Hoddinott 2000.

ACE, Absolute consumption expenditure.

formance, taking into account the political economy of delivering services.

Though the 1990s started with the conviction that retrenching governments and expanding the private sector would benefit virtually all areas of the economy, it is now seen that these expectations were unrealistic, and that government has a key role to play in at least three areas: education, health, and infrastructure. Further, it is increasingly seen that *how* to organize these services so that they are effective and reach the poor is the key question.

Answering this question will require a better understanding of the reasons behind failures and successes. The developing world is littered with dysfunctional services—schools with no books or no teachers, or teachers who are absent; clinics with no drugs, without functional equipment, with staff that does not attend or provides low-quality care; and water services that operate only sporadically. At the same time there are services that do work well.

As *WDR 2004* emphasized, the effective provision of services depends on relationships of accountability from the providers of services to citizens, politicians, and policy makers. Related to this, the Shanghai Conference of May 2004 on Scaling Up Poverty Reduction, in its attempt to clarify the reasons for success, produced four key messages:[6]

(1) *Get the economics right*—and get the politics behind the economics right. Poverty reduction depends on growth, which in turn needs sustained political support for implementation of growth-promoting policies and institutions.

(2) *Get the focus on clients right—and keep the focus on clients.* One message relevant across different types of activities was that without a focus on clients, even the best-intentioned efforts can go astray and break down in the field.

(3) *Get the implementation right*—the devil is in the details. There is no single recipe for a successful education project or health project: implementation must be adapted to the circumstances.

(4) *Get the support for innovation right—and back the right leadership and management.* "Scaling up" is not simply a matter of more resources but rather of support for innovations that lead to better ways of doing things, that are tailored to circumstances and can be scaled up once they have been shown to be successful. This requires a rigorous means of separating successes from failures, to scale up the former and shut down the latter.

## It Is Important to Clarify the Causes and Consequences of Inequality

Rising inequality in some industrialized and developing countries has brought inequality to the fore of policy discussions. Whether inequality should be a matter of public policy, and how to address it, depends on the underlying economic, social, and political forces causing inequality and their relationship to social equity. This is not straightforward, however. Not only is the relationship between inequality and other key economic variables such as growth, or poverty reduction, nonlinear, but its sign probably changes over time (Timmer and Timmer 2004).

Some evidence is emerging, for example, thus far at the microeconomic level more than in the aggregate, that inequality can negatively affect the functioning of institutions, the efficiency of resource allocation, and collective decision-making processes, leading to a negative impact on growth (Acemoglu, Johnson, and Robinson 2001; Aghion 1998).

The interpretation of narrow indicators of income inequality is not straightforward, however. Income inequality is not a good indicator of opportunities for the poor, and its use as a focus of analysis may miss—just as narrow definitions of poverty did—key issues of the reality and social perception of fairness, opportunity, legitimacy, and equity (box C.1). *WDR 2006* will take up the issues of equity and development and explore them in depth.

This section outlines six reasons why inequality has become such a visible issue and the importance of conceptual clarity in interpreting its significance.

First, growth-oriented reforms have winners and losers; and there is an inclination to believe that the losers are the poor, that their losses constitute a severe loss of welfare and an obstacle to reforms, and that if the poor could be compensated for their losses, political support for reform would be greater. Therefore, the reforms of the 1990s inevitably raised the issue of the distribution of gains and costs of reforms, and how they affect income distribution. Over the 1990s, however, as it became clear that the poor are vulnerable continuously, not only during episodes of reform, the concern of policy makers began to evolve away from episodic forms of compensation toward providing more permanent forms of social protection. Meanwhile, studies have also suggested that it may be naïve to believe that mitigating the impacts on the poor will reduce the opposition to reform. Research by Graham and Pettinato (2002) indicates, for instance, that people who have benefited from reforms are as likely to report themselves opposed to reform as people whose incomes have stagnated or fallen. The formation of attitudes toward reforms is complex, and clearly needs further research.

Second, in some transition countries such as China or the former Soviet Union, inequality has increased significantly. A view has emerged that inequality is on the agenda because the resentment generated by higher inequality is a powerful political factor and creates social pressures that slow reforms and create uncertainty about policy continuity. Resentment about rising inequality needs to be disentangled, however, from the perception that the *process* by which fortunes were accumulated was *unfair*. Perceptions of process and procedural fairness are important influences on an individual's attitudes toward outcomes, and there is no simple association between inequality of outcomes and perceptions of the fairness of those outcomes—perceptions that go to much deeper issues of equity. In Sri Lanka, for example, there was widespread resentment at the politicization of civil service employment, because the process for allocating civil service jobs was perceived as unfair. The key issue was less whether civil servants were overpaid than whether the opportunities to access those

jobs were legitimate (box C.1). Just as important as the inequality in outcomes is the perception of the fairness of the process that generates the outcomes. This implies that examining increases in income inequality alone, without considering the equity of the process behind the increase, will not capture the true meaning of a rise in inequality and its policy consequences.

Third, it is often asserted that inequality is increasingly on the international agenda because "global" inequalities are rising. Changes in inequality are not a unique feature of the 1990s; Bourguignon and Morrison (2002) suggest that inequality rose steadily from 1880 to 1980 and stopped rising in the 1980s and 1990s (see figure 1.4 in chapter 1). Yet the issue is complex empirically, because much depends on what estimates of inequality are used and how the data are weighted: whether by country, to estimate the cross-national distribution of income; or by population, to estimate the global personal distribution of income; or by using national accounts or household data, to estimate the growth of income. This has engendered debates on the extent of cross-national inequality and the reduction in global poverty, between Bhalla (2002) and Sala-i-Martin (2003) on the one hand and Milanovic (2004) on the other; see also exchanges in *The Economist* (2004). A recent review by Bourguignon (2004a) shows that even using the same data, different measures of inequality can show falling or rising inequality.

Fourth, measures of inequality fail to capture the significance of underlying economic and poverty conditions. For instance, Ethiopia is a relatively unequal country in which the income of the richest 10 percent of the population is 10 times that of the poorest 10 percent. Should inequality be the primary policy issue in Ethiopia, or should the country focus on generating higher average income? Currently even "the rich" in Ethiopia (except for perhaps the very few) have incomes and indicators of physical well-being well below those of "the poor" in industrial countries, and per capita income in Ethiopia is *50 times* lower than that in the U.S.

Fifth, while rising inequality is sometimes equated with rising poverty, the poverty impact

**BOX C.1**

## Perceptions of Fairness in Allocating Opportunity Are Central  (Case Study: Sri Lanka)

Sri Lanka's Presidential Commission on Youth was appointed in late 1989 to examine the causes of youth discontent and unrest that led to the Marxist rebellion of 1987–89. The Commission's report highlights that meritocratic processes are critical for maintaining social and political stability. The Commission reported a strong consensus within the country that politicization and abuse of power and injustice were the main causes of youth unrest in Sri Lanka. The Commission felt that the politicization of employment, through the "chit system" (the practice of receiving a letter from one's Member of Parliament in order to find public sector employment), was deemed by youth as incompatible with the basic norms of fairness, equity, and merit. This was based on the representations made by civil society before the Commission suggesting an alarming degree of public dissatisfaction in this sphere of recruitment to the public service. Hence, the Commission stated that the 1972 Constitution, which removed the power of appointment vested in the Public Service Commission and brought such appointments within the purview of the Cabinet of Ministers, triggered a politicization process that had far-reaching social repercussions in a country where the public sector accounts for the bulk of formal employment.

*Source: Report of the Presidential Commission on Youth, 1990* (as cited in World Bank 2000h).

of changes in inequality is not self-evident but depends on the causal interpretation of events. Policies that improve both the growth and the distribution of income are "win-win," but even policies that worsen the distribution of income can be "win" policies for improvement in poverty if their effects on growth are large enough.

As detailed in Bourguignon (2004b) there is a poverty-growth-inequality triangle, and income poverty, income distribution, and changes in mean income are linked by an "arithmetic identity"—which, however, alone does not reveal the underlying causal forces, including policies, that drive both growth and its distribution. For example, in China, as an arithmetic matter, the worsening inequality in the 1990s partially offset the rate of growth of mean income, so that the growth-elasticity of poverty declined. Poverty did not worsen, but the rate of poverty reduction was slower than it would have been if inequality had remained constant. With an equal society and no growth there was very little poverty reduction. With rapid growth there has been a massive reduction in poverty *and* an increase in inequality.

From this it could be deduced that poverty has fallen "in spite of" increasing inequality. However, understanding the impact of China's policies makes it important to differentiate "constructive" inequality (which provides the incentives needed to move resources to their most efficient use) from "destructive" inequality (which generates envy and socially unproductive distribution) (Timmer and Timmer 2004). Thus it may be more causally correct to say that poverty in China went down *because* inequality was allowed to go up. This would be the case if the policy changes that led to a rapid increase in average incomes needed to allow inequality to rise in order to provide incentives for investment and innovation. Discussion at an international meeting in 1987 with Chinese, Korean, and Indian economic policy makers illustrates this point:

After the other delegations [from India, Korea] presented their experiences in managing a market economy, the Chinese Vice Minister presented an outline of the Chinese reform program. At the end of this presentation, Manmohan Singh, in his usual gentle but forceful tone, asked: "Would not what you are trying to do result in greater inequality in China?" To that the Vice Minister replied, with firm conviction: "We would certainly hope so!"

—Edwin Lim, World Bank (2005a)

Vietnam has seen the same combination of rising inequality and spectacularly declining poverty as China. Vietnam lifted a third of its population out of poverty between 1993 and 2002—achieving what may be the greatest reduction in poverty in a single decade in the history of mankind. Vietnam confirms the conventional wisdom reflected in *World Development Report 1990*: poverty reduction was rapid because it began when poverty was high, incomes were equal, and growth was intensive in unskilled labor. Inequality in consumption expenditures rose modestly over this period: the Gini coefficient was .34 in 1993, and .37 in 2002.

Thus, while it is analytically appropriate to say that "if the growth of consumption expenditures had not changed and if inequality had not increased, poverty reduction would have been more rapid," this arithmetic fact is not dictated by causality in the sense that a feasible (economically, administratively, and politically) policy that would have accomplished that goal may simply not exist. It is perhaps unlikely that the fastest reductions in poverty in history, such as those in Vietnam in the 1990s (or in Indonesia and China in the 1970s, 1980s, and 1990s) could have been even faster.

Sixth, there is some emerging, though as yet inconclusive, evidence that more equal societies are able to be more efficient: they adopt better policies, provide public goods more efficiently, allocate capital more efficiently, and reduce crime and insecurity. There is evidence from the United States, for example, that appropriately designed social safety nets can improve both distribution and efficiency (Blank 2002). The new view (discussed in chapter 1) is that by reducing poverty countries can improve the functioning of markets and that of institutions in a manner that is both "pro-poor" and "pro-growth"—social policies can increase the

opportunities of the poor to invest and hence can raise both equity and growth.

This is an enormous shift from the view, prevailing until the late 1970s, that concentrating income among the rich increases savings (because the rich have a lower propensity to spend), and hence capital accumulation and hence growth, so that more inequality is good for growth. That view has an element of truth but it ignores some key issues that are now back on the theoretical and empirical agenda (see, for example, Aghion 1998; Banerjee and Duflo 2003): that inequality can lead to underinvestment by the poor, and that unequal income distributions tend to encourage the persistence of poor policies and the protection of rents.

Bourguignon (2004b) reviews theoretical ways in which more equal income distribution could raise growth, but finds that the "available aggregate evidence is inconclusive." The scenarios and policies in which improved equity and growth are complementary are increasingly on the table.[7]

## Notes

1. http://planningcommission.nic.in/plans/planrel/fiveyr/welcome.html; Bhagwati and Srinivasan (2002).

2. The early focus was on inequality because few countries (with the prominent exception of India) had well-defined poverty lines, or systematic measurements of poverty. By many standard measures of poverty, growth, inequality, and poverty are arithmetically linked, but the research was not explicitly about absolute measures of poverty.

3. The *World Development Reports* of 1990 and of 2000–01 benchmark the evolution of thinking about poverty over the decade. More recent sources of insights are *WDR 2004* on *Making Services Work for the Poor* and the Global Learning Process on Scaling up Poverty Reduction, which culminated in the Shanghai Conference of May 2004. Both examine modes of improving services to low-income groups that were developed mostly during the 1990s.

4. Any poverty line is a social convention. There is no right or wrong choice, and no technocratic standard, for establishing a poverty line, but only ways to make comparisons consistently across households, regions, and over time for a given poverty line. For international comparisons the World Bank has con-

ventionally used a "one dollar a day" poverty line, derived from the official poverty lines prevailing in some of the poorest countries in the early 1990s, and "two dollars a day" as another standard for the poverty line. Each country usually uses its own poverty line, and in some countries the poverty line is defined in relation to average incomes and hence automatically evolves with changes in average incomes. On the technical complexities of setting poverty lines, see Ravallion (1994) and Pradhan et al. (2001).

5. *Measured* is a very important caveat. Suryahadi et al. (1999) and Luttmer (2001) and others have demonstrated that measurement error in income or consumption expenditures can account for a substantial fraction of these measured transitions.

6. The global learning process that led up to this conference emphasized hearing directly from practitioners from the South. It produced more than 100 case studies of projects in all regions of the world in areas from education to health to community development to targeted programs, and sponsored field visits across projects to promote South-South learning.

7. These will be addressed in *World Development Report 2006* on equity.

*Chapter 5*

# Trade Liberalization: Why So Much Controversy?

ECONOMISTS HAVE LONG RECOGnized the gains from international trade; the study of these gains is where modern economics began. Over centuries, international trade has brought together remote parts of the world and different civilizations, helped disseminate knowledge and ideas, and shaped the course of regions and nations. Rapid reductions in transport and communications costs accelerated this trend in the 19th century, and international trade reached unprecedented levels at the beginning of the 20th century. Trade declined, however, following the two World Wars, the 1929 crisis, and the worldwide increase in protectionism.

A reversal in protectionism started after World War II among the industrialized countries, and spread to the developing countries in the 1970s. Trade reforms were further expanded and consolidated in the 1980s and 1990s across the developing world: in South Asia, East Asia, Latin America, Eastern Europe, and, to a lesser extent, in Africa and the Middle East. Yet in the 1990s, the results of trade reform have varied and sometimes fallen short of expectations. Critics of the economic and social effects of globalization have also become more vocal. Why have some trade liberalizations been reversed, and why have others brought prosperity, opportunities, and economic diversification? Is there still a role for the protection of infant industries in growth strategies? Does trade liberalization lead to economic growth? Finally, does trade liberalization improve or reduce poverty?

Drawing on the experience and academic research of the 1990s, this chapter identifies five lessons:

- Openness to trade has been a central element of successful growth strategies. In all countries that have sustained growth the share of trade in gross domestic product (GDP) has increased, and trade barriers have been reduced.

- Trade is an opportunity, not a guarantee. While trade reforms can help accelerate integration in the world economy and strengthen an effective growth strategy, they cannot ensure its success. Other elements that address binding constraints to growth are needed, possibly including sound macroeconomic management, trade-related infrastructure and institutions, and economywide investments in human capital and infrastructure.

- There are many possible ways to open an economy. The challenge for policy makers is to identify which best suits their country's political economy, institutional constraints, and initial conditions. As these vary from country to country, it is not surprising that there is a striking heterogeneity in country experiences regarding the timing and pace of reforms. Different countries have opened up different sectors at different speeds (for example, Bangladesh and India); others have achieved partial liberalization through the establishment of export processing zones (for example, China and Mauritius); and yet others have combined unilateral trade reforms with participation in regional trade agreements (for example, Estonia).

- The distributive effects of trade liberalization are diverse, and not always pro-poor. Trade reforms were expected to increase the incomes of the unskilled in countries with a comparative advantage in producing unskilled-intensive goods. Yet evidence from the 1990s suggests that even in instances where trade policy has reduced poverty, there are still distributive issues. One important policy lesson is that countries need to help workers affected move out of contracting (import-competing) sectors into expanding (exporting) sectors. This is an issue relevant to both developing and industrialized countries.

- The preservation and expansion of the world trade system hinges on its ability to strike a better balance between the interests of industrialized and developing countries. Global markets are the most hostile to the products produced by the world's poor—such as agricultural products and textiles and apparel. The problems of escalating tariffs, tariff peaks, and quota arrangements systematically deny the poor market access and skew the incentives against adding value in poor countries. These problems can be addressed through collective action, best pursued through the Doha Round and the World Trade Organization. Although there is a role for nonreciprocal preferences and for reciprocal regional approaches, this comes at a cost to excluded countries, is arbitrary and political, and thus is not first best in terms of generating the right incentives for investment.

## 1. Trade Reform as a Component of a Successful Growth Strategy

This chapter begins by reviewing key changes in trade policy, trade volumes, and the composition of trade in the 1990s. One striking fact is that

trade—measured as a share of exports in GDP—is now larger in developing than in developed countries. Another important trend is the shift in the composition of developing-country exports toward manufactures. Countries whose incomes were low in 1980 have managed to raise their exports of manufactures from about 20 percent of their total exports to more than 80 percent.[1]

Virtually all successful economies have increased their openness to trade. In part because successful trade reforms have been introduced in conjunction with other policy initiatives, it is difficult empirically to identify the growth effect of trade policy alone, compared with the growth effect of other policy initiatives, and to disentangle whether trade causes growth or growth causes trade. As an economy accumulates physical and human capital, shifts its comparative advantage toward more capital-intensive activities, and becomes internationally competitive in a wider range of goods and services, it will inevitably trade more. But is higher trade the result or the cause of its growth? Most likely both processes are at work. This section reviews the evidence on these questions and then argues for the need to pursue trade reform as part of a comprehensive growth strategy. Openness to the global economy has helped efficiency and growth in many cases (East and South Asian countries, Botswana, Chile, Mauritius, Tunisia), but it has failed to do so in many others. These experiences do not necessarily imply that less trade reform would have been desirable, but that trade reform must be done and sequenced sensibly, as part of an effective growth strategy.

### The 1990s: An Overview

Reforms in the 1980s and 1990s were the origin of a strong expansion in international trade (box 5.1). As detailed in chapter 3, developing countries are now more integrated with the world economy than are high-income countries.

The integration of labor emerged as another important issue on the globalization agenda during the 1990s. In 2001, developing countries received some US$71 billion in migrants' remittances—a sum that was nearly 40 percent more

**BOX 5.1**
**Trade Policy over the Centuries**

Protection of domestic industries has a long history. In the 12th century, for example, to maintain the competitive edge of their textile industries, Flanders and England restricted the movement of experienced weavers. In the 13th century, England enacted laws restricting the types and origin of fabrics certain individuals could wear. In 16th and 17th century France, the state promoted selected industries, through import protection, direct ownership, or subsidies, as did Japan later during the Meiji period. While the protection of domestic industries took various forms—such as subsidized capital, or monopoly or monopsony rights—protection from imports was the most widely used and became particularly important after the start of the industrial revolution. During the 1800s and the first half of the 1900s, tariffs on imports in industrial countries were as high as 30–50 percent (World Bank, *World Development Report 1991*).

Many developing countries pursued import substitution industrialization strategies in the three decades that followed World War II, but by the mid-1980s, most developing countries were seeking to reduce their import protection and liberalize trade. Three developments had raised doubts about the long-run effectiveness of strategies based on import protection. First, in the 1960s, the Republic of Korea and Taiwan (China) had begun adopting export-oriented growth strategies that not only yielded superior economic performance, but also helped these two economies to withstand the severe interest rate and oil price shocks of the 1970s. Second, high tariffs, administrative restrictions, and rationing of foreign exchange and of import licenses created high returns to rent seeking, reinforcing vested interests and an environment that stimulated corruption and weakened national institutions. The results, including state capture by vested interests and the misuse of government discretion, discredited import substitution strategies even among economists who believed in the strategic importance of import substitution in the initial phases of industrialization. Third, growth strategies based on import substitution proved difficult to implement in practice, and the practical and political aspects of implementation often negated most of the expected gains (Balassa 1971; Little, Scitovsky, and Scott 1970). High nominal tariffs often provided negative protection to emerging activities and protection to activities with negative value added, and contributed to misallocation and underutilization of capital in capital-scarce economies. Overvaluation of the exchange rate resulting from import restrictions discouraged exports and penalized agriculture—further reducing the size of the market for import-competing industries.

As a result, during the 1980s and 1990s virtually all developing countries followed the examples set by Singapore, Hong Kong (China), Korea, and Taiwan (China): encouraging exports and reducing levels of protection. Industrialization based on import protection was gradually discredited and, starting in the mid-1980s, most developing countries sought to reduce levels of import protection and liberalize trade. Chile and Sri Lanka were among the first liberalizers, having started already in the 1970s. Argentina and Uruguay followed shortly thereafter. By the early 1990s, researchers and policy makers generally accepted the superiority of outward orientation over import substitution as a development strategy.[a] Trade liberalization expanded in the 1990s, leading to increased integration of developing economies in world trade. The fall of communism in Central and Eastern Europe, together with the collapse of the former Soviet Union, reinforced this view. Countries that had not already embarked on liberalization began to do so now, while others scaled up their efforts. They included hitherto very highly protected and inward-looking economies such as India, and countries in Sub-Saharan Africa that looked to integration with the world economy as a key instrument for reversing hitherto dismal growth performance.

*(Box continues on the following page.)*

While some of the reforms were unilateral, others were accomplished in the context of multilateral trade agreements such as the Uruguay Round. Important components of those reforms included large tariff reductions and the elimination of quotas, as well as the relaxation of restrictions on foreign investment. Looking at the improvement in market access for the developing countries, tariff cuts in industrial countries accounted for about a third of the improvement and tariff cuts in the developing countries themselves accounted for two-thirds (World Bank, *Global Economic Prospects 2004*).

[a] See Krueger (1997) and Baldwin (2003) for expositions on the evolution of economic thinking over this issue during the second half of the 20th century.

than all official development assistance and significantly more than net debt flows to developing countries in that year.[2] However, such remittances went to only a few developing countries, and their importance for developing countries as a group declined over the 1990s, from slightly above 4 percent of all foreign exchange receipts to slightly below.[3]

Remittances would provide a much larger share of foreign exchange receipts for developing countries were it not for industrial-country restrictions on labor migration. If rich countries were to permit the temporary immigration of up to 3 percent of their total labor force, developing countries would gain as much as $160 billion a year (Walmsley and Winters 2003).

Virtually all commitments under the General Agreement on Trade in Services have focused mainly on the first three modes of international service delivery rather than on mode 4, the "movement of natural persons," which involves the temporary movement of labor to provide services. Mode 4 accounts for only 1.4 percent of services trade (figure 5.1). The lack of liberalization in labor services has been particularly costly to developing countries, whose comparative advantage lies in the export of medium- and low-skilled, labor-intensive services.

## Trade Reform, Exports, and Economic Growth

For decades, researchers have been debating the merits of economic openness and its association with growth. Academic debates on whether openness to trade causes higher growth are riddled with problems of measurement, reverse causation (faster growing countries tend to open their markets more quickly), and omitted variable bias (countries that successfully lower tariffs also adopt other complementary policies).[4] Notwithstanding difficulties in interpreting country experiences during the1990s, almost all economists agree that liberal trade is important for growth over the long run (box 5.2).

Research that focuses on the relationship between trade reforms and economic growth in the 1990s also finds that trade reforms are associated with higher growth, although the strength of the association varies across different studies.[5] Yet trade liberalization by itself is not enough for economic growth. Studies show that trade policy is most likely to be associated with positive outcomes when it is conducted in a favorable eco-

FIGURE 5.1

**Temporary Labor Mobility, Underused Mode of Trade in Services**

(value of world trade in services by mode; percent)

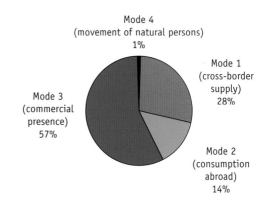

*Source:* World Bank, *Global Economic Prospects 2004.*

**BOX 5.2**
**The Trade and Growth Debate**

The debate among economists and policy makers over the relationship between trade and growth has risen to prominence during the last few years, owing on the one hand to the mixed growth outcomes of developing countries that have undergone extensive trade liberalization and, on the other hand, to differences over data, econometric techniques, and model specifications among professional economists.

The resurgence of interest in the 1990s among economists on the impact of trade on growth can be attributed to the significant improvements that have taken place in endogenous growth theory as well as to the availability of more comprehensive data and new econometric techniques. According to the new growth theory (attributed to Romer 1986; Lucas 1987; and Grossman and Helpman 1992), whether import protection raises or lowers the growth rate depends on the pattern of imports and exports. Economists on both sides of the debate accept that as a matter of theory the relationship between trade and growth is ambiguous. The issue is hence an empirical one, which has become the focus of the debate in the last few years.

The launching of the debate can be attributed to Rodriguez and Rodrik (2000) (RR) and Harrison and Hanson (1999) (HH), who reviewed a number of empirical studies in the 1990s. While HH showed that the Sachs and Warner (1995) study reflected the gains from macroeconomic stability rather than trade reform, RR reviewed a number of studies, including Dollar (1992), Sachs and Warner (1995), and Edwards (1998). RR expressed doubt "that there is a strong negative relationship in the data between trade barriers and economic growth, at least for levels of trade restrictions observed in practice," viewing "the search for such a relationship futile." A unique feature of the HH and RR analyses was their use of the various authors' actual data sets in testing the robustness of their results. HH and RR criticized the empirical studies on data grounds, on model-specification grounds, and on grounds of econometric techniques. Data problems included, among others, the use of poor measures of trade barriers (including the World Bank's classification of trade regimes, which they criticized as subjective in Edwards' paper), and the use of measures that are highly correlated with other sources of bad economic performance such as poor exchange rate management (as in Dollar's and Sachs and Warner's papers). Separately, Rodrik also criticized one of the more recent papers on the topic, Dollar and Kraay (2001), on data and model-specification grounds. The data problem arises from the combination of policy measures (tariff averages) with outcome measures (imports as a share of GDP). The model specification problem arises from regressing income on trade shares when both are endogenous (outcome variables).

- Notwithstanding these criticisms, it would be safe to say that most authors agree on the following: First, that *trade protection is not good for economic growth*. Even RR themselves state in their paper that they have seen no credible evidence to support the notion that trade protection is good for economic growth, at least for the post-1945 period.

- Second, that *trade openness by itself is not sufficient for growth*. RR argue in their paper that researchers and policy makers have been overstating the systematic evidence in favor of trade openness, when what is really necessary is to further identify the connection between trade and economic growth.

nomic environment,[6] and that while lack of regulations can undermine the growth effects of trade, in countries with effective regulation the effects of trade reforms are positive for growth.[7]

In developing countries that successfully integrated into the global economy in the 1990s, a variety of factors reinforced each other: a stable investment climate, greater market access, complementary macroeconomic policies, and unilateral or multilateral trade reforms. Table 5.1 illustrates how the trade intensity of economies changed in response to reductions in tariffs. In the countries that began the 1990s with very high tariffs, and reduced them the most, the share of imports plus exports in GDP rose significantly. But in countries that began the decade with more moderate tariffs and lowered them further, the responses varied widely. One possibility—consistent with the evidence presented in table 5.1—is that at more moderate levels of protection, other changes in the economy play a growing role in determining changing trade shares.

One important avenue through which tariff reductions in the 1990s contributed to economic growth is through their impact on exports. Figure 5.2 shows that tariff reductions in the 1990s were positively and significantly associated with developing countries' export shares. The positive association between tariff reductions and export growth is consistent with so-called Lerner symmetry, whereby taxing imports has the same effect on international trade as does taxing exports.[8] This means that reducing tariffs promotes exports. Cross-country regressions also suggest that in the 1990s real export growth was higher in countries with greater macroeconomic stability, countries that reduced tariffs more, and countries that had more effective government.[9]

Detailed case studies reinforce these lessons on the determinants of export activity. Studies using detailed plant-level data have shown that manufacturing firms that move into exporting are frequently the most productive in an economy. Consequently, policies that encourage investments in human and physical capital, and that support technological change, are likely to promote export growth. Evidence for Morocco suggests that many exporters are new enterprises, so that policies that encourage new plant entry and at the same time ease the exit of inefficient enter-

TABLE 5.1

## Tariff Reductions and Changes in Goods Trade Integration, 1990–2000

| % changes in tariffs, from late 1980s to late 1990s | Change in integration, 1990–2000 | | | |
|---|---|---|---|---|
| | <1 time | 1–1.5 times | 1.5–2 times | >2 times |
| 40–70 reduction | | India | Bangladesh | Sudan |
| 20–30 reduction | Pakistan, Burkina Faso Peru, | Benin, Ecuador, Kenya, Thailand | China | |
| 10–20 reduction | Egypt, Arab Rep. of, Iran, Mauritania, Mauritius, Zambia | Republic of Congo, Indonesia, Turkey, Uganda, Venezuela | Argentina, Colombia, Costa Rica, El Salvador, Guatemala, Nicaragua, Sri Lanka | Philippines |
| 0–10 reduction | Tanzania, Paraguay, Senegal | Chile, Côte d'Ivoire, Bolivia, Jamaica, Malaysia, Nigeria, South Africa | Ghana, Nepal | |
| 0–2 increase | Mozambique | | Madagascar, Trinidad and Tobago | Mexico |
| 2–10 increase | Tunisia | Jordan, Morocco, Oman, Saudi Arabia | | |
| >10 increase | Syrian Arab Rep. | | | |

Source: World Bank staff calculations, available at http://sitesources.worldbank.org/INTRANETTRADE/Resources/tar2002.xls.

Note: Trade integration, defined as the share of goods exports plus imports in GDP, is measured in real terms and excludes services trade.

FIGURE 5.2

## Changes in Export Shares of GDP and Changes in Tariffs, 1990–2000

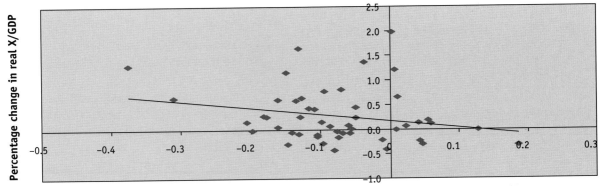

Source: World Bank staff calculations, available at http://siteresources.worldbank.org/INTRANETTRADE/Resources/tar2002.xls.

Note: Changes are for the entire 10-year period 1990–2000, not annual changes. The correlation coefficient is –0.25 and statistically significant.

prises are likely to play an important role. Evidence from Mexican and Indonesian censuses suggests that exporters are likely to use skilled labor, which suggests that policies supporting the development of human capital are important.

Plant-level studies and anecdotal evidence also point to the importance of foreign investors in helping developing-country exporters to break into new markets. Recent studies control for the possibility of reverse causality, taking into account the fact that foreign firms may create or take over the most efficient firms.[10] Even if the importance of foreign investment is difficult to identify in cross-country studies, plant-level studies provide ample evidence that foreign ownership has been associated with export activity (box 5.3). Studies on Indonesia, Mexico, and Morocco show that joint ventures and foreign-owned plants are significantly more likely to export than other types of enterprises. Although the mechanism is not completely clear, foreign firms are likely to provide knowledge of foreign markets and customer preferences, as well as access to new technology and financing opportunities.

### The Need for Effective Growth Strategies

While trade integration opens new opportunities and can strengthen an effective growth strategy, it cannot ensure that the strategy is effective. Liberalization of trade in Argentina in the 1980s and 1990s, and in Chile in the early 1980s, for example, was accompanied by an appreciation of the real exchange rate, which reduced the competitiveness of domestic industries and incentives to export—with adverse consequences for the balance of payments and real economy. In many countries of the former Soviet Union and some in Eastern Europe in the 1990s, trade was liberalized while property rights were not well defined and the institutional base for a market economy was not well developed. These, and other institutional issues preventing the free movement of resources, often meant that trade reforms did not expand economic opportunities but restricted them instead (Bolaky and Freund 2004).

Trade reforms are most likely to stimulate growth when they are part of a comprehensive strategy. Important elements of an effective growth strategy can include sound macroeconomic management, building of trade-related infrastructure and institutions, economywide investments in physical and human capital, greater access to developed- and developing-country markets, and maintenance of a sound rule of law. Because these elements are often difficult to implement, there has been excessive emphasis on trade policy alone, rather than as a component of an overall growth

**BOX 5.3**

## The Impact of Foreign Direct Investment on Growth

Foreign direct investment (FDI) has been an important force in the global integration of national economies. Countries welcome FDI for many reasons. Capital-scarce countries benefit from the infusion of a less volatile source of capital. Greater investment financed by incoming FDI should also translate into higher growth. Foreign investors are expected to provide employment opportunities, better wages and working conditions, and more training. Many countries give foreign firms and joint ventures special treatment in the expectation that these firms will transfer new technology and knowledge to domestic workers and firms.

The cross-country evidence on the relationship between FDI and growth is mixed, in part because incoming FDI as a share of GDP is typically quite small. A cross-country study using data for 72 countries for 1960–95 (Carkovic and Levine 2002) finds no evidence that FDI exerts a positive impact on economic growth independent of other growth determinants (openness, black market premium, financial development, initial income, years of schooling). However, Bosworth and Collins (1999) find that FDI, by raising total factor productivity, raises a country's rate of output growth. Borenzstein et al. (1998) find that FDI adds to capital accumulation and raises the efficiency of investment, but only where the host country has a minimum level of human capital—an indicator of absorptive capacity. The Borenzstein study is consistent with evidence that suggests FDI can promote growth if the country has complementary institutions such as developed financial markets

(Alfaro et al. 2000) or is open to trade (Balasubramanyam, Salisu, and Dapsoford 1996).

A number of studies use micro-data to analyze the role of FDI in promoting technology transfer and raising host country wages (see, for example, World Bank, *Global Development Finance 2000*; Aitken and Harrison 1999; Haddad and Harrison 1993; Djankov and Hoekman 2000; Konings 2000; and Damijan et al. 2003). They provide a mixed picture. However, they all agree that affiliates of foreign firms are more productive than indigenous firms. While part of these results could reflect the fact that foreign firms acquire more efficient domestic enterprises, anecdotal evidence also suggests that local firms acquired by foreign investors undergo restructuring and improve their performance as a result of the takeover. This direct effect should not be ignored, because its magnitude may be significant. Other evidence also suggests that foreign enterprises pay higher wages (Aitken, Hanson, and Harrison 1997) and are more likely to comply with local labor standards (Harrison and Scorse 2003).

In sum, while quite a lot of evidence suggests that FDI is positively associated with growth, there is no consensus on the issue, and in particular no consensus on the direction of causality. Regardless of whether FDI independently contributes to growth, it is clear that policies and institutions that are important for growth would also be the ones that would attract FDI as well as enhance the impact of FDI on growth. Therefore, countries should focus on such policies and institutions rather than narrowly on how to attract FDI.

strategy. In addition to freeing markets and ensuring the institutional foundation of a market economy, governments may also need to address market failures that impede a supply response. Identifying which industries warrant special treatment is highly risky, and the experience of the last few decades is riddled with attempts to correct market failures that became more costly than the

failures themselves. At the same time, however, governments have learned how to structure interventions in a manner that can reduce the risks of capture and failure.

Although many factors contributed to the rise in trade integration in the 1990s, as discussed above, for brevity the following discussion is selective. It focuses on two critical complementary areas: macroeconomic stability and trade-related infrastructure and institutions.

## Macroeconomic Stability

Macroeconomic stability is an important element in successful outcomes from trade reforms.[11] Macroeconomic stability entails low levels of inflation and a stable and competitive exchange rate. Exchange rate volatility creates a risky business environment in which future profits and payments are uncertain, and these risks are higher in the many developing countries that have not developed financial instruments for hedging against foreign exchange risk.

Successful exchange rate management requires, among other things, appropriate sequencing of trade reforms and capital account liberalization. Experience has shown that capital account liberalization should follow, not precede, the liberalization of trade, because the large inflows of capital that generally follow the freeing of the capital account could cause a large appreciation of the real exchange rate, leading to large import surges that destabilize domestic industries and the balance of payments.

India's appropriate sequencing of trade reforms, as well as its maintenance of a stable macroeconomic framework, contributed to its impressive export and growth performance in the 1990s (World Bank 1994b). Before starting to liberalize trade, in the early 1990s India allowed a significant depreciation of the real exchange rate, which served to increase export incentives and cushion the impact of lower import barriers on domestic industry. Trade liberalization preceded the opening of the capital account. Since 1992, India's real effective exchange rate has remained at more or less the same level, facilitating trade reforms.

In Zambia, by contrast, macroeconomic instability undermined the potentially positive effects of structural reforms. Trade and other structural reforms in the early 1990s gave Zambia one of the most liberal trade regimes in Africa, but export performance has been lackluster. An important reason is macroeconomic instability, with high inflation and high real interest rates, as well as a highly volatile real exchange rate. The latter reflected Zambia's unsuccessful management of the large declines that took place in 1995 and 1997 in the prices of copper, its main export (World Bank 2003n). In Malawi, too, macroeconomic instability undermined export and growth performance. During the 1990s, high and volatile inflation, averaging 31 percent, resulted in an overvalued and highly volatile real exchange rate, seriously undermining domestic production, investment, and exports. Malawi's manufacturing sector contracted by 9 percent during 1995–96. These developments hindered Malawi's efforts to diversify its exports out of tobacco, where they remain highly concentrated (World Bank 2003h).

## Trade-Related Infrastructure and Institutions

Successful trade integration requires supportive infrastructure and institutions—the so-called behind-the-border agenda.[12] A comparison of Jamaica and Mauritius illustrates the importance of institutions, as well as macroeconomic stability (box 5.4). Two other important constraints are transport infrastructure and institutional capacity for meeting product standards. Globally, improvements in transport and communications, in conjunction with developing-country reforms, have allowed the production chain to be broken up into components, with some developing countries playing a key role in global production sharing, as noted in chapter 3.

In many other countries, however, transport remains a key bottleneck. Markets that are isolated may feature little competition and may fail to realize economies of scale or scope. The result is typically a vicious cycle of low productivity and low profitability. Such constraints severely limit the growth potential of the poorest countries, where agriculture supplies 15 to 52 percent of GDP. In addition, since most of the poor reside in rural areas, these constraints have serious negative effects on poverty. For exporters in some developing countries, transport is the single most important component of cost.[13] The main issues related to transport are lack of competition and inadequate investments. Transport costs are further raised by formal and informal fees and checkpoints. Poor transport particularly affects agricultural producers (mainly small-

**BOX 5.4**

## Jamaica and Mauritius: Institutions and Macroeconomic Stability Make the Difference

Jamaica and Mauritius had nearly the same per capita GDP in 1984. But between 1984 and 2000, real per capita GDP grew at about 4.8 percent a year in Mauritius, compared with only 0.7 percent in Jamaica. This is a dramatic difference in performance, given the many similarities between the two countries.

Both countries have similar natural endowments and historical legacies. Both are island economies, have tropical climates, are subject to natural shocks (hurricanes in Jamaica and cyclones in Mauritius), and are former British colonies with English as the official language. Their economic structures are similar, with about 6 percent of GDP from agriculture, about one-third from industry, and the remaining 60 percent or so from services. Sugarcane is widely grown in both countries, and both enjoy preferential access to the European Union and the United States for sugar exports. Both established export-processing zones centered on garment manufacturing, with the primary impetus provided by East Asian investors.

The disparate growth performance cannot be attributed to differences in trade: between 1985 and 2000, real annual growth of exports was 3.9 percent in Mauritius and 3.6 percent in Jamaica, and by 2000, trade accounted for a larger share of GDP in Jamaica than in Mauritius. Jamaica has geographic advantages for trade, being much closer to the United States and the European Union than Mauritius is to either. Jamaica surpasses Mauritius in education enrollment indicators. And through the 1990s, Jamaica enjoyed higher FDI as a share of GDP than Mauritius.

Two factors that may explain the difference in growth performance are institutional quality and macroeconomic stability. Subramanian and Roy (2001) point to Mauritius's superior institutions (democracy and strong participatory institutions), and ethnic diversity, which provided important links to the rest of the world (68 percent of the population is Indian), and the need for participatory political institutions that were important for maintaining stability, rule of law, and mediating conflict. Looking at indicators of institutional quality (Kaufmann, Kraay, and Zoido-Lobaton 2002), Mauritius outperforms Jamaica in all but one (regulatory quality): Mauritius does better in government effectiveness, political stability, rule of law, control of corruption, and voice. The rule of law is a particular problem in Jamaica, with crime and violence costing at least 4 percent of GDP (excluding dynamic costs) (World Bank 2003g). Unlike Mauritius, Jamaica has lacked a social/political compact; though recently the labor unions have agreed with the government to limit their wage increases in response to the grave economic situation.

Mauritius outperformed Jamaica in macroeconomic stability for the two decades from 1980 to 2000, in terms of the level of inflation and the stability and competitiveness of the real exchange rate. In the 1990s, Jamaica's poor management of adverse macroeconomic developments seemed to more than offset the potentially positive effects of a substantial trade (and capital account) liberalization. Financial crisis in the mid-1990s worsened the already deteriorating fiscal performance, and dramatically enlarged the ratio of debt to GDP. This has dampened private sector confidence, government investment, interest rates, and growth.

holder farmers and herders) who have difficulty accessing markets both domestic and external. In Malawi, for example, high transport costs have weakened the competitiveness and profitability of firms and farmers. Malawi is an efficient producer of sugar, but domestic transport costs account for 15 percent or more of local consumer prices, and for sugar exports, regional and international transport costs add nearly 50 percent to the ex-mill production costs (World Bank 2003i). Lack of competition in road transport (where Malawi has restrictions on foreign operators) and high transport taxes add substantially to transport costs.

Product standards in international trade have proliferated and become more stringent in recent years. Consumers in developed countries are demanding stricter food standards, while major food retailers, food manufacturers, and restaurant chains have been adopting codes of practice, standards, and other forms of supply-chain governance as part of their commercial strategies of differentiation. Increasingly, middle-income and some low-income countries are also raising their product standards, in part through the investments undertaken by multinational supermarket or restaurant chains and competitive responses by local firms.

Prospects are dim for "special and differential treatment" that would require less stringent standards from poorer countries (Jaffee and Henson 2004). Developing countries need to develop and improve their food safety and agricultural health management systems to position themselves competitively and to enhance their export performance. Building such capacity is not beyond the reach of developing countries, and some very poor countries are meeting exacting international standards. Examples include Peruvian exports of asparagus to the United States and the European Union, and low-income African countries' exports of fish products that meet EU hygiene standards. Countries that meet strict export standards are generally those where the private sector is well organized and the public sector well focused to meet exporters' needs, such as through out-grower programs for smallholder farmers, systems of training and oversight for small and medium-size enterprises through associations and groups, and twinning and regional networking for small countries.

## 2. Different Paths to Trade Reform

This section discusses issues related to the path of liberalization, including the success of different partial approaches to trade liberalization, managing the political economy of trade reform, whether there is a limited role for infant industry protection, and the pros and cons of regional trade agreements.

One element is common to almost all of the success stories: despite the diversity of approaches to trade reform, all successful liberalizations either explicitly or implicitly promoted export growth. Exporters were given incentives to ensure that selling on international markets was as attractive as domestic sales. This required establishing a regime that offset the anti-export bias. In turn, this required an effectively functioning bureaucracy to implement the offsetting regulation—as with the "indirect duty drawbacks" in Korea. This proactive approach is not generally prescribed. Since most countries lack the institutional capacity that is required to implement offsetting regulation, classic trade liberalization—through low, uniform tariffs and the elimination of quantitative restrictions—has been the more conventional recommendation.

### Partial Trade Liberalization: China and India

China opted for partial trade liberalization, pursued through a dual-track approach. Special economic zones (SEZs)—one of the drivers in China's export and growth success—were set up in the 1980s to give the firms established within them access to duty-free imported inputs. Firms outside the SEZs faced much higher tariffs on imports, at 56 percent in 1982, falling to 44 percent in 1991and 16 percent in 2000 (Lardy 2002).

China established its first four SEZs in 1980 in two coastal provinces (Guangdong and Fujian), selected for their location.[14] The success of the initial zones led to the addition four years later of 14 coastal cities (including Shanghai) as "coastal open cities," with authority similar to that of the SEZs. By 1992, most cities along the Yangtze River and the borders of China had been granted special privileges as coastal cities, with Shanghai being granted even more autonomy. These developments, in turn, spurred the establishment of "development zones" in many inland cities that extended tax benefits and autonomy to foreign and domestic investments.

In many cases, such zones were established with-out the approval of the central government.[15] In 1993 China became the world's second-largest destination for FDI, next to the United States. Compared with other regions, the SEZs enjoy lower tax rates and greater authority in approv-ing foreign investment projects. The removal of administrative barriers had nearly as great an effect in spurring trade as China's tariff reduc-tions, which did not really begin until the 1990s. Exports grew at an annual average of 15 percent in the 1980s, and at 19 percent in the 1990s.[16]

India followed a different model of partial liberalization, liberalizing trade across all regions of the country but relaxing protection one sec-tor at a time. After piecemeal efforts at liberaliz-ing trade during the 1980s, India launched a coherent trade reform program in 1991, with some faltering during 1997–2001.[17] The reforms entailed concurrent reductions of some of the highest tariff and nontariff barriers (NTBs) in the world. A large reduction in NTBs and the streamlining of a very complex import licensing regime came early in the reform pro-gram, while tariffs were reduced in a phased manner, with reductions continuing today. Cur-rently, the maximum customs tariff for nonagri-cultural goods is 30 percent, scheduled to be reduced to 20 percent or less in the near future.[18] Capital and intermediate goods imports were liberalized first, and consumer goods (which were effectively banned) not until several years later. It was not until 2001 that all consumer goods imports were liberalized.[19]

India's sequencing of trade liberalization, which entailed earlier liberalization of capital and intermediate goods than for consumer goods, and much steeper reduction in tariffs for some of them, was intended to discourage the deferment of investments that might occur if domestic pro-ducers expected further reductions in capital goods tariffs.[20] The response was rapid: in dollar terms, exports were growing by 20 percent annu-ally within three years of the start of the reform program. The strong export supply response pro-vided impetus for a continued response, not least because the new export receipts alleviated the pressures on the balance of payments.

Factors that were clearly important for the trade reforms adopted by China and India were the credibility of reforms and the importance of strong institutions. Some ways to achieve reform credibility are discussed below.

## Political Economy of Trade Reforms

The success of trade reforms is not automatic. Political economy considerations need to be taken into account at the design stage if reforms are to be sustainable. The key elements on the political economy front are ensuring that the costs of adjustment arising from reforms are eased, and that reforms are credible.

### Easing the Costs of Adjustment

Easing the costs of adjustment is clearly important to generate social and political support for reforms. One way to ease adjustment costs is to ensure that safety nets are adequate to compen-sate losers. But, as discussed earlier, a more effica-cious way is to design a reform program that minimizes adjustment costs.

China and Mauritius provide good examples in this regard, by creating new profit opportuni-ties at the margin while leaving old opportuni-ties undisturbed. The upshot was that there were no identifiable losers. In China, few vested inter-ests opposed the SEZs because these were set up outside the scope of central planning and did not disrupt planned production and allocation. China's approach also maximized political sup-port for the reforms as the number of winners grew over time. Mauritius partially liberalized trade by establishing export processing zones (EPZs) and segmenting the labor market (Subra-manian and Roy 2001). Labor market rules were much less stringent in the EPZs than elsewhere in the economy. Until the mid- to late 1980s, employers had greater flexibility in dismissing workers in the EPZ sector, and in the 1980s, EPZ wages were about 36–40 percent lower than wages in the rest of the economy, with the differ-entials narrowing to 7–20 percent in the 1990s. Aside from acting as a subsidy to exports, the seg-mentation of the labor market also prevented the expansion of the EPZs from driving up wages in the rest of the economy and disadvantaging the import-substituting industries.

## Ensuring Credibility

At the very least, reforms should be publicly communicated so that economic agents are aware of them and can respond accordingly. Mozambique lifted export restrictions on cashew nuts but with very little communication to those directly affected by the reforms, so that few cashew nut farmers were aware that substantial reforms had been undertaken.[21] As a result, much of the price increase that resulted from the reforms went to the traders, and the supply response was constrained. Had farmers been told of the reforms, they could have strengthened their bargaining power in relation to the traders, making it difficult for the latter to pay low prices. Public communication of reforms also diminishes the possibility of reform reversals, boosting their credibility.

Another way to boost the credibility of reforms is to undertake measures that are less easy to reverse than price changes. In Mozambique, another reason why the supply response was poor was that cashew nut processors did not make investments to improve their efficiency, in part because they expected the reforms to be reversed. The overall reform program would have been more credible had the price reforms been accompanied by nonprice reforms, such as government investment in transport, better access to credit, promotion of competition in cashew marketing, and the creation of incentives to adopt improved technologies for cashew growing. Such nonprice interventions strengthen credibility by signaling to the public a government's commitment to the reforms.

Further ways to promote credibility include the establishment of institutions such as India's Tariff Commission, which is charged with the design and implementation of the trade reform program and has a tenure that outlasts governments. Such long tenure helps to enhance the credibility of reforms, as it diminishes private sector expectations that the reform program will be reversed by successive governments. Finally, credibility can also be achieved through signing on to regional trade arrangements that lock in reforms.

## Should Emerging Industries Be Protected?

Although import substitution policies have been largely discredited, the need to address market failures that prevent the development of internationally competitive industries has continued to provoke debate. Suggestions have been made to grant temporary modest levels of import protection where there is a demonstrated need (Williamson 2004a). Other authors have focused on choosing the right form of protection, advocating subsidies to the initial entrants rather than the use of import duties (Baldwin 2003).

Another suggestion is to approach development as a process of "self-discovery," since the key challenge that a modernizing economy faces is learning what it is good at producing (Hausmann and Rodrik 2002). The entrepreneur who first discovers what the country should specialize in can capture only a small part of the social value that this knowledge generates, because other entrepreneurs will quickly emulate such discoveries. Thus this type of entrepreneurship will typically be undersupplied and economic transformation delayed. There may be a role for government involvement to provide incentives to induce such investments, as well as to exert discipline in pruning investments that turn out to be costly.

A key challenge for countries that choose to pursue such a strategy is to structure the right combination of incentives (inducements) and discipline (competitive pressures, resistance against special interests). Some of the world's most successful economies during the last four decades (Korea and Taiwan [China] since the early 1960s; China since the late 1970s) prospered by pursuing policies that gave inducements for investment and risk taking while expanding competitive pressures that ensured efficient allocation by investors. During their industrial drives in the 1960s and the 1970s, Korea and Taiwan (China) provided export subsidies contingent on export performance. This strategy allowed policy makers to distinguish firms and sectors that were highly productive from those that were not. The subsidies included supplying inputs, providing working capital, imposing import restrictions, and—in Taiwan's (China) textile industry in the 1950s—buying the resulting output. Local production grew spectacularly as a result. But the government also pruned nonproductive firms subsequently.

Asia's successful experiences in this regard contrast with the generally failed experiences of Latin America. Pursuing import substitution strategies in the 1960s and the 1970s, Latin American governments provided incentives without sufficient discipline, with the result that too many low-productivity firms operated alongside the high performers. When trade openness and domestic competition brought discipline in the 1990s, producers received too little support (Hausmann and Rodrik 2002). Without a good balance between promotion and discipline, Latin American countries' industrial performance fell short of that in East Asian countries during these decades.

Chile has often been touted as a miracle of free-market economics. In fact, public-private collaboration strategies have played a key role in fostering structural change and stimulating non-traditional activities (box 5.5). Yet identifying the conditions for successfully assisting new activities is not easy. Rodrik and Hausmann (2003) emphasize the importance of creating an institutional architecture that resists the pull of special interests, and the importance of political leadership from the top. Whatever institutions are employed to support new activities, they must be transparent and accountable, or selective support is likely to evolve into a new mechanism for supporting private interests in the name of public gain. The promotion of new activities should conform to a set of design principles that include the following: (1) incentives should be provided only for new, "sunrise" activities, not sunset ones; (2) there should be clear benchmarks for success or failure; (3) support must have a predetermined end (a so-called sunset clause); (4) public support should target *activities* such as worker training or infrastructure investment, rather than *sectors* such as electronics; (5) subsidized activities should provide clear potential for externalities; and (6) agencies involved in these activities should be autonomous enough to avoid capture by private

interests, but should maintain links with the private sector to maximize economywide gains. This is not a prescription for creating new state enterprises, promoting existing activities, or giving governments authority to expand their bureaucratic reach. Clearly, the institutional and administrative requirements for success are formidable.

## A Role for Regional Agreements?

Some countries have achieved greater integration and strong growth by adopting unilateral or multilateral trade reforms combined with participation in regional trade agreements. Signing on to regional trade agreements provides countries with access to the markets of fellow members, and can help improve their domestic institutions. But evidence suggests that as many as half of regional trade agreements are substantially trade-diverting. Trade and investment diversion cause significant economic losses to the countries excluded from the agreements.

Regional integration has yielded good results for Central and Eastern European countries that signed Europe Agreements in the 1990s with the European Union, and for Mexico, which joined the North American Free Trade Agreement (NAFTA). For the Central and Eastern European countries, the institutional harmonization aspect of the Europe Agreements has been very important for successful trade integration and growth (World Bank 2000d); agreements on harmonization of investment policies, regulatory rules, and institutions with those of EU members have encouraged export-oriented foreign direct investment into the Central and Eastern European countries. In Mexico, NAFTA has had positive effects on trade, foreign direct investment, technology transfer, and growth, and is also associated with productivity improvements in manufacturing. But although NAFTA has contributed to institutional harmonization between Mexico and the United States in the areas that it covers—in particular intellectual property rights, investor protection, and environmental standards—it has not helped to narrow other institutional gaps, especially in the areas of rule of law and corrup-

**BOX 5.5**

**Behind Chile's Success: A Less than Orthodox Approach**

Chile appears to be the exception among Latin American countries by striking the right balance of inducements and discipline in promoting domestic industry.

Fruits and salmon, Chile's two largest export items after copper, have both benefited from private-public sector partnerships. The foundations of the fruit industry were laid in the early 1960s through the efforts of the *Corporacion de Fomento*, the University of Chile, and the National Institute of Agricultural Research (INIA). INIA, established in 1964 with highly paid, skilled researchers, initiated the fruit research program. The public sector carried out much of the development of scientific personnel and knowledge to achieve technological transfer; identification and planting of new varieties suitable for export to foreign markets; improvements in orchard and postharvest management; and the development of the infrastructure necessary to export fruit to foreign markets. Private investment and exports took off after the reforms of the mid-1970s once uncertainties regarding land reform, macroeconomic stability, and labor militancy were resolved. These investments and exports were further boosted by the sharp real depreciation of the currency in the mid-1980s.

The salmon industry, which generates $600 million in annual exports and provides jobs for more than 100,000 people in this country of 15 million, also benefited significantly from public interventions. It was created single-handedly by *Fundacion Chile*, a nonprofit institution created by the Chilean Government in 1976. *Fundacion Chile* brought the technology of salmon farming to Chile, adapted it and made it commercially viable, formed private sector businesses to use it, and eventually sold its participation to Japanese investors at a great profit.

*Sources*: Rodrik and Hausmann 2003; Ocampo 2004; and *Washington Post*, January 21, 2004.

tion, which are nonetheless important for income convergence between the two countries (Perry et al. 2003).

Evidence suggests that for developing countries, signing on to regional trade agreements with developed countries, particularly large developed countries, is most useful. Agreements should also strive to ensure that barriers that apply to nonagreement countries are kept low. Signing such agreements will not generate positive export and growth responses unless the countries themselves also pursue other necessary economic, political, and social reforms. Among the EU accession countries in the 1990s, benefits only accrued to those countries that were also undertaking the necessary economic, political, and institutional reforms to transform their economies into market-based ones.[22] For example, Bulgaria and Romania signed Europe Agreements in 1993, in advance of several other accession countries, but they lagged behind in the transition process and fared much worse in economic performance compared to Estonia and Slovenia, which signed such agreements in 1995 and 1996, respectively.

Most important, regional trade agreements can divert attention away from the multilateral World Trade Organization (WTO) process, and result in higher costs than benefits for developing countries.[23] This will be especially true if the agreed upon protection relative to third parties remains high. Recent experience with the Free Trade Area of the Americas, the Central American Free Trade Agreement, and the U.S.-Australia Free Trade Agreements suggests that regionalism will not help the developing countries much with their market access priorities: trade-distorting agricultural support in the North, contingent protection, and liberalization of temporary migration of labor. Further, the high costs of negotiating such agreements divert resources away from such larger multilateral issues.

## 3. Trade Liberalization, Poverty, and Income Distribution

Despite expected gains for the economy in the longer term, trade reform generates both winners and losers in the short run.[24] The critical question is whether the short-run costs of trade reform fall disproportionately on the poor. Economists in the 1990s expected trade and foreign investment reforms to help developing countries reduce poverty. Trade liberalization was expected to increase demand for goods produced by developing countries' poor or low-skilled workers, leading to higher wages for unskilled workers and ameliorating poverty. Trade reforms were also expected to raise the prices of the agricultural products produced by the poor and to reduce prices of goods that the poor consume. Is the emerging evidence from the 1990s consistent with these expectations? How much of the decline in poverty rates and increasing within-country inequality can be attributed to the trade reforms of the 1990s?

### Effects of Trade Reform on Aggregate Growth and Poverty

#### Direct Effects

If opening up to trade is associated with higher growth, it may be associated with a decline in poverty as well. This argument rests on two assumptions: first, that opening up to trade leads to higher growth, and second, that growth raises the incomes of the poor as much as the incomes of the rich.

What actually occurred? There is widespread evidence that GDP growth reduces poverty.[25] In other words, evidence suggests that growth benefits those at the lower end of the income distribution. If trade liberalization contributes to growth—as discussed earlier in this chapter—it should be associated with reductions in poverty. China and India, for example, have both experienced tremendous increases in trade integration and growth, as well as large reductions in poverty. From 1980 to 2000, real per capita GDP grew at an annual average of 8.3 percent in China and

3.6 percent in India, while trade integration (trade in goods and services in real terms as a share of GDP) rose from 23 to 46 percent of GDP in China, and from 19 to 30 percent in India. Over this period, both countries massively reduced the incidence of poverty—from 28 to 9 percent between 1978 and 1998 in China, and from 51 to 27 percent between 1977–78 and 1999–2000 in India.[26] Since a large share of the world's poor lives in these two countries, these large reductions have served to reduce or mitigate overall inequality in the world, even though inequality has risen within both countries (Ravallion 2003b; Sala-i-Martin 2003).

Nevertheless, Harrison (2005) suggests that policy makers need to be cautious about expecting large gains in poverty reduction from trade reforms.[27] Many economists expected that developing countries with a comparative advantage in unskilled labor would benefit from liberalization of trade through increased demand for their unskilled labor–intensive goods, which in turn should reduce inequality and poverty. However, the evidence in this volume—which includes 15 separate studies of the links between poverty and globalization—suggests that the story is more complex. One reason is that labor is not nearly as mobile as simple trade models assume. If comparative advantage is to increase the incomes of unskilled workers, they need to be able to move out of contracting sectors and into expanding ones. A second reason is that developing countries have historically protected their unskilled-intensive sectors, so that trade reforms may lead to less protection for unskilled workers relative to skilled. A third reason is that even firms in countries with a comparative advantage in producing goods that use unskilled labor need to use skilled workers in order to compete in global markets.

#### Indirect Effects

Trade reforms can also affect poverty indirectly—for example, by influencing (1) the job opportunities and wages of the poor, (2) the prices that poor consumers pay for the goods that they buy, (3) government revenues and in turn social expenditures that particularly affect the poor, and (4) income instability as well as workers' chances of becoming poor (Winters et al. 2004). Even if aggregate poverty falls or remains constant, many households may move into or out of poverty as a result of trade liberalization.

*Effects on jobs and wages.* Some studies have found that trade reforms reduce employment in the short run, but others have found that trade reforms increase employment over the long run, as expanding sectors create new employment opportunities. Trade explains much of the decline in Singapore's unemployment rate, from more than 9 percent in the 1960s to close to 2 percent in the late 1990s. A study of 18 countries in Latin America and the Caribbean over the period 1970–96 found that trade liberalization had a negative, though small, direct effect on employment.[28] The negative effect was greater in countries where the real exchange rate appreciated as a result of capital inflows that followed the economic reforms. Similarly, in Brazil during 1990–97, trade liberalization slightly reduced employment in the short run, but the more labor-intensive output mix that resulted over the long run increased employment.[29] Much larger negative effects on output and employment have been found in some African countries. One study for Kenya, Tanzania, and Zimbabwe found that most firms responded to import competition pressure by contracting rather than upgrading aggressively.[30] Among the suggested reasons for such behavior are the firms' lack of preparation for competition, absence of policies to promote technological improvement (especially among small and medium enterprises), and poor technological and human infrastructure.

Trade reforms of the 1990s in Latin America and the Caribbean reduced employment in previously protected industries and augmented it in others (De Ferranti et al. 2001). Argentina lost much of its automobile industry while seeing an expansion in more sophisticated chemicals and capital- and labor-intensive manufactures. Brazil lost much of its cereals industry to Argentina under Mercosur, and its manufacturing industry suffered more generally. Costa Rica lost much of its labor-intensive manufacturing to Mexico after NAFTA, but it also substantially increased its

manufacturing of computer chips. In each case, substantial numbers of workers lost their jobs, and some experienced very long periods of unemployment or large wage losses, or both.

As emphasized by De Ferranti et al. (2001), such dislocations are transitional and do not imply a permanent increase in the unemployment rate. Chile, for example, experienced double-digit rates of unemployment for several years after liberalization, but from 1986 to 1997 its unemployment rates were among the lowest in the region. Mexico's present rate of unemployment is roughly at its traditional level, despite that country's dramatic economic integration with the United States.

Although most studies find that the unemployment effects of trade liberalization tend to be temporary, even short-term costs can be high in human terms. Such costs must be addressed through a variety of policy approaches, including stronger social safety nets, in order to ensure that trade reforms succeed.

*Effects on prices.* An emerging literature using household-level data suggests that, via changes in factor and goods prices, trade liberalization can lead to poverty reduction. For instance, a recent study of trade liberalization in Argentina using household survey data found that Mercosur has benefited the average Argentine household across the spectrum of income distribution.[31] The same study also finds that Mercosur has had a pro-poor bias, benefiting poor households more than middle-income households, and that its impact on rich families is positive but not statistically significant. The reason behind these results is that Argentine trade policy protected the rich over the poor prior to the reforms, and granted some protection to the poor after the reforms.

*Effects on social spending.* Social spending is another avenue through which liberalization may affect income distribution, but there is no direct evidence for such a relationship. The available evidence, relating mostly to the 1980s,[32] suggests that many trade reforms had no revenue costs. Some of the main reasons were that temporary tariff surcharges were introduced when quantitative restrictions were removed, and that changes in the import/export base arising from the trade reforms enhanced revenues. For example, Kenya's trade liberalization between 1989 and 1999 (which entailed halving the simple average import duty rate over the period and abolishing import licensing requirements and foreign exchange controls) led to increases both in duty as a share of imports and in import duty revenues as a share of GDP. The increase in revenues reflected the expansion of the revenue base, tighter exemption management, higher duty rates on certain products, a shift in imports to the higher duty classes, and possibly also improvements in customs administration and the introduction of a preshipment program (Glenday 2000, cited in Winters et al. 2004).

Even in cases in which revenues are cut, available evidence suggests that public spending important to the poor can be protected. There are alternative sources of revenues—though caution needs to be exercised to ensure that replacement taxes do not hurt the poor. And, with political will, social spending, particularly that oriented toward the poor, may be shielded.

*Effects on vulnerability and income volatility.* When Indonesia, Korea, and Thailand opened up to trade in the late 1980s and early 1990s, no strong negative effects on poverty and vulnerability resulted.[33] It remains an open question whether openness made the 1997–98 Asian financial crisis much more serious than the shocks that had hit the three countries in the 1980s. It is clear, however, that financial crises are very costly to the poor. In Indonesia, the financial crisis of 1997 led to a 50 percent reduction in real wages.[34] In Mexico, the peso crisis of the mid-1990s led to a stagnation in real wages that lasted nearly a decade. A recent study of financial deregulation across countries emphasizes the need for complementary policies, such as the creation of reliable institutions and macroeconomic stabilization policies (Prasad et al. 2003). While financial crises resulting from unrestricted capital flows are associated with a higher likelihood of poverty, foreign direct investment inflows are associated with a reduction in poverty. The poverty-reducing effects of FDI are clearly documented in several recent studies on India and Mexico.

## Summarizing the Links between Trade Reforms and Poverty

What lessons emerge from cross-country and more detailed case studies using household data? First, the poor are more likely to share in the gains from globalization where complementary policies in place. Case studies of India and Colombia in Harrison (2005) suggest that globalization is more likely to benefit the poor if trade reforms are implemented in conjunction with labor market deregulation.[35] In Zambia, poor farmers are only expected to benefit from greater access to export markets if they also have access to credit, technical know-how, and other complementary inputs.[36] The same volume also points to the importance of social safety nets. In Mexico, trade reforms in the 1990s hurt the poorest corn farmers; without support from the government, these farmers' real incomes would have been halved.[37] The same result has been found more recently in Ethiopia.[38]

Second, while financial crises are associated with increasing poverty, reforms in trade and foreign investment in a number of countries have helped to reduce poverty. In Mexico, the poor in the most globalized regions have weathered the macroeconomic crises the best.[39] In India, opening up to foreign investment was associated with a decline in poverty. In Colombia, increasing export activity was associated with an increase in compliance with labor legislation and a fall in poverty. In Poland, unskilled workers—who are the most likely to be poor—have gained from the country's accession to the European Union.[40]

Clearly, globalization produces both winners and losers among the poor. Winters, McCulloch, and McKay (2004); Ravallion and Lokshin (2004); and Harrison (2005) all emphasize this heterogeneity in outcomes. It should not be surprising that the results defy easy generalization. The poor can gain from one set of policy reforms, if those lower the prices they pay for consumption goods, and lose from other trade reforms that lower the prices of the goods they produce. Poor wage earners in exporting sectors or in sectors with incoming foreign investment gain from trade and investment reforms; conversely, workers in previously protected sectors are likely to lose.

This emerging evidence on the links between trade reforms and poverty points to the need for carefully targeted social safety nets and complementary policies to ease the transition of workers from contracting to expanding sectors.

## Trade Liberalization and Inequality

Though inequality has been increasing in both rich and poor countries we still lack a comprehensive understanding of why. A popular explanation is that technological change—which may or may not be associated with opening up to trade—has led employers to demand more skilled labor. This phenomenon, referred to as skill-biased technical change, has occurred in both developed and developing countries. Some economists argue that the demand for more skilled workers is unrelated to trade liberalization, since the same trend has been documented in services that are not traded on world markets, but others argue that skill-biased technical change is itself an outcome of globalization.

One reason why trade reforms may be associated with increasing inequality is that many countries—Colombia, Mexico, Morocco, and Poland, for example—have traditionally protected the sectors that use mainly unskilled labor.

Another possible reason is that exporters—who benefit from trade reforms—need to hire skilled workers to succeed in world markets. A number of studies have shown that exporters are more likely to use a high proportion of skilled workers, suggesting that as countries turn to exporting, the demand for skilled workers will rise, pushing up their wages relative to those of unskilled workers.[41] Foreign firms in developing countries tend to hire more skilled workers than do domestic firms. In Mexico, increasing inequality is most evident in the border region—the region most affected by increasing trade with the United States.

Nevertheless, the evidence on trade liberalization and wage inequality remains inconclusive. In Argentina, Brazil, Costa Rica, the Dominican Republic, and Mexico, the industries that are most exposed to international competition pay the highest wages. It is difficult to distinguish the impact of globalization from that of technical change, since the adoption of new technologies could be stimulated by external competition via trade. In Mexico, for example, the tripling of manufactured exports during the 1990s has been associated with increased rates of adoption of modern production technologies, an acceleration of productivity growth, a relative increase in the demand for skilled labor, and an increase in inequality.

There is no evidence that trade liberalization permanently worsens income distribution. As noted above, however, there *is* evidence that trade liberalization has been associated with—at times significant and prolonged—adjustment costs in the form of employment losses. In Mexico, trade integration through NAFTA, while reducing poverty, has also increased income inequality between regions: regions with lower per capita GDP and higher telephone density grew faster, while regions with high public employment grew more slowly (Perry et al. 2003).

Governments need to help the disadvantaged by strengthening social safety nets and by providing education and training for the unskilled. As attested by the industrialized countries, it is a daunting task to build up the administrative and institutional capacity required to design and implement safety nets that are well targeted and that avoid leakages. More innovative approaches to trade reforms and trade reform assistance packages may be needed.

## 4. Issues of Differential Market Access

After the reforms of the 1990s the world trade system has been more supportive of development. But it remains strongly biased against the poor. Global markets are most hostile to the products the world's poor produce—agriculture, textiles, and labor-intensive manufactures. Escalating tariffs, tariff peaks, and quota arrangements maintained by both developed and developing countries systematically deny the poor market access and skew incentives against adding value in poor countries. In both rich and poor countries, protection remains heavily concentrated in the most politically sensitive areas—textiles, clothing, other labor-intensive manufactures, and agriculture.

Differential treatment by developed countries still constrains the expansion of trade by developing countries, particularly the poorest. In developed countries, the relatively low average tariffs mask the sometimes high protection in the form of tariff peaks, tariff escalation, specific duties, and production subsidies.

Developed-country protection is much more pronounced in agriculture than in manufacturing (World Bank, *Global Economic Prospects 2004*). Since most of the world's poor live in rural areas and work in agriculture, rich-country subsidies combined with trade protection to domestic agriculture worsen world poverty. Farm production subsidies in the United States, for example, are distributed overwhelmingly to the richest farmers, exacerbating income

inequality in agriculture and favoring wealthy landowners. Developed countries impose higher tariffs on agricultural imports from developing countries than from other industrial countries (table 5.2). Developed countries impose an average tariff of 15 percent on agricultural imports from other industrial countries, but average tariffs ranging from 20 percent (for Latin America) to 35 percent (for Europe and Central Asia) on agricultural imports from developing countries. The issue of agricultural protection, in particular in cotton, has risen in prominence in multilateral trade talks, and was one of the main reasons for the failure of the most recent round of WTO talks in Cancun in September 2003. Since then, Brazil has gone to the WTO with charges that U.S. subsidies on cotton are inconsistent with WTO obligations, and the WTO ruling on April 2004 affirmed Brazil's charges.[42]

On manufactured goods, tariffs are on average lower in developed than in developing countries,

TABLE 5.2

## Rich Countries Levy Higher Tariffs on Poor Countries' Exports
(1997 protection rates facing exporters in each region, in percentage points)

| Exporting region | Importing region | | | | | | |
| --- | --- | --- | --- | --- | --- | --- | --- |
| | East Asia | Europe and Central Asia | Latin America | Middle East | South Asia | Sub-Saharan Africa | Industrial countries |
| Agriculture | | | | | | | |
| Industrial countries | 33.3 | 43.7 | 20.1 | 65.4 | 16.4 | 24.0 | 15.3 |
| East Asia | 31.0 | 30.3 | 15.5 | 45.3 | 38.4 | 19.0 | 30.5 |
| Europe and Central Asia | 24.2 | 36.4 | 23.8 | 55.3 | 34.2 | 12.7 | 35.1 |
| Latin America and the Caribbean | 42.1 | 36.0 | 14.8 | 50.3 | 29.7 | 24.7 | 20.4 |
| Middle East | 23.0 | 43.4 | 14.9 | 76.4 | 31.8 | 18.9 | 23.4 |
| South Asia | 16.6 | 34.6 | 13.7 | 41.1 | 27.7 | 11.0 | 25.8 |
| Sub-Saharan Africa | 26.7 | 20.3 | 14.4 | 39.1 | 30.9 | 33.6 | 23.6 |
| Nonagriculture | | | | | | | |
| Industrial countries | 7.4 | 9.6 | 8.5 | 10.4 | 25.2 | 12.2 | 1.0 |
| East Asia | 8.2 | 13.8 | 15.1 | 12.2 | 28.1 | 14.5 | 5.1 |
| Europe and Central Asia | 6.4 | 6.4 | 11.4 | 8.6 | 25.8 | 12.8 | 5.9 |
| Latin America and the Caribbean | 4.3 | 6.7 | 15.4 | 8.9 | 19.4 | 11.9 | 2.1 |
| Middle East | 5.4 | 11.5 | 8.8 | 11.4 | 33.6 | 11.7 | 6.0 |
| South Asia | 7.1 | 11.0 | 13.6 | 10.2 | 19.0 | 17.4 | 8.1 |
| Sub-Saharan Africa | 4.4 | 6.1 | 11.7 | 6.1 | 27.6 | 20.6 | 4.2 |

*Source*: Weighted averages calculated using GTAP Version 5 database (www.gtap.org). Most-favored-nation rates except for major free-trade blocs such as the European Union and the North American Free Trade Area.

but the types of goods exported by poor countries face higher tariffs in the rich countries. For example, while exporters of manufactures from industrial countries face, on average, a tariff of 1 percent on their sales to other industrial countries, exporters from developing countries pay anywhere from 2 percent if they are from Latin America (where NAFTA weighs heavily) to 8 percent if they are from South Asia.

Overall, rich countries collect from developing countries about twice the tariff revenues per dollar of imports that they collect from other rich countries. Protection also takes forms other than tariffs—among them quotas, specific duties, and contingent protection measures such as antidumping duties. As with tariffs, these measures tend to be used more frequently against labor-intensive products from developing countries. Antidumping duties are on average 7 to 10 times higher than tariffs in industrial countries, and around 5 times higher in developing countries. Developing countries are also hampered in other critical areas, including access for their agricultural and textile exports, and restrictions on international labor migration.

To continue the momentum toward greater global integration, high-income countries must further open their markets to developing-country exports. Industrial countries' unfair tariff treatment of developing countries must be addressed in the upcoming Doha round of trade negotiations.

## Notes

1. These changes were not just due to declines in the prices of agricultural and resource commodities relative to manufactures—the strong shift in the composition of exports shows up even when price changes are removed. Further, it was not just due to a few, large high-growth exporters such as China and India. Excluding China and India, the share of manufactures in developing-country exports grew from one-tenth in 1980 to almost two-thirds in 2001. It increased sharply, but not equally, in all regions. The laggards included Sub-Saharan Africa and the Middle East and North Africa, which have yet to reach 30 percent. Many countries, particularly the poorest, remain dependent on exports of agricultural and resource commodities.

2. World Bank (*Global Economic Prospects 2004*, 139). These statistics are based on remittances sent through official channels. Existing payment systems make remittances difficult and costly, especially in and to Africa and Central America. To many parts of the world, unofficial remittances far outweigh official ones.

3. From 1990 to 2000, income from migrant workers overseas (including workers' remittances and employees' compensation) as a share of foreign exchange receipts (measured as exports of goods, services, and workers' income) fell from 4.3 to 3.8 percent for all developing countries. Conceptually it makes sense to compare income from migrant workers with receipts from exports of goods and services since labor could be viewed as one form of a country's service exports. Almost all of the drop for the developing world as a whole can be attributed to the decline in migrant workers' income in the Arab Republic of Egypt, which in 1990 had enjoyed the largest amount of this income in nominal terms in the developing world. The decline in migrant workers' income in Egypt during the 1990s was related to the Gulf War. Excluding Egypt, the ratio fell from 3.7 to 3.6 percent over the decade. Countries where incomes from migrant workers have become quite important—ranging between 20 and 46 percent of total foreign exchange receipts in 2000—and where such income increased significantly over the 1990s (increases ranging from 10 to 46 percent) include Albania, Ecuador, Jamaica, Jordan, Nicaragua, Sudan, and Uganda. At the same time, however, countries including Benin, Cape Verde, Egypt, Lesotho, and Pakistan experienced declines in such incomes, ranging from 10 to 30 percent.

4. Properly identifying the causal impact of changes in trade policies on growth needs to take into account other factors associated with GDP growth, and the possibility of reverse causality (that is, if GDP growth causes changes in trade policies). This means that the variable for trade policy should be "instrumented" or represented with measures that affect trade policy but are not correlated with GDP growth. Since most reforms are driven by initial protection levels, one way to get around the problem is to instrument the changes in tariffs in the 1990s with the initial tariffs that prevailed during 1986–90. The initial tariffs were found to explain 36 percent of the changes in tariffs during the decade: countries with high tariffs in the late 1980s and early 1990s reduced tariffs by a higher percentage, while countries with already low tariffs reduced them less. The results also control for some other policies that affected growth in the 1990s, including exchange rate policies, government consumption, and inflation.

5. For example, Dollar and Kraay (2001, 2003); Lee, Ricci, and Rigobon (2004); and Alcala and Ciccone (2004) all show a positive relationship between trade

and growth, whereas Rigobon and Rodrik (2004) get mixed results. Wacziarg and Welch (2003) find a positive relationship between a composite measure of economic reforms and economic growth, but that relationship is not significant for the 1990s; nor do they isolate the role of trade policy per se, but look at the composite measure including exchange rate reforms. Their analysis is done in a panel context, since they measure the impact of changes in trade policy on economic growth.

6. See Wacziarg and Welch (2003) and Baldwin's (2003) summary of the recent debate on the topic.

7. See Bolaky and Freund (2004). The authors measure excessive regulation using a World Bank survey on labor regulations and business entry regulations. They find that the benefits of expanding trade (as measured by trade shares) are offset by excessive regulations in the most regulated economies in the 1990s.

8. Lerner symmetry in the two-good case can be illustrated as follows: $Px/Pm(1 + t) = [Px/(1 + t)]/Pm$, where $Px$ = price of exports; $Pm$ = price of imports; $t$ = tariff.

9. Macroeconomic stability refers to the stability of the real effective exchange rate, as measured by the standard deviation, and average inflation. Government effectiveness refers to combined perceptions of the quality of public service provision, the quality of the bureaucracy, the competence of civil servants, the independence of the civil service from political pressures, and the credibility of the government's commitment to policies. The government effectiveness indicator is taken from Kaufmann, Kraay, and Mastruzzi (2003), and based on 17 separate sources of subjective data on perceptions of governance constructed by 15 different organizations.

10. See Aitken, Hanson, and Harrison (1997).

11. See Thomas and Nash (1992); and Nash and Takacs (1998).

12. Tsikata (2003). This study summarizes the findings of diagnostic trade integration studies undertaken during 2001–03 for 12 least developed countries (Burundi, Cambodia, Ethiopia, Guinea, Lesotho, Madagascar, Malawi, Mali, Mauritania, Nepal, Senegal, and the Republic of Yemen).

13. The discussion in this paragraph is based on Jaffee and Sutherland (2003).

14. Information in this paragraph is from Qian (2000).

15. The autonomy given to local governments in China is a very important factor in this development. This autonomy is provided in the form of the "fiscal contracting system" introduced between 1980 and 1993, under which provincial governments are provided incentives to build up local economies and their own revenue bases. Specifically, the incentives arise from allowing the provinces to keep the lion's share of the increases in revenues at the margin. Data from the reform period of 1982–91 show that the correlation coefficient between the provincial budgetary revenue and expenditure is 0.75, compared to 0.17 in the prereform period of 1970–79 (Qian 2002). Another study (Jin, Qian, and Weingast 2001) found that such incentives were indeed significant—for the growth of employment of nonstate enterprises and in the reform of state enterprises.

16. Qian (2002); Jin, Qian, and Weingast (2001).

17. A result of the increasing import competition from East and Southeast Asian countries that devalued their currencies in the aftermath of the Asian financial crisis.

18. These tariffs underestimate true import competition since there are also specific tariffs.

19. However, imports of several agricultural goods, making up 40 percent of Indian agricultural GDP, continue to be controlled by state trading enterprises.

20. World Bank (1994b).

21. See McMillan, Rodrik, and Welch (2002).

22. Much of the benefits came in the form of export-oriented FDI from the EU member countries (World Bank 2000d).

23. This discussion is taken from World Bank (2004d); see also Stiglitz and the Initiative for Policy Dialogue (2004).

24. See Harrison (forthcoming); Winters, McCulloch, and McKay (2004); Goldberg and Pavcnik (2005, forthcoming) for comprehensive surveys.

25. See, for example, the survey papers by Berg and Krueger (2003); Winters, McCulloch, and McKay (2004); and papers by Dollar and Kraay (2001, 2003). The general conclusion of these papers is that growth increases the incomes of the poor, although whether or not the effect is neutral across different incomes is subject to debate.

26. Asian Development Bank (2000), cited by Bhagwati and Srinivasan (2002).

27. Papers from this volume, which was commissioned by the National Bureau of Economic Research, can be viewed online at www.nber.org.

28. Marques and Pagés (1998).

28. Moreira and Najberg (2000). The appreciation of the real exchange rate during the period contributed to the negative employment effect by encouraging imports and undermining exports.

30. Lall (1999).

31. Porto (2003).

32. See Winters et al. (2004) for studies cited.

33. World Bank (2003e).

34. See Thomas (2004).

35. For the study on India, see Topalova (2005). For the study on Colombia, see Goldberg and Pavcnik (2005).

36. Balat and Porto (2004).

37. Ashraf, McMillan, and Peterson-Zwane (2005).

38. Levinsohn and McMillan (2004).
39. Hanson (2004).
40. Goh and Smarzynska Javorcik (2004).
41. For a review of recent evidence on these links, see Hanson (2004); Goldberg and Pavcnik (2004).
42. U.S. subsidies on cotton amounted to $3.7 billion in 2002 (three times the U.S. aid to Africa).

# The Middle East and North Africa: Performing below Potential

Earlier parts of this report highlighted that sustained growth experiences result from four functions of growth being met, and that at different moments, different functions are more relevant than others and their absence poses more binding constraints. Fulfilling only some of the functions of growth results in performance well below potential. Countries in the Middle East and Northern Africa illustrate this point: while they have succeeded in accumulating capital, both physical and human, and have also succeeded in ensuring equitable distribution, they have not sufficiently emphasized efficient allocation of resources through openness and liberalizing their domestic economies.

The 12 developing countries[1] of the Middle East and North Africa have a total population of 260 million, of which the two most populous, the Arab Republic of Egypt and the Islamic Republic of Iran, account for about half.[2] While the countries of the region vary widely in their natural resources, population density, and stage of economic and political development, they share a common history and cultural heritage. They also share a common approach to economic policies: relatively high import protection and a large role of government in the economy. Their experiences highlight the role of natural endowments in growth processes, and the role of openness and domestic liberalization.

Countries in the region have generally followed prudent macroeconomic management principles and have avoided extreme instability of the kind seen in Latin America. Inflation has been moderate and relatively stable, and Argentina-like fluctuations in output have been exceptional. But the fundamentals have in many cases weakened and the region now faces a number of serious macroeconomic vulnerabilities. In particular, contingent liabilities have been building up in many countries, from sources such as pension systems, banking sectors, public enterprises, and a variety of implicit and explicit government guarantees.

Although intraregional trade and financial flows are small, the countries in the region are tied together by large-scale labor migration. Other common characteristics include rapid gains in social indicators over the last two decades, starting from extremely low levels (table D.1). Poverty declined rapidly in the 1960s, 1970s, and 1980s, but changed little in the 1990s. Income inequality remained relatively low throughout the period. Also, in the last two decades, countries in the region experienced one of the highest labor force growth rates in the developing world. Between 1990 and 2020, the growth of the economically active population (ages 15–64) will exceed that of the economically dependent population by a much greater amount than in any other region. As experience elsewhere has shown, this rapid growth presents an opportunity, but also poses the challenge of responding to the employment expectations of an increasingly urbanized labor force.

For most of the last century, because of its oil and natural gas reserves, the world's largest, the region has been the focus of attention from industrialized superpowers. Possibly as a result of such strategic importance, armed conflicts have been frequent over the past four decades.[3]

## Growth Performance

Though the region has escaped extreme instability, its high output growth of the 1960s and 1970s

TABLE D.1

## Progress on Social Indicators, Middle East and North Africa, 1980–2000

|  | 1980 | 1985 | 1990 | 1995 | 2000 |
|---|---|---|---|---|---|
| Headcount poverty rate, % | — | 16.9 | 17.2 | 15.9 | — |
| Life expectancy, % | 59 | 64 | 67 | 69 | 70 |
| Infant mortality rate, % | 83 | — | 42 | 36 | 32 |
| Adult literacy rate, % | 42 | 49 | 57 | 64 | 72 |
| Secondary school enrollment, % gross | 33 | 45 | 49 | 59 | 69 |
| Literate female to literate male ratio, ages 15–24 | 62 | 69 | 79 | 86 | 92 |

*Source*: World Bank 2004f; Adams and Page 2003.

*Note*: Table shows medians of the regional social indicators. Headcount poverty rate is a simple arithmetic average, because the sample size is small: long enough series are available for only five countries: Egypt (1981–82, 1990–91, 1995–96, 1997, 1999–2000); Jordan (1986–87, 1992, 1997); Morocco (1984–85, 1990–91, 1998–99); Tunisia (1984–85, 1990–91, 1998–99); and the Islamic Republic of Iran (1986, 1990, 1994, 1998). Though not reflected in the table, in 2000 poverty rates continued to decline in the countries for which data are available (Egypt and the Islamic Republic of Iran), and rose only in Morocco. Data shown on adult literacy rate and literate female-to-male ratio do not include Djibouti and Lebanon, for which no data are available.

—. Not available.

gave way to stagnation in the 1980s (figure D.1 and table D.2). Except for Egypt and Tunisia, the countries of the region have not grown fast enough to reduce the income gap with more advanced industrial economies (Country Note B, *Lessons from Countries That Have Sustained Their Growth*). Per capita income declined over the 1980–2000 period in several countries, including Algeria, Jordan, and virtually all of the Gulf countries.

Natural resources have not ensured economic performance (World Bank 2004f). Indeed, over the last two decades, countries without large oil resources have generally performed better than those rich in oil (tables D.3 and D.4).

Labor-abundant countries have performed better than those where labor is scarce. In particular, in the 1980s, when practically all oil-rich economies shrank as oil prices collapsed, the oil-poor, labor-abundant countries were able to sustain growth: Egypt, Morocco, and Tunisia grew annually at 2.9, 1.6, and 1.1 percent, respectively, during that decade (table D.3). Jordan was an exception: because of its dependence on remittances and financial support from oil-exporting countries, its growth in the 1980s dwindled, trailing that of resource-rich countries.

The 1990s saw improvements in performance virtually everywhere, except in Saudi Arabia (whose

FIGURE D.1

## Median and GDP-Weighted Economic Growth in the Middle East and North Africa, 1961–2000

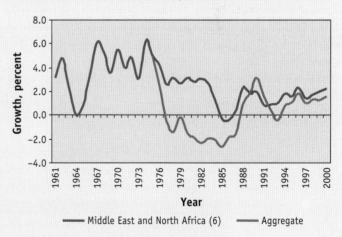

*Source*: World Bank, *World Development Indicators (WDI)*.

*Note*: Median growth rates for samples of countries that have complete GDP series. Aggregate is growth rate for the region (regional GDP over regional population). All data are smoothed with three-year moving averages. Extending the sample of the region's countries to six more does not significantly change the results in the later decades.

income per capita declined to the point that the country is now classified as a developing country) and Oman. The return to peace accounted for much of the improvement in the Islamic Republic of Iran, after the Iran-Iraq war, and in Lebanon and Yemen,

TABLE D.2

## Economic Growth in the Middle East and North Africa, 1960–2003
(median GDP per capita growth)

|  | 1960 | 1970 | 1980 | 1990 | 1990s* |
|---|---|---|---|---|---|
| 6 countries | 2.4 | 3.6 | 1.3 | 1.4 | 1.5 |
| 9 countries |  |  | −0.2 | 0.6 | 0.9 |
| 12 countries |  |  |  | 1.2 | 1.2 |
| All developing countries (69) | 2.0 | 1.8 | −0.5 | 1.3 | 1.0 |
| Developing countries (78) | — | 1.9 | −0.3 | 1.0 | 1.0 |
| Developing countries (93) | — | — | −0.2 | 1.0 | 0.9 |

*Source: WDI.*

*Note:* Different country groups correspond to the periods for which data exist for all countries. For example, there are only 6 countries in the Middle East and Northern Africa for which GDP statistics exist since 1960, 9 for which they exist since 1980, and 12 for which they exist since 1990. 1990s* means 1990s including 2001 and 2002.
6 countries: Egypt, Arab Rep. of; Morocco; Tunisia; Algeria; Syrian Arab Rep.; Oman.
9 countries: Egypt, Arab Rep. of; Morocco; Tunisia; Jordan; Algeria; Syrian Arab Rep.; Iran, Islamic Rep. of; Oman; Saudi Arabia.
12 countries: Egypt, Arab Rep. of; Morocco; Tunisia; Jordan; Lebanon; Djibouti; Algeria; Syrian Arab Rep.; Iran, Islamic Rep. of; Yemen, Rep. of; Oman; Saudi Arabia.
—. Not available.

TABLE D.3

## Three Major Middle Eastern and North African Country Groups

|  | Abundant labor | Scarce labor |
|---|---|---|
| Rich in resources | Algeria, Syrian Arab Rep., Iran, Islamic Rep. of, Yemen, | Oman, Saudi Arabia |
| Poor in resources | Egypt, Arab Rep. of, Morocco, Tunisia, Jordan, Lebanon, Djibouti | |

*Source:* World Bank 2004f.

after civil conflicts. In Jordan, improvement took place as the result of ambitious reforms that opened and liberalized the economy in the 1980s, even though political uncertainties and restrictions on the country's access to external markets kept the country's growth below its potential (Khalaf Hunaidi, in World Bank 2005b).

## Fulfilled and Unfulfilled Functions of Growth

Recent World Bank reports have highlighted the importance of governance reforms, to enable the countries in the region to grow faster and more equitably (World Bank 2003a–d). Middle Eastern and North African countries have benefited from public institutions that are able to maintain law and order and exert the state's authority. The energy of the bureaucracy, however, has often focused more on controlling the allocation of resources than on supporting private sector initiatives and a competitive economy. Many countries in the region have been hesitant to embrace economic openness and competition, and some analysts believe that political liberalization is needed to address governance issues and create an investment climate that is more predictable and more conducive to growth.

Middle Eastern and North African countries have generally fulfilled two of the central functions of growth: accumulation and distribution. Their investment rates have been high compared with those of other developing-country groups (figure D.2). The Middle East and North Africa's "social contract," with the state dominating the economy, allowed it to mobilize significant resources for investment, particularly when oil prices skyrocketed in the 1970s. Throughout the 1970s and early 1980s, investment rates in the region were comparable with those in the eight high-performing East Asian economies. Investment rates were high not only in the oil-rich countries—such as Algeria with a two-decade average of 38 percent of gross domestic product

TABLE D.4

## Economic Growth in the Middle East and North Africa: Impact of Natural Resources

|  | 1990 | 1980 | 1970 | 1960 |
|---|---|---|---|---|
| Resource-poor with abundant labor |  |  |  |  |
| Egypt, Arab Rep. of | 2.3 | 2.9 | 4.4 | 2.9 |
| Morocco | 0.4 | 1.6 | 2.7 | 2.0 |
| Tunisia | 3.1 | 1.1 | 5.0 | 2.8 |
| Jordan | 0.6 | −1.8 | — | — |
| Lebanon | 5.3 | — | — | — |
| Djibouti | −4.0 | — | — | — |
| Resource-rich with abundant labor |  |  |  |  |
| Algeria | −0.3 | −0.2 | 2.8 | 1.2 |
| Syrian Arab Rep. | 2.1 | −1.1 | 6.4 | 2.0 |
| Iran, Islamic Rep. of | 2.5 | −0.7 | — | — |
| Yemen, Republic of | 1.7 | — | — | — |
| Resource-rich, labor importing |  |  |  |  |
| Oman | 0.6 | 4.7 | 1.2 | 16.2 |
| Saudi Arabia | 0.0 | −5.7 | 7.9 | — |

Source: WDI.

—. Not available.

(GDP)—but also in Jordan (31 percent), Tunisia (28 percent), and Egypt (26 percent). From an international perspective, these investment rates are extremely high. Even after the collapse of oil prices, and ensuing declines in investment rates in recent years, they have been comparable to those in the high-performing East Asian economies.

Middle Eastern and North African countries have also invested large amounts in human capital. They have dramatically reduced infant mortality, raised life expectancy, and expanded school enrollment. Their literacy rates have increased significantly, including for women in countries such as Algeria, the Islamic Republic of Iran, Jordan, and Tunisia, and are now above those in many developing countries at similar levels of income.

Most governments in the Middle East and North Africa, perhaps with the exception of Morocco, have been highly redistributive. Distribution took place through a variety of programs, including provision of health and education, subsidies for housing and for consumption items including bread and transport, scholarships, and even jobs in the public sector. In the 1990s, how-

FIGURE D.2

## Investment in the Middle East and North Africa, 1960–2002

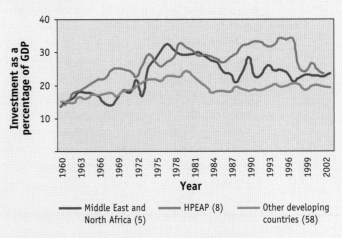

Source: WDI.

Note: HPEAP designates high-performing East Asian economies; Other developing countries (58) is the sample of 58 countries for which data are available for this period. Extending the sample of Middle East and North African countries to six more does not significantly change the results in the later decades.

ever, as part of fiscal adjustment programs, many of the subsidies were phased out.

Macroeconomic stabilizations in the late 1980s reduced inflation and debt and reduced the need for external inflows. Fiscal positions were consolidated and economies recovered from recessions. But for a number of reasons growth in the region has failed to regain its pre-1979 levels.

Combined with the high investment rates in physical and human capital, the disappointing growth performance suggests that productivity growth was negative. Negative productivity growth may be the most important reason why countries in the Middle East and North Africa have performed less well than countries in, for example, East and South Asia.

There are three main reasons for the low productivity of investments in the Middle East and North Africa. First is the dominance of production by the state, which typically uses resources less efficiently than the private sector.

Second, the region's tariff barriers are among the highest in the world. For countries with limited domestic markets, import substitution policies quickly outlive their usefulness. In the early 1980s, the region's tariffs were quite low compared with those in other developing regions. But they have remained at these levels, while those in other regions have now been dramatically reduced. Average tariff rates in Algeria, the Islamic Republic of Iran, Jordan, Libya, Morocco, Saudi Arabia, the Syrian Arab Republic, and Tunisia have either increased somewhat or remained constant since the late 1980s (figure D.3) (Oliva 2000).[4]

Third, Middle Eastern and North African countries maintain domestic restrictions on private investments. Domestic restrictions on private investments are not always explicit and the lack of a vibrant and developing private sector is not always the result of state monopolies. Red tape, the inefficiency of the judiciary, corruption, and state capture of government regulation all work to deter private investment. And the absence of clear directions on the future evolution of policy creates uncertainty, which further limits private investment.

FIGURE D.3

**Tariffs in the Middle East and North Africa, 1980–2000**

(median of unweighted average tariffs)

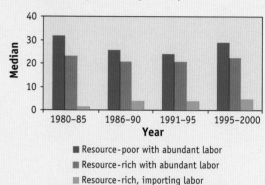

■ Resource-poor with abundant labor
■ Resource-rich with abundant labor
■ Resource-rich, importing labor

*Source:* World Bank, World Integrated Trade Solution database.

The low productivity of investments belies several waves of reform in the region's trade regimes. Notwithstanding the reforms, investments tended to be allocated inefficiently and as a result, the growth payoff to large investments was low.

Tunisia, Egypt, and Morocco introduced their first trade-related reforms in the 1970s (figure D.4). Tunisia was able to significantly accelerate its growth rate in the 1970s by creating export-processing zones insulated from the rest of the economy, and it continued with gradual but persistent steps to liberalize the economy (Oliva 2000). Egypt followed the route of internal liberalization first, drawing on the potential of its large internal market; the pace of reform was much slower and the approaches more sporadic. During the 1990s, trade volume rose in Tunisia but fell in Egypt. Morocco joined the General Agreement on Tariffs and Trade in 1987 and proceeded to liberalize its financial sector, privatize state-owned enterprises, and rationalize its tax system. Openness steadily increased in both Morocco and Tunisia, as did the share of manufactured goods in these countries' exports, but only in Tunisia did increased openness translate into high growth (figure D.5).

In Lebanon and in labor-abundant and resource-rich economies—Republic of Yemen, Algeria, Syria, and the Islamic Republic of Iran—

FIGURE D.4

**Trade Outcomes in Egypt, Morocco, and Tunisia, 1960–2000**

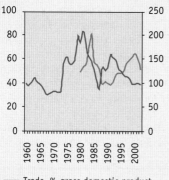

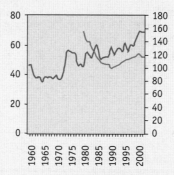

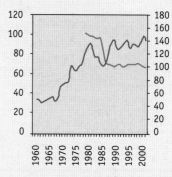

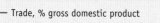

— Trade, % gross domestic product
— Real effective exchange rate, 1990 = 100

— Trade, % gross domestic product
— Real effective exchange rate, 1990 = 100

— Trade, % gross domestic product
— Real effective exchange rate, 1990 = 100

*Source: WDI.*

FIGURE D.5

**Diversification in Egypt, Morocco, and Tunisia, 1960–2002**
(manufactured exports as a percentage of exports of goods and nonfactor services)

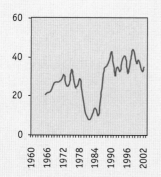

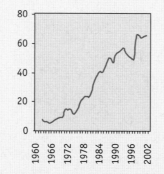

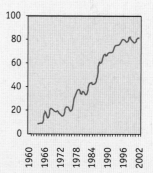

*Source: WDI.*

the approach to trade reform has been more gradual and haphazard. The Islamic Republic of Iran, after the Iran-Iraq war, implemented some internal liberalization that, as in Egypt, resulted in high output growth but not much international integration. In the Islamic Republic of Iran, it is difficult to disentangle the effects of liberalization from those of postwar "reconstruction," dismantling of wartime price controls, gradual and sporadic reforms, and higher oil revenues. But despite decades of state support to manufacturing, the

Islamic Republic of Iran's exports remain completely undiversified and the manufacturing sector itself shows little sign of viability (Tabibian 2003). The sustainability of the country's liberalization measures is unclear (Esfahani 2002).

*Conclusion*

The experience of developing countries in the Middle East and North Africa illustrates the importance of maintaining a balance among the different functions of growth, and that if a country succeeds in fulfilling one function, it may not achieve its full potential unless it can fulfill the other functions as well. The achievement of sustained high growth in the region will require more clarity on the future directions of policies and considerable domestic and external liberalization.

## Notes

1. Algeria, Syrian Arab Republic, Islamic Republic of Iran, Republic of Yemen, Arab Republic of Egypt, Morocco, Tunisia, Jordan, Lebanon, Oman, Djibouti, Saudi Arabia.

2. The region's performance and development challenges have been analyzed in a series of World Bank reports (World Bank 2003b, 2003f, 2003j, 2003l), on which this country note draws extensively.

3. The number of conflicts is at par with that in Sub-Saharan Africa, where the number of countries is three times that in the Middle East and North Africa (World Bank 2003b, 2003f, 2003j, 2003l).

4. Tariffs increased for various reasons. Those in Saudi Arabia rose by between 8 and 12 percent a year in response to balance of payments pressures, and those in Morocco rose as the result of quota tariffication.

*Chapter 6*

# Privatization and Deregulation: A Push Too Far?

Governments in the 1990s traded the commanding heights of their economies for more nearly free marketplaces. Despite many successes, state-owned firms had frequently become inefficient, overstaffed, and a drain on public budgets. Earlier attempts short of privatization had failed to improve their operations. Governments recognized that they might have taken on a role that they could not adequately fill and that a greater reliance on markets would be beneficial.

Privatization and deregulation were often parts of a broader set of reforms to improve economic efficiency, and their speed and extent reflected individual countries' convictions and circumstances. More rapid and widespread in Latin America than in Africa or South Asia, the privatization process also varied by sectors. Its proximate causes differed. Some countries sought greater operating efficiency; others, fiscal revenues, and many acted under pressure from international lenders. Utilities were sold because capacity was fast becoming a bottleneck and governments lacked the needed funds to invest. In Eastern Europe and the former Soviet Union, privatization was central to the transition to market economies, and was part of a much wider process of societal change.

Many observers now ask if privatization and deregulation were pushed too far. Today's dissatisfaction is not limited to countries where, as in the Russian Federation, a few well-connected people took over some large firms cheaply. Two-thirds of the respondents to a 2002 survey in 17 Latin American countries agreed that "privatization of state companies has *not* been beneficial" (up from 43 percent in 1998). Even in the United States, some commentators ask if current bankruptcies in airlines and telecom can be traced to earlier deregulation. Skeptics cite the impressive economic growth of India and China, where the government's role in allocating resources has been reduced and this change has been popular.

This chapter first describes the background to the deregulation movement (in section 1) and then outlines the efforts made during the 1990s to privatize state-owned firms, especially in the transition countries (section 2). Studies that evaluate the experience with privatization are reviewed in section 3; they all find that benefits have followed. Section 4 focuses on the privatization of infrastructure and other utilities. It finds that, contrary to some perceptions, privatizing utilities did not hurt the poor. Consumers with access (a few of them poor) paid more when prices were raised, but they benefited when service improved, as it did by any physical measure of performance. Expectations on the role that the private sector could play in infrastructure clearly proved unrealistic, however. Section 5 analyzes recent attempts in Latin America and Eastern Europe to increase the private sector's involvement in the provision of pensions and social security; it finds instances where privatization may have been pushed too far. Section 6 concludes the chapter.

# 1. Privatization in Market Economies

In the 1950s and 1960s, governments in developing countries sought the commanding heights of their economies to promote economic development, and many newly independent countries, seeking to assert their authority, nationalized firms that belonged to their erstwhile colonial masters. State ownership was also thought to promote development in areas where the private sector was too risk-averse or myopic to see the latent, untapped profit. State-owned firms coexisted with privately owned ones. Even in the United States, the government had been taking a major role in the economy since the 1930s' Great Depression, but generally did so through regulation, not outright ownership.[1]

The move to privatize stemmed more from pragmatism than ideology. Attempts to improve failing public enterprises, for example, through professional managers, independent boards of directors, or performance contracts, had not succeeded. By the end of the 1980s, reformers had reached broad agreement that nothing short of privatization would do.

## The (American) Regulatory Revolution

The impetus behind the privatizations of the 1990s began decades earlier in the United States, where a regulatory revolution starting in the late 1970s won over many economists, and visibly improved consumer prices and services in air travel, telecom, and other industries.

The first bold step was the deregulation of the airline industry, starting with the abolition of the Civil Aeronautics Board in 1978. Real fares halved between 1978 and 2000, and service improved in ways the public valued, such as flight schedules and frequency. Airlines became more efficient in a variety of unforeseen ways. They bought more fuel-efficient fleets and developed computer reservation systems and statistical models to price-discriminate among different types of passengers to fill all flights. They developed the hub-and-spoke system to balance the public demand for frequent flights against the capacity and fuel economy of their fleets. Their

productivity increased: passenger miles doubled with only half as many more employees between 1977 and 1987. Sometimes it took strikes and bankruptcy filings to shake off inefficient working practices that were embedded in company cultures and union agreements. Some aviation pioneers could not adapt—Pan Am, TWA, and Eastern went out of business—but others emerged such as Southwest, with its vigorous low-cost and customer-friendly culture.

This success emboldened the U.S. government to tackle AT&T. In 1984 the Department of Justice broke up American Telephone and Telegraph (or "Ma Bell") into one long-distance and seven regional firms (the Baby Bells) offering local services. Figure 6.1 shows how customers switched in increasing numbers to MCI and other competitors. By 1996, the price of a telephone call per minute was only 40 percent of its 1984 level.

When mobile telephony arrived, eliminating the rationale to regulate (there was no longer a fixed line creating a natural monopoly), the Federal Communications Commission had already learnt its regulatory lesson: it auctioned the necessary radio spectrum, enriching the U.S. Treasury by $9 billion, and ensured that there was adequate competition. Most of the 100 largest metropolitan areas in the United States now have at least five cellular telephone providers. Public awareness of the benefits from deregulation greatly increased.[2]

## Spread of the Privatization Trend

The United Kingdom followed the United States' lead. In the 1970s and 1980s, the government privatized firms in coal, steel, railroads, telecom,[3] electricity, and even water, despite fierce opposition from militant trade unions, and when the initially skeptical public was won over, the Labor government that succeeded Mrs. Thatcher's Conservatives did not reverse course. The rest of Europe was slower to privatize, but the rules introduced by the European Union to create a single market limited subsidies to loss-making firms, and this led to many firms being sold. Italy dismantled and began selling parts of

FIGURE 6.1

**Market Shares of Revenues for U.S. Long-Distance Carriers, 1984–98**
(percent)

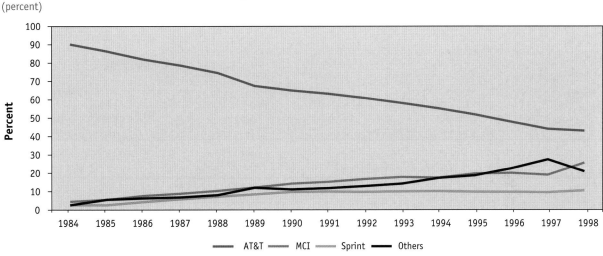

*Source:* Crandall and Hazlett 2000.

IRI, and France and Germany sold part of their telecom stakes in the late 1990s.[4]

Some Latin American countries began a deregulation and privatization process as early as the 1970s. Chile removed a panoply of controls that had accumulated over decades, and privatized utilities and even social security, in part because of its economic plight in the 1970s and the reformers' academic links to American universities. Chile's subsequent economic growth emboldened Mexico, Brazil, and Argentina to follow suit, developing techniques such as debt-to-equity swaps to extinguish their accrued external debts. Countries tended to privatize firms in competitive industries before tackling infrastructure and utilities. Chile privatized telephones in 1990, and Mexico had sold 361 of some 1,200 state-owned enterprises by 1992, thereby virtually eliminating subsidies that had amounted to almost 14 percent of its gross domestic product (GDP).[5]

Countries in Africa have privatized much less than Latin American or transition countries, and more reluctantly. Between 1991 and 2001, roughly 2,300 privatizations worth $9.1 billion affected fewer than 40 percent of Africa's state-owned enterprises. Just four countries—Ghana, Côte d'Ivoire, Nigeria, and Zambia—accounted for a third of these transactions. Nellis (2003a)

observes that in Africa often "the principal motivation for privatization has been to placate the international financial institutions." An ideological suspicion of capitalism, perceived to be hand in glove with colonialism, or the influence of vested interests, and sometimes both, delayed beneficial changes. But as governments abandoned trade protection and indirect subsidies (for example, directed lending from banks that the state controlled), the firms' losses and inefficiencies became more apparent.

Thus by the start of the 1990s, privatization and deregulation were well under way in Latin America along with a growing, if controversial, move to do the same elsewhere.[6] The trickle became a flood with the collapse of central planning in Eastern Europe and the former Soviet Union.

## 2. The Great Transition Sale: Haste to Avoid Waste[7]

The scale and speed of privatization in the transition countries of Eastern Europe and the former Soviet Union were vastly greater than in the market economies, and the process spawned new techniques.

When centrally planned economies collapsed and turned to markets, the need for privatization was self-evident, and most of the discussion centered on *how* this should be accomplished. Advocates of rapid privatization won the day, but critics now question the haste and point to mistakes that were made: assets were sold to cronies at low prices, and the many institutions that are vital to supporting the market have been slow to develop.[8] Minority shareholders have few protections, and privatization sometimes resulted in the new owners stripping assets and spiriting them abroad rather than investing to improve their working.

Before judging this experience, however, it is important to appreciate how chaotic and dysfunctional state ownership had been.

## Opening Pandora's Box

State ownership in the former Soviet Union countries was far murkier and complicated than the term suggests. There was a fundamental difference between selling state-owned firms in countries where markets function and supporting institutions exist and doing the same in countries where the state collectively owns all assets.[9] In the latter, laws protecting private property could be readily passed, but enforcing them required a daunting array of institutions that communism had destroyed. A state that is strong enough to protect private property is also strong enough to confiscate it, especially when its finances are desperate. The former East Germany could rely on West Germany's institutions after the unification, but other transition countries did not have this advantage.

While the law may state that the state owns something (or everything), somebody (it is never clear who) controls its use, and such usufructuary rights have value despite the absence of a market. In the former Yugoslavia, for example, a firm's workers "clearly" owned the firms, and a portion of their wage funds financed the investments, but did retirees who had financed the older machines also have claims? The land under the firm "clearly" belonged to the state, not the firm, but did the usufructuary rights transfer automatically and would they pass with the firm or with the building? State ownership of the land is a meaningless concept if the land is automatically transferred with either the enterprise or the structure, but if the land is not part of the package, how can the firm be sold?

Restitution claims added another dimension of complexity and confusion. Communist governments had confiscated properties and their former owners and heirs wanted them back. Some claimants had left the country but were willing to return; many others had remained, some of them still working on the confiscated farms and firms. The situation was even more complicated in countries such as Hungary, Poland, and Ukraine where earlier rounds of confiscation under Nazi occupation made it harder to determine whose claims to honor and, where national boundaries had also shifted during and after World War II, whose laws applied. Sometimes the records were unclear or lost. Firms were the more pressing issue because they were struggling for survival: GDP in transition countries was falling rapidly and people were undergoing great hardship. Since the Soviet Union had often located firms strategically, ignoring transport costs, its division into 15 republics wreaked havoc on firms that were freed to buy or sell as they pleased. Many found that their suppliers and/or buyers had become foreigners overnight. Borders were erected where none existed, and tolls were extracted as each republic sought revenues from customs duty to pay for basic services such as the police.

Firms scrambled to cope. Many managers were part of the *nomenklatura*, and while some sought political protection and favors on the firm's behalf, others did the reverse. Some managers resisted the changes, others adapted, and some exploited the situation to their personal advantage. Survival often required laws to be broken, and smugglers and criminals prospered, corroding values, politics, and societies. The breakdown of credit and central plans led to the increasing use of barter, shortfalls in cash led to workers being paid in shoes or commodities, and machinery was scavenged to produce products that could actually be sold.

This then was the background against which the discussions on privatization took place.[10] The situation did not allow for a fully informed debate, and even participants who agreed about what to do often disagreed over the reasons. Some argued that the creation of a market to replace central planning did not necessarily require firms to be privatized, or at least not immediately. Janos Kornai (1990), the eminent Hungarian economist, warned that the state should guard the wealth it was entrusted with until a more responsible owner came along, but such a course was impossible in countries where the government had lost effective control. Other protagonists favored rapid privatization: some to prevent the asset stripping that was becoming blatant, and others because it was "necessary to create a market economy" in the sense that privatization was expected to create a demand for more market-supporting institutions.[11] Some who favored restructuring the firms before selling them to raise more revenue were opposed by those who lacked confidence in the managers.

The experience of the *Treuhand*, created to sell the state-owned assets of East German firms after the fall of the Berlin Wall in 1989, provided early lessons. The *Treuhand* had to cope with the economic effects of the political decision to unify the two Germanys: an overvalued currency that reduced competitiveness and inflexible labor laws and practices that exacerbated the resulting unemployment. Asset values eroded quickly through neglect. Simple and quick sales were better, and imposing additional and largely unenforceable requirements (employment maintenance clauses and/or investment requirements) greatly reduced potential buyers' interest. It was inefficient and pointless for the government to restructure a firm in hopes of a better price, as restructuring could often be done better by buyers.

China's experience was often cited to argue that transformation and growth could be achieved without privatization, but the difference may lie more in labels than in substance (box 6.1), for China's experience in practice underscores the importance of incentives and the growth of private enterprise. The fundamental difference between China and most countries in Eastern Europe and the former Soviet Union was the continuing power of China's Communist Party despite the internal political turmoil. Changes in the relations between the central and local governments and in their control over enterprises often amounted to privatization in all but name, and the process was just as turbulent and nontransparent as privatization in the transition countries.

## The Process

The "when" to privatize was quickly settled: the sooner the better, although the "how" really set the pace.

The decision on what to privatize was also perfunctory: as much as possible. No distinction was drawn between regulated industries and competitive ones, although a few countries enacted but could not properly enforce antimonopoly laws.[12] Indeed, economists' forays into political science were unchallenged when they claimed that windows of opportunity might soon slam shut.[13] Telecom, particularly licenses for cellular telephony, was an especially lucrative business to privatize, and thus many telecom licenses were sold with exclusivity provisions to increase revenue despite the lower welfare implied.

Transition countries did not privatize their banks as they did firms, not because of a grand plan but more because buyers would not be forthcoming until governments dealt with the mountains of nonperforming loans and the banks' negative net worth. Inflation reduced the stock of deposits, and the public was wary of entrusting banks with savings. As a result, banks had little to lend—a condition that may have helped harden the budget constraint on firms, quite independently of firms' privatization per se.

Diverse decisions were made on how to privatize. Conventional techniques were clearly inadequate to the task at hand. The United Kingdom divested 20 firms in 10 years and Mexico 150 in six. The transition countries required an approach that could do much more, and faster. Poland had 8,400 state-owned enterprises accounting for 70

**BOX 6.1**
## China: Stealth Privatization

Before 1978, China's plans covered almost every decision of a state-owned firm—output, pricing, investment, working capital, labor use and wagesæbut unlike the Soviet system, China allowed a great deal of local autonomy in practice. Although the state-owned enterprises (SOEs) were owned by the central government, many were effectively controlled by provincial or municipal governments, because the center set highly aggregated production targets and credit flows.

Reforms began in agriculture with the "household responsibility system." The initial move was to allocate land among the 20 constituent households of a commune and allow each to sell more than the contracted grain-procurement quota at uncontrolled prices, and to keep the proceeds. Deng's now famous remark that the color of the cat did not matter so long as it caught mice assuaged fears that this small move away from collectivist orthodoxy would be crushed. Output and incomes rose, and by 1982, this system had been adopted by 80 percent of China's rural households and had spread to manufacturing.

Similarly in manufacturing, the "management responsibility system" evolved to give state enterprises more autonomy over their operations. Firms negotiated their own arrangements for limited profit retention, dual-track pricing, and some investment autonomy, which gave them incentives. Within firms, the relations and authority of technical managers and party officials shifted to reflect personalities and changes in the powers of central and provincial governments. Municipality-owned township and village enterprises (TVEs) expanded their production of highly profitable light industrial products and SOEs were permitted to have joint ventures with private foreign investors.

These joint ventures amounted to a form of stealth privatization. SOEs contributed productive assets or space in exchange for equity in a joint venture; foreign investors provided funds, newer machinery, and management expertise. SOEs often hold social assets (such as cafeterias, housing) and show losses that mask the joint ventures' profitability.

While many observers have credited TVEs as the driver of China's growth, comparative studies of provinces show that (1) TVEs flourished more when genuine private firms were prevented from emerging, and (2) provinces with genuine private firms grew faster (Huang 2003). This "private sector" (both private firms and firms in the government's statistical category that includes TVEs) emerged before legal restrictions on its existence were eased. Provincial governments often tolerated, and sometimes encouraged, its operations, notwithstanding laws to the contrary. The TVEs could not obtain financing from banks, but nevertheless managed to thrive. Although the state-owned banks only lend to SOEs, the SOEs in turn fund private suppliers and joint ventures.

China's experience also illustrates De Soto's (2000) important distinction between de facto and de jure ownership. While it would be ideal if both were congruent, China illustrates the importance of de facto protection. In contrast, most East European transition countries emphasized de jure protection. Perhaps the absence of laws in China did not deter entrepreneurship because the presence of laws had not protected people during the Great Leap Forward, the Cultural Revolution, or other tumultuous episodes.

to 80 percent of GDP at the outset; but many spun off subsidiaries, and it was hard to keep track of the changing numbers and sizes.

Since many firms were too large for any small group of investors to buy, and—more important—workers and managers could disrupt and deter unwelcome buyers, employee ownership arose almost out of necessity in all transition countries. Poland's 1990 Privatization Law, for example, required managers and the workers' council to agree before a firm could be sold. Disputes then arose over whether diffused ownership in general, and employee ownership in particular, was a good idea. While most commentators conceded that workers should be given *some* shares, especially if doing so would stave off unrest and opposition, only a few wanted all firms given entirely to their employees—especially since this would shortchange workers in those firms facing a bleak future who would, besides losing their jobs, have only worthless scrip.

Having mutual funds as intermediaries seemed sensible, and it was heroically thought that the funds would jumpstart a stock exchange that would permit holdings to be subsequently reshuffled, should owners so desire (Bell 1995). This proposal satisfied the proponents of broadly based share distribution as well as those who sought incentives for committed owners. It was a source of pride that the Warsaw Stock Exchange, first established in 1871, was reopened in the former Communist Party headquarters in 1991 to trade the equity of five privatized firms. But although the U.S. Agency for International Development (USAID) and other donors lavished technical assistance, most of the exchanges that were established in the transition countries have since atrophied.[14]

All these discussions took place separately but not simultaneously or identically in each country, with everyone looking over others' shoulders to see what was being done elsewhere. Many countries adopted similar techniques with some variations.

## Mass Privatization through Vouchers

Mass privatization through vouchers is simple in concept even though its administration is com-plex. The government prints and distributes vouchers (free or, to prevent their being scorned, for a token sum), perhaps unequally to favor some groups (such as military veterans, widows). The vouchers are then used in lieu of cash or as supplements, to bid for firms being auctioned to the highest bidders (with many variants—for example, allowing sealed bids for controlling interests). The government thereby exchanges its equity in state firms for vouchers that are then extinguished.

Many commentators extolled the virtues of mass privatization,[15] noting that auctions allowed a firm to be sold to the buyers most likely to add value, and that vouchers allowed governments to separate distributive from efficiency considerations. Vouchers could be allotted to reflect the government's distributive desires, and secondary market trading (of vouchers or of shares on the stock exchange) would result in efficient clustering of owners and holdings of firms. It was hoped that voucher schemes would act as the seedling of the stock exchange.[16]

Poland was the first to consider vouchers, in 1989, but it did not introduce them until 1995, so in practice the use of vouchers is indelibly associated with the Czech Republic. Many other countries, including Albania, Estonia, Georgia, Mongolia, and Russia, introduced variants of the Czech voucher scheme that each differed in important details. The Czech Republic allowed, and tacitly encouraged, the creation of mutual funds so that the public need not have to select from among the thousands of firms for sale. It was thought that these 20 or so funds would oversee the firms, because their expertise and sizable stakes would help ensure that firms were well run. In contrast, Poland's government organized the funds itself, but critics contend that this procedure was hardly an improvement over the ministries that had overseen firms in the previous era.

The outcomes attributable to voucher schemes are not impressive. The redistribution of wealth that is possible through vouchers is minor and may not have been worth the effort. Benefits were not as widely distributed as might appear: most recipients sold their vouchers for a fraction of their face value,[17] often to the firms' incumbent managers.

Privatization created value, but it generally accrued to the controlling owner, and other owners received little.

## 3. The Results: Gains, but Controversies As Well

In general, large benefits followed privatization, even though they differed across countries and stakeholders. Workers and consumers could benefit through higher wages and lower product costs even where firms were sold too cheaply, but there is also evidence that the benefits have been greater when privatization has been transparent and conducted fairly.

Because many things changed simultaneously, however, the benefits that followed privatization are not proof that privatization was their cause. More studies will not resolve the debate because empirical work cannot disentangle the effects of each of the many changes that accompanied privatization, and theory is not decisively against government ownership.

Nor is it clear *how* the benefits arose: for example, did owners oversee managers better or did lenders stop financing losers? Was it because managers had the freedom (or incentive) to do their job, or because private owners demanded (and so obtained) better managers, or because overstaffing was reduced, or because soft budget constraints were hardened? The reasons could differ by firm, but if so, they cannot be gleaned from aggregate data. Even if privately owned firms fare better than state-owned firms, is this performance due to a selection bias, whereby only those firms with a better potential were sold?

Evaluating benefits is also a complex task because the substantial transfers among different stakeholders vary over time, often for reasons, such as business cycles, that are unrelated to the sale. Owners' gains can be measured by profits, dividends, and/or equity prices (which may not move together); workers' gains can be measured through wages, but one must also correct for changing employment and skill mix, which is hard to do. Workers losing their jobs often find alternative employment, but tracking these

changes requires data that are difficult to compile. Hence reliable studies are difficult and expensive, and lag privatization by several years.

The discussion below draws on comprehensive literature surveys by Megginson and Netter (2001); Djankov and Murell (2002); and Nellis (2002, 2003a, 2003b). One strand looks at how firms in market economies fared after privatization and who gained and who lost. Another strand looks less carefully (because data are less complete and reliable) at outcomes in transition economies.

### Evidence from Market Economies

In a thorough study of the privatization of 12 major firms in four different countries, Galal et al. (1994) find substantial net gains (averaging 30 percent of predivestiture sales) in all but one (table 6.1). Workers always gained, as did owners and governments, and consumers benefited in half the cases.

Megginson, Nash, and van Randenborgh (1998) examine a different but larger sample and find substantially the same results. The postprivatization performance of 61 firms in 18 countries (6 developing and 12 industrial) showed substantial improvements in different measures of efficiency: profit margins were higher and so were inflation-adjusted sales per employee, as well as the ratio of capital expenditures to sales. Employment increased after privatization by an average of 6 percent.

Boubakri and Cosset (1998) find similar results from the same type of study, covering more firms. Their sample of 79 newly privatized firms between 1980 and 1992 included many from low-income countries. While profitability and efficiency rose significantly, they rose more in upper middle-income countries than in low-income countries.

Nellis (2003b) surveys studies of Latin American privatization, one of which, dealing with Mexico, can be singled out to illustrate the typical findings. LaPorta and López de Silanes (1999) analyze the pre- and postprivatization performance of 218 Mexican firms in 26 different industries that were privatized between 1983 and 1991.

TABLE 6.1
## Winners and Losers from Divestiture in 12 Case Studies
(percent)

| Country and enterprise | Domestic | | | | | | Foreign | | | World net welfare change |
|---|---|---|---|---|---|---|---|---|---|---|
| | Govt. | Buyers | Consumers | Workers[a] | Others | Net welfare change | Buyers | Consumers | Others | |
| **U.K.** | | | | | | | | | | |
| British Telecom | 2.7 | 3.1 | 4.9 | 0.2 | −0.1 | 10.8 | 1.2 | 0.0 | 0.0 | 12.0 |
| British Airways | 0.9 | 1.4 | −0.9 | 0.3 | 0.0 | 1.7 | 0.4 | −0.5 | 0.0 | 1.6 |
| National Freight | −0.2 | 0.8 | 0.0 | 3.7 | 0.0 | 4.3 | 0.0 | 0.0 | 0.0 | 4.3 |
| **Chile** | | | | | | | | | | |
| CHILGENER | −1.4 | 2.0 | 0.0 | 0.1 | 0.0 | 0.7 | 1.4 | 0.0 | 0.0 | 2.1 |
| ENERSIS | −1.6 | 7.6 | 2.2 | 3.9 | −7.4 | 4.6 | 0.6 | 0.0 | 0.0 | 5.2 |
| CTC | 8.0 | 1.0 | 131.0 | 1.0 | 4.0 | 145.0 | 10.0 | 0.0 | 0.0 | 155.0 |
| **Malaysia** | | | | | | | | | | |
| Malaysian Airline Systems | 5.2 | 2.0 | −2.9 | 0.4 | 0.0 | 4.6 | 0.8 | 0.8 | 15.8 | 22.1 |
| Kelang Container Terminal | 37.6 | 11.5 | 6.2 | 7.0 | −11.9 | 50.4 | 2.9 | 3.1 | −3.0 | 53.4 |
| Sports Toto Malaysia | 13.6 | 10.7 | 0.0 | 0.0 | −13.0 | 10.9 | 0.0 | 0.0 | 0.0 | 10.9 |
| **México** | | | | | | | | | | |
| Teléfonos de México | 13.3 | 11.4 | −62.0 | 15.6 | 28.3 | 6.6 | 25.1 | 0.0 | 17.9 | 49.5 |
| Aeroméxico | 62.3 | 3.9 | −14.6 | 2.4 | −2.3 | 52.9 | 1.8 | −6.2 | 0.0 | 48.5 |
| Mexicana de Aviación | 3.5 | −1.4 | −7.7 | 0.0 | 3.2 | −2.4 | −1.3 | −3.3 | 0.0 | −7.0 |

*Source*: Galal et al. 1994.

*Note*: All figures are the annual component of the perpetuity equivalent to the welfare change, expressed as a percentage of annual sales in the last predivestiture year.

a. Includes workers both in their role as wage earners and as buyers of shares.

The authors find a 24 percent increase in average profitability, as measured by the ratio of operating income to sales, arising from increases in productivity (57 percent), labor retrenchment (33 percent), and price increases (10 percent) (table 6.2). Profitability rose more in competitive sectors than in noncompetitive sectors; so these gains did not arise from an increase in monopoly power. Mexico had some 1,155 state-owned firms in 1982, accounting for about 14 percent of GDP; and the government sold 150, liquidated 260, and merged an additional 400 firms by 1988—all before the privatization wave in the 1990s with infrastructure firms including telecom.

In Argentina, some 150,000 workers were dismissed between 1987 and 1997 following privatization; 90,000 workers were dismissed when Brazil privatized the railroads. Not all countries have ways to ease workers' transition from one job to another; certainly finding alternative employment that adds value is easier in a growing economy. To find the full effects, one must look at employment beyond the privatized firms. No study has tracked displaced workers in such a manner

Nellis (2003a) surveys the studies of African privatization and finds impressive benefits. A 2001 study commissioned by the Zambian Privatization Agency found that 235 of the 254 enterprises privatized since 1991 continued to operate. The investments in nonmining firms were worth more than $400 million; but the largest deals had been in mines where improvements did not materialize, a result that warrants a brief explanation. Zambia nationalized its copper mines shortly after independence in 1964. The mines benefited from the copper boom in the 1970s and suffered with its crash (fiber optics had

TABLE 6.2
## Performance Changes in Privatized Firms in Mexico

| | N | Changes in industry-adjusted performance | | | | Competitive vs. noncompetitive industries (according to prospectus) | | | | Competitive vs. noncompetitive industries (according to market share) | | | |
|---|---|---|---|---|---|---|---|---|---|---|---|---|---|
| | | Mean change | s.s. (%) | Median change | s.s. (%) | N c | nc | Mean change (difference) | s.s. (%) | N c | nc | Mean change (difference) | s.s. (%) |
| *Profitability* | | | | | | | | | | | | | |
| Operating income/sales | 168 | 0.353 | 1 | 0.153 | 1 | 134 | 32 | 0.061 | | 104 | 62 | 0.108 | |
| Net income/sales | 168 | 0.412 | 1 | 0.211 | 1 | 134 | 32 | −0.146 | 10 | 103 | 62 | −0.026 | 10 |
| *Operating efficiency* | | | | | | | | | | | | | |
| Cost per unit | 168 | −0.183 | 1 | −0.152 | 1 | 134 | 32 | 0.106 | 1 | 104 | 62 | −0.049 | |
| Log(sales/employees) | 166 | 0.935 | 1 | 0.896 | 1 | 134 | 32 | 0.151 | | 106 | 62 | 0.33 | 5 |
| *Labor* | | | | | | | | | | | | | |
| Log(# of employees) | 169 | −19.05 | 10 | −24.47 | 1 | 136 | 33 | −0.273 | 5 | 107 | 62 | −0.069 | |
| *Assets and investment* | | | | | | | | | | | | | |
| Investment/sales | 168 | −0.048 | 1 | 0.067 | 1 | 134 | 32 | −0.005 | | 104 | 62 | −0.005 | |
| *Output* | | | | | | | | | | | | | |
| Log(sales) | 170 | 0.489 | 1 | 0.424 | 1 | 136 | 33 | −0.215 | | 105 | 61 | 0.206 | |
| Net taxes | | | | | | | | | | | | | |
| Taxes | 168 | 26,441 | 5 | 2,161 | 1 | 135 | 33 | −7,024 | 1 | 106 | 61 | 1,013.6 | |

*Source:* LaPorta and López de Silanes 1999.

*Note:* N = number in sample; s.s. (%) = statistical significance to a % level; c = competitive, nc = noncompetitive. The columns that compare competitive versus noncompetitive show the difference in mean change (Δcompetitive − Δnoncompetitive). There are two definitions of competitive: (1) according to privatization prospectus, and (2) according to market share (>10 percent is considered noncompetitive).

reduced the demand for copper worldwide).[18] The state-owned Zambia Consolidated Copper Mines (ZCCM) was too poorly managed to adjust and was a burden on the rest of the economy. Early privatization may have helped save the mines, but the government was loath to give up a source of corruption and patronage. As a result, privatization discussions that began in 1991 (under donor prodding with a new government) dragged on through the decade, despite losses averaging US$15 million a month. A $1 billion offer during 1996–97 from a consortium of experienced mining firms was rejected, and ZCCM was finally sold in 1999 after the assets had further deteriorated.[19] The consortium is reported to have invested more than $350 million in the Konkola Copper Mine,[20] but no one seems to know whether the Treasury received any cash proceeds or what happened to them. Even this sale was subsequently canceled when the Anglo-American consortium abandoned the purchase. Privatization can improve how a firm

operates but not the world prices for commodities it produces. Even so, earlier privatization could have prevented the mines from deteriorating to a point where massive outlays were needed before they could operate. The outlays were uneconomical with low copper prices, resulting in the mines being closed.

Nellis also cites studies by Boubakri and Cosset (2002) examining 16 privatizations (10 in Morocco and 6 in Tunisia) where investments and profitability were found to have risen. Jones, Jammal, and Gokgur (1998) examine 81 privatizations in Côte d'Ivoire and find better performance with net benefits for about 25 percent of predivestiture sales. Appiah-Kubi (2001) finds benefits from the 212 privatizations in Ghana. Andreasson (1998) finds improved performance of divested firms in Mozambique and Tanzania. Temu and Due (1998) find that of the 158 firms Tanzania divested through 1999, two-thirds were sold to nationals (South African firms that buy larger-value firms and breweries are resented) and that government revenues rose and subsidies to state-owned enterprises fell.

## Evidence from Transition Countries

Across 27 transition economies, more than 150,000 large enterprises and several times as many small firms have not been merely sold but transformed. Despite the assertions that outcomes would have been better had privatization been done differently, the fact that it *was* done is a remarkable achievement, and numerous studies show that it was beneficial.

These studies vary in quality, however. The early ones were more scorecards than evaluations, and as better studies became available they showed some of the early bloomers of privatization fading. For example, the Czech Republic, long the darling of the advocates of speed, stumbled in 1997, and its GDP recovery was delayed until 2000.[21] Poorly managed privatization was held partly responsible, because firm managers and funds were allegedly too busy looting from noncontrolling shareholders to focus on adding value. The Russian loans-for-shares scandal and other shenanigans such as coercive purchases of workers' shares by managers have also muted the initial enthusiasm for privatization.

Pohl, Anderson, and Djankov (1997) examine firm-level data, and find that countries that privatized more and faster restructured better.

Weiss and Nitkin (1997) find that *who* bought the firms seemed to matter. Djankov and Murell (2002) find the greatest gains arose when firms were sold to outsiders rather than workers. This pattern could be the result of adverse selection; workers were often sold firms that outsiders thought unviable, and the findings would follow if the outsiders were correct on average. Frydman et al. (1999) correct for such adverse selection by examining a random sample of mid-sized manufacturing firms in the Czech Republic, Hungary, and Poland. They too find that selling to outsiders resulted in greater gains. So who buys the firms does seem to matter, although we do not quite understand why.

Moving from firms to the aggregate, the conclusions are also not clear-cut. Endowments (initial conditions), policies, and institutions all matter for economic growth. Output recovered sooner in some countries than in others; and critics make much of the fact that the swiftest sellers did not grow the fastest, but this argument ignores the role that endowments and other factors play.

One important lesson from the experience is that market-supporting institutions—well-functioning courts, credit agencies, accounting firms—did not spring up in response to the demand that privatization created. Advocates of speed countered critics' arguments at the time by pointing out that such institutions would not emerge without a demand for them. Even if they were right, however, privatization should not necessarily have been slower, given the propensity for asset-stripping mentioned earlier. In the Czech Republic, it was not the speed of privatization but the government's disregard of provisions to protect minority equity holders' interests that drove investors away from the Prague Stock Exchange and turned voucher funds into untrustworthy mutual funds.

Even the features now recognized as mistakes were not viewed at the time as critical flaws.[22] Incentives operate through people; and if people perceive unfairness or fear social turmoil, they may not invest for the future and the gains may not follow. While the incentives for privatization normally are to create and increase value, the fears that ownership of the large Russian firms (that were unfairly purchased) would be reversed have encouraged asset-stripping and capital flight. So although privatization has been beneficial when viewed as a whole, the manner of the sale matters.

## 4. Utilities: Why the Disappointments?

Utilities is the collective label for a range of disparate industries (telecom, electricity, roads, railroads). Their privatization is discussed separately in this section because of the more complex regulatory issues involved. The outcomes have often been disappointing, and this section examines why.

Utilities in developing countries had often failed to invest enough to keep pace with improving technology or growing populations. Most of them were short of funds because, in turn, governments kept prices low, thinking that the poor could not pay for the services the utilities provided. Indeed, few of the poor did pay, because few of the poor had access to the services (figure 6.2). Underpriced services such as electricity and piped water were overused by the nonpoor. Nor did governments compensate utilities for the financial shortfalls that low prices and unpaid bills implied, because the owner (the state) either did not know or did not care and sought to retain power and/or patronage. Utilities operated erratically because revenues rarely covered their costs: funds would dribble in from belated price increases, erratic budget transfers, and/or forced loans from government-controlled banks when the enterprises were in danger of shutting down. This instability played havoc with maintenance and planning and reinforced poor

management. The facilities deteriorated even as population grew and, with it, demand.

## The Invisible Burden on the Poor

The true costs of neglecting infrastructure are enormous and the financial shortfall in the utilities is only the tip of the iceberg. But even the tip is huge: public monopolies in power, water, roadways, and railways have annual losses of almost $180 billion ($55 billion in technical losses and $123 billion due to pricing), equivalent to almost the total infrastructure investment in all developing countries.

Taxpayers pay the costs of underpriced power and water, but people without access bear a larger invisible burden because alternatives are much costlier. A familiar sight in many developing-country cities is the array of water tanks on the rooftops of homes—the costly individual response to erratic city water supply. Investment in such tanks is a social waste: the storage is inefficient and the overall water supply is not augmented. The poor suffer more: lacking the funds (or land titles) to invest in storage, they pay dearly for water delivered by truck. Similarly, lighting with a paraffin or kerosene lamp costs 10 to 20 times as much as running an electric lamp; powering radios is far more expensive with batteries than with electricity; and so on (Brook and Irwin 2003). Almost all types of infrastructure are desperately needed, and while the returns from such investments are high, the magnitude of the investments needed is daunting.

Governments began to privatize utilities because they could not cope with the attendant problems and were emboldened by the euphoria over privatization in general and by the specific successes of some countries. Chile broke up and privatized its electric utilities in 1978; the United Kingdom did so in 1989, Argentina and Norway in 1991, and New Zealand in the mid-1990s.

In developing countries the scale of utility and infrastructure privatization was immense: between 1990 and 2001 more than 2,500 private infrastructure projects worth $805 billion were privatized (Harris 2003). Latin America and the Caribbean accounted for almost half ($397 bil-

FIGURE 6.2

**Access to Basic Services, by Income Group—Ghana, Mexico, and Peru**

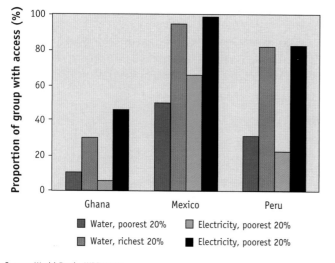

*Source:* World Bank, *WDR 1994.*

lion), followed by East Asia, Eastern Europe, South Asia, with the Middle East and Sub-Saharan Africa tying for the rear (table 6.3). By sector, the bulk was in telecom ($356 billion) and electricity ($268 billion).

These often-cited data sum up the value of infrastructure *transactions* (actually commitments), rather than physical *investment*. The transactions benefited developing countries' fiscal and/or balance of payments accounts, but additions to capacity were likely far lower than the buyers' outlays to buy existing utilities. Figure 6.3 shows the breakdown by divestiture and greenfield projects, but even these data may not accurately represent physical investments in additional capacity. Calderón, Easterly, and Servén (2002) report that aggregate infrastructure investments declined as a share of GDP in Latin America between 1980–84 and 1995–98: from 3.1 to 0.2 percent of GDP (itself often falling) in Argentina, 5 to 2 percent in Bolivia, 3.7 to 0.6 percent in Brazil, 3.1 to 1.7 percent in Chile, 2.5 to 0.4 percent in Mexico, and 2.0 to 0.6 percent in Peru. This aggregate decline is still consistent with increased investments in the privatized firms (separate data are harder to compile), but if expectations of

improvements were based on transaction commitments, the disappointment is not surprising.

### Differences across Sectors

The value of privatization transactions led to great expectations, but since meager investments did not ease the capacity bottlenecks, disappointments inevitably ensued. Experience varied greatly by sectors. Although few transactions have been reversed,[23] many are being renegotiated: some 74 percent of transport and 55 percent of water concessions in Latin America. The examination below illustrates the issues involved.

### Telecommunications

Telecommunications was a clear privatization success. While technology provided the impetus, the size of the gains was influenced by the competition that regulation encouraged. Privatization and new entries expanded the network, increasing operating efficiency and labor productivity. The productivity gains did not reduce employment, and network expansion absorbed overstaffing. Figure 6.4 shows the gains from competition, among both cellular providers and

TABLE 6.3

## Investment in Infrastructure Projects with Private Participation in Developing Countries, 1990–2002
(2002 US$ billions, by region or sector)

| Region or sector | 1990 | 1991 | 1992 | 1993 | 1994 | 1995 | 1996 | 1997 | 1998 | 1999 | 2000 | 2001 | 2002 | Total |
|---|---|---|---|---|---|---|---|---|---|---|---|---|---|---|
| East Asia and Pacific | 2.7 | 4.3 | 9.7 | 13.7 | 17.1 | 22.2 | 32.1 | 39.0 | 10.6 | 9.8 | 15.0 | 12.4 | 9.7 | 198.4 |
| Europe and Central Asia | 0.1 | 0.4 | 1.4 | 1.5 | 4.4 | 9.5 | 12.4 | 16.0 | 13.1 | 10.0 | 23.2 | 7.3 | 9.7 | 109.0 |
| Latin America and the Caribbean | 14.9 | 12.9 | 16.5 | 19.3 | 19.5 | 20.2 | 29.6 | 55.3 | 77.0 | 39.9 | 40.5 | 34.3 | 17.3 | 397.2 |
| Middle East and North Africa | 0.0 | —a | 0.0 | 3.6 | 0.4 | 0.1 | 0.4 | 5.7 | 3.4 | 3.2 | 4.1 | 3.9 | 1.6 | 26.4 |
| South Asia | 0.4 | 0.8 | 0.1 | 1.4 | 3.4 | 4.2 | 6.6 | 6.8 | 2.8 | 5.0 | 4.2 | 4.6 | 5.5 | 45.8 |
| Sub-Saharan Africa | 0.1 | 0.0 | 0.1 | 0.0 | 0.8 | 0.9 | 1.6 | 4.8 | 2.7 | 4.8 | 3.4 | 5.0 | 3.5 | 27.8 |
| Energy | 1.3 | 1.3 | 13.1 | 15.9 | 17.2 | 25.4 | 34.2 | 51.6 | 30.5 | 18.0 | 28.4 | 14.9 | 16.5 | 268.3 |
| Telecommunication | 6.3 | 13.7 | 8.0 | 9.9 | 18.8 | 20.2 | 28.5 | 44.3 | 56.3 | 38.7 | 47.3 | 40.2 | 23.7 | 355.8 |
| Transport | 10.5 | 3.4 | 4.7 | 5.8 | 9.0 | 9.7 | 18.1 | 22.1 | 19.3 | 9.0 | 9.9 | 10.0 | 5.2 | 136.6 |
| Water and sewerage | —a | 0.1 | 2.0 | 8.0 | 0.5 | 1.8 | 2.0 | 9.4 | 3.5 | 7.0 | 4.9 | 2.5 | 1.9 | 43.6 |
| Total | 18.0 | 18.5 | 27.7 | 39.6 | 45.6 | 57.1 | 82.8 | 127.5 | 109.6 | 72.7 | 90.5 | 67.6 | 47.3 | 804.5 |

*Source:* World Bank, PPI Project Database.

a. No private participation in infrastructure occurred.

FIGURE 6.3

**Infrastructure Projects with Private Participation, 1990–2001**
(2001 US$ billions)

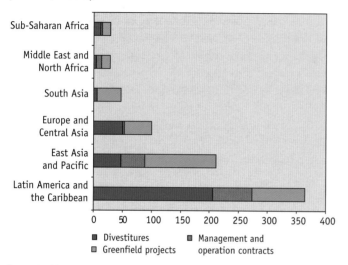

Source: World Bank PPI Project Database.

FIGURE 6.4

**Growth in Latin American Telecom Lines**
(percent per year)

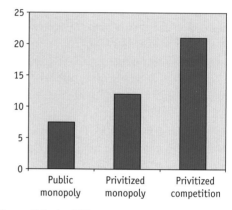

Source: Wellenius 1997.

those with fixed lines. Latin American countries that granted monopoly rights of 6 to 10 years to their privatized telecommunications operators expanded their networks to 1.5 times the size under state ownership. Countries that retained the right to issue competing licenses did even better.

These gains were within the reach of all countries, including those that had not traditionally benefited from much foreign investment.

Box 6.2 describes how the increase in access was financed in Bangladesh. Cellular telephone costs also declined; but the potential for future gains remains immense: although the number of GSM (Global System for Mobile Communication) phone sales doubled in 2003 to almost 21 million in India, only 7 percent of India's 1 billion people have access to any type of phone. China already has 200 million cellular phone users (more than the United States' 140 million). Despite the recent bursting of the dot.com and telecom bubble, the potential is still immense.

The gains in telecommunications were the result of (1) technological changes that almost eliminated natural monopolies; (2) low coverage in most developing countries, which allowed

substantial gains from expansion; and (3) inequitable cross-subsidies in pricing, which allowed higher overall prices, benefiting the poor through increased access and the well-off with new and better services. The private sector's better financial, technical, and managerial resources have a distinct advantage in keeping abreast of this increasingly complex industry.

## Electricity

Electricity restructuring and privatization are more complicated because unique characteristics determine how the market functions. Electricity is the ultimate real-time product with its production and consumption occurring at virtually the same instant. Peak-time supply is very inelastic near full capacity and demand shifts seasonally as well as during the day, depending on such factors as temperature.

Recent technological advances affecting location and hence transmission capacities have dramatically changed the cost structure of electricity generation (figure 6.5). Technological improvements in gas turbines allow smaller, less-polluting generators to be built more quickly near cities. Similar developments in wind generators and photo-voltaics may change the competitive potential of electricity in many countries, both developed and developing. These developments have allowed the market for generation to become

**BOX 6.2**

**Cellular Phone Operators in Rural Bangladesh**

Around the world, new service providers have taken advantage of drastically reduced economies of scale to enter global and local markets, increasing competition and reducing prices. Women in Bangladesh have taken the possibilities of cellular technology further than in most countries. Using microloans of little more than US$30, women in rural areas have set themselves up as small-scale operators in a business that can offer a net annual income of over US$600, or more than twice the 1997 per capita GDP. Grameen Bank, which provides microcredit to small-business investment, financed the purchase of payphones by entrepreneurial women in villages from Grameen Telecom, its subsidiary. Starting in March 1997, within three years of its first operation Grameen Telecom had provided phone access to nearly 2.8 million people in 1,100 villages. Access to phone services has brought many benefits to poor communities beyond the additional income to operators: it reduced communication costs (particularly transport) and raised farmers' income by providing information on market prices that increased their bargaining power with middlemen.

FIGURE 6.5

## Optimal Size of U.S. Generating Plants

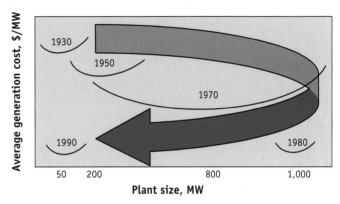

*Source*: Bayless 1994.

ure 6.6). Most reforms attracted considerable private investment in generation and distribution (though much less in transmission) thus reversing the underinvestment of recent decades. Electricity prices have fallen in many Latin American countries as wholesale markets have developed and new generators with lower costs have augmented supplies. As retail prices start to reflect underlying costs, cross-subsidies have been reduced and in some countries eliminated.

Not every country is equally well positioned to gain through new technology and attendant restructuring of ownership. Brazil, for instance, has a largely hydro-based power system, and box 6.3 illustrates why uncertain rainfall and multiuse dams preclude substantial gains from privatization, even of its nonhydro generators. In other situations, as in Norway, privatizing hydro-based power yielded substantial benefits.

Reaping the potential gains that technology now allows, however, requires countries to change the thrust and manner of regulation. Electricity prices have been kept so low in most developing countries for so long that raising them to reflect underlying costs will be politically difficult. In several developing countries, attempts to raise tariffs in the face of acute power shortages have led to street riots that have caused the increases to be reversed. Although private entrants will naturally demand a credible commitment that future prices will be adequate

competitive, and many countries have benefited from allowing such competition.

Of the many countries that reformed their electricity sectors in the 1990s, most achieved good outcomes. When done properly—with vertical and horizontal restructuring, privatization, and effective regulation—reform significantly improved operating performance: labor productivity rose, sometimes dramatically in generation and distribution; technical and nontechnical losses fell; and service quality rose (fig-

FIGURE 6.6

## Postprivatization Labor Productivity in Electricity Distribution in Chile, Argentina, and the United Kingdom

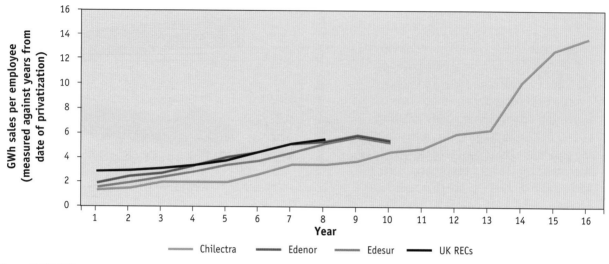

*Source:* Pollitt 2003.

before investing, few countries provide such an undertaking.

### Potential Problems in Power Markets

Two additional issues deserve greater attention: (1) many developing countries are too small to benefit from competition in the power sector, and (2) the single-buyer model (since the gains are from generation) entails great risks.

Privatization is not always appropriate and its suitability depends on the country's circumstances. Many developing countries are relatively small: 60 have a system peak load below 150 megawatts (MW), 30 have a load between 150 and 500 MW, and another 20 a load between 500 and 1,000 MW. Under the most favorable circumstances, the opportunities for introducing competition in such small systems are limited, as suggested by the market shares shown in table 6.4. Some of the smaller countries may benefit by linking their grids where possible to those of their neighbors (small, distant islands obviously cannot) and pursuing a regional as opposed to a national approach to regulation.

The Asian financial crisis exposed the risks involved when independent power producers (IPPs) sell to a state-owned utility through long-

term power-purchase agreements (PPAs). In Indonesia, Malaysia, the Philippines, and Thailand, rapid economic growth during the late 1980s and early 1990s increased the demand for electricity, but central governments were unable to finance the needed physical infrastructure investments. So the single state-owned utilities signed purchase agreements with independent power producers, typically contracted in dollars with government guarantees, since default proceedings against a state-owned utility were often not allowed.

At first the stratagem seemed successful: Southeast Asia attracted $65 billion in transactions for the private provision of infrastructure between 1990 and 1997—more than half the total for all developing countries and substantially more than the other major destination, Latin America (with $45 billion).

But the Asian crisis in 1997 caused GDP, electricity demand, and the currencies' value in foreign exchange markets to fall. In Indonesia, electricity prices doubled in local currency under the PPAs, but state utilities did not pass the increase on to final consumers. So the power purchasers could not honor the PPAs, and even the government guarantee could not be honored

**BOX 6.3**
**Brazil: No Rain or Privatization Gains**

Brazil's experience illustrates that the specifics of each country's situation should guide whether to include privatization in the reform strategy. Brazil faced an acute power shortage during 2002–03 despite reforms that began in the 1990s, including privatizing some of its generation. Like many countries, Brazil had underinvested in capacity for decades: annual investment had declined steadily from a 1982 peak of $12 billion to $3 billion by 1999 although demand continued to grow with the economy.

Brazil was heavily influenced by the British model of separating distribution and transmission from generation, which would then be privatized. Unlike the United Kingdom's, however, Brazil's generation is predominantly hydroelectric. The massive costs of dams are incurred upfront (and are sunk), and the running (marginal) costs are negligible. And in Brazil, even the long-run average costs of power are lower than even those of combined-cycle gas turbines, because the gas network and market are not well developed and the sunk costs of the dam are not fully included.

Multiuse dams further complicate the functioning of competitive, privately owned generation. Rainfall fluctuations and the need to maintain adequate water reserves for irrigation and water uses other than electricity require basinwide coordination between water management authorities and power dispatch. Furthermore, if hydro is used to satisfy peak, as opposed to base-load, demand—and it is difficult to forecast how much this demand will be (especially when rainfall also fluctuates year to year)—it is very difficult to price power correctly. Spot markets for electricity will not clear supply and demand and simultaneously provide investors with adequate returns.

These difficulties with hydro power inevitably also spill over into nonhydro generation. Even if combined-cycle gas turbines were economical for peak provision, or coal-fired generators for base load, the presence of a large hydro system with unpredictable rainfall would make them unremunerative without special payments for their role as emergency capacity or reserve. If such capacity were privately owned, rules that determine such transfers would be important and would be influenced by rainfall.

Hence the private ownership of generation in Brazil brought few gains, and endless disputes with private investors. The situation would differ if dams' sole use were for electricity (as in Norway), or if the cost of thermal plants determined electricity prices (as in Chile and Argentina). While dams may be privately owned, the efficiency gains in Brazil are greater during their construction than in operation.

because of the effects of the crisis on the balance of payments and the government budget. There were strong pressures to renege on, delay, or renegotiate PPAs, resulting in protracted and acrimonious disputes, especially when allegations of corruption surfaced (box 6.4).

Although power-purchase agreements create the same type of liabilities as foreign debts, these liabilities were not explicitly recognized even when governments guaranteed them. Furthermore, such contracts did not address the underlying problem of electricity tariffs not reflecting cost; if anything, the currency crisis made the gap worse. Promoting rapid investment in an unreformed electricity sector by offering independent power producers long-term PPAs with state-owned, single-buyer utilities involves substantial risks both to the investors and to the public interest, and investors often exact a substantial premium for the risks they incur. Hence such contracts are rarely cheap even if they are entered into competitively. They are an expensive way to expand capacity quickly.

TABLE 6.4

## Market Shares of the Three Largest Generation, Transmission, and Distribution Companies in Various Countries, 2000

(percent)

| Country | Generation | Transmission | Distribution |
|---------|-----------|--------------|--------------|
| Argentina | 30 | 80 | 50 |
| Bolivia | 70 | 100 | 70 |
| Brazil | 40 | 60 | 40 |
| Chile | 67 | 100 | 50 |
| Colombia | 50 | 100 | 60 |
| Czech Republic | 71 | 100 | 49 |
| El Salvador | 83 | 100 | 88 |
| Hungary | 74 | 100 | 65 |
| Indonesia | 100 | 100 | 100 |
| Malaysia | 62 | 100 | 97 |
| Pakistan | 95 | 100 | 100 |
| Panama | 82 | 100 | 100 |
| Peru | 100 | 100 | 100 |
| Poland | 45 | 100 | 21 |
| Thailand | 100 | 100 | 100 |

*Source:* Jamasb 2002.

## Transport

In many segments of the transport sector (rail, ports, trucking, airlines, interurban busing), the pressures of inter- and intramodal competition are sufficient in most countries to justify substantial liberalization and privatization. It is difficult for regulators or service providers to predict what are efficient and market-responsive vertical relationships and combinations of logistical roles among various rail entities, truckers, barge operators, port operators, air carriers, warehouses, forwarders, and so forth.

Experience confirms what theory predicts: markets freed from excessive regulatory controls find efficient and innovative ways to serve transport needs. It is important to distinguish transport *services*, which are generally competitive or contestable, from physical infrastructure *facilities*, which may have natural monopoly characteristics. The case for privatizing transport infrastructure is less compelling than that for services. Rail track, basic and access port infrastructure, and certain portions of airport facilities, where monop-

BOX 6.4

## Controversial Power Purchases in Indonesia

Before 1990, the budget (oil revenues) and development assistance funded power investments in Indonesia. The private sector played only a small role. The power company (*Perusahaan Listrick Negara* or PLN) was an integrated, state-owned firm with problems typical of such entities. In the mid- to late 1980s, a shortfall in oil revenues made the lure of private investments in generation (funded by export credits) irresistible. In 1990, Indonesia needed an estimated 12,000 megawatts of additional capacity by 2000, implying a need for investment of about $20 billion.

With such needs, PLN embarked on a vigorous expansion, entering what has been termed "a gold rush for the invited elite and their foreign partners."* Between 1990 when the first IPP project was solicited and 1997 when the East Asian crisis broke, PLN signed 26 power-purchase agreements and energy-sales contracts covering 10,800 megawatts for some $13 billion. The terms appeared very favorable to the investors, many of whom sought these concessions with a well-connected local partner that opened doors in exchange for an equity stake (that the foreign investor often financed): the tariffs were in the 5.7–8 cents/kilowatt-hour range, well above the prevailing average tariff, with "take or pay" clauses that shifted most risks to the purchasing utility.

* World Bank 2003c. This report focuses more on the absence of accountability and reports more on egregious skimming of contracts by the well-connected than on the underlying problems of the sector.

oly is unavoidable or substantial amounts of sunk capital are involved, must be regulated or even operated by the public sector.

*Reforming rail regulation.* Railroads have been in decline since the early 1950s in almost all countries; but better regulation has revived them when and where they are economical. Figure 6.7 shows the decline in Eastern Europe, but the U.S. experience points to ways in which their potential could be realized.

Railroads lost their historical dominance as carriers of high-value freight because of poor service and unreliability. Passenger traffic switched to roads and air. Misguided regulatory policies exacerbated the problems of the rail industry. Pricing restrictions and cross-subsidies from freight to passengers accelerated the loss of rail's freight market-share to trucking. The combination of public ownership and exclusive monopoly dulled incentives to control costs. Railroad productivity has been especially poor relative to latent technological opportunities.

In the United States, regulatory reform freed the industry from many arcane and ruinous rules. The 1980 Staggers Act substantially deregulated the railroads, allowing pricing flexibility and the abandonment of unproductive and redundant track. The effects were dramatic: productivity

gains exceeded those in nearly every other U.S. industry. From 1981 through 2000, labor and locomotive productivity increased by 317 and 121 percent, respectively. Lower rail rates—down 59 percent, on average, in real terms from 1981 to 2000—have saved shippers and their customers more than $10 billion annually. After decades of steady decline, rail market share (measured in ton-miles) has trended slowly upward, from 35.2 percent in 1978 to more than 40 percent today.

Nor was the United States an isolated case: Japanese National Railways began its restructuring in 1986. In the early 1990s, British Rail was split vertically and horizontally (box 6.5). The British government subsequently privatized the freight businesses and the entire infrastructure and competitively awarded several franchises in the passenger segment.

In developing countries, virtually all the rail systems were owned by the state at the beginning of the 1990s, but private operators obtained concessions in most Latin American and several African countries.

The gains from privatizing railroads depend on the manner of regulation. There will be no gains if private operators are as constrained as their state-owned predecessors.

FIGURE 6.7
## Railroad Cargo in the Transformation Period, 1985–97

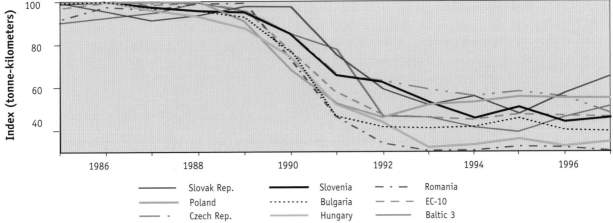

*Source:* von Hirschhausen and Meinhart 2001.

A country can choose from a continuum of ownership and market structure reform options, but the choice should be based on many country- and industry-specific characteristics: size, level of development, institutional capacity, density of the rail network, condition of fixed rail facilities, strength of intermodal competition, and efficacy of public finances. Thus an uncritical choice, especially of the extreme options (entirely private or public, complete vertical integration or separation), does not serve the public interest.

*Toll roads.* Private sector participation in toll roads increased dramatically during the 1990s. About $61 billion of private investment was committed to 279 such projects between 1990 and 1999 in 26 developing countries. Many of these projects, however, encountered difficulties and were either renegotiated or canceled: of the 279, 21 projects in Hungary, Indonesia, Mexico, and Thailand, accounting for $9.5 billion in total private investment, were taken over by governments.

More than a third of the canceled projects were part of the Mexican toll-road program. The Mexican toll roads were built on the basis of very optimistic traffic projections—especially regarding the price elasticity of users' demand, which is relatively difficult to predict. The tolls that were needed to cover project costs drove much of the traffic on to parallel, nontoll roads with the result that revenue was inadequate to service the debts incurred (from government-owned development banks). The government therefore took over the project and lowered the tolls.

The Mexican failure, as does the France-U.K. Channel tunnel, illustrates an inherent difficulty with some types of infrastructure projects: that the state cannot avoid certain types of risks, regardless of the clauses in the contract. Once built, the marginal cost of allowing additional users is low until the point of congestion, but if the toll charged is low, to allow for optimal use, it cannot cover a project's average costs. Alternatives determine the price charged—Mexican law requires nontoll alternative roads, and the Channel tunnel faces competition from ferries—and these prices result in financial losses that are often

## BOX 6.5
## Problems with Unbundling in Railroads

The United Kingdom separated the ownership of infrastructure (track) and operations (trains) to permit competition among rail operators without the need for regulation; but the action gave rise to serious coordination problems, loss of economies of scope, and unnecessary transaction costs.

Many innovative rail services require specific investment in infrastructure (for example, constructing loading and transshipment facilities, building spur tracks to reach a shipper's location), and operators find it difficult and inefficient to coordinate this work with the infrastructure owner, especially if their investment incentives are poorly designed. This is what happened when the British railway system was vertically unbundled and the core infrastructure was transferred to a privatized company, Railtrack plc. The operating companies and Railtrack frequently disagreed on the type, magnitude, and timing of needed track repairs. A frequent complaint was that Railtrack focused too much on commercial concerns and not nearly enough on engineering: so the tracks were not properly maintained, leading to breakdowns that interrupted operator service, jeopardized safety, and prompted public complaints.

borne by taxpayers because of their sheer size. Even if lenders were not state-owned banks (as with Mexican toll roads) or pension funds (with government standing behind them), assets of this size and no alternative use should not be allowed to rust and decay, and governments should open their purses to put them to their intended use.

Inaccurate projections of demand (especially of the cross-elasticity of demand) create serious problems that compound the underlying difficulty of most infrastructure projects. Rather than handing over a project entirely, it may be better to involve the private sector in some aspects of the project, such as the construction phase of roads (if the quality could be specified, monitored, and verified) or the collection of tolls (where new scanning technology to pay could be used). Private participation is also easier with projects, such as road bridges or ring roads, where substitutes are few and where less elastic demand allows full cost recovery.

## Water

The scope for introducing competition in the supply of water and sewerage services is much more limited than that in the other network utilities. Local networks of pipes and sewers remain the quintessential natural monopolies. Moreover, unbundling is not as attractive because the benefits resulting from increased competition in supply are likely to be considerably less than in other network utilities. The costs of producing water are relatively low in relation to the value added at the transport stage, although this relationship may vary across countries. The opportunities for introducing competition in sewage treatment, on the other hand, are of greater significance. Overall, franchising is likely to be the most effective way of increasing competition in the sector.

*Technological change in water supply systems.* A significant difference between the water sector and most other infrastructure is that technological change in the past couple of decades has been much less dramatic or rapid and has had less impact on the underlying economics of supply. The most significant technological innovation in conventional water systems has been the widespread introduction of metering at the point of consumption, which permits the utility to set a tariff reflecting the marginal cost of water used and to bill for actual consumption.

*Difficult political economy.* Part of the reason why the water sector is behind electricity, telecoms, or transport in restructuring or privatization is that in many countries the political economy of water

has not been highly favorable to reform. Major water reforms have tended to be provoked by public health crises, and to some extent by declining real water revenues owing to inflation—factors that led to reforms in Buenos Aires, Lima, Conakry, Santiago, and Mexico City in the late 1980s and early 1990s.

The reforms in these cities depended on the relative political power of potential winners and losers, not on social benefits. The political benefits may come from expanded service to the unconnected population, typically the urban poor, and from better service to middle-income groups. But vested interests include those consumers who already have access and stand to be charged more, workers with patronage employment in publicly owned utilities, and the lucrative businesses that provide services inefficiently (for instance, private trucks that haul water in Indian cities). Water sector reforms have been politically most difficult to sustain in cities where the marginal supply price of water is increasing steeply and where wastewater creates large externalities—such as Lima and Mexico City. In Buenos Aires, by contrast, the lower cost (and bids that reflected this) of renewable water resources have made it possible to reduce water prices and still generate enough return to attract private investment.

*Reform outcomes.* After a few years of reform (1988–93) in six cities, the initial results showed improvements in the coverage indicators (except in Lima), often dramatically (Abidjan and Conakry). Unaccounted-for water—a measure combining physical losses due to poor maintenance and commercial losses due to poor financial management or illegal use—fell significantly in Buenos Aires, Lima, and Santiago. Financial performance and labor productivity improved, and revenues exceeded costs in all cases except Mexico City (figure 6.8).

Nevertheless, the well-publicized problems with the Cochabamba concession in Bolivia underscore the unpopularity of such reforms (especially price increases) and reveal the deep distrust with which the private sector is viewed, especially when there are nontransparent deals with poorly overseen governments. Such opposition is less likely if the public realizes that, regardless of whether the provider is public or private, costs must be covered—if not through prices, then through subsidies that many governments cannot afford, and that the alternative to higher prices is having no piped water at all.

## Utility Regulation: Some Lessons of Experience

Privatization makes good regulation both more important (because private owners care for profits, even at the public's expense) and more difficult (because firms have a greater incentive and ability to misrepresent costs and market conditions). The recent experience in some countries shows that better regulation is possible though not inevitable. Three lessons emerge.

### 1. Regulatory Reform Should Promote Competition, Not Control

Improving regulations has traditionally meant giving greater legal powers to regulators, perhaps training them and trying to make them independent of politics. Absolute regulatory independence is neither feasible nor desirable. Regulators will always report to politicians who

pass the laws, and politics will always play a role in what is regulated and how.

Regulation should promote competition and ensure access to bottleneck facilities, not attempt to control a firm. Information asymmetries and regulatory capture make attempts at control counterproductive. Competition is the most effective regulator, and regulatory reform implies focusing on ensuring competition and access to physical infrastructure.

Ensuring competition implies allowing entry, a goal that unbundling services sometimes helps to advance, although experience shows how coordination problems arise when the effort is overdone. Attempts to control prices are invariably distorting, especially with rapidly changing technology and privatization of parts of the infrastructure system.

The importance of ensuring access is illustrated in figure 6.9, which compares several Latin American countries that opened their telecommunications markets to private competition. No new entrants gained more than 15 percent of the market, even in Chile, where they operated for more than 20 years, because regulators were unable to ensure access to bottleneck telecommunications facilities (such as the local loop).

Even under technically competent regulators, regulatory interventions often fail. It is ironic that when the World Bank and other multilateral institutions helped developing countries set up regulatory agencies they gave considerable attention to the organization and legal independence of these agencies but not to their mandate: many operate without any controlling principles. Their present structure accentuates the tendency to expand regulatory jurisdiction, often with dysfunctional consequences.

India's experience illustrates the difficulties in staffing a regulatory agency (box 6.6), even in a country with considerable administrative abilities and a vast pool of competent potential staff.

### 2. Regulatory Reform Should Focus on Getting the Underlying Economics Right

Understanding the source of benefits helps in structuring reform. A pricing policy that does not allow adequate revenue cannot improve the

FIGURE 6.8

**Labor Productivity in the Water Sector**

(year of reform = 0)

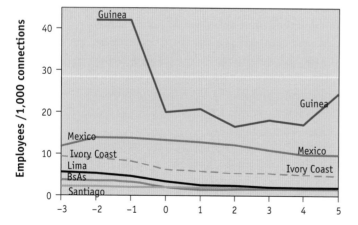

*Source:* Shirley and Menard 2002.

BsAs, Buenos Aires.

FIGURE 6.9

## Local Exchange Carriers in Latin America

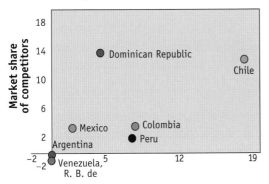

*Source:* Pyramid Research 2001.

situation, no matter if the industry is privatized or an independent regulator is established. For example, as of 2000, in almost all Commonwealth of Independent States (CIS) countries, household electricity prices covered less than 50 percent and industrial prices less than 70 percent of the long-run marginal costs of supply (figure 6.10).

Similarly, imposing social service obligations on only some providers will not promote efficient investment, even when institutional mechanisms provide a credible commitment to policy stability.

Neglecting the underlying economics is also why social security reform has gone astray: there are some risks that the private sector simply cannot handle adequately. While some governments may find it difficult to socialize these risks adequately, it is a mistake to think that they could be borne by the private sector. Despite potential gains from others sharing these risks, they may have to be borne by individuals until better institutions develop.

## 3. Regulatory Structures Should Reflect Country Differences

Countries differ greatly in their economic structures and in their institutions. These institutional differences—including courts (where appeals are made), legislatures (where laws are passed), the

### BOX 6.6
### India's Regulatory Capacity versus Effectiveness

India's power sector is overseen by states, but its regulatory problems do not stem from center-state jurisdictional issues. As in the United States, India's 1998 reforms created independent electricity regulatory commissions in each state, with the Central Electricity Regulatory Commission (CERC) dealing with national and interstate issues (for example, the National Electricity Grid Code). The State Electricity Regulatory Commission (SERC) sets tariffs, enforces licensing conditions, and monitors compliance.

To ensure the independence of these commissions, their mandate to protect the public interest is clearly defined and members have reasonable job security (they cannot be dismissed unless impeached for unethical conduct). With funding coming through special provisions in the consolidated central and state budgets, the commissions are freed from the Ministry of Power's direct financial control.

Nevertheless, a recent review of state and central electricity regulators showed inadequate staffing, which sharply limited regulatory capabilities (Prayas Energy Group 2003). CERC and most of the SERCs (Orissa and Andhra Pradesh are possible exceptions) could not fill their specialist positions. Government pay scales are insufficient to attract capable professionals, and requests for professional and technical staff appointments are routinely delayed for months or years. All but two SERCs had only three or fewer professional and technical staff when they were supposed to have 8 to 10, and 8 of the 12 SERCs studied had no permanent professional and technical staff at all. They often relied on temporary staff from the incumbent utilities they were ostensibly regulating.

press (which informs the electorate), an engaged public (demanding more from governments), academia (training regulators and encouraging studies of problems)—determine why what is sound regulation in one country is ineffectual in another.[24]

Although countries can learn from the mistakes of others, important differences among them make it hard to replicate others' successes.

FIGURE 6.10

## Cost-Coverage Ratios of Electricity Prices in the CIS Countries

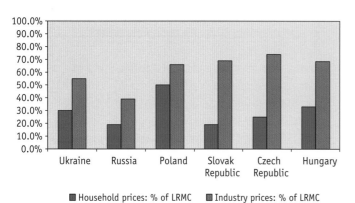

■ Household prices: % of LRMC    ■ Industry prices: % of LRMC

*Source:* von Hirschhausen and Opitz 2001.

LRMC. Long-run marginal cost.

Countries often adopt regulatory reforms in name but not in substance, to satisfy international agencies that sometimes require this reform as a condition for aid or loans. Developing countries looked to the experience of Canada, New Zealand, the United Kingdom, and the United States in formulating their regulations, often ignoring their big differences from those countries.[25] Rash attempts to regulate can be far more dangerous and costly than inaction. There is good reason to be concerned that regulations could thwart competition, not promote it.[26]

## 5. Privatizing Social Security

Several countries, primarily in Latin America and Eastern Europe, reformed their social security systems by moving to a multipillar system and giving a prominent role to privately managed individual accounts. We describe their experiences, after defining key terms in pensions and social security (box 6.7).

### Three Pillars for Stability?

Countries sought to reform social security for different reasons. Chile's privatization of parts of

its social security system attracted many imitators in Latin America and Eastern Europe, and the World Bank provided a three-pillar model of pension reform in an influential report, *Averting the Old Age Crisis* (1994a). The experience of the 12 Latin American and 8 East European countries,[27] however, calls into question the universal applicability of this model.

Each pillar of the three-pillar model is best described by its function, since the method of financing and determining benefits can differ. The first pillar seeks to prevent old-age poverty, usually through a defined-benefit PAYG pension. All countries with social security systems have this pillar, and in many it is the only one. The second pillar aims to smooth consumption over the life cycle and prevent a dramatic decrease in income during retirement. Consumption smoothing requires retirement payments linked to previous income, so this pillar tends to be a fully funded,[28] defined-contribution pension. Funding purports to protect against demographic changes and insulate recipients from the vagaries of budget appropriations. The third pillar augments income in old age and is essentially a voluntary savings scheme for retirement, often with tax advantages. A need-based cash-transfer system financed by general (not wage) taxes is sometimes called a zero pillar.

### The 1990s Reforms

Most of the social security reforms of the 1990s took place in Latin America and Eastern Europe, but the two regions differ starkly. Latin America's large young population contrasts with the higher proportion of the aged in Europe (figure 6.11).

Social security coverage is low in Latin America, but almost universal in Eastern Europe. Fiscal sustainability is a concern for both regions, though particularly acute in Eastern Europe (figures 6.12 and 6.13). Reforms in the two regions erected the second and third pillars. Many Latin American countries sought to phase out the first pillar completely, thereby privatizing social security. But most governments in Europe and Central Asia (except Kazakhstan) retained at least a small first pillar, not only because of their legacy of protecting the aged

**BOX 6.7**
**Definitions**

A pension is deferred compensation that employers pay. As employers, some governments have long provided pensions for civil servants and military veterans and their widows and orphans, but very few firms did so until well into the 20th century. Banks were an exception, perhaps to avert malfeasance (bankers making bad loans before they retired). Pension coverage in private firms rose in the United States during the 1930s and further during World War II, perhaps to circumvent wage controls. The expansion coincided with increasingly progressive income tax rates, and spreading income over a lifetime reduced the total taxes paid.

Pensions are of two types: a *defined-benefit* scheme specifies the amounts (generally related to years of service and the last few years' salary) while a *defined-contribution* scheme invests employees' (and employers' matching) contributions and links the payouts to the investment value. Funds are generally set aside in both types of schemes; but employers bear the investment risk in defined-benefit schemes and employees decide the investment allocation and bear the risk in defined-contribution schemes. Defined-contribution schemes are more portable, allowing employees to change jobs without worrying about qualifying for or losing pension eligibility, and are displacing defined-benefit schemes in many countries.

**Social security** also grew in the 20th century. Some governments began paying the elderly, not just their former employees, but required the recipients to have worked and earned in order to qualify, thereby giving such transfers pension-like features. Social security payments are often based on need, capped to favor the nonrich, and only loosely tied to wages/earnings, giving them safety net–type features. Social security began as a pay-as-you-go (PAYG) system, either unfunded or with partial funding, with payroll taxes usually financing payouts. Rising prosperity made for increasingly generous systems, and

greater mobility and declining ties to the extended family and community made social security a safety net that the public valued.

In most OECD countries, problems with social security have arisen because of demographic changes. Increased longevity and declining fertility led to an increase in the proportion of the elderly in the population, meaning that fewer workers had to support more pensioners. This imbalance required either a reduction in benefits or an increase in tax rates (coverage was already almost universal) or a delay in retirement age or some combination of the three. Alternatively, the projected shortfalls could be funded* (by moving from a PAYG scheme to generating a cash flow surplus). But projections are error-prone, depending not just on demography but also on economic growth, and many governments, including those of the United States, have been reluctant to set aside as much as was needed. Often, they spent even those funds.

Many developing countries, especially in Latin America, introduced social security early in the 20th century, but they generally limited coverage to government employees and the unionized formal sector—a small fraction of the labor force. Unlike those of OECD countries with aging populations, developing countries' social security problems do not arise from demography—half the population consists of children who will soon enter the labor force—but from poorly defined and enforced eligibility rules and overly generous payments. The high tax rates encourage evasion not just from coverage but from the formal sector altogether: many employees work in smaller businesses that remain in, or migrate to, the informal economy.

The situation is different in the transition countries of Eastern Europe.** The demography and benefit coverage are similar to those of OECD countries, but the massive decline in output (outlined in Country Note E on Eastern Europe's Transition) and the

*(Box continues on the following page.)*

**BOX 6.7**

**(continued)**

difficulties in administering taxes made it difficult for governments to honor their promises to the unemployed, the retirees, and the elderly. Their solution was to cap benefits or build up pension arrears in the first instance and to then cut costs in a variety of ways: increasing contribution rates, raising the retirement age, or experimenting with different forms of indexing benefits.

*"Funding" (by generating a surplus that is invested *before* the "demographic bulge" retires) requires a country to save in the aggregate, which it can do only by running a current-account surplus. Barr (2000) points out that many discussions make this fallacy of composition, and several countries seeking to reform social security run current account deficits that prevent funding.

** China's demography differs from those of both Latin America and the Caribbean and Eastern Europe, and its social security system covers about 18 percent of the population. But the immediate problem seems to be clarifying whose liabilities these are: while they are being transferred from the enterprises to the government, it is not clear which level of government will ultimately be responsible, and how intergovernmental transfers will take place.

but also because of concerns about the future. Many of these countries seek membership in the European Union, and for labor to move freely within the European Union, the social protection systems of its members should be compatible. Most EU countries provide the first pillar, although harmonizing their systems does not appear to be a high priority, and bilateral agreements among EU members govern workers moving from one member country to another.

Pensions and social security are long-term contracts, and any change involves an extended transition. In Latin American countries, covered workers were given a short period in which to choose between a reduced first pillar (a defined-benefit pension in what remained of the pay-as-you-go system) or a new second pillar with the privately managed individual accounts that were

being established. The third pillar allowed, but did not mandate, additional savings with tax advantages. In Latin America, new entrants to the system were only offered the second and third pillars: thus, once workers who were already covered retired and died, the system would be completely private.

## Results

Figure 6.14 shows how the reforms reduced the governments' projected liabilities, but the transition was unexpectedly costly.[29] In Argentina and Bolivia, a poorly managed switchover increased payouts by more than expected because of fraudulent claims and a lax interpretation of the rules. Figure 6.15 shows that Bolivia's budget deficit rose instead of falling. The transition costs were also high in Eastern Europe because the newly created private sector evaded the taxes when rates were high to finance both the first-pillar payouts and the second pillar's funding.

There were other disappointments too. Despite the reforms, coverage remains low in Latin America, notwithstanding predictions that a closer link between contributions and benefits in a funded system would improve incentives to participate (figure 6.16). It is unclear whether this is because workers mistrust social security or simply evade the payroll tax.

Capital markets did not develop either, contrary to predictions.[30] Pension funds have simply held government bonds, not commercial paper or equities. Perhaps this development should not be surprising since equity markets require the principal-agent problem to be effectively overcome—which usually takes much longer than the accumulation of funds. But placing government bonds in captive funds does not create a market. Mandating private savings have led to more, and occasionally better, financial sector and capital market regulations. Countries that run a current account surplus could invest in foreign markets; but most developing countries run current account deficits.

Surprisingly, private pension funds proved more expensive to administer than the previous state-run systems. Although private competition was expected to reduce administrative costs, these

FIGURE 6.11

## Eastern Europe's Population Is Significantly Older than Latin America's
(percentage of total population in each age cohort)

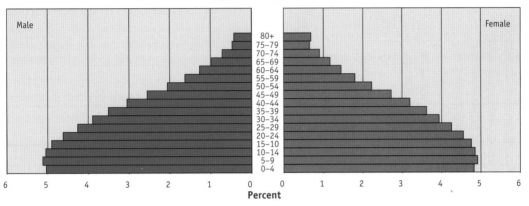

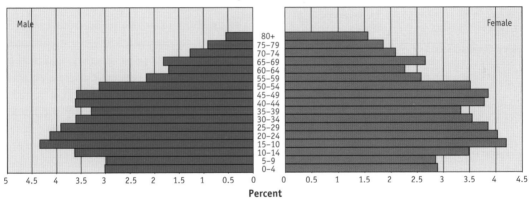

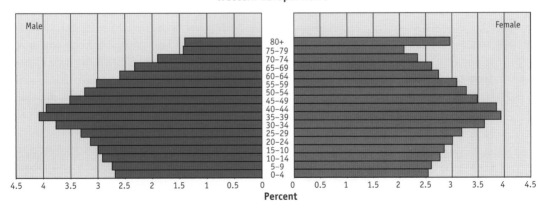

*Source*: U.S. Census Bureau, International Programs Center.

FIGURE 6.12

**Coverage is Greater in Europe and Central Asia than Latin America and the Caribbean, but Intraregional Variation is Wide**

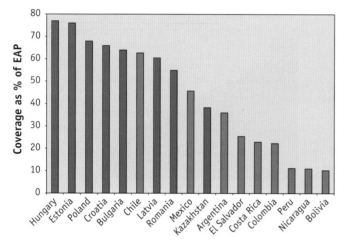

*Sources*: Palacios and Pallares-Miralles (2000) for Europe and Central Asia; recent household surveys for Latin America and the Caribbean.

EAP Economically active population.

FIGURE 6.13

**Eastern Europe Has Greater Fiscal Need for Reform than Latin America**

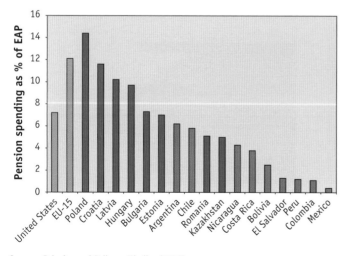

*Sources*: Palacios and Pallares-Miralles (2000).

EAP Economically active population.

costs increased in Latin America as part of the transition from centralized to decentralized management in an industry with possible scale economies. Even in Eastern Europe, where centralized records were maintained for the privately managed funds, charges have been comparable to those in decentralized Latin American systems. Moreover, private fund managers could collude since they were few and entry was difficult. Regulation did not focus on ensuring competition, and rents to incumbents came at workers' expense.

*Government's Role in Pension Systems*

Although privatization is often appealing, governments have a necessary role in pension systems. People can save for old age (to smooth consumption) in a variety of different ways, including investing in their children and buying real estate or claims on other assets, but these choices are limited in many countries. People may be unable to diversify against catastrophes such as droughts or famines, especially if all members of their family and community are affected. Besides, community and family ties fray with urbanization and economic development. The question is whether governments or markets can protect against such risks better than personal and/or private initiatives.

The government may have a role in keeping the elderly out of poverty, especially as societies prosper. Since private markets to insure against poverty may not develop because of adverse selection and moral hazard, the government essentially provides this insurance through the first pillar.

Though insurance markets develop to pool the risk of infrequent large but predictable losses from, say, fire and automobile accidents, other losses are better managed through prevention and self-insurance (Ehrlich and Becker 1972). Old age is predictable and self-insurance means saving. Governments have a clear role in enforcing contracts for savings and investment vehicles, but it is less clear why the second pillar should be mandated, if this forces savings through a poorly developed financial system. In many developing countries, relying on investments in a family

FIGURE 6.14

## Reforms in Latin America Reduced Debt: Projected Pension Debt (Explicitly Accumulated after 2001)

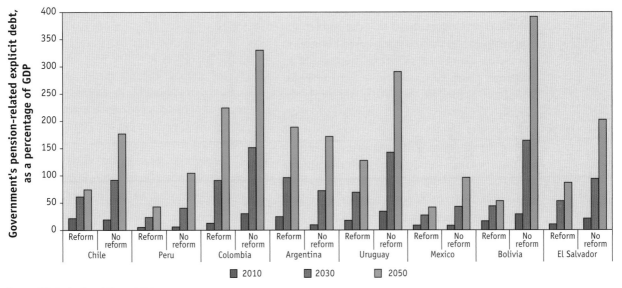

*Source:* Gill, Packard, and Yermo 2004.

FIGURE 6.15

## Bolivia's Pension Reform Was Unexpectedly Costly

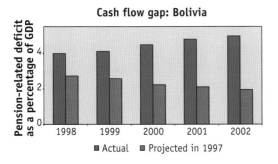

*Source*: Gill, Packard, and Yermo 2004.

business, or in children, may be a better choice for all concerned.

The third pillar may not be necessary but, as it is voluntary, it is not harmful. It should be viewed in conjunction with the tax system. The tax break for such savings tends to move the tax system from taxing (realized) income to taxing consumption—a shift that economists since Kaldor (1955) have long favored.

FIGURE 6.16

## No Marked Rise in Participation in Latin America

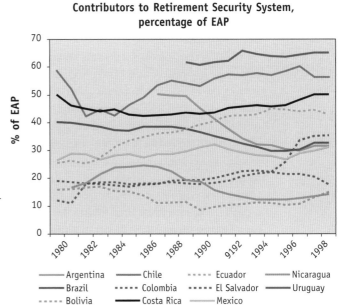

*Source*: Gill, Packard, and Yermo 2004.

The experiences of Latin America and Eastern Europe differ greatly, but common lessons emerge. The multipillar model may be suitable for some countries, but clearly not for all. Latin America's experience shows that the problems in the first pillar—that is, a need-based pension to the aged—cannot be solved by simply adding additional pillars, or by switching from a pay-as-you-go to a funded system. In Argentina the default on government bonds has essentially destroyed the second pillar, which was meant to replace the first (box 6.8). A government cannot resolve the fiscal implications arising from the first pillar by "privatizing" it: a better choice may be to scale back the benefits, administer it well, and ensure that it is financially sound.

Whether a second pillar (mandated individual accounts) is advantageous depends on a country's circumstances. Financial markets are not equally developed in all countries, and the second pillar may be unsuitable and administratively costly in many. Government bonds will likely remain the main asset in such funds, meaning that the second pillar, like the first, will rely on the promises of a financially strapped government. The government will always have a role in any mandated pillar, and without competition, "private provision" may merely be an expensive decoration.

Many transitions have proved unexpectedly expensive because of fraud and poor administration of the rules. Governments should be especially wary with social security and pension reforms, because mistakes are difficult to undo. Those with an existing system may be better advised to keep it simple and make it sound than to add pillars on a shaky fiscal foundation. Countries without social security should be especially wary about introducing such measures, because once established, a pension system cannot be easily dismantled.

## 6.  Conclusions

The 1990s experience shows how difficult both privatization and regulation are. There is no universally appropriate reform model. Every

### BOX 6.8
### Argentina: Private Accounts Do Not Protect Workers from Government Risk

Privately administered mandatory individual retirement accounts were thought to protect workers against political interference inherent in a public PAYG system; but the 2001 crisis in Argentina showed otherwise.

Argentina's private pension system was vulnerable even before the 2001 crisis. Since the system began in 1994, nearly half the assets were invested in government bonds, making pensions vulnerable to the government's fiscal problems. Indeed, converting implicit PAYG government liabilities into explicit debt (having a funded system) contributed significantly to Argentina's declining fiscal position: the bonds benefited from high interest rates, but this gain increased the overall fiscal deficit.

Argentina's return to the *peso* and the default on its debts left pensioners in the lurch. The events of 2001–02 so eroded confidence in any mandated retirement system that participation in any system will likely suffer.

*Source*: Rofman 2002.

restructuring and privatization program needs to consider explicitly the underlying economic attributes and technology of each sector and its institutional, social, and political characteristics.

Clear gains have followed the privatization of nonutilities (with the possible exception of large extractive industries). With extractive firms and utilities (or with social security), the government will play a role through taxes or regulatory controls, and the benefits from their privatization will depend greatly on how effectively this is done.

Privatization is less about finding better owners than the government than it is about separating commerce from politics. Government ownership does not blur this distinction in OECD countries as much as in developing countries where oversight over governments is weaker. Privatization helps to achieve the separation but does not automatically ensure it, because governments retain other powers they could abuse and, without institutions to check such conduct, still influence firms they do not own. The transition countries' experience shows that market-supporting institutions do not emerge quickly in response to demand. And in infrastructure utilities the commercial cannot be separated from the political, regardless of the adequacy of institutions.

If privatization is oversold as a means of separating commerce from politics, restoring the link through regulation is underappreciated. There are huge potential gains from privatizing infrastructure, but inappropriate regulation has sometimes prevented these from being realized. In particular, when prices are controlled at levels that do not cover costs, owners will not invest in new capacity. Regulation must also respond to technical changes, which make today's sensible regulation distorting tomorrow. California's misadventures in electricity show how even sophisticated regulators can make mistakes that leave the public confused about what really happened. And in countries where the public already distrusts markets, privatization bears the opprobrium.

Experience shows that it is possible for regulation to focus less on control than on ensuring access to bottleneck facilities and encouraging competition and entry, in turn encouraging innovation. Redirecting regulation in this manner requires a good understanding of technology and economics. It also calls for modesty, especially in settings where politics can undercut regulators' competence.

In social security, privatization has not eliminated the government's role, and administrative costs have sometimes increased. The purpose and nature of such contracts may always require government involvement. Changes in these arrangements have large consequences that are difficult to reverse.

## Notes

1. The Tennessee Valley Authority was an exception; it promoted rural electrification to tackle poverty in the depressed Appalachian region.
2. Kahn (2004) reflects on and summarizes the deregulation of airline and telecommunications industries and the current controversies (such as the Baby Bells being allowed into the long-distance market).
3. In 1984, the privatization of British Telecom was the largest stock market flotation ever.
4. The (West) German government sold a majority stake to the public in Volkswagen in 1961 and in VEBA (a major energy/industrial corporation in Germany), but later bailed out shareholders when stock prices collapsed. German banks rather than individuals or mutual funds own most industrial equity. Similarly, there was modest privatization in France during the 1980s, but not on the same scale as in Britain.
5. Nellis (2003b) summarizes the many descriptions and studies of Latin America's privatization.
6. Nellis and Shirley (1991).
7. *World Development Report 2003* covers the role of the private sector in the provision of many services that governments traditionally provide and are not discussed here. This chapter focuses primarily on privatization in the transition economies and the regulation of utilities, not changes in the various agricultural marketing boards (primarily in Africa) or the deregulation of nonutilities in developing countries.
8. See Country Note E, "Eastern Europe's Transition: Building Institutions."
9. Even human capital could be considered state-owned since wages were administratively set, migration was restricted, and the choice of professions was constrained. The freeing of wages and other restrictions implicitly meant that this capital was restituted to individuals.
10. The specifics differed by country, but an account of Russian privatization by Boycko, Shleifer, and Vishny (1996), who were advisors to the privatization agency—with its elements of political intrigue, clash of personalities, and the need to make important decisions quickly without adequate information—would resonate with anyone who worked in transition countries at the time.
11. More was done to establish stock exchanges than to establish institutions protecting property rights. More was done to pass new laws than to help courts function better.
12. Some of the least market-oriented countries avidly passed such laws, so the few times they were used were to shake down efficient firms that increased their market shares.

13. Kogot and Spicer (2002) describe how the small group of influential economists were unaware or dismissive of the work of political scientists, many of whom were knowledgeable about the countries. Dani Rodrik (2003c) makes a similar point in http://ksghome.harvard.edu/~.drodrik.academic.ksg/ Stiglitzconference notes.pdf.

14. Claessens, Djankov, and Klingebiel (2001) offer a bleak outlook for equity markets and suggest that efforts are better directed at improving creditor protection.

15. Some did so for fallacious reasons. Lieberman and Nellis (1994) provided a premature endorsement of Russian experiments with vouchers, arguing that vouchers give the public purchasing power. Ramachandran (1997) sought to dispel some of the many fallacies that arose by pointing out that vouchers cannot provide purchasing power or be inflationary, and that their main advantage was to effectively reduce the "minimum value" that governments often placed that would have prevented their sale.

16. Although the privatization agencies disbanded, their employees often found work in the securities and exchange commissions that were created (and later atrophied when trading volumes could not justify their continuation).

17. Little empirical work has been done on this. When valued at the secondary market price for vouchers, a mere $40 million could have bought all firms in Georgia in 1994.

18. Copper prices fell from $7,000 a tonne in 1996 to $3,000 in the mid-1990s to about $1,500 in the early 2000s. Production had fallen from its peak of about 800,000 tonnes of finished copper a year to under 300,000 tonnes.

19. Anglo-American headed the consortium through its subsidiary, Zambia Copper Investments, which held 65 percent of the shares. ZCCM Holdings had 20 percent, IFC took a 7.5 percent stake, and the Commonwealth Development Corporation took the remaining 7.5 percent, while the Government of Zambia held a golden share.

20. Konkola Copper Mine's December 2003 statement to the Extractive Industries Evaluation (describing efforts to find alternative employment and activities for the affected miners).

21. *World Development Report 1996: From Plan to Market* concluded that "the Czech Republic's mass privatization program has been the most successful to date."

22. Except for the loans-for-shares scheme in Russia where major assets were practically given away to a cabal of cronies.

23. Some 48 contracts worth $24 billion (that is, 1.9 percent by number and 3.2 percent by value) were canceled, a third of them dealing with the Mexican toll road program. Water and sanitation had higher cancellation rates than telecom or ports.

24. Analogously, the performance of state-owned firms is disappointing in some countries (India, Mexico) but not in others (Sweden, France).

25. Sophisticated rate-of-return rules are meaningless if firms do not keep accounts adequately, and recourse to courts for remedies may not be possible. Some notable examples include the adoption of the quasi-judicial U.S. model for telecommunications and energy in the Philippines, a country with a notoriously weak judiciary, where reform led to regulatory failure; and the adoption of a U.S.-style Public Utility Commission in Jamaica, where without the constitutional protections and administrative due process prevalent in the United States, the result was regulatory instability and the nationalization of telecommunications in 1975.

26. The World Bank's recent *Doing Business 2004: Understanding Regulation* report (World Bank 2004c) shows that the biggest and most common mistake is to regulate too much, and to do so poorly.

27. Chile pioneered the multipillar system in 1981. The system was adopted (with its many variants) during the 1990s by seven countries in Latin America and the Caribbean (Peru, Colombia, Argentina, Uruguay, Mexico, Bolivia, and El Salvador) and three in Europe and Central Asia (Hungary, Poland, and Kazakhstan). Costa Rica, the Dominican Republic, Latvia, Romania, Bulgaria, Croatia, and Estonia adopted it in the 2000s, and Nicaragua and Ecuador plan to do so.

28. Several countries provide some form of minimum pension guarantee to the funded pillars, however, adding a defined benefit component to an otherwise defined contribution pension.

29. This section is based on Gill et al. (2004). Lindemann, Rutkowski, and Sluchynskyy (2000); Kritzer (2001); and World Bank (2003a) describe the experience in Europe and Central Asia.

30. For further discussion, see chapter 7, section 2.

# Eastern Europe's Transition: Building Institutions

The economic and political consequences of the end of Communism in Eastern and Central Europe and the collapse of the Soviet Union have changed the lives of 400 million people in 27 countries. The transition was without precedent, and vividly illustrates how complex is the transformation and establishment of institutions, even in societies that are well endowed with human capital and rich cultural traditions.[1]

## Legacy

Fifty years of communism left a relatively large stock of physical capital—in the form of infrastructure, manufacturing industries, and housing (much of it technically obsolete)—and of human capital. Literacy and health indicators were comparable with those of industrialized countries, and the scientific and intellectual cadres were among the world's best. But resources had been inefficiently used because prices were administratively set and the state owned everything. Centrally made decisions on production and pricing disregarded preferences and scarcity. For example, Uzbekistan grew cotton extensively, drying up the rivers that fed the rapidly diminishing (inland) Aral Sea. Energy was as wastefully consumed in industry as water and fertilizer were in agriculture.[2] Many industries subtracted rather than added value: at world prices, their inputs were worth more than their outputs. Despite Soviet scientific achievements, machinery often embodied obsolete technologies because prices did not signal value and influence resource allocation.

All East European countries faced the same transition issues: to reorganize production and reallocate resources better. The expectation was that market allocation provided better incentives, leading to less waste, and economic prosperity would follow, especially with the end of the costly arms race following the demise of communism,.

Transformation was a daunting task, and some economic turmoil was anticipated, but the countries' prospects were not bleak. Most advisers—including international financial institutions, think tanks, and academics—advocated rapid reform, meaning open trade with low tariffs, rapid removals of controls over the economy in general, and quick privatization. As reformers have highlighted (notably the Russian Federation's former Minister of Finance Gaidar, in World Bank 2005b), speed was essential. The political and administrative collapse that accompanied the transition virtually everywhere meant that gradual trade liberalization, or carefully planned and sequenced privatization, was simply not possible.

## Outcomes

Output in all countries declined much more sharply than expected. The 12 Central and Southeastern European countries and the 3 Baltic countries (CSB) fared better than the 12 countries of the Commonwealth of Independent States (CIS).[3] Over four years, CSB had a cumulative average output decline of 22 percent, or 12 percent when weighted by population. By contrast, CIS output fell 50 percent over 6.5 years, or by 45 percent when weighted by population.

Recovery diverged more sharply. Output in CSB now exceeds its pretransition levels, but that in the CIS is still one-third lower, or one-fifth lower when weighted by population at the end of 2003. Within the CIS, there are differences as well (figure E.1). For example, Georgia's output declined by roughly 75 percent between 1990 and 1994, and at the end of 2003 it was no more than 40 percent of its pretransition level, partly because of civil war. Incomes are more unequal now within countries (the Gini coefficient almost doubled in Bulgaria, Armenia, and several other countries). More worryingly, absolute poverty has risen.

Private enterprise overtook the state sector in most countries; but its share of output varies from more than 80 percent in Hungary to a mere 20 percent in Belarus. Newly established private firms account for much of the growth, although many are spinoffs from older firms. International trade expanded, especially with countries outside the former Soviet bloc. Exports from the CSB have outpaced those from the CIS (8.8 percent annual growth versus 3.2 percent during 1993–98). This was partly because these countries had ports or had good roads to connect them but also because foreign firms invested there, since the countries were expected to join the European Union. Whether it is a cause or consequence, CSB governments have introduced policies that provide a better investment climate that fostered domestic firms and attracted inflows of direct foreign investment: Hungary has attracted foreign investments of more than 5 percent of its gross domestic product (GDP) since 1995, among the highest rates of foreign direct investment (FDI) in the world. Russia, Poland, and the Czech Republic have also attracted substantial FDI, although the amounts were smaller fractions of their GDP.

The transition buffeted government finances. Revenues fell. Collecting taxes requires a different administration than does commanding resource transfers, and developing new tax administrations was difficult and slow. Meanwhile fiscal deficits ballooned. Concomitantly, government spending rose, because unemployment called for additional outlays and because firms requested funds (subsidies, guarantees, or loans) to restructure their operations. Cutting government spending was risky: police officers easily organize protection rackets, and members

of the military at the borders with weapons and transport are tempted to smuggle contraband.[4] Domestic borrowing was difficult because savings fell, and foreign lenders were not always forthcoming. Printing money created inflation that hurt the poor, who (unlike in Africa or Asia) had no extended families to fall back on.

Reorganizing the real sector involved more than freeing prices. Every firm had to decide how and what to produce and how much to charge, which workers to retain, and so forth, but neither governments as owners nor state-owned banks as creditors could oversee the firms' managers. Mechanisms such as hard budget constraints were needed for this purpose and to discipline firms. Some firms were slow to restructure and continued operating as before, building up inventories and interenterprise arrears. Some governments (for example, Romania, twice) sought to break the logjam, thereby loosening the hard budget constraint.[5] Utilities posed special problems: their finances were often sapped by the unpaid bills of energy-intensive industries, but shutting them down could be a death sentence for consumers in cold climates, because workers lived in company housing. Many governments made mistakes when tackling issues such as this, but some recognized and corrected the mistakes more quickly than others.

Problems were similar in agriculture: although farmers could switch crops and use inputs more efficiently in theory, those growing cash crops (for example, Uzbek cotton growers) faced problems similar to those in industry when they could not easily adapt irrigation and the marketing infrastructure. De-collectivizing agriculture was not easy: even when restitution claims were sorted out and land was redistributed, farmers sometimes had to continue operating collectively because they lacked their own equipment and access to credit.

Financial intermediaries did not develop quickly. Countries licensed many new banks, often creating so-called commercial banks with the stroke of a pen, but developing a credit culture takes time, and in any event banks had little to lend. As incomes fell, so did savings rates, and few savers entrusted their savings to banks, espe-

## Key Indicators for Transition Countries

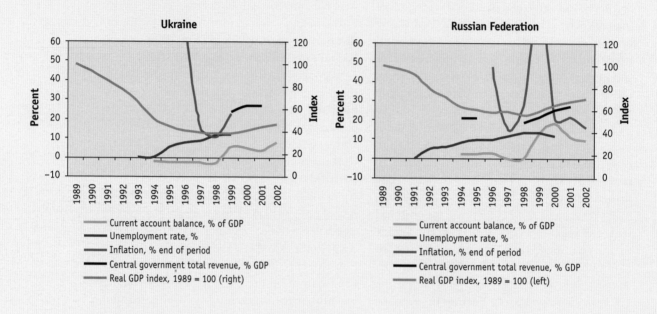

**Ukraine**

**Russian Federation**

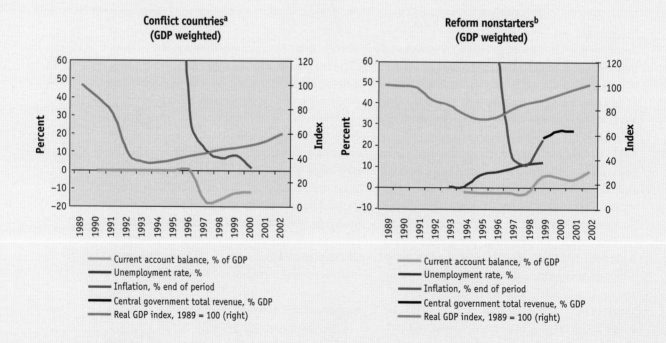

**Conflict countries[a]**
**(GDP weighted)**

**Reform nonstarters[b]**
**(GDP weighted)**

*Source:* World Bank, *WDI;* EBRD 2003.

a. Georgia, Armenia.
b. Belarus, Uzbekistan.

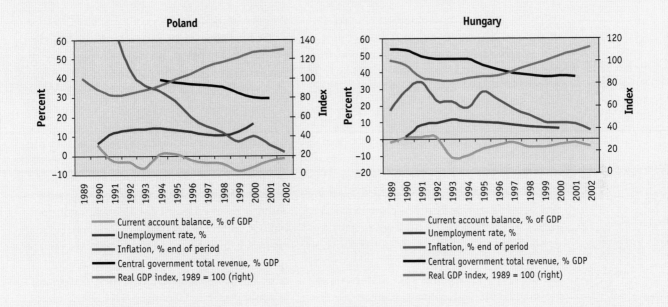

**Poland**

Current account balance, % of GDP
Unemployment rate, %
Inflation, % end of period
Central government total revenue, % GDP
Real GDP index, 1989 = 100 (right)

**Hungary**

Current account balance, % of GDP
Unemployment rate, %
Inflation, % end of period
Central government total revenue, % GDP
Real GDP index, 1989 = 100 (right)

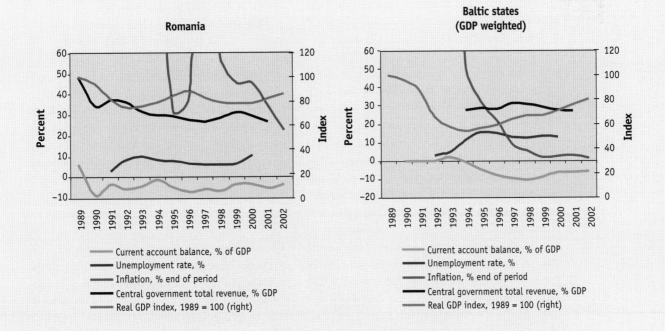

**Romania**

Current account balance, % of GDP
Unemployment rate, %
Inflation, % end of period
Central government total revenue, % GDP
Real GDP index, 1989 = 100 (right)

**Baltic states
(GDP weighted)**

Current account balance, % of GDP
Unemployment rate, %
Inflation, % end of period
Central government total revenue, % GDP
Real GDP index, 1989 = 100 (right)

cially since they lost much of their deposits to high inflation during the early years of the transition. Banking deposits now range from 3 percent of GDP (Georgia) to 60 percent (Czech Republic); those in most transition countries are in the 10–20 percent range. Some countries (Albania, Romania, and Russia) suffered from destructive pyramid schemes that added to depositors' distrust and to the liabilities of governments that intervened. The inexperienced central banks found it difficult to oversee financial systems or to resist government demands that led to inflation.

Privatization was only one of the many real-sector issues that governments tackled. Allowing new firms to emerge required changes at many levels in the bureaucracy, including company registration and tax collection. As noted above, in countries with no tradition of voluntary tax compliance, developing tax administration proved difficult. Governments traditionally collected payroll taxes, but relying heavily on this method implied high tax rates that deterred new business formation or forced activities into the untaxed informal sector.

Thus, although social concerns were important, funds for schools, health care, and pensions had to be cut. Spending on education declined to 2–8 percent of GDP and on health care to 1–6 percent of GDP. Many social services that were formerly provided by enterprises (such as housing and childcare) had to be transferred to local governments, but their costs far outstripped the governments' ability to raise revenues. When spending on such services declined, it was difficult to protect vulnerable groups, especially when there were large regional disparities and no transfer mechanisms in place. Some of the spending cuts were accomplished by eliminating overly generous provisions: Poland, for example, had been spending twice as much on disability pensions as the Organisation for Economic Co-operation and Development (OECD) average.

Pensions and unemployment insurance were provided centrally, and these amounted to a high 10–13 percent of GDP—double their pretransition proportion, and unsustainable. Because tax rates on wages were already high, encouraging

evasion, most countries made it harder to qualify for pensions, unemployment insurance, and other benefits by raising the retirement age and other eligibility requirements. Improving the efficient delivery of social services will take time.

Many people were adversely affected by the changes taking place, and their perceptions now mattered because most countries were becoming democracies. (The few that remained authoritarian were not among the economic reformers.) It did not help when newly prosperous citizens flaunted their wealth, especially when this wealth had been "legally stolen" through noncompetitive privatization. The hardships caused many citizens to resent the harshness of markets, but no country has reverted to communism, and more impressively, there has been no significant policy reversal.[6] But democracy's roots have yet to spread, especially in the CIS; media criticism is new; and politicians are unseasoned. Georgians, and more recently Ukrainians, took to the streets to oust an unpopular president after a rigged election, but their new heroes face familiar constraints and cannot work miracles.

Despite the difficulties, the achievements are impressive and the outlook is bright: by the end of 2003, real GDP in the CIS (weighted by population) was 50 percent higher than in 1998, and citizens of the Balkans enjoy peace after years of war and civil conflict. Eight transition countries have joined the European Union, and this has spurred their own efforts and those of other prospective members to improve their societies in all their dimensions.

## Lessons

Though endowments matter, so do policies. The countries that prospered most were not those that many observers had predicted. For example, the former East Germany's endowments did not lead to prosperity, and the Czech Republic's progress belied expectations stemming from its "reforms" (soft budget constraints and the resulting lack of industrial restructuring precipitated the Czech crisis during 1996–98).

East Germany's experience, in particular, shows the importance of sound policies. The East was fortunate to be well located, sharing West Germany's language, culture, and history (except during the communist years). East Germany could quickly and smoothly adopt laws and organizations from the West, and it obtained considerable financial assistance: 40–60 percent of its GDP from the West as cumulative transfers during 1991–97 and only slightly less thereafter. Nevertheless, East Germany's output fell substantially, and remains more depressed than that of many transition countries whose disadvantages are greater. Unifying the German currency at an overvalued level, and adopting West Germany's rigid labor laws and generous welfare benefits, resulted in too much of East Germany's capital being scrapped and too few investments being made, leading to high unemployment. Foreign direct investors leapt over East Germany into countries such as Poland that had better economic policies.

The transition countries show no consistent statistical association between particular types of reform policies and growth.[7] This should not be surprising: even if the policy reform index chosen identifies and measures the right policies, the response of the economy to reform also depends on many other factors including government credibility, institutions, and social cohesiveness, which differ greatly across countries (and perhaps also over time in each of them).

Even so, some observations are notable.

First, as discussed further in chapter 6, some slow privatizers have fared better than fast ones, yet the issue is not speed per se, but a rapid move to a market economy. Although studies have found that growth has come disproportionately from newly created firms, privatizing existing firms ensures that these new firms have assets with which to work (McMillan and Woodruff 2002).

Second, building a consensus is important and takes time. As noted above, many reforms perforce had to be done quickly. Prices had to be freed, and firms had to be sold rapidly, especially if the state had lost control and firms operated in limbo. But other changes, such as improving accounting or a court system, take time to accomplish. Accelerating such reforms precludes the discussions

needed for compromises and consensus building. Even if such reforms are not reversed, they may not bear fruit if complementary measures are not taken. As Larry Summers put it, "Well executed policies that are 30 degrees off are much more effective than poorly executed policies that are spot on…. the ability to do things we take for granted in modern market economies is actually a crucial part of success [in the transition economies]" (World Bank 2005b). Some political systems seem to enable consensus building better than others (World Bank 2002a, 2002c). And competitive democracies (such as the Czech Republic, Hungary, Poland, Slovenia) have sustained reforms better than noncompetitive political regimes (such as Belarus, Uzbekistan, Turkmenistan), though here it is hard to distinguish the effect of new leaders from the effect of new political regimes.

Third, policies and endowments, including institutions, are not entirely independent of each other. Societies take many years to change, and in retrospect it was unrealistic to have expected market-supporting institutions to emerge rapidly in response to demand. If policies are effective only when there is a broad consensus about them—rather than any particular reform measure per se, or the zeal and speed with which it is implemented—this also depends on endowments and institutions. Assured of broad support for the reform course, governments can change the implementation of policies to respond to opportunities and shocks (for example, by speeding up or slowing privatization, or adjusting budget deficits), with good results, as in Poland and Hungary.

## Notes

1. The large literature on the transition includes the World Bank's *World Development Report 1996* and a report examining the first 10 years of transition (World Bank 2002c). Looking at the ingredients for successful transition, the World Bank's 2002 report emphasized the role of policies facilitating the entry of new firms and limiting the flow of resources to old industries; and the role of market institutions that, among other things, enforced property rights and ensured good governance. It also indicated that

competitive democracies (that is, those that established and protected civil liberties and political rights permitting multiparty democratic elections) recovered sooner and grew faster than others. While recognizing the importance of initial conditions, the report concluded that after the first few years, policy and institutional reforms had been more important than those conditions in explaining performance.

2. For example, in 1985 the Soviet Union used 0.95 ton of oil equivalent per $1,000 of GDP, nearly double the 0.5 ton used by OECD countries (IMF, World Bank, OECD, and EBRD 1991).

3. The 14 CSB countries are Albania, Bosnia and Herzegovina, Bulgaria, Croatia, the Czech Republic, Estonia, Hungary, Latvia, Lithuania, the Former Yugoslav Republic of Macedonia, Poland, Romania, the Slovak Republic, and Slovenia. The CIS comprises Armenia, Azerbaijan, Belarus, Georgia, Kazakhstan, the Kyrgyz Republic, Moldova, the Russian Federation, Tajikistan, Turkmenistan, Ukraine, and Uzbekistan.

4. In several countries, high excise taxes on tobacco and cigarettes attracted well-organized smuggling operations that also moved drugs, weapons, and people (illegal immigrants and victims of bondage).

5. Condon and Ramachandran (1993) show that this buildup would plateau and that the situation would correct itself.

6. As measured by the European Bank for Reconstruction and Development's transition indicator.

7. Selowsky and Martin (1998) use panel data to measure the effect of reforms (using a liberalization index) on growth after controlling for initial conditions and other factors (such as dummies for war). The coefficient on the liberalization index is statistically significant. However, Heybey and Murell (1999) find that correcting for its possible endogeneity (using initial level, share of industry, and the like as instruments) the liberalization index does not explain growth during the first four years of the transition. Brown and Earle (2004) find that interfirm reallocation of output, labor, and capital are not related to productivity, although privatization improves such reallocation.

*Chapter 7*

# Financial Liberalization:
# What Went Right, What Went Wrong?

THE FINANCIAL LIBERALIZATION that took place in the developing countries in the 1980s and 1990s was part of the general move toward giving markets a greater role in development. It was also a reaction to several factors specific to finance: the costs, corruption, and inefficiencies associated with using finance as an instrument of populist, state-led development; a desire for more financial resources; citizens' demands for better finance and lower implicit taxes and subsidies; and the pressures exerted on repressed financial systems by greater international trade, travel, migration, and better communications.

The financial reforms went beyond the interest rate liberalization that had been recommended by the so-called Washington Consensus. To varying degrees, governments also allowed the use of foreign currency instruments and opened up capital accounts. Domestic markets developed in central bank and government debt, and international markets expanded in government and private bonds. Capital markets developed, but less rapidly, and were most successful in the larger, already rapidly growing, East and South Asian countries. State banks continued to have a major role for much of the 1990s; their privatization was gradual and often proved costly. Central banks moved away from trying to finance development; they became more independent and successfully focused on keeping inflation low, but their debt increasingly absorbed bank deposits.

Certainly the reforms produced some gains. But the growth benefits of the financial and nonfinancial reforms in the 1990s were less than expected. Financial crises raised questions of whether financial liberalization was the wrong model, what had gone wrong, and the appropriate direction of future financial sector policy. Overall, the 1990s is probably best considered a precursor of better things that will take some time to achieve.

Section 1 of this chapter describes why and how financial liberalization occurred. Section 2 discusses the outcomes of financial liberalization during the 1990s, including the crises that occurred and their relation to macroeconomic policies, financial liberalization, and the overhangs of old economic and political systems. Section 3 summarizes the lessons from the experience of the 1990s, and section 4 draws suggestions for future policy. Section 5 concludes the chapter.

## 1. From Financial Repression to Financial Liberalization

The financial repression that prevailed in developing and transition countries in the 1970s and 1980s reflected a mix of state-led development, nationalism, populism, politics, and corruption. The financial system was treated as an instrument of the treasury: governments allocated credit at below-market interest rates, used monetary policy instruments and state-guaranteed external borrowing to ensure supplies of credit for themselves and public sector firms, and directed part of the resources that were left to sectors they favored. State banks were considered necessary to carry out the directed credit allocations,[1] as well as to reduce dependence on foreigners. Bank supervisors focused on complying with the often intricate requirements of directed credit rather than with prudential regulations. Interest rates to depositors were kept low to keep the costs of loans low. In some cases, low deposit and loan rates were also populist measures intended to improve income distribution.[2]

Repressed finance was thus an implicit tax and subsidy system through which governments transferred resources from depositors receiving low interest rates (and from those borrowers not receiving directed credits) to borrowers paying low rates in the public sector and to favored parts of the private sector. Governments had to allocate credit because they set interest rates that generated excess demand for credits. Capital controls were needed not (as often argued) to protect national saving, but to limit capital outflows fleeing low interest rates and macroeconomic instability, and to increase the returns from the inflation tax.[3] In effect, capital controls were a tax on those unwilling or unable to avoid them and they encouraged corruption (Hanson 1994).

## Factors behind Financial Liberalization

Three general factors provided an impetus for the move to financial liberalization: poor results, high costs, and pressures from globalization. This section discusses each in turn.

### Poor Results

Together, the limited mobilization and inefficient allocation of financial resources slowed economic growth (McKinnon 1973; Shaw 1973). Low interest rates discouraged the mobilization of finance, and bank deposit growth slowed in the 1980s in the major countries (figure 7.1). Capital flight occurred despite capital controls (Dooley et al. 1986). Allocation of scarce domestic credits and external loans to government deficits, public

FIGURE 7.1

### Increase in Average Deposits/GDP in Major Countries, by Regions, 1960s–90s

(difference between 3-year average of bank deposits/GDP at the end of each decade)

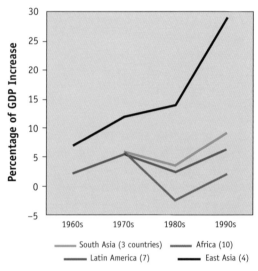

*Source*: IMF, *International Financial Statistics.*

*Note*: Countries and regions covered are:
East Asia: Indonesia, Republic of Korea, Malaysia, the Philippines, Thailand.
Latin America: Argentina, Brazil, Chile, Colombia, Mexico, Peru, República Bolivariana de Venezuela.
Africa: Burkina Faso, Cameroon, Côte d'Ivoire, Ghana, Kenya, Mali, Nigeria, Senegal, Tanzania, Uganda.
South Asia: Bangladesh, India, Pakistan.

sector "white elephants," and unproductive private activities yielded low returns, crowded out more efficient potential users, and encouraged wasteful use of capital.

Financial repression also worsened income distribution. Subsidies on directed credits were often large, particularly in periods of high inflation, and actual allocations often went to large borrowers.[4] The low interest rates led to corruption and to the diversion of credits to powerful parties. Diversions tended to grow over time, particularly when inflation reduced real interest rates on credits, and rising fiscal deficits and directed credits absorbed more of the limited deposits.

### High Costs

The repressed systems were costly. Banks, particularly state banks and development banks, periodically required recapitalization and the takeover of their external debts by governments. Political pressures and corruption were widespread. Loan repayments were weak because loans financed inefficient activities, because loan collection efforts were insufficient, and because borrowers tended to treat loans from the state banks simply as transfers. Typically, banks and other intermediaries rolled over their nonperforming loans until a period of inflation wiped out depositors' claims and permitted a general default. Since intermediaries were not forced to follow reasonable prudential norms or mark their portfolios to market, the losses were nontransparent, even to the governments that often owned them. Inflation also helped to conceal the problems of commercial banks through their earnings on low interest deposits. The hidden costs of the repressed systems became more apparent once financial liberalization began.

## Pressures from Globalization

Perhaps most important, financial repression came under increasing pressure from the growth of trade, travel, and migration as well as the improvement of communications.[5] The increased access to international financial markets broke down the controls on capital outflows on which the supply of low-cost deposits had depended.[6] Capital controls may be effective temporarily, but over time mechanisms (such as overinvoicing imports and underinvoicing exports) develop to subvert them (Arioshi et al. 2000; Dooley 1996). These mechanisms became more accessible as goods and people became more internationally mobile.

## *The Evolution of Financial Liberalization*

The shift in policies differed in timing, content, and speed from country to country and included many reversals. Broadly:

- African countries turned to financial liberalization in the 1990s, often in the context of stabilization and reform programs supported by the International Monetary Fund and

World Bank, as the costs of financial repression became clear.

- In East Asia, the major countries liberalized in the 1980s, though at different times and to different degrees. For example, Indonesia, which had liberalized capital flows in 1970, liberalized interest rates in 1984, but the Republic of Korea did not liberalize interest rates formally until 1992. Low inflation generally kept East Asian interest rates reasonable in real terms, however. In most countries, connected lending within industrial-financial conglomerates and government pressures on credit allocation remained important.

- In South Asia, financial repression began in the 1970s with the nationalization of banks in India (1969) and Pakistan (1974). Interest rates and directed credit controls were subsequently imposed and tightened, but for much of the 1970s and 1980s real interest rates remained reasonable. Liberalization started in the early 1990s with a gradual freeing of interest rates; a reduction in reserve, liquidity, and directed credit requirements; and liberalization of equity markets.

- In Latin America, episodes of financial liberalization occurred in the 1970s but financial repression returned, continued, or even increased in the 1980s, with debt crises, high inflation, government deficits, and the growth of populism (Dornbusch and Edwards 1991). In the 1990s, substantial financial liberalization occurred, although the degree and timing varied across countries.

- In the transition economies, financial liberalization took place fairly rapidly in the 1990s in the context of the reaction against communism (Bokros, Fleming, and Votava 2001; Sherif, Borish, and Gross 2003).

The earliest policy changes generally focused on interest rates. In many instances governments raised interest rates with a "stroke of the pen" to mobilize more of the resources needed to finance budget deficits and to enable the private sector to play a greater role in development. (Some interest rate increases, designed to curb capital flight, were intended more for stabilization than for liberalization.) New financial instruments were introduced that had freer rates and were subject to lower directed credit requirements. Some countries also began admitting foreign currency deposits, to attract offshore funds and foreign currency holdings into the financial system as well as to allow residents legal access to foreign currency assets (Hanson 2002; Honohan and Shi 2003; Savastano 1992, 1996).

Partial interest rate liberalizations soon generated pressures for more general freeing of interest rates (albeit in some cases after reversals of liberalization). As borrowers directed funds into deregulated instruments and sectors, demand for low-cost loans increased and repayments on them deteriorated.[7] Unfortunately, when the macroeconomic situation was unstable and interest rates were freed, very high real interest rates developed, creating corporate and banking problems that added to the overhang of weak credits that were exposed by liberalization.

At very different speeds in different countries, interest rate liberalization came to be supplemented by other changes:[8]

- Central banks were made more independent. They abandoned their earlier developmental role to focus on limiting inflation, often in the context of stabilization programs.

- Reserve requirements and directed credit were eased.

- Capital accounts were liberalized, even in countries where domestic foreign currency instruments remained banned. Foreigners were allowed to participate in capital markets[9] and private corporations were allowed to raise funds offshore.

- Markets were set up for central bank debt and government debt. Equity markets were set up in the transition countries and liberalized where they already existed.

- In some countries, pension systems added defined contribution/defined benefits elements, often operated by private intermediaries.

- Gradually, state banks were privatized. Banking competition increased, as a result of the entry of new domestic and foreign banks and, in some cases, nonbank intermediaries.

In general, however, the financial reforms of the 1990s focused on freeing interest rates and credit allocations, and made much less effort to improve the institutional basis of finance—a much harder, longer task.

## 2. Outcomes in the Financial Sector during the 1990s

Private sector credit is a key factor in growth.[10] Banks can intermediate funds and take risks only if private credit is not crowded out by government debt. Over the 1990s, deposits grew faster than in the previous decade, but in many countries bank credit to the private sector from domestic sources grew only slowly. The increase in loanable funds was largely absorbed by the public sector.

### Deposit Growth

Bank deposits grew as a share of the gross domestic product (GDP) in the 1990s, unlike in the 1980s (figure 7.1 above and Hanson 2003b). Thus, most major countries and most regions achieved a major objective of financial liberalization. And in India and some East Asian and Latin American countries, nonbank deposits supplemented the rapid growth in bank deposits.

Box 7.1 discusses the resumption of deposit growth in India as it gradually liberalized, as well as the growth of India's capital market.

Many factors contributed to the deposit growth, including the slowdown in inflation in the 1990s,[11] the positive real deposit rates, and new deposit instruments. Another factor was the legalization of foreign currency deposits. Deposits in foreign currency grew as a share of total deposits in many countries in the 1990s, and in some cases they supplied more than half the total by the end of the decade (Honohan and Shi 2003).[12] Not surprisingly, the foreign cur-

**BOX 7.1**

## India—A Successful Liberalizer with Strong Capital Markets

India liberalized its financial sector gradually over the 1990s, with particular success in capital markets, while avoiding any major crisis. In the 1980s, India had a repressed financial system (Hanson 2001, 2003a). This, plus increasing macroeconomic instability, slowed deposit growth. Financial liberalization was part of greater reliance on the private sector after the 1991 foreign exchange crisis. Interest rates were raised and gradually freed, bank regulations and supervision were strengthened, and nonbank financial corporations (NBFCs) were allowed under easier regulations (Hanson 2003a). After a 1991 capital market crisis, regulations were strengthened, listings were liberalized, foreign investors were allowed in, and infrastructure was substantially improved (Shah and Thomas 1999; Nayak 1999).

Bank deposits of nationals and nonresident Indians resumed their growth and NBFC deposits grew sharply after 1992. The stock, bond, and commercial paper markets became among the most vibrant in developing countries, providing nearly one-fourth of India's corporate funding from 1992 to 1996 (Reserve Bank of India 1998) with listings more than doubling from 2,000 in 1991 to over 5,000 (Standard and Poor's 2003). The post-1997 economic slowdown led to a stock market fall, problems in the NBFCs (which were wound down), and crises in the government development banks and mutual fund, though public sector commercial banks performed surprisingly well. Recently, large capital inflows and higher growth have led to low interest rates and better bank performance.

Although India's approach to financial liberalization served it well, three major issues remain: (1) crowding out, with government debt now absorbing more than 37 percent of bank deposits compared to about 24 percent at the end of the 1980s; (2) a weak information and legal framework, which, despite efforts at improvement, still contributes to nonperforming loans and limits access to credit; and (3) the still-dominant role of public sector banks.

India: Money (M3 in Sept.)/GDP, Deposit Rate and Inflation

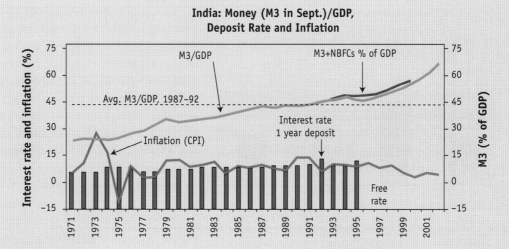

*Source*: Reserve Bank of India data.
CPI. Consumer price index.
GDP. Gross domestic product.

rency deposits were popular with members of the public, many of whom had lost their savings and pensions in inflation and repressed financial systems.[13] But foreign currency loans were also popular with borrowers.[14]

The reforms reduced the burden on banks, widening their discretion over the allocation of resources and lowering required reserves. Now that governments could raise resources from newly developing debt markets, they had less need to require banks to invest in government debt or to hold low-return reserves with the central bank that were invested in government debt. In many of the 25 largest developing countries, the average ratio of reserves to deposits fell over the 1990s (Hanson 2003b). Directed credit requirements were reduced, interest rates were raised on remaining directed credits, and nominal market rates fell.

## Credit: Absorption of Deposits by the Public Sector

Bank credit to the private sector grew much less than bank deposits and other bank liabilities in the 1990s (figure 7.2).

Access to credit expanded less than many observers hoped after the financial reforms, though it improved toward the end of the1990s. Panel studies had suggested that financial liberalization would make more credit available to a wider group of borrowers. (See, for example, Schiantarelli et al. 1994, and works cited there.) After liberalization there was some growth, but in practice government and central bank debt crowded out many borrowers. In some countries where nonbank intermediaries (henceforth, nonbanks) grew, they did increase lending to nontraditional borrowers. But both banks and nonbanks were hindered by the lack of information on borrowers and weaknesses in the legal and judicial systems in the areas of collateral and creditors' rights.

Instead of increasing private credit, the rise in bank deposits over the 1990s tended to be absorbed by government and central bank debt, and by banks strengthening their offshore positions. In particular, in the 25 developing and transition countries with the largest banking systems, the average ratio of net government debt to bank deposits rose by more than 60 percent, from about 13 percent in 1993 to about 21 percent in 2000 (Hanson 2003b).[15] Similar patterns prevailed in the larger African countries.[16]

The main reason for the rise in government debt was postcrisis bank restructurings, involving replacement of weak private credits, particularly in Brazil, Indonesia, Jamaica, Mexico, and some African countries. But growing government deficits also played a key role in some cases, notably India and Turkey. In general, the increases in banks' holdings of government debt reflected rises in the stock of government debt, rather than any increased attractiveness of government debt to banks, or decreased willingness of banks to take risks.[17]

Banks also increased their net holdings of central bank debt—substantially in some countries—despite falling reserve requirements. On average in the 25 developing countries with the largest financial systems, banks' net holdings of central bank debt rose by nearly 5 percentage points of GDP over the 1990s (Hanson 2003b). As a monetary policy instrument, central bank

FIGURE 7.2

## Changes in the Ratios of Bank Assets and Liabilities Plus Capital to GDP, 1990s

(averages by country group)

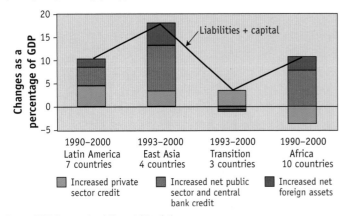

Source: IMF, International Financial Statistics.

Note: Countries covered are the same as in Figure 1. South Asia is excluded because countries in that region do not report private credit or capital separately.

debt had advantages over the previous instruments of credit controls on individual banks, changes in reserve requirements, and variations in central bank lending, which had tended to limit competition, to affect banks bluntly, and to affect weak banks heavily. But the use of central bank debt had costs, in that it crowded out would-be borrowers. Central banks often sold their debt to sterilize capital inflows as well as to tighten money when capital flowed out.[18] Central banks may also have sold debt to mop up some of the liquidity that arose from lowered reserve requirements, or when they needed to fund their own quasi-fiscal deficits that arose from negative spreads between their assets and liabilities.

Another reason for the slow growth of private credit was that banks themselves increased their net holdings of foreign assets for hedging purposes (see figure 7.2 above). Those in the largest 25 developing-country markets went from essentially a balanced foreign position in 1990, on average, to net borrowing of nearly 1 percent of GDP in 1993 and nearly 3 percent of GDP in 1997, before reverting to being net holders of foreign assets in 2000 (Hanson 2003b). After 1997, external lenders cut credit lines, banks wound down their external borrowings, and banks increased their external assets.[19]

Given the limited growth of private sector credit, a variable that has been shown to be linked with economic growth,[20] it is not surprising that the rise in GDP growth associated with the financial (and general) liberalization of the 1990s was less than hoped for.

However, the story is more complex than the slow growth of private credit. In the major developing countries, especially in East Asia, the average growth of private sector credit (especially including external credits) and of GDP was much faster before 1996 than after. About 1995, some countries began to experience financial crises. Much of the private credit extended by banks and nonbanks proved to be unproductive, in the sense that it became nonperforming before or during the crises. During bank restructurings, these credits were replaced with government debt (to ensure depositors were paid); when eventually

executed, the associated collateral was usually worth less than 30 percent of the face value of the loans, suggesting how unproductive the growth in private sector credit had been. In the transition countries and African countries the quality of credit issues was typically more related to the public sector's use of the credits.[21]

## Bond and Equity Markets

Government and central bank bond market development was fairly successful in the 1990s. By 2000, more than 40 developing countries, including all but one of the 25 with the largest financial systems, had government bond markets (Del Valle and Ugolini 2003), and more than 20 had central bank debt markets. The government bond markets allowed governments to reduce their reliance on foreign borrowing. The supply of this debt was inelastic, but it was attractive to banks for several reasons: its interest rates had been freed, it carried a low capital requirement, it was less risky than private debt, and it had liquidity once the markets became active.

The growth of domestic equity and bond markets contributed to private sector financing in East Asia and India during the 1990s. In the major East Asian equity markets, market capitalization exceeded $20 billion in 2000, having risen 80 percent or more (except in Thailand) since 1990. Turnover averaged more than 50 percent and listings in the individual countries rose at least 40 percent between 1990 and 2000, to the point where they all exceeded listings in every Latin American country except Brazil (Standard and Poor's 2003). The Indian market was even more successful in providing resources to a wide group of firms after listing regulations were eased (see box 7.1 above). Chile's market also did reasonably well, though its turnover was low because of the pension funds' buy-and-hold policies. However, even in these countries, banks remain the main source of finance.

Elsewhere, equity markets were less successful. On the seven largest Latin American stock exchanges, listings have declined since 1997, and on five of those seven they have declined ever since 1990; turnover in all seven is less than 50 percent of market capitalization (Standard and Poor's 2003). In transition countries, equity markets were created as part of the privatization process,[22] often with only belated recognition of the importance of regulatory frameworks. Listings declined in most of these markets as some privatized companies were taken off the market. Market capitalization is less than $20 billion, except in Poland and the Russian Federation, and turnover exceeds 50 percent only in Hungary (Standard and Poor's 2003).

Several factors lie behind the slow development of equity markets in developing and transition countries. The first is that potential investors are deterred by the low turnover in these markets (usually much less than 75 percent compared with 85 percent in even the smaller deciles of traded companies on the U.S. NASDAQ) and by low liquidity, which reflects the small sizes of the listed companies as well as the low turnover (Shah and Thomas 2003). Second, listings on stock exchanges have been reduced by takeovers of firms by multinational corporations, and trading has been reduced by the migration of major firms' listings to industrial-country markets. In 2000, companies listed offshore accounted for about 55 percent of the market capitalization in 15 middle-income countries, and for 27 percent of the market capitalization in 25 low-income countries; much of the trading in these stocks also takes place offshore (Claessens, Klingebiel, and Shmuckler 2003). Family firms that could list often do not, partly because the benefits are not great, partly because these firms often have privileged access to credit through related banks, and partly because they fear that dilution of ownership will reduce their control. Third and more fundamentally, weak institutional factors—poor information, poor treatment of minority shareholders, and weak regulation of market participants—weaken the interest of investors, both domestic and foreign, in many equity markets (Glaeser, Johnson, and Shleifer 2001; LaPorta, López de Silanes, and Shleifer 2002b; Black 2001).

The better performance of the East Asian and Indian markets seems to result more from superior economic performance than from any obvious institutional advantage. This suggests that in the short run, equity market growth mainly reflects general economic performance, which attracts foreign investors willing to risk sums that are small to them but large relative to the market. Simply setting up a market may not add much to growth or allow firms to raise funding. Over time, however, as institutions improve, equity markets do seem to contribute to economic growth (Levine 2003; Levine and Zervos 1998). Another important element in equity market performance seems to be foreign investor participation (Bekaert, Harvey, and Lundblad 2003).

Private bond markets grew even less than equity markets in the 1990s. They share the problems of equity markets as well as having some of their own. Concerns about potential future macroeconomic instability have led bond buyers to demand high returns for committing funds for the long term, and deterred issues of long-term bonds. Often only public sector firms issued long-term bonds, and then only in a few countries, notably in South Asia. Potential buyers of private bonds were also deterred by lack of protection in law and in fact for bondholders' rights, and by the lack of good bankruptcy legislation and enforcement. Nonetheless, some private bond markets have developed, for example, in India, and in Mexico, recently, for securitized housing finance.

## External Finance for the Private Sector

Within the private sector in developing countries, external borrowing grew faster than domestic borrowing in the first part of the 1990s, as large private companies increasingly drew on external credits. For example, in 17 of the countries with the largest financial markets, the ratio of private sector foreign borrowing (of more than one year's maturity) to borrowings from domestic banks increased fairly steadily, from 16.5 percent in 1990 to 27 percent in 1997.[23] Short-term borrowing also grew substantially. However, after 1997 these credits slowed in dollar terms. In the same 17 countries, external credit to the private sector changed little in dollar terms. However, the ratio of these credits to domestic credit rose by 50 percent by 2000, reflecting crisis-related devaluations and the removal of private sector credits from banks in restructurings in these countries.

The external credits to the private sector were narrowly distributed. They went only to internationally creditworthy borrowers, and four countries accounted for the bulk of private sector external borrowing (in dollars) in 2000: Brazil (27 percent), Mexico (12 percent), Indonesia (9 percent), and Thailand (7 percent).

Offshore equity sales were another source of capital for many large private companies in the 1990s. The numerous developing-country companies that were listed offshore in 2000 largely reflected issues of global depository rights and American depository rights during the 1990s. Of course, this source of capital was also narrowly distributed.

While financial liberalization benefited large, well-run companies and, indirectly, other borrowers in developing countries, it raised banks' risks. The best firms obtained loans and equity finance offshore at less cost than in the domestic market, albeit with currency risk.[24] This left a larger portion of the limited domestic private credit available to other borrowers, but it also increased the average risk in the banks' loan portfolios. Moreover, banks in developing and transition countries increased their net intermediation of external loans up to 1997, especially in East Asia, and they also guaranteed some direct external borrowings by the corporate sector, typically off their balance sheets.

The external borrowings were a major factor in the East Asian external payments crises and were also important in other crises of the 1990s. As external borrowings grew, lenders shortened maturities, creating maturity mismatches for borrowers. Further, loans made by financial intermediaries based on their own external borrowing, though typically matched in terms of currency, entailed substantial risks when the borrowers lacked an assured source of foreign exchange. Eventually, lenders refused to roll over their credits because they considered the risks too high. This generated both a banking crisis and a foreign exchange crisis. The resulting sharp devaluations increased debt-servicing problems on many foreign currency loans and led to calls on the guarantees, worsening the difficulties of firms and banks.

## Financial Intermediaries

Most of the impact of financial reforms on the institutional structure of the financial sector was not felt until the latter half of the 1990s. This limited the gains from liberalization during the decade and contributed to crises.

State banks, with their well-known problems (LaPorta, López de Silanes, and Shleifer 2002a), decreased in importance only after 1995, and indeed still dominated many financial systems in 2000 (figure 7.3). The continued large state bank presence meant that credit allocations changed only slowly, despite liberalization. The problems of state banks after liberalization were most obvious in the transition countries,[25] where the banks often simply continued to lend to traditional clients or were captured by politically powerful groups; as a result, their loans were unproductive and their already large portfolios of nonperforming loans increased. State banks in other countries had similar problems. The continued dominance of these banks, the associated weakness in credit allocation, and the implied state guarantees that allowed them to raise increasing deposits despite their high incidence of nonperforming loans, all limited the gains from liberalization and accounted for a substantial part of the cost of crises in the 1990s.

Private banks changed gradually with liberalization, entry of foreign banks, and fiercer competition, but their deficiencies also contributed to unproductive lending and crises. Their credit management skills did not keep pace with changes in the environment such as the growth of foreign currency operations and the greater competition that their traditional borrowers were facing in the real sector. Moreover, many private banks in East Asia and some Latin American countries were parts of industrial-financial conglomerates and continued to provide funding to their increasingly unprofitable industrial partners. State banks that were privatized to local buyers in weak institutional

FIGURE 7.3

**State Ownership in Banking, 1998–2000**

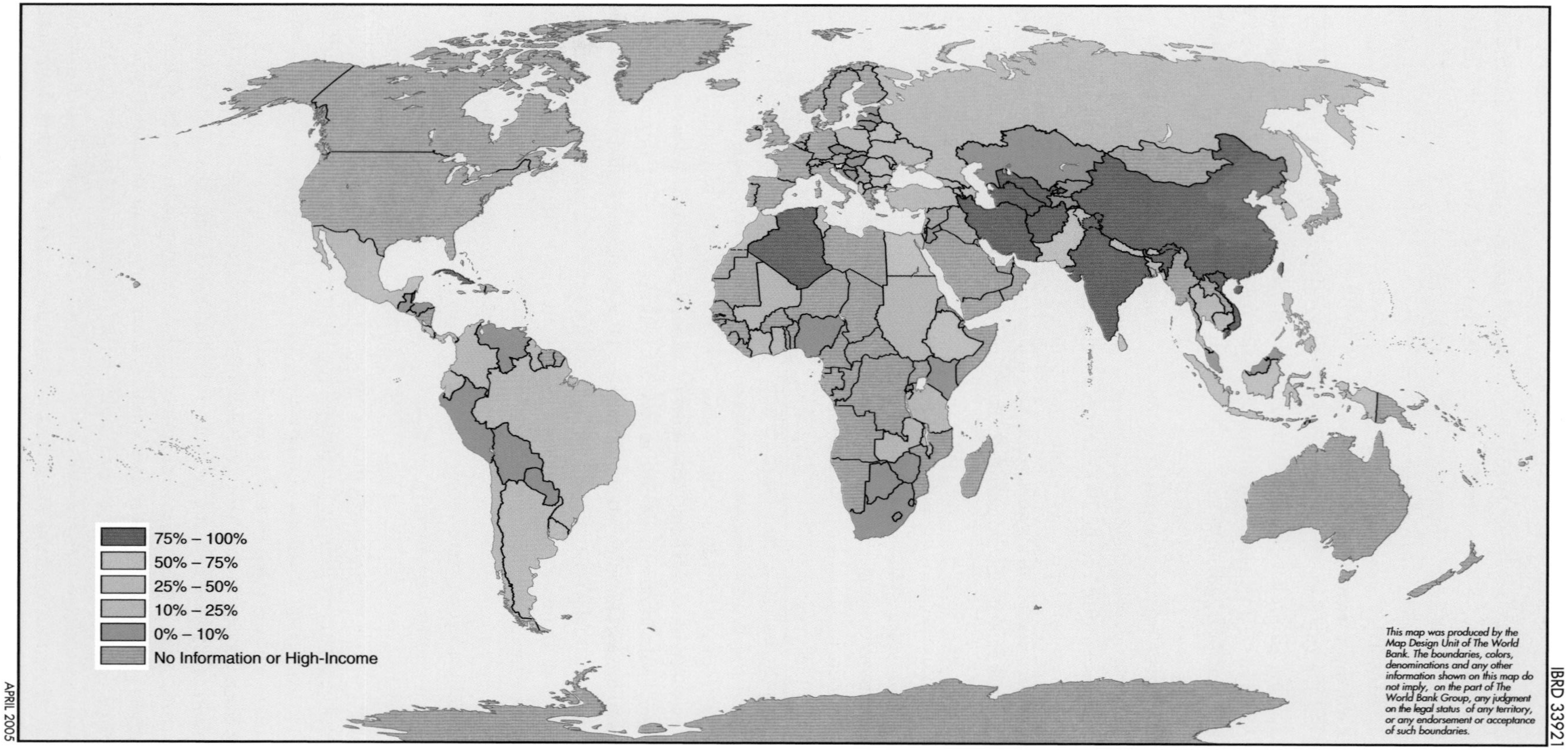

75% – 100%
50% – 75%
25% – 50%
10% – 25%
0% – 10%
No Information or High-Income

IBRD 33921

*This map was produced by the Map Design Unit of The World Bank. The boundaries, colors, denominations and any other information shown on this map do not imply, on the part of The World Bank Group, any judgment on the legal status of any territory, or any endorsement or acceptance of such boundaries.*

APRIL 2005

*Source:* Map Design Unit, World Bank.

environments often suffered similar problems and had to be renationalized.

Foreign banks enlarged their role as new policies eased restrictions on their entry in the latter half of the 1990s, particularly in transition countries but also in Latin America and Africa.[26] Their entry increased competition in banking and cut costs for bank clients. They competed fiercely for the best clients and drove down profits on business with them, and they also competed in lending to small firms.[27]

A second approach to increasing competition, taken by a few countries, was to simply allow more banks, by lowering entry requirements.[28] Unfortunately, many of these new banks were "pocket banks," capturing deposits to lend to their owners' businesses and often suffering problems. A third approach was to allow the growth of nonbank financial corporations (box 7.2). These intermediaries also often suffered from problems of risky and connected lending and were often the first to fail when credit tightened.

Greater competition can also create problems for banks by cutting their profits (Caprio and Summers 1996; Dooley 2003). Although this problem seems to be mainly one of adjusting to competition (Demirgüç-Kunt and Detragiache 1998), it does force owners to decide whether they should continue costly competition, try to exit, or loot the bank. Thus regulation and supervision, particularly with regard to bank intervention and exit, are important issues when liberalization increases competition.

## Regulation, Supervision, and Deposit Insurance

### Banking Regulation and Supervision

Improvements in the prudential regulation and supervision of banks lagged behind the liberalizations of the 1990s and contributed to crises. The oversight of banks in developing countries started from a low base in the 1990s because, during the period of financial repression, bank supervisors had focused on compliance with directed credit rules.

International standards for supervision—the 25 Basel Core Principles—were not agreed upon until September 1997. Countries did enact their own prudential regulations and upgraded supervision,

**BOX 7.2**
**Nonbank Financial Intermediaries (NBFIs) in the 1990s**

NBFIs such as finance companies, co-op banks, and nonbank financial corporations exist in many countries and in the 1990s some of them were an important factor in private sector credit and deposit mobilization. For example, India eased restrictions on nonbank financial corporations in 1992 and by 1996 their deposits were equal to more than 5 percent of broad money (box 7.1 above). In Thailand and Malaysia, finance companies' deposit and credit growth picked up in the early 1990s. In Latin America, co-op banks and housing banks in Colombia have been important for some time. NBFIs usually offered higher deposit rates and credit in different forms and to different clients than banks—for example, loans for construction, consumer credit, and small borrowers. NBFIs also were often subject to easier regulations on interest rates, reserves, and capital than were banks, as well as less supervision. However, NBFIs had a history of periodic crises in Latin America and East Asia, as, for example, in Thailand in the 1980s (Sundararajan and Balino 1991, 47–48). After 1997, many NBFIs in India, Malaysia, and Thailand went bankrupt, depositors shifted to banks, and, to some degree, banks increased their loans to the former NBFI borrowers.

but implementation—a political as well as a technical issue—often lagged, even after costly crises. Enforcement was patchy, even of weak regulations on income recognition, provisioning, capital, and connected lending, and weak banks continued in operation. International standards on minimum bank capital were not set until

1988, in the Basel agreements between industrial countries for internationally active banks.

The issues in improving regulation and supervision were not just technical but also political. The crises of the 1990s did engender attempts to improve regulation and supervision. But even then, regulations were often not strengthened immediately and forbearance was used to limit the capital injections that governments otherwise would have had to make. For example, in East Asia, regulations on capital, income recognition, and provisioning lagged behind international standards after the 1997 crisis (Barth, Caprio, and Levine 2001), and actual capital in many Indonesian and Thai banks was still well below the Basel standard in 2000.

By letting weak banks overexpand, the poor oversight contributed to the crises of the 1990s. In developing countries, weak banks that were allowed to continue operations often opted for a high-risk/high-return lending strategy or, in the worst case, were looted, as has also occurred in industrial countries. Market discipline, which might have restrained the expansion of weak banks, was limited by poor information and implicit or explicit deposit insurance.

## Deposit Insurance

Deposit insurance and, in crises, blanket guarantees, were standard recommendations of many financial advisors, and formal deposit insurance was initiated or improved in nearly 40 countries in the 1990s, mostly in transition and West African countries (Demirgüç-Kunt and Kane 2002; Demirgüç-Kunt and Sobaci 2001). In addition, countries such as Ecuador, Indonesia, Korea, Malaysia, Mexico, Thailand, and Turkey introduced blanket guarantees of bank liabilities. Deposit insurance and blanket guarantees are mainly attempts to reduce the risk of bank runs. Deposit insurance also has the secondary, consumer protection benefit of protecting unsophisticated depositors. Governments liked deposit insurance as it appeared to give benefits yet had no costs, at least until a crisis arrived. Local private banks, often politically important, liked it because it improved their competitiveness with state and foreign banks.

The actual impact of deposit insurance and guarantees has been mixed. The statistical evidence suggests that the gains from deposit insurance depend on its particular features, its credibility, and the institutional environment (Demirgüç-Kunt and Kane 2002; Demirgüç-Kunt and Detragiache 2002). In many cases, the insurance created large contingent guarantees, increased moral hazard, and reduced market discipline (Demirgüç-Kunt and Kane 2002; Demirgüç-Kunt and Sobaci 2001; Demirgüç-Kunt and Huizinga 1999). Large lender-of-last-resort support and blanket guarantees in effect provided unlimited insurance not only for depositors but for owners, many of whom looted their banks. They were particularly ineffective in the context of open capital markets and political and economic turmoil: for example, in Ecuador (IMF 2004b) and in Indonesia, liquidity support to banks was almost as large after the introduction of blanket guarantees as it was before. One reason may be that as the likelihood increases that the deposit insurance or a blanket guarantee will be used, its cost and credibility come into question, and runs on banks and the currency may increase (Dooley 2000).

Various attempts have been made to adjust deposit insurance so as to reduce moral hazard and increase market discipline ex ante, but usually depositor losses have been socialized ex post. For example, insurance limits have been placed on large deposits and on deposits carrying the high rates that are often offered by weak banks, but often the limits have not prevented the insurance from extending to all depositors in a crisis. Another approach has been to use risk-based deposit insurance premiums, in an attempt to offset the moral hazard and market discipline problem, but in practice the differentials in premiums have been substantially smaller than the differentials in bank risk (Laeven 2002a, 2000b, 2000c). This probably reflects the political power of the local bank owners who benefit most from deposit insurance.

To sum up, the schemes that were introduced for the support of depositors tended to create large contingent liabilities and to increase moral hazard while reducing market discipline. They contributed to crises and volatility by encouraging the funding of weak institutions after liberalization. Depositors and external lenders, expecting to be bailed out of any problems by a government guarantee, tended to supply too much funding, particularly to state banks and well-connected financial-industrial conglomerates. Market discipline, which might have limited this funding, was negligible, not just because of weak information but also because of the implicit and explicit guarantees.

## Equity and Bond Market Regulation

Improvements in equity and bond market regulation began in the 1990s and also proved difficult to implement. Even improving trading rules was difficult because of the difference between the interests of buyers and sellers, on the one hand, and the short-run interests of market operators, on the other. Also difficult to resolve has been the conflict between the interests of majority and minority shareholders. Attempts to create markets overnight have had only limited success, not only in cases of limited regulation (Czech Republic), but also where investor protection rules appeared to be reasonably good (Russia). Regulation in Poland seems to have been relatively successful, however (Black, Kraakmen, and Tarassova 2000; Glaesner, Johnson, and Shleifer 2001). As with bank regulation and supervision, the issues are not merely technical but also political.

## *Pensions*

As described in chapter 6, a major change in pension systems occurred in the 1990s, with many countries shifting from pay-as-you-go systems to systems in which at least part of pension income is based on full funding for individual accounts. Chile was the first developing country to adopt this approach, in 1981. Among the countries with large financial systems, Argentina, Colombia, Mexico, and Peru in Latin America, plus Hungary, Poland, and Thailand, all adopted variants of this system after 1994 (Fox and Palmer 2001). The new systems gave individuals much better access to their pensions and held the promise of generating demand for long-term financial instruments and thereby stimulating capital markets.

The results were not as good as anticipated. First, all systems had to cope with the change-over problem of paying existing pensioners while investing the contributions to the new system into assets. Without large fiscal surpluses, the change-over generated a large increase in government debt that the new pension system had to hold, as occurred in Argentina. As a result, the demand for long-term private instruments did not rise much. Thus the initial impact of pension reforms was simply to make the government's liability transparent. A second issue is that because capital markets typically are small, pension funds either generated price rises, as happened even in Chile, and/or had to invest in bank debt, as happened in Peru. Third, costs have been high in many of the private pension funds, reflecting set-up costs, insurance linked to the pensions, and a response to advertising that encouraged excessive shifts between funds. Some of these problems could have been reduced and country risk decreased for the individual accounts by allowing the funds to invest externally, but countries have usually tried to retain pension contributions and avoid possible balance of payments pressures.

## *Financial Sector Crises*

Financial sector and external payments crises were features of the 1990s.[29] Costly crises occurred in Mexico, the East Asian "Miracle" countries, Russia, Brazil, and some Eastern European and African countries. The new millennium began with crises starting in Argentina and Turkey and high nonperforming loans in China. Africa also suffered costly financial crises (figure 7.4).

What role did financial liberalization play in the financial and currency crises of the 1990s, dubbed the "twin crises" by Kaminsky and Reinhart (1999)? The discussion below first assesses the roles played by macroeconomic problems, financial liberalization, and weak lending by state banks and financial-industrial conglomerates and then outlines the difficult tradeoffs that policy makers faced in responding to crises over a short time horizon.

FIGURE 7.4

## Selected Financial Crises, 1980–99

**Estimated starting year and restructuring cost**

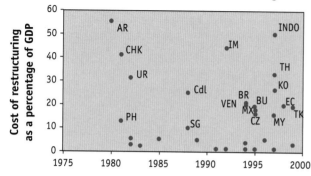

*Source:* Caprio et al. 2003.

*Note:* The figure illustrates the estimated financial costs of restructuring after selected crises, but not the losses in GDP.

## Macroeconomic Problems

Most crisis countries had high debt and larger than usual current account deficits and were pursuing exchange rate–based stabilization policies.[30] Many also had open capital accounts, but a causal association with crises is not clear: not all countries with open capital accounts experienced crises and, in the 1980s, crises had developed even in countries whose capital accounts were nominally closed.

The combination of high debt and exchange rate–based stabilization seems to be associated with unsustainable booms in capital inflows, imports, and GDP and shifts in relative prices, followed by reversals in these variables as financing slows and maturities shorten, while interest rates rise. The slowing of inflows reflects both the inherent characteristics of portfolio adjustment and the growth of investor concerns regarding debt-servicing capacity and exchange rate pegs.[31] The rises in interest rates may reflect a combination of smaller inflows, growing concerns about the sustainability of the exchange rate peg, and attempts to defend the peg with tight money, often for long periods. Eventually, the exchange rate depreciates and debts need to be restructured. Not surprisingly, the financial sector suffers a crisis in the downward phase of

such cycles, reflecting liquidity squeezes on banks that have borrowed externally; problems with borrowers, especially those indebted in foreign currency; and runs on the banks to speculate on the currency.

Various events may trigger a crisis. External shocks include deteriorating terms of trade, increases in international interest rates, and increases in risk premiums in industrial-country markets that automatically affect developing-country debt.[32] Contagion in financial markets has also been cited.[33] Domestically, unstable or inconsistent macroeconomic policies sooner or later lead to pressures against banks and the currency. Political developments, such as the ouster of presidents Marcos in the Philippines in 1986 and Soeharto in Indonesia in 1998, lead connected parties to liquidate their assets, putting pressure on banks and lenders with whom they did business.

## Financial Sector Liberalization

Financial sector liberalization seems to have been a factor in crises (Demirgüç-Kunt and Detragiache 1998, 2001; Kaminsky and Reinhart 1999). It increased capital inflows and deposits, which allowed rapid growth in credit to weak public and private enterprises and the government, as well as to real estate. Over time, the quality of the lending deteriorated. This may be one explanation for the lags between liberalization and financial crises (Demirgüç-Kunt and Detragiache 2001), and between financial crises and currency crises (Kaminsky and Reinhart 1999).[34] Eventually, corporate bankruptcies, banking problems, and runs on banks and currencies developed, particularly when the rapid credit growth and inflows slowed, real growth declined, and real interest rates rose.[35] These problems were often connected to unsustainable fiscal policy and the defense of unsustainable currency pegs with long periods of high interest rates. Problems in the timing and sequencing of liberalization, sometimes related to political issues, also contributed to the crises (box 7.3).

In assessing the role of financial liberalization in the 1990s crises, an important question is why international lenders and domestic depositors

**BOX 7.3**
**Problems with the Process of Financial Liberalization**

In the late 1980s Nigeria liberalized interest rates and bank entry but retained a multiple exchange rate regime that was accessible only through banks. This raised the demand for bank licenses, many of which went to well-connected parties who were interested in arbitraging foreign exchange between the multiple rates, not in banking. Though the number of banks tripled, the ratio of deposits and credit to GDP fell, and, by the 1990s, banks were experiencing significant distress (Lewis and Stein 2002).

In Korea, the de facto rapid liberalization of short-term borrowings in the early 1990s, both internationally and internally, led the heavily leveraged corporations to be increasingly financed by short-term inflows and through less regulated intermediaries. In the run-up to joining OECD, Korea had opened its capital account by freeing short-term foreign borrowings, but left longer-term borrowings subject to restrictions in an attempt to limit total capital inflows (Cho 2001). This policy encouraged a maturity mismatch in lending and a currency mismatch on the part of borrowers, especially since rates were much lower on foreign currency loans than domestic ones. Although deposit rates were formally liberalized in 1993, their rise was limited by moral suasion, government guidance, and high reserve requirements until 1996. New intermediaries (finance companies converted to merchant banks) sprang up to meet demands for funds by inter-

mediating external inflows. Bank trust accounts were liberalized and grew relative to bank deposits; they also were allowed to take short-term commercial paper, which had relatively free interest rates. Finally, the freeing of interest rates on consumer loans contributed to a shift of loanable funds to these activities and may have dampened Korea's saving rate, augmenting the country's increased reliance on (short-term) external borrowing.

Thailand set up its "offshore"/onshore Bangkok International Banking Facility in 1993 with tax and regulatory advantages that were justified as an attempt to create a regional financial center operated by national banks. The facility allowed locals to deposit in foreign currency and local borrowers to escape (albeit with short-term loans) from the government's tight money policy and foreign currency–denominated loans. Its operations became a major factor in the expansion of Thailand's external debt (Bordo et al. 2001; Alba, Hernandez, and Klingebiel 1999). Pressure on the government from these borrowers was probably a factor in the government's lengthy, costly attempt to defend the *baht* even as it supported the borrowers, taking a monetary stance inconsistent with the fixed exchange rate. After the devaluation, these obligations were a major factor in the banks' problems and in the closure of many finance companies.

supplied so much funding. Part of the large increases in loanable funds may have reflected a natural overshooting tendency in financial markets (Kindleberger 2000; Minsky 1992). But any such tendency was certainly exaggerated by the explicit and implicit guarantees that governments provided to lenders. Government debt was directly guaranteed (although after crises it was sometimes restructured). Growing private external debt, funneled through banks or guaranteed by them, and growing deposits carried at least an implicit guarantee, which ex post often became

explicit. Moreover, when liberalization led banks to lose franchise value and capital, weak regulation and supervision did not prevent bank owners from engaging in high-risk/high-return lending or even looting. Nor did it limit banks' overexposure to related borrowers. Thus market discipline was eroded by government guarantees, implicit or explicit, while weak regulation and supervision did not limit moral hazard.

Guarantees and their credibility may also explain why the crises in the 1990s seem to have happened relatively quickly (Dooley 2000).

According to this explanation, avoiding a crisis depends on maintaining foreign investors' and depositors' perceptions that the guarantees (and the exchange rate peg) are credible. Events, including fears of political change, can quickly change these perceptions, leading to shifts into foreign exchange, curtailment of short-term credits, and rollovers of maturing loans, triggering banking and exchange rate crises.[36]

### Weak Lending

A third factor in the 1990s crises was the weak lending, old and new, by the old financial intermediaries, notably state banks and industrial-financial conglomerates. Before liberalization these intermediaries had large overhangs of bad debt, which had been rolled over several times to favored borrowers. Financial liberalization made

these debts worse because of higher real interest rates and lower inflation. Moreover, lower protection and increased competition reduced traditional borrowers' ability to service their debts. However, the increased deposits and capital inflows associated with financial reform provided new funds that enabled the banks to roll over their loans again, adding to the ultimate volume of nonperforming loans. For example, in the early stages of liberalization in the transition countries, "most state banks continued to lend as instructed or for patronage purposes" (Sherif, Borish, and Gross 2003, 21). In East Asia, banks expanded their lending to related industrial conglomerates, which were increasingly overleveraged (Claessens, Djankov, and Lang 1998). In addition, crises tended to generate a shift of deposits to state banks, because of expectations of government

---

**BOX 7.4**

**Indonesia: Early Liberalization and Weaknesses Related to Political Connections**

In Indonesia the freeing of interest rates and easing of capital and reserve requirements contributed to large deposit growth, as well as a doubling of the number of commercial banks (Hanson 2001). By 1996, competition and the expansion of 10 private banks had reduced state banks to about 45 percent of the system. However, all banks were very weak (World Bank 1996, 1997a). Despite the rules, state banks were overexposed to well-connected borrowers, and private banks to their owners. State banks reported low capital and their reported nonperforming loans, though high, were understated, given the rollover of bad loans and other maneuvers. At least two state banks were insolvent. Loans were often inflated by "commissions" to loan officers. Private banks reported better figures but weak supervision provided no check on them. Exposure limits were not enforced and many small banks were bankrupt.

The spillover from the July 1997 Thai devaluation exposed these weaknesses and the dependence of

finance on the political regime. Capital outflow developed and rollovers of the large amount of short-term external loans stopped as investor concerns mounted (despite the imposition of limits on currency speculation). Monetary policy was loosened to ease borrowers' problems. The November IMF program brought little relief—runs on private banks and the currency speeded up with the closure of 16 banks (small depositors did not begin to be paid until January 1998) and the December illness of Soeharto. State banks, which benefited from shifts in deposits, made loans to well-connected borrowers on the basis of projected exports that did not materialize. In January 1998, outflows increased with the poor reception of the 1998–99 budget, panic buying of goods, riots that frightened Indonesians of Chinese origin, and the possibility of introducing a currency board. The exchange rate fell to less than one-seventh of its precrisis level. Massive central bank liquidity support, often well in excess of banks' capital and in some cases up to 75 percent of their assets, would guarantees.[37] This allowed further increases in lending to favored clients who often used the loans to buy foreign exchange and then defaulted on the loans.

The overhang and growth of state banks' non-performing loans, and their cleanup, were substantial elements in the crises of the 1990s. A notable example is Indonesia (box 7.4). In Thailand, more than 80 percent of Bank Krung Thai's loans became nonperforming. Brazil's BANESPA (the state bank of São Paulo) was estimated to have more than 90 percent nonperforming loans; the estimated cost of the federal government's 1997 cleanup, prior to privatizing the bank, was about $20 billion or nearly 3 percent of GDP. The Finance Ministry has estimated that restructuring Banco do Brasil and Caixa Economica Federal may cost $50 billion. In Argentina, the bankrupt state of the smaller provincial banks was exposed by the spillover of Mexico's "Tequila" Crisis; the support needed for their privatization amounted to about half their assets (Clarke and Cull 1999). In Eastern Europe, the cost of the public sector banks' bad debt overhang was enormous—for example, about 16 percent of GDP in Bulgaria and about 18 percent of GDP in the Czech Republic (Sherif, Borish, and Gross 2003). In China, official estimates of the nonperforming loans of the four largest state banks exceeded 20 percent of loans in 2003; various private estimates were much higher.

Privatization is often considered as a remedy for the weak lending of public sector banks, but it has been costly in cases where the state has retained a controlling interest or where sales have been made to weak owners whose operations

have doubled the money base had reserves not fallen (Kenward 2002; World Bank 2000c). Imposition of a blanket guarantee at the end of January temporarily slowed outflows. Soeharto's reelection in March was followed by severe riots, often directed against Indonesians of Chinese origin and Soeharto cronies. Capital outflows rose once again, as did liquidity support. In May 1998 Soeharto resigned but pressures on banks continued.

In sum, liberalization encouraged deposit growth and foreign inflows, but credit access depended not on profitability but on political connections, including access to external loans from international banks (corporations did much of Indonesia's external debt borrowing; the state banks' external borrowing was limited by policy). Lenders and depositors looked at connections, not at risk and corporate leverage. The easing of bank licensing and the lack of enforcement of exposure limits worsened this problem. Then, when political concerns developed, the well-connected tried to withdraw their assets and an outflow developed, exacerbated by the concerns of the middle-class Indonesian Chinese. As a result, the blanket guarantee stopped the bank runs only temporarily—total liquidity support was nearly as large after the blanket guarantee was imposed as before, according to the figures in Enoch et al. (2001). Of the US$20 billion liquidity support that went mostly to private banks, 96 percent was unrecoverable and a substantial amount was diverted into foreign exchange speculation, according to an ex post study by the National Auditor. The cost of the crisis is estimated at more than 50 percent of GDP. Bank Mandiri, a merger of four state banks of which at least two were bankrupt before the crisis began, accounted for about 30 percent of the cost of the crisis (more than 17 percent of GDP). More than 70 percent of the losses in the state banks were in loans that had to be taken off the books. The poor quality of these loans is shown by the eventual recovery rate of less than 30 percent, most of which was realized four to five years after the crisis.

were poorly regulated and supervised. Mexico's 1991 privatization is perhaps the best known example. Soon after privatization, partly because of the currency crisis, the Mexican government was forced to renationalize the banks; it then cleaned up their balance sheets at an estimated cost of more than US$70 billion and reprivatized them to international banks, beginning in 1998 (box 7.5).

In Eastern Europe, the initial bank privatizations went poorly, particularly where governments retained a controlling interest (Clarke, Cull and Shirley 2003). In Africa, too, the experience with bank privatization was often bad, with long delays and sales eventually made to undercapitalized owners who did not improve credit management and abandoned the banks when they lost their capital (box 7.6).

## Difficulties in Policy Responses to Crises

The crises presented difficult new policy problems. Traditional macroeconomic policies of tighter fiscal and monetary policy and devaluation were appropriate for reducing excess demand and current account deficits to financeable levels. But the financial sector problems, and their implications for the balance of payments, raised a new set of more complicated issues and tradeoffs, for which no single best practice exists.

To deal with an individual bank's problems, the standard recommended response is to provide liquidity support at high interest rates and then intervene with protection for small depositors. But banks become insolvent well before they become illiquid, and owners of insolvent banks may then choose a risky lending strategy or even attempt to loot the bank (de Juan 2002).[38] Moreover, prob-

---

**BOX 7.5**
**Bank Privatization in Mexico**

Mexico nationalized its commercial banks in 1982. It decided to privatize them in 1991, as part of liberalization and to raise fiscal resources. At the time, the privatization was acclaimed as a resounding success, fetching higher prices than predicted. Although open only to domestic purchasers, the sale was considered technically well designed and executed. Bidders were first qualified, and the auctions were transparent and quick, without scandal.

The macroeconomic (Tequila) crisis of 1995 took the shine off this success: loan defaults increased sharply with the collapse of the *peso* and the rise in interest rates. Failing banks were found to have made poor loans under the relaxed regulatory framework, often to politically powerful groups connected to their controlling owners (Haber and Kantor 2003; LaPorta and López de Silanes 2003). The connected lending meant that the banks had effectively financed much of their own purchase. Taking into account loans from development banks, the buyers actually had minimal equity, but this had not pre-

vented their purchase of the banks. The government renationalized the failed banks and protected the depositors but taxpayers were left with a huge bill, estimated at 18 percent of GDP.

The features of the sale that were praised earlier are now often criticized: the privatization for being too hasty and the purchase prices as too high. Yet a sale was considered necessary to raise fiscal resources and sustain the government's commitment to reform. The main mistakes were the exclusion of foreigners and the acceptance of purchases by politically powerful but heavily leveraged buyers. The exclusion of foreign bidders was partly a calculated risk to shore up domestic support in a nationalistic country. Even with foreign participation, highly leveraged locals might have bid more for the banks through their access to loans. Thus, above all, the Mexican experience illustrates not just a flawed privatization but the complicated issues that bank privatizers must juggle, including the difficult problems associated with dealing with local elites in a sector as sensitive as banking.

## BOX 7.6
## Bank Restructuring and Privatization in Sub-Saharan Africa

At the end of the 1980s many African banks were insolvent and illiquid. Governments undertook major restructuring programs over the 1990s to deal with these problems. A gradual return to macro-stability and balanced government budgets—a prerequisite for bank restructuring—occurred in programs supported by the International Monetary Fund (IMF) and the World Bank. Directed credits were abandoned and interest rates liberalized. Government arrears to the banking sector were often securitized on various terms, with debt service often guaranteed. Money markets were established. Many countries issued new banking laws, overhauled regulations, and set up supervisory authorities.

Bank restructurings were both organizational and financial and sometimes led to privatization, but the process also often required multiple restructurings and was hesitant (World Bank 2001c). Some banks, particularly public sector banks, were closed or weak branches were turned into agencies. In Benin, the extreme case, all public sector banks were closed in 1990, leaving the country without banks for some months until new private banks entered the market. In other cases, bad assets were provisioned and losses were absorbed by existing shareholders (governments and the private sector); in a few cases, new capital was injected by the private sector; and in others, bad loans were removed from banks. Asset recovery corporations were set up to manage bank liquidations and/or to recover loans and reimburse depositors/creditors (for example, in Cameroon, Côte d'Ivoire, Ghana, Uganda, and Senegal) with mixed results. Management was changed, staff retrenched, internal controls were put in place, and new loan procedures were gradually developed.

Treatment of depositors in failed banks varied from country to country. In some, the government left the deposits in the restructured bank or reimbursed all depositors. In others, repayment of depositors depended on the asset recovery of the failed institutions. Priority was given to compensation for small depositors. Depositors incurred substantial losses in Cameroon and the Republic of Congo, for example. Some countries introduced deposit insurance in the late 1990s, but it is unclear whether these systems could handle banking crises as large as those of the 1990s.

Privatizations generally went to a major institutional partner, often foreign. In some cases the foreign banks were large and well known, with a reputation to protect. African private banks that operate in several countries have developed (Ecobank, Bank of Africa, Financial Bank, CBC, Stanbic) as a result of privatization involving foreign partners. However, in some cases, the foreign banks provided little improvement.

As a result of the restructurings, African commercial banks have become more solvent, liquid, and profitable and a safer haven for deposits, but many problems remain. In many countries, banks are still weak in their lending and operations. Bank deposits have declined in some countries, probably reflecting a mix of bank closures, discouragement of small deposits, and civil strife. Commercial bank lending has generally been limited, reflecting crowding out of government debt and bankers' selectivity in lending.

lems in one bank typically indicate more widespread problems, and closing a bank without promptly compensating depositors may trigger runs on other banks and looting by bank owners.

As a bank problem becomes systemic, bank runs turn into currency runs and pose severe problems for which there is no standard answer. The government faces the unpleasant choice of either intervening in weak banks, thus possibly provoking runs on other banks,[39] or providing liquidity support—loose money—that will spill over into pressure on the exchange rate and international reserves, especially in open economies (World Bank 2000c).

Another choice is that of how much to support the exchange rate with reserves and tight money (offsetting the loose money from liquidity support) versus how much to allow a depreciation. Tight money helps to protect the exchange rate, as in the traditional policy response, and thus helps borrowers in foreign currency, but it hurts borrowers in local currency and it hurts banks, particularly if it is maintained for a long time. Liquidity support and loose money will help borrowers in local currency, but put additional pressure on the exchange rate that will hurt borrowers in foreign currency. Use of reserves delays this problem, but reserves are finite and their decline can provoke a speculative attack on the currency.

Nontraditional policies have had only mixed success. Capital controls have not been effective in stopping currency runs.[40] A blanket guarantee may or may not halt bank or currency runs, depending on how it affects concerns about the credibility of the guarantee and the burden of future costs (Dooley 2000). A few countries, including Argentina and Ecuador, have tried to stop bank runs by freezing deposits and devaluing, but the disruption to the payments chain has led to massive recessions. If deposits are to be written down, in parallel with loans, it is probably best to make a politically unpalatable exchange of tradable bonds, as Argentina did in its January 1990 Bonex plan. Whatever is done, GDP growth is almost certain to slow if not decline (Frankel and Wei 2004).

In sum, the crises of the 1990s appear to be related to macroeconomic problems, but also to financial liberalization in the context of the overhang of old political and economic relationships, manifested in state banks and politically powerful financial-industrial conglomerates. Government guarantees encouraged a rise of funding for these intermediaries, which they channeled into weak loans. Eventually crises developed and the depositors and external creditors were bailed out by governments. Privatization in these environments did not solve the problems, and often required costly renationalizations.

## 3. Lessons of the 1990s

In the 1980s and 1990s the approach to finance shifted from the repression of prices and markets

and the use of government credit allocations to a more market-based, internationally open system. Yet this shift, along with the other reforms, had less than the expected effects on growth. Access to financial services does not seem to have improved substantially in the 1990s, though there are indications of improvements recently. Expectations may well have been too high. Another reason was an apparent "boom in bust[s]" (Caprio 1997), related to macroeconomic policies but also to financial liberalization in the context of an overhang of weak institutions—financial intermediaries, financial markets, and informational, legal, and judicial frameworks. Problems in these areas reduced the impact of liberalization and in some cases led to perverse results.

The weaknesses of institutions were not just a technical issue: they reflected the difficulty of changing the previous state-led development system and, more fundamentally, its underlying political-economic basis within a short period, while restraints on markets could be and were quickly lifted. The overhang of these factors during the 1990s was an important reason behind the following:

- Credit allocation was weak and continued to go to the public sector, well-connected individuals, financial-industrial conglomerates, and traditional state bank clients.

- Bank privatization was slow and partial privatizations left control of intermediaries in the hands of government in many transition and African economies, leading to continued preferential treatment of the traditional borrowers from state banks.

- Privatizations and restrictions on foreign entry in the financial sector often allowed local elites to retain or increase their economic and political power.

- Implicit and explicit guarantees of deposits and international loans supported local elites' ability to raise resources.

- Liberalization of bank licensing led to "pocket" banks that mainly engaged in connected lending or regulatory arbitrage, not expansion of access (the record of nonbank intermediaries is somewhat better but they too were often linked to industrial-financial conglomerates).

- Development of the framework for capital markets—such as reasonable information, legal and judicial treatment of bankruptcy, treatment of minority shareholders, conduct rules for market participants—was slow, compounding the problems that capital markets in developing countries face in terms of concerns about macroeconomic stability, high costs, and low liquidity.

The process of liberalization and the limited nature of the results in the 1990s suggest four major lessons, discussed next.

## Finance Depends on Institutions

Perhaps the most important lesson of the 1990s for finance is that the financial sector's contribution to development depends not just on resource mobilization but also on attention to institutions: intermediaries, markets, and the informational, regulatory, legal, and judicial framework. Resources need to be allocated to those that offer the best combination of return and risk, and this depends on the quality of institutions. Building up these institutions is not easy, takes time, and requires political support.

In the 1990s, the traditionally weak loans of state banks and financial institutions linked to industrial conglomerates were further weakened by the higher interest rates that followed liberalization, as well as by increased import competition and real appreciations that cut the profitability of traditional borrowers. Explicit and implicit guarantees allowed these financial institutions to obtain much of the liberalization-induced increase in deposits and capital inflows, and to substantially expand lending to their traditional borrowers, private and public. Regulation and supervision did not prevent this; their weaknesses reflected not just technical but political issues. Market discipline was eroded by poor information and, more important, by implicit and explicit guarantees. Better capital market development could have relieved some risks and

absorbed part of the shocks. However, the capital markets faced competition from implicitly or explicitly guaranteed deposits and external loans. Market development also was hindered by the inherent problems of capital markets in developing countries and the difficulties of building up a reasonable institutional framework quickly.

By the end of the 1990s, it became clear that much of the increased deposits and capital inflows had gone into (1) unproductive private borrowing or state enterprise debt that had to be replaced by government debt in order to bail out depositors and lenders, (2) deficit finance, and (3) central bank debt to stabilize the economy. Thus it is not surprising that the financial liberalizations of the 1990s did not live up to the high expectations regarding sustained increases in growth or credit access.

Focusing on the poor quality of credits exposes a common thread in the slow growth and financial crises of the 1990s: the continuation of preferential access, related to the overhang of old institutions, that was changed only slowly by the financial reforms. In many countries in the 1980s and 1990s, public sector borrowing, with its implicit guarantee from future tax revenues, was excessive and eventually led to crises and slow growth. But even in countries with smaller public sectors and relatively limited fiscal problems, such as Chile in the late 1970s and East Asian countries in the 1990s, loans to industrial conglomerates—made from the guaranteed deposits in the private financial intermediaries that they controlled or from state banks and international lenders, to which they had preferential access because of the institutional setup—eventually became nonperforming and contributed to crises. As noted earlier, the poor contribution of such loans to sustained growth is shown by the low value of the associated collateral when it was eventually sold.

## Delaying Needed Policies Is Costly

Limiting the incidence and cost of financial crises depends on resisting political pressures to prolong unsustainable booms and to delay action on weak banks,[41] as well as on avoiding socializing their losses. In the 1990s, governments often tried to prolong booms and did not limit the expansion of weak banks.[42] Unfortunately, such policies increased the ultimate volume of bad loans and the size of the crises. Then, after crises occurred, governments typically responded by bailing out depositors and external investors through liquidity support, expansion of whatever deposit insurance existed, and blanket guarantees, all of which generated large increases in government debt and contingent liabilities.

Expectations that losses would be socialized, through explicit and implicit guarantees, also contributed to crises and volatility by encouraging weak institutions to mobilize funds after liberalization. Depositors and external lenders, expecting to be bailed out of problems by a government guarantee, supplied funding to state banks and financial intermediaries that were part of financial-industrial conglomerates. The funding was well in excess of what could be used productively. Market discipline, which might have limited this funding, was weakened by the implicit and explicit guarantees.[43] The process was unstable, however. When a rise occurred in the subjective probability that the guarantees would be called, net capital outflows developed, as depositors and investors became concerned about how the guarantees would be paid and funded.[44] The capital flight was facilitated by the liquidity support to weak banks and the support of the exchange rate by reserve sales. The combination of high initial returns, limited losses on the funds that were taken out of the countries just before the crises, and the ultimate provision of government guarantees left the depositors and investors with good returns during the 1990s.[45]

Improvements in these policies will depend not just on new measures but also on strong implementation, which has been difficult even in industrial countries.

## Financial Liberalization Increases Financial Resources

A financially liberalized economy tends to generate more financial resources than a repressed economy. This is an old lesson (McKinnon 1973; Shaw 1973) that had been forgotten during the finan-cially repressed 1980s. During the 1990s, the growth in bank deposits (relative to GDP) speeded up in many countries. This acceleration reflected lower inflation, more realistic interest rates, and a wider menu of financial instruments, including foreign exchange–denominated instruments. In addition, domestic capital markets were started and developed and private firms increased their external borrowing and external equity issues.

Deposits and domestic capital markets performed best where growth was already rapid, where there was a history of high deposit mobilization, and where investors were willing to take risks to get equity shares in rapidly growing corporations: East Asia and India. Elsewhere, deposit growth was less and capital market performance was less good. Deposit growth picked up much less in Latin America, reflecting the region's history of inflation and government intervention. Also, much of the growth was in foreign currency deposits that complicated policy making. The decline in listings in equity markets in Latin American and transition economies suggests that access to finance through equity issues did not widen much. Even where capital market performance was better, access suffered from the lack of scale and liquidity in the markets; multinational takeovers of major firms; migration of listings to less costly, more liquid industrial country markets; and, more fundamentally, weak institutional frameworks—in particular the lack of information, regulatory protection of minority shareholders, and bankruptcy protection for bond holders. Private external borrowing and offshore equity issues did provide lower-cost funding but only to larger corporations in a few countries, and the loans were subject to currency and rollover risk. The slowdown in net private-to-private disbursements and short-term loans was a major factor in the crises. Though it will be difficult, better development of domestic capital markets, even in the countries that have done relatively well, would reduce the impact of future crises.

## Successful Finance Depends on Macroeconomic Stability

Another old lesson is that successful financial liberalization and successful finance depend on macroeconomic stability (World Bank, *World Development Report 1989*). If anything, open capital accounts and volatile international capital flows place a larger premium on sound macroeconomic management. However, financial reforms, or at least more market-based interest rates, were often put in place in the 1990s in the midst of macroeconomic imbalances, complicating what was already a technically difficult problem.[46] For example, countries with unsustainable fiscal policies often used financial liberalization to continue their debt buildup and delay adjustment.[47] Even when fiscal deficits were smaller than in the 1980s, the countries that liberalized finance often had large external and internal debt overhangs that contributed to volatility.

Even a strong financial system has difficulty protecting itself against default by an overindebted government, as the recent Argentine crisis illustrates.[48] Also, many countries that liberalized were pursuing exchange rate–based stabilization, or had relatively fixed exchange rates. These macroeconomic policies, and the tight monetary policy and the credibility issues associated with them, often meant extended periods of high real interest rates and burdensome external borrowing, which eventually contributed to countries' inability to service debt and to financial crises. Thus, the problems with financial liberalization, the crises, and the limited results from financial liberalization in the 1990s often reflected macroeconomic policy deficiencies and the overhang of large external debts.

## 4. The Future of Finance

Looking ahead, the general pattern seems likely to remain one of more market-based finance. In most countries the financial liberalizations of the 1990s are unlikely to be reversed in their broad aspects, barring large macroeconomic policy errors. A widespread return to financial repression is probably now untenable for two reasons. One reason is political: lower inflation and a more market-based, more open financial system

became political imperatives in the 1990s. Repressed finance had high costs and regressive distributional effects. Over time, increasingly politically active households have demanded protection for their savings and access to the investment opportunities that were once available only to political and economic elites. A second reason, noted earlier, is that the increased access to external financial markets brought about by the enormous growth in trade, travel, and migration and by improvements in communications has made financial repression difficult.[49]

Although macroeconomic stability, on which good finance depends, seems to exist in many countries, macroeconomic issues remain. First, in today's open economies, slow policy responses or policy errors quickly translate into macroeconomic instability. Second, large government debt overhangs and/or large unfunded pension liabilities are problems in many countries. The burden of these problems has been eased by low world interest rates, but rising world interest rates, as well as other shocks, may lead macroeconomic policy astray. As the 1980s and 1990s show, excessive government debt can interact with inconsistent exchange rate and monetary policy to lead to massive capital flight, large currency depreciations, and costly financial sector collapses. When the government goes bankrupt, the financial system and the whole economy suffer.

The financial liberalizations of the 1990s have created a sounder basis for finance in at least six ways:

- Crises cleared away the "debris" of past non-performing loans, although they left large holdings of government debt that created problems.

- Intermediaries and capital markets have improved. In Eastern Europe, Latin America, Africa, and even East Asia, many financial intermediaries were gradually replaced by reputable foreign banks. Such banks have better lending skills, are more able to engage in arms-length lending and resist government pressures, and, potentially, impose fewer demands on government for bailouts than the intermediaries they replaced. Capital markets have also been set up or improved, but they still face many structural and institutional challenges.

- Government and central bank debt markets have developed. They allow central banks to carry out monetary policy more efficiently, increase banks' liquidity, and allow less inflationary finance of fiscal deficits. The growth of government debt markets also helps provide a benchmark that can make private debt markets more efficient.

- Access to credit is growing in some countries, from foreign banks (Clarke et al. 2004), new domestic banks, and bank-like intermediaries. With the closure of the old intermediaries, bad credit no longer drove out good credit. New intermediaries that hold the promise of a sustainable increase in small-scale lending were able to grow. In Ecuador, for example, the collapse of the public sector intermediaries has left room for dramatic growth in private banks' small credits in the last two years.

- Information is improving. The accounting and auditing of intermediaries and borrowers is improving. So is information on small borrowers—public credit bureaus have been established in 23 (mostly transition countries) since 1994 and the private credit bureaus that already existed in many countries are improving (World Bank 2003d).

- Prudential regulation and supervision seem to be improving and, in a few cases, the combination of regulation, supervision, and a better safety net has limited the impact of crises in individual banks, for instance in Peru, although supervision has also missed major weaknesses in some countries, such as the Dominican Republic.

## Improving Finance

Further improvements in the contribution of finance to development depend on improving the key tradeoff between safe and sound finance and risk taking in the financial sector's intermediation between savers and investors. The crises

of the 1990s naturally have raised concerns about financial instability that can lead to poor growth. Governments, attempting to reduce the future costs of crises, have often tended to emphasize prudence. But there is a tension between stability and the ability of the financial system to carry out the key intermediary roles for development—mobilizing funds from savers, allocating these funds to investors that will yield the best combination of return and risk, reducing risk, and shifting risk to those most willing to bear it. A financial system that does these tasks well will contribute greatly to development.

Improving the tradeoff between stability and intermediation in finance depends not just on maintaining the systems of market-based interest rates and credit allocations that arose during the 1990s, but also on the following:

- Reducing the crowding out of private credit by the current large overhang of government debt;

- Reducing the volatility of resource flows, particularly on the upside of cycles and to weak institutions;

- Improving intermediaries and markets; and

- Widening access to credit.

The discussion below addresses each in turn. Progress will depend heavily on countries' success in building institutions, improving their informational and legal frameworks, and, ultimately, achieving more competitive political systems that will reduce the power of political-economic elites.

## Reducing the Crowding out of Private Credit

Perhaps the most immediate obstacle to the ability of the financial system to carry out its intermediary role, as well as a threat to stability, is the large overhang of government debt in many countries.[50] It is often said that private credit is currently limited by the unwillingness of banks and markets to take risks. In fact, it is limited by the large volume of inelastically supplied government debt. This is because, to ensure that all government debt is held (either by financial intermediaries or by individuals), the spread between interest rates on government debt and private debt has to be big enough to crowd out enough private debt. Hence the way to expand the supply of private credit is not to try to make government debt less attractive but to leave more space for funds for the private sector in the financial system, or to make private debt and equity more attractive, so that more financial resources can be raised in total.

## Reducing the Volatility of Flows and Its Impact

Governments have made various efforts to reduce the volatility of flows, especially on the upside of a boom, and to ease the impact of volatility, particularly by building up international reserves to offset shocks and, within banks, by externally hedging foreign currency liabilities.

But much remains to be done. Some analysts have argued for reducing incentives to excessive capital inflows that can easily turn into excessive outflows. They argue, for example, that India's success in avoiding the 1997 crisis was related to its limits on banks' (and firms') offshore borrowing, even as it allowed inflows into the stock market and liberalized direct foreign investment regulations. Chile's implicit taxes on short-term inflows also appear to have had some success in reducing inflows, extending their maturities, and in limiting the impact of shocks, but at the cost of reducing credit availability to the private sector (Edwards 1999; Forbes 2003).

Another approach would be to reduce the incentives to banks for increasing their net offshore borrowings. This would involve at least leveling the playing field through application of the same reserve, liquidity, directed credit requirements, and premiums for "deposit insurance" as on domestic deposits. Here, too, little has been done. In the area of international bond issues, some countries have begun to try to reduce the bias in bond buyers' beliefs that any restructuring will favor them, by making restructurings easier in terms of lowering the percentage of bond holders that is needed to accept a restructuring offer (the Collective Action Clause). However, it remains to be seen how this change will oper-

ate—U.S. courts have often allowed individual creditors to seek preferential treatment. In the case of Elliot Associates vs. Peru, settled in 2000, Elliot Associates obtained a restraining order on the payments on the restructured debt to which Peru had agreed with other creditor representatives. Peru eventually settled by paying Elliot Associates $56 million for the debt that they had bought for $11 million in 1996. Ultimately, all attempts at limiting excessive inflows depend on political will to limit a boom, while in practice, countries often have eased restrictions on capital inflows in order to prolong a boom.

Internally, governments have tried to develop capital markets as a shock absorber for the volatility of external and internal flows. Funds invested in equity or long-term domestic government and private debt represent much less of a threat to the economy than do volatile short-term external capital flows.[51] Thus, capital market development could contribute to stability as well as assisting the allocation of funds to promising activities. One problem, of course, is that investors in such instruments demand high returns under the current environment in developing countries, so such instruments are often unattractive to potential issuers. This problem adds to the structural problems of small size, lack of liquidity, and high costs that limit capital market development. Domestic capital markets, particularly in the larger countries, could be stimulated by improvements in institutional factors, such as better information on firms, better rules on market conduct and corporate treatment of minority shareholders, and better legal and judicial treatment of bankruptcy. Generally, such improvements require substantial time and effort.

Better market discipline is another approach to enhancing both intermediation and stability. Market discipline means ensuring that depositors and international lenders have appropriate incentives to limit their funding to weak intermediaries, by ensuring that they stand to receive lower returns on deposits and investments if problems occur. Market discipline complements government regulation and supervision and evidence exists that it can work in developing countries (Martinez-Peria and Shmuckler 2001; Calomaris and Powell 2001). Unfortunately, market discipline depends on good information. Though accounting and auditing are improving, much remains to be done. For example, regulations could encourage prompt dissemination of accurate information and impose stiff penalties for failure to do so.

Perhaps more important, market discipline is blunted by widespread implicit and explicit government guarantees that developed in the 1990s. To make market discipline work, governments face the difficult task of establishing credible limits on liquidity support, blanket guarantees, and deposit insurance, so that at least the holders of banks' large obligations consider themselves at risk. One way to begin improving market discipline might be to limit payoffs to large providers of funds, especially since the latter can be expected to have relatively good information about the strength of individual banks. It would also help to prevent problems in one bank from contaminating the rest of the system. However, the policy would immediately pass the problems of a weak bank on to the central bank as lender of last resort—a role that also would need to be limited, to contain costs. Deposit insurance would also come into play, and would need to be truly limited to small deposits. Premiums for deposit insurance would need to reflect differences in risk in different classes of banks. Unfortunately, the systems of risk-based premiums that have been adopted have largely copied the pricing from industrial economies and, though better than flat, premiums still provide substantial subsidies to domestic private banks, probably because of the banks' political power.

When banks' problems have become more systemic, the past responses—large lender of last resort support and blanket guarantees—have undermined future market discipline and been costly to future generations. In effect, they have provided nearly unlimited insurance not only for depositors but also for owners who can loot their banks. Alternative options for dealing with crises would need to begin with a different approach to dividing the costs of the crises between current holders of liabilities and future generations. Lengthy suspensions of deposit withdrawals have

proved to be undesirable: they break down the payments chain and have contributed to large declines in output, as has happened in Argentina and Ecuador. But brief suspensions of deposit withdrawals, while term deposits are replaced by long-term, marketable instruments that involve a substantial discount (in present value terms), are a possible alternative that would make current depositors bear part of the cost of the crisis (Beckerman 1995; IMF 2004b). Of course, such policies are politically difficult to implement. But they would not only limit the burden of crises that future generations would have to pay, they might also reduce the size of future crises, by strengthening market discipline.

To limit weak lending and crises, governments have also improved their banking laws and prudential regulation and supervision. Since the strengthening of prudential regulation and supervision only began in the later 1990s, not much evidence has accumulated on how well it can work to prevent crises. At the simplest level, regulators and supervisors in developing countries may lack the technical skills even to deal with loan quality and provisioning, not to speak of more complicated aspects of banking, such as evaluating complex operations in capital markets and foreign exchange, swaps and derivatives that are poorly valued in imperfect markets, and risk management models. Deficiencies exist in the consolidated supervision of financial-industrial conglomerates and in the supervision of offshore activities—important areas in developing countries that will not be improved simply by giving supervisors more power.

Partly these problems reflect incentives: typically supervisors are poorly paid and have an incentive to shift into banking, especially once they have been trained to handle tasks well. Often supervisors are subject to lawsuits by bankers, even for actions in performance of their duties—which makes them hesitant to raise issues.[52] Protecting supervisors completely from legal action raises another issue—the risk that they will engage in malfeasance. Hence a tribunal separate from the court system is needed to deal with accusations of malfeasance by supervisors.

More fundamentally, improvements in regulation and supervision face substantial political roadblocks, which have arisen in industrial as well as developing countries. For example, from time to time, U.S. financial economists have raised concerns about some U.S. banks being too big to fail. Also in the United States, political forces and regulatory forbearance are often cited as a contributory factor in the U.S. savings and loan crisis. In many developing countries a few large banks dominate the system, and bankers and major borrowers are often one and the same. In this context, regulatory capital does not have even the minimal incentives that it does in arms-length transactions between intermediaries and borrowers. The industrial-financial groups are the principal entrepreneurs in many countries, even large ones, so limits on connected lending are not feasible. If problems of loan quality develop, the strength of the economic and political elite is likely to lead to regulatory forbearance. Even if supervisors can identify capital insufficiencies and other regulatory violations, it would be difficult for them to stand up to monolithic political elites, particularly when the alternative is simply to ignore a problem in return for a supplement to their small salaries. Finally, the potential strength of regulation and supervision is limited by the still-important role of large state banks that carry out government policies and are nontransparent almost by design. In sum, regulation may not be successful unless it also empowers the market to monitor banks better, by encouraging market discipline.

## Improving Intermediaries

The entry of reputable foreign banks is one way to improve intermediation as well as to limit the cost of crises. Reputable foreign banks bring better-trained staff to the country and generally have better systems for evaluating and managing credit risk than local banks. These advantages often spill over into the local banking system, from competitive pressures and the movement of personnel. In addition, reputable foreign banks also are likely to cover any losses on their loans or operations without demanding government support, so as to avoid damaging their reputations.

Reputable international banks have entered many countries in recent years, but losses and, in some cases, their own lack of capital have limited their interest in further expansion. Some banks that expanded in Eastern Europe, in hopes of establishing a presence before countries acceded to the European Union, suffered losses as competition developed. Some that expanded in Latin America have suffered losses from operations and from the developments in Argentina. In the recent re-privatizations of Indonesian banks, only one bid came from a well-known global bank. Lesser-known banks have been expanding internationally, but such banks can generate more supervision problems than local banks, because of the problems with international supervision. Moreover, without reputations to lose, such banks may pull out when things go bad in the country or in their home market, leaving governments to bear the costs.

## Improving Access to Finance

Increasing small clients' access to finance is a critical issue for the financial sector in its support of development. It involves the tradeoff between making banks safe and sound and making sure they continue to intermediate. A prerequisite to increasing access is to reduce the absorption of loanable resources by the government and the central bank.

Pressures remain great to direct low-cost credit to small borrowers. Historically, however, these efforts have usually been unsuccessful, undermining sustainable finance for rural and small and medium-sized enterprises, just as occurred under financial repression.

A few intermediaries have successfully sustained loans to small borrowers (box 7.7). The more traditional banking operations among them have common features that explain their success: interest rates that cover costs, good deposit mobilization, containment of administrative costs, and a high rate of loan collection, all backed by appropriate internal incentives for good staff performance (Yaron, Benjamin, and Piprek 1997). Their example needs to be followed. The informational infrastructure for small lending also improved toward the end of the 1990s with the founding and improvement of credit bureaus.

Greater competition in banking services, through greater entry of banks and nonbanks and

**BOX 7.7**

**Extending Credit for Small Borrowers**

In addition to the well-known examples of the Grameen Bank (begun in 1976) and Bank Rakyat Indonesia after its 1983 reform (Robinson 2002), other successful lenders began to expand toward the end of the 1990s. These included CrediFe in Ecuador, MiBanco in Peru, CrediAmigo in Brazil, and, in India, SEWAH (which uses a Grameen-type approach) and self-help groups that use a mixture of the Grameen approach and traditional banking. Some of these intermediaries received support from donors. The Grameen approach relies on the social responsibility of borrowers who belong to a narrow group—an approach that has also been used by some banks.

looser regulations and supervision, is sometimes recommended to improve access and lending in general. Certainly, regulations should provide room for intermediaries that take funds from groups of well-informed investors/depositors and "nip at the heels" of banks, by offering better returns to depositors (though with greater risk), along with better service and innovation in products and lending.

Exactly how these entities should function— for example, as venture capital funds or deposit takers—and where the lines should be drawn between them and "banks," are country-specific details. Such intermediaries operated in some East Asian and Latin American countries and in India in the 1990s, and the outcomes illustrate their positive and negative sides. Before they fell victim to crises in 1997, the nonbank intermediaries increased finance for underbanked sectors such as consumer durables and construction. But to some extent their success was not in competition and innovation but based on regulatory arbitrage relative to banks, which were constrained by interest rate controls (in India) or tight money policy (in Thailand). A critical issue with such

intermediaries is whether politically they can be denied access to the bank safety net, or whether they should be regulated and supervised in the same manner as banks to protect taxpayers as well as depositors. India appropriately resisted bailing out depositors, but Thailand's attempt to offer these intermediaries access to liquidity funding contributed to an easing of monetary policy that was inconsistent with the pegged exchange rate.

Another related issue is the size of the investor/depositor base: as it widens, the distinction blurs between these institutions and banks, the pressures for claims on the safety net increase, and the government may be drawn into supervision and regulation. Such problems have occurred in co-op banks in India and in countries such as Indonesia, Nigeria, and Russia, where banks were allowed to set up with negligible capital. In Indonesia, 48 of these banks, many run by the politically well-connected, borrowed from the lender-of-last-resort facility well in excess of their capital during the crisis (Kenward 2002), and used the funds to support foreign exchange purchases and related businesses (see box 7.4 above).

Improving access, as well as the quality of credit allocation in general, depends heavily on improving the informational, legal, and judicial framework. The poor supply of information about borrowers, though improving, limits lending to smaller clients. In some countries, this problem has been circumvented by lending through third parties that in effect guarantee the loans.[53] More generally, however, better information would enhance competition for sound borrowers while giving borrowers an incentive to service their loans to maintain good credit records. Thus, the continued spread and improvement of credit bureaus will be an important development in improving access to credit as well as the quality of loans. Important issues that need to be addressed in this process are banking secrecy; how to make banks comply promptly and accurately with the requirement to provide information; whether the credit bureau is to be private or public; the inclusion of related information such as installment purchases; and consumers' rights to challenge and amend the information.

Improvements in the legal and judicial framework, notably the definition and execution of collateral and bankruptcy laws, are also important in improving credit access and lending in general. Financial intermediaries prefer not to execute collateral—they are mobilizers and allocators of funds, not managers of firms—but the threat of executing collateral gives an incentive for prompt debt service. Good bankruptcy laws make the survival of viable firms easier and allow shifts of physical capital from nonviable firms to others, with creditors receiving the maximum settlement. The potential to improve credit access through better information, contract enforcement, and technology is great: in the United States, the cost of processing a small loan is now below the price of a modest lunch.

Good access to financial services also involves efficient deposit and payments services—important facilities given the increase in domestic and international migration. In Africa, unfortunately, the strengthening of the banking system has in some cases reduced access to deposit and payments services for small transactions. In other parts of the world, payments services are often limited and uncompetitive. Post office banks—narrow banks, holding only government debt—with better technology, and banks providing only these services (for example, in Tanzania and Mongolia) are examples of innovative ways to serve these needs.

## 5. Conclusion

While financial liberalization delivered in some aspects during the 1990s, its benefits are likely to lie in the future and to depend on further institutional reforms. The crises of the 1990s, and the limited contributions of liberalization to growth and access to finance, reflect to a large degree the continuation of the weak institutional framework related to the overhang of the old financial system and, more fundamentally, the persistence of old political and economic power centers. The freeing of interest rates and credit allocation increased resource mobilization. But the persistence of the former institutional framework

meant that resource allocation improved less rapidly. Implicit and explicit guarantees, by removing market discipline, contributed to excessive expansion of lending for the low-productivity projects of well-connected borrowers. Weak regulation and supervision reflected not just technical problems but also political pressures for regulatory forbearance. Large, generalized liquidity support during the crises often went to favored parties that bought foreign exchange with it. Information, which might have helped market discipline and limited excessive lending had guarantees been less, was not a focus of regulation, and it suffered from the lack of transparency typical of many developing countries. Limited credit access reflected the crowding out of public sector and central bank borrowing. In addition, it reflected a lack of information related not only to technical issues but also to the unwillingness of established intermediaries to share information on their borrowers. Weak legal and judicial frameworks, designed to protect borrowers and often responsive to economic and political elites, reduced the incentives to service debts and made it difficult for new borrowers to gain access to finance by pledging collateral effectively. Capital markets, which might have absorbed some of the shocks, grew slowly because of the weak institutional framework and underlying structural problems.

The lessons of the 1990s are that improving the contribution of finance to growth depends heavily on macroeconomic stability, governments that are willing to take steps to limit unsustainable booms, a market-based approach, and the quality of institutions (financial intermediaries, information, and the quality of the legal and regulatory framework). The quality of institutions was not changed much by the stroke-of-the-pen liberalizations of interest rates and credit allocations. Improving these institutions, and thereby improving financial intermediation, will depend on institution building, better informational and legal frameworks, and, ultimately, more competitive political systems. Success will depend on a mix of increased market discipline and limiting guarantees, better regulation and supervision that includes encouraging greater market discipline of intermediaries, greater participation of reputable foreign banks, and capital market development. Government is needed to support better markets, without intervening excessively in them, backed by an open political process that limits the distortions of finance in favor of well-connected parties.

## Notes

1. As Lenin cogently put it, "The big banks are the state apparatus which we need to bring about socialism and which we take readymade from capitalism" (quoted in LaPorta, López de Silanes, and Shleifer 2002a, 266). Thus communist, socialist, and planned economies nationalized domestic and foreign commercial banks. Gerschenkron (1962) was among the first to provide academic support for the provision by government and state banks of funds for industrialization and long-term credit. In addition to state banks, specialized development finance intermediaries, generally public, were set up to provide credits for small-scale industry, agriculture, housing, and long-term industrial credit. They were financed by government-guaranteed external borrowing, including bilateral and multilateral loans; by low-cost directed credits from banks and other intermediaries; and by government revenues. Often these intermediaries went bankrupt, reflecting failures to collect debt service and dependence on unhedged external borrowing.

2. For example, Brownbridge and Harvey (1998) describe such financial repression in Africa.

3. Dornbusch and Edwards (1991); Alesina, Grilli, and Milesi-Ferreti (1994); and Garrett (1995, 2000).

4. Estimates of aggregate subsidies range from 3 to 8 percent of GDP annually (World Bank, *World Development Report 1989*; Hanson 2001). Regarding allocations, in Costa Rica in the mid-1970s for example, the public Banco Nacional's interest rate subsidy on agricultural credits was equal to about 4 percent of GDP and 20 percent of agricultural value added. About 80 percent of the credit went to 10 percent of the borrowers; the average subsidy on these loans alone would have put each recipient into the upper 10 percent of the income distribution (World Bank, *World Development Report 1989*). The situation in other countries was similar. See Adams and Vogel (1986); Adams, Graham, and Von Pischke (1984); Gonzalez-Vega (1984); and Yaron, Benjamin, and Piprek (1997). Larger firms often accessed directed credit and on-lent it to their suppliers, capturing the spread between repressed and free rates. Directed

credits were also diverted into loans with free rates, for example, through curb markets, or, when some deposit rates were freed, into deposits that paid higher rates than the loan rates on directed credits.

5. Abiad and Mody (2003) note the link between greater openness to trade and financial liberalization.

6. Capital controls, particularly in the context of macroeconomic imbalances, increase incentives for corruption, worsen the income distribution, and, because they fail, create disrespect for laws. Even in the 1970s, a high proportion of the massive capital inflows into Latin America leaked out (Dooley et al. 1986). More recently, in China, net short-term outflows of capital and errors and omissions in the balance of payments were very large (World Bank 1997a, 2000c).

7. For example, in Mexico after the post-1982 high inflation, the limits on interest rates on agricultural loans were below the rates on some deposits for a period. Rural borrowers often simply took their loan proceeds and deposited them, earning a positive return on the loans with much less effort than by farming.

8. Abiad and Mody (2003).

9. Stock markets were opened to foreign investors between 1986 and 1993 in the major East Asian and Latin American countries and in India and Pakistan (Bekaert, Harvey, and Lundblad 2003).

10. Levine and Zervos (1998); Levine, Loayza, and Beck (2000).

11. The sharp fall in inflation in the 1990s made interest rates more realistic, even with declines in nominal rates; it also reduced other financial distortions associated with inflation. Among the 25 developing countries with the largest financial systems, those with hyperinflation at the beginning of the 1990s reduced inflation sharply (in some cases, such as Argentina, to single digits), while most of those with initial inflation of 10–50 percent annually reduced inflation to single digits by 2000. In Africa, inflation also fell and in most transition countries, inflation fell sharply from initial high levels.

12. Foreign currency holdings also were often large relative to financial systems (Hanson 2002).

13. As an example of the popularity of these measures, in Peru after hyperinflation at the end of the 1980s, the 1993 Constitution (Article 64) guaranteed citizens the right to hold and use foreign exchange. More than 50 percent of deposits are in dollars, even in the non-Lima savings banks.

14. The interest rates on foreign currency credits avoid the high, up-front cost of an expected depreciation that may not occur for some time—the "peso problem"(Hanson 2002). This improves cash flows (lower deficits for governments using cash accounting) and increases a loan's effective maturity. Moreover, when a depreciation does come, the cost is spread out in

the amortization period. Not surprisingly, governments borrow externally, and many countries, for example, Mexico in 1994 and Brazil and Turkey recently, have indexed some domestic debt to foreign currency. For private firms, there is also the hope that a depreciation may lead to a government bailout, either by a favorable takeover of their foreign loans or an asymmetric conversion of domestic foreign currency debts and deposits to local currency, as occurred in Mexico (1982) and Argentina (2002). However, foreign currency loans do increase bank risks, even when matched with foreign currency deposits, since the borrowers may not have easy access to foreign currency earnings. Banks could have adjusted the foreign and domestic currency proportions of their balance sheets by varying interest rate differentials, but, given the demand for foreign currency deposits, the spread probably would have been high, creating moral hazard problems in loans in domestic currency.

15. These figures understate the relative growth of public sector debt because they include China, where deposit growth was large and banks' accumulation of government debt was relatively small, but the accumulation of state enterprise debt was large. In those transition countries for which relevant data are available, privatization reduced borrowing by public enterprises, thereby offsetting the rise in government debt, but deposits grew only slowly and were largely absorbed by increased central bank debt.

16. Note that these figures understate the growth of private credit in India and East Asia before 1997 and overstate it after 1997, because of the growth and decline of the nonbank sector.

17. Government debt was either injected into the banks as part of restructurings or, in the case of deficit finance, sold at whatever rates would ensure its purchase. Thus, as a first-order approximation, the supply was inelastic (except for changes in the proportions sold internally and externally). The liquidity, low risk, and low capital requirements on government debt affected only the rate differential between the debt and private credit that was needed to crowd out the equivalent amount of private credit, rather than the amount of government debt held, which was determined by the inelastic supply.

18. In some cases, the central banks also temporarily acted as large lenders of last resort.

19. The increase in external assets probably reflected an attempt to hedge the risks from their foreign currency liabilities, including deposits (Honahan and Shi 2003). Although banks' net external positions were small in 2000, gross external assets and liabilities were much larger than earlier (Hanson 2003b), suggesting that financial liberalization had increased banks' ability to diversify themselves.

20. For statistical evidence on the importance of private sector credit in growth see Levine and Zervos (1998); Levine, Loayza, and Beck (2000). The evidence of the link between savings/investment and financial sector liberalization is mixed (see, for example, Bandiera et al. 2000), but the investment ratio does seem to have risen in the 1990s in the larger Asian countries, though not in the larger Latin American countries, and it actually declined in the larger African countries. The difference between saving and investment ratios may, of course, reflect differences in capital inflows.

21. Crises, unproductive credits, and their links to the unreformed institutional and political framework that remained after liberalization are discussed in the section below on financial crises.

22. Stock markets were reported as of 1991 in Hungary and Poland; in 1994 in Croatia, the Czech Republic, Romania, Russia, the Slovak Republic, and Slovenia; in 1995 in Bulgaria, Latvia, Lithuania, and Mongolia; in 1996 in the Former Yugoslav Republic of Macedonia, Moldova, and Uzbekistan; and in 1997 in Estonia, Kazakhstan, and Ukraine (Standard and Poor's 2003).

23. This average is for the 17 of the 25 largest financial markets for which data are available on banks' domestic credit to the private sector. It excludes China, India, and Korea, which do not report separate data on private sector credits. These three countries are large external borrowers in absolute terms but are likely to have smaller ratios of private external borrowings to bank credit than the average for the 17 countries.

24. The additional currency risk of these funds was less than it might seem, as domestic credit in many countries was increasingly denominated in foreign exchange.

25. "[The state banks'] commercialization as joint stock companies was not accompanied by sufficient commercialization of their credit management, product development, service levels, operational efficiency, or risk management. All this meant poor loan performance and eventually insolvency. Many factors worked against early detection of such problems—poor accounting and auditing standards, inexperienced supervisory personnel, inadequate prudential regulations, decentralized and incomplete information systems (often branch accounts not consolidated with headquarters accounts) and the traditional reliance on the government for additional funding when liquidity became short . . . . Management information systems were weak. All these factors worked against timely and effective scrutiny of management behavior" (Sherif, Borish, and Gross 2003, 21–22).

26. Western European banks entered Eastern Europe hoping to gain market shares before the European

Union expanded. The shares of foreign banks in the number of banks and in total bank assets grew rapidly in Bulgaria, the Czech Republic, Hungary, and Poland. In Russia and Ukraine, however, foreign banks represented only a small fraction of the total number of banks, even in 2000 (Sherif, Borish, and Gross 2003). In Latin America, Spanish banks became a major force by taking over state and private banks. In Africa, foreign banks reentered and South African banks were playing an increasing role in southern Africa at the end of the 1990s.

27. Research suggests that in Latin America foreign banks are at least as good as domestic banks at lending to small firms (Clarke et al. 2004), and in India foreign banks' lending to small and medium-size firms has grown faster than that of state banks.

28. Indonesia took liberalizing bank entry to an extreme, with almost "free banking" (box 7.4). Russia and Nigeria later followed a similar approach. Most new banks in these countries were "pocket" banks, capturing funds for their owners' firms. In Indonesia, these banks were hit hard by the crisis and proved costly to the government when deposits were guaranteed.

29. Caprio and Klingebiel (2002) list 117 systemic financial crises (in which most of banks' capital was exhausted) in 93 countries and 51 borderline crises in the period 1970–99. See also Sundararajan and Balino (1991) and World Bank, *World Development Report 1989*.

30. Argentina, Russia, and some African countries had high public sector debt compared to public revenues (IMF 2004a). Other countries, notably in East Asia, had high private debt, including high external private debt, relative to GDP. Variants of exchange rate–based stabilization were being used by Argentina, Chile, and Uruguay in the late 1970s and by Argentina, Brazil, and Mexico in the 1990s. Other countries, notably the East Asian countries and Turkey in the 1990s, limited the flexibility of their exchange rates. The relation between the 1990s crises and the current account deficits is similar to but not the same as "Generation I" models of balance of payments crises (Krugman 1979). In the 1990s crises, the problem was not just financing the current account deficit but net amortizations of long- and short-term loans, which could change suddenly.

31. Portfolio adjustments to improved investment opportunities generate rapid inflows initially, followed by a slowdown in inflows and net negative foreign exchange flows (because of interest payments that require internal adjustment).

32. See, for example, Demirgüç-Kunt and Detragiache (2002); and Kaminsky and Reinhart (1999). In the crises of the early 1980s, high U.S. interest rates, as well as the fall in petroleum prices, probably played a

role, while lower interest rates contributed to the large capital inflows to developing countries in the early 1990s and again recently. The rise in international interest rates that started in 1993 probably contributed to a gradual tightening of credit conditions for developing countries.

33. A substantial literature has evolved over the possibility that the crises in the 1990s, particularly those in East Asia, reflected contagion in financial markets, not fundamentals; see Claessens and Forbes (2001) and works cited there. Contagion is one explanation of "Generation II" models of crises in which there are multiple equilibria, associated with high and low rates of capital inflow. No doubt international investors exhibit some herding behavior for various reasons. Another explanation is that events in one country could lead external investors to reevaluate the subjective risks in others and reduce their exposures. This also would seem like contagion.

34. The lag between liberalization and crises seems fairly long (Demirgüç-Kunt and Detragiache 2001, 105). The lag may also reflect the difficulty of pinpointing liberalization and crises, both of which occur over time, as discussed in Eichengreen (2001). Demirgüç-Kunt and Detragiache (2001) date liberalization from the removal of some interest rate controls and note that the estimated lag may reflect the gradualness of interest rate liberalization. Of course, the initial rise in deposit interest rates may also reflect part of a defense against a run on the currency, as, for example, in India in 1991. The lag between financial crises and currency crises may reflect liquidity support to weak banks at the start of financial crises, as discussed below.

35. See Diaz-Alejandro (1985); the capsule discussions of country experience in Sundararajan and Balino (1991, 40–49); and the descriptions of financial crises in Kindleberger (2000).

36. Of course, this explanation is related to Generation II models of crises, discussed in footnote 33.

37. State banks have not been closed without paying off depositors, except in a few African countries.

38. The United States has required intervention in weak banks well before capital is exhausted, and explanations if bank failures lead to deposit insurance payments (Benston and Kaufmann 1997). It is unclear how well this approach would work in developing countries.

39. Even if small depositors are promptly paid off, large depositors may switch to foreign exchange.

40. Arioshi et al. (2000); Dooley (1996). The Malaysian controls are often cited as an example of effective controls, but they were put in place after the crisis was largely over (World Bank 2000c).

41. To paraphrase William McChesney Martin, former chairman of the U.S. Federal Reserve Board, the role

of governments is to take away the punchbowl before the party gets too wild.

42. Such government behavior occurs not only in developing countries but also in industrial countries, for example, in the U.S. savings and loan sector before its crisis.

43. This weakness would have existed even if good information had been available.

44. Interestingly, additional deposits often flowed into state banks during these periods. Despite the weakness of their lending, the public typically considered them to have better guarantees. These banks, in turn, often made additional loans to weak borrowers.

45. See, for example, Klingen, Weder, and Zettelmeyer 2004.

46. Financial liberalizations, even gradual ones, are not easy to manage. Errors in liberalization are not always technical; they sometimes reflect pressures by influential groups.

47. Financial liberalization also tended to increase the fiscal deficit and make it more costly to finance, as the government lost seigniorage revenues and had to pay more market-based interest rates on its debt.

48. World Bank (1998a) describes the substantial strengthening of Argentina's financial system in the mid-1990s.

49. Some policies and some countries will of course deviate from the general trends. Some governments where democracy is limited may attempt to impose capital controls and return to the inflation tax as a means of capturing resources. And many countries remain concerned about the narrowness of credit access for their citizens, and seek ways to provide funds for rural and small and medium-size enterprise lending at below-market rates through specialized intermediaries, notwithstanding the past failures of this approach and the increases in access that are occurring.

50. Such debt is not completely bad—it can serve as a liquid asset to improve the payments system and as a way for individual banks to deal with limited runs. However, governments' low revenue-generating capacities make it difficult to service these debts, lead to cuts in public social and infrastructure spending, and divert governments from developmental issues by the day-to-day problem of rolling over the debt, raising the risk of a return to inflationary finance. These potential problems have been eased by the fall in interest rates worldwide. However, when interest rates begin to rise again, and the costs of debt service correspondingly increase, the problems may reappear.

51. International equity markets can also act as a shock absorber, but only the largest and most transparent firms can list in these markets. Offshore bond markets also are developing in private as well as public bonds; they reduce the risk of credit crunches but increase currency risk.

52. Protecting supervisors completely from legal action raises another issue, the risk that they will engage in malfeasance. Hence, a tribunal separate from the court system is needed to deal with accusations of malfeasance by supervisors.

53. For example, making loans for scooters, cars, and homes to workers in the formal sector who often cannot be fired; making loans to farmers that are repaid by deductions from the contracts the farmers have with crop buyers; and lending to small and medium-size enterprises either through larger firms or by discounting their orders from such firms.

## Country Note F

# Lessons and Controversies from Financial Crises in the 1990s

Since financial markets came into being, financial crises have been their costly companions (Kindleberger 1984). But the 1990s, loosely interpreted, will be remembered for the severity of the crises that shook Mexico in 1994, East Asia in 1997, Brazil and the Russian Federation in 1999, Turkey in 2000, and Argentina and Uruguay in 2002. This country note looks at the origins and costs of these crises and at how they have changed opinions on the use of capital controls, the choice of exchange rate regimes, and approaches to crisis management.

In the early 1980s, high real interest rates, declining export prices, and a global slowdown combined to raise the costs of debts that had been contracted in the 1970s, when real interest rates were negative and the external environment was more favorable. Rising costs of debt accompanied by declining debt-service capacity and inadequate response to shocks produced the debt crisis of the 1980s.

Many of the crises of the 1980s had a common origin. Countries attempted to stabilize inflation through programs anchored on a preannounced, fixed, or only slowly depreciating nominal exchange rate, while delaying needed fiscal adjustments. As adjustments in the nominal exchange rate lagged behind inflation, the real exchange rate appreciated even when inflation declined. Attempts to defend the nominal exchange rate while the real rate was appreciating led to increases in current account deficits and declines in reserves, which ultimately triggered external payments crises, with capital outflows and large and sudden devaluations. In Argentina, Chile, and Uruguay, where banks were allowed to hold deposits in foreign cur-

rency, currency mismatches on the banks' or borrowers' balance sheets made the banks vulnerable to devaluations. When the devaluations came, balance sheet losses were often larger than the banks' entire capital, and compounded the currency crisis with a banking one.

Governments and creditors in Turkey and some countries in Latin America and in East Asia responded with deflationary policies that increased their net exports and some write-down of the debt. This, together with an improvement in the external environment, eventually brought the debt crisis to an end. The adjustment was turbulent, however, and the costs were high. The output collapses during the "lost decade" of the 1980s were comparable to those in the 1929 crisis: the gross domestic product (GDP) declined by 7 percent in Turkey during 1979–80, 15 percent in Chile during 1982–83, 20 percent in Uruguay during 1982–83, 11 percent in Argentina during 1981–82, and 12 percent in Bolivia during 1982–86. By the end of the 1980s, the per capita incomes of most countries in Latin America and in Turkey were only marginally higher, and in some cases lower, than at the beginning of the decade.

Governments, banks, and economists learned important lessons from the experience of the 1980s. Except in Argentina, governments reduced their recourse to external financing and increased their reliance on domestic capital markets to finance their budgets. Commercial banks in industrialized countries reduced their lending to foreign governments. Economists learned that attempts to reduce inflationary expectations through reliance on a nominal exchange rate anchor could not be credible if they were accompanied by adverse balance of payments developments. They also learned, or relearned, that episodes of real exchange rate appreciation could have devastating effects on the real economy if not driven by sustainable long-term increases in productivity (the Balassa-Samuelson effect). Last but not least, they learned that domestic banks' exposure to exchange rate fluctuations could devastate the banks' balance sheets, and that this risk of currency mismatches stemmed not only from their own balance sheets but also from those of their borrowers.

Capital flows increased significantly in the late 1980s and 1990s, reflecting the worldwide shift to market-oriented policies, the decline in industrial countries' interest rates, the fall of the Soviet Union, the spread of international standards of banking supervision and accounting, progress in information technology, and regulatory changes in industrialized countries that allowed mutual and pension funds, insurance companies, and banks to invest abroad. The resulting rise in flows to emerging markets was massive (Tirole 2002). Capital flows to developing countries, including the Republic of Korea, reached US$265 billion in 1996, six times their volume at the beginning of the 1990s, and four times the peak reached during the 1978–82 commercial lending boom. Though these amounts were small in relation to the economies of industrialized countries, they were extremely large in relation to those of developing countries: 9.4 percent of Brazil's GDP (1992–95), 25.8 percent of Chile's (1989–95), 9.3 percent of Korea's (1991–95), 45.8 percent of Malaysia's (1989–95), 27.1 percent of Mexico's (1989–94), and 51.5 percent of Thailand's (1988–95).

The expectation was that these inflows would help developing countries integrate themselves into the global economy, while diversifying financial risks and reducing economic fluctuations. In the first half of the 1990s, it frequently became part of the International Monetary Fund's (IMF) advice to developing countries not only to remove restrictions on their current accounts (in line with the IMF's Article VIII) but also to remove restrictions on their capital accounts. It was also perceived that these developments would help diversify the risks to investors in industrialized countries, improve developing countries' access to finance, and raise developing countries' investment levels and growth.

The results challenged expectations. Financial crises occurred more often than in the 1980s (figure 4.21 in chapter 4) and the costs were, once again, staggering, with declines in GDP similar to those of the 1980s. The 1990s will be remembered as a decade of macroeconomic crises and turbulence in emerging markets.

The average cost of a crisis has been put at about 8 percent of GDP, and that of a financial crisis accompanied by a banking crisis at 18 percent.[1] Bank restructuring costs reached 50 percent of GDP in Indonesia, and one-third of GDP in Korea and Thailand. The output collapses were, for example, 6 percent of GDP in Mexico in 1994, 11 percent in Thailand in 1997, 13 percent in Indonesia in 1997, and 15 percent in Argentina in 2002. Even though in East Asian countries, Turkey, and Russia per capita incomes have returned to their precrisis levels and growth has been relatively rapid, and Argentina has experienced two years of rapid growth, the cost of the crises has been simply staggering.

In some countries, the crises of the 1990s were similar to those of the 1980s in several respects. As in the 1980s, large and unsustainable current account deficits played an important role in Argentina, Brazil, Mexico, Thailand, and Turkey, though they were not significant in the other crisis countries. As in the 1980s, these deficits were often the result of stabilization programs anchored on a nominal exchange rate. And as in the 1980s, in some countries (Argentina, Indonesia, Korea, Thailand, Turkey) the currency crisis triggered a banking crisis, itself the result of currency and maturity mismatches either on commercial banks' balance sheets, or on their borrowers'.

The crises of the 1990s were much more difficult to predict than the crises of the 1980s. While many observers warned of impending crises in Argentina or Mexico, few anticipated those in East Asia. In general, interest rate spreads remained remarkably low in the months preceding the crises (figure F.1).

FIGURE F.1

## Interest Rate Spreads and Real Exchange Rates in Crisis Countries

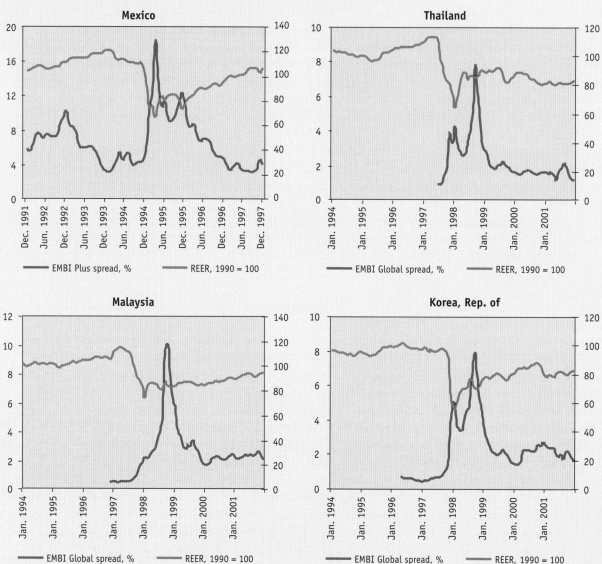

*Source:* JP Morgan, EMBI+ database; World Bank, *WDI.*

*Note:* EMBI = Emerging Markets Bond Index; REER = real effective exchange rate.

The crises of the 1990s differed from those of the 1980s in three other important respects. First, indebtedness by the private sector played a more important role than in the 1980s, both in terms of imbalances between saving and investment and in terms of external debt. Whereas in the 1980s the current account deficits in the balance of payments always reflected negative public sector savings, in several of the crises of the 1990s they reflected negative private sector savings-investment balances. There is consensus that fiscal deficits were not a serious source of vulnerability in Indonesia, Korea, Mexico, or Thailand (Summers 2000). But in some countries—for example, Indonesia, Korea, and Turkey—fiscal accounts did not reflect the full

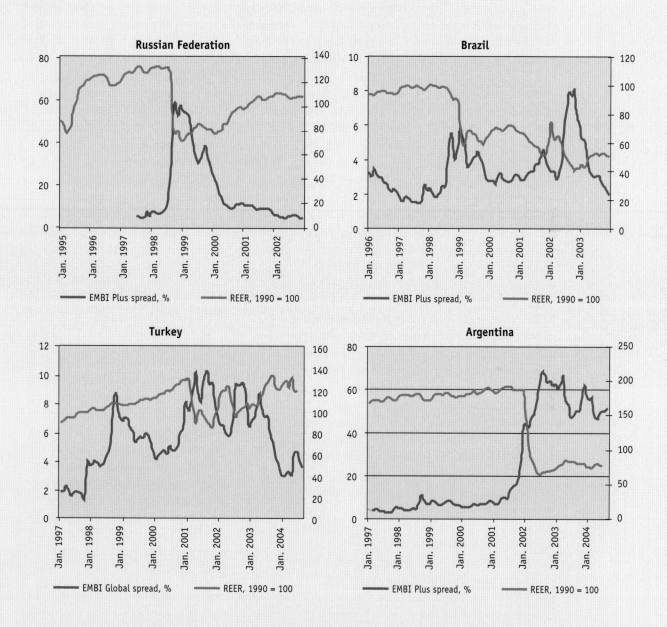

consolidated fiscal and quasi-fiscal picture, and some observers have argued that *prospective* deficits—that is, those that the government would incur if it had to bail out the banks or the private firms, or if an exchange rate collapse took place—were key to understanding these crises (though on this reasoning every country is vulnerable to a crisis). Politically motivated

lending weakened the balance sheets of commercial banks, whose quasi-fiscal cost ultimately increased the domestic public debt. In Turkey, a significant portion of the costs of the banking crisis stemmed from state banks lending to politically connected borrowers.

Second, the 1990s made it clear that not only the stock but the terms of external debt mattered, and especially the maturity structure. In many of the crises of the 1990s, rollover risks stemming from excessive short-term debt played a more important role than did an unsustainable stock of debt or unsustainable current account deficits in the balance of payments. Russia ran surpluses in the current account of the balance of payments both in the year of the crisis and in the years preceding it. Indonesia and Korea's current account balances were negative, but relatively small, and under normal circumstances their financing would not have been a problem (Summers 2000).

Third, twin crises (currency and banking) were much more frequent than in the 1980s, even though banking supervision and bank capitalization were no worse than in the 1980s, and were much better in some cases (such as Argentina's).

The novel features of the crises of the 1990s led to a reexamination of beliefs, regarding among others capital controls, exchange rate regimes, and crisis management. Though debates will continue, the balance of opinion seems to be that the crises of the 1990s altered the conventional wisdom that prevailed in these three areas at the beginning of the 1990s (see Feldstein 2003 and Williamson 2004b for syntheses and alternative views). Essentially, the crises emphasized the so-called impossible trinity, whereby it is impossible for a government to simultaneously maintain an open capital account, an exchange rate target, and an independent monetary policy.

## Capital Account Policies

Controls on capital inflows can reduce the risk of currency crisis, but their desirability and feasibility remain controversial. In the world that emerged from the 1929 crisis and World War II, sources of international finance were extremely limited. Most countries severely restricted capital outflows. France, for example, controlled capital outflows well into the 1980s. In the late 1980s and 1990s, countries whose policies had traditionally focused on managing the scarcity of foreign exchange suddenly faced liquidity surges stemming from large inflows of debt and equity.

In theory, these inflows should have been beneficial, enabling countries to increase their investment rates. In practice, they were not an unmitigated blessing. The impossible trinity posed complex choices for the authorities and often threatened the competitiveness of real exchange rates. Even small adjustments in international portfolio allocations to emerging markets caused swings that were very large in relation to the size of these economies. In addition, the availability of cheap finance encouraged external borrowing beyond prudent limits. Indicative of this, 7 of the top 10 recipients of private capital flows during the 1990s suffered financial crises (table F.1); the exceptions were Chile, China, and India.

- Some let finance flow in freely to the national economy, allowing the nominal exchange rate to bear the full brunt of the adjustment. The advantage of this policy is that it allows the authorities to maintain discretion over monetary policy. The disadvantage is that it implies appreciation of both the nominal and the real exchange rate, an increase in the relative price of nontradables, a loss in the competitiveness of exports, a reduction in the price of imports and a consequent increase in the current account deficit of the balance of payments, and an adverse real shock to the economy as the tradable sector loses competitiveness with imports. No country pursued this policy to the letter, but many let their nominal exchange rates appreciate to some extent, or lag behind inflation.

- Some countries let financial flows flow in freely but mitigated the impact on the nominal exchange rate by building up reserves. This policy has the advantage that it prevents nominal appreciation of the exchange rate, but its cost is a loss of monetary control. In countries with a fixed nominal exchange rate, whether by law (Argentina), or in practice (China, Thailand), this came at the cost of a large expansion of credit, which in turn put upward pressure on the prices of nontradables. Typically, central banks tried to sterilize increases in liquidity through open market operations.

TABLE F.1

## Financial Inflows and Major Financial Shocks

| Financial crises (country, year) | Rank of recipients, by absolute volume of private flows, 1990–96 | Private capital flows 1990–96, % GDP (in 1996) | FDI flows, 1990–96, % private capital flows |
|---|---|---|---|
| Mexico 1994–95 | 2 | 33.0 | 42.8 |
| Thailand 1997 | 6 | 27.1 | 22.7 |
| Indonesia 1997 | 7 | 17.7 | 22.7 |
| Korea, Rep. of 1997 | — | — | — |
| Malaysia 1997 | 5 | 62.7 | 47.2 |
| Russian Federation 1998 | 11 | 4.8 | 18.7 |
| Brazil 1999 (2002) | 3 | 12.6 | 20.7 |
| Turkey 2000–01 | 10 | 12.1 | 22.1 |
| Argentina 2001–02 | 4 | 23.9 | 33.4 |
| China | 1 | 25.2 | 68.2 |
| India | 8 | 7.6 | 20.6 |
| Chile | 9 | 39.4 | 37.2 |

*Source*: IMF and Bank staff estimates.

—. Not available.

While this reduced monetary expansion, the resulting increase in real interest rates was, again, the cause of an adverse real shock to the economy. Further, it generated a vicious cycle of rising inflows, higher interest rates, even more inflows, and so on. Also, because central banks earned less on reserves than on domestic treasury bonds, sterilization came at a high cost—and in turn threatened fiscal stability (Calvo 1998).

- Some countries restricted capital inflows, using a variety of methods. The advantage of this policy is that it leaves the authorities in control of monetary policy, and reduces pressure for the exchange rate to appreciate. In 1990 Indonesia imposed a ceiling on total external borrowing by domestic banks and public enterprises and Thailand restored a 10 percent withholding tax on the interest paid on foreign loans. Chile first introduced restrictions on capital inflows in 1991, in the form of an unremunerated reserve requirement of 20 percent of inflows for all portfolio inflows; for maturities of less than a year, the reserve requirement applied for the duration of the inflow, and for longer maturities, it applied for one year. In July 1992, Chile

increased the requirement to 30 percent and the holding period to one year, regardless of the duration of the inflow. As the volume of inflows continued to grow, Chile continued to gradually extend the coverage, up until 1998 (Edwards 2003). In 1992, Mexico limited commercial banks' foreign liabilities to 10 percent of their total liabilities. India, in 1994, introduced guidelines restricting issues of equity abroad and setting annual aggregate ceilings on private borrowing abroad.

In retrospect, it is important to distinguish controls on capital outflows from controls on inflows. Countries that restricted capital inflows performed better than those that did not. Chile, China, and India all introduced controls on capital inflows that helped them maintain some degree of control over monetary policy and helped to mitigate upward pressure on the exchange rate.. Though their banking systems were not without weaknesses, China and India avoided a financial crisis and also maintained strong growth. Their experience is consistent with the view of some economists (Williamson 1995; Bhagwati 1998; Feldstein 2003) that the efficiency gains from liberalizing capital movements are small in relation to the risks this liber-alization introduces. There is nonetheless an opposite view, holding that controls on capital movements are not only inefficient (Summers 1999, 2000), but also difficult to implement in practice. In the case of Chile, some studies sug-gest that the controls were less effective than gen-erally believed and that they did not succeed in increasing the average maturity of debt. Perhaps more important, there is no guarantee that capi-tal controls will work in other nations as effec-tively as they did in Chile.[2]

## Exchange Rate Policies

Few economic issues were more hotly debated in the 1990s than that of the appropriate exchange rate regime for developing countries. Maintaining competitive real exchange rates is central for financial stability and growth, and it now appears that this can best be achieved through flexible regimes that prevent real appre-ciation from running ahead of a country's pro-ductivity gains. Flexible regimes are also more likely to discourage currency mismatches at the level of firms or banks, and to provide a more accurate picture of public indebtedness.

After a period of relative disfavor, fixed nomi-nal exchange rates made a comeback in academic and policy circles in the late 1980s and early 1990s (Edwards 2003). Notwithstanding Mexico's costly experience with a rigid exchange rate regime in 1994, there was a belief that in countries facing inflation, a fixed exchange rate could provide a nominal anchor and keep interest rates lower than they would be if there were a currency risk. The four major East Asian countries that ran into crises in 1997 (Indonesia, Korea, Malaysia, Thailand), Russia in 1998, Brazil in 1999, and Argentina and Turkey thereafter, had all adopted fixed exchange rate regimes. The fixed rates encouraged domestic companies and banks to borrow in foreign exchange even when their revenues were in domestic currency.

As domestic price and external developments (notably the appreciation of the U.S. dollar against the yen before the 1997 East Asia crisis) made their exchange rates unsustainable, govern-

ments typically attempted to defend the rates using foreign exchange reserves. When the reserves eventually ran out, governments had no choice but to let their currencies go. The result-ing exchange rates were often a small fraction of the fixed rates: half in Thailand and Brazil, and one-fourth in Argentina, at least initially, before it stabilized at one-third.

For the many companies and banks that were highly leveraged in foreign exchange and depended on domestic currency earnings to pay their liabilities, the doubling or trebling of their debt meant bankruptcy. Banks that had lent to these companies, whether in foreign exchange or in domestic currency, also went bankrupt. The economic implosion that followed was stagger-ing. Among the countries shown in table F.1 above, Brazil was the only one that escaped a dra-matic decline in GDP. This was mostly because Brazilian companies were much less leveraged than those of Indonesia, Korea, or Thailand, where corporate debt-equity ratios were in the range of 250–500 percent (Dornbusch 2001). This experience suggests that

> . . . the existence of large amounts of pri-vate debt denominated in dollars or other hard currencies is the most serious source of economic hardship facing the economy. . . . Avoiding large amounts of dollar-denominated debt, and particularly private dollar debt, is probably the most useful thing that a country and corporation can do to reduce the serious consequences of a currency fall. This is true of financial institutions as well as of non-financial companies. (Feldstein 2003)

The balance of opinions has now moved away from rigid exchange rates and, except for China, most developing countries have adopted flexible regimes. These are not clean floats. Korea, for example, has accumulated reserves of US$140 bil-lion since the crisis, which suggests that the gov-ernment has intervened extensively to avoid nominal appreciation. In India, the Reserve Bank (RBI) has often stated that the exchange rate will be determined by market fundamentals, which it has been careful not to define. At times, RBI used the stabilization of the real effective exchange rate as a guide to set nominal rates, but at times the real rate has been only one of the factors in deciding the nominal rate, reflecting the fact that this "constructive ambiguity" is perhaps unavoidable when operating a managed floating exchange rate regime. The prevailing opinion is that RBI has tried to avoid nominal appreciations more forcefully than it has tried to avoid nominal depreciations—which is one of the reasons for the large buildup of reserves. In the case of China, the stability of the nominal rate is based on a continuous buildup of reserves that prevents a nominal appreciation. There is an expectation, however, that the Chinese currency will need to appreciate in nominal terms to reflect increases in productivity: in the long run, as an economy develops, productivity and real wages rise, and incomes approach those of industrialized economies, its exchange rate will inevitably appreciate—as did the Japanese yen in the last two decades, or the European currencies in the 1960s in relation to the U.S. dollar.

The large nominal devaluations that followed the crises had four consequences of economy-wide proportions. These consequences highlight the risks associated with appreciation of the real exchange rate, even if temporarily.

First, the devaluations led to banking crises, even where banks were sound.[3] The banks' open positions, or the borrowers', were simply too large to withstand a devaluation as large as witnessed in Argentina, Indonesia, or Uruguay. In Argentina the problem was compounded after the devaluation by an asymmetric conversion of assets and liabilities, with assets converted at a lower rate than liabilities, but the devaluation was so large that even a well-capitalized bank with modest exposure could not have withstood the shock. Even a well-supervised banking system cannot be sounder than the economy in which it operates. Where there were weaknesses in the banking system, as in Indonesia and in Turkey's state banks, the problem was compounded by the poor quality of the portfolio. Last but not least, governments raised interest rates, sometimes to extremely high levels, in order to moderate the extent of devaluation and prevent "overshoot-

ing" (Blejer, in World Bank 2005b), and this created another source of stress on the banks.

Second, the devaluations caused public debts to rise. While their direct impact on the public debt was not always large, their effect was also felt through two other channels (table F.2): the costs of bailing out and recapitalizing banks, and the impact on foreign-currency-denominated debt and the compounding of real interest rates. Real interest rates exceeded 100 percent in the days and weeks following the devaluation as the authorities sought to prevent the devaluation from overshooting. Such high interest rates were not sustained for long, but even the more moderate rates that succeeded them for a period of months or years had a large impact on the buildup of debt (table F.2). In Argentina, the bailout of banks and the impact of the devaluation accounted for most of the very large increase in public debt. In Turkey, it was the recapitalization of banks and the impact of real interest rates that contributed most.

Third, the devaluations led private external debt to be nationalized through a variety of channels. In principle, borrowing abroad by domestic private firms or private banks without government guarantees is a strictly private transaction. In practice, widespread bankruptcies, or the threat of them, inevitably involved government interventions and the socialization of part of the costs. This constitutes one of the earliest arguments advanced for controls on capital inflows: individual creditors have no exact knowledge of the exposure by other creditors while every increase in exposure causes an increase in the currency risk. A large share of the increase in public debt in table F.2 refers to the socialization of the costs of crises, mostly in the form of bank bailouts and recapitalization.

Fourth, in the presence of foreign debt, the devaluations limited the effectiveness of monetary policies. The presence of large foreign-denominated liabilities can reverse the effect of monetary policies and deepen a crisis (Mishkin 2001). Where the government's foreign-denominated debt is large, as in Brazil, a monetary expansion weakens the government balance sheet and thus prompts a rise in interest rate spreads, thereby

TABLE F.2

## Debt Dynamics in Crisis Economies, Cumulative Change, Three Years Before . . .

|  | Mexico, 1991–93 | Indonesia, 1994–96 | Korea, Rep. of, 1994–96 | Malaysia, 1994–96 | Russian Federation, 1995–97 | Brazil, 1995–97 | Turkey, 1997–99 | Argentina, 1999–2001 |
|---|---|---|---|---|---|---|---|---|
| Change in public sector debt | −22.8 | −11.6 | −2.6 | −16.6 | −8.8 | 6.3 | 14.5 | 21.5 |
| Primary deficit (− surplus) | −12.9 | −7.5 | −2.1 | −22.1 | 9.3 | 0.7 | 1.8 | 1.7 |
| Rec. of contingent liab. (net of privatization) | 0.0 | 0.0 | 0.0 | −2.0 | −9.3 | 4.0 | −0.7 | 0.7 |
| Contribution from real GDP growth | −3.9 | −7.3 | −3.1 | −16.0 | 4.0 | −3.0 | −2.4 | 4.2 |
| Contribution from real interest rate | 3.4 | 3.7 | 0.0 | 7.0 | −7.4 | 3.6 | 20.7 | 10.7 |
| Contribution from real exchange rate change | −5.9 | −2.2 | −0.6 | −1.2 | −29.7 | −1.6 | −0.4 | 2.4 |
| Contribution from debt indexation | 0.4 | 0.0 | 0.0 | 0.0 | 0.0 | 1.4 | 0.0 | 0.0 |
| Residual | −4.0 | 1.6 | 3.3 | 17.6 | 24.3 | 1.3 | −4.5 | 1.9 |

## . . . and Three Years After

|  | Mexico, 1994–96 | Indonesia, 1996–99 | Korea, Rep. of, 1997–99 | Malaysia, 1997–99 | Russian Federation, 1998–2000 | Brazil, 1998–2000 | Turkey, 2000–03 | Argentina, 2002–03 |
|---|---|---|---|---|---|---|---|---|
| Change in public sector debt | 28.0 | 68.6 | 30.3 | 14.9 | 4.2 | 15.7 | 19.1 | 83.7 |
| Primary deficit (− surplus) | −16.8 | −2.7 | 6.0 | −19.6 | −7.0 | −6.7 | −12.6 | −3.9 |
| Rec. of contingent liab. (net of privatization) | 0.0 | 0.0 | −0.7 | 6.9 | −5.9 | 5.0 | 15.4 | 0.3 |
| Contribution from real GDP growth | −0.6 | 2.0 | −2.9 | −2.5 | −9.4 | −2.6 | −6.4 | −5.6 |
| Contribution from real interest rate | 12.5 | 4.3 | 2.3 | 7.8 | −4.8 | 17.1 | 21.7 | 1.3 |
| Contribution from real exchange rate change | 6.5 | 10.8 | 1.8 | 8.7 | 30.9 | 2.8 | 3.3 | 40.6 |
| Contribution from debt indexation | 4.4 | 0.0 | 0.0 | 0.0 | 0.0 | 4.9 | 12.2 | 0.0 |
| Residual | 22.1 | 54.3 | 23.8 | 13.6 | 0.4 | −4.9 | −14.5 | 51.0 |

*Source*: World Bank 2005c.

*Note*: The residual captures the recognition of implicit liabilities, such as banking sector bailouts, implicit social security and pension debts, and so on, for which no hard data exist, and which thus are not included directly in the calculations. It also includes various cross-products assumed away with the approximations made. For Argentina, data are available for only two postcrisis years: 2000 and 2001.

opening the possibility that interest rates will rise rather than fall. Similarly, foreign-denominated debt in domestic *private* balance sheets makes it more difficult for a country to recover from a financial crisis because expansionary monetary policies will likely cause a nominal depreciation of the domestic currency. This will hurt the balance sheets of firms and banks and reduce their net worth. In a country without foreign-denominated debt issued by the private sector, expansionary monetary policies can help shore up balance sheets of financial and nonfinancial firms, and increase their net worth.

## Monetary and Fiscal Policies

There is a view, though highly controversial, that the management of the crises of the 1990s relied on excessive fiscal adjustment; that excessively high real interest rates have in some instances forced unnecessary bank closures; and that international financial institutions often forced crisis countries to undertake structural reforms that were not directly related to resolving the crises—which would have been better done through countries' own national decision-making processes (Feldstein 2003; Stiglitz 2001; Ahluwalia 2003).

The least controversial of these statements is that fiscal policies were unnecessarily tight, as acknowledged in the IMF's own evaluation (IMF 2003b). A common explanation for this is that capital account crises were dealt with as current account crises.

"Weak" banks have often been blamed for the crises. However, while poorly run banks can exacerbate a crisis, and perhaps even cause one, well-capitalized banks cannot guarantee against a financial crisis. Even well-capitalized banks can quickly lose their equity in the face of large swings in exchange rates, or the collapse of the real economy.

## Notes

1. World Bank, *Global Economic Prospects 1998*.
2. Although the reasons as to why they would work better in Chile than elsewhere are not clear (Edwards 2003).
3. Argentina, for example, following the Mexico crisis in 1994 in which many banks had failed, considerably improved the financial soundness of its banking system by restructuring and shifting the ownership of banks to foreign private banks (primarily from the United States and Spain).

*Chapter 8*

# Policy Reforms and Growth Performance: What Have We Learned?

THIS CHAPTER SYNTHESIZES THE lessons from the review of experience with policy reform in macroeconomics, trade, privatization, and finance. As the preceding chapters illustrate, each of these areas of policy reform is complex and an attempt to draw lessons in any one of them creates vigorous debate. Nevertheless, three key cross-cutting lessons seem to emerge:

- Most market-oriented reforms have had positive payoffs, though their impact on growth was not as large as some of the exorbitant claims made both in academic and policy circles.

- Experience shows the importance of creating institutional constraints on the exercise of discretion in policy implementation. Institutions and rules should be seen as a means to facilitate the predictable, credible, and beneficial use of discretion, rather than as a substitute for discretion.

- The expectations of the various actors in the markets play a crucial role in the success or failure of reforms, and their evolution can lead to either virtuous or vicious circles in the reform process.

These lessons are discussed in section 1. They create three suggestions for a way forward, examined in section 2:

- While the basic economic principles behind most of the reforms of the 1990s were cor-

rect, there was a tendency to believe that they could only be implemented in certain ways. Going forward, more emphasis is needed on common principles, along with a more pluralistic approach to implementing those principles.

- Growth strategies, focused on initiating and sustaining episodes of rapid growth, are the key to reaching much higher levels of income. Such strategies focus on attacking the binding constraints on growth, rather than addressing many weaknesses simultaneously.

- Creating the institutional conditions for a favorable climate for investors, both large and small, is essential. Government actions and their design should be scaled to match the country's institutional capability. "Do no harm" is a wonderful guide, and the potential for government action to improve on market outcomes needs to be balanced against the ability of existing institutions to sustain good practices.

## 1. Cross-Cutting Lessons of the 1990s

For each of the three cross-cutting lessons, this section uses a common organizational structure: it diagnoses previous successes and failures, reviews the conventional wisdom of the 1990s that lay behind the reform efforts, and describes the lesson itself.

*Lesson 1*

*Most market-oriented reforms have had positive payoffs*, though their impact on growth was not as large as some of the exorbitant claims. And the benefits of reform were, in general, predicted correctly by microeconomists and sectoral experts, though not by crude applications of the "new growth" theory.

## Diagnosis before the 1990s: Conflicting Interpretations of the Relationship of Growth to Policy

Understanding the lessons of the 1990s for economists requires a little background on the professional state of play in the early 1980s. At that time, growth theory was still dominated by the Solow-Swann model (Solow 1956, 1971; Swann 1956). According to that model, in the steady-state equilibrium, long-run growth rates are completely unaffected by national policies. That is, while national policies could affect the *level* of income they could not permanently affect the *growth rate*.[1] Meanwhile, the analysis of sectoral reforms—for example, in trade, privatization, or the financial sector—was dominated by microeconomic models in which gains resulted from policy reforms but were typically only small fractions of the gross domestic product (GDP).[2]

This match—of the unresponsiveness of long-run growth rates to national policies in macroeconomics, and the apparently small efficiency gains to be had from sectoral reforms in microeconomics—was a stable but increasingly unhappy marriage. Stable because these were both very robust features of their respective analytical approaches. Unhappy because by the early 1990s this combination of approaches clearly could not explain some basic facts about the world, particularly the developing world:

- Since some countries are very rich and others are very poor, differences in growth rates must have been sustained and substantial. Indeed, as chapter 2 showed, growth rate differences of nearly 2 percentage points a year have been sustained for more than 100 years.

- The differences in growth rates across countries over periods of a decade or more were

too large to be "steady-state" differences, but they also seemed too large to be transitional differences in adjusting to efficiency gains.

- Countries' growth rates change dramatically: some countries have growth rates that propel them rapidly out of poverty traps while others go from rapid growth to stagnation or bust.

## Conventional Wisdom in the 1990s: "New Growth" Theory and Large Gains from Reform

This inability of the standard theory of steady-state growth to explain the facts perhaps explains the love affair of academic and policy-making circles with "new growth theory" models in the 1980s. Advances in the modeling of noncompetitive equilibria (Romer 1983, 1986) allowed the development of a new set of endogenous growth models in which national policies could influence not just the level of income but also countries' steady-state growth rates (Grossman and Helpman 1992; Aghion and Howitt 1998). These led to the conventional wisdom of the 1990s—that policy reform could affect economic growth—but they never made quite clear why this should be so. Often, authors did not make clear whether their growth regressions were intended to identify differences in steady-state growth or, instead, to identify impacts of policy on the level of income. Such lack of clarity pervades discussions of growth. It is useful to dispel this confusion by keeping the gains in levels with "growth" as a transitional phenomenon and gains in "growth" in the steady state. In the end, the hope was dashed that there were large policy-driven gains in *steady-state* growth. Even so, this does not imply that policy reform cannot yield large growth gains when it has a large impact on the *level* of income.

Trade policy reform illustrates this point. Many growth regressions related growth in output per person in the $i$th country over some period of $n$ years to the lagged level of output and some indicator of trade policy during some period:

Figure 8.1 shows the path of annual growth stemming from a hypothetical trade reform that increases the sustainable level of output. Let us

$$g^i_{t,t-n} = y^i_t - y^i_{t-n} = \alpha + \lambda \star y^i_{t-n}$$
$$+\beta \star \textit{Trade Policy}^i_f(t, t-n)$$
$$+ \textit{Other factors} + \textit{error term}$$

assume for now that "trade policy" at any point in time can be adequately represented by a single number. The graph shows a hypothetical economy growing at a steady-state rate of 2 percent a year. In year $t = 5$ there is a permanent improvement in trade policy from TP to TP★. If trade policy raises the *steady-state* growth rate immediately and permanently by 2 percentage points, the measured growth rate over any five-year period will increase from 2 to 4 percent and will remain at that higher level. In this case the impact of the trade reform on the *level* of output will be infinitely large.

Figure 8.1 also shows the impact of a trade reform that affects only the *level* of output. In each case we assume some dynamics for illustration—that the impact on the level of output takes 10 years to be fully felt and that the adjustment from the baseline to the higher level of output is linear. In this case, the reform has an impact on measured five-year growth rates that increases as output adjusts to its new level, and then decreases to zero; that is, the economy returns to its steady-state growth path. The graph shows the impact on annual growth rates of a trade reform, using three possible magnitudes of the cumulative impact of the reform on the level of output: 5 percent, 25 percent, and 50 percent (under certain assumptions about adjustment dynamics). If the cumulative impact of the trade reform on the equilibrium level of output is only 5 percent, the impacts on measured growth rates are small and disappear quickly, compared to the impact of a 2 percentage point increase in steady-state growth rates. In contrast, if the cumulative impact of trade reform on the level of output is 25 percent, over a 10-year horizon the effect of the reform on the observed growth rate is virtually indistinguishable from the effect of an increase in the steady-state growth rate— and only over long periods does it become possible to distinguish one (an impact on level with transitional growth) from the other (an increase

### FIGURE 8.1

### Simulated Impacts of Policy Reform on the Level and Growth Rate of Output

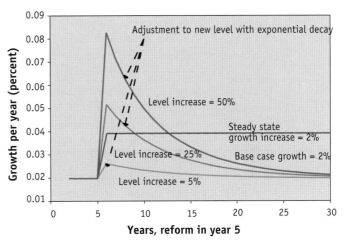

*Source:* Author's elaboration.

in steady-state growth). Finally, if the impact of the trade reform on the equilibrium *level* of output is as large as 50 percent, the impact on observed five-year growth rates is much larger for a reform that "only" affects the level than it is for a reform that has a large impact on steady-state growth.

This technical excursion clarifies that over the horizon of a decade or more the impact of an economic reform on observed growth rates does not depend at all on whether the reform raises steady-state growth or "only" raises the long-run level of output with no impact on steady-state growth. What matters is the size of the gain and the speed of adjustment. Over the medium term, if the effects on the level of output are small, the effects on steady-state growth will also be small, and if the effects on the level of output are large, the effects on growth will be large.

Whether growth regressions in the 1990s were estimating growth effects or level effects mattered less than how the regressions were interpreted. In practice they were widely seen as producing estimates of gains from policy reform that were whole orders of magnitude larger than the microeconomic estimates of those gains. The example of trade liberalization again illustrates this point. The original microeconomic ("Harberger triangle") estimates of the welfare gains were on the order of 1 to 5 percent of GDP for an ambitious reform of tariffs from moderately high levels. With moderate adjustment speeds, such a reform would increase growth rates temporarily by not more than half a percent a year. Even when models introduced general equilibrium effects and plausible links from trade reform to productivity improvements, the apparent gains from trade reform were too small to cause sustained growth increases of more than 1 percent a year, over a period as long as a decade. By contrast, it was frequently claimed that growth regressions, such as those of Sachs and Warner (1995a), supported the view that trade liberalization could raise the rate of economic growth by 2 percent a year over a 30-year horizon. This implies a rise of 80 percent in the level of output. Even if trade policy reform were to raise the economic growth rate by only 1 percent a year, sustaining these effects for a very long period—as implied by the very small adjustment coefficients—would produce gains of as much as 50 percent of GDP.

Interpreting the "aggregate" and "growth regression" evidence concerning the impacts of trade policy on output is nearly impossible, because even though many studies take growth as the variable to be explained, the interpretation of the magnitude of the resulting coefficient depends entirely on how the dynamics of the regression are specified: the same reported coefficient on a variable representing trade policy could imply either a small or an infinitely large effect on the level of output.

## Lesson of the 1990s: Policy Reform Produced Mixed, and Modest, Gains

The 1990s showed that the long-run impact on output[3] of most policy reform actions in the areas considered—macro, trade, privatization, financial liberalization—was positive and roughly as large as claimed by microeconomic or general equilibrium studies.

In particular, from most microeconomic-based models we would expect that the gains would be larger, the larger the initial policy distortion, because the welfare gains from distortions increase as the square of the distortion. Chapter 5 emphasized that countries that made very large reductions in tariffs (Bangladesh, India, Pakistan) achieved large gains in integration, while those that made smaller reductions in tariffs achieved smaller gains. Similarly, chapter 4 showed that the potential gains from taming hyperinflation are much larger than the potential gains from reducing inflation from more moderate levels. And in the financial sector, the gains from interest rate liberalization depend on the severity of the initial financial repression: thus for countries with very negative real interest rates, liberalization should produce large gains, while for countries with moderate financial repression the gains would be more modest.

These relationships would also lead one to expect large gains in countries that are very poor when reforms begin, since many of these countries are much less productive than they could be if they had good policies and institutions. The very fast growth achieved by countries such as China, India, and Vietnam is consistent with the view that reform can have enormous effects on the level of output, which in turn lead to rapid growth in the course of transition to the new higher levels of equilibrium output.

That said, the claims that policy reforms would raise growth rates permanently, or by as much as 1 or 2 percentage points a year, were almost certainly exaggerated. The disappointment with the returns to policy reform stems partly from the fact that regressions have suggested that some policy variables, such as budget deficits, outward orientation, and privatization, are associated with economic growth. If such an empirical association represents a stable, uniform, causal relationship between the policy variable and growth, it is puzzling if, at least on average, the relationship does not hold for policy reforms. However, the magnitudes of the impact of the policy variables on immediate growth rates were never very clear.

To sum up, the gains from more effectively and efficiently provided infrastructure services will not be infinite but they are important, as are the gains from better allocation of financial resources.[4] Finally, not everything that is called "market-friendly" reform will work to increase output. The details do matter and it is perfectly possible to make large and costly mistakes, as attested by some of the examples in this volume.

## Lesson 2

*Institutional limits are needed on the exercise of discretion in policy implementation.* Government discretion cannot be squeezed out of policy making, and the presence of government discretion implies the need for a solid institutional foundation to control it. Creating effective institutions that will play this role depends not just on technocratic design, but also on an underlying "shared mental model" (North 1990).

## Definitions

For purposes of this discussion we define "policy," "organization," and "institutions" to mean very specific things.

A policy is a mapping from states of the world to actions. That is, a policy is not a single action but the description of a process that produces a sequence of policy actions. The policy actions may be contingent on facts: for example if a country has a fiscal policy of running a cyclically adjusted surplus of 1 percent of GDP, this requires a budget (policy action) that is tailored to the state of the business cycle (fact).

To implement a policy, translating it into practice, requires an organization of policy making.

The direct organization of policy making includes the following:

- The organization that has authority to take policy action;

- The range of feasible policy actions;

- The process to be followed in taking policy actions;

- The objectives of the policy;

- A model that determines the relevant facts (or states of the world); and

- Some indication of the policy mapping from facts to actions, given the objectives and the model. These policy mappings can take one of three archetypical forms: objectives with discretion, conditional rules, and unconditional rules.

The background institutions of policy making are the legal and political environment into which the direct institutions are embedded. The background institutions include not just governmental organization of checks and balances on the discretion of organizations and on the government itself—but also rules such as the freedom of the press and the ability of citizens to organize.

Figure 8.2 illustrates these basics. The organization responsible for implementation is the agent, to which the principal delegates the power to take policy actions. If for simplicity we imagine the organization as a single agent,[5] we can imagine a positive model of policy actions. One such model is that the organization will take policy actions that maximize its *own* objective function subject to the constraints and incentives it faces. In this sense the notional policy (proposed objectives, model, relevant facts, and proposed mapping) and the background institutions are what establish the incentives and constraints on the maximization problem of the agency.

Table 8.1 gives examples of how these descriptive terms fit into a specific area, such as monetary policy, as a component of macroeconomic policy. Each of the policy areas discussed in the previous chapters, from trade to financial sector regulation, can be understood using this same vocabulary.

## Diagnosis before the 1990s: Government Discretion Is the Problem

Up to the 1990s, a prominent diagnosis of development experience had two components. First, policy mappings were seen to consist mainly of multiple objectives with discretion. Hence in macroeconomic, trade, financial, infrastructure, and regulatory policy the organizations with direct responsibility for policy actions were often given multiple (unclear) objectives, while at the same time they were given control over a wide range of policy actions. Second, while discretion was seen to be used well in some times and

FIGURE 8.2

## The Elements of Policy Action

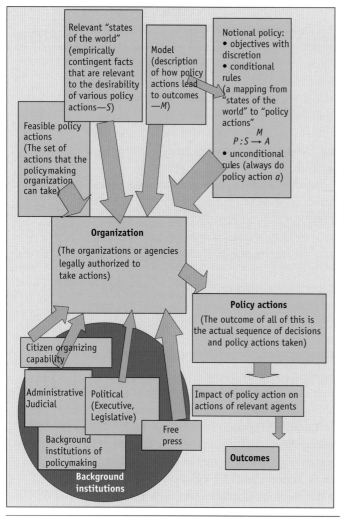

places, it was also seen to be misused, in a variety of ways (table 8.2):

- Inadequate information led to wrong decisions.

- Technical capacity was insufficient to take correct decisions.

- Multiple objectives led to ineffective actions.

- Policy actions were politicized in a way that sacrificed effectiveness for political expediency.

- Public officials had inadequate incentives to be dynamic or to innovate.

- Corruption was rampant.

## Conventional Wisdom in the 1990s: Create Market-Friendly Conditions by Reducing or Eliminating Government Discretion

Given that the diagnosis was "too much discretion," the conventional-wisdom goal of the 1990s was to reduce public sector discretion as much and as fast as possible. Reformers pursued this goal in three ways (table 8.3):

- First, reducing the scope of government activities that required discretion, by removing the government from direction over production (by divesting the public sector of productive assets), and by eliminating unnecessary regulations.

- Second, in whatever regulatory or policy activity remained under the government, reducing government discretion, by pursuing rules-based formulas for decision making based on clear "objective" criteria and by granting autonomy to regulatory agencies.

- Third, making binding international commitments that limited the scope of domestic discretionary action, for example, multilateral or regional international trade agreements, and agreements limiting exchange rate flexibility.

## Lesson of the 1990s: Proper Exercise of Discretion in Policy Implementation Is Key

The attempts to reduce government discretion had two phases: a rationalization phase followed by an optimization phase.

The rationalization phase, which happened mainly in the 1980s, was needed and beneficial. It eliminated accretions of actions, regulations, and decisions that had often resulted in policies that served nobody's best interests.[6] Examples included reducing the variability and capriciousness of tariff rates, closing down and consolidating many special-purpose and money-losing financial intermediaries, and selling off assets in competitive industries.

By the 1990s, reforms were moving into the optimization phase. These "second generation"

TABLE 8.1

## Sectoral Example of Direct and Background Institutions of Policymaking

| Item | Definition | *Objectives with discretion* | *Conditional rule— inflation targeting* | *Unconditional rule* | *Unconditional rule— no discretion(free banking)* |
|---|---|---|---|---|---|
| | | *Examples from monetary policy* | | | |
| Feasible policy action | A legally authorized act by a public sector authority | Money supply | Money supply | Money supply | None |
| "Model" | Specification of causal chain from policy action to outcome | Money lowers interest rates, stimulates output | | | |
| Relevant state of the world | Relevant facts for the application of policy | State of the business cycle | Prices | None | None |
| Policy mapping | A model-informed mapping from states of the world to policy actions | Increase money when output temporarily low | | Always increase money supply by *k* percent | Match outstanding obligations to foreign assets |
| Direct organization of policymaking | Public sector organization authorized to act | Central bank | Central bank | Central bank | Currency board |
| Indirect institutions of policymaking | Formal and informal checks on policy-making decisions | Procedures for administrative appeal<br>Courts<br>Executive<br>Legislature<br>Media<br>Interest groups | | | |

*Source:* Author's elaboration.

reforms (Naim 1995, 1999) constituted a move to conditional rules governing the actions of a wide range of policy makers—monetary authorities, regulators of banks and utilities, and private contractors providing public services. In essence, many of the reforms were shaped by the view that institutions should play the role of eliminating discretion wherever possible, rather than facilitating effective decision making. The reforms had to grapple with the question of how core government responsibilities were to be carried out. In a number of sectors there is a core of public responsibility that governments cannot avoid. For example, while there is no compelling reason for government to own and operate commercial or investment banks, government does have a core, unavoidable responsibility and interest in the soundness of the banking sector. And while there is no compelling reason why government should run an electricity company, government does have a core, unavoidable

responsibility and interest in the soundness of the electricity grid.

The attempts to reduce government discretion by imposing rules-based policies had much less impact than was hoped. In retrospect, there were two reasons why.

First, the risk that the public sector will abuse its discretion is a necessary consequence of the monopoly nature of state power over the means of coercion. If performance is poor because the public sector has incentives to abuse discretion (whether by failing to respond to problems, making mistakes, capricious enforcement and corruption, or outright predation), it is unlikely to be sharply improved by reforms that limit the scope of government. Policy conditionality cannot be effective except in those rare cases in which the policy action is unequivocal and compliance is easily observed. Easterly (2000) provides an insightful analysis of attempts to limit fiscal deficits through the application of rules.

TABLE 8.2

## Examples of Misuse of Discretion

| Policy area | Motivation for public sector engagement | Examples of ways in which policymaking discretionary power was misused | Negative consequences of discretion |
|---|---|---|---|
| Macro | Control of the money supply<br>Maintenance of system of external payments (exchange rate) | Central banks forced to "print money" to finance deficits through high seigniorage<br>Overvalued exchange rates maintained with preferential access to foreign exchange for government and parastatals | Money creation, high and variable inflation<br>Lack of fiscal discipline led to high debts<br>Mismatch of monetary and exchange rate policy led to overvaluation with periodic crises and "maxi" devaluations |
| Trade | Revenue mobilization, industrial promotion, control of trade balance | Firms lobbied to obtain protection for politicians' "pet" projects<br>Bribery in customs to evade trade restrictions | Industries, once protected, never grew up from "infant" status<br>Discretionary controls over imports led to "rent seeking" in the creation and allocation of import restrictions |
| Privatization and regulation | Supply of infrastructure | Governments used firms for patronage (for example, placement of executives)<br>Placement of facilities was politically motivated<br>Outright corruption in the placement of contracts | Underpricing and lack of autonomous control over adequate cash flow led to underinvestment in maintenance<br>Multiple and unclear objectives (no "bottom line") led to productive inefficiencies and technological stagnation |
| Financial sector | Private sector capital markets could not provide long-term credit | Allocation of credit to politically preferred activities<br>Rollover of debt for favored borrowers (for instance, parastatals)<br>Selective enforcement of repayment obligations | Large losses for banks<br>Low deposit rates (often negative in real terms)<br>High borrowing rates for nonpreferred borrowers<br>Capital did not flow to new, promising industries |

*Source:* Author's elaboration.

TABLE 8.3

## Efforts to Limit Government Discretion

| | Reduce the scope of government activity | "Rules not discretion" with "independent" regulation | Binding international agreements |
|---|---|---|---|
| Macroeconomic | | Dollarization, currency boards, inflation targeting, independent central banks | Monetary unions |
| Trade | Elimination of barriers to trade | Moving to uniform tariffs; eliminating nontariff barriers in favor of tariffs | Bilateral (NAFTA), regional (EU, Mercosur), multilateral (WTO) |
| Privatization/ regulation | Privatization | Using contracts as a means of engaging with private sector providers | |
| Financial sector liberalization | Privatization of state-owned banks; elimination of regulations | Adopting supervisory standards (for example, Basel) | Allowing entry of foreign banks |

*Source:* Author's elaboration.

Suppose, as is not unusual, that a government wants to overspend—specifically, to bring expenses into the present and to push the generation of revenues into the future, hence reducing net public assets. Then suppose some outside agency wants the country to limit its fiscal deficit to a level lower than the government wants. Will a "policy" change that limits the fiscal deficit to some specified amount staunch the reduction in net assets? No. The government can reduce net public assets in hundreds of ways that do not increase the recorded fiscal deficit.[7] This ability exposes the mirage of so-called rules-based policies, because by the time one has a means to prevent all the tricks by which a simple rule such as "no fiscal deficits" can be subverted, one actually has the institutional conditions in place for good expenditure management.

The second reason why attempts to reduce government discretion by imposing rules-based policies had less impact than hoped for is that the difference between "rules" and "discretion" proved much murkier than supposed. The first round of the rules-versus-discretion debate generally ignored the key difference between conditional and unconditional rules.

The 1990s brought home that if incentives remain unchanged, and there are no background institutions to check the findings of fact, the use of conditional rules can produce exactly the same policy actions as the use of discretion. Conceptually, and often in practice, the process of policy actions with conditional rules can be divided into two stages: a findings-of-fact stage and a policy action stage; as noted above, the findings of fact dictate the policy action (or narrow range of actions). The scope for exercising discretion can then be pushed back from the policy action stage to the findings-of-fact stage.

A telling example comes from Indonesia's attempt to create bankruptcy courts. In the wake of the financial crisis, many observers felt that the lack of a credible judiciary was limiting creditors' ability to enforce their contracts or even to force debtors to negotiate resettlements. Because judicial reform is a slow process, a new bankruptcy law was passed that attempted to remove all discretion from the courts in bankruptcy

cases. The only role left to the courts was to declare a debtor bankrupt,[8] and after the judicial declaration of bankruptcy all future jurisdiction passed to the group of creditors. The result was that in the first few high-profile bankruptcy cases the judges did not declare bankruptcy because they found that a "legal" debt did not exist. Instead they used various criteria to show that otherwise apparently ironclad debt contracts did not in fact constitute debt. The new law had not changed anyone's incentives. There were no credible checks on the courts' findings and hence the exact same result—lack of a credible creditor threat of bankruptcy—was reached even in the face of determined attempts to remove discretion from the legal process.

This conceptual framing may help us to understand several elements of the experience of the 1990s:

- Why the success of reforms differed so widely across countries, and the significance of new evidence about the importance of institutions over policies;

- The evolution of concerns from policy reform to governance and institutions;

- The mixed popularity of growth reforms and importance of perceptions in the success of reform; and

- The evolution toward policy recommendations designed to fit specific institutional capabilities, as opposed to the application of universal best practices.

We discuss each of these elements in turn.

*Intercountry differences in the success of reform.* Why did the success of reforms differ so widely across countries? The answer may lie in the combination of a country's initial level of income and its institutional capability to implement complex reforms.

Many of the biggest successes of the 1990s were achieved by countries that were much less productive than they could be with good policies and institutions, so that modest reforms whose implementation was not institutionally demanding were able to produce large gains in expected future income. Examples are China's liberalization of agriculture and India's dismantling of very high trade barriers.[9]

The varied experience of the transition countries illustrates the difficulty of achieving the right mix between declared policies and institutional capability. A viable financial sector that channels resources to productive investments is key to a market economy. Reform efforts in this direction sometimes had acceptable results—for instance, in Hungary. In Albania, by contrast, financial sector liberalization with essentially no government control led to a giant Ponzi scheme,[10] and after a brief bubble, to massive losses that forced the government out of power. In some countries of Eastern Europe, privatization worked reasonably well. In others, privatization was achieved rapidly but it was followed by a shake-out, because the institutional capability for regulating the basics of corporate governance did not exist. Another group of East European countries pursued a so-called policy of privatization without any credible central authority, any mechanisms of public sector accountability or corporate governance, or any means of legal enforcement of contracts. This concentrated assets in the hands of those who were able to operate in such an environment.

Latin America's experience was mixed. By and large, the countries of the region began with a base of better policies and more advanced institutions, offering less "low hanging fruit" for reformers than in Asian and transition countries. Most Latin American countries had to grapple with institutionally intensive reforms—financial sector regulation, and regulation of privatized infrastructure—in the 1990s. Not surprisingly, therefore, some reforms worked well and were widely popular, some worked well and were unpopular (such as the privatization of water utilities in Argentina), and some worked badly with recriminations all around (for example, the first round of Mexican toll roads).

*Evolution of concerns from policy reform to governance and institutions.* Current discussions about the investment climate differ from 1991 discussions of "market-friendly" policies. The recognition today is that, except for a very few macroeconomic policies that can be executed with the stroke of a pen and easily observed, policies are meaningless unless they are backed by controls that make the policy actors sufficiently accountable.

Take the example of replacing the public provision of an infrastructure service with private provision by a contractor. The public agency responsible for awarding the contract must announce the winning bidder. Most of the second generation reforms in infrastructure dealt with extremely complex services, for which the evaluation of bids inevitably involves some discretion (one does not merely want to choose the lowest bidder without prequalification, consideration of the full range of services included in the contract, and so forth). But the necessary discretion that is created by complexity can lead to inefficiency, malfeasance, or corruption. The same is true with the transition from concern with fiscal discipline to a broader concern with budgetary institutions. While it is easy to place conditions (either via rules or outside agencies) that govern easily observable policy variables such as the fiscal deficit, it is impossible to mandate that public monies be well spent. Similarly, sensible regulation of banks requires the use of considerable judgment. Because of the importance of trust between borrowers and lenders, especially in environments in which the formal mechanisms of contract enforcement are weak, close continuing relationships between banks and firms tend to be the norm. From a regulator's perspective this makes it difficult to distinguish between a perfectly rational business decision to carry a long-term customer over a difficult spot by rolling over loans and a bank's unwillingness to realize and write off bad debts. The regulator's problem in observing the "true" facts about any given loan is of course compounded when a regulatory agency is held accountable for thousands of such decisions made every day.

*The mixed popularity of growth reforms and importance of perceptions.* Analyzing the institutional conditions for policy implementation may also help to explain why many market-oriented reforms—even those for which there is evidence of success—have not been altogether popular. In Latin America, for example, bringing more market forces into the provision of infrastructure has improved the quality of services and expanded their coverage, but prices have risen and "privatization" is widely unpopular. A possible explanation is that a lack of public confidence in the regulatory institutions means that the public may perceive deals as fixed or corrupt and price increases as simply leading to high and unjustified profits for firms, which have regulators "in their pockets." This is a hard problem to deal with.

*The evolution toward policy recommendations designed to fit institutional capability.* Suppose that some goods have dynamic externalities, so that greater domestic production of these goods raises a country's overall output, and that other goods do not, so that their protection and greater domestic production cause overall output to be lower.[11] Assuming that tariff rates can change relative prices, a possible tariff policy would be to place a high tariff on the good with dynamic externalities and no tariff on the growth-reducing good. This policy is a conditional rule that depends on distinguishing which good is which. In practice, however, this distinction might be difficult to draw and to verify. Now suppose that producers of the growth-reducing good offer a larger bribe than producers of the growth-enhancing good.

In such a situation the optimal policy depends entirely on the institutions of policy making. If we define good tariff policy institutions as those providing institutional conditions in which the conditional rule, "high tariffs on growth-promoting goods," will be applied correctly, with good institutions the best policy to choose is a conditional rule. But the institutions of tariff policy could be weak. They might lack the technical capacity necessary to assess which goods are growth-promoting and which are not. Or, if they were faced with discretion or a conditional rule, their findings of fact might be susceptible to political influence or outright bribery. If the direct and indirect institutions of policy making are weak, the optimal policy is an unconditional rule of uniform tariffs, and perhaps even zero tariffs (table 8.4).

More generally, if it is perceived that corruption is the central problem in public sector action, the tendency will be to force all discretion out of policy implementation—for example, by removing the government from bank regulation. Good regulation is better than no regulation. But no regulation is better than bad regulation, and where mechanisms are not available to control the discretion that is inherent in attempts to implement reasonable policies, "no regulation" may be the appropriate choice. Similarly, if the central problem is that private investors fear predation by the state, strong preconditions to prevent predation are needed— even if their introduction sacrifices otherwise desirable regulations or actions.

The debate today is no longer about whether "the market" or "the state" is always superior, nor is it about "the proper role of the state" in the abstract.[12] As theorists, most prominently Joseph Stiglitz, have shown, one can always create a theoretical model in which state action can improve on the free market outcome—if the state action is perfect. But, as Pigou pointed out nearly a century ago, the real choices are not

TABLE 8.4

## Example of the Dependence of Appropriate Policy on Institutional Conditions

|  | "Bad" institutions | "Good" institutions |
|---|---|---|
| Differentiated tariffs (either discretion or "conditional rules") | Can lead to lobbying, rent seeking, corruption, and mistakes and result in complex, distorting tariffs with no positive effects | Can allow trade policy instruments to promote nascent industries with possible dynamic externalities |
| Uniform tariffs | Forgoes possible benefits of differentiation, but avoids losses from rent seeking |  |
| Better policy | Uniform/precommitment | Differentiation |

*Source:* Author's elaboration.

between the best the economist can imagine and "the market." The choice is between the market such as it is and what will actually happen if a given policy is adopted—which in turn depends on the actual policy decisions that will be taken, which in turn depend on the quality of institutions for controlling the discretion used in policy implementation.[13]

This discussion points forward to the problems addressed in chapters 9 and 10. If the key problem is policy implementation, and the key problem with implementation is to create the conditions for the effective exercise of government discretion, the organizations of the public sector are vitally important (chapter 9) and so are the background institutions of policy making, especially the ways in which citizens are able to monitor the performance of government (chapter 10).

## Lesson 3

*Expectations play a crucial role in the success of policy reform.* And political and social legitimacy and continuity are important in promoting expectations of a more stable investment climate.

If the gains from policy reform are to be realized, individuals and firms must believe that if they invest in response to the opportunities created by the policy reforms, they will reap the gains of their investment. Investment is always about the future, and about the future there are no certainties, only beliefs and expectations.

### Diagnosis before the 1990s: Policies Had Put Too Much Faith in Government as the Driver of Growth

As detailed above, the key explanation for the slowdown in growth in the late 1970s and early 1980s was that policy makers had simply been wrong in their attempt to extend the scope of government action beyond the government's implementation capacity.

### Conventional Wisdom in the 1990s: Fixing Policies Would Ignite Growth

The conventional wisdom of the 1990s was that fixing policies would ignite growth. The belief was threefold:

- Get the policies right and investors will respond.

- Bold action upfront signals the seriousness of reform.

- Signaling to the market requires ambitious reform agendas.

### Lesson of the 1990s: Expectations Are Central

Not only does the investment climate need to improve, but also investors (small and large, domestic and foreign) need to believe that the improvement in investment climate is here to stay. The 1990s emphasized that expectations are central, not only as regards stabilization during crises, but also as regards the supply response to policy reform. We discuss these two aspects in turn.

*Crisis management.* Restoring expectations is often the single most important factor in turning around a crisis.

> To restore credibility [after a crisis] you have to show that your word is your bond . . . [I]t is crucial to choose targets that can be and are met. This is more important than issuing unrealistic projections . . . .
> —Kemal Derviş in World Bank (2005b)

Our strategy at the Central Bank was based on the view that, given the lack of reference for the correct exchange rate, exchange rate expectations had to be stabilized for the bank to develop a market for its sterilization instruments. Otherwise, the interest rates needed to induce significant demand for the new instruments would reach unreasonable levels. In other words, an interest rate defense and active foreign exchange market intervention were complementary rather than substitute policies. These three policies were popularly characterized as a Central Bank attempt to increase demand for domestic assets—and in this way stop the bank run and the currency run—by inducing greed to overcome panic. The bank's main consideration was that greed (interest rate policy) cannot overcome panic unless panic is also reduced by controlling chaotic conditions in the foreign exchange market through active intervention.

—Mario Blejer (World Bank 2005b)

There is disagreement on two big issues. The first is that of the proper scope of a reform program in the midst of the stabilization of a financial crisis. One view is that the reform should be limited and feasible, because an overambitious reform can backfire by creating expectations that cannot be met. The other is that the reform should be big, broad, and aggressive, because that convinces the markets that the government is serious about reform. But if in fact the big broad and aggressive measures are ad hoc and not institutionalized, there is a risk that meeting the targets will not create confidence, while missing them will create damage. This is particularly true of implementation-intensive reforms incorporated into crisis stabilization packages.

The second big issue is whether expectations can be positively affected by tying a government's hands. For example, in the early 1990s there was a view that countries should move to either fixed or completely flexible exchange rates to show evidence of the complete removal of government discretion. But since the Argentina crisis, some observers believe that removing discretion by creating mechanisms that impose large penalties may itself undermine expectations. Velasco and Neut (2003) argue that if the world is uncertain and there are situations in which the lack of discretion will cause large losses, a precommitment device can actually make things worse.

*Achieving a supply response.* The supply response to any given policy action depends on how credibly that policy action signals a sustained rise in the level of income. Many of the benefits of trade liberalization, privatization and/or deregulation, and financial sector reform depend on the responses of private investors. The gains come with new export industries, new expansions of industry, improvements in efficiency and productivity (which often require investments), and new activities. Small reforms may have big impacts if they are seen as harbingers of future reforms, while large reforms may have little impact if investors perceive the results as temporary.[14] Though the supply response to a policy reform is limited by credibility, larger supply responses make for greater support for continuing the policy, creating a virtuous circle in which successful reform leads to continued reform.

Many problems may interpose themselves between policy reform and the faster growth it is designed to achieve (table 8.5).

The first possibility, which has received a great deal of attention, is that policy actions may or may not signal policy reform. For example, if the budget deficit is cut from 5 percent to 2 percent, does this signal macro-stability or merely reluctant compliance with external pressures? Certainly expectations about future macroeconomic stability will differ dramatically depending on which of the two is perceived to be the case. Conventional wisdom holds that part of the reason why policy conditionality had a disappointing impact on growth was that the conditioned changes in policy actions did not change investors' expectations about the long run. As a result, the 1990s saw a growing emphasis on the ownership of reforms as key to a successful investment and supply response. Without ownership, current policy actions may not signal future policy actions and hence do not create a powerful investment response.

Even if a policy shift is owned by the current government, the shift may not change expectations if it appears likely to be reversed by either the current or a future government. And even if investors believe that current policy actions signal a true shift in policy, and even if they do not expect the policy to be reversed, the fact that new policies often call for new organizations and direct institutions of policy making implies that investor confidence may be difficult to build.

This can create a particularly difficult dynamic, particularly in the interaction between government and providers of infrastructure. This dynamic is that, even if investors would invest at existing profits/prices if they were confident these prices would persist, they fear the government may renege on its commitment to price regulations and attempt to squeeze their profits in the future.

TABLE 8.5
## Policy Reform and Growth: Sources of Differential Impacts

| Question | Effect | Possible slips between policy action and growth/output response |
|---|---|---|
| By how much does a policy action raise growth? | $\partial \dot{y}_t^j / \partial \text{Policy action}_t$ | |
| Does policy action change anticipated *policy*? | $\partial AP_{t,T} / \partial \text{Policy action}_t$ | • Policy action conditioned<br>• Policy action unsustainable (either economically or politically)<br>• Policy actions not institutionalized |
| Do changes in trajectory of policy change the trajectory of distributions of profitability? | $\partial R_{t,T} / \partial AP_{t,T}$ | • Changes in returns not large<br>• Policy is "wrong" |
| Do changes in trajectory of profitability raise desired capital stocks? | $\partial k_{t,T}^{j*} / \partial R_{t,T}$ | • Expected profitability higher but uncertainty higher (and investors not risk neutral)<br>• Policy changes *lower* profitability in the short run (adjustment costs) but raise it in the long run<br>• Complementarities |
| Do changes in desired capital stock(s) lead to investment responses? | $\partial \dot{k}_t^j / \partial k_{t,T}^{j*}$ | • Financial system does not accommodate<br>• Other aspects of investment climate unfavorable to investment |

*Source:* Pritchett 2003a.

If that is so, investors will be willing to invest only at a large risk premium over and above profitability. But—particularly in a weak political and institutional climate—the likelihood that a government will renege is higher, the higher the ex post profitability. The risk of reversal alone can block an investment response, given that the only profit rate at which investors would be willing to risk their capital in new investments is one at which governments cannot resist public pressure to lower prices. Hence the risk of policy reversal can itself create a self-fulfilling prophecy of failure.

These dilemmas explain the continuing search for mechanisms with which to signal a government's commitment to the irreversibility of reforms. The temptation has been to argue that the lack of a supply response meant that reforms had to be pushed harder, faster, and deeper. But this is not necessarily so. If the problem is that the reforms are not expected to be sustained because they are too aggressive, pushing them harder might further undermine expectations of their sustainability. To sum up, acknowledging the importance of expectations does not imply that either big bang or gradualism is the right approach to policy reform, but it is a reminder

that excessively ambitious reforms that are delayed in implementation can hinder the formation of positive expectations.

## 2. The Way Forward

Taking on board the lessons of the 1990s, what is the way forward? Three guidelines are discussed in what follows:

• Accept that there are many ways to implement common principles.

• Pursue growth strategies—not just stabilization or the avoidance of problems.

• Create the institutional conditions for a favorable investment climate.

### Common Principles—And Many Ways to Implement Them

Perhaps the most important and difficult lesson of the 1990s is that there is no one right way to achieve development.

The 1990s have not proved mainstream economists wrong; indeed the basic principles of eco-

POLICY REFORMS AND GROWTH PERFORMANCE: WHAT HAVE WE LEARNED?

nomics have proved remarkably resilient. In countries such as Poland, the Czech Republic, and the Slovak Republic, where the introduction of incentives proved feasible, they have worked remarkably well. In China and Vietnam, the introduction of stronger incentives has led to the most rapid poverty reductions in history.

What was wrong, and never should have been part of economics, was the belief that the first principles of economics had to be implemented in a particular way (Rodrik 2002a). This point can be illustrated with regard to four economic principles:

- *Expectations about future claims.* Investors need certainty that they will reap the gains of their investment. But this stability of expectations can be sought in a variety of ways. For example, do favorable investor expectations depend on property rights? Do property rights rest on the same definition of property and the same means of enforcing those rights as have developed in some particular industrial country? Experience with land titling has shown that, in some cases, holding the title to land increases a farmer's incentives, but in other cases the existing informal systems have provided adequate security. One way of providing property rights is through a well-functioning legal system, but many countries achieved decades of rapid growth with very little legal certainty, when stability was embodied in the political system.

- *Openness.* The principle of openness to ideas, trade, and investments with the rest of the world need not entail free trade. There are many ways of engaging productively in international markets. Even the four East Asian Tigers, all famed for being outward oriented, differed widely in the extent to which their governments intervened in the economy and in international trade. While Hong Kong (China), as a trading center, was always open, the Republic of Korea opened its markets to imports only quite late in its growth process. While some economies invited foreign investors, Korea had very little direct foreign investment.

- *Competition.* The principle that competition from alternative suppliers promotes productive efficiency does not dictate that competition has to take any particular form. China's experience with township and village enterprises, which were not private enterprises in the usual sense but created effective competition, is instructive (see box 6.1 in chapter 6).

- *Macroeconomic stability.* The view that this or that particular arrangement is needed in order to create macroeconomic stability is belied by the diversity of experience of countries that tried the same thing, and the similarity of experience of countries that tried different things.

To conclude this discussion of the different modalities for implementing common principles, it should be emphasized that "one size does not fit all" should not be interpreted as "anything goes." A vast array of policies in the world are not fundamentally sound, and are not heterodox implementations of sound orthodox principles. A vast array restrict competition in order to protect existing owners (private and public), and create investor uncertainty through arbitrary and capricious behavior by state officials. What is needed is not less economics but more and better economics, to identify the exact set of policies and institutional changes needed to address binding constraints on growth, based on first principles in each instance.

## Growth Strategies

If policy reform, while beneficial, does not explain the bulk of the variation in growth performance across countries and time, something else must. As discussed in chapter 2, recent research has emphasized that there are large numbers of extended episodes of rapid growth— some sustained and some not. How these growth episodes are initiated and sustained is a key question. While "policies," as represented by standard growth-regression measures, do increase the likelihood of a growth episode, they are far from sufficient to explain growth. And what causes the start of a sustained episode of rapid growth is not well understood.

In any developing country, nearly everything is far from ideal. The 1990s have shown that to achieve rapid growth, countries do not need to get everything right but they do need to get the *right* things right. Identifying those right things is the purpose of devising a growth strategy, which is a coherent set of actions designed to initiate and sustain rapid growth.

Devising a growth strategy requires a clear diagnosis of the obstacles to growth—in particular, the binding constraints, which will vary widely depending on countries' initial conditions. To illustrate, figure 8.3 from Hausmann, Rodrik, and Velasco (2004) maps the possible explanations of slow growth in a country in which the slow growth is associated with low rates of investment and entrepreneurship.[15] The figure emphasizes that starting from fundamental principles can lead one's search for binding constraints in many directions. For example, starting from the condition that profitability must exceed the cost of investment, perhaps the cost of capital

is too high; perhaps investors fear macroeconomic instability; perhaps too few profitable opportunities are discovered; or perhaps infrastructure deficits raise costs.

One problem, particularly with strategies that involve donors, is that governments face pressure to act on all fronts simultaneously. In creating an all-encompassing document such as a poverty reduction strategy paper it is very easy to justify anything as being important to growth—from low human capital, poor health conditions, judicial insecurity, weak infrastructure, a weak civil service, to stagnant investments in agriculture. Thus too often a proposed strategy becomes a menu, not a meal. To be sure, all of these problems will at some stage need to be addressed. But identifying the binding constraints on growth and focusing on them is the essence of strategy.

## Institutional Conditions for a Favorable Investment Climate

For investors, the launch of any new public policy initiative raises the question, How will policy

---

FIGURE 8.3

### Diagnosing the Problem of Low Levels of Investment and Entrepreneurship

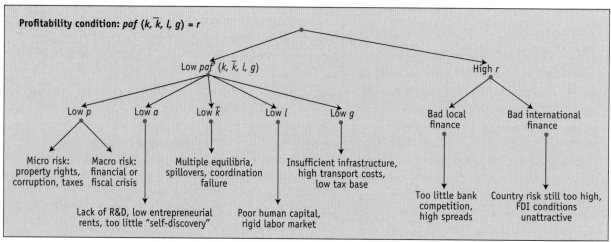

*Source:* Adapted from Hausmann, Rodrik, and Velasco 2004.

*Note:* $p$ = private appropriability of investment; $l$ = labor input; $a$ = total factor productivity; $g$ = government "input" (e.g., infrastructure); $f$ = production function for an individual investor or firm; $paf'$ = expected private return to investment; $k$ = firm-level capital; $r$ = real interest rate; $\bar{k}$ = economywide capital; FDI = foreign direct investment; R&D = research and development.

actions evolve with this new policy? For governments and societies at large, a key question going forward is, How does one develop the institutions of policy that reliably lead to the (mostly) positive use of discretion in policy implementation?[16]

First, continuity in the background institutions of policy making is conducive to success in pursuing individual reforms. One of the problems with the transition in Eastern Europe and former Soviet Union countries is that investment depends on expectations of policy implementation, that policy implementation depends on background institutions, and that when institutions are in flux no one can say with certainty what will happen. The fact that Indonesia has had much more difficulty than Korea and Thailand in restoring growth after crisis is almost certainly because Indonesia's background institutions have shifted, so that no one can predict quite where they will lead, while those of Korea and Thailand have not. Often shifts in background institutions are seismic political events beyond the control of any policy maker. But experience does suggest that new governments that are in the midst of an institutional shift should consider it a priority to establish credibility around a few key areas, rather than undertaking a broad array of new policy initiatives whose success may depend on expectations.

Second, if the key problem is that credible background institutions that can limit predation by the state, such as an independent judiciary or electoral accountability, do not exist and the government cannot make a credible commitment to resist predatory behavior, it is possible that no amount of institutional reform will sufficiently reassure investors. Acemoglu, Johnson, and Robinson (2001) have argued strongly that what is meant by "institutional quality" is not the state's ability to regulate transactions between individuals, but rather a country's ability to limit the state's temptation to expropriate. Since economic elites often benefit from controlling the state and existing institutions (Hellman, Jones, and Kaufmann 2000; Acemoglu, Johnson, and Robinson 2001), there may be little internal impetus for reform, precisely when it is needed most.

Third, the capability of the direct organization of policy making is often a key issue in

debates about reform. For example, should one privatize when there is no regulator? Should banks be liberalized while prudential regulation is weak? Particularly with the large fiscal losses in the financial sector in the 1990s, should reforms have been more gradual, with greater attention paid to prudential regulation? In some cases "the use of all deliberate speed" is hard to distinguish from "never." Another school of thought argues that capacity only develops in response to need, and so if one delays the privatization of utilities until one has developed an adequate regulatory capability one might delay forever. Indeed, it is hard to build experience in regulation if there is nothing to regulate.[17]

A fourth area of debate about creating favorable expectations is the tension between attempting to reassure specific investors and improving the overall investment climate. Some would argue that since the costs of investment are so high, and improvement in organizations and institutions is so slow, the best way to attract investment in the short run is to nurture individual investors, either on a deal-by-deal basis or in special regimes (such as for foreign investors). The latter approach, bypassing the weaknesses in the overall investment climate, is attractive because initiating a new industry or endeavor often requires attracting a large investor. Certainly this approach has been made to work, but it has dangers. Complex special deals can be conspicuously opaque and a perfect vehicle for corruption. Particularly when their negotiated terms are contested, special deals can undermine the perception of social and political legitimacy of a government's overall policy approach (the deal with Enron in the Indian state of Maharashtra and the water deal in the Bolivian city of Cochabamba are examples). Particularly in infrastructure, the renegotiation of individual deals has proven be an enormous challenge (World Bank 2004e). Finally, cutting deals for specific investors or specific classes of investors can undermine the pressures for systemic improvement for all investors. De Soto (forthcoming) is eloquent on the fact that most Latin American investors exist outside the scope of the formal legal economy.

# Notes

1. This feature, "Solow invariance" (Hall 1999), is robust and driven by basic features of these models.

2. The classic example (perhaps because it was there that the theory had been the most clearly worked out) was the calculation of the welfare losses that resulted from the differences between international and domestic prices induced by border restrictions on trade, such as a tariff. The standard analysis showed that a tariff raised prices, which benefited producers and hurt consumers, but that the efficiency losses from "too little" consumption caused an overall net social loss. Graphically this loss of consumer surplus was a triangle—in fact the estimates of the losses from price distortions were known as Harberger triangles (after Arnold Harberger 1971). The "partial equilibrium" estimates suggested that a move from the current level of restrictions to completely free trade would produce welfare gains on the order of 1 to 5 percent of GDP. These small estimates implied that the temporary "growth" effects caused by the transition from lower to higher levels of (properly measured) output from efficiency-improving reforms were quite limited.

3. That is, $\left. \dfrac{\partial \gamma \star}{\partial A} \right|_{\infty}$ .

4. Many proponents of the efficiency case for the welfare gains from trade (as opposed to the "growth" arguments) are strong supporters of free trade. Jagdish Bhagwati frequently points out that there was never any theoretical support for growth-regression-based claims on behalf of trade liberalization—but that theory and evidence on the microeconomic level provide all the support one needs.

5. Of course, in reality each organization will have its own "principal-agent" problems.

6. For instance, in trade policy an original policy would be set, restrictions would be added, and then exceptions granted, and then new categories created, and then other new restrictions added. Many countries had reached the point where few people actually knew what the trade regulations were (in many cases, even customs officials did not possess fully up-to-date copies of the tariff code) and where, taken as a set of interventions, the trade policy was "irrational." Similar accretions—taking over firms that had gone bankrupt here, making a firm a parastatal in order to obtain official financing there—often led to government ownership of a variety of businesses and activities for which there was no coherent rationale.

7. Suppose that to meet the fiscal deficit target the government simply lengthens payments to suppliers. This does not change net public assets. One could imagine then putting limits on both the cash fiscal deficit and the payment of suppliers. A government could then defer spending on the maintenance of public assets, causing potentially the same (or an even larger) reduction in the value of net assets while meeting the same target for the fiscal deficit plus payables. One could then set conditions that specify a cash deficit target, a limit on payables, and a limit on the reductions in maintenance. But there are still many other ways to reduce net public assets—for example, freezing the nominal wages of public sector workers at lower than sustainable levels, or underfunding future pension obligations, or authorizing expenditures (such as guarantees of lending) that create a quasi-fiscal obligation.

8. The new law attempted to remove every vestige of judicial discretion by declaring that if any creditor petitioned for a bankruptcy and a debtor was more than a certain number of days overdue on a contractual payment, the judge must declare bankruptcy.

9. For instance, in the early 1990s tariffs in India were four to five times as high as in most Latin American countries.

10. A Ponzi scheme refers to any investment that pays off initial investors unsustainably large returns not out of actual returns from investment but from flows of funds from new investors. These depend on rapid growth in new investors, but in the end not every investor can be paid the promised high returns.

11. This would be the case, for example, for a good that is an input into many other goods and is produced by a domestic monopoly.

12. No one can look at the experience of Singapore or the Republic of Korea (and earlier Japan) without being convinced that purposive government action to promote rapid development can succeed. Conversely, no one can review the tragic experience in many African countries and believe that purposive government action (at least ostensibly) to promote rapid development cannot fail.

13. Comparing industrial countries with poorer countries, it is noticeable that government action is much more pervasive in industrial countries—tax rates are higher, and regulation is pervasive—and that the exercise of discretion is explicit, and that much of the infrastructure is owned and operated by the public sector. A frequent practice has been to attempt to transplant more or less wholesale the policies of industrial countries—including the direct institutions of policy making—without adequate consideration for whether the transplants could survive in entirely different conditions. For example, every industrial country regulates banks. But can banks be successfully regulated without an effective legal system that can enforce creditor rights? Without a strong tradition of an autonomous civil service that can resist political pressures? Without effective legislative oversight? Without transparency and an

aggressive free press? Without a police force that can protect impartially against threats of violence?

14. These observations are part of the same overall story as the first two common lessons in this chapter—the question of large- versus small-level effects and the importance of institutional quality for successful policy implementation.

15. If investment were high and growth slow, a different diagnostic would be appropriate.

16. This is the main question in chapter 9, which reviews efforts in the 1990s on several fronts.

17. Countries with parastatal firms had decades in which they could have created regulatory capability—but they did not do so, in part because it was not perceived as necessary. Similarly with financial sector regulation: developing the capability for "arm's length" regulation when the government embraces the entire sector is conceivable, but difficult.

# Africa's Growth Tragedy: An Institutional Perspective

Africa's slow growth was unexpected (Easterly and Levine 1997; Collier and Gunning 1997). In the 1960s, most African countries were richer than their Asian counterparts, and their stronger natural resource base led many to believe that Africa's economic potential was superior to overpopulated Asia's. This view was shared by renowned economists, from Gunnar Myrdal in his well known *Asian Drama*, to Andrew Kamarck, the founding director of the World Bank's economic analysis complex, who listed seven African countries that he thought could grow at annual rates of 7 percent or more (Enke 1963; Kamarck 1967). More recently, many economic reports, including several by the World Bank, foresaw rapid growth in Africa.

The continent's growth record, however, has fallen well short of expectations. Over the last four decades, in the 28 countries that have complete gross domestic product (GDP) series for this period, the median growth rate has gradually but persistently declined (figure G.1) and 11 countries now have income levels lower than at the time of their independence.

Ranked by their growth performance since 1960, 15 of the world's 20 slowest performers and only 2 of the 20 best performers are in Africa (table G.1). Perspectives on Africa have thus become much more guarded (Easterly and Levine 1997; Acemoglu, Johnson, and Robinson 2002).

As noted earlier in this report, growth has been poorly predicted not only in Africa but in the developing world in general. Growth is difficult to predict because it reflects processes of change, and complex historical and political forces. Social scientists and historians have limited

FIGURE G.1

## Africa: Getting Poorer over Decades

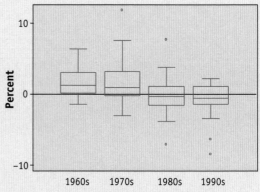

*Source*: World Bank, *World Development Indicators 2004.*

*Note*: Box-and-whisker plot for decadal growth rates of 28 African countries that have GDP series from the 1960s onward. The plots show averages as well as the dispersion around them: median, first and third quartiles, and outliers.

predictive power particularly when it comes to breaks with past trends—which are the essence of development processes.

Seeking to understand the deep forces influencing Africa's growth performance, researchers have increasingly looked into structural factors: geography (Sachs and Warner 1997; Bloom and Sachs 1998; Mellinger, Sachs, and Gallup 1999); ethno-linguistic polarization and inequality (Easterly and Levine 1997); and institutions.

The effect of institutions on growth has been a particularly fertile area of research in the last 10 years, bringing new analytical insights and perspectives (Acemoglu, Johnson, and Robinson 2001, 2002). For example, some see the origin of Africa's institutional weaknesses in the long-lasting effects of European colonial rule, which had little incentive to develop African local institu-

TABLE G.1

## African Growth in Context: Average Annual Growth Rates of Real per Capita GDP, 1960–2001

| Best performers | | Worst performers | |
|---|---|---|---|
| Botswana | 6.4 | Guyana | 0.5 |
| Korea, Rep. of | 5.8 | Argentina | 0.5 |
| Singapore | 5.6 | Côte d'Ivoire | 0.5 |
| China | 5.6 | Bolivia | 0.3 |
| Oman | 5.4 | Zimbabwe | 0.3 |
| Hong Kong, China | 5.2 | Burundi | 0.3 |
| Thailand | 4.5 | Nigeria | 0.2 |
| Ireland | 4.2 | Rwanda | 0.2 |
| Japan | 4.1 | Ghana | −0.1 |
| Malaysia | 3.9 | Senegal | −0.2 |
| Portugal | 3.8 | Chad | −0.4 |
| Lesotho | 3.6 | Venezuela, R. B. de | −0.5 |
| Indonesia | 3.5 | Central African Republic | −0.7 |
| Spain | 3.3 | Zambia | −1.1 |
| Hungary | 3.2 | Haiti | −1.1 |
| Greece | 3.2 | Sierra Leone | −1.1 |
| Norway | 3.1 | Madagascar | −1.3 |
| Egypt, Arab Rep. of | 3.0 | Niger | −1.5 |
| Finland | 2.9 | Liberia | −3.2 |
| Italy | 2.8 | Congo, Dem. Rep. of | −3.3 |

*Source:* World Bank, *World Development Indicators 2005.*

*Note:* Real GDP per capita growth rates (only for countries with GDP per capita series since 1960).

tions and focused instead on developing extractive institutions (Crawford 1994). As discussed in Country Note H on natural resources, the so-called natural resource curse has been another factor emphasized in the literature (Sachs and Warner 1995b, 2001).

Recently, the focus has been on the African state. Scholarly research and policy-making circles increasingly view poorly functioning state institutions as the root cause of Africa's development problems, and believe that solutions are to be found within the state itself and political institutions that link the state and society (Davidson 1992; Chege 1998; Herbst 2000; van de Walle 2001).

Post–World War II geopolitics played a role in many countries. The system of international relations polarized by the Cold War, which Africa's new democracies had to face after their independence, turned much of Africa into an arena of political struggle between the two superpowers.

Cold War politics did not encourage the development of effective state institutions and good governance in Africa. In many instances, the United States and the Soviet Union supported political regimes and leaders intent on preventing such institutions from emerging (Herbst 2000).

From a longer historical perspective, the deeper cause may be the pattern of state formation in Africa (Herbst 2000). For geographical reasons, state power was particularly costly to consolidate in Sub-Saharan Africa: population densities were low and barriers to long-distance transport too numerous. Thus Africa's pattern of state formation and consolidation differed from those in some other parts of the world.

In Europe, for example, land was scarce relative to labor, and therefore incentives to exert control over land were strong, even if at the cost of wars. Nation-states that could efficiently perform key functions—mobilize fiscal and human resources, organize and finance an army, provide public goods through effective administrations, and establish legitimacy, not least though their ability to deal with citizens through representative institutions—were able to thrive. States that could not, disappeared.

Herbst argues that this Darwinian process of state selection and survival did not take place in Africa, where it was labor that was scarce, not land. The drawing of national borders by former colonial powers, independent of the new states' ability to exert their authority over their territories, worsened the problem by enabling "weak" states to persist without requiring them to strengthen their institutional foundations, effectiveness, or political legitimacy. Because their countries lacked the external threat of war or territorial conquest that had driven much of European state-building, postcolonial African leaders never faced significant incentives to extend their power—including power related to the provision of public goods on the entirety of their territory. States that did not have to fight to survive had no need to invest in effective administrative and fiscal institutions, to control domestic opposition, or to make political concessions to their citizens. Aid and the Cold War accentuated this state of affairs in some countries.

Other observers have emphasized the emergence of the African state, not as an organic evolution of existing societal and institutional arrangements, but as an artificial creation oblivious to those arrangements. Mamdani (1996), for instance, pointed out that European colonial rule created state institutions relying on customary law under a regime of "decentralized despotism," which was exerted through indigenous chiefs. The population was ill-prepared to participate as citizens in the modern states that succeeded colonial rule. Hence, Mamdani argues, most of Africa's postcolonial history is to be understood as citizens' struggle for their rights. Davidson (1992) emphasized that the nation-state as a mode of social organization was ill-suited to African realities. A European creation, it ignored the checks and balances embedded in indigenous power structures and their evolution in the years before colonial rule. It alienated political structures from the lives and needs of the population. As a result,

following decolonization, modes of governance rapidly shifted to "neopatrimonial" systems of rule, characterized by "client-patron" relationships (Joseph 1998).

Seeking a solution to Africa's states' inability to exercise their authority across the territories they are to control, Herbst (2000) suggested rethinking colonially imposed borders. While this is a highly controversial solution, Davidson (1992) also suggests that creative thinking is needed to find alternatives to nation-states, that can incorporate indigenous African forms and traditions of governance. Recent reports suggest looser political arrangements, to enable greater autonomy in divided societies (World Bank 2000g; Ndegwa and Levy 2003).

While different forms of explanation—geographical, political, institutional—all provide useful insights and perspectives, it is unlikely that any single approach will be able to respond to all the questions that the continent's performance raises. For example, none is able to explain the differential growth within the continent. Why has Botswana been able to grow at the world's fastest rate for the past four decades, notwithstanding one of the highest rates of income inequality in the world and a reliance on natural resources, which has been a curse in many other developing countries? Why has Tanzania been able to maintain corruption at relatively modest levels, and to create a national ethic? Why has political stability been elusive in Côte d'Ivoire in the past 10 years, but not in Ghana? Among Africa's largest economies, why have some countries been able to grow so much faster than others (figure G.2)? As emphasized throughout this report, specificity is important for accurate analysis of growth and for design of effective growth strategies: depending on the country, or the time, some factors may be more important than others.

Recent improvements in policies seem to account for improvements in performance starting in the second half of the 1990s, when the median growth rate rose from −0.6 to a positive 0.9 percent—a significant 1.5 percentage point increase (figure G.3). Yet behind these policy improvements were improvements in political governance in some cases (Ghana, Kenya, Mali,

Tanzania, Uganda) while in others there were improvements in security (Mozambique, Sudan), making it difficult to see a stable causal relationship. Although some studies (Gelb, Ngo, and Ye 2004) show that structural reforms and the quality of their implementation track African performance quite well (table G.2), there is in Africa a strong sense that improvements in the economic fortunes of the continent will depend on its ability to establish effective political governance structures and to ensure security—from which better policies will necessarily emerge. This perception is confirmed by the focus of new leaders on dealing with weak institutions—in, for example, Ethiopia, Ghana, Mali, Mozambique, Tanzania, South Africa, and Uganda (World Bank 2000g).

Expectations that the improvement noted above indicates a break with past trends need to be balanced with the knowledge that few developing countries have been able to transform episodes of growth into sustained and prolonged growth. As discussed in Country Note B, "Lessons from Countries That Have Sustained Their Growth," the key is countries' ability continuously to adjust and reform institutions in a manner that enables them to sustain higher levels of income and lay the basis for further growth.

FIGURE G.2

## Africa's Seven Biggest Economies: Volatile and Unstable
(indexes, 1960 = 100)

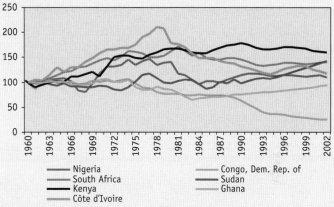

Source: World Bank, *World Development Indicators 2004*.

Note: African countries with the largest populations and with GDP per capita series starting in the 1960s.

FIGURE G.3

## Africa: Rebounding in the Late 1990s
(median of GDP per capita growth rates)

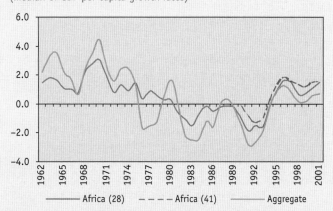

Source: World Bank, *World Development Indicators 2004*.

Note: Numbers of countries in each sample are in parentheses. "Aggregate" is total Sub-Saharan African GDP over total population. Three-year moving averages.

TABLE G.2
## Annual Growth in 17 African Countries, 1975–2003

| Country | 1975–84 | 1985–89 | 1990–96 | 1997–2003 |
|---|---|---|---|---|
| Six sustained reformers | 0.3 | 0.9 | 1.5 | 2.2 |
| Six later adjusters | −2.3 | 0.1 | −2.2 | 1.8 |
| Five governance-polarized countries | −0.9 | 0.3 | −0.6 | −1.6 |

*Source:* World Bank, *World Development Indicators 2004.*

*Note:* Median of the real GDP per capita growth.
Eight (six) sustained reformers: Benin, Burkina Faso, Ghana, Malawi, Mali, Mozambique, Uganda, and Zambia (Mozambique and Uganda do not have a complete 1975–2003 GDP per capita series).
Eight (six) later adjusters: Cameroon, Chad, Guinea, Madagascar, Mauritania, Niger, Senegal, Tanzania  (Guinea and Tanzania do not have a complete 1975–2003 GDP per capita series).
Five governance polarized countries: Côte d'Ivoire, Kenya, Nigeria, Togo, and Zimbabwe. This classification is from the 1994 World Bank study, *Adjustment in Africa.*

# Chapter 9

# Improving Public Sector Governance: The Grand Challenge?

MANY GOVERNMENTS IN developing countries face the challenge of delivering a wide range of services essential for development—from infrastructure and social services to the functioning of the legal system and enforcement of property rights—all of which pose the challenge of how to get governance "right."

States have responded with varying degrees of success. At one end of the spectrum are the failed states, where governments barely exist, and where they do, provide hardly any services. At the other extreme are a handful of countries where governments and their leaders are doing well by most development measures. In between are weak or predatory states that "consume the surplus they extract, encourage private actors to shift from productive activities to unproductive rent seeking, and fail to provide collective goods" (Evans 1995, 24); young democracies managing simultaneous political and economic liberalization with weak bureaucracies and few checks and balances; and more mature democracies where governments face the same difficulties as advanced countries when it comes to political corruption and abuse of office. Then there are the large, continent-size polities such as India and Brazil, within whose national boundaries can be found the entire range of governance configurations.

Though extensive research had probed the causes and impact of poor governance, and in particular of corruption,[1] it was not until the mid-1990s, with improvements in data and econometric techniques, that large, cross-country analyses emerged on the impact of governance institutions on investment and growth. This research has shown that corruption—which is both a symptom and cause of bad governance—discourages private investment and, more generally, that the quality of governance institutions has a significant impact on economic growth (Mauro 1995; Knack and Keefer 1995; Wei 1996, 2000; World Bank, *World Development Report 1997*; Kaufmann, Kraay, and Zoido-Lobaton 1999; Kaufmann 2003; Kaufmann, Kraay, and Mastruzzi 2003; Rodrik, Subramanian, and Trebbi 2002). Further, the research provides evidence that corruption distorts the allocation of resources in ways that hurt the poor (Mauro 1998a, 1998b; Tanzi and Davoodi 1998; Gupta, Davoodi, and Alonso-Terme 2002).[2]

Combined with urbanization and the spread of democracy, and also the extensive public awareness efforts of international organizations such as Transparency International and the World Bank,[3] the empirical research gave rise to governance reforms in developing countries. These ranged from very focused technical reforms of budgetary and civil service systems to more encompassing efforts such as decentralization and the overhaul of legal and judicial systems.

This chapter reviews these reform efforts and the lessons they yield. Section 1 introduces key governance concepts and discusses why governance reforms are particularly challenging, and section 2 draws emerging lessons. Recognizing that one size does not fit all, section 3 presents a heuristic approach to identifying avenues for reforms depending on broad country characteristics. Section 4 concludes the chapter.

# 1. Understanding the Governance Conundrum[4]

Public sector governance refers to how the state acquires and exercises the authority to provide and manage public goods and services.

The quality of governance (and thus the nature and extent of corruption) depends fundamentally on institutions. As discussed in chapter 1, institutions are the "rules of the game" that shape the behavior of organizations and individuals in a society (North 1990, 3). Institutions can be formal rules, such as a country's constitution, its laws and regulations, contracts, and internal procedures.[5] Or they can be informal rules, such as the values and norms that drive bureaucratic behavior. Scholarly research and concern with institutions is not new, but a strong interest in institutions reemerged in the 1990s, largely because the stronger macroeconomic policies of the 1980s had not achieved more rapid progress in development and poverty reduction. Interest moved from "getting the policies right" to "getting the institutions right" and had a particular focus—the rules of the game on which the governance of the public sector is grounded.

Fundamentally, public sector governance is about the nature and quality of three principal relationships: between citizens and politicians, between politicians as policy makers and the bureaucracy (those responsible for providing public goods and services), and between the bureaucracy as delivery agents and the citizenry as clients (figure 9.1).[6]

## Citizens and Politicians: The Heart of Governance

In an ideal world, citizens can hold politicians accountable for their actions and for policy outcomes, both through elections and through checks and balances on the abuse of power. Periodic elections provide the basic means through

FIGURE 9.1

## Citizens and Politicians

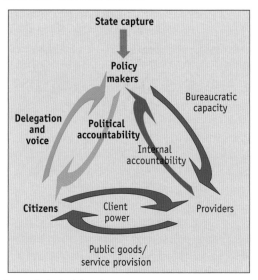

Source: Author's elaboration.

which citizens can hold politicians' feet to the fire. Restraints in the form of court adjudication of disputes among contracting parties, especially between government and the citizenry, and legislative oversight of executive or ruling party decisions and actions, foster accountability between elections. In well-functioning democracies, these latter features are embodied in the constitution and promote the rule of law: everyone, politicians included, behaves in accordance with agreed rules as embodied in laws and regulations and no one is above the law.

However, many countries are not democratic and even in those that are, as discussed in the next chapter, the conditions needed to make democracy function well are very demanding. In many countries, the formal trappings of democracy do not translate into accountable decision making for a variety of reasons—from the lack of a truly independent parliament or judiciary to electoral market imperfections. Even in countries with regular competitive elections among multiple political parties or candidates, elections often do not have the desired effect, so that politicians can easily renege on campaign promises and responsibilities.[7] In either case, the relationship between citizens and politicians is typically governed by weak institutions—whether political institutions (rules or arrangements that define, govern, and influence how leaders and other politicians are selected and replaced) or institutions of restraint (rules or arrangements that establish checks and balances on the abuse of power and authority). Courts are easily swayed by influential politicians; the legislature rubber-stamps the narrowly focused special interest initiatives of the executive; high-ranking officials abuse their authority for private gain; and enforcement agencies prey on the citizenry. In other words, the rule of law is weak.

When the rule of law is weak, the risk of state capture is high. State capture "refers to actions of individuals, groups, or firms . . . in the public and/or private sectors to influence the formation of laws, regulations, decrees, and other government policies to their advantage, through the illicit and nontransparent provision of private benefits to politicians and/or civil servants" (World Bank 2000a)[8] and is a serious problem in many developing countries (Kaufmann 2003). When pervasive, it becomes the principal stumbling block for efforts to reform governance institutions.

## Politicians and Policy Makers and the Bureaucracy: The Core Principal-Agent Problem

Politicians make policy and are responsible to the citizenry for the policies that are promulgated and implemented, but they delegate the implementation of policy to an army of bureaucrats. In delegating, they establish the rules and regulations that govern the operations of the civil service. These include, for example, formal institutions such as the civil service code, the budgeting system, and reporting systems as well as informal institutions (such as the practice of *amakudari* in Japan).

Delegation almost always gives rise to the principal-agent problem. The principal delegates the implementation of a task to an agent but will need to monitor the agent efficiently to confirm exactly what has been accomplished.

To delegate implementation, policy makers establish a compact with bureaucrats that has two major features. First, it provides the means through which the bureaucracy can develop and enhance its capacity to implement policies and deliver public goods and services. Capacity in this context refers to (1) the skills bureaucrats need to deliver on various mandates, (2) the resources (capital and financial) to support the needed efforts, and (3) the processes and systems (such as the budgeting system and the procedures for using it) that enable large numbers of individuals to function efficiently together. Second, the compact establishes means through which bureaucrats can be held accountable to policy makers for performing their tasks. That is, the bureaucrats are responsible to policy makers for accomplishing certain tasks and are prepared to explain and face the consequences of deficiencies or failures. Accountability mechanisms typically involve checks and balances internal to government agencies, such as internal audit, ex post program evaluations, and ex post reporting, as well as external restraints such as exercised by an ombudsman, supreme audit institutions, and anticorruption commissions.

Adequate capacity is needed if accountability is to work. Auditing, performance evaluation, reporting, investigations, and prosecution require information. And to produce the right information requires processes, skills, and resources to provide appropriate infrastructure and create appropriate incentives. In the same vein, more effective accountability helps strengthen capacity because policy makers are more willing to grant greater flexibility and because resources make the bureaucracy even more effective. Figure 9.2 highlights the salient features of the compact.

The nature of the compact between policy makers and bureaucrats critically determines the outcomes of policies. When the compact is defective, because capacity is weak or accountability is poor, administrative (or bureaucratic) corruption typically emerges. Weak capacity and accountability translate into numerous opportunities for soliciting or extracting bribes and other illicit payments.[9]

The compact is itself partly conditioned by the extent of state capture. Administrative corruption differs fundamentally from state capture but is inextricably linked to it. Politicians are at

FIGURE 9.2

**Politicians and Policy Makers and the Bureaucracy**

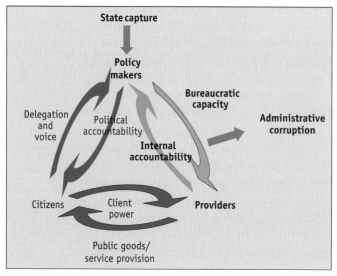

Source: Author's elaboration.

that the representative will intercede with or pressure the bureaucracy on their behalf. If they are generally unhappy with the response, they can vote the person out of office. But they cannot penalize or punish bureaucrats directly or officially.[10]

Citizens acquire leverage over the bureaucracy if they can organize themselves into nongovernmental organizations (Rose-Ackerman 2004). The capacity to organize gives citizens "voice" (the ability to monitor the performance of the bureaucracy, generate valuable information, and pressure politicians for action) and "client power" (the ability to engage directly with the providers of services). Both of these attributes strengthen the compact between politicians and the bureaucracy and thus help to improve the delivery of public goods and services.[11] Figure 9.3 highlights the role of voice and client power in the triad.

Citizens generally find it difficult to organize themselves, however. Collective action is costly and thus does not always emerge naturally. A weak link between citizens and politicians, as when electoral processes are flawed, can exacerbate the problem of administrative corruption: desperate for service, citizens may ultimately offer bribes to

the heart of state capture—whether as perpetrators or as willing respondents to the captors—but since it is bureaucrats who implement the distorted policies that result from capture, corrupt politicians need at a minimum the acquiescence of at least some segments of the bureaucracy. In practice this implies that politicians constrain the capacity of bureaucrats or weaken their accountability. For instance, in many developing countries, the annual budgets allocated to the ombudsman or to the supreme audit institution are inadequate and the personnel appointed to key posts are rarely the most qualified (Heilbrunn 2002). Moreover, politicians will prefer to sustain clientelistic practices within the bureaucracy rather than to introduce formal, transparent merit-based recruitment processes (World Bank 2000b).

## *Bureaucrats and the Citizenry: Where the Rubber Hits the Road*

Most citizens' immediate contact with the state is through the bureaucracy. Citizens can complain to their congressman or mayor about the poor quality or inadequacy of some service and hope

FIGURE 9.3

**Bureaucrats and the Citizenry**

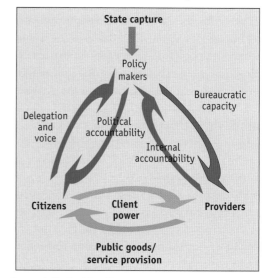

Source: Author's elaboration.

bureaucrats or give in to bureaucratic demands for bribes. The inability to organize can thus worsen an already defective compact.

## 2. Public Sector Governance Reforms in the 1990s

Using the three-part analytical framework outlined in section 1 as a guide, this section identifies some potential lessons from the governance reforms of the 1990s.

### *Enhancing Political Accountability: Legal and Judicial Reforms*

Democracies, particularly nascent ones, face dilemmas in promoting genuine political competition, and thus in establishing political accountability. When the citizenry cannot clearly attribute responsibility for poor outcomes to politicians, elections—already blunt instruments for accountability—become distorted, and this enables non-performing or poorly performing politicians to remain in power (see also chapter 10).[12]

Perhaps partly because of the immense difficulty of addressing problems in political institutions, countries in the 1990s turned to the other channel of political accountability: reforming legal and judicial systems, which seemed more amenable to technical solutions.[13] Two trends—the privatization thrust and the new emphasis on private sector development—helped to make legal and judicial reform an imperative in many developing countries.[14] Several other factors also provided an impetus: globalization and trade, drug trafficking, human rights, immigration, protection of intellectual property, suppression of terrorism, and the consolidation of emerging democracies (Messick 1999). Law reform and development activities skyrocketed during the decade, encouraged by support from the international financial institutions and key donors.[15]

### Pragmatic Approaches Have Been More Effective and Are More Likely to Succeed

Most reforms affecting private sector law were supported through short-term technical assistance involving foreign law professors or expert practitioners (Kovacic 1995; deLisle 1999). The foreign experts typically brought the text of their own country's laws, either as a basis for drafting a country-specific statute or simply for adoption wholesale.[16]

Many of the new laws have had little or no effect on behavior. For example, several former Soviet nations have statutes that on paper provide corporate shareholders more protection than under French or German law, but in practice, as capital flows attest, investor rights in France and Germany are much more secure (Pistor, Raiser, and Gelfer 2000, 65). Albania and Romania have enacted statutes governing the posting of collateral for a loan and the regulation of banks and securities markets, but businesses report that the statutes are ineffective (Gupta, Kleinfeld, and Salinas 2002, 13–14). And although new laws in Bangladesh, Benin, and Pakistan require bank debtors to repay their outstanding loans immediately, most debts remain unpaid (Messick 1999).

Experience emphasizes the need for pragmatism in legal reform. First, a new law must reflect the realities of the institutional environment within which it is to be inserted, including in particular the state of the institutions that will enforce it—judiciary, ministry of justice, the police, and regulatory agencies (box 9.1). When the agencies that will enforce a new law are corrupt, technically incompetent, or insufficiently independent of political authorities, the law must compensate for these deficiencies.

Second, implementation is easier if a new law incorporates customs, or norms that citizens are already observing. Hernando de Soto, for instance, spearheaded several law reforms in Peru that incorporated the norms and practices of street vendors, urban transit operators, and small landholders (de Soto 1989). Peru's new land law, granting urban squatters property rights to their land, relies on customary methods of showing possession to establish these rights.

Experience also shows that a transparent and inclusive reform process reduces opposition to a new law and enhances compliance with it. In its projects, the European Bank for Reconstruction and Development has included representatives

## BOX 9.1
## Bright Line Rules versus Standards

An early lesson that law reformers learned was the importance of substituting bright line rules for standards wherever possible. A bright line rule specifies the exact conduct expected (for example, a law establishing a 45-mile-per-hour speed limit) whereas a standard leaves the question of violation to the enforcement agency (for example, a law that makes a "reasonable speed" the limit). Bright line rules put less of a burden on enforcers than standards. Determining whether a driver was exceeding 45 mph is straightforward, whereas deciding whether a speed was reasonable requires investigation into such factors as time of day, weather conditions, and the presence of pedestrians and other traffic. Bright line rules leave enforcers with little or no discretion and so reduce opportunities for bribery. Since the enforcement of bright line rules is far easier to monitor, this can provide openings for self-help and other means of enforcing the law without resort to the authorities.

not only of government ministries, regulators, judges, and legislators but also of businesses and other civil society groups.

### Poor Incentives Rather than Weak Capacity Have Been the Root Cause of Poor Judicial Performance

Concern to improve the implementation of laws gave rise to parallel reforms of the judiciary. Early in the 1990s, reforms focused on contract enforcement, influenced by seminal work on institutions and economic growth that emphasized the important role that contract enforcement plays in economic development (North 1990; Weingast 1995; see also Oliver Williamson 1985). The rationale for judicial reform broad-

ened as the decade unfolded, and with increasing frequency a better-functioning judiciary was linked to, if not equated with, the rule of law.[17] This broader emphasis coincided with the growing recognition in the international community that a well-performing judiciary was part of the solution to many development problems. By the close of the 1990s, judicial reform had, in the words of one practitioner, become "the big tent for social, economic, and political change generally." Because it lent itself more readily to technical solutions, judicial reform became the entry point for addressing a problem that was fundamentally political in nature.

The widening of objectives caused significant changes in judicial reform programming among assistance agencies. At the World Bank, for example, judicial reform projects to create commercial courts and support similarly focused interventions gave way to much more ambitious undertakings: supporting new institutions to assume responsibility for governing the judicial branch, revising rules on the selection and promotion of judges, overhauling the management of the judiciary's human and physical resources, rooting out corruption, constructing new courthouses and equipping them with modern communications and computer technology, training lawyers and judges, providing programs to reach out to women and the poor, and establishing administrative courts.

Judicial reform proved to be a far greater challenge than expected. As did the attempted reforms of other public sector institutions during the 1990s, most of these interventions produced little change (Burki and Perry 1998). As experience grew, it became clear that the roots of poor performance in the judicial system lay much less in a lack of resources and skills than in the behavior of judges, clerks, lawyers, and litigants. For example, India has created an enormous number of tribunals to handle civil service, tax, land, and consumer cases, to reduce the burden on the regular civil courts and speed up the disposition of cases, but these reforms have had little effect (Moog 1997). The reason is that lawyers, clerks, and many litigants have an interest in court delays and thus continue to frustrate reform efforts.

State capture has compromised the proper functioning of formal institutions.

## Development of Complementary Institutions Is Essential for Reform

The absence of parallel institutional reforms will tend to negate any progress in judicial reform. For example, efforts to improve the judiciary will be hindered if they are not complemented by reforms of the police and the public prosecutor offices (box 9.2).

While most efforts at judicial reform focused on improving court systems, some dealt with alternative dispute resolution mechanisms, offering arbitration, mediation, and other dispute-resolution methods as a way to channel disputes away from the courts to private fora. These projects tended to overestimate the potential of alternative dispute resolution methods. Unlike state-sponsored courts, private dispute resolution fora cannot induce the parties to appear or to comply with the resulting decision. For private methods to substitute effectively for resolution by the courts, the parties must have some incentive to submit their dispute and to be bound by the outcome.

At the same time, the projects largely ignored that many disputes could be avoided altogether if more information were available on the creditworthiness and reliability of potential contracting parties. The importance of credit bureaus and other devices for sharing information is beginning to be recognized. For instance, recent research has shown the significance of information availability for deepening credit markets (World Bank, *World Development Report 2003*, 101–103).

Improving information sharing is a relatively apolitical approach to improving the rule of law, but by itself it cannot solve the problems of credible commitment that are inherent in contracting among private parties. The question that then arises is what else a country can do to make an investment environment more predictable, while waiting for the courts-based rule of law to emerge.

## Reforms to the Legislature Deserve Greater Attention

In most countries, the legislature is the constitutionally mandated institution through which the

---

**BOX 9.2**

**Integrated Justice Sector Reforms: The Jamaican Case**

The justice sector plays a critical role in enforcing the rule of law and protecting property rights and the rights of citizens. Safeguarding the accountability mechanisms that underpin the justice sector requires effective collaboration between the courts and the police. Successful violence reduction programs substantially increase the cost of crime by combining a high probability of capture (by the police) with a high probability of conviction (by the judicial system).

Jamaica's fairly well-developed judicial system has been criticized because of dramatic increases in political and criminal violence. To have an effective crime prevention strategy, Jamaica would need to match the effectiveness of its judicial system with better police capabilities; it would need to increase police accountability and improve police-community relations.

*Sources*: U.S. Library of Congress country study and study by the World Bank Group Jamaican country team, 2004.

---

electorate holds government to account. In doing so, the legislature can use several means, including approval of budgets, the questioning of senior government officials, the review and confirmation of executive appointments, impeachment and/or the power to dismiss the government, the establishment of parliamentary committees, and the formation of commissions of inquiry.

Relatively few attempts were made to reform legislatures during the 1990s (Manning and Stapenhurst 2002). The reasons included the more political and controversial nature of such reforms, donors' lack of experience with such reforms, and the nascent state of many legislatures (Lippman and Emmert 1997).

Nevertheless, the spread of democracy created the space for legislatures to evolve into independent political institutions that could oversee the executive and, with or without foreign assistance, legislatures ventured slowly to build their oversight capacity. Numerous organizations, including bilateral donors, multinational organizations, and international financial institutions, supported these efforts. Their assistance ranged from supplying office and other equipment to helping establish legislative budget offices and strengthening committees.

The decade saw a trend toward legislative budget activism in developing and transition countries, reflecting the process of democratization and the opening up of possibilities for legislative involvement in what were previously closed budgetary systems. In Brazil, for example, where Congress had historically played no significant role in the budget process, constitutional changes gave Congress powers to modify the budget. In Africa, too, changes occurred. For example, South Africa and Uganda passed financial administration or budget acts that give more influence to the legislature during the budget formulation and approval processes.

The experience to date suggests that developing-country legislatures have a long way to go before they can adequately perform their oversight functions, especially over national budgets. Building oversight capacity involves, among other things, strengthening "money committees," establishing dedicated research staff, enhancing complementary institutions such as national audit offices, and encouraging public input at the various stages of the budget cycle.

In assistance for democracy, it is support to legislatures that most often falls short of its goals, and legislative strengthening efforts should be seen as complements to related improvements in governance. In the case of money committees, this means dovetailing reform activities with broader efforts to enhance government accountability and strengthen public financial oversight, and ensuring that training activities include participants from other stakeholder organizations, such as the ministry of finance, the auditor general's office, and representatives from civil society.

## Strengthening the Compact

For more than two decades now, public sector reforms have focused strongly on improving the compact between politicians as policy makers and civil servants as implementers of policy and providers of services. With the fiscal crunch arising from the debt crisis of the 1980s, efforts to prune and rationalize the role of the state led to privatization of state-owned enterprises. Budget and financial management reforms were initiated, and even challenging and controversial New Public Management reforms were undertaken in a great number of developing countries.[18]

The public sector reforms had essentially two thrusts. The first was to build the capacity of the public sector—personnel skills, systems, and processes—to formulate and implement policies. The second, whose emphasis increased during the 1990s, was to instill clearer and more binding accountabilities in civil servants to policy makers and politicians. Underpinning both of these trends was the move toward greater democratization of politics, which sought to strengthen political accountability. This often took the form of a major decentralization of financial and functional authority to local governments, to bring governments closer to the people.

Three caveats apply to the lessons offered below. First, given the slow pace at which institutions change, and the fact that most of these reform efforts are rather recent, it is too early to reach definitive conclusions about successes or failures. Second, very little systematic research has evaluated results and outcomes. Third, since reforms imply changes in formal and informal rules, both of which are deeply rooted in a country or organization's culture and history, it is not obvious that successful reform efforts in one organization can be transplanted into other circumstances.

### Fiscal Management

*Governments faced with populist pressures can strengthen fiscal discipline by tying their own hands.* During the 1990s, governments attempted to improve fiscal discipline in a number of ways. As noted in chapter 4, the most high-profile efforts granted independence to central banks, as a means to clarify the banks' direct responsibility for controlling inflation and to grant them the flexibility to meet this mandate. Recent research suggests that the central bank's ability to play this role depends heavily on the nature and efficacy of checks and balances in the larger environment (Keefer and Stasavage 2003, 407).

On the public expenditure side, the experience of the 1990s suggests that institutions define and constrain the political bargaining that affects fiscal outcomes.[19] Well-defined antideficit rules, especially when coupled with credible limits on government borrowing, induce smaller deficits and more rapid adjustment of taxes and spending to unexpected fiscal shortfalls.[20] In recent years, a number of developing countries and subnational governments have passed fiscal responsibility acts to strengthen fiscal management. These laws enhance transparency, as well as the accountability of the executive to the legislature and the accountability of both the executive and the legislature to the citizenry, by stimulating discussion of fiscal policies and their implications before and after budget deliberations. Although no studies have yet assessed their effects, the new laws are expected to strengthen fiscal discipline.

*Fiscal transparency is essential for maintaining fiscal discipline.* The Asian financial crisis highlighted the importance of budget transparency, since hidden contingent liabilities can destroy the fabric of fiscal discipline. Greater budget transparency provides a basis for informed debate about budgetary policy among the public and the legislature, and within the executive; it also increases the chances that fiscal risks will be identified and policy responses put in place. But the adoption of more transparent practices has often been slow, partly because of capacity constraints and partly for political reasons (box 9.3).

*A medium-term expenditure framework (MTEF) will work only if politicians embrace it.* Many countries adopted MTEFs during the 1990s, as a way to increase the transparency of budgeting and enhance the predictability of agency budgets. The primary function of an MTEF is to infuse a multiyear perspective into budgeting, enabling policy makers to recognize the implications of current budgetary decisions for future government finances and creating a more disciplined, sequenced budget process that clarifies the deliv-

erables and accountabilities of both central and line ministries.[21] Part of an MTEF's value comes from the discussion, debate, and agreement that it generates among different parties engaged in the budget process—in particular the legislature—about the tradeoffs that need to be made among programs, activities, and projects. To be effective, an MTEF needs to be integrated into the budget process and budget documents.

Among Organisation for Economic Cooperation and Development (OECD) countries, few have adopted the full plethora of features of MTEFs, whether by choice or by circumstance.[22] Their adoption of multiyear features evolved gradually, usually as technical improvements to the budget process. Their experience suggests that an MTEF may be better used as a conceptual framework for thinking how elements of budget reform fit together, rather than as a reform in and of itself. Pursuing the key features of an MTEF individually appears to be a more effective approach than wholesale adoption of the full gamut of features.

Largely through donor initiatives, developing countries have introduced the MTEF as a process technically superior to annual budgeting. In Africa, implementation has been slow and MTEFs have not produced the expected results. As of 2002, 19 countries had MTEFs at some stage of implementation, but only five had integrated MTEFs in a meaningful way into their budget processes. In most cases, MTEFs have operated in parallel to the general budget process (Le Houerou and Taliercio 2002). Only four countries had submitted MTEFs to both cabinet and parliament and, in some cases, the MTEF has remained strictly a technical document of the ministry of finance (Le Houerou and Taliercio 2002, 13).

Just as is the budget, an MTEF is fundamentally political. Its effectiveness depends heavily on the willingness of politicians to embrace it as a reformed budget process and to accept the discipline it brings.

## Organizational and Human Resource Management

*Capacity constraints are binding: strategic incrementalism may be the only option for many developing coun-*

**BOX 9.3**

**Fiscal Transparency and Developing Countries**

The International Monetary Fund introduced the Code of Good Practices on Fiscal Transparency in 1998 as a response to the financial crises of the late 1990s, and updated it in 2001. The Code is based on the following objectives: roles and responsibilities in government should be clear; information on government activities should be provided to the public; budget preparation, execution, and reporting should be undertaken in an open manner; and fiscal information should attain widely accepted standards of data quality and be subject to independent assurances of integrity.

The IMF helps countries to implement the fiscal transparency code through participating voluntarily in fiscal modules of reports on the observance of standards and codes (ROSCs). These assess the availability and quality of fiscal data and evaluate the fiscal management framework, including relations between levels of government and accountability for fiscal activities outside the budget. As of end-2003, ROSCs had been completed in 63 countries; 58 of these reports had been posted on the IMF Web site.

Countries electing to have a fiscal ROSC are often those already engaged in fiscal management reform, yet in developing countries the reports have identified pervasive problems of data quality (unreconciled accounts, lack of clarity in accounting policies, weak external audit); excessive discretion in tax administration and poor enforcement; unrealistic budgeting; weak internal controls; significant payment arrears; and lack of clear responsibilities at various levels of government. In a number of developing economies, the scope and extent of off-budget activities (including quasi-fiscal activities) is an issue to be addressed. Further, except for a few industrial countries, most countries do not quantify tax expenditures. Many of these problems reflect underlying institutional problems.

*Source*: IMF 2003e.

---

*tries. World Development Report (WDR) 1997* argued that the state should match its role to its capacity, since taking on too much makes the state less effective. This was certainly evident from the various reforms that were pursued in public expenditure management, but it is perhaps most salient in the attempts of many developing countries to adopt New Public Management (NPM) approaches.

NPM reforms are a challenge even in countries with strong capacity. In environments where the basics are very weak, resort to NPM-style performance management techniques has been associated with poorer performance, as measured by increases in administrative corruption (Anderson, Reid, and Ryterman 2003; Schick 1998). These authors found that the most significant factor contributing to better performing public organizations is the creation of merit-based personnel management practices: putting in place recruitment and selection systems, performance evaluation procedures, promotion procedures, salary-setting rules and procedures, wage bill controls, and due process protections, and ensuring that they function as planned.[23] The implication is that these core systems and practices are preconditions for effective performance management.

Performance-based budgeting emerged as a corollary reform of NPM, and over the past 20 years OECD countries have gradually shifted the focus of their public sector budgeting and management from inputs to outputs. Arguably this development has enhanced public sector management and increased the effectiveness and efficiency of governments. But, as has the multiyear expenditure framework, it has taken many years to mature. And the experience has debunked the earlier belief that performance measurement can often be an effective catalyst for organizational change (Schick 2003). An important lesson for developing countries is the fact that OECD countries already had basic personnel management systems that functioned very well, many in the Weberian tradition, before they launched into performance management and budgeting.

*Capacity constraints and political imperatives can severely impede civil service reform.* In many developing countries, establishing basic personnel management systems requires overhauling the civil service. A malfunctioning civil service creates disillusionment among the citizenry, and a depoliticized, reasonably well-compensated, and skilled civil service can serve as a credible commitment mechanism signaling that better public services are on the way (Shepherd 2003). Thus one might expect politicians to be interested in improving the internal incentive mechanisms that affect the civil service. However, many developing countries attempted civil service reforms under conditions where clientelist politics of one form or another were already deeply entrenched. Hence the reforms met formidable opposition and, not surprisingly, their results have been quite discouraging (World Bank 2000a; Levy and Kpundeh 2004). A key part of the difficulty is that such efforts must inevitably transfer some authority from the political echelons (legislators, ministers, and their political appointees) to a cadre of depoliticized officials (civil servants) (Manning and Parison 2003). In many developing countries, the political history and environment make this a gargantuan task.

*Enclaving is a potential path to sustained reforms of the civil service.* The challenges of politics and capacity constraints have led some countries to experiment with enclave approaches to civil service reform, spinning off selected government entities from central government ministries.

Increased autonomy for revenue collection agencies became a key feature of governance reforms in Latin America in the early 1990s, starting with Peru in 1991, followed by República Bolivariana de Venezuela, Mexico, Bolivia, Guatemala, Argentina, and Colombia. Such reforms became popular in Africa in the late 1990s, with 12 countries experimenting with revenue boards or semi-autonomous agencies. In Asia, by contrast, only Malaysia and Sin-

gapore have given greater autonomy to their tax administrations, although other countries in the region are beginning to consider this.[24] In general, an autonomous revenue agency has more flexibility in managing personnel and finances and more control over corporate governance than does the typical government agency. At the same time, it also has clearer and more transparent accountabilities. The introduction of such agencies implied that collections would increase and service would be more taxpayer friendly.

In practice, the performance record of these agencies has been mixed.[25] Performance problems have resulted mainly from lack of political support, tensions between the autonomous revenue agency and the ministry of finance, and poor organizational design, including weaknesses in the new accountability regime. Nonetheless, on the whole the record suggests that, with enough political push and proper design, these agencies can improve tax administration and be sustainable (box 9.4).[26]

Given the immense difficulty of overhauling the whole of government, for many developing countries enclave reforms may be the only game in town. The important lesson is that enclaving must be strategic if it is not to constrain and/or distort the capacity-building efforts of government (box 9.5).[27] Part of the reason why autonomous revenue agencies have been modestly successful in some countries is that revenue collections dictate government budget envelopes.

In Africa, narrowly focused strategic interventions tended to be more successful than broader reforms over the long run, and among the more narrowly focused reforms, the capacity-building initiatives that focused on improving expenditure accountability were considerably more successful than those that focused on human resource management, according to Engberg-Pedersen and Levy (2004). These authors conclude that the expenditure accountability reforms, given their more technical nature, may have been less threatening to vested interests than the more politically sensitive administrative reforms, and, perhaps more important, that expenditure reforms produce more readily

## BOX 9.4
## SUNAT in Peru: A Modest Success

In the late 1980s, Peru decided to set up a semi-autonomous revenue authority (SUNAT), since tax administration was riddled with corruption and on the verge of collapse, with revenue collections dropping to a record low of 9 percent of GDP in 1988. A comprehensive staff screening and replacement program was initiated, and less than one-third of the original tax administration staff was rehired by the new organization. A modern human resource management system was introduced and SUNAT was allowed to operate under private sector labor laws and without undue political interference. Salaries were adjusted to private sector levels. A new financing mechanism provided financial stability. By 1997 tax revenues had recovered to 14 percent of GDP.

After its successful start, however, SUNAT suffered from decreasing political support for efficient revenue collection; a decline in the quality of the tax policy framework, which made fair and efficient tax collection more difficult; and increased interference by the Ministry of Finance. As a consequence, SUNAT has suffered a loss of standing in public opinion. Despite these problems, however, its creation has permitted the launch of far-reaching efficiency- and integrity-enhancing reforms, which are having an ongoing impact. Revenue collection, at 12 percent of GDP in 2001, remains far above the pre-reform level.

## BOX 9.5
## The Enclave Conundrum in Uganda

The Government of Uganda now has to decide the fate of more than 70 enclave units, most of which are outgrown project implementation units and semiautonomous organizations called secretariats. These were set up at the behest, or with support, of donors who doubted line ministries' capacity and were dissatisfied with ministries' procurement practices. The enclave units were allowed to set their own wage rates, above ministry levels, based on the premise that the necessary skills would not be available at the public service's low salary levels.

Ironically, with these higher salaries, the enclaved units recruited substantial numbers of skilled personnel from within the public service, depleting the capacity of ministries and demoralizing competent ministry staff.

Enclaving has also undermined the budget process. First, although budgeted under development expenditures, two-thirds (71 percent) of the enclave units' expenditure is of a recurrent nature. These recurrent expenditures come from the government's 10 percent contribution to donor-funded projects. While this may seem a nominal proportion of any project's total budget, the total constitutes nearly one-third (28 percent) of the government's own generated funds. This significant share is spent without the rigor that is associated with allocating other government expenditures.

*Source*: Draft report, "Affording Uganda's Public Administration Sector" (December 2003), World Bank. The report is currently being reviewed by the Government of Uganda.

observable results that generate the general public support needed to counter vested interests.

*Values, commitment, and pride in public service matter as much as controls and compliance.* NPM reforms sought to introduce stronger market-based incentives as a means of reforming government bureaucracies. Emulating the experiences of developed countries such as New Zealand and the United Kingdom, developing-country governments adopted performance management techniques that grew out of reforms in the private corporate sector and sought to enhance the autonomy and accountability of public sector managers and staff. Such reforms have arguably led to improved service and performance in developed countries, but have had little success in developing countries.

Industrial countries' experience with industrial performance and workplace transformation shows that workers' dedication to the job is an important explanation for improvements in performance (Tendler 1997). Recognition of this relationship has caused firms that perform well to pay close attention to innovative practices that increase worker dedication. Tendler contrasts this with the development literature, which has been rife with suspicion that "civil servants are self-interested, rent-seeking, and venal, unless proven otherwise." Her research in Ceará, Brazil, demonstrates that the creation of a sense of calling and ownership around public service by a committed leadership, a dedicated work force, and an informed and engaged civil society can increase acceptance of reform and improve service delivery (box 9.6).

*The effectiveness of information and communications technologies (ICT) depends on the reengineering of underlying processes and the proactive use of change management.* To increase transparency and efficiency in the delivery of front-line services, many countries in the 1990s began adopting ICT in such varied areas as tax collection, customs valuation, procurement, treasury and cash management, issuance of licenses, land registration and titling, passport issuance, and other focused front-line public services. This trend, which has come to be known as "e-government," involved significant experimentation with the application of ICT to internal processes (box 9.7).[28]

In a wide range of countries, e-government has been a powerful tool for enhancing the efficiency and effectiveness of public services (table 9.1).[29]

Experience nonetheless suggests that e-government is not a panacea for basic problems. First,

---

**BOX 9.6**

## Building a Sense of Calling and Commitment in Public Service Delivery: Ceará, Brazil

Ceará has substantially improved its preventive health services, as reflected in indicators such as infant mortality and vaccination coverage. Agriculture programs have raised output and productivity. Spillover effects from procurement reform programs have resulted in local economic development, in addition to increasing output and productivity for small-firm suppliers. Public works construction has created more jobs in the economy than usual, resulting in a greater share of public expenditure being allocated to labor.

Four closely intertwined explanations can be offered for this improved performance:

First, civil servants in these programs showed high dedication to their jobs. Either they were dedicated entrants into civil service, and work conditions perpetuated that dedication, or the circumstances of the jobs elicited their commitment.

Second, the government repeatedly and publicly demonstrated admiration and respect for the civil servants by regularly announcing successes and openly rewarding good performance, building a sense of calling and pride around the workers and creating a sense of chosen elite in the public service. Publicity also increased citizen awareness and public monitoring of civil servants and local governments, and created a new constituency that would help leaders and agencies overcome political opposition.

Third, innovative organization of tasks for workers in the public programs resulted in often voluntary ownership of varied and multiple tasks. These multiple tasks often coalesced into client-centric, problem-solving approaches to service delivery.

And fourth, repeated messages from the government and reorganization of tasks kept rent-seeking behavior under control by creating a sense of pride, ownership, and recognition around public service, in the eyes of society and civil servants alike.

*Source:* Tendler 1997, 135–65.

**BOX 9.7**

**Mexico's e-SAT Program for More Efficient Tax Administration**

Inspired by the early successes of Argentina, Brazil, and Chile in using ICT to improve the delivery of government services, the Mexican government (as part of its OECD-based program of regulatory and administrative reform), began moving government information and services online. Mexico's federal tax administration (*Servicio de Administración Tributaria*, or SAT) embarked on e-SAT, a program to offer tax services online. Starting in 1995, e-SAT has evolved gradually. By 1998, SAT had established an interactive Web page that contained basic information on tax laws and procedures and permitted taxpayers to file their annual declarations electronically. The main beneficiaries of the first phase of this new system were large corporations. During 2000–03, SAT expanded the nucleus of online tax services to allow taxpayers to (1) obtain a personal form of electronic identification, (2) obtain a corporate tax ID for new entities via the Internet, (3) submit a tax declaration and other relevant forms, (4) enquire into the status of a taxpayer account, and (5) schedule an appointment with a SAT tax counselor. In August 2002, SAT promulgated a new regulation requiring the electronic submission of most individual and corporate taxpayer declarations (through SAT's portal) and payments (through the portal of the taxpayer's bank). SAT is now working to develop and make operational online systems for the receipt and processing of credit card payments and payment of tax refunds. e-SAT has greatly reduced the amount of paperwork previously managed by Mexico's tax registry, declaration, and collection units.

*Source*: Kossick 2003.

for real gains to be made, processes need to be simplified and automated in ways that reduce the discretion of government officials. For example, a study of the effectiveness of efforts to introduce computerized integrated financial management systems in Africa concludes that "technology can only add value in the context of an underlying commitment to disciplined decision making, and internal management systems geared to monitoring compliance" (Dorotinsky and Floyd 2004). Second, most e-government projects have faced substantial resistance from public servants who tend to see such projects as a threat to their jobs; publication and easier access to information dilute their control and diminish their responsibility as information brokers. Hence, reform projects can stall unless adequate change management processes are adopted.[30] Third, political support from top leadership is critical. In Andhra Pradesh, India, for example, top leadership publicly pushed for e-government and allocated resources accordingly for an ambitious program. Several services are now delivered online and the state secretariat

is moving to a paperless office and electronic workflow. In the Republic of Korea, the success of the OPEN project has been largely due to the support of the mayor of Seoul, who took a multipronged approach to curbing corruption.[31] In Gujarat, India, with strong support from the leadership, computerized check posts trebled the fines collected from overloaded trucks, but when this support waned, the verve to reduce corruption weakened, and new forms of extortion hampered the overall effectiveness of the program.

## External Restraints

*To combat corruption, prevention may be more effective than investigation and prosecution.* With the spiraling concern over corruption in the public sector, developing countries began to establish institutions of restraint that focused mainly on enhancing internal accountability: supreme audit agencies, the ombudsman function, and anticorruption agencies.

Among these, anticorruption agencies gained most currency, in countries from Latin America

TABLE 9.1

## Examples of Efficiency Gains from ICT

| Country, region | Type of government application | Time to process before application | Time to process after application |
|---|---|---|---|
| Brazil | Registration of 29 documents | Several days | 20–30 minutes per document, one day for business licenses |
| Chile | Taxes online | 25 days | 12 hours |
| China | Online application for 32 business services | 2–3 months for business license Several visits to multiple offices for filings | 10–15 days for business license Several seconds for routine filing for companies |
| India, Andhra Pradesh | Valuation of property | Few days | 10 minutes |
| India, Andhra Pradesh | Land registration | 7–15 days | 5 minutes |
| India, Karnataka | Updating land registration | 1–2 years | 30 days for approval, request completed on demand |
| India, Karnataka | Obtaining land title certificate | 3–30 days | 5–30 minutes |
| India, Gujarat | Interstate check posts for trucks | 30 minutes | 2 minutes |
| India, Andhra Pradesh | Statutory certificates on caste | 20–30 days | 15 minutes |
| Jamaica | Customs online | 2–3 days for brokers to process entry | 3–4 hours |
| Philippines | Customs online | 8 days to release cargo | 4 hours – 2 days to release cargo |
| Singapore | Issue of tax assessments | 12–18 months | 3–5 months |

*Source*: Bhatnagar and Deane 2003.

to Africa. These agencies have had mixed results. The successes of Singapore's CPIB and Hong Kong's ICAC are widely known. More often, however, such agencies have been seriously impeded by resource constraints, weaknesses in complementary institutions such as the judiciary and the police, and multiple goals (Meagher 2002). Some have been set up to satisfy a political need—such as an outcry from a corruption scandal or loan conditionality—but lack enough resources or political backing to actually do their work. They have served to deflect demands for action against corruption while the authorities fail to undertake any real responses (Heilbrunn 2002). Box 9.8 outlines the demanding requirements for an effective anticorruption agency.

Supreme audit agencies are crucial for enforcing the financial accountability of the government, and during the 1990s such agencies were established or restructured in many developing countries. Their effectiveness has been highly variable (Heilbrunn 2002). In many countries, the auditor general's independence is compromised by an executive that seeks to prevent the opposition from learning of possible cases of illicit enrichment. For instance, reports from the auditor general are submitted to the president, who then determines when and how to release the information. Too often, the information is not released.

Focusing on cure rather than prevention of corruption has rarely worked in developing-country contexts, at least not in the short to medium term. As the 1990s ended, it became clear that the gestation period for such reforms would be much longer than had been expected and that, over the medium term, better results could probably be obtained from preventive measures that achieve the following:

• *Reduce the likely benefits from corruption.* Promoting competition in the private sector, through lowering barriers to entry and reforming regulations where there are natural monopolies, serves to reduce rents and rent seeking. Ensuring competition in procurement through nationwide advertising and efforts to prevent collusion can also greatly reduce corruption. More radical measures include calling for a referendum for the pub-

## BOX 9.8
## What It Takes to Create a Successful Anticorruption Agency

*Establishment*: Carefully situate the agency within a set of well-defined supports: a comprehensive anticorruption strategy, careful planning and performance measurement, realistic expectations, and strong enough political backing (across class and party lines) to make it effective regardless of political and personal consequences. Agencies that score high on these measures are those in Hong Kong (China), Singapore, Malaysia, Uganda, and Australia's New South Wales.

*Focus*: Define the agency's focus in a way that will maximize its effectiveness. For example, an agency could focus on prevention and monitoring government implementation of anticorruption policy, forgoing a comprehensive mandate (as in Korea); or its jurisdiction could be mainly prospective, with only limited concern with past cases (as in Hong Kong, China); or it could choose cases selectively, based on clear standards (as in Argentina and New South Wales); or it could deal only with the probity and reputation of the public service (as in the United States and India). Clarity of focus seems to be consistently associated with success, except where massive resources are available.

*Accountability*: Promote the agency's accountability through such factors as the application of legal standards, the availability of judicial review, systems of public complaint and oversight, a requirement that the agency answer to all branches of government and the public, and precise and comprehensive expenditure accountability. Some commentators also suggest minimizing the agency's size, as well as the "free" support given by aid donors. Accountability is not uniformly associated with success. Many successful anticorruption agencies are strongly accountable, but this is probably an outgrowth of the rule of law, which seems to be more consistently associated with success (see below).

*Independence*: Independence arises in some cases simply from outside accountability, and in others from the agency's placement and line of responsibility, the appointment and removal procedures for top officials, or some forms of fiscal autonomy. The most important sign of independence is the absence of political intrusion into the agency's operations. De facto autonomy enables anticorruption agencies to operate on a consistent and professional basis with relatively little partisan intrusion. In most environments, this mode of operation is important to success.

*Powers*: A successful anticorruption agency will have strong research and prevention capabilities, along with the authority to do the following: access documents and witnesses, freeze assets and seize passports, protect informants, monitor income and assets, propose administrative and legislative reforms, and exercise jurisdiction over the head of state. Many agencies have most or all of these powers on paper but frequently cannot put them into effect owing to lack of coordination, weak capacity in cooperating institutions, and political factors.

*Resources*: Agencies in this field, as in others, depend on well-trained personnel, including sufficient numbers with highly specialized skills. Staff should also be well compensated, subject to integrity reviews and quick removal, and endowed with a strong ethic of professionalism, integrity, and high morale. Also important are sufficient funds, adequate facilities and assets, high-level information sharing, and coordination with other government bodies.

*Complementary institutions:* Anticorruption agencies do not succeed without the basic features of the rule of law: functioning courts, free and active media, an active community of nongovernmental organizations (NGOs) and public interest groups, and other capable institutions such as supreme audit agencies and central banks. Civic factors such as free media and capable nongovernmental watchdogs are not as clearly associated with their success.

*Source*: Meagher 2002.

lic to approve large projects and the tax and expenditure allocation choices these imply.

- *Reduce the number of transactions that create opportunities for graft*—for example, by liberalizing imports, removing price controls, removing industrial and trade licensing requirements, or making such licensing automatic. For example, when India liberalized industrial licenses in the early 1990s, a large industry aimed at obtaining licenses disappeared, along with the corruption associated with it. Similarly, when Indonesia liberalized its trade regime in the 1980s it radically reduced corruption in import licensing. Streamlining bureaucracy by reducing the number of approvals required for particular transactions, reducing bureaucratic instructions, simplifying rules, improving service standards, and decentralizing services all have this effect.

- *Increase information, transparency, and public oversight.* Corruption often occurs because of lack of information. Governments lack information on what their agents are doing on the ground. Consumers of government services are not aware of what rules or charges are legitimate. Clarifying rules and increasing transparency helps to reduce opportunities for corruption, as does involving beneficiaries in the oversight of government programs. Indonesia's Kecamatan Development Program is a good example of this (World Bank 2003c).

- *Establish time-tested, basic systems of personnel management.* Merit-based recruitment systems and long-term career path arrangements—essential attributes of a Weberian system—significantly reduce bureaucratic corruption (Evans and Rauch 2000), and there is evidence that smaller pay differentials between the public and private sectors lead to lower levels of bureaucratic corruption (Van Rijkeghem and Weder 2001).

Much current thinking about fighting corruption is influenced by the principal-agent problem. The above lessons assume that the principal (the politician or the head of a government agency) is himself or herself not corrupt, and that he or she has an interest in ensuring that his or her agents are not corrupt. But most principals, that is, politicians, even if they themselves are honest, need money to stay in power, fight election battles, or buy off opposition. Those who contribute such money can then influence the way power is exercised. If politicians are beholden to special interests or are captured by various interest groups, fighting corruption becomes rather difficult (see the discussion in section 3 on reform strategies in captured states).

## Nurturing Voice and Client Power

By the mid-1990s, it was clearly seen that civil society organizations—such as NGOs and religious organizations—could play an important role in inducing better performance from government. In many developing countries, the introduction of elections opened the way for citizens to hold politicians accountable for the performance of the public sector. Homegrown experiments sprouted throughout the developing world, showing that active civil society participation in reform can potentially lead to much needed improvements in the compact.[32] For example:

- Citizen report card surveys, which originated in Bangalore (box 9.9), have spread to other parts of India and are now being tried in other developing countries including Peru and the Philippines. This instrument has channeled the collective voice of citizens seeking better public services.

- Different forms of participatory budgeting have emerged in parts of the developing world including Brazil and South Africa. At its core, participatory budgeting engages citizens and their elected representatives, such as the mayor or governor, in a partnership to determine the priorities of the community and what projects will be funded from the local budget during the coming fiscal year. Typically, this process has been launched by forward-looking local politicians as a means of locking future politicians into a transparent

**BOX 9.9**

**The Report Card Survey in Bangalore, India: Stimulating Administrative Reforms**

The 10-year experience of the Public Affairs Centre (PAC) in Bangalore, India, illustrates the potential of using client surveys as a lever to induce upstream public management reforms and an improvement in service delivery. Established in 1994 to improve public sector governance in India, PAC's primary focus and strength lies in assisting citizen groups in "using knowledge as a basis for collective action" (Paul 1995). In 1994, the PAC conducted its first report card survey, effectively an opinion poll, of citizens in Bangalore on their perceptions of the quality of services provided by eight key government organizations. Citizens showed themselves generally dissatisfied with the delivery of public services. The results of the survey were published in a leading newspaper, raising their visibility and leading public officials in a number of agencies to discuss their agencies' problems with PAC and citizens' groups. PAC offered to help these agencies address some of the problems. Further surveys, undertaken in 1999 and 2003, show that over 10 years the public has become much more satisfied with the service delivery across all eight agencies. The lesson: demand pressures can lead to needed public sector reforms.

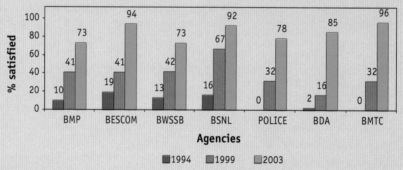

**Citizen satisfaction with various agencies across three report cards**

*Source*: Paul 2003.

budget process for which they can be held accountable.

• NGO advocacy for greater transparency and fairness in public procurement and monitoring of procurement processes has become more common as well. So-called integrity pacts developed by Transparency International have now been used in several countries as part of huge procurement contracts, for example, in Colombia and Mexico.[33]

Most demand-driven reforms have taken place in the delivery of public services, because service delivery is where the state meets the aver-

age citizen. Changes in quality, quantity, and access to services affect everyday lives and thus make citizens more prone to support, if not to seek, reforms in governance.

Interventions to improve service delivery are a potential entry point for broader governance reforms (box 9.10). In the Middle East and North Africa, there are few democracies and the governance gap is significantly wider than in other developing regions, largely as the result of weaknesses in public accountability (World Bank 2003c). Though there appears to be much less governance reform activity than in other regions, civil society efforts to address poor service deliv-

BOX 9.10

### Service Delivery and Civil Society in the West Bank and Gaza

A 1998 review of service delivery in the West Bank and Gaza asked a representative sample of beneficiaries about the provision of health and education services by NGOs, the private sector, and the Palestinian Authority. Meanwhile, specialists carried out institutional reviews of education and health facilities. The findings show that beneficiaries often select a particular provider because its service is better or easier to access—areas in which NGOs and the private providers ranked higher than the government. The findings were presented at dissemination workshops that were attended by ministers, senior civil servants, and senior representatives from NGOs and private organizations. The ministers of health and education reacted by using the findings to improve the quality of health and education services across the board and to improve coordination among the government, the NGOs, and the private sector.

*Source*: World Bank 1999.

BOX 9.11

### Procurement Watch: Working with the "Enemy"

In the Philippines, Procurement Watch Inc (PWI) was born in part out of the need to harness citizens' collective anger and frustration about widespread corruption. It was organized as a nonprofit institution with encouragement from the government Department of Budget and Management (DBM) and seed funding from the World Bank's Asian Emergency Trust Fund (ASEM) grant facility, along with private contributions. To establish its credibility with citizen groups and legislators, PWI quickly developed technical expertise in the area of procurement. With well-trained and experienced staff and an active board of directors, it drew attention from the media to the need for a procurement reform bill. It secured advocacy support from different citizen groups throughout the country, was invited to participate actively in the three technical working groups formed to formulate the law—one in the executive, another in the House of Representatives, and the third in the Senate—and was sought after for advice by proponents of the bill in both the House and the Senate. With technical assistance from donors and advocacy support coordinated and managed by PWI, DBM secured the enactment of the Government Procurement Reform Act of 2002. The President signed the bill into law on January 10, 2003, almost four years after the effort was initiated.

ery appear to be sprouting at the community level. All regimes care about their legitimacy, and one way that nondemocratic regimes can maintain their legitimacy is by providing adequate public services.[34] To do this, they need information about service delivery problems. Civil society organization efforts such as report card surveys provide such information.

If demand-raising efforts are to be effective, public officials and civil society groups must be willing to work closely together (box 9.11). Civil society organizations need partners inside the public sector, since they have the knowledge and understanding needed to move a reform agenda within the government. Likewise, reform-minded politicians and civil servants need civil society organizations to galvanize public support.

## Decentralization

Many developing countries embarked on wide-ranging decentralization efforts in the 1990s (*WDR 2000*; Litvack, Ahmad, and Bird 1998; Burki, Perry, and Dillinger 1999b; Ebel and Yilmaz 2002). In developing countries on average, the share of subnational governments in total government spending increased by 20 percent from the 1980s to the 1990s.[35] Although some of the decentralization efforts may have been indirectly stimulated by fiscal crisis, as in Indonesia, most were inspired by changes in the political landscape: the collapse of long-standing highly centralized regimes and the emergence of strong global pressures for democratization. In many countries, including Thailand, pent-up distaste among the citizenry for tight, unchecked central control and a greater desire to hold political leaders accountable provided the impetus.

*Decentralization is a political choice, whose design and implementation may not improve service delivery.* Designed well, decentralization can move decision making closer to the people, enhance the efficiency and responsiveness of service delivery (Faguet 1997; Kahkonen and Lanyi 2001; Bardhan and Mookherjee 2000), support economic growth, and offer a potentially powerful tool for alleviating poverty. But designed inappropriately, or introduced without strong local participation and accountability (of local officials to local citizens), it can lead to macroeconomic instability, declining service levels (Martinez-Vazquez and Boex 2001), heightened regional disparities or conflicts (Smoke 2001), and increased corruption (Brueckner 1999).

Because the ultimate objective of devolved arrangements is to provide needed public services in an equitable and technically efficient manner, the most critical concern is the political accountability of locally elected officials to local residents. Political representation appears to be insufficient, however, reflecting capture by elites and the weaknesses of local political processes (Crook and Manor 1998; Conning and Kevane 2001). Experience also shows that even if local elected officials are strongly com-

mitted to responding to local needs, the intended services may not be forthcoming without appropriate inputs by the bureaucracy (Schroeder 2002).

A local government should be just as accountable for funds transferred to it as for funds collected directly from local taxpayers. Instruments for ensuring financial accountability are often in place, but their implementation is often poor. Financial audits of local accounts, for example, tend to be delayed for long periods, and as a result, they have not become effective instruments of accountability. Experience has varied widely across countries, but emphasizes the importance of imposing credible, hard budget constraints on local governments (Rodden, Eskeland, and Litvack. 2003). Otherwise local governments may borrow recklessly to fund local initiatives or find other ways to transfer liabilities and potentially expose the national government to unwanted fiscal risks.

Throughout the 1990s, decentralization efforts featured intergovernmental fiscal reforms. Argentina's experience highlights the challenges in the design and evolution of a good intergovernmental fiscal system (box 9.12).

*The administrative aspects of decentralization are as important as the fiscal aspects.* The details of implementation arrangements ultimately determine outcomes. The challenges that have emerged fall into three categories: (1) adoption of a more systematic view of decentralization (Bahl 2000); (2) balancing of responsibility with resources, capacity, and accountability; and (3) creating incentives for implementation to match formal decentralization arrangements. Experience shows the value of pragmatism in implementing decentralization (Litvack, Ahmad, and Bird 1998; Bahl 2000; Bahl and Smoke 2003). A pragmatic strategy would be unique to each country undertaking decentralization, but should include a general vision and framework for reform, mechanisms for coordination and resolving conflicts, a prioritization of reforms and a plan for sequencing them, information to monitor outcomes and adjust the reform program, and incentives to change central and local behavior.

---

**BOX 9.12**

**Hard Budget Constraints: The Challenge of Fiscal Decentralization in Argentina**

Provinces in Argentina depend on federal transfers for the bulk of their fiscal resources. Revenue sharing (*coparticipaciones*) was introduced in the 1930s to compensate provinces for the introduction of national income and sales taxes, and in 2000, 56 percent of provincial resources came from this common pool. The majority of provinces (roughly 60 percent) relied on their own resources for less than 30 percent of their spending.

The challenge of ensuring hard budget constraints under fiscal decentralization depends on a country's social, cultural, and institutional features. Experience in countries such as Argentina and Brazil underscores that central commitment problems and limitations in effective regulation can conspire to weaken subnational hard budget constraints. Strong efforts by the central government to regulate can exacerbate problems, as, for example, when subnational governments circumvent the spirit of regulations through recourse to affiliated state-owned enterprises, including regional banks. Argentina's experience shows that such problems have no quick fixes. They require the evolution of credible policies—and political will—buttressed by effective institutional arrangements, whether predominantly market based or hierarchical and dependent on central oversight.

*Sources*: Eaton 2003; Perry and Servén 2002; Rodden, Eskeland, and Litvack 2003; Saiegh and Tommasi 1999; Tommasi 2002; Webb 2003.

---

## Information and Media Help Build Citizen Power

The media can be a powerful instrument for galvanizing citizen action. A free press raises popular awareness of inappropriate actions by elected and appointed officials. When people are aware of corrupt officials or networks, their reaction may include voting against incumbents, protests, and manifestations of unrest, or disengagement from the formal economy.[36] Widespread press coverage was notable in the deposition of former Brazilian President Collor in the early 1990s, which brought citizens to the streets to protest (Stapenhurst 2000). It was also instrumental in building the people power movement in the Philippines to depose then-President Estrada in 2001, and widespread protests in Ecuador to oust then-President Bucharam in the late 1990s.

Media pressure (more precisely, from progressive elements), can create the impetus for reform. Just as brave reporting brought down the Nixon administration in the United States, so too it can shake the foundations of corruption in developing countries.

The power of good research that feeds into the media should not be underestimated (box 9.13). Experience in Uganda illustrates how access to information can galvanize civic action. The Ministry of Finance launched a public expenditure tracking survey to monitor the flow of funds from the budget for per capita education grants to local school districts. The survey showed that, in 1994, the local districts received on average only 13 percent of the funds due them. Alarmed by the huge leakage, the ministry launched a nationwide awareness program that informed communities of the funds that were due their respective districts, thus giving communities a benchmark for monitoring the flow of funds. As a result, the leakage has fallen to less than 20 percent of the budgeted funds.[37]

Laws on the right to information empower NGOs, business organizations, and civil society more generally. For example, a grassroots campaign in Rajasthan, India, led by a local nongovernmental organization, MKSS, used information gleaned from government files to expose and then combat massive corruption at the local level, showing how public officials

**BOX 9.13**

**Investigative Journalism: Lifestyle Checks of Public Officials**

In 2003, over an intense period of six months, a team of researchers from the Philippines Center for Investigative Journalism (PCIJ) conducted a lifestyle check on personnel from the Bureau of Internal Revenue (BIR) and published their findings in a three-part report, "BIR Officials Amass Unexplained Wealth," which later was picked up by the daily newspapers. Throughout the years, survey after survey has indicated that the Bureau is one of the most corrupt government agencies.

The research produced a wealth of information on the lavish lifestyles of BIR officials and employees, ranging from grand houses in highly exclusive neighborhoods to expensive luxury vehicles, despite modest official incomes. The research covered 25 officials at various levels and found that many of them could not explain how they acquired their assets, including shares in businesses and companies. As the report stated, "One regional director, for example, lives in a big house in posh Ayala Alabang,

yet he earns less than P300,000 (approximately $5,400) a year. Parked in his garage on the day PCIJ visited were a Ford Expedition, a Toyota Land Cruiser, and a brand new BMW."

The report also uncovered interesting schemes, such as BIR officials petitioning the Civil Service Commission to change their birth records so that they could delay retirement and hang on to their lucrative postings. The PCIJ team discovered 24 such applications from the BIR between 1989 and 2001.

Since the publication of the report, one senior official has resigned and several have been suspended pending investigation by the ombudsman. It remains to be seen whether any of the officials under investigation will be indicted and convicted of corruption, as many challenges still confront the legal and judicial system. But lifestyle checks have now been added to the arsenal of the anticorruption agencies, making it more difficult for public officials to enjoy illicit wealth.

*Sources:* Bacalla 2003; Porcalla 2004; Nocum 2004.

skimmed money off the wages of workers and paid friendly contractors for work never done. A recently passed freedom of information law made it possible for MKSS to conduct this vigorous and successful campaign.[38]

## 3. Strategy and Implementation: The Challenge for Governance Reforms

Governance reform strategies in the 1990s typically fell into two broad categories: "big bang" or ad hoc incrementalism. Big bang approaches proved to be largely inconsistent with capacity constraints and political realities—in Hirschman's words, countries with the wherewithal to carry out a coordinated big push "would not be underdeveloped in the first place." The main

results of these approaches were major changes in formal rules: new or amended constitutions, new legislation, ostensibly independent courts and audit institutions, and so forth. Such changes are not unimportant. But in practice they rarely shape behavior unless there is an equal commitment to better aligning *informal* rules to improve the incentives that face politicians, bureaucrats, and citizens (Burki and Perry 1998).[39]

Ad hoc incrementalism has also been problematic. With few exceptions, the ad hoc reforms were often symbolic, intended to preserve the old rules and informality while pretending to reform. In some cases they represented well-motivated attempts of individual or small groups of reformers that, for lack of support, were undermined by jealousy, intrigue, or fatigue. More important, they tended to be unrelated to a more coherent reform strategy and thus over time many lost their steam.

What may be needed instead is highly focused, pragmatic interventions that may be termed "strategic incrementalism." These interventions are opportunistic because they exploit the willingness to reform, but they are better grounded in political realities and consistent with the capacity constraints of the country concerned. Knowing what is appropriate in which country situation is often half the battle. Though providing a detailed road map to guide strategy is a task requiring fundamentally new research and analysis, the following discussion suggests a possible approach to governance reform strategies in developing countries.

A recent survey of firms conducted by the World Bank in Eastern Europe and Central Asia provided information that can be used to array the countries of that region along a two-dimensional matrix, with an administrative corruption index on one axis and a state capture index on the other.[40] Since administrative corruption reflects the quality of the compact and state capture affects the strength of political accountability, the quality or state of governance in a country can be broadly characterized by these two indexes.[41] The matrix in figure 9.4 suggests a classification of countries into four possible types: capable, weak, captured, and restrained. Each type faces different challenges and different opportunities for reform.

*Capable*: In capable states, administrative corruption tends to be low and state capture not heavily entrenched. Examples are Korea, Chile, Hungary, and the Czech Republic. To a lesser extent, Botswana and the Indian states of Andhra Pradesh and Karnataka may fall into this category. In capable states, the challenge is usually to increase the quality and efficiency of public services, so as to best utilize limited public resources. Episodic scandals, reported by vigilant media or civil society organizations, usually result in public dialogue and ultimately in a set of actions to reduce opportunities for corruption. In these countries it is often possible to undertake difficult systemic reforms using a more or less technocratic approach, providing there is leadership

FIGURE 9.4

## Classification of States by Governance Profile

*Source:* World Bank Business Environment and Enterprise Performance Survey (BEEPS), 1999 and 2003.

and support that coalesces around the reform objective.

*Weak*: Weak states lack many of the basic structures needed to manage the public sector. Many have only recently emerged from conflict or attained statehood. Bureaucratic capacity and accountability are weak, and administrative corruption is high. Often weak states have largely escaped capture by business interests, not because accountability mechanisms are effective, but because the state is itself insufficiently developed to be captured. In fact, as these basic structures are established, the risks of state capture quickly increase. Examples of such states are Albania (in 1999) and Armenia (in 1999). Nepal and Tanzania may also be examples, as may many low-income countries under stress.[42] In weak states, the primary challenge is to ensure that taxes are collected, key services are delivered, and budget execution is sufficiently controlled. Given limited bureaucratic capacity, it is especially important that reform efforts be targeted and that international support for these reforms be highly coordinated.

*Captured*: These states have serious problems of administrative corruption and their environment makes them highly subject to capture. Many have an urgent need to build capacity in the public sector, but investments in capacity are unlikely to produce sustainable improvements, because political corruption (grounded in rents) permeates the system at all levels. Examples of such states include Azerbaijan (in 1999), the Russian Federation (in 1999), and the Kyrgyz Republic. States that are weak but resource-rich or dominated by a few valuable industries can fall easily into this category. The challenge in these states is to break the stranglehold of special interests—for example, by breaking up powerful monopolies if capture is by private interests, or by reducing military expenditures if capture is by the military. Not surprisingly, these types of reforms are the least likely to be adopted while vested interests remain strong.

*Restrained*: The bureaucracy in these states tends to have sufficient capacity and accountability so that administrative corruption is relatively mild. Political accountability is likely the weakest link in the chain, which results in a high level of state capture. Examples of such states are Croatia (in 1999), the Slovak Republic (in 1999), Serbia and Montenegro (in 1999), Latvia, and possibly Argentina, the Philippines, and some states in India. Reform options are limited in such states while the existing leadership is well entrenched. When a genuine change in leadership occurs, as in Croatia, Latvia, Serbia and Montenegro, and the Slovak Republic, and where civil society is relatively robust and can play an important role in stimulating demand for change, reforms can emerge fairly fast and can potentially be sustained.

Table 9.2 highlights the potential entry points for strategic interventions in each of the four types of states. "Breaking through" a captured state may be the most difficult strategic challenge in governance reform.

## 4. Conclusion

Improvements in governance are critical to ensuring sustainable development. Perhaps the most important lesson of the 1990s is that technocratic responses to improve governance work only in very auspicious settings—where there is committed leadership, a broadly based coalition in support of reform, and sufficient capacity to carry the reform process forward. Clearly, these conditions exist in only a minority of developing countries and rarely in those countries in most urgent need of governance reform. This is the crux of the challenge for the decade ahead.

Meeting the challenge requires a good understanding of the political dimensions of reform, and, in particular, of how reform can be used to identify and build constituencies that are capable of sustaining the reform momentum. This requires fundamental changes in current methods of analysis. In this context, a focus on "drivers of change" is promising (Duncan 2003). While the particular drivers will naturally vary from country to country, the common thread of this approach is a focus on solving the specific, highly salient problems facing individual communities—for example, in health care, sanitation, or business regulation. These are problems around which constituencies for reform both inside and outside government may be easier to build and maintain than, say, upstream reforms in civil service reform or financial management.

Almost all successful reform efforts have been shepherded through by dynamic leaders (World Bank, *World Development Report 1997*, 154). In many countries, the drivers of change may be a group of young, perhaps inexperienced, leaders in need of training and support.

The challenge is creating and nurturing an environment that encourages dynamic, forward-looking individuals to push much needed reforms. In some cases, this may be achieved through political decentralization and economic liberalization, where the former gives local public officials autonomy over their localities and the latter creates pressures for competition among localities. In other cases, the pressure for reform may come from outside. Civil society groups, media, business associations, and/or religious organizations are fertile sources of change. While these groups are often plagued by collective action problems, experience shows that they are fully capable of overcoming these problems. The challenge they face is one of sustainability, a problem that donors and private foundations can address through technical assistance and funding. Because better governance is a

TABLE 9.2

## Types of States and Entry Points for Strategic Interventions: A Governance Typology

| Type of state | Governance profile | Main implications for the triad | Key challenge | Possible entry point |
|---|---|---|---|---|
| Capable state | Low to modest administrative corruption<br>Mild state capture | Some gaps in bureaucratic capacity and internal accountability | Increasing efficiency of public service delivery | Technocratic reforms in public administration, as needed; comprehensive reform strategy may be feasible |
| Weak state | High levels of administrative corruption<br>Mild state capture | Very weak bureaucratic capacity and/or internal accountability | Ensuring delivery of basic public goods | Highly targeted reforms in key sectors only, supplemented by limited reforms in budget execution to ensure financial accountability |
| Captured state | High levels of administrative corruption<br>High state capture | Very weak political and internal accountability; possibly weak bureaucratic capacity | Breaking hold of vested interests on the process of policy and institutional reform | Build demand for reforms; possibly explore opportunities at subnational level |
| Restrained state | Low to modest administrative corruption<br>High state capture | Very weak political accountability | Increasing "voice" | Build demand for reform; await change in leadership caused by crisis related to corruption, after which technocratic reforms to increase political accountability may be possible |

*Source:* Author's elaboration.

public good, groups working on governance reforms will generally find it more difficult to solicit contributions from the general public.

Whether this focus on problem solving and results-oriented drivers of change will help countries to navigate the difficult terrain of governance reform in the next decade remains to be seen. What is certain is that governance reform will retain a high place on the reform agenda.

## Notes

1. See, for instance, Rose-Ackerman (2004) and Klitgaard (1988). Much of the literature on rent seeking from the mid-1970s to the 1980s, for example, Bhagwati (1978), essentially tackled conceptual issues.
2. The causality can work both ways, with growth also perhaps inducing better governance. Some recent studies address this (Rodrik and Subramanian 2003; Subramanian and Roy 2001).
3. The 1996 "Cancer of Corruption" speech given by World Bank President James Wolfensohn is considered a watershed in the Bank in the fight against corruption and the push for reforms of governance institutions in developing countries. The publication

of Transparency International's Corruption Perception Index made governments and their constituent publics more aware of problems of corruption and helped trigger the development of cross-country empirical studies and survey-based diagnostic work on corruption (see, for instance, Kaufmann, Kraay, and Zoido-Lobaton 1999; Reinikka and Svensson 2003).
4. This section builds on an analytical framework from the World Bank's *World Development Report (WDR) 2004.*
5. Formal organizations such as the central bank are also often referred to as institutions. In the abstract, an organization is a collectivity functioning within a predetermined set of formal rules. That is, it is an agglomeration of rules that affects the behavior of a given set of individuals.
6. *WDR 2004* characterizes the bilateral relationship as one of accountability (of agents to principals). But the relationship can also be affected by other factors—in particular, capacity issues. If the agent lacks the ability or the resources to perform his or her task, then no matter how strong the accountability link, he or she will be unable to deliver on his or her mandate. If, for instance, bureaucrats have a poor financial management information system to work with, they cannot produce adequate information upon which to judge their performance.

7. See also *WDR 2004,* chapter 5.

8. More specifically, the possibility of obtaining rents drives influential groups and/or individuals to bribe politicians or high-ranking civil servants. In turn, the latter introduce and maintain bad laws, policies, or regulations in order to perpetrate their illicit earnings. In this context, corruption causes bad governance.

9. Several empirical studies have shown that deficiencies in civil service processes and procedures tend to increase administrative corruption (Van Rijkeghem and Weder 2001; Evans and Rauch 2000; World Bank, *World Development Report 1997*) and have confirmed the findings of numerous case studies (for instance Rose-Ackerman 1978; Wade 1985; Klitgaard 1988, 1990). The relation between public sector pay and corruption is controversial: it is commonly presumed that the lower is public sector compensation, the greater is administrative corruption, but various empirical studies suggest that other factors confound this relationship. See http://www1.worldbank.org/publicsector/civilservice/ineffectivemon.htm#4.

10. Citizens can use shame tactics to pressure local-level civil servants who live within the same community.

11. "Client power" also includes the ability of citizens to choose among different providers of the same service. This does not require collective action on their part; rather it requires policy decisions to promote some form of competition among service providers. Voice (and thus organization) can play a role in getting politicians to promulgate such policies.

12. Political accountability during elections can be enhanced by independent electoral commissions. However, such institutions may themselves also be subject to capture.

13. Work has been done on reforming political institutions, including attempts at reform in political campaign finance. But such efforts have been far fewer than those devoted to legal, judicial, and legislative reforms.

14. The heightened concern with improving legal and judicial systems in the 1990s was predated by similar concerns and reform efforts in the 1960s—some of which are only now beginning to bear fruit.

15. The World Bank's first significant effort was a 1990 adjustment loan to Bangladesh, followed two years later by support to Tanzania for training judges, upgrading legal libraries, and publishing court decisions. In 1992 the Bank also extended a $30 million loan to Venezuela solely for judicial reform. This was the first of 11 investment loans totaling close to $200 million that the Bank extended principally for judicial reform during the 1990s. Data from other organizations show a similar increase in judicial reform activities. Starting from scratch in the 1990s, the Inter-American Development Bank had made 18 loans totaling $418 million by June 2001, and entered into 65 technical cooperation agreements comprising another $43 million to support reform of judicial institutions (Biebesheimer and Payne 2001, 12).

16. For example, in the early 1990s the Ukrainian legislature was asked to enact a verbatim translation of the Uniform Commercial Code—a lengthy American statute governing sales, leasing, and related transactions—and advisors to the Mongolian government suggested that to create a stock market Mongolia simply copy U.S. securities laws.

17. This Anglo-Saxon concept—and related ones in use in Europe, Latin America, Asia, and Africa—can mean many different things. But in the parlance of the development community the rule of law became synonymous with a state where laws effectively restrained rulers from opportunistically seizing private property and simultaneously promoted welfare-enhancing cooperation among the citizenry.

18. Though there are differing interpretations of the composition of New Public Management reforms, there is general agreement that the key components include deregulation of line management, conversion of civil service departments into free-standing agencies; performance-based accountability, particularly through contracts; and competitive mechanisms such as contracting-out and internal markets. Various authors also include privatization and downsizing as a part of the package (Polidano 1999).

19. See Poterba (1996) for a review of the literature circa 1996.

20. Alesina and Perotti (1996) discuss institutions in terms of the degree of centralization of authority in the budget process and the degree of transparency. Von Hagen (1992) provides summary information on the budget process in European Community nations. Von Hagen and Harden (1996) suggest that tighter budget rules are associated with smaller budget deficits and lower levels of government borrowing.

21. An MTEF has five key features: (1) a top-down process for establishing hard budget constraints at the aggregate and sectoral level; (2) a bottom-up process in which line ministries prepare forward estimates of expenditures over a three- or four year period; (3) a system for reconciling the forward estimates and the hard budget constraints, which includes processes for making intersectoral reallocations; (4) a transparent system for incorporating changes to the forward estimates during rollovers to the following year; and (5) a tractable system for undertaking program evaluation (World Bank 1998b).

22. World Bank/OECD Survey on Budget Practices and Procedures (2003). Available online at http://ecde.dyndns.org.

23. Their finding is consistent with related work by Evans and Rauch (2000), and with research at the sector level. Gunnarsson et al. (2004) find strong evidence indicating that the granting of autonomy to local district school principals (akin to delegation under NPM) improves student performance only if the principal and the school staff have adequate capacity to take advantage of the increased autonomy.

24. In related reforms, more than 40 developing and transition countries have set up special large taxpayer units to improve the tax compliance of the largest taxpayers and to pilot new organizational structures, systems, and procedures.

25. For a particularly strong critique, see Fjelstad (2002); and for a more general country survey and balanced assessment, see Taliercio (2003).

26. The same political support might perhaps have achieved the same results without the move to an autonomous revenue agency, but in some instances introducing such an agency has energized and crystallized support for more wide-ranging administrative and civil service reform.

27. Harding (2003) analyzes different approaches to health care provision: direct provision by the public sector, through nonprofit providers, through for-profit providers, and through informal providers. The lessons suggest possibilities for focused strategic interventions in the health sector.

28. E-government applications have normally evolved through a four-stage process. The first stage includes the publication of information on a Web site for citizens to seek knowledge about procedures governing the delivery of different services; the second stage is interactivity online, allowing clients to download applications for receiving services; the third stage involves electronic delivery of documents; and the fourth results in electronic delivery of services, which may involve more than one department in processing a service request or service.

29. E-government can also enhance transparency. For instance, the use of electronic bulletin boards in government procurement has made information on government contracts much more widely available (Bhatnagar and Deane 2003).

30. Bhatnagar and Deane (2003) estimate that roughly 40 percent of an e-government project's cost must be allocated to managing the change process.

31. http://www1.worldbank.org/publicsector/egov/seoulcs.htm.

32. *WDR 2004* provides examples and indicates the extensiveness of citizen-based mechanisms for raising the demand for better governance.

33. An integrity pact embodies a transparent process of procurement that all participating bidders agree to bind themselves to. A civil society organization, such as a local chapter of Transparency International, monitors the process step by step to assure all bidders that each has kept to the joint commitment.

34. For examples see John Pomfret, "SARS Reported in Rural China," available online at http://stacks.msnbc.com/news/904928.asp?cp1=1, and John Pomfret, "China to Open Field in Local Elections," *Washington Post,* June 12, 2003. In Cuba, while dictatorial tactics have certainly kept the Castro regime in power for almost four decades, the high quality of health services—which are among the best in the developing world—is a factor that has contained citizen dissent.

35. Based on IMF *Government Financial Statistics.*

36. An excellent study that analyzes the effect of type of electoral system on policy outcome is Myerson (1999). Persson, Tabellini, and Trebbi (2000) assess the impact of corruption and voting in different electoral systems.

37. Reinikka and Svensson (2003, 2004).

38. For more on lessons on freedom of information laws, see World Bank (2004a).

39. There is "often a vicious circle whereby the failure of the state breeds more corrective rules which both reformer and opportunist applaud—the reformer under mistaken formalistic notions about how to reform and the opportunist in the knowledge that reform will be frustrated and his opportunism can continue" (Burki and Perry 1998, 128). This is not to imply that in developed-country settings there are no informal rules. These never disappear. But they tend to be better aligned with formal institutions rather than being inconsistent with them (North 2002).

40. This is the Business Environment and Enterprise Performance Survey (BEEPS) conducted first in 1999 and most recently in 2003. The findings of the 1999 survey were analyzed and published in World Bank (2000a).

41. Ideally, a third dimension measuring client power would be desirable. This dimension could be constructed using available data on citizen voice.

42. World Bank data suggest that 25 to 30 countries qualify as low-income countries under stress. In these countries, securing law and order and ensuring the delivery of very basic public services remain the primary governance tasks. Beyond this, the evidence suggests that comprehensive and/or more technically demanding governance reforms are unlikely to be feasible.

# Natural Resources: When Blessings Become Curses

Since at least the time of Adam Smith and David Ricardo there has been a belief that natural resources are a blessing: that countries richly endowed with natural resources have an advantage over countries that are not. For centuries, people moved to where natural resources were abundant: to the Americas, to Australia, to oil-rich countries in the Middle East. Natural resource endowments have helped many countries, including Australia, Canada, Finland, and Norway, to grow and diversify, in part by providing a basis for developing associated technologies and capital goods industries (World Bank 2001b).

Since the end of World War II, however, and particularly since the 1960s, evidence has accumulated that natural resources are less often a blessing than a curse[1] (see figure H.1). This finding is statistically robust, invariant to changes in specification, variable definitions, or inclusion of additional explanatory variables—including those commonly used in empirical growth studies, such as geography and climate. After controlling for all possible influences and interactions, the evidence is that countries rich in natural resources grow more slowly.

Not only economic growth is affected negatively (Gelb 1988). Controlling for country income level, countries that are rich in natural resources have more unequal income distribution and a larger share of their population in poverty; they exhibit greater corruption, have more authoritarian regimes, spend more on the military, and face a higher probability of an armed conflict (Palley 2003). The probability of a civil conflict is 0.5 percent in a country with limited natural resources, but 23 percent in a country where natural resources account for 26 percent of GDP (Collier and Hoeffler 1998, 2001). In far too many countries, including Iraq, Nigeria, Sierra Leone, Venezuela, former Zaire, Zambia, and many others, enormous oil or mineral wealth has not translated into economic and social well-being for the majority of the population.

The natural resources that depress countries' long-run growth are those whose rents are technically easy to appropriate: so-called point-source natural resources such as diamonds, gold, oil, and minerals. Other resources, such as land or human resources, have more diffuse rents and do not seem to have such an effect.

Two lines of explanation have emerged to explain the "natural resource curse." The first focuses on how natural resources affect the economy, and the second on how they affect institutions (Eifert, Gelb, and Tallroth 2003).

## Economic Effects

The so-called Dutch disease is perhaps the most well-known effect of natural resource rents on the real economy. High exports of natural resources cause an appreciation of a country's real exchange rate, which moves its productive resources away from tradables such as manufactured goods. If manufacturing produces significant positive externalities that are crucial for long-term development, such as learning-by-doing, the country's economic growth rate will suffer (Sachs and Warner 1997).

Another well-known problem of resource-rich economies is volatility, with cycles of boom and bust. For example, the high resource prices of the 1970s led resource-rich countries to borrow heavily, and the collapse of prices that ensued

FIGURE H.1

## Natural Resources and Growth, 1970–89

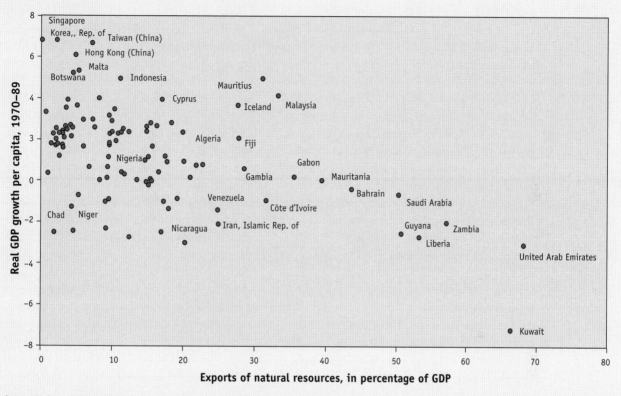

*Source:* Sachs and Warner 1997.

in the early 1980s left them with large debts and little capacity to service them (Manzano and Rigobon 2001). The countries affected ranged from Bolivia to República Bolivariana de Venezuela to Côte d'Ivoire and Nigeria; many resource-rich countries have not yet recovered.

Equally serious, unless a resource-rich economy has a large non-resource-based tradable sector to begin with, the uncertainty associated with cycles of boom and bust can reinforce a downward cycle. The smaller the nonresource tradable sector, the fewer opportunities workers have to find new jobs when resource prices decline; as a result, a price decline can cause the whole economy to contract. Interest rates will reflect the risks associated with this volatility: the greater the volatility, the higher is the interest rate, and, in turn, the smaller are investments in nonresource tradables. These two effects combine to cause the economy to specialize away from production of

nonresource tradables. In turn, the less the economy produces nonresource tradables, ". . . the greater the volatility of relative prices, the higher the interest rate the sector faces, causing it to shrink even further, until it disappears" (Hausmann and Rigobon 2002).

Saving rates in oil-exporting countries are much higher than in other developing countries. But even so, these relationships mean that without corrective policies, volatility causes oil-exporting economies to specialize inefficiently in the production of nontradables, retarding their long-term growth. Thus, it has been argued that República Bolivariana de Venezuela's growth implosion in the early 1980s was the result of the high real interest rates facing the nonresource tradable sector, and of uncompetitive and volatile exchange rates, which caused the country to specialize almost exclusively in resource extraction and nontradables (Hausmann and Rigobon 2002).

## Institutional Effects

These economic explanations do not answer questions about the differences in performance across resource-rich countries, such as why diamonds have been a curse for Sierra Leone but a blessing for Botswana, or why oil has been a blessing for Indonesia. Neither can they explain why point-source natural resources affect growth differently from natural resources with more diffuse rents. Such differences in performance have given rise to a large literature offering political and institutional explanations of the resource curse.

Large and concentrated rents, easier to appropriate than the more diffuse rents associated with land or human resources, make societies less entrepreneurial by increasing the private returns to unproductive rent-seeking. Several studies focus on the "voracity effect," or common pool problems, that move an economy into a low-growth equilibrium because of political fights over resource rents (Lane and Tornell 1999; Mehlum, Moene, and Torvik 2003). In Nigeria, for example, governance institutions were weak and large oil resources were wasted. Large windfall oil profits corrupted Nigeria's institutions and changed its politics, which came to be shaped by the incessant fight over resource revenues. Public spending turned into outright patronage, crippling the civil service. Starting with the Biafra war in the late 1960s, successive military dictators plundered Nigeria's oil wealth, wasting resources on an enormous scale; the country's total factor productivity has declined by 1.2 percent a year over the last few decades (Sala-i-Martin and Subramanian 2003).

Numerous econometric studies confirm that countries rich in natural resources have weaker institutions, measured in terms of checks and balances on the executive, rule of law, and corruption (Sala-i-Martin and Subramanian 2003; Isham et al. 2003; Sala-i-Martin, Doppelhofer, and Miller 2003; Robinson, Torvik, and Verdier 2002; Mehlum, Moene, and Torvik 2003). These studies also show that, controlling for institutions, natural resources have no effect on long-term growth. That is, institutions are not just the principal but the *only* channel through which resources influence the course of the economy.

While natural resources were a curse for Nigeria, the discovery of diamonds became a blessing for development in Botswana, as did oil in Indonesia.

Botswana has effectively maintained law and order, limited state predation, and enforced hard budget constraints on its parastatal organizations (Acemoglu, Johnson, and Robinson 2003). The government has invested heavily in the expansion of infrastructure and efficient delivery of education and health services. While AIDS has reversed some of the health gains, and led to a sharp decline in life expectancy, Botswana's other social indicators are among the better in Africa and in the developing world. The bureaucracy is largely meritocratic, relatively noncorrupt, and efficient. Fiscal revenues from resource rents have been used to smooth revenue over commodity price cycles, rather than financing consumption booms; indeed, Botswana was one of the first countries to establish a stabilization fund, which it managed well. One of the reasons behind Botswana's success is believed to be its benign neglect by colonial powers: Botswana was on the periphery of the British empire, not known to have valuable resources, and hence of little interest. Thus, unlike in most other African countries, colonialism had a negligible effect on traditional social and political institutions. Botswana's pastoral traditions traditionally encouraged broad-based participation and constraints on political leaders; rural interests, chiefs, and cattle owners retained their political power throughout the colonial period. They have been the source of checks on the executive, and explain why diamond rents have been exceptionally well managed.

Indonesia did not have democratic and participatory institutions, at least until very recently. But although corruption and governance problems were widespread, Soeharto's regime focused on economic and social development. On the one hand, it provided checks on state and individual predation and, on the other, it provided predictability and consistency in policy making (Temple 2003). Internal accountability mechanisms enabled the bureaucracy to deliver a wide array of social and infrastructure services, and antipoverty programs. Growth in Indonesia was not only rapid but quite widely shared, through programs such as the Instruction of the President (INPRES), a rural development program that was started at the time of the first rise in oil prices in 1973 and subsequently expanded. INPRES included village support grants, rural infrastructure, and a massive expansion of schooling (World Bank 1993). One reason for Indonesia's success was that the Soeharto regime shielded technocrats from political pressures: the group of high-level technocrats responsible for policy making (the "Berkeley mafia") was empowered to make economic policy decisions with long-term growth and development objectives in mind. Thus, the response to a fall in oil prices in the early 1980s was a textbook adjustment that triggered comprehensive microeconomic reforms—from competition policy to exchange rate adjustments and trade liberalization (see also Country Note B, "Lessons from Countries That Have Sustained Their Growth").

Economic and political explanations are difficult to disentangle. In the course of development, economic institutions are shaped by economic incentives and opportunities, and political dynamics respond to underlying economic forces (Engerman and Sokoloff 2002). Political and other institutions may be the main explanatory forces, but economic forces also play a role in explaining why the institutions are the way they are.

## Conclusion

Simply copying or adopting policies that have been effective elsewhere rarely succeeds. Many resource-rich developing countries have experi-mented with oil funds or stabilization programs—with disappointing results. Successful management of a natural resource curse calls for a combination of policies and institutions. On the economic policy front, countercyclical stabilization policies have a critical role to play, as do policies that maintain the competitiveness of the real exchange rate for the nonresource tradable sector, and financial policies that encourage investments in that sector. On the institutional front, institutions such as transparency, and checks and balances on the use of rents, that increase the costs of nonproductive activities can help countries to move away from rent-seeking equilibria to more dynamic, diversified, and growing economies. East Timor's oil stabilization fund illustrates this approach. While it is too early to determine how the fund will work in practice, the intent of the fund is to rely on institutional improvements that ensure resource rents are effectively used for long-term development. It emphasizes transparency and public awareness of the issues that concern the good use of oil revenues, thus developing constituencies in support of prudent policies.

## Note

1. Sachs and Warner (1995b, 1997, 2001); Lane and Tornell (1999); Auty and Mikesell (1998); Gylfason (2001); Leite and Weidmann (1999); Dalmazzo and de Blasio (2001). While there are many ways to define natural resource abundance—for example as the share of natural resources in the gross domestic product (GDP) or exports (as in figure H.1), with further breakdown for fuel, ores, and metals; or oil-producing versus other developing countries—they all suggest that countries rich in resources grow more slowly.

*Chapter 10*

# Does Democracy Help?

A STRIKING PHENOMENON OF
the 1990s was the rise in the
number of countries selecting
their leaders through competitive elections.[1] The
number rose from 60 countries in 1989 to 100 in
2000. Among poorer countries (those with less
than the median country's per capita income),
the number nearly tripled, from 11 in 1989 to 32
in 2000; 15 percent of the poorer countries
elected their governments in 1989 and 42 percent in 2000.

Unfortunately, democratization does not
ensure economic development. The simple fact
of competitive elections did not enable Haiti's
government to contain predation by the powerful or to establish minimal law and order. Nor
did it prevent Kenya's government from exerting
its authority to benefit a small, privileged elite.
Certainly, most poor democratic countries control predation better and treat citizens more gen-
erously than in these examples. But typically
contractual and property rights, widely recognized as fundamental for investment and economic growth, are less well enforced in poorer
democracies than in richer ones. Similarly, while
rent seeking and corruption are higher in poorer
democracies, public services such as education,
critical for both growth and poverty alleviation,
are less well provided.

Accelerating economic development in
developing countries with elected leaders stands
as one of the important challenges of the 2000s.
Why are democratic institutions less accountable—more vulnerable to narrow interests, rent

seeking, and venality—in some countries than in
others? Why are commitments by some governments more credible than others?

To answer these questions, this chapter focuses
on two propositions. First, elected governments
are most likely to make policies favoring narrow
segments of the population at the expense of the
majority when citizens are ill informed, or cannot
trust promises made prior to elections, or are
deeply polarized. Second, elected governments
are most credible and most likely to respect private property rights when they confront checks
and balances on their decision making.[2] These are
not the only explanations for democratic performance. For example, outside forces direct the
policies of some countries, and the consequences
of a country's history and culture are surely
important.[3] But the arguments in this chapter
suggest that it is through their effects on political
credibility (party development), clientelism, citizen information, and social polarization that these
other forces probably operate.

Section 1 looks at the relationship between
democracy and development, finding that competitive elections have only a modest effect on the
quality of government; elected governments do
not exhibit a systematic advantage in achieving
economic development. Section 2 examines reasons why political decision makers do not always
adopt policies in the broad public interest. Imperfections in electoral markets—lack of voter information, the inability of political competitors to
make credible promises, and social polarization—
are important to understanding policy formula-

tion and explaining differences in economic performance between rich and poor democracies. Section 3 looks at reasons for the lack of credibility of government commitments. It finds evidence that imperfections in political markets have a significant impact on economic growth and hence need to be taken into account in designing strategies to speed growth and development. Section 4 discusses reform strategies for remedying some of the fundamental distortions that can plague democratic decision making. Adjustments in the way that governments and their development partners approach the more traditional development agenda, from service delivery improvements to broader public sector reforms, can go a long way toward mitigating the shortcomings in information and credibility that otherwise undermine government accountability and performance. Section 5 concludes the chapter.

## 1. Elections Have an Uneven Impact on Development

Intuitively, one might expect that in countries where most of the public cannot hold the government accountable, government decision making will tend to disregard the public interest. Moreover, the richest countries in the world (the countries with the longest record of sustained growth) have experienced relatively long periods of uninterrupted elections. Thus the political upheaval and democratization in the 1990s offered reasons for optimism regarding economic development.

Some policy progress could be seen among the democratizing countries. For example, among countries that lacked competitively elected governments in 1988 but had them by 1998, secondary school enrollment rose by about 14 percentage points. Similarly, a measure of the rule of law—capturing the extent to which government acts arbitrarily—improved by three-quarters of a point on a six-point scale.

Cross-country analysis shows, however, that there is little association between competitive elections and the quality of government. The modest improvements that took place in the poli-

cies of newly democratized countries are better explained by increases in income per capita. Among all countries that held competitive elections in the 1990s, purchasing power parity (PPP)–adjusted incomes rose by a third during the decade.[4] Using a six-point scale to compare the quality of government in these countries, three points separated the lowest-scoring 25 percent of countries from the highest-scoring. And in half of these countries, the rule of law was no better than it was in the median country lacking competitive elections. Among countries that had competitively elected governments in 1995, gross secondary school enrollment varied more than 140 percentage points from the minimum to the maximum, and 60 percentage points separated the top and bottom quartiles. After accounting for the effect of income per capita, 40 percent of the countries lacking competitive elections exhibited higher gross secondary school enrollment than 40 percent of the countries that held them.

Consistent with these findings, a large literature finds no consistent, significant effect of elections on economic growth. For example, Przeworski et al. (2000) find no difference in growth rates between countries that have competitive elections and those that do not.

Another factor that blurs the distinction between democracies and nondemocracies is the heterogeneity of the latter group. Some autocrats find that they can extract more rents and stay in office longer if they encourage investment and promote long-run economic growth; indeed, in countries with nonelected leaders, property rights become more secure the longer the leaders have been in office (Clague et al. 1996).[5] But many autocrats are unable to trigger this virtuous circle: investors are deterred by the fear that profits will be expropriated, the rents obtained by the autocrat fall, economic performance drags, and threats to the autocrat's tenure grow. It appears that in nondemocracies in which the likely rates of return to investment are low (for example, countries with uneducated workforces and no easy access to foreign markets), or in which the rates of return to natural resource exploitation are high, leaders are less likely to curb their own authority to attract greater investment.

Beyond geographic explanations, nondemocracies that emerge from broad social movements appear to place more controls on their leaders. In Mexico, for example, during the period that it dominated politics, the *Partido Revolucionario Institucional* (PRI) provided checks on the behavior of presidents. Nondemocracies also differ in the extent of their institutionalized sources of authority (even within a single party) that might counterbalance the authority of the top leader. Even nondemocracies with an unelected legislature have significantly less corruption and greater rule of law than countries without an unelected legislature.[6] Gandhi (2003) finds that nondemocracies with unelected legislatures grow faster than those without such legislatures.

## 2. Characteristics of Democracies That Influence Policy Success and Failure

In all settings where people come together to act collectively, complaints of high-handed behavior by leaders and of its converse, endless consensus-building, are endemic. Whether in town councils, sports clubs, or *Musikvereinen*, issues of fairness and equity, efficiency, and consistency regularly arise. Special interests curry favor in every country in the world, and individuals everywhere succumb to the temptations of venality and rent seeking.

Why, though, are rent seeking, special interest influence, and venality—the effects of government inefficiency—worse in poor countries than in rich? As shown in the following discussion, the activities of special interest groups explain policy outcomes generally, but they do not explain why policy outcomes in developing countries differ from those in developed ones. Similarly, differences in political and electoral institutions explain variations in policy outcomes across countries, but they do not explain the divergence between policies in developing and developed countries.

Instead, there are three other explanations, all related to imperfections in electoral markets, for why policies are more likely to neglect the public interest in poor democracies but not rich ones: lack of voter information, the inability of political competitors to make credible promises and be trusted, and social polarization. Each of these is important to understanding policy formulation and reform.

### Special Interests

Before the 1990s, attempts to explain government policy failures centered on the role of special interests. The logic—"the logic of collective action," as Mancur Olson coined it in 1965—is clear. Small, homogeneous groups with much at stake confront relatively low costs to acting collectively in their common interest. In competing for benefits from government, this gives them advantages over large groups whose interests are heterogeneous. Unfortunately, narrow interests rarely benefit from public goods, such as the provision of universal education or an improved court system, as much as they do from diverting some fraction of societal resources to themselves. Hence, to the extent that government incentives encourage targeting of benefits to special interest groups, policy failure—the underprovision of public goods and the overprovision of regulations and laws that benefit special interests at the expense of the whole society—is more likely.

Ample evidence points to the importance of collective action considerations in the making of public policy in all countries. Bates (1981, 1983) and Frieden (1991) make compelling cases for the role of special interests, indigenous or foreign, in shaping policies in Africa and Latin America, for example.

There is no strong evidence, however, that the logic of collective action can explain differences in development outcomes. For example, there is no indication that the intrinsic characteristics of special interests differ in developing countries, better enabling special interests in these countries to extract rents from the unorganized majority. Nor is there evidence that special interests in developing countries are more unified than in developed countries, and therefore less likely to "cancel out" their respective influences.

## Formal Rules

Great attention has focused on the role of institutions in development. The formal rules determining how politicians attain office and make decisions decisively influence policy outcomes. However, it is less clear that institutional differences can explain the differences in development performance among democracies.

Substantial research in the 1990s focused precisely on the effects of political and electoral institutions on the magnitude of government spending, broad public goods, and rent seeking.[7] Researchers found that under some conditions majoritarian rules (first-past-the-post electoral systems with small electoral districts) lead politicians to focus on pivotal narrow constituencies, biasing spending downwards and away from broadly based public goods.[8] Comparisons of presidential and parliamentary forms of government yielded similar predictions: parliamentary systems, under some conditions, promote greater allocations to broad public goods than do presidential systems.[9] These findings are potentially important for our understanding of development, to the extent that public goods such as universal education or law and order are essential to economic growth.

Do poorer democracies, with less robust provision of public goods and greater rent seeking, exhibit the electoral and political institutions that are thought to promote these outcomes?

In 2000, of the countries with competitively elected governments, plurality or first-past-the-post rules dominated among the electoral systems of the poorer countries but not among those of the richer (figure 10.1).[10] Similarly with respect to political systems, presidential systems were much more common among the poorer democracies than among the richer (figure 10.2).

Though these associations might suggest an institutional explanation for the differences in the policy experiences of the two sets of countries, the evidence is weak that these institutions are *responsible* for the differences. As researchers have predicted, spending on education is about 2 percentage points of gross domestic product (GDP) greater in parliamentary democracies with

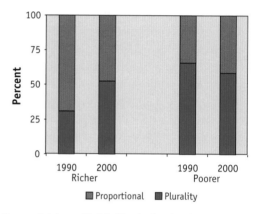

FIGURE 10.1

### Electoral Rules in Richer and Poorer Democracies

*Sources*: Database of Political Institutions (Beck et al. 2001) and World Bank, *World Development Indicators*.

*Note*: Countries represented are those that held competitive elections for executive and legislative elections (the Legislative and Executive Indexes of Competitive Elections from the Database of Political Institutions were both equal to seven).

proportional electoral systems than in presidential democracies with majoritarian systems.[11] However, the key public good is education itself, not education spending, which turns out to have little effect on gross secondary school enrollment.[12] Political and electoral institutions are insignificant determinants of secondary school enrollment precisely because they have less of an influence in poorer countries.[13] Among the richer democracies in 1997, school enrollment was about 38 percentage points greater in parliamentary than in presidential systems. In the poorer democracies, it was essentially the same regardless of political systems.[14]

Corruption is another indicator of the extent to which government decisions on spending or policy are likely to translate into improved social welfare. There is little evidence that political and electoral institutions can explain the greater prevalence of corruption in developing countries than in developed ones. Arguments formulated in the 1990s (for example, by Persson and Tabellini 2000) suggested that under some conditions, presidential systems would reduce corruption. However, there is little evidence of this in either rich or poor countries (Adserà, Boix, and Payne 2003).

FIGURE 10.2

## Political Systems in Richer and Poorer Democracies

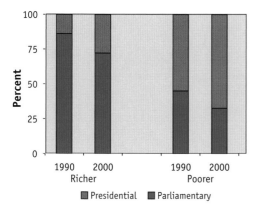

Source: Database of Political Institutions (Beck et al. 2001) and World Development Indicators.

Note: Countries represented are those that held competitive elections for executive and legislative elections (the Legislative and Executive Indexes of Competitive Elections from the Database of Political Institutions were both equal to seven).

There is more evidence that electoral systems affect corruption, but the effect is subtle. Adserà, Boix, and Payne (2003) find no effect. But Persson, Tabellini, and Trebbi (2003) break down electoral institutions into their component parts—district magnitude (measured by the number of seats up for election in the district) and voting rule—and argue that the larger the district, the lower are the barriers to entry faced by competing parties and the more likely it is that voters can drive out corrupt parties. When voters can express a preference for individual candidates, as in plurality systems, they are better able to remove corrupt legislators. Persson, Tabellini, and Trebbi (2003) find evidence that both effects are at work. In practice, however, the two effects cancel each other out, since countries with proportional electoral rules generally require voters to choose parties rather than candidates. Hence, electoral rules cannot explain the greater levels of corruption in poor countries.

There is, then, no strong evidence that either special interest group organization or formal differences in political and electoral institutions account for the different policy choices of developed- and developing-country democracies. Still,

the arguments that these elements *should* matter are persuasive and seem to have great validity in richer countries. Their relative weakness in explaining outcomes in poorer countries suggests that the underlying conditions of political competition in these countries differ from those in richer countries. We explore these conditions and their effects next.

### Imperfections in Electoral Markets

Differences in economic performance across democracies can be explained with respect to imperfections in electoral markets. Numerous imperfections in electoral markets make it difficult for citizens to hold politicians accountable for policies. The discussion below focuses on three imperfections—uninformed voters, noncredible political competitors, and social polarization—that offer powerful insights into the underperformance of many democracies.

### Uninformed Voters

In political markets, the information that voters have about the characteristics of political competitors and government performance is crucial. Without information about the attributes of political competitors, about what politicians are doing, and how their doings affect citizens' well-being, citizens cannot easily reward high-performing politicians. This encourages poor performance. Politicians confronting uninformed voters can invest resources to persuade them of their accomplishments, through advertising or meetings, for example. But financing these efforts, whether from their own pockets or those of special interests, or from government funds, carries a social cost: special interests demand policies that diverge from the social interest in exchange for campaign financing, while government funding diverts resources away from the provision of goods and services to the electorate.

No data directly measure how well informed citizens are about the contributions that their representatives make to their welfare. One commonly used proxy for citizen information is newspaper circulation per 1,000 as a proportion of population.

In 1995, among countries that hold competitive elections, newspaper circulation was, not unexpectedly, considerably higher in richer than in poorer countries (figure 10.3).

Controlling for income and other factors, higher newspaper circulation is associated with lower corruption (Adserà, Boix, and Payne 2003), and with greater rule of law, better bureaucratic quality, and greater secondary school enrollment (Keefer 2003a). As discussed later in this chapter, newspaper circulation and access to radios increase the probability of receiving government transfers (Besley and Burgess 2002 and Strömberg 2002, respectively).

Figure 10.4 illustrates these effects, showing how newspaper circulation, controlling for other influences, suppresses corruption.[15]

## Credibility of Politicians

When challengers cannot make credible policy commitments to citizens, citizens have no reason to prefer them over incumbents. Even if incumbents do badly, citizens have no reason to believe

FIGURE 10.4

**Newspaper Circulation and Corruption**

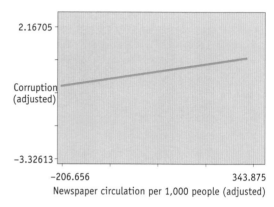

Source: Database of Political Institutions (Beck et al. 2001) and *World Development Indicators*.

Note: The figure depicts the effect of the component of newspaper circulation that is uncorrelated with the other explanatory variables on the component of corruption that is uncorrelated with the other explanatory variables (the orthogonal component of each), based on the regression below. The sample is of countries that exhibit competitive elections (LIEC = EIEC = 7 from the Database of Political Institutions), 1990–2000; economic variables are from *World Development Indicators*; t-statistics are in parentheses; ordinary least squares regression controls for clusters of observations from the same country that artificially inflate statistical significance.

*Corruption* = 3.85 + 0.00002*PPP-adjusted income/capita* + (2.25e–08) *land area–5.33) (0.66)(0.65)* (9.3e–10) *population –0.44 electoral system* – 3.87*percent population young* + 1.2 *percent rural (–1.14) (–2.49) (–1.98)* – 0.01 *political system* + 0.02 *continuous years competitive elections* + 0.002 *newspaper circulation per 1,000 (2.62) (–0.07) (3.94) (2.88)*.

FIGURE 10.3

**Indicators of Political Market Imperfections in Countries Holding Competitive Elections, 1995**

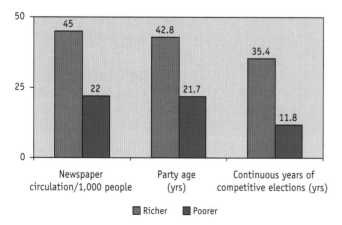

Source: Newspaper circulation from *World Development Indicators*; party age (the average age of parties under their current name); and continuous years of competitive elections, are from the Database of Political Institutions.

Note: Countries are all those with Legislative and Executive Indexes of Electoral Competition (LIEC and EIEC) equal to the highest score of seven (see Figure 10.1). The income per capita threshold between richer and poorer democratic countries, dividing them into roughly equally sized groups, is US$6,193.

that challengers will do better.[16] This insulates incumbents from pressure to perform.

In practice, politicians never entirely lack credibility. Some political competitors are credible on only one or a few issues unrelated to economic development, such as a country's struggle for independence, or issues of religious importance, but in such cases, the votes they attract do not provide a motivation for better economic policy performance.

Credibility may also be partial in the sense that politicians can make credible promises to some voters only. Credibility resides in individual politicians or in "patrons" rather than in political parties. The problem of credibility is therefore closely related to the phenomenon of clientelism, which is widely argued to characterize political relationships in poorer countries, and involves patrons and clients who are bound together by reciprocal, long-lasting patterns of exchange. These exchanges form the foundation of reputations that allow patrons to deliver votes at election time. Unfortunately, narrowly based credibility gives politicians incentives to under-provide public goods and to extract large rents (box 10.1).

A dysfunctional public sector limits the ability of politicians to make credible promises. This is the problem of capability that was discussed in chapter 9. If an education ministry is deeply dysfunctional and is likely to take years to reform, and if citizens cannot observe changes in the ministry until these are reflected in schools, even favorably inclined politicians are unlikely to make promises about education. For example, when Alberto Fujimori became President of Peru in 1990, he privatized enterprises, revamped

---

**BOX 10.1**
## Clientelism, Credibility, and Politics

Only since the late 1990s have scholars begun to understand why clientelism is a more dominant characteristic of public policy in some countries than in others. One explanation derives from the struggle to make credible promises to citizens. Clientelism in public policy prevails when average citizens cannot believe the promises of political competitors with whom they have no personal connection. Such a connection emerges most strongly in the context of patron-client relations. Scholars have long noted that these relations have two important characteristics: patrons and clients interact over a long period and they exchange goods and favors. Bista (1991, 91–92) describes the key role of reciprocity in the operation of clientelism in Nepal (where it is called *chakari*): "The gift donor in chakari has certain rights. There is an obligation on the part of the recipient to respond to the chakariwal when the chakariwal so determines. . . . Ultimately, there has to be a balance in exchange relations."

Scholars of clientelism from Africa to Southern Europe to East Asia confirm this pattern (Lemarchand 1972; Powell 1970; and Scott 1972). Extended compliance with reciprocal obligations forms a basis for credible commitment, which patrons can use if they decide to become politically active.

In fact, Scott (1972) quotes Wurfel as pointing out that "the Filipino politician . . . does favors *individually*

rather than collectively because he wishes to create a personal obligation of clientship." He cites the work of Nash on the 1960 elections in Burma: "When a local patron was approached to join U Nu's faction of the AFPFL on the promise of later patronage, he was able to get thirty-nine others—his relatives and those who owed him money or for whom he had done favors, i.e., his clients—to join as well." The rents to patrons were potentially high, since parties often had to give a local patron significant authority over local administrative and development decisions in exchange for vote delivery (Scott 1972, 110).

Patron-client relations drive politicians to focus on targeted favors and goods over broad public goods and public policy: to the extent that only clients believe patron promises (given the absence of well-developed political parties, for example), political competition concerns primarily targeted transfers to clients rather than public policy issues more generally. Wilder (1999) quotes former members of the Pakistani National Assembly from the state of Punjab as saying, "People now think that the job of an MNA and MPA is to fix their gutters, get their children enrolled in school, arrange for job transfers. . . . [These tasks] consume your whole day. . . ." (p. 196). "Look, we get elected because we are *ba asr log* [effective people] in our area. People vote for me because they perceive me as someone who can help them" (p. 204).

*Source:* Keefer 2002.

the tax administration, removed price controls, reformed the customs system, and built up a large and successful social fund, but he explicitly ignored education, which was at least as troubled as the sectors that he did address.

The credibility of preelectoral promises is difficult to measure empirically. However, it is likely to be associated to some extent both with the number of years that countries have experienced continuous elections and with the age of their political parties. The passage of time allows (though it does not require) political competitors and parties to build up a reputation for their stances on policy issues. Among countries that hold competitive elections, as figure 10.3 illustrates for 1995, both of these factors are considerably higher in richer countries than in poorer ones.

Similarly, where political reputations are sturdier, the effects of clientelism should be reduced, public good provision should be greater, and rent seeking lower, since political competition encourages politicians to provide high-quality public services. Keefer (2003a) finds that this is the case in practice: the longer a country's unbroken series of elections, the greater are secondary school enrollment, the rule of law, and bureaucratic quality, and the less are corruption and public investment as a fraction of GDP (public investment having the greatest political payoffs to targeted constituencies). These effects are often large. The number of continuous years of elections has a greater impact on corruption than do any of the other usual determinants, from newspaper circulation to formal constitutional rules to demographics (figure 10.5). It has a greater impact on secondary school enrollment than do education spending and primary school enrollment (figure 10.6).[17]

Figure 10.6 also indicates that education spending, which has little effect on gross secondary school enrollment in general, has a strong conditional effect: once one controls for continuous years of competitive elections, education spending has a significant positive effect on enrollments. This is a clear indication of an increasingly well-identified phenomenon: that without appropriate political incentives, financial resources do little to improve government performance.[18]

FIGURE 10.5

## Continuous Years of Competitive Elections and Corruption

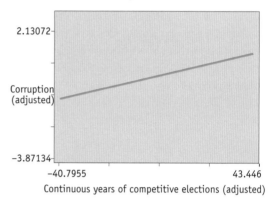

*Source:* Database of Political Institutions (Beck et al. 2001) and *World Development Indicators*.

*Note:* See note to Figure 10.4 for specification, data sources, and estimation methodology. Figure drawn from regression below:

*Corruption* = 3.85 + 0.00002*PPP income/capita* + (2.25e-08)*land area* − (9.3e-10)*total population (5.33) (0.66) (0.65) (−1.14) −* 0.44 *electoral rule* − 3.87 *percent pop. young* + 1.2 *percent pop. rural* − 0.01 *political system (−2.49) (−1.98) (2.62) (−0.07) +* 0.02 *continuous years competitive elections* + 0.002 *newspaper circulation per 1,000 (3.94) (2.88).*

Taken together, then, the evidence suggests that the divergent performances of rich and poor democracies can be traced to differences in their exposure to electoral market imperfections.

## Social Polarization

Social polarization undermines the accountability of government to citizens. One type of social polarization emerges when substantial groups of citizens have deeply opposing interests on most salient political issues. These divisions can run so deep that one group of citizens cannot contemplate electing a representative from the other. Elected representatives from one group then have no incentive to satisfy the concerns of citizens in the other. Moreover, they may have little incentive even to satisfy the concerns of citizens from their own group; this can happen if groups choose their candidates in a distorted manner (for example if backroom deals determine who will be the candidate from each group for the general election).

FIGURE 10.6

## Gross Secondary School Enrollment and Continuous Years of Competitive Elections

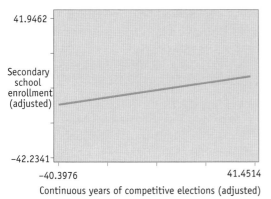

Continuous years of competitive elections (adjusted)

*Source:* Database of Political Institutions (Beck et al. 2001) and *World Development Indicators.*

*Note:* See Figure 10.4 for interpretation. Specification and estimation as in Figure 10.4 and Figure 10.5 , with the addition of primary gross school enrollment and education spending.

*Gross secondary school enrollment* = 82.23 + 0.0009*PPP income/capita* – (3.68e–07) *land area (6.96) (2.21) (–0.59)* – (1.87e–08) *total population* – 176.7 *percent pop. young* – 16.78 *percent pop. rural (–1.23) (–8.53) (–1.79)* + 0.99 *electoral rule* + 0.89 *political system* + 0.16 *continuous years of competitive elections (0.39) (0.52) (1.56)* + 0.001 *newspaper circulation per 1,000* + 0.34 *gross primary enrollment* + 77.7 *total education spending/GDP (0.11) (3.7) (2.29).*

Majority disdain for the interests of identifiable minorities is another manifestation of social polarization. The more pronounced the disdain, the greater the distortion in the provision of public goods, and the more likely that minorities will be excluded from government services. There is substantial evidence for these effects, and not only in developing countries. In the United States, Alesina, Baqir, and Easterly (1999) find that the more ethnically fragmented is a community (the smaller is the white majority), the more limited is the provision of public goods. In such cases, the failure of political accountability does not show up as an excessive willingness to serve special interests at the expense of average citizens, but as the opposite: an exceptional unwillingness to protect the rights of minorities. Subjective measures of ethnic tensions are dramatically higher in poorer democracies than in richer ones.[19] Outright

abuse of minorities has been documented in a wide range of countries.

Both the nature and consequences of social polarization depend on the political environment. In the first case above, of "classic" polarization, there may be third groups that are indifferent to the ideological divide between the other two groups and whose support is needed to win elections. In the second, political institutions and circumstances can mitigate or exacerbate the effects of discrimination against minorities. For example, scheduled tribes and castes in India received greater benefits once they were guaranteed seats on local legislative bodies. Wilkinson (2000) finds that Hindu–Muslim violence was less common and elicited a more aggressive government response in those Indian states in which Muslims were pivotal voters. Rodrik (1999b) argues that ethnically fragmented countries had the greatest difficulty reaching the agreement necessary to emerge from crisis, though countries with a better governance environment were able to offset this effect.

The consequences of social polarization can be worsened by all the factors that undermine voters' ability to hold politicians accountable. If voters are better informed about actions taken by members of their own social groups, or if they are more likely to trust promises by members of their own social groups, relative to members of other groups, the effects of social polarization are likely to be worsened, and the rewards from controlling the government are more likely to flow to the groups whose representatives control government. By contrast, where the information and credibility gap between own-group and other-group representatives is smaller, social polarization is less likely to have damaging effects.

Controlling for numerous other factors, including income per capita, analysis shows that a common subjective measure of ethnic tensions is significantly worse, the lower are the average age of political parties (one measure of the credibility of political competitors) and newspaper circulation.[20] The extent to which there are multiple large ethnic or linguistic groups in a country, though, has no effect on ethnic tensions.

Another key element of social polarization is the ability of competing groups to make credible commitments to each other. Previously quiescent intergroup relationships can suddenly explode into conflict when the foundation for credible commitment crumbles. Bates, de Figuereido, and Weingast (1998) point to key events—such as the election of Slobodan Milosevic in the former Yugoslavia—that disrupt arrangements that all groups believe have protected them from aggression by other groups. The interaction of political and ethnic effects explains why social identity (ethnic, tribal, religious, geographic) is often *not* politically salient and has no discernible effect on policy. It also explains why, as Posner (forthcoming) shows for Africa, the "identities" that matter for politics often shift within the same population.

## 3. Government Credibility as a Prerequisite for Development

All of the foregoing relates to the reluctance or inability of political decision makers to adopt policies in the broad public interest. A related problem for development emerges when policies, once enacted, are not credible.

### Lack of Government Credibility Undermines Growth . . .

The most notable effect of credibility is on investment and growth. Investors rely on government promises to respect investors' rights to their assets. When those promises are not credible, investments slow down or take inefficient forms: power plants are set up on barges rather than on land; older machinery is used at the expense of greater efficiency; innovation falls, in part because production techniques are not at the cutting edge and in part because the fruits of innovation are themselves vulnerable to expropriation. The growth effects are immediate: annual growth in income per capita in poor countries with the most secure property rights is between 2 and 4 percentage points faster than in poor countries with the least secure property rights (Keefer and Knack 1997). Earlier chapters in this report attribute the weak effects of policy reform on growth partly to insti-

tutional weaknesses in countries. The inability of countries to secure property and contractual rights is a core element of these weaknesses.

Controversy emerged in the 1990s regarding two issues surrounding the growth–property rights debate: whether trade or other factors matter more to growth than does the security of property rights, and whether the security of property rights is rooted in countries' more fundamental geographical features. The first debate is not resolved and may not be, bound up as it is in intractable problems (Rodrik, Subramanian, and Trebbi 2002; Dollar and Kraay 2003).[21] The implications of the second debate loom larger. If geography determines the security of property rights—that is, if geography is fate—the range of options for accelerating development is more limited. The role of geography is discussed below, in the context of institutional and other determinants of government credibility.

### . . . and Undermines Policy

A vast array of government policies need to be credible to be effective. A key problem in monetary policy, for example, is the threat that the government will enact a surprise increase in the money supply at the expense of economic agents that have signed long-term contracts. Anticipating this, economic agents factor extra inflation into their contracts, raising the long-term rate of inflation (Barro and Gordon 1983).

Lack of government credibility also dampens incentives to invest in public infrastructure or to make other social investments. The payoffs to these investments depend on the willingness of economic actors to make complementary investments that take advantage of them. Where expropriation is more likely, private investors are slower to respond to improved public infrastructure, and governments correspondingly reduce their allocations to these investments. Keefer and Knack (2002) show that in countries with insecure property rights, measured public investment is largely rent seeking. When property rights are insecure, an additional percentage point of public investment as a fraction of GDP significantly *reduces* the rate of growth of income per capita;

when property rights are secure, it adds 0.3 percentage point to the growth rate.

The security of property rights has a similar effect on other long-term investments. In the 1990s, improved security of property rights increased gross secondary school enrollment by an amount as large as did a similar increase in government expenditure.[22] Confirming the link between rent seeking and public sector performance, Rajkumar and Swaroop (2002) find that child mortality rates and primary school attainment improve in response to increased public health and education spending only in countries with low corruption and high bureaucratic quality.

## Sources of Low Government Credibility: Lack of Reputation and Short Time Horizons

What makes government policies credible? Certainly the elements of political competition that allow political competitors to make credible pre-electoral promises help to ensure the credibility of the policies they implement after they take office. There is some evidence of this, if one accepts that the number of years that countries with competitively elected governments have continuously had such governments corresponds to the opportunities that political competitors have had to build reputations. The greater the number of years of uninterrupted competitive elections, the more established is the rule of law.[23]

However, many policies are not the subject of preelectoral debate. Even when they are, the gains from reneging on policies, once implemented, are often greater than the gains from reneging on pre-electoral promises to implement them in the first place.[24] Finally, investors are always concerned about a change in political control, from politicians who have promised to support a particular policy to those who have not.

The horizons of political actors—how long they expect to be in power or to be competing for power—can mitigate these additional threats to credibility. Governments that expect to be in office many years have more to lose from current policies that upset future growth, such as investment-deterring expropriation, than do governments with short horizons. As noted earlier, Clague et al. (1996) show that among nonelected leaders, the longer is their horizon, the more likely they are to respect property rights. These results do not imply that governments should be immune to threats of removal. They do imply that in countries where accountability mechanisms are flawed, extending the horizons of governments by making them more secure in office may be the only means to create sufficient incentives to maintain secure property rights.

## Sources of Low Government Credibility: Political Institutions

Multiple institutional arrangements have been proposed to solve the problem of government credibility, but in the end, only political institutions— particularly institutional checks and balances—have demonstrated a consistent effect on the credibility of government decision making. For example, Keefer and Stasavage (2003) find that only in countries that exhibit political checks and balances does the legal independence of central banks suppress inflation. Moreover, even in countries without legally independent central banks, political checks and balances can inhibit governments from reneging on monetary commitments. Inflation is lower in countries with political checks and balances than in countries without them.

This finding is consistent with a large body of research on institutions and government credibility. North and Weingast (1989) argued that the introduction of checks on the English monarchy after the Glorious Revolution reduced the monarchy's ability to renege on sovereign debt obligations to foreign creditors, and eventually brought down interest rates.[25] Acemoglu, Johnson, and Robinson (2002) point, though less explicitly, to the role of the right to vote and political checks and balances as the key link between the economic drivers of political power (relative prices and natural resource endowments) and the ultimate security of property rights.[26]

Engerman and Sokoloff (2002) make similar arguments. These authors highlight the role of natural endowments and other exogenous factors in determining the types of institutions that countries exhibit. The essential logic is that in countries where ownership of economic activity is concentrated in the hands of a few, and assuming that political power follows control of the country's most valuable assets, there is no incentive for the politically and economically powerful to enfranchise the powerless. The gains that the elite could reap—in the form of increased productivity of the masses, whose greater political rights would protect them from expropriation—would not offset the losses that the elite would face in being forced to share the high returns from their plantations, mines, or oil wells. Hence, these countries grow slowly, and the price of slow growth is borne by the disenfranchised.

If geography were the main determinant of institutional development, there would be little purpose in institutional reform, and development possibilities would be limited. But in practice many countries have made institutional changes that seem to represent an escape from geographically determined destinies. One example is the wave of democratization in the 1990s. Another is the spread of democracy in Latin America in the 1980s and 1990s, precisely where conditions for democracy are supposed to have been the least propitious.

In all of these cases, the question remains why the introduction of formal institutions is not sufficient to ensure sustained development across countries. Our earlier analysis suggests that the reason may be rooted in the underlying conditions of political competition. Improvement in these conditions, therefore, is likely to be an important complement to institutional reform.[27]

### Growth and Accountability

Boiled down to its essence, the foregoing argues that elections alone are insufficient to ensure accountability of governments to citizens. If this is true, one might expect to find a stronger relationship between growth and democracy if one takes account of the different accountability mechanisms used in different democracies. In fact, there

is evidence that the extent of imperfections in political markets has a significant impact on economic growth.

Easterly and Levine (1997) look at the effects on growth of one measure of social polarization: ethnolinguistic fractionalization. Although they do not explicitly consider the role of elections, they find that their polarization variable has a significant impact on economic growth. Keefer (2003b) provides evidence that newspaper circulation, checks and balances, and the number of continuous years of elections have a significant impact on economic growth. Gerring, Brandt, and Bond (2003) similarly find that—controlling for whether a country is democratic or not (which has no impact on growth)—the total number of years that a country had elected governments through most of the 20th century had a significant impact on growth.

Taken together, these results make a compelling case for reformers and development activists to take political market imperfections into account in designing strategies to speed growth and development.

## 4. Lessons: Making Politics Work for Policy When Governments Are Not Credible and Electoral Markets Are Imperfect

How should we formulate strategies of policy reform, given imperfections in the market for political office and limitations on the credibility of government commitments? And what reforms might mitigate these political and institutional problems directly?

The traditional answer to the first question is to buy off the opposition to reform. This formula requires political leadership: buying off the losers who are in a position to block reform, and exploiting windows of opportunity such as crisis or a change in government. However, nothing in the traditional formula hints at the fact that reform may be systematically more difficult in some countries and policy areas than in others.

## Political Market Imperfections Explain Why Buying off Reform Losers Usually Fails

That compensation strategies have rarely succeeded is not surprising. First, the compensation needed to persuade reform losers to support reform can be prohibitively high; for example, the benefits to the fertilizer industry of fertilizer subsidies in India amount to 0.7 percent of GDP each year (Panagariya 2003). Even large payouts may be feasible if the gains are correspondingly large. But when the imperfections in the market for political office loom as large as they do in many countries, or when political institutions provide few checks on opportunistic behavior by politicians, adequate compensation may be impossible. If politicians cannot make credible promises to voters, they cannot make credible promises of compensation to losers from reform. And if citizens are poorly informed about what politicians do in office, losers may be unable to observe whether governments have actually delivered the promised compensation. Hence remedying the underlying imperfections in electoral markets is a prerequisite for successful reform.

Second, institutional deficiencies can also undermine compensation strategies. If reform losers control government decision making, they cannot credibly promise to refrain from introducing inefficient policies that benefit them at the expense of others: once they have received compensation, nothing prevents them from reverting to policies that run counter to the public interest. In this case, institutional reform is an essential prerequisite of policy reform.

Third, a reform itself can undermine the bases for making credible agreements. Consider an effort to downsize a ministry or to close a money-losing state-owned enterprise. If they are well organized, threatened workers can oppose these efforts by demonstrating, targeting contributions to politicians who will help them, and purchasing advertisements to sway public opinion. To offset this opposition, reform proponents could offer the workers a large pension. Should this proposal be accepted, the workers will be sent home. Once scattered, they cannot easily

block subsequent efforts to reduce the generous pension. Reform has undermined the political power that would allow them to enforce the agreement.[28] Realizing that they would then be vulnerable to government efforts to recapture the pension from the now-disorganized workers, workers therefore reject the proposal.

Dramatic increases in prices are relatively easy to attribute to political failure (Keefer and Khemani, forthcoming). But some other types of policy reforms—banking and social service delivery, for example—are more vulnerable to political market imperfections and institutions that fail to solidify government credibility.

Banking crises emerge after years of regulatory neglect and imprudent lending practices. It is difficult to assign political responsibility for them because these practices may occur under multiple governments, and because politicians can easily blame regulators for shirking and bankers for criminal behavior. Such claims are difficult for voters to evaluate in every country, so it is not surprising that the fiscal costs of banking crises are almost exactly the same in poorer and richer countries.[29]

Social services are also vulnerable to electoral market failure. The goal of universal education is exactly contrary to clientelist political motivations.[30] It is quite difficult for citizens to assign blame to politicians for health and education failures, which could be due to idiosyncrasies of individual health status, or to shirking by service providers, or to the fact that the country lacks resources.

The essential lesson is that for policies and countries in which electoral market failures loom large, reform efforts should focus on mitigating these failures rather than on paying off losers or encouraging leadership or awaiting the opening of windows of opportunity. Where market failures are too large, the first may be too expensive, the second unrealistic, and the third may never occur.

## Mitigating Electoral Market Failures

What measures might alleviate imperfections in the markets for political office?[31] Mitigating electoral market failures essentially means reducing politicians' incentives to engage in clientelist behavior. How to shift political competition away from clientelism is a key challenge of institutional reform that is not yet well understood. Some steps are probably key to reform, however: increasing public information, and increasing the credibility of political promises.

## Increasing Public Information

An important step is to encourage, or remove impediments to, nongovernmental sources of information on reform needs and direction. If their credibility is established, such sources can validate reform strategies outlined by interested political actors. The report cards undertaken in India by the Public Affairs Centre of Bangalore, mentioned in chapter 9, are one way in which nongovernmental organizations (NGOs) can credibly collect information about the performance of public officials and use it to stimulate reform.

The media also appear to be key for increasing government responsiveness. Research on India and the United States during the Great Depression highlights how information can improve access to government assistance. Between 1933 and 1935 in the United States, federal assistance to low-income households was significantly greater in those counties where more households had radios and were thus more likely to be informed about government policies and programs. The spread of the radio particularly improved information access for rural voters, who had previously been disadvantaged relative to urban voters, with the latter's ready access to other information sources such as newspapers. It accounted for as much as 20 percent greater allocation of social assistance funds to a rural county as compared to an identical urban county (Strömberg 2001). Besley and Burgess (2002) find that state governments in India are significantly more responsive to declines in food production and crop flood damage via public food distribution and calamity relief expenditure where newspaper circulation, particularly in local languages, is greater.

These findings raise some unresolved issues. The studies suggest that information (newspaper circulation) seems to have only a limited effect on

the provision of public goods (gross secondary school enrollment). This result, consistent with those of other studies, suggests that the availability of information has its greatest impact on the provision of transfers to voters, who can easily monitor such transfers with the assistance of a thriving media industry. For example, even in societies with educated societies and unrestricted media, voters tend to be relatively uninformed about the specifics of government performance. While government-controlled media are more likely to limit citizens to information favorable to the government, private media can be controlled by special interests that have their own biases. This is less problematic if there are low barriers to entry into the news business, but even if barriers to entry are low, it might be the case that other types of news are more profitable to report than information on government performance (Strömberg 2002). For example, the media might prefer to report extreme outcomes that are not typical of the government's performance and that bias voter perceptions.

Indirect evidence of this emerges from work on campaign finance reporting in the United States. The research suggests that newspapers systematically bias the information that citizens receive about campaign finance. Specifically, newspaper reporting conveys the impression that politicians receive more contributions overall and a higher fraction from corporations than they in fact do. In turn, college-educated Americans—those who are most likely to read newspapers—believe campaign financing flows are approximately what newspapers report, while less educated Americans believe they are considerably less (Ansolabehere, Snowberg, and Snyder 2004).

The media may solve the following coordination problem: voters unhappy with a government, for whatever reason, may be reluctant to oppose the government if they think their own experience is isolated. By conveying a general impression of government performance to which all voters are exposed, individual voters who share that impression can be more confident that others share it as well. This reduces their reluctance to support or oppose performing or nonperforming governments.

Information reforms must also grapple with the conditions under which politicians respond to the revelation of information about their performance. Scandalous information frequently has no political impact: even public knowledge of criminal behavior by politicians is not a sufficient condition for politicians to leave office, in either developed or developing countries. Newspaper circulation can reduce corruption, as seen earlier in this chapter, but appears to have no effect in countries that lack competitive elections. Among countries with competitive elections, the influence of newspaper circulation on corruption depends, though less robustly, on the existence of political checks and balances.[32] Competing political forces inside government, each with the right to influence government decisions, have both the incentive and ability to use evidence of each other's mal- or misfeasance for their own political advantage.

The efficacy of other information reforms also depends on the political environment. A key characteristic of government in many developed countries is the transparency with which new regulations emerge from the executive branch of government. These range from the issuance of white and green papers in the United Kingdom to open meeting requirements and freedom of information laws. These transparency requirements are almost always imposed by politicians on themselves, and are potentially but not always enforceable by courts. This means, however, that the requirements have less effect to the extent that there is little political cost to politicians who decide not to abide by them and to the extent that the courts are reluctant to require adherence to them. Unfortunately, the political costs of ignoring transparency laws are likely to be lowest precisely where government performance in general is likely to be poor: where there are few political checks and balances, and where political competition is organized around clientelist favors rather than overall government performance.

## Increasing the Credibility of Political Promises

The other major electoral market imperfection—the lack of credibility of political competitors—is more difficult to address. In principle, political credibility should provide political competitors with a competitive advantage. Clientelism (the default option for political competition when politicians cannot make credible promises) is expensive. The resources needed to give 50 voters jobs could finance broad public goods, such as improved education, offering equivalent benefits to hundreds of voters. That is, politicians who can offer credible policy or public goods to a large number of voters can defeat politicians who can only operate in a patronage mode.

However, moving out of clientelism is risky for politicians. Shifting resources to public goods may leave clients sufficiently dissatisfied to desert their patron, while public good benefits may materialize too slowly to attract new bases of political support before the next round of political competition. In any case, the beneficiaries of improved public services may not credit the incumbent politician for the improvements.

How can politicians build the credibility of their promises to improve the quality of public goods? Leaders can build credibility by being vocal, emphatic, and specific about their reform goals. Specificity makes it easier for citizens to judge when leaders have failed. Emphasis makes it clear that leaders expect to be judged on their performance regarding these goals, rather than on other issues, and independent of shocks or difficulties that might emerge. Together these improve credibility. As is often the case, there may be a tradeoff between reform success and building up credibility. Publicizing reform may incite resistance that stifles reform, while successful reform undertaken unpublicized has fewer political benefits and may be less sustainable.

Public sector reform can help too. A political competitor is unlikely to promise improved provision of public goods if the organization needed to supply those goods is dysfunctional, since citizens cannot easily distinguish whether reform failure is caused by bureaucrats or politicians.[33] Unfortunately, public sector reform is itself an arduous process that requires political commitment. In systems where politicians have a strong political interest in satisfying clientelist demands, their incentives to improve the functioning of the civil service are weak. Cox (1987) demonstrates that the professionalization of the justly acclaimed British Civil Service *followed*, rather than preceded, the shift in the basis of political competition from clientelism to partisan or policy differences.

Donors can help developing-country governments with this dilemma by coordinating their assistance for public sector reforms with their assistance for improving the provision of public goods, while being sensitive to the political timetable according to which citizens express their judgments about these reforms. A successful reform strategy is one that devises and links "on-the-ground" outcomes to intermediate stages of public sector reform, such that politicians can get credit for reform in a timely fashion. (Again, government leaders need to be vocal in promising results, or the credibility effects will be diminished and voters will have little reason to change their judgments about incumbents based on the reform experience.)

Donor strategies for project implementation are relevant here. A donor focus on specific projects touching a fraction of the population, rather than on broad policy goals and public good improvements that affect most of the population, may accelerate project implementation, but it reinforces patterns of political accountability in which voters expect only targeted or clientelist benefits from their leaders. Donors also often agree with governments to set up enclaves of bureaucratic excellence to carry out particular tasks. As discussed in chapter 9, while enclaving can assure governments that promises will be carried out, enhancing the sustainability of reform, this potential benefit is rarely realized, since the end of a task often means the dissolution of the enclaved agency.

The development community is also doing considerable work to "institutionalize" political parties, improving their ability to communicate with voters or to organize at the grassroots level. This is potentially important for achieving the ultimate goal of improving policy credibility and voter information about the policy stances of political competitors. However, it has no guarantee of success, since party leaders may prefer to construct patronage machines or vehicles for personal advancement rather than rely on the institutionalization of their party's stance on policy issues (box 10.2).

## Mitigating Political Market Failures: Institutional and Legal Reforms

Even though institutional factors do not systematically explain the underperformance of some democracies relative to others, institutional reforms can promote policy reform. Such reforms include changing electoral rules, reinforcing checks and balances, introducing laws that regulate campaign contributions, and decentralization.

### Electoral Reforms Can Spur Sustainable Policy Reform

Reform of electoral laws can both spur reform and serve as a vehicle for mitigating electoral market imperfections. One indication of the policy effects of such reform emerged in the 1990s in Japan. Prior to its 1994 reform, the electoral system in Japan was a mix of plurality voting and multimember districts that essentially compelled candidates from the same political party to compete with one another. Because they could not use party labels to distinguish themselves from competitors, candidates spent considerable sums of money distinguishing themselves in other ways, thereby building up personal constituencies. These constituencies had clientelist attributes. Politicians, for example, would appear at weddings and funerals, making cash contributions to the newly married or bereaved. Their need for financial resources led incumbent politicians to be especially generous toward special interests, including the banking industry. The lax regulatory standards to which banks were held contributed to soaring nonperforming loans. These were exposed when rapid economic growth ground to a halt in 1990.

The electoral reform of 1994 introduced single-member districts and changed rules in multimember districts to proportional rather than plurality electoral rules. These changes raised the electoral value of partisan affiliation and reduced

**BOX 10.2**
**Political Parties and Reform**

In many countries political parties are suppressed or limits are placed on the extent to which they can make ethnic appeals. Candidates in some elections in Pakistan and Uganda have been prohibited from running under a party affiliation. In Bulgaria, ethnically based parties have been excluded.

While parties are far from a sufficient condition for eliminating electoral market imperfections, they may be necessary. Mature political parties with well-defined positions on economic and social issues help solve problems of both information and credibility that otherwise plague competition for political office. Mature parties convey information to voters on the policy stances of party members, particularly relative to members of other parties. Unlike individual candidates, they are more likely to have policy reputations that allow them to make credible promises to voters. When parties are credible entities, vot-

ers can more easily assign blame and credit to the parties in control, relieving them of the need to identify specific individuals to hold responsible.

Unfortunately, history is replete with parties hijacked by personal interests or dedicated to patronage politics or serving as a locus for ethnic rivalry or religious conflict. Parties often fail to offer voters a credible choice in terms of economic policies.

At the same time, policy-based political parties can emerge from or succeed in a clientelist milieu, as may be indicated by the fall of the PRI in Mexico from dominance and the persistence of the *Partido dos Trabalhadores* (Workers Party) in Brazil. Nor is policy reform impossible in clientelist environments—the most effective means for politicians to capture the vast majority of disaffected voters who do not benefit from clientelist payoffs is to develop a reputation for policy performance that benefits the majority.

the need for money in campaigns. Soon after, in 1996, the ruling Liberal Democratic Party forced banks to bail out their mortgage-lending subsidiaries and absorb huge losses rather than socialize the losses with taxpayer-financed bailouts.[34] Policy reforms that had been urged on Japan for years finally occurred, but only after the adoption of institutional reforms that changed political incentives. Whether such reforms would have an equal effect in countries without well-established political parties and informed voters is less clear.

## Checks and Balances: Difficult to Introduce, Easy to Undermine

Political checks and balances have a significant effect on government credibility and, as a consequence, on the effects of policies in areas ranging from taxation to public investment and monetary policy.[35] It is difficult to introduce political checks and balances where none exist, however. They require both formal institutions that endow multiple branches or individuals of government with

authority over government decision making; and they require that those individuals or branches enjoy independent sources of political authority. The first is relatively easy to accomplish, through statutory or constitutional amendment. The second is difficult.

When formal institutions of checks and balances are present (formal legislative, judicial, and executive branches of government, for example), steps can be taken to reinforce checks and balances even when the branches do not enjoy independent sources of political authority, as is often the case. Their effects are likely to be small, however, until political authority is more equally shared among the branches.

For example, public sector financial management reforms increase the information available to legislators inside government. Often, though, legislators have no incentive to act on this information: their prospects for reelection depend on maintaining good relations with the executive branch, such that the executive branch will fund projects in their constituencies, and this weakens their incentives to supervise the executive's over-all performance. This dependency is less important in countries (such as the United Kingdom) where strong parties provide an offsetting check on political excess. But without strong political parties, budget rules that deny legislator influence over spending undermine political checks and balances.

Moreover, formal institutions are often incomplete in these circumstances: budget-making procedures deny them the policy-making leverage they need to act on the information. Legal and constitutional changes that endow legislatures with very limited authority over spending prevent them from imposing budgetary sanctions on government ministries that diverge from agreed allocations and amounts.

Where political checks and balances are weak, implementation of reforms—or of donor-supported projects—is more likely to be undermined. Closer donor supervision is the most effective short-run response to avoid this. At the same time, political checks and balances are not a substitute for solving electoral market failures. Among countries that exhibit political checks and balances, the rule of law and corruption are still strongly affected by variables that capture the effects of some of these failures. However, their absence undermines prospects for sustainable reform and their development is therefore important.

## Campaign Finance Reform: Attacking the Symptom, If Not the Disease

Other institutional reforms can reduce both electoral market failures and the lack of credibility—although they can potentially exacerbate them as well. One is campaign finance reform. Popular in both developed and developing countries, the general notion is that to prevent special interests from using money to distort political outcomes, one must place caps on campaign finance or increase public financing of elections. The evidence is not in on the efficacy of either solution, though the latter is likely to be more effective than the former.

Evasion and enforcement have everywhere been a serious problem with campaign finance reforms. In the United States, caps on one form of contribution have led to dramatic increases in other forms. Even when caps are comprehensive, as in France and Germany, reports on campaign finance scandals suggest that the flows continued nonetheless. Evasion and nonenforcement are more likely in countries in which politics is clientelist and large policy issues are not germane to political competition.

Even where caps are binding, some observers argue that they actually *increase* the returns to lobbying. Drazen, Limão, and Stratmann (2004) argue that moderate caps on political contributions can induce more lobbyists to enter the political market, offsetting the reduction in contributions by existing groups. They find some evidence for this, moreover, across U.S. states, which exhibit sharply different campaign finance regulations.

## Decentralization: Finding More Perfect Political Markets

Decentralization embraces a range of institutional reforms that have the possibility both of upsetting clientelist political patterns and of reinforcing them. To the extent that political competition and decision making are less subject to political market imperfections—information, credibility, or social polarization—in subnational than in national governments, policy outcomes are likely to be more conducive to development. Similarly, by splitting up issues between national and subnational governments, decentralization facilitates voter efforts to hold politicians accountable for specific policy areas, and also assists political efforts to develop policy reputations that go beyond clientelism.[36] However, these preconditions for successful decentralization are frequently absent, and in their absence decentralization can exacerbate the policy distortions of clientelism.

## 5. Conclusion

The arguments in this chapter paint a broad picture of the role of political economy in development and highlight a few characteristics of political systems that help explain some development outcomes:

- Can voters observe the decisions of government officials and the effects of these decisions? Can even informed observers attribute political responsibility for policy failure? They cannot if political parties are amorphous and individual participation in political decision making is opaque.

- Are policy differences at all relevant to political competition? Do party platforms exist and, if so, do they diverge? Can the average citizen recognize and rely on policy differences among the parties? If not, political competition is sure to focus on the allocation of narrowly targeted benefits—projects, jobs, exemptions from onerous regulations—and promises of broadly based reform are unlikely to be credible.

- Are checks and balances present and operative?

These questions are important in seeking to understand societies' collective decision-making process.

## Notes

1. Countries are regarded as having competitively elected governments if they are reported in Beck et al. (2001), Database of Political Institutions, as having the highest score (seven) on the Executive Index of Electoral Competition (EIEC) and on the Legislative Index of Electoral Competition (LIEC), where seven implies that there are multiple parties competing and no party gets more than 75 percent of the vote. The rule of law measure is from Political Risk Services' *International Country Risk Guide*.

2. These same sources of heterogeneity, especially information and social polarization, may also matter in nondemocracies. This possibility is not explored below—there is little evidence bearing on the question—but future work needs to explore the overarching determinants of good government performance that might be common to both democracies and nondemocracies.

3. Banerjee and Iyer (2002) show that British colonial practices affect land tenure relationships and land productivity in parts of India to this day. Acemoglu, Johnson, and Robinson (2002) argue that a complex interaction of relative price changes, natural endowments, and institutional choice has consequences that last for generations.

4. These results persist even when countries in Eastern Europe and Central Asia are excluded.

5. The effect is nearly as large as that of a standard and always powerful control, income per capita: an increase of one standard deviation in the years a non-elected leader is in office reduces the risk of expropriation almost as much as does one standard deviation in a country's income.

6. Controlling for total population, population living in rural areas, land area, population under the age of 16, and purchasing power parity–adjusted income per capita, and looking only at countries that did not exhibit fully competitive elections in 1995, the absence of a legislature of any kind, elected or not, was associated with a one standard deviation worsening of the rule of law and corruption measures.

7. Persson and Tabellini (2000).

8. Kontopolous and Perotti (1999) and Persson, Roland, and Tabellini (2003) argue that proportional representation systems encourage small parties, which increases the prevalence of minority governments or multiparty coalition governments, which in turn increases taxes and spending. Majoritarian systems, as argued by Milesi-Ferretti, Perotti, and Rostagno (2002) and others, should lead to greater attention to pivotal voters, and therefore more targeted spending, rather than spending on broad-based public goods or redistributive programs.

9. Persson and Tabellini (2000) argue that vote of confidence procedures in parliamentary democracies bind legislative majorities together, allowing them to make credible agreements that taxes raised will serve the interests of the majority. This encourages them to establish higher taxes and spending. In presidential systems, legislative minorities (for example, chairpersons of legislative committees) are more powerful, but they are assumed to be unable to make credible agreements with each other. Spending is targeted to the constituencies of these legislative minorities, but because they cannot credibly agree with one another that higher tax revenues will be targeted to their constituencies, overall spending is lower.

10. Elections in which there were multiple competing candidates or parties, more than one party contesting, and no candidate or party winning more than 75 percent of the vote, taken from the Legislative and Executive Indexes of Electoral Competition, in Beck et al. (2001).

11. This result uses institutional data from Beck et al. (2001) and economic and social data from *World Development Indicators*.

12. Education spending, controlling for primary school enrollment, has a small effect on secondary school enrollment. One estimate suggests that a full percentage point increase in education spending as a fraction of GDP (where the average country spends

approximately 3.3 percent of GDP) increases gross secondary school enrollment by fewer than 5 percentage points (where gross secondary school enrollment in the average country is approximately 65 percent).

13. These results are from an ordinary least squares regression of gross secondary school enrollment on PPP-adjusted income per capita; the percentage of the population that is young; land area; gross primary school enrollment; whether a system is parliamentary, presidential, or semipresidential; the voting rule used to elect the majority of representatives in the lower chamber of the legislature; and the average district magnitude of the chamber. The data are yearly, from 1990 to 2000. Significance tests based on robust standard errors assuming country observations from different years are not independent. The economic variables are from *World Development Indicators*; the political variables from the Database of Political Institutions (Beck et al. 2001).

14. In neither group are electoral institutions a significant determinant of gross secondary school enrollment. Specification is as described in footnote 15. Standard errors are White-corrected (robust). The economic variables are from *World Development Indicators*; the political variables from the Database of Political Institutions (Beck et al. 2001).

15. The sample includes only country-years in which countries had competitive elections, since for countries for which this is not the case, there is no obvious reason that would impel a government to allow a free press that reports on how well the government is performing.

16. A common refrain of voters in many countries is, "All politicians are the same, and none is interested in the people." Uninformed voters would naturally express this opinion. So too would voters confronting politicians who cannot make credible promises.

17. From cross-sectional regressions using democratic episodes (1975–2000) as the units of observation, controlling for land area, total population, percentage of the population that is young, and political and electoral systems.

18. See, for example, Rajkumar and Swaroop (2002). It is possible that the relationships between continuous years of competitive elections and corruption or education, for example, are due to omitted effects that in turn influence both of these. One can control for this possibility by identifying instrumental variables that explain competitive elections but not education or corruption. Results are robust to instrumental variable estimation. using the share of nonmanufacturing activity in total industrial activity in a country in 1965 and/or 1975. These capture reliance on natural resources (especially mining), which in turn is often thought to discourage politi-

cal development. It does not explain either corruption or secondary school enrollment but is strongly related to years of continuous competitive elections.

19. One and one-half standard deviations higher, using a measure of ethnic tensions from the *International Country Risk Guide*.

20. The regression controls for income per capita, percentage of the population that is young or rural, land area, and total population of a country, for all years since 1989.

21. Rodrik, Subramanian, and Trebbi (2002) argue that the security of institutions (measured as the security of property rights, the rule of law, and so on) matters more for economic development than geography and trade. Dollar and Kraay (2003) show that the instrumental variables used to control for the endogeneity of both trade and measures of governance or the security of property rights yield a high correlation between the two, making their independent effects difficult to assess.

22. Results from regressing yearly data on gross secondary school enrollment from 1990 to 1997 on gross primary school enrollment, PPP-adjusted income per capita, land area, the fraction of the population that is young, total population, education spending as a fraction of GDP, and expropriation risk.

23. Controlling for PPP-adjusted income per capita, total population, the fraction of the population that is young, land area, whether the political system is presidential or parliamentary, whether the electoral system is proportional or plurality, and the average district magnitude (yearly data only for countries that have leaders chosen by competitive elections).

24. For example, the gains from reversing tax cuts meant to encourage investment are potentially substantial after fixed investments have been made in response to the tax cut.

25. Stasavage (2003) revisits this episode and concludes that parliament only restrained opportunistic behavior by the government when the minority of parliamentary members who favored honoring sovereign obligations were able to make a deal involving religious freedom with those who were less favorable. That is, he shows that not only did institutions matter, but so did politics.

26. This point is explicit in the theoretical work of Acemoglu and Robinson (2001), who argue that only by sharing power can the disenfranchised be persuaded that the enfranchised will not expropriate them.

27. Acemoglu and Robinson (2001) explain the poor performance of some democracies by arguing that, in countries exhibiting high inequality, as in Latin America, democratization would give rise to significant redistribution and lay the groundwork for democracy's collapse as the elites aimed to take back power. Certainly, Latin American democracy

throughout the 20th century has been notably unstable. However, simple averages of government expenditure as a fraction of GDP and of education spending specifically, as a fraction of GDP, show little difference between democratic and nondemocratic periods since 1975. If anything, government spending was slightly higher in the nondemocratic country–years than in the democratic; education spending was almost identical.

28. See, for example, Acemoglu and Robinson (2000).

29. The total cost is 12 percent of GDP. Data from Honohan and Klingebiel (2000), data on real incomes from Aten, Heston, and Summers (2001).

30. Social funds, in contrast, which are intended to distribute resources to particular groups, are potentially useful to clientelist politicians. Schady (2000), for example, shows that the Peruvian social fund, FONCODES, was well targeted to the poor, conditional on the poor residing in areas where President Fujimori thought political transfers would be most useful. The poor in opposition strongholds were particularly unlikely to receive funds.

31. In advocating efforts to organize the demand for reforms, chapter 9 points out that reform winners are often disorganized and confront significant barriers to the collective action that would make them effective supporters of reform. Lowering these barriers is one recommendation of chapter 9. The political market imperfections and institutional deficiencies discussed here are additional obstacles to successful reform, and also undermine the efforts of reform proponents to shift government policy.

32. Controlling for income per capita, population variables, and the years that elections have been continuously held, the effect of an increase in newspaper circulation on corruption approximately doubles, moving from a parliamentary political system in which the party of the prime minister party controls the legislature to one in which a four-party coalition government is in power.

33. See Shepherd (2003) for a thorough review of the argument that meritocratic and well-performing civil servants improve government credibility.

34. Rosenbluth and Thies (2001).

35. Development assistance can have the unfortunate side effect of undermining political checks and balances where they do exist. Chapter 9 described a number of reforms, particularly medium-term expenditure frameworks, that are meant to ensure that all public spending is subjected to the scrutiny of multiple actors in the political system. It also identifies the hazards of funneling outside resources directly to line ministries, outside the normal budget processes.

36. Besley and Coate (2001) argue in the context of citizens' initiatives that a key problem in politics is that governments make decisions on numerous policy dimensions, but voters can only cast votes for a single politician or party. They are confronted, therefore, with an "all or nothing" offer: politicians can shirk on some margins, but still be reelected if they are sufficiently forthcoming on the "salient" dimensions of policy. Decentralization eases this problem by splitting issues between multiple levels of government, allowing more policies to become politically salient than would otherwise be the case.

# Bibliography

Aalt, J., and D. Lassen. 2003. "Fiscal Transparency and Fiscal Policy Outcomes in OECD Countries." Economic Policy Research Unit Working Paper 2003-02.

Abiad, Abdul, and Ashoka Mody. 2002. "Status Quo Bias in Financial Reform." IMF Working Paper (October). Washington, D.C.: International Monetary Fund.

————. 2003. "Financial Reform: What Shakes It? What Shapes It?" IMF Working Paper WP/03/70 (April). Online at http://www.imf.org/external/pubs/ft/wp/2003/wp0370.pdf.

Abramovitz, Moses. 1956. "Resource and Output trends in the United States since 1870." *American Economic Review* 46(2): 5–23.

Acemoglu, Daron, and James Robinson. 2000. "Why Did the West Extend the Franchise? Democracy, Inequality, and Growth in Historical Perspective." *Quarterly Journal of Economics* 115(4): 1167–99.

————. 2001. "A Theory of Political Transitions." *American Economic Review* 91(4): 938–63.

Acemoglu, Daron, Simon Johnson, and James A. Robinson. 2001. "The Colonial Origins of Comparative Development: An Empirical Investigation." *American Economic Review* 91(5): 1369–1401.

————. 2002. "Reversal of Fortune: Geography and Institutions in the Making of the Modern World Income Distribution." *Quarterly Journal of Economics* 117(4): 1231–94.

————. 2003. "An African Success Story: Botswana." In Dani Rodrik, ed., *In Search of Prosperity: Analytic Narratives on Economic Growth*. Princeton, N.J.: Princeton University Press.

Adams, D., and R. Vogel. 1986. "Rural Financial Markets in Developing Countries: Recent Controversies and Lessons." *World Development* 14: 477–87.

Adams, D., D. Graham, and J. D. Von Pischke, eds. 1984. *Undermining Rural Development with Cheap Credit*. Boulder, Colo.: Westview Press.

Adams, Richard, Jr., and John Page. 2003. "Poverty, Inequality, and Growth in Selected Middle East and North African Countries, 1980–2000." *World Development* 31(12): 2027–48.

Adelman, Irma, and Cynthia Taft Morris. 1965. *A Factor Analysis of the Interrelationship between Social and Political Variables and per Capita Gross National Product*. Evanston, Ill.: Northwestern University Press.

Adserà, Alícia, Carlos Boix, and Mark Payne. 2003. "Are You Being Served? Political Accountability and Governmental Performance." *Journal of Law, Economics, and Organization* 19(2): 445–90.

Aghion, Philippe. 1998. "Inequality and Economic Growth." In Philippe Aghion and Jeffrey G. Williamson, *Growth, Inequality, and Globalization: Theory, History, and Policy* (5–102). Raffaele Mattioli Lectures, Cambridge. New York and Melbourne: Cambridge University Press.

Aghion, Philippe, and Peter Howitt. 1998. *Endogenous Growth Theory*. Cambridge, Mass.: Massachusetts Institute of Technology Press.

Aghion, Philippe, Eve Caroli, and Cecilia Garcia Penalosa. 1999. "Inequality and Economic Growth: The Perspective of the New Growth Theories." *Journal of Economic Literature* 37(4): 1615–60.

Ahluwalia, M. S. 2003. "IMF Operations and Democratic Governance: Some Issues." Online at http://www.imf.org/external/np/ieo/2003/sp/110103.htm.

Ahmed, Belal. 2001. "The Impact of Globalization on the Caribbean Sugar and Banana Industries." Society for Caribbean Studies Annual Conference Papers, Vol. 2.

Aitken, Brian J., and Ann E. Harrison. 1999. "Do Domestic Firms Benefit from Direct Foreign Investment? Evidence from Venezuela." *American Economic Review* 89.

Aitken, Brian J., Gordon Hanson, and Anne E. Harrison. 1997. "Spillovers, Foreign Investment, and Export Behavior." *Journal of International Economics* 43: 103–32.

Aizenman, Joshua, and Brian Pinto. 2004. "Managing Volatility and Crises." Draft chapter (March) for *Managing Volatility and Crises: A Practitioner's Guide*. Online at

http://www-wbweb.worldbank.org/prem/prmep/
economicpolicy/documents/mv/pgchapter00.pdf.

Alba, P., L. Hernandez, and D. Klingebiel. 1999. *Financial Liberalization and the Capital Account: Thailand 1988–1997.* World Bank Policy Research Paper No. 2188.

Alcala, Francisco, and Antonio Ciccone. 2004. "Trade and Productivity." *Quarterly Journal of Economics* 119(2): 613–46.

Alesina, A., V. Grilli, and G. Milesi-Ferreti. 1994. "The Political Economy of Capital Controls." In L. Liederman and A. Razin, eds., *Capital Mobility: The Impact on Consumption, Investment, and Growth.* Cambridge, U.K.: Cambridge University Press.

Alesina, Alberto, and Roberto Perotti. 1996. "Budget Deficits and Budget Institutions." NBER Working Paper No. 5556. National Bureau of Economic Research, Cambridge, Mass.

Alesina, Alberto, and Lawrence Summers. 1993. "Central Bank Independence and Macroeconomic Performance: Some Comparative Evidence." *Journal of Money, Credit and Banking* (May 25): 151–62.

Alesina, Alberto, Reza Baqir, and William Easterly. 1999. "Public Goods and Ethnic Divisions." *Quarterly Journal of Economics* 114(4): 1243–84.

Alesina, Alberto, Sule Ozler, Nouriel Roubini, and Philip Swagel. 1996. "Political Instability and Economic Growth." *Journal of Economic Growth* 1: 189–211.

Alfaro, Laura, Areendam Chanda, Sebnem Kalemli-Ozcan, and Selin Sayek. 2000. "FDI and Economic Growth: The Role of Local Financial Markets." Working Paper 01-083, Harvard Business School.

Allen, Donald S., and Michelle T. Gyles. 1995. "Trade, Growth, and Capital: A Case Study of Jamaica." Working Paper 1995-012B, Federal Reserve Bank of St. Louis.

Allen, Richard, Salvatore Schiavo-Campo, and Thomas Columkill Garrity. 2004. *Assessing and Reforming Public Financial Management: A New Approach.* Washington, D.C.: World Bank.

Anderson, J., and D. Marcouiller. 1999. "Trade, Insecurity, and Home Bias." NBER Working Paper 7000. National Bureau of Economic Research, Cambridge, Mass.

Anderson, Jim, Gary Reid, and Randi Ryterman. 2003. "Understanding Public Sector Performance in Transition Countries: An Empirical Contribution." World Bank, Washington, D.C.

Andreasson, Bo. 1998. "Privatization in Sub-Saharan Africa: Has It Worked and What Lessons Can Be Learnt?" Swedish Development Advisers, Gothenburg, Sweden. Online at www.swedevelop.com.

Ansolabehere, Steven, Erik Snowberg, and James Snyder. 2004. "Statistical Bias in Newspaper Reporting: The Case of Campaign Finance." Paper presented at the 2004 Meeting of the Public Choice Society, Baltimore.

Appiah-Kubi, K. 2001. "State-Owned Enterprises and Privatization in Ghana." *Journal of Modern African Studies* 39(2).

Arioshi, A., K. Habermeier, B. Laurens, I. Otker-Robe, J. Canales-Krijenko, and A. Kirilenko. 2000. "Capital Controls: Country Experiences with Their Use and Liberalization." Occasional Paper No. 190. International Monetary Fund, Washington, D.C.

Ashraf, Nava, Margaret McMillan, and Alix Peterson-Zwane. Forthcoming. "My Policies or Yours: Have OECD Agricultural Policies Affected Incomes in Developing Countries?" In Harrison (forthcoming).

Asian Development Bank. 2000. *Asian Development Outlook.* Manila, Phillippines: Asian Development Bank.

Aten, Bettina, Alan Heston, and Robert Summers. 2001. *Penn World Tables 6.0.* Philadelphia: University of Pennsylvania, Center for International and Interarea Comparisons.

Auty, R., and R. Mikesell. 1998. *Sustainable Development in Mineral Economies.* Oxford: Clarendon Press.

Bacalla, Tess. 2003. "BIR Officials Amass Unexplained Wealth." Philippine Center for Investigative Journalism. Reprinted in *Malaya, Manila Times, Manila Standard, Cebu Daily News* and *Sun-Star Daily Cebu,* May 12–14; in *Abante* and *BusinessWorld,* May 13–14. Online at http://www.pcij.org/stories/2003/bir.html.

Bahl, R. 2000. "How to Design a Fiscal Decentralization Program." In S. Yusuf, W. Wu, and S. Evenett, eds., *Local Dynamics in an Era of Globalization.* New York: Oxford University Press.

Bahl, R., and Paul Smoke. 2003. *Restructuring Local Government Finance in Developing Countries; Lessons from South Africa.* Cheltenham, U.K.: Edward Elgar.

Baier, Scott L., and Jeffrey H. Bergstrand. 2001. "The Growth of World Trade: Tariffs, Transport Cost, and Income Similarity." *Journal of International Economics* 53.

Balassa, Bela. 1971. *The Structure of Protection in Developing Countries.* Baltimore: Johns Hopkins University Press.

———. 1978. "Exports and Economic Growth: Further Evidence." *Journal of Development Economics* 5: 181–89.

Balasubramanyam, V. N., M. Salisu, and D. Dapsoford. 1996. "Foreign Direct Investment and Growth in EP and IS Countries." *Economic Journal* 106.

Balat, Jorge, and Guido Porto. 2004. "Globalization and Complementary Policies. Poverty Impacts in Rural Zambia." In Harrison (forthcoming).

Baldwin, E. Robert. 2003. "Openness and Growth: What's the Empirical Relationship?" NBER Working Paper No. 9578. National Bureau of Economic Research, Cambridge, Mass. Published (2004) in Robert E. Baldwin and L. Alan Winters, eds., *Challenges to Globalization: Analyzing the Economics.* Chicago: University of Chicago Press.

Balino, T., A. Bennett, E. Borensztein, and others. 1999. "Monetary Policy in Dollarized Economies." IMF Occasional Paper No. 171. International Monetary Fund, Washington, D.C.

Bandiera, Oriana, Gerard Caprio, Patrick Honohan, and Fabio Schiantarelli. 2000. "Does Financial Reform Raise or Reduce Saving?" *Review of Economics and Statistics* 82(2) (May): 239–63.

Banerjee, Abhijit, and Esther Duflo. 2003. "Inequality and Growth: What Can the Data Say?" *Journal of Economic Growth* 8: 267–99.

Banerjee, Abhijit, and Lakshmi Iyer. 2002. "History, Institutions, and Economic Performance: The Legacy of Colonial Land Tenure Systems in India." Working Paper, Department of Economics, Massachusetts Institute of Technology.

Banerjee, Abhijit V., Paul J. Gertler, and Maitreesh Ghatak. 2002. "Empowerment and Efficiency: Tenancy Reform in West Bengal." *Journal of Political Economy* 110(2): 239–80.

Banerjee, Abhijit, Dilip Mookherjee, Kaivan Munshi, and Debraj Ray. 2001. "Inequality, Control Rights, and Rent Seeking: Sugar Cooperatives in Maharashtra." *Journal of Political Economy* 109(1).

Bardhan, Pranab. 2002. "Decentralization of Governance and Development." *Journal of Economic Perspectives* 16(4): 85–205.

Bardhan, Pranab, and Dilip Mookherjee. 2000. "Capture and Governance at Local and National Level." *American Economic Review* 90(2): 135–39.

Barr, Nicholas. 2000. "Reforming Pensions: Myths, Truths, and Policy Choices." IMF Working Paper WP/00/139. International Monetary Fund, Washington, D.C.

Barro, Robert J. 1991. "Economic Growth in a Cross-Section of Countries." *Quarterly Journal of Economics* 106(2): 407–43.

———. 1996. "Democracy and Growth." *Journal of Economic Growth* 1: 1–27.

Barro, Robert, and David Gordon. 1983. "A Positive Theory of Monetary Policy in a Natural Rate Model." *Journal of Political Economy* 91: 589–610.

Barth, J., G. Caprio, and R. Levine. 2001. *Regulation and Supervision of Banks around the World: A New Data Base.* World Bank Policy Research Paper No. 2588.

Barzel, Yoram. 1989. *Economic Analysis of Property Rights.* Cambridge, U.K.: Cambridge University Press.

Bates, Robert H. 1981. *Markets and States in Tropical Africa: The Political Basis of Agricultural Policies.* Berkeley: University of California Press.

———. 1983. *Essays on the Political Economy of Rural Africa.* Cambridge, U.K.: Cambridge University Press.

Bates, Robert H., Rui de Figueiredo, and Barry Weingast. 1998. "The Politics of Interpretation: Rationality, Culture, and Transition." *Politics and Society* 26: 603–42.

Baulch, Robert, and John Hoddinott. 2000. Economic Mobility and Poverty Dynamics in Developing Countries. *Journal of Development Studies* 36: 1–24.

Bayless, Charles E. 1994. "Less Is More: Why Gas Turbines Will Transform Electric Utilities." *Public Utilities Fortnightly* 132(22): 21–25.

Beck, Thorsten, George Clarke, Alberto Groff, Philip Keefer, and Patrick Walsh. 2001. "New Tools in Comparative Political Economy: The Database of Political Institutions." *World Bank Economic Review* 15(1): 165–76.

Beckerman, P. 1995. "Central-Bank 'Distress' and Hyperinflation in Argentina, 1989–90." *Journal of Latin American Studies* 27: 663–82.

Bekaert, G., C. Harvey, and C. Lundblad. 2003. "Equity Market Liberalization in Emerging Markets." *Federal Reserve Bank of St. Louis Review* 85: 53–74.

Bell, Stuart. 1995. FPD Note, "Privatization through Broad-Based Ownership Strategies." World Bank, Washington, D.C. March.

Ben-David, Dan. 1993. "Equalizing Exchange: Trade Liberalization and Income Convergence." *The Quarterly Journal of Economics* 108(3): 653–79.

Ben-David, Dan, and David H. Papell. 1994. "The Great Wars, the Great Crash, and the Unit Root Hypothesis: Some New Evidence about an Old Stylized Fact." NBER Working Paper No. 4752. National Bureau of Economic Research, Cambridge, Mass.

Benston, G., and G. Kaufmann. 1997. "FDICIA after Five Years." *Journal of Economic Perspectives* 11: 138–58.

Berezlin, Peter, Ali Salehizadeh, and Elcior Santana. 2002. "The Challenge of Diversification in the Caribbean." IMF Working Paper No. 02/196. World Bank, Washington, D.C.

Berg, Andrew, and Anne Krueger. 2003. "Trade, Growth and Poverty: A Selective Survey." IMF Working Paper No. 03/30. International Monetary Fund, Washington, D.C.

Bernard, Andrew, and J. B. Jensen. 1999. "Exceptional Export Performance: Cause, Effect, or Both?" *Journal of International Economics* 47(1): 1–25.

Besley, Tim, and Robin Burgess. 2002. "The Political Economy of Government Responsiveness: Theory and Evidence from India." *Quarterly Journal of Economics* 117(4): 1415–52.

Besley, Tim, and Stephen Coate. 2001. "Issue Unbundling via Citizens' Initiatives." Center for Economic Policy Research Paper No. 2857 (June), Washington, D.C.

Bhagwati, Jagdish. 1978. *Foreign Trade Regimes and Economic Development: Anatomy and Consequences of Exchange Control Regimes.* Cambridge, Mass.: Ballinger.

———. 1998. *A Stream of Windows: Unsettling Reflections on Trade, Immigration, and Democracy.* Cambridge, Mass.: Massachusetts Institute of Technology.

———. 2002. "Globalization and Appropriate Governance." 2000 WIDER Annual Lecture. World Institute for Development Economics Research, the United Nations University, Helsinki.

Bhagwati, Jagdish N., and T. N. Srinivasan. 2002. "Trade and Poverty in the Poor Countries." *American Economic Review* 92(2): 180–83.

Bhalla, Surjit S. 2002. *Imagine There's No Country: Poverty, Inequality, and Growth in the Era of Globalization.* Washington, D.C.: Institute for International Economics.

Bhatnagar, Subash, and Arsala Deane. 2003. "Building Blocks of e-Government: Lessons from Developing Countries. World Bank, Washington, D.C. Online at http://www1.worldbank.org/prem/PREMNotes/premnote91.pdf.

Bhattasali, Deepak, Li Shantong, and Will Martin. 2002. "Impacts and Policy Implications of WTO Accession for China." Draft, World Bank, Washington, D.C.

Biebesheimer, Christina, and J. Mark Payne. 2001. "IDB Experience in Justice Reform." Technical Paper, Sustainable Development Department. Washington, D.C.: InterAmerican Development Bank. Online at http://www.iadb.org/sds/doc/sgc-IDBExperiences-E.pdf.

Birdsall, Nancy. 2002. "From Social Policy to an Open-Economy Social Contract in Latin America." Center for Global Development Working Paper No. 21, December. Online at http://www.cgdev.org/docs/cgd%20wp021.pdf.

Bista, Dor Bahadur. 1991. *Fatalism and Development.* Calcutta: Orient Longman.

Black, B. 2001. "The Legal and Institutional Preconditions for Strong Securities Markets." *UCLA Law Review* 48: 781–858.

Black, B., R. Kraakmen, and A. Tarassova. 2000. "Russian Privatization and Corporate Governance: What Went Wrong?" *Stanford Law Review* 52: 1781.

Blair, Harry, and Gary Hansen. 1994. "Weighing in on the Scales of Justice: Strategic Approaches for Donor-Supported Rule of Law Programs." Program and Operations Assessment Report 7. U.S. Agency for International Development, Washington, D.C.

Blanchard, O., and F. Giavazzi. 2003. "Improving the Stability and Growth Pact through Proper Accounting of Public Investment." Center for Economic and Policy Research Discussion Papers No. 4220, Washington, D.C.

Blank, Rebecca M. 2002. Evaluating Welfare Reform in the United States. National Bureau of Economic Research, NBER Working Papers: 8983.

Blomstrom, Magnus. 1986. "Foreign Direct Investment and Productive Efficiency: The Case of Mexico." *Journal of Industrial Economics* 15.

Blomstrom, Magnus, Robert Lipsey, and Mario Zejan. 1994. "What Explains the Growth of Developing Countries?" In William J. Baumol, Richard R. Nelson, and Edward N. Wolff, eds., *Convergence of Productivity: Cross-National Studies and Historical Evidence.* Oxford and New York: Oxford University Press.

Bloom, D., and J. Sachs. 1998. "Geography, Demography, and Economic Growth in Africa." *Brookings Papers on Economic Activity*, 2. Washington, D.C.: Brookings Institution.

Bloom, David E., Ajay Mahal, Damien King, Aldrie Henry-Lee, and Philip Castillo. 2001. "Globalization, Liberalization, and Sustainable Human Development: Progress and Challenges in Jamaica." UNCTAD/UNDP Global Program Occasional Paper.

Bloomberg database. Bloomberg Financial Services, New York.

Bokros, L., A. Fleming, and C. Votava. 2001. *Financial Transition in Europe and Central Asia: Challenges of the New Decade.* Washington, D.C.: World Bank.

Bolaky, Bineswaree, and Caroline Freund. 2004. "Trade, Regulations, and Growth." Draft (March). University of Maryland and World Bank.

Bordo, M., B. Eichengreen, D. Klingebiel, and M. S. Martinez-Peria. 2001. "Is the Crisis Problem Growing More Severe?" *Economic Policy: A European Forum* 32 (April): 51–82.

Borensztein, Eduardo, Jose De Gregorio, and Jong-Wha Lee. 1998. "How Does Foreign Direct Investment Affect Economic Growth?" *Journal of International Economics* 45, June.

Bosworth, Barry, and Susan M. Collins. 1996. "Economic Growth in East Asia: Accumulation vs. Assimilation." Brookings Papers in Economic Activity, 2. Brookings Institution, Washington, D.C.

———. 1999. "Capital Flows, Investment, and Growth." Tokyo Club Papers, Vol. 12.

———. 2003. "The Empirics of Growth: An Update." Unpublished paper (March 7). Brookings Institution, Washington, D.C.

Boubakri, Narjess, and Jean-Claude Cosset. 1998. "The Financial and Operating Performance of Newly Privatized Firms: Evidence from Developing Countries." *Journal of Finance* 53(3) (June): 1081–1110.

———. 2002. "Does Privatization Meet the Expectations? Evidence from African Countries." Forthcoming in *Journal of African Economics.*

Bourguignon, François. 2004a. "Global Distribution and Redistribution." Keynote Address, the 16th Annual Bank Conference on Development Economics (ABCDE), held at World Bank Headquarters in Washington, D.C., May 3–4.

———. 2004b. "The Poverty Growth Inequality Triangle." Paper presented at the Indian Council for Research on International Economic Relations, New Delhi, February 4.

Bourguignon, Francois, and Christian Morrison. 2002. "Inequality among World Citizens, 1820–1992." *American Economic Review* 92(4): 727–44.

Boycko, Maxim, Andrei Shleifer, and Robert Vishny. 1996. "Privatizing Russia." Cambridge, Mass.: MIT Press.

Brook, Penelope J., and Timothy C. Irwin. 2003. "Infrastructure for Poor People." World Bank.

Brown, David, and John Earle. 2004. "Economic Reform and Productivity-Enhancing Reallocation in the Post-Soviet Transition." Upjohn Institute, Staff Working Paper No. 04-98.

Brownbridge, M., and C. Harvey. 1998. *Banking in Africa.* Trenton, N.J.: Africa World Press.

Brueckner, Jan. 1999. "Fiscal Decentralization in LDCs: The Effects of Local Corruption and Tax Evasion." Unpublished manuscript, Department of Economics, University of Illinois at Urbana-Champaign.

Bruno, Michael, Martin Ravallion, and Lyn Squire. 1995. "Equity and Growth in Developing Countries: Old and New Perspectives on the Policy Issues." In V. Tanzi and K. Chu, eds., *Income Distribution and High-Quality Growth.* Cambridge, Mass.: MIT Press.

Buiter, W. 1990. *Principles of Budgetary and Financial Policy.* Cambridge, Mass.: MIT Press.

Buiter, W., Akram Esanov, and Martin Raiser. 2001. "Nature's Blessing or Nature's Curse? The Political Economy of Transition in Resource-Based Economies." EBRD Working Paper No. 65. London: European Bank for Reconstruction and Development.

Burkhart, Ross, and Michael Lewis-Beck. 1994. "Comparative Democracy: The Economic Development Thesis." *American Political Science Review* 88: 903–10.

Burki, Shahid Javed, and Guillermo Perry. 1998. *Beyond the Washington Consensus: Institutions Matter.* Washington, D.C.: World Bank.

Burki, Shahid Javed, Guillermo E. Perry, and William R. Dillinger. 1999a. *Beyond the Center: Decentralizing the State.* Washington, D.C.: The World Bank.

————. 1999b. "Mas Alla Del Centro: La Descentralizacion Del Estado." World Bank, Washington, D.C.

Burnside, Craig. 2004. "Currency Crises and Contingent Liabilities," *Journal of International Economics* 62(1): 25–52.

Burnside, Craig, and David Dollar. 2000. "Aid, Policies, and Growth." *American Economic Review* 90(4): 847–868.

Calderón, C., R. Duncan, and K. Schmidt-Hebbel. 2003. "The Role of Credibility in the Cyclical Properties of Macroeconomic Policies in Emerging Economies." Draft. Central Bank of Chile.

Calderón, C., William Easterly, and Luis Servén. 2002. "How Did Latin America's Infrastructure Fare in the Era of Macro-Economic Crises?" Working Paper No.185. Banco Central de Chile.

Calomaris, C., and A. Powell. 2001. "Can Emerging Market Regulators Establish Credible Market Discipline?" In F. Mishkin, ed., *Prudential Supervision: What Works and What Doesn't.* Chicago: University of Chicago for the National Bureau of Economic Research.

Calvo, G. 1998. "Capital Flows and Capital Market Crises: The Simple Economics of Sudden Stops." *Journal of Applied Economics* 1: 35–54.

Calvo, G., and C. Reinhart. 2000. "When Capital Inflows Come to a Sudden Stop: Consequences and Policy Options." In P. Kenen and A. Swoboda, eds., *Key Issues in Reform of the International Monetary System.* Washington, D.C.: International Monetary Fund.

Campillo, M., and J. Miron. 1997. "Why Does Inflation Differ across Countries?" In C. Romer and D. Romer, eds., *Reducing Inflation: Motivation and Strategy.* Chicago: University of Chicago Press.

Campos, J. Edgardo, ed. 2001. *Corruption: The Boom and Bust of East Asia.* Quezon City, Philippines: Ateneo de Manila University Press.

Caprio, Gerard. 1997. "Safe and Sound Banking in Developing Countries: We're Not in Kansas Anymore." *Research in Financial Services: Private and Public Policy* 9: 79–97.

Caprio, Gerard, and Patrick Honohan. 2001. *Finance for Growth: Policy Choices in a Volatile World.* Oxford and New York: Oxford University Press.

Caprio, Gerard, and D. Klingebiel. 2002. "Episodes of Systematic and Borderline Banking Crises." In D. Klingebiel and L. Laeven, eds., *Managing the Real and Fiscal Effects of Banking Crises.* World Bank Discussion Paper No. 428.

————. 2003. "Bank Insolvencies: Cross-Country Experience." Draft. World Bank, Washington, D.C.

Caprio, Gerard, and L. Summers. 1996. "Financial Reform: Beyond Laissez Faire." In D. Papadimitriou, ed., *Stability of the Financial System.* New York: McMillan Press (earlier version published as World Bank Policy Research Working Paper 1171, August 1993).

Caprio, Gerard, P. Honohan, and J. Stiglitz, eds. 2001. *Financial Liberalization: How Far, How Fast?* Cambridge, U.K.: Cambridge University Press.

Caprio, Gerard, D. Klingebiel, L. Laeven and G. Noguera. 2003. Banking Crises database. Updated October 2003. Available online at http://www1.worldbank.org/fin ance/html/database_sfd.html.

Carkovic, Maria, and Ross Levine. 2002. "Does Foreign Direct Investment Accelerate Economic Growth?" Draft (October). University of Minnesota, Department of Business Finance and Carlson School of Management.

Cespedes, Luis Felipe, Roberto Chang, and Andres Velasco. 2002. "IS-LM-BP in the Pampas." Working Paper, John F. Kennedy School of Government, Harvard University. Online at http://ksghome.harvard.edu/~.avelasco.academic.ksg/Files/Research/pam pasimf.pdf.

Chang, Ha-Joon. 2001. "Institutional Development in Developing Countries in a Historical Perspective—Lessons from Developed Countries in Earlier Times." Paper presented at the European Association of Evolutionary Political Economy Annual Meeting, November 8–11.

Chari, V., and P. Kehoe. 2003. "Hot Money." *Journal of Political Economy* 111(6): 1262–92.

Chege, Michael. 1998. *Liberal Democracy and Its Malcontents: Contrasting Perspectives of a Democratic Capitalist World Order from Sub-Saharan Africa in the 1990s.* Cambridge, Mass.: Harvard Academy for International and Area Studies, Weatherhead Center for International Affairs.

Chen, Shaohua, and Martin Ravallion. 2004. "How Have the World's Poorest Fared since the Early 1980s?" *World Bank Research Observer* 19(2): 141–70.

Cho, Y. 2001. "The Role of Poorly Phased Liberalization in Korea's Financial Crisis." In G. Caprio, P. Honohan, and J. Stiglitz, eds., *Financial Liberalization: How Far, How Fast?* Cambridge, U.K.: Cambridge University Press.

Chong, Alberto, and Cesar Calderón. 2000. "On the Causality and Feedback between Institutional Measures and Economic Growth." *Economics and Politics* 12(1): 69–81.

Chuang, Yih-Chyi, and Chi-Mei Lin. 1999. "Foreign Direct Investment, R&D, and Spillover Efficiency: Evidence from Taiwan's Manufacturing Firms." *Journal of Development Studies* 35(4).

Claessens, Stijn, and K. Forbes. 2001. *International Financial Contagion.* Boston: Kluwer Academic Press.

Claessens, Stijn, Simeon Djankov, and Daniela Klingebiel. 2001. "Stock Markets in Transition Economies." In *Financial Transition in Europe and Central Asia.* Washington, D.C.: World Bank.

Claessens, Stijn, Simeon Djankov, and L. Lang. 1998. *Corporate Growth, Financing, and Risks in the Decade before East Asia's Financial Crisis.* World Bank Policy Research Paper No. 2017.

Claessens, Stijn, D. Klingebiel, and S. Shmuckler. 2003. "Explaining the Migration of Stocks from Exchanges in Emerging Economies to International Centers." Working Paper No. 168, Center for Research on Economic Development and Policy Reform, Stanford University, Palo Alto, Calif.

Clague, Christopher, Philip Keefer, Stephen Knack, and Mancur Olson. 1996. "Property and Contract Rights under Democracy and Dictatorship." *Journal of Economic Growth* 1(2): 243–76.

Clark, Ximena, David Dollar, and Alejandro Micco. 2002. "Maritime Transport Costs and Port Efficiency." Working Paper No. 2781. World Bank, Washington, D.C.

Clarke, G., and R. Cull. 1999. "Why Privatize? The Case of Argentina's Public Provincial Banks." *World Development* 27: 865–88.

———. 2002. "Political and Economic Determinants of the Likelihood of Privatizing Argentine Banks." *The Journal of Law and Economics* 45: 165–89.

Clarke, G., R. Cull, and M. Shirley. 2003. "Empirical Studies of Bank Privatization." Paper presented at the World Bank Conference on Bank Privatization, November 21–23.

Clarke, G., R. Cull, M. Martinez Peria, and S. Sanchez. 2004. "Bank Lending to Small Businesses in Latin America: Does Bank Origin Matter?" Forthcoming, *Journal of Money, Credit, and Banking.*

Clement, Jean A. P., Johannes Mueller, Stephane Cosse, and Jean Le Dem. 1996. *Aftermath of the CFA Franc Devaluation.* IMF Occasional Paper No. 138 (May).

Clerides, Sofronis K., Saul Lach, and James R. Tybout. 1998. "Is Learning by Exporting Important? Micro-Dynamic Evidence from Colombia, Mexico, and Morocco." *Quarterly Journal of Economics* 113(3): 903–47.

Coase, Ronald H. 1937. "The Nature of the Firm." *Economica* 4: 386–405.

———. 1960. "The Problem of Social Cost," *Journal of Law and Economics* 3: 1–44.

Cohen, Avi, and G. C. Harcourt. 2003. "Whatever Happened to the Cambridge Capital Theory Controversies?" *Journal of Economic Perspectives* 17(1): 199–214.

Cohen, D., and R. Portes. 2003. "Dealing with Destabilizing 'Market Discipline.'" Center for Economic and Policy Research Discussion Paper No. 4280.

Cole, David C., and Betty F. Slade. 1998. *Building a Modern Financial System: The Indonesian Experience.* Cambridge, U.K.: Cambridge University Press.

Collier, Paul, and J. Gunning. 1997. "Explaining African Economic Performance." Center for Study of African Economies Discussion Paper, University of Oxford.

Collier, Paul, and Anke Hoeffler. 1998. "On the Economic Causes of Civil War." *Oxford Economic Papers* 50.

———. 2001. "Greed and Grievance in Civil War." World Bank, Washington, D.C.

Collins, Susan, and Robert Z. Lawrence, eds. 2000. "Brookings Trade Forum 1999." Brookings Institution, Washington, D.C.

Condon, Timothy, and S. Ramachandran. 1993. "Cash Constraints and Credit Corsets: The Chimera of Inter-Enterprise Credits."

Conning, J., and M. Kevane. 2001. "Community-Based Targeting Mechanisms for Social Safety Nets." World Bank, Washington, D.C.

Cox, Gary W. 1987. *The Efficient Secret: The Cabinet and the Development of Political Parties in Victorian England.* New York: Cambridge University Press.

Crandall, R., and T. Hazlett. 2000. "Telecommunications Policy Reform in the United States and Canada." Working Paper 00-9, American Enterprise Institute–Brookings Joint Center for Regulatory Studies, Washington, D.C.

Crawford, Young. 1994. *The African Colonial State in Comparative Perspective.* New Haven, Conn.: Yale University Press.

Crook, R., and J. Manor. 1998. *Democracy and Decentralization in South Asia and West Africa*." Cambridge, U.K.: Cambridge University Press.

Cukierman, A., G. Miller, and B. Neyapti. 2001. "Central Bank Reform, Liberalization, and Inflation in Transition Economies: An International Perspective." Center for Economic and Policy Research Discussion Paper No. 2808.

Cukierman, A., S. Webb, and B. Neyapti. 1992. "Measuring the Independence of Central Banks and Its Effect on Policy Outcomes." *World Bank Economic Review* 6(3): 353–98.

Dalmazzo, A., and G. de Blasio. 2001. "Resources and Incentives to Reform: A Model and Some Evidence on Sub-Saharan African Countries." IMF Working Paper No. 86. International Monetary Fund, Washington, D.C.

Damijan, Joze P., Mark Knell, Boris Majcen, and Matija Rojec. 2003. "Technology Transfer through FDI in Top-10 Transition Countries: How Important Are Direct Effects, Horizontal and Vertical Spillovers?" William Davidson Institute Working Papers Series 549. William Davidson Institute at the University of Michigan Business School.

Davidson, Basil. 1992. *The Black Man's Burden: Africa and the Curse of the Nation State.* New York: Times Books.

De Ferranti, David, G. Perry, I. Gill, and L. Servén. 2000. *Securing Our Future.* Washington, D.C.: World Bank.

De Ferranti, David, Guillermo E. Perry, Daniel Lederman, and William Maloney. 2001. *From Natural Resources to the Knowledge Economy: Trade and Job Quality.* Washington, D.C.: World Bank.

De Haan, J., and W. Koi. 2000. "Does Central Bank Independence Really Matter? New Evidence for Developing Countries Using a New Indicator." *Journal of Banking and Finance* 24(4): 643–64.

De Juan, A. 2002. "From Good Bankers to Bad Bankers." In G. Caprio, P. Honohan, and D. Vittas, eds., *Financial Sector Policy for Developing Countries—A Reader.* Oxford: Oxford University Press.

De la Torre, A., and S. Schmukler. 2003. "Coping with Risk through Mismatches: Domestic and International Financial Contracts for Emerging Economies." Draft. World Bank, Washington, D.C.

De la Torre, A., E. Levy-Yeyati, and S. Schmukler. 2003. "Living and Dying with Hard Pegs: The Rise and Fall of Argentina's Currency Board." *Economía: Journal of the Latin American and Caribbean Economic Association* 3(2): 43–99.

De Long, J. Bradford, and Andrei Shleifer. 1993. "Princes and Merchants: European City Growth before the Industrial Revolution." *Journal of Law and Economics* 36: 671–702.

De Soto, Hernando. 1989. *The Other Path: The Invisible Revolution in the Third World.* New York: Harper and Row.

———. 2000. *The Mystery of Capital.* New York: Basic Books.

———. Forthcoming. "Missing Ingredients of Globalization." In Ernesto Zedillo, ed., *The Future of Globalization: Explorations in Light of Recent Turbulence.* Princeton, N.J.: Princeton University Press.

Deaton, Angus. 2003a. "Health, Inequality, and Economic Development." *Journal of Economic Literature* 41(1): 113–58.

———. 2003b. "Household Surveys, Consumption, and the Measurement of Poverty." *Economic Systems Research* 15(2): 135–59.

———. 2003c. "Measuring Poverty in a Growing World (or Measuring Growth in a Poor World)." NBER Working Paper No. 9822. National Bureau of Economic Research, Cambridge, Mass.

deLisle, Jacques. 1999. "Lex Americana? United States Legal Assistance, American Legal Models, and Legal Change in the Post-Communist World and Beyond." *Journal of International Economic Law* (University of Pennsylvania) 20: 179.

DeLong, J. B. 2000. "Cornucopia: The Pace of Economic Growth in the 20th Century." NBER Working Paper No. 7602. National Bureau of Economic Research, Cambridge, Mass.

Del Valle, C., and P. Ugolini. 2003. "Development of Domestic Markets for Government Bonds." In R. Litan, M. Pomerleano, and V. Sundarajan, *The Future of Domestic Capital Markets in Developing Countries*, 45-76. Washington, D.C.: Brookings Institution.

Demirgüç-Kunt, A., and E. Detragiache. 1998. "The Determinants of Banking Crises: Evidence from Industrial and Developing Countries." *IMF Staff Papers* 45: 81–109.

———. 2001. "Financial Liberalization and Financial Fragility." In G. Caprio, P. Honohan, and J. Stiglitz, eds., *Financial Liberalization: How Far, How Fast?* Cambridge, U.K.: Cambridge University Press.

———. 2002. "Does Deposit Insurance Increase Banking Stability? An Empirical Investigation." *Journal of Monetary Economics* 49(7): 1373–1406.

Demirgüç-Kunt, A., and H. Huizinga. 1999. "Market Discipline and Financial Safety Net Design." World Bank Policy Research Paper No. 2183.

Demirgüç-Kunt, A., and E. Kane. 2002. "Deposit Insurance around the Globe: Where Does It Work?" *The Journal of Economic Perspectives* 16(2): 175–96.

Demirgüç-Kunt, A., and T. Sobaci. 2001. "Deposit Insurance around the World: A Data Base." *World Bank Economic Review* 15(3): 481–90.

Demsetz, Harold. 1964. "The Exchange and Enforcement of Property Rights." *Journal of Law and Economics* 7: 11–26.

Diamond, Jared. 1997. *Guns, Germs, and Steel: The Fates of Human Societies.* New York: Norton.

Diaz-Alejandro, C. 1985. "Good-Bye Financial Repression, Hello Financial Crash." *Journal of Development Economics* 19(1–2): 1–24.

Djankov, Simeon, and Bernard Hoekman. 2000. "Productivity Growth and Foreign Investment in Czech Enterprises." *World Bank Economic Review* 14: 49–64.

Djankov, Simeon, and Peter Murell. 2002. "Enterprise Restructuring in Transition: A Quantitative Survey." *Journal of Economic Literature* XL (September): 739–92.

Dollar, David, and Aart Kraay. 2001. "Trade, Growth, and Poverty." Draft (June). World Bank, Washington, D.C.

———. 2003. "Institutions, Trade, and Growth: Revisiting the Evidence." World Bank Policy Research Working Paper No. 3004 (March).

Dooley, M. 1996. "A Survey of Literature on Controls over International Capital Transactions." *International Monetary Fund Staff Papers* 43(4): 639–87.

———. 2000. "A Model of Crises in Emerging Markets." *Economic Journal* 110: 256–73.

———. 2003. "Financial Policies." In M. Feldstein, ed., *Economic and Financial Crises in Emerging Market Economies.* Chicago: University of Chicago Press for the National Bureau of Economic Research.

Dooley, M., W. Helkie, R. Tyron, and J. Underwood. 1986. "An Analysis of External Debt Positions of Eight Countries through 1990." *Journal of Development Economics* 21(2): 283–318.

Dornbusch, Rudi. 2001. "A Primer on Emerging Market Crises." NBER Working Paper 8326. National Bureau of Economic Research, Cambridge, Mass.

Dornbusch, Rudi, and S. Edwards, eds. 1991. *The Macroeconomics of Populism in Latin America.* Chicago: University of Chicago for the National Bureau of Economic Research.

Dorotinsky, William, and Robert Floyd. 2004. "Expenditure Accountability in Africa: Progress, Lessons and Challenges." In Brian Levy and Sahr Kpundeh, eds., *Building State Capacity in Africa: New Approaches, Emerging Lessons.* Washington, D.C.: World Bank Institute.

Drazen, Allan, Nuno Limão, and Thomas Stratmann. 2004. "Political Contribution Caps and Lobby Formation: Theory and Evidence." Paper presented at the 2004 Meeting of the Public Choice Society, Baltimore.

Duncan, Alex. 2003. "Drivers of Change: Reflections on Experience to Date." Discussion Note. U.K. Department for International Development.

Easterly, William. 1999. "When Is Fiscal Adjustment an Illusion?" *Economic Policy* 14(28): 55–76.

———. 2000. "Small States, Small Problems? Income, Growth, and Volatility in Small States." *World Development* 28(11): 2013–27.

———. 2001. "The Lost Decade: Developing Countries' Stagnation in Spite of Policy Reform 1980–1990." *Journal of Economic Growth* 6: 135–57. Online at http://www.cgdev.org/fellows/easterly_lostdecades.pdf.

———. 2002. "How Did Heavily Indebted Poor Countries Become Heavily Indebted? Reviewing Two Decades of Debt Relief." *World Development* 30(10): 1677–96.

———. 2003a. "Can Foreign Aid Buy Growth?" *Journal of Economic Perspectives* 17(3): 23–48.

———. 2003b. "National Policies and Economic Growth: A Reappraisal." CGD Working Paper No. 27, May. Center for Global Development, Washington, D.C.

Easterly, William, and S. Fischer. 2001. "Inflation and the Poor." *Journal of Money, Credit, and Banking* 33: 160–79.

Easterly, William, and Ross Levine. 1997. "Africa's Growth Tragedy: Politics and Ethnic Divisions." *Quarterly Journal of Economics* 112(4) (November): 1203–50.

———. 2003. "Tropics, Germs, and Crops: How Endowments Influence Economic Development." *Journal of Monetary Economics* 50 (1): 3–39.

Easterly, William, and L. Servén, eds. 2003. *The Limits of Stabilization: Infrastructure, Public Deficits, and Growth in Latin America.* Palo Alto, Calif.: Stanford University Press.

Easterly, William, R. Islam, and J. Stiglitz. 2001. "Volatility and Macroeconomic Paradigms for Rich and Poor." In J. Dréze, ed., *Advances in Macroeconomic Theory.* New York: Palgrave.

Easterly, William, Michael Kremer, Lant Pritchett, and Lawrence Summers. 1993. "Good Policy or Good Luck? Country Growth Performance and Temporary Shocks." NBER Working Paper No. 4474. National Bureau of Economic Research, Cambridge, Mass.

Eaton, K. 2003. "Menem and the Governors: Intergovernmental Relations in the 1990s." In S. Levitsky and M. N. Murillo, eds., *Rethinking Dual Transitions: Argentine Politics in the 1990s in Comparative Perspective.* Manuscript online at http://www.wws.princeton.edu/keaton.

Ebel, Robert D., and Serdar Yilmaz. 2002. *On the Measurement and Impact of Fiscal Decentralization.* Washington, D.C.: World Bank Institute.

*Economist.* 2004. "More or less equal?" March 11.

Edison, H., R. Levine, L. Ricci, and T. Sloken. 2002. "International Financial Integration and Economic Growth." NBER Working Paper No. 9164. National Bureau of Economic Research, Cambridge, Mass.

Edwards, Sebastian. 1998. "Openness, Productivity and Growth: What Do We Really Know?" *Economic Journal* 108(March): 383–98.

———. 1999. "How Effective Are Capital Controls?" *Journal of Economic Perspectives* 13(4): 65–84.

———. 2003. "Exchange Rate Regimes, Capital Flows, and Crisis Prevention." In Feldstein (2003).

Ehrlich, Isaac, and Gary Becker. 1972. "Market Insurance, Self-Insurance and Self-Protection." *Journal of Political Economy* 80: 623–48.

Eichengreen, Barry. 2001. "Capital Account Liberalization: What Do Cross-Country Studies Tell Us?" *World Bank Economic Review* 15(3): 341–66.

———. 2002. *Financial Crises and What to Do About Them.* Oxford: Oxford University Press.

Eifert, Benn, Alan Gelb, and Nils Borje Tallroth. 2003. "The Political Economy of Fiscal Policy and Economic Management in Oil-Exporting Countries." In J. M. Davis, R. Ossowski, and A. Fedelino, eds., *Fiscal Policy Formulation and Implementation in Oil-Producing Countries.* Washington, D.C.: International Monetary Fund.

Engberg-Pedersen, Poul, and Brian Levy. 2004. "Building Governance Capacity: Learning from Performance and Results." In Brian Levy and Sahr Kpundeh, eds., *Building State Capacity in Africa: New Approaches, Emerging Lessons.* Washington, D.C.: World Bank Institute.

Engerman, Stanley, and Kenneth Sokoloff. 2002. "Factor Endowments, Inequality, and Paths of Development among New World Economics." NBER Working Paper 9259. National Bureau of Economic Research, Cambridge, Mass. Published in *Economia* 3(1): 41–88.

Enke, Stephen. 1963. *Economics of Development.* London: Denis Dobson.

Enoch, C., B. Baldwin, O. Frecaut, and A. Kovanen. 2001. *Indonesia: Anatomy of a Banking Crisis. Two Years of Living Dangerously, 1997–1999.* International Monetary Fund Working Paper No. 01/52.

Esfahani, Hadi Salehi. 2002. "Political Economy of Growth in Iran, 1963–2002." Draft (September). University of Illinois at Urbana.

EBRD (European Bank for Reconstruction and Development). 2003. *Transition Report 2003.* London.

Evans, Peter. 1995. *Embedded Autonomy: States and Industrial Transformation.* Princeton, N.J.: Princeton University Press.

Evans, Peter, and James Rauch. 2000. "Bureaucratic Structure and Bureaucratic Performance in Less Developed Countries." *Journal of Public Economics* 75: 49–71.

Faguet, Jean-Paul. 1997. "Decentralization and Local Government Performance." World Bank, Washington, D.C.

Feenstra, Robert C., and Hiau Looi Kee. 2003. "On the Measurement of Product Variety in Trade." Draft. University of California and World Bank.

Feenstra, Robert C., Dorsati Madani, Tzu-Han Yang, and Chi-Yuan Liang. 1999. "Testing Endogenous Growth in South Korea and Taiwan." *Journal of Development Economics* 60: 317–41.

Feldstein, M., ed. 2003. *Economic and Financial Crises in Emerging Market Economies.* Chicago: University of Chicago Press for the National Bureau of Economic Research.

Fernandez-Arias, E., and P. Montiel. 2001. "Reform and Growth in Latin America: All Pain and No Gain?" *IMF Staff Papers* 48(3) (December): 522–46.

Fischer, Stanley. 2001. "Exchange Rate Regimes: Is the Bipolar View Correct?" *Journal of Economic Perspectives* 15(2): 3–24.

———. 2003. "Globalization and Its Challenges. Richard T. Ely Lecture." *American Economic Review* 93(2): 1–30.

Fjelstad, O-H. 2002. "Fighting Fiscal Corruption: The Case of the Tanzania Revenue Authority." Working Paper 2002.3. Bergen, Norway: Christian Michelsen Institute.

Forbes, K. 2003. "One Cost of the Chilean Capital Controls: Increased Financial Constraints for Smaller Trade Firms." NBER Working Paper No. 9777. National Bureau of Economic Research, Cambridge, Mass.

———. 2004. "Capital Controls: Mud in the Wheels of Market Discipline." NBER Working Paper No. 10284. National Bureau of Economic Research, Cambridge, Mass.

Fox, L., and E. Palmer. 2001. "New Approaches to Multi-Pillar Pension Systems: What in the World Is Going On?" In R. Holzmann and J. Stiglitz, eds., *New Ideas about Old Age Security.* Washington, D.C.: World Bank.

Frankel, Jeffrey A., and David Romer. 1999. "Does Trade Cause Growth?" *American Economic Review* 89(3) (June): 379–99.

Frankel, Jeffrey A., and A. Rose. 1996. "Currency Crashes in Emerging Markets: Empirical Indicators." NBER Working Paper No. 5437. National Bureau of Economic Research, Cambridge, Mass.

Frankel, Jeffrey A., and Shang-Jin Wei. 2004. "Managing Macroeconomic Crises: Policy Lessons." NBER Working Paper No. 10907. National Bureau of Economic Research, Cambridge, Mass.

Frankel, Jeffrey A., E. Fajnzylber, S. Schmukler, and L. Servén. 2001. "Verifying Exchange Rate Regimes." *Journal of Development Economics* 66(2): 351–85.

Frieden, Jeffry A. 1991. *Debt, Development, and Democracy.* Princeton, N.J.: Princeton University Press.

Friedman, Lawrence. 1985. *A History of American Law.* New York: Simon and Schuster.

Frydman, Roman, Cheryl Gray, Marek Hessel, and Andrzej Rapaczynski. 1999. "When Does Privatization Work? The Impact of Private Ownership on Corporate Performance in the Transition Economies." *Quarterly Journal of Economics* (November):1153–91.

Funke, Michael, and Ralf Ruhwedel. 2001. "Export Variety and Export Performance: Empirical Evidence from East Asia." *Journal of Asian Economics* 12: 493–505.

Furman, J., and J. Stiglitz. 1998. "Economic Crises: Evidence and Insights from East Asia." *Brookings Papers on Economic Activity*, 2: 1–135.

Furtado, Celso. 1963. "The Concept of External Dependence in the Study of Underdevelopment." In Kenneth P. Jameson and Charles K. Wilber, eds., *Political Economy of Development and Underdevelopment.* New York: McGraw-Hill.

Galal, Ahmed, Leroy Jones, Pankaj Tandon, and Ingo Vogelsang. 1994. *Welfare Consequences of Selling Public Enterprises: An Empirical Analysis.* New York: Oxford University Press.

Galasso, Emanuela, and Martin Ravallion. 2000. "Distributional Outcomes of a Decentralized Welfare Program." World Bank Policy Research Working Paper No. 2316, World Bank, Washington, D.C.

Gallup, John Luke, Jeffrey D. Sachs, and Andrew Mellinger. 1999. "Geography and Economic Development." CID Working Paper No. 1. Center for International Development, Harvard University. Online at http://ideas.repec. org/s/wop/cidhav.html.

Gandhi, Jennifer. 2003. "Dictatorial Institutions and Their Impact on Economic Performance." Draft, Department of Politics, New York University. Presented at the Meetings of the American Political Science Association, Philadelphia, September.

Garrett, G. 1995. "Capital Mobility, Trade, and the Domestic Politics of Economic Policy." *International Organization* 49(4): 657–87.

———. 2000. "Capital Mobility, Exchange Rates, and Fiscal Policy in the Global Economy." *Review of International Political Economy* 7(1): 153–70.

Gavin, M., and Ricardo Hausmann. 1996. "The Roots of Banking Crises: The Macroeconomic Context." Working Paper 318, Office of the Chief Economist, InterAmerican Development Bank, Washington, D.C.

Gelb, Alan, ed. 1988. *Oil Windfalls: Blessing or Curse?* New York: Oxford University Press.

Gelb, Alan, Brian Ngo, and Xiao Ye. 2004. "Implementing Performance-Based Aid in Africa: The Country Policy and Institutional Assessment." Africa Region Working Paper Series No. 77, November.

Gerring, John, William T. Brandt, and Philip Bond. 2003. "Democracy and Economic Growth: A Historical Perspective." Draft, Political Science Department, Boston University, September.

Gerschenkron, Alexander. 1962. *Economic Backwardness in Historical Perspective: A Book of Essays.* Cambridge, Mass.: Belknap Press of Harvard University.

Ghirmay, Teame, Richard Grabowski, and Subhash C. Sharma. 2001. "Exports, Investment, Efficiency, and Economic Growth in LDCs: An Empirical Investigation." *Journal of Applied Economics* 33: 689–700.

Gill, Indermit S., Truman G. Packard, and Juan Yermo. 2004. *Keeping the Promise of Social Security in Latin America.* Washington, D.C.: World Bank.

Glaeser, Edward, and Andrei Shleifer. 2001. "Legal Origins." NBER Working Paper No. 8272. National Bureau of Economic Research, Cambridge, Mass.

———. 2003. "The Rise of the Regulatory State." *Journal of Economic Literature* 41(2): 401–25.

Glaeser, E., S. Johnson, and A Shleifer. 2001. "Coase versus the Coasians." *Quarterly Journal of Economics* 116: 853–99.

Glenday, G. 2000. "Trade Liberalization and Customs Revenues: Does Trade Liberalization Lead to Lower Customs Revenues? The Case of Kenya." African Economic Policy Discussion Paper No. 44. John F. Kennedy School of Government, Harvard University.

Goh, Chor-Ching, and Beata Smarzynska Javorcik. 2004. "Trade Protection and Industry Wage Structure in Poland." In Harrison (forthcoming).

Goldberg, Penny, and Nina Pavcnik. 2004. "Trade, Inequality, and Poverty: What Do We Know? Evidence from Recent Trade Liberalization Episodes in Developing Countries." NBER Working Paper No. 10593. In Susan Collins and Carol Graham, eds., *Brookings Trade Forum.* 2004. Washington, D.C.: Brookings Institution Press.

———. 2005. "The Effects of the Colombia Trade Liberalization on Urban Poverty." In Harrison (forthcoming).

Gonzalez-Vega, Claudio. 1984. "Credit Rationing Behavior of Agricultural Lenders: The Iron Law of Interest Rate Restrictions." In D. Adams, D. Graham, and J. D. Von Pischke, eds., *Undermining Rural Development with Cheap Credit.* Boulder, Colo.: Westview.

Goodpaster, Gary. 2003. "Law Reform in Developing Countries." *Transnational Law and Contemporary Problems, A Journal of the University of Iowa College of Law* 13 (2): 659–98.

Graham, Carol, and Stefano Pettinato. 2002. *Happiness and Hardship: Opportunity and Insecurity in New Market Economies.* Washington, D.C.: Brookings Institution Press.

Graham, Carol, and Sandip Sukhtankar. 2004. "Does Economic Crisis Reduce Support for Markets and Democracy in Latin America?" *Lessons from Surveys of Public Opinion and Well Being* 36 (May): 349–77.

Grossman, Gene, and Elhanan Helpman. 1992. *Interest Groups and Trade Policy.* Princeton, N.J.: Princeton University Press.

Gunnarsson, Victoria, Peter Orazem, Mario Sanchez, and Aimee Verdisco. 2004. "Does School Decentralization Raise Student Outcomes? Theory and Evidence on the Roles of School Autonomy and Community Participation." Unpublished manuscript. World Bank and InterAmerican Development Bank, Washington, D.C.

Gupta, Poonam, Rachel Kleinfeld, and Gonzalo Salinas. 2002. *Legal and Judicial Reform in Europe and Central Asia.* Washington, D.C.: World Bank Operations Evaluation Department.

Gupta, Sanjeev, Hamid Davoodi, and Rosa Alonso-Terme. 2002. "Does Corruption Affect Income Inequality and Growth?" *Economics of Governance* 3(1): 23–45.

Gutiérrez, E. 2003. "Inflation Performance and Constitutional Central Bank Independence: Evidence from Latin America and the Caribbean." IMF Working Paper 03/53. International Monetary Fund, Washington, D.C.

Gylfason, T. 2001. "Nature, Power, and Growth." CESinfo Working Paper No. 413.

Haber, S., and S. Kantor. 2003. "Getting Privatization Wrong: The Mexican Banking System 1991–2003." World Bank Conference on Bank Privatization, Nov. 20–21. Online at http://www.worldbank.org/research/projects/ bank_privatization_conference.htm.

Haddad, Mona, and Ann Harrison. 1993. "Are There Positive Spillovers from Direct Foreign Investment?" *Journal of Development Economics* 42.

Halac, M., and S. Schmukler. 2003. "Distributional Effects of Crises: The Role of Financial Transfers." Policy Research Working Paper 3173. World Bank, Washington, D.C.

Hall, Robert E., and Charles I. Jones. 1999. "Why Do Some Countries Produce So Much More Output per Worker Than Others?" *Quarterly Journal of Economics* 114: 83–116.

Hall, Thomas. 1999. "Economic Reform and Financial Sector Regulation in Emerging Markets." Ph.D. dissertation, University of Southern California, Los Angeles.

Hanson, Gordon. 2004. "Globalization, Labor Income, and Poverty in Mexico." In Harrison (forthcoming).

Hanson, J. 1994. "An Open Capital Account: A Brief Survey of the Issues and Results." In G. Caprio, I. Atiyas, and J. Hanson, eds., *Financial Reform: Theory and Experience*. Cambridge, U.K.: Cambridge University Press.

———. 2001. "Indonesia and India: Contrasting Approaches to Repression and Liberalization." In G. Caprio, P. Honohan, and J. Stiglitz, eds., *Financial Liberalization: How Far, How Fast?* Cambridge, U.K.: Cambridge University Press.

———. 2002. "Dollarization, Private and Official: Issues, Benefits, and Costs." In G. Caprio, P. Honohan, and D. Vittas, *Financial Sector Policy for Developing Countries— A Reader.* Oxford: Oxford University Press.

———. 2003a. "Indian Banking: Market Liberalization and the Pressures for Institutional and Market Framework Reform." In A. Krueger and S. Chinoy, eds., *Reforming India's External, Financial, and Fiscal Policies*. Stanford, Calif.: Stanford University Press.

———. 2003b. *Banking in Developing Countries in the 1990s.* World Bank Policy Research Paper No. 3168.

Hanson, J., and Sanjay Kathuria, eds. 1999. *India: A Financial Sector for the Twenty-First Century.* Washington, D.C.: World Bank and New York and Oxford: Oxford University Press.

Hanson, J., P. Honohan, and G. Majnoni, eds. 2003. *Globalization and National Financial Systems.* New York and Oxford: Oxford University Press for the World Bank.

Harberger, Arnold C. 1971. "Three Basic Postulates for Applied Welfare Economics: An Interpretive Essay." *Journal of Economic Literature* 9(3): 785–97.

———. 2004. "Exploring the Process of Economic Growth." Draft.

Harding, April. 2003. "Service Delivery Reforms: A Key Ingredient for Accelerating Progress toward MDGs." Draft. World Bank, Washington, D.C.

Harris, Clive. 2003. "Private Participation in Infrastructure in Developing Countries: Trends, Impacts and Policy Lessons." Working Paper No. 5. World Bank, Washington, D.C.

Harrison, Ann, ed. Forthcoming. *Globalization and Poverty.* Chicago: University of Chicago Press for National Bureau of Economic Research.

Harrison, Ann, and Gordon H. Hanson. 1999. "Who Gains from Trade Reform: Some Remaining Puzzles." NBER Working Paper No. 6915. National Bureau of Economic Research, Cambridge, Mass.

Harrison, Ann, and Jason Scorse. 2003. "The Impact of Globalization on Compliance with Labor Standards: A Plant-Level Study." Brookings Trade Forum, Brookings Institution, Washington, D.C.

Harrison, Lawrence, and Samuel Huntington. 2000. *Culture Matters: How Values Shape Human Progress.* New York: Basic Books.

Hausmann, Ricardo. 2003. "Good Credit Ratios, Bad Credit Ratings: The Role of Debt Structure." Working Paper, John F. Kennedy School of Government, Harvard University. Online at http://ksghome.harvard .edu/~.rhausma.cid.ksg/publication.htm.

Hausmann, Ricardo, and Barry Eichengreen. 2002. "Original Sin: The Pain, the Mystery, and the Road to Redemption." Working Paper, John F. Kennedy School of Government, Harvard University. Online at http://ksghome.harvard.edu/~.rhausma.cid.ksg/pub lication.htm.

Hausmann, Ricardo, and Roberto Rigobon. 2002. "An Alternative Interpretation of the 'Resource Curse': Theory and Policy Implications." NBER Working Paper No. 9424. National Bureau of Economic Research, Cambridge, Mass.

Hausmann, Ricardo, and Dani Rodrik. 2002. "Economic Development as Self-Discovery." NBER Working Paper No. 8952. National Bureau of Economic Research, Cambridge, Mass. Published (2003) in *Journal of Development Economics* 72(2): 603–33.

Hausmann, Ricardo, D. Mathieson, and J. Roldos. 2003. "Trends in Developing Country Capital Markets Around the World." In R. Litan, M. Pomerleano, and V. Sundarajan. eds., *The Future of Domestic Capital Markets in Developing Countries.* Washington, D.C.: The Brookings Institution.

Hausmann, Ricardo, Ugo Panizza, and Ernesto Stein. 2001. "Original Sin, Pass Through, and Fear of Floating." Working Paper, John F. Kennedy School of Government, Harvard University. Online at http:// ksghome.harvard.edu/~rhausma/paper/OSpasstrhro ughfearoffloating.pdf.

Hausmann, Ricardo, Dani Rodrik, and Lant Pritchett. 2004. "Growth Accelerations." NBER Working Paper

10566. National Bureau of Economic Research, Cambridge, Mass. Online at www.nber.org/papers/w10566.

Hausmann, Ricardo, Dani Rodrik, and Andres Velasco. 2004. "Growth Diagnostics." John F. Kennedy School of Government, Harvard University. Online at http://ksghome.harvard.edu/~drodrik/barcelonasep20.pdf.

Heilbrunn, John. 2002. "Anti-Corruption: Lessons from the 1990s." Draft, PREM Public Sector. World Bank, Washington, D.C.

Helliwell, John. 1994. "Empirical Linkages between Democracy and Economic Growth." *British Journal of Political Science* 24: 225–48.

Hellman, Joel, G. Jones, and Daniel Kaufmann. 2000. "Seize the State, Seize the Day: State Capture, Corruption, and Influence in Transition." World Bank Institute Working Paper. Washington, D.C.

Herbst, Jeffrey. 2000. *States and Power in Africa: Comparative Lessons in Authority and Control.* Princeton, N.J.: Princeton University Press.

Heron, Tony. 2002. "Export Processing Zones and Policy Competition for Foreign Direct Investment: The Offshore Caribbean Development Model." July.

Heybey, Berta, and Peter Murell. 1999. "The Relationship between Economic Growth and Speed of Liberalization during Transition." *Journal of Policy Reform* 3: 121–37.

Hirschman, Albert O. 1958. *The Strategy of Economic Development.* New Haven, Conn.: Yale University Press.

Hnatkovska, V., and N. Loayza. 2004. "Volatility and Growth." Policy Research Working Paper 3184. World Bank, Washington, D.C.

Hoekman, Bernard, Constantine Michalopoulos, Maurice Schiff, and David Tarr. 2001. "Trade Policy Reform and Poverty Alleviation." Developed as part of the World Bank's Poverty Reduction Strategy Sourcebook (December). Washington, D.C.

Hoff, Karla. 2003. "Paths of Institutional Development: A View from Economic History." *World Bank Research Observer* 18(2): 205–26.

Hoff, Karla, and J. E. Stiglitz. 2001. "Modern Economic Theory and Development." In Gerald Meier and J. E. Stiglitz, eds., *The Future of Development Economics in Perspective.* Oxford: Oxford University Press.

Holzmann, Robert, Robert Palacios, and Asta Zviniene. 2001. "Implicit Pension Debt: Issues, Measurement, and Scope in International Perspective." Pension Reform Primer. World Bank, Washington, D.C.

Honohan, Patrick, and Daniela Klingebiel. 2000. "Controlling Fiscal Costs of Banking Crises." Policy Research Working Paper No. 2441, World Bank, Washington, D.C.

Honohan, Patrick, and A. Shi. 2003. "Deposit Dollarization and the Financial Sector." In J. Hanson, P. Honohan, and G. Majnoni, eds., *Globalization and National Financial Systems.* New York and Oxford: Oxford University Press for the World Bank.

Huang, Yasheng. 2003. "One Country, Two Systems: Foreign-Invested Enterprises and Domestic Firms in China." *China Economic Review* 14(4): 404–16.

Huang, Yasheng, and Tarun Khanna. 2003. "Can India Overtake China?" *Foreign Policy* (July).

Hutchison, M., and I. Noy. 2002. "Sudden Stops and the Mexican Wave." Working Paper Series No. 02-12. Economic Policy Research Unit, Copenhagen.

Huther, Jeff, and Anwar Shah. n.d. "Anti-Corruption Policies and Programs—A Framework for Evaluation." Draft, 13 pp. World Bank, Washington, D.C.

Inter-American Development Bank (IDB). 1995. *Overcoming Volatility in Latin America.* Washington, D.C.: Inter-American Development Bank.

———. 1997. "Latin America after a Decade of Reforms." In *Economic and Social Progress in Latin America.* Washington, D.C.: IDB.

International Monetary Fund (IMF). 2001. "Jamaica: Staff Report for the 2001 Article IV Consultation." International Monetary Fund, Washington, D.C.

———. 2002a. "Jamaica Staff Report for the 2002 Article IV Consultation." International Monetary Fund, Washington, D.C.

———. 2002b. "Financial Stability in Dollarized Economies." Draft.

———. 2003a. *Fiscal Adjustment in IMF-Supported Programs.* Washington, D.C.: IMF.

———. 2003b. *The IMF and Recent Capital Account Crises.* Washington, D.C.: IMF.

———. 2003c. "Redrafting the Reform Agenda." *Finance and Development* (September). Washington, D.C.: IMF.

———. 2003d. *World Economic Outlook.* Washington, D.C.: IMF.

———. 2003e. "Assessing and Promoting Fiscal Transparency: A Report on Progress." Fiscal Affairs Department, International Monetary Fund, March 5 (online at http://www.imf.org/external/np/pdr/sac/2003/030503s2.htm).

———. 2004a. *World Economic Outlook.* Washington, D.C.: IMF.

———. 2004b. *Sovereign Debt Restructurings and the Domestic Economy: Experience in Four Recent Cases.* Washington, D.C.: Policy Development and Review Department, IMF.

International Monetary Fund (IMF), World Bank, OECD, and EBRD. 1991. "A Study of the Soviet Economy."

Isham, Jonathan, Thomas Kelly, and Sunder Ramaswamy, eds. 2002. *Social Capital and Economic Development: Well-Being in Developing Countries.* Cheltenham, U.K. and Northampton, Mass.: Elgar.

Isham, Jonathan, Michael Woolcock, Lant Pritchett, and Gwen Busby. 2003. "The Varieties of Resource Experience: How Natural Resource Export Structures

Affect the Political Economy of Economic Growth." Middlebury College Working Paper Series 0308. Department of Economics.

Islam, Roumeen. 2002. "Institutional Reform and the Judiciary: Which Way Forward?" World Bank Institute Working Paper No. 3134. World Bank, Washington, D.C.

Ize, A., and E. Levy-Yeyati. 1998. "Financial Dollarization." IMF Working Paper No. 1998/28. International Monetary Fund, Washington, D.C.

Jaffee, Steven, and Spencer Henson. 2004. "Agro-Food Exports from Developing Countries: The Challenges Posed by Standards." Prepared as chapter for book edited by Ataman Aksoy, forthcoming, World Bank.

Jaffee, Steven, and Jeanette Sutherland. 2003. "Integrated Framework Trade Diagnostic Studies: Findings and Lessons from Agricultural Sector Analysis." Draft. World Bank, Washington, D.C.

Jalan, Joyotsna, and Martin Ravallion. 1998. "Transient Poverty in Post-Reform China." *Journal of Comparative Economics* 26: 338–57.

Jamasb, T. 2002. "Reform and Regulation of the Electricity Sector in Developing Countries." University of Cambridge, Department of Applied Economics, Cambridge, U.K.

Jin, Hehui, Yingyi Qian, and Barry R. Weingast. 2001. "Regional Decentralization and Fiscal Incentives: Federalism, Chinese Style." Draft. Stanford University.

Johnson, S., and T. Mitton. 2002. "Cronyism and Capital Controls: Evidence from Malaysia." *Journal of Financial Economics* 67(2): 351–82.

Jones, Charles. 2004. "Growth and Ideas." Forthcoming in *Handbook of Economic Growth*. Amsterdam: North Holland.

Jones, E. L. 1981. *The European Miracle*. Cambridge, U.K.: Cambridge University Press.

Jones, Leroy P., Yahya Jammal, and Nilgun Gokgur. 1998. "Impact of Privatization in Cote d'Ivoire." Draft final report, Boston Institute for Developing Economies, Boston University.

Joseph, Richard A. 1998. "Patrons, Clients, and Factions: New Dimensions of Conflict Analysis in Africa." In Peter Lewis, ed., *Africa: Dilemmas of Development and Change*. Boulder, Colo.: Westview Press.

JP Morgan. Emerging Market Bond Index Plus (EMBI+) database.

Kahkonen, Satu, and Anthony Lanyi. 2001. "Decentralization and Governance: Does Decentralization Improve Public Service Delivery?" PREM Note (June). World Bank, Washington, D.C.

Kahn, Alfred. 2004. "Lessons from Deregulation: Telecommunications and Airlines after the Crunch." American Enterprise Institute and Brookings Institution, Washington, D.C.

Kaldor, Nicholas. 1955. *An Expenditure Tax*. London: George Allen and Unwin.

Kamarck, Andrew. 1967. *Economics of African Development*. New York: Praeger.

Kaminsky, G., and C. Reinhart. 1999. "The Twin Crises: The Causes of Banking and Balance of Payments Problems." *American Economic Review* 89(3): 473–500.

Kanbur, Ravi. 2000. "Aid, Conditionality, and Debt in Africa." In Finn Tarp, ed., *Foreign Aid and Development: Lessons Learned and Directions for the Future*. London: Routledge.

———. 2001. "Economic Policy, Distribution, and Poverty: The Nature of Disagreements." *World Development* 29(6): 1083–94.

———. 2002. "Conceptual Challenges in Poverty and Inequality: One Development Economist's Perspective." Draft (April), Cornell University, Ithaca, N.Y.

Karl, Terry Lynn. 1997. *The Paradox of Plenty: Oil Booms and Petro-States*. Berkeley: University of California Press.

Kaufmann, Daniel. 2003. "Rethinking Governance: Empirical Lessons, Challenge Orthodoxy." Discussion draft, March 11. Washington, D.C.: World Bank.

Kaufmann, Daniel, Aart Kraay, and Massimo Mastruzzi. 2003. "Governance Matters III: Governance Indicators for 1996–2002." World Bank Institute Working Paper. Online at http://www.worldbank.org/wbi/governance/pdf/ govmatters3_wber.pdf.

Kaufmann, Daniel, Aart Kraay, and Pablo Zoido-Lobaton. 1999. "Governance Matters." Policy Research Working Paper No. 2196. World Bank, Washington, D.C.

———. 2002. "Governance Matters II: Updated Indicators for 2000/01." Working Paper No. 2772. World Bank, Washington, D.C.

Keefer, Philip. 2002. "Clientelism, Credibility and Democracy." Draft, Development Research Group, World Bank.

———. 2003a. "Democratization and Clientelism: Why Are Young Democracies Badly Governed?" Draft, Development Research Group, World Bank.

———. 2003b. "All Democracies Are Not the Same: Identifying the Institutions That Matter for Growth and Convergence." Draft, Development Research Group, World Bank.

Keefer, Philip, and Stuti Khemani. Forthcoming. "Democracy, Public Expenditures, and the Poor." *World Bank Research Observer*.

Keefer, Philip, and Stephen Knack. 1997. "Why Don't Poor Countries Catch Up?" *Economic Inquiry* 35 (July): 590–602.

———. "Boondoggles and Expropriation: When Are Property Rights Secure and Public Investment Growth-Promoting?" Policy Research Working Paper No. 2910, World Bank (October).

Keefer, Philip, and David Stasavage. 2003. "The Limits of Delegation: Veto Players, Central Bank Independence, and the Credibility of Monetary Policy." *American Political Science Review* 97(3): 407–23.

Kenward, L. 2002. *From the Trenches—The First Year of Indonesia's Crisis 1997/98 As Seen from the World Bank's Office in Jakarta.* Center for International and Strategic Studies, Jakarta.

Keynes, John Maynard. 1931. *Essays in Persuasion.* London: Macmillan.

Khan, Mushtaq H. 2002. "State Failure in Developing Countries and Strategies of Institutional Reform." Draft paper for ABCDE conference, Oslo, June 24–26.

Kharas, H., and B. Pinto. 2001. "An Analysis of Russia's 1998 Meltdown: Fundamentals and Market Signals." *Brookings Papers on Economic Activity*, 1: 1–50.

Kikeri, Sunita, John Nellis, and Mary Shirley. 1992. "Privatization: The Lessons of Experience." World Bank, Washington, D.C.

Kindleberger, Charles P. 1984. *A Financial History of Western Europe.* London: Allen and Unwin.

———. 2000. *Manias, Panics, and Crashes: A History of Financial Crises.* New York: Wiley.

King, R., and R. Levine. 1993. "Finance and Growth: Schumpeter Might Be Right." *Quarterly Journal of Economics* 108(3): 717–37.

Klenow, Peter J., and Andres Rodriguez-Clare. 1997. "The Neoclassical Revival in Growth Economics: Has It Gone Too Far?" In Ben S. Bernanke and Julio J. Rotemberg, eds., *NBER Macroeconomics Annual 1997.* Cambridge and London: MIT Press.

Klingen, Christoph, Beatrice Weder, and Jeromin Zettelmeyer. 2004. "How Private Creditors Fared in Emerging Debt Markets, 1970–2000." IMF Working Paper WP/04/13. International Monetary Fund, Washington, D.C.

Klitgaard, Robert. 1988. *Tropical Gangsters.* New York: Basic Books.

———. 1990. "Cleaning Up and Invigorating the Civil Service." *Public Administration and Development* 17(5): 487–509. Online at http://wbln0018.worldbank.org/Network/PREM/PREMDocLib.nsf/58292AB451257BB9852566B4006EA0C8/256D2F1ADB2AE2F085256713000468E0.

Klitgaard, Robert, Ronald Maclean-Abaroa, and H. Lindsey Parris. 2000. *Corrupt Cities: A Practical Guide to Cure and Prevention.* Oakland, Calif.: Institute for Contemporary Studies and Washington, D.C.: World Bank Institute.

Knack, Stephen, and Philip Keefer. 1995. "Institutions and Economic Performance: Cross-Country Tests Using Alternative Institutional Measures." *Economics and Politics* 7: 207–27.

Kogot, Bruce, and Andrew Spicer. 2002. "Capital Market Development and Mass Privatization Are Logical Contradictions: Lessons from Russia and the Czech Republic." *Industrial and Corporate Change* 11(1): 1–37.

Kokko, Ari. 1994. "Technology, Market Characteristics, and Spillovers." *Journal of Development Economics* 43.

Kokko, Ari, Ruben Tansini, and Mario C. Zejan. 1996. "Local Technological Capability and Productivity Spillovers from FDI in Uruguayan Manufacturing Sector." *Journal of Development Studies* 32.

Konings, Jozef. 2000. "The Effects of Foreign Direct Investment on Domestic Firms: Evidence from Firm-level Panel Data in Emerging Economies." William Davidson Institute Working Papers Series 344. William Davidson Institute at the University of Michigan Business School. Also published as CEPR Discussion Paper No. 2586, Centre for Economic Policy Research, London.

Kontopolous, Yoannis, and Roberto Perotti. 1999. "Government Fragmentation and Fiscal Policy Outcomes: Evidence from the OECD Countries." In James Poterba and Juergen von Hagen, eds., *Fiscal Institutions and Fiscal Performance.* Chicago: University of Chicago Press.

Kornai, Janos. 1990. *The Road to a Free Economy: Shifting from a Socialist System—The Example of Hungary.* New York: Norton.

———. 1992. "The Postsocialist Transition and the State: Reflections in the Light of Hungarian Fiscal Problems." In Robert E. Goodin and Deborah Mitchell, eds., *The Foundations of the Welfare State,* Volume 2. Cheltenham, U.K and Northampton, Mass.: Edward Elgar.

———. 2000a. "Making the Transition to Private Ownership." *Finance and Development* 37(3): 12–13.

———. 2000b. "What the Change of System from Socialism to Capitalism Does and Does Not Mean." *Journal of Economic Perspectives* 14(1): 27–42.

———. 2000c. "Ten Years after 'The Road to a Free Economy': The Author's Self-Evaluation." *Economic Systems* 24(4): 353–59.

Kose, A., E. Prasad, and M. Terrones. 2003. "Financial Integration and Macroeconomic Volatility." IMF Staff Paper No. 50: 119–142. International Monetary Fund, Washington, D.C.

Kossick, Roberto M. 2003. "Modernizing Mexico's Tax Administration: The Development and Implementation of the E-Sat Mexico." Case study, E-Government Thematic Group. World Bank, Washington, D.C.

Kovacic, William. 1995. "Procurement Reform and the Choice of Forum in Bid Protest Disputes." *Administrative Law Journal* (American University) 9: 461.

Kraay, Aart. 2004. When Is Growth Pro-Poor? Cross-Country Evidence." IMF Working Paper 04/47. International Monetary Fund, Washington, D.C.

Kraay, Aart, and V. Nehru. 2003. "When Is External Debt Sustainable?" Policy Research Working Paper 3200, February. World Bank, Washington, D.C.

Kritzer, Barbara E. 2001. "Social Security Reform in Central and Eastern Europe: Variations on a Latin American Theme." *Social Security Bulletin* 64(4). Washington, D.C.: U.S. Social Security Administration.

Krueger, Anne O. 1978. *Foreign Trade Regimes and Economic Development: Liberalization Attempts and Consequences.* Lexington, Mass.: Ballinger.

———. 1983. *Trade and Employment in Developing Countries.* Chicago: University of Chicago Press.

———. 1997. "Trade Policy and Economic Development: How We Learn." *American Economic Review* 87(1): 1–22.

———. 2004. "Meant Well, Tried Little, Failed Much: Policy Reforms in Emerging Market Economies." Roundtable Lecture (March 23), Economic Honors Society, New York University.

Krugman, Paul. 1979. "A Model of Balance of Payments Crises." *Journal of Money, Credit, and Banking* 11(3): 311–25.

———. 1998. "Firesale FDI." Working Paper, Massachusetts Institute of Technology.

———. 1999. "Balance Sheets, the Transfer Problem and Financial Crises." In P. Isard, A. Razin, and A. Rose, eds., *International Finance and Financial Crises.* Washington, D.C.: International Monetary Fund. Partly reprinted from *International Tax and Public Finance* 6(4). Boston: Dordrecht and London: Kluwer Academic.

Kuznets, S. 1955. "Economic Growth and Income Inequality." *American Economic Review* 65: 1–28

Laeven, L. 2002a. "Pricing of Deposit Insurance." Working Paper No. 2871. World Bank, Washington, D.C.

———. 2002b. "Bank Risk and Deposit Insurance." *World Bank Economic Review* 16: 109–37.

———. 2002c. "International Evidence on the Cost of Deposit Insurance." *Quarterly Review of Economics and Finance* 42(4): 721–73.

Lall, S. 1999. *The Technological Response to Import Liberalization in Sub-Saharan Africa.* London: Macmillan.

Landes, David. 1998. *The Wealth and Poverty of Nations: Why Some Are So Rich and Some So Poor?* New York: Norton.

Lane, Philip R. 2003. "The Cyclical Behavior of Fiscal Policy: Evidence from the OECD." *Journal of Public Economics* 87: 2661–75.

Lane, Phillip R., and Aaron Tornell. 1999. "Voracity and Growth in Discrete Time." *Economic Letters* 62(1): 139–45.

LaPorta, Rafael, and López de Silanes. 1999. "The Benefits of Privatization: Evidence from México." *Quarterly Journal of Economics* 114(4): 1193–1242.

———. 2003. "Related Lending." *Quarterly Journal of Economics* CXVII: 231–68.

LaPorta, Rafael, F. López de Silanes, and A. Shleifer. 2002a. "Government Ownership of Banks." *Journal of Finance* 57(1): 265–301.

———. 2002b. "What Works in Securities Laws? Lessons for Latin America." Draft, Harvard University and Yale University.

Lardy, Nicholas R. 2002. *Integrating China into the Global Economy.* Washington, D.C.: Brookings Institution Press.

Lau, Lawrence J., Yingyi Qian, and Gerard Roland. 2000. "Reform without Losers: An Interpretation of China's Dual Track Approach to Transition." *Journal of Political Economy* 108(1).

Laursen, T., and S. Mahajan. 2004. "Volatility, Income Distribution and Poverty." In J. Aizenmann and B. Pinto, eds., *Managing Volatility and Crises: A Practitioner's Guide.* Washington, D.C.: World Bank.

Le Houerou, Philippe, and Robert Taliercio. 2002. "Medium-Term Expenditure Frameworks: From Concept to Practice. Preliminary Lessons from Africa." Africa Region Working Paper No. 28 (February). World Bank, Washington, D.C.

Lee, Ha Yan, Luca Anotnio Ricci, and Roberto Rigobon. 2004. "Once Again, Is Openness Good for Growth?" *Journal of Development Economics* 75(2) (December): 451–72.

Leite, C., and J. Weidmann. 1999. "Does Mother Nature Corrupt? Natural Resources, Corruption, and Economic Growth." IMF Working Paper No. 85. International Monetary Fund, Washington, D.C.

Lemarchand, Rene. 1972. "Political Clientelism and Ethnicity in Tropical Africa: Competing Solidarities in Nation-Building." *American Political Science Review* 66(1): 68–90.

Levine, David. 1995. *Reinventing the Workplace: How Business and Employees Can Both Win.* Washington, D.C.: Brookings Institution.

Levine, R. 1998. "Financial Development and Economic Growth: Views and Agenda." *Journal of Economic Literature* XXXV(2): 688–726.

———. 2003. "More on Finance and Growth: More Finance, More Growth?" *Federal Reserve Bank of St. Louis Review* 85: 31–46.

Levine, R., and S. Zervos. 1998. "Stock Markets, Banks, and Economic Growth." *American Economic Review* 88(3): 537–88.

Levine, R., N. Loayza, and T. Beck. 2000. "Financial Intermediation and Growth: Causality and Causes." *Journal of Monetary Economics* 46(1): 31–77.

Levinsohn, James. 1999. "Employment Responses to International Liberalization in Chile." *Journal of International Economics* 47: 321–44.

Levinsohn, James, and Margaret McMillan. 2004. "Does Food Aid Harm the Poor: Household Evidence from Ethiopia." In Harrison (forthcoming).

Levy, Brian, and Sahr Kpundeh, eds. 2004. *Building State Capacity in Africa: New Approaches, Emerging Lessons.* Washington, D.C.: World Bank Institute.

Lewis, P., and H. Stein. 2002. "The Political Economy of Financial Liberalization in Nigeria." In H. Stein, O. Ajakaiye, and P. Lewis, eds., *Deregulation and the Banking Crisis in Nigeria.* London: Palgrave.

Lieberman, Ira, and John Nellis. 1994. "Russia: Creating Private Enterprises and Efficient Markets." World Bank, Washington, D.C.

Lim, Ewe-Ghee. 2001. "Determinants of, and the Relation between, Foreign Direct Investment and Growth: A Summary of Recent Literature." IMF Working Paper 01/175. International Monetary Fund, Washington, D.C.

Lindemann, David, Michal Rutkowski, and Oleksiy Sluchynskyy. 2000. "The Evolution of Pension Systems in Eastern Europe and Central Asia: Opportunities, Constraints, Dilemmas, and Emerging Practices." World Bank, Washington, D.C.

Lippman, Hal, and Jan Emmert. 1997. "Assisting Legislatures in Developing Countries: A Framework for Planning, Programming, and Implementation." Center for Development Information and Evaluation, USAID, Washington, D.C.

Little, Ian, Tibor Scitovsky, and Maurice Scott. 1970. *Industry and Trade in Some Developing Countries: A Comparative Study.* London and New York: Oxford University Press for the Development Centre of the Organisation for Economic Co-operation and Development.

Litvack, J., J. Ahmad, and R. Bird. 1998. "Rethinking Decentralization at the World Bank." World Bank, Washington, D.C.

Loayza N., P. Fajnzylber, and C. Calderón. 2002. "Economic Growth in Latin America and the Caribbean. Stylized Facts, Explanations, and Forecasts." Draft, World Bank (June). Online at http://wbln0018 .worldbank.org/lac/lacinfoclient.nsf/8d6661f6799ea 8a48525673900537f95/92400b44aeb50a0185256cad 00708a4a/$FILE/N.Loayza.pdf.

Lora, Eduardo. 2001a. "Structural Reforms in Latin America: What Has Been Reformed and How to Measure It." Inter-American Development Bank, Washington, D.C. (December).

————. 2001b. "El crecimiento económico en América Latina después de una década de reformas estructurales." Draft. InterAmerican Development Bank, Research Department, Washington, D.C.

Lucas, Robert E., Jr. 1987. *Studies in Business-Cycle Theory.* Cambridge, Mass. and London: MIT Press.

Luttmer, Erzo F. P. 2001. "Measuring Poverty Dynamics and Inequality in Transition Economies: Disentangling Real Events from Noisy Data." Working Paper No. 2549. World Bank, Washington, D. C.

Maddison, Angus. 1995. *Monitoring the World Economy: 1820–1992.* Paris: Development Centre of the Organisation for Economic Co-operation and Development.

————. 2002. *The World Economy: A Millennial Perspective.* Paris: Development Centre of the Organisation for Economic Co-operation and Development.

Mamdani, Mahmood. 1996. *Citizen and Subject: Contemporary Africa and the Legacy of Late Colonialism.* Princeton, N.J.: Princeton University Press, 1996.

Manning, Nicholas, and Neil Parison. 2003. "International Public Administration Reform: Implications for the Russian Federation." World Bank, Washington, D.C.

Manning, Nicholas, and Richard Stapenhurst. 2002. "Strengthening Oversight by Legislatures." *PREM Note* No. 74 (October). World Bank, Washington, D.C.

Manzano, Osmel, and Roberto Rigobon. 2001. "Resource Curse or Debt Overhang?" NBER Working Paper No. 8390. National Bureau of Economic Research, Cambridge, Mass.

Marques, Gustavo, and Carmen Pagés. 1998. "Trade and Employment: Evidence from Latin America and the Caribbean." IDB Working Paper No. 366. Inter-American Development Bank, Washington, D.C.

Martinez-Peria, M. S., and S. Shmuckler. 2001. "Do Depositors Punish Bank for Bad Behavior? Market Discipline, Deposit Insurance, and Banking Crises." *Journal of Finance* 56(3): 1029–51.

Martinez-Vazquez, Jorge, and Jameson Boex. 2001. "Russia's Transition to a New Federalism." WBI Learning Resources No. 97. World Bank Institute, Washington, D.C.

Masson, P. 2001. "Exchange Rate Regime Transitions." *Journal of Development Economics* 64(2): 571–86.

Mauro, Paolo. 1995. "Corruption and Growth." *Quarterly Journal of Economics* 110: 681–712.

————. 1997. "Why Worry about Corruption?" *Economic Issues* No. 6. Washington, D.C.: International Monetary Fund.

————. 1998a. "Corruption: Causes, Consequences, and Agenda for Further Research." *Finance and Development* 35(1) (March).

————. 1998b. "Corruption and the Composition of Public Expenditures." *Journal of Public Economics* 29: 263–79.

McKinnon, R. I. 1973. *Money and Capital in Economic Development.* Washington, D.C.: Brookings Institution.

McMillan, John, and Christopher Woodruff. 2002. "The Central Role of Entrepreneurs in Transition Economies." *Journal of Economic Perspectives* 16(3): 153–70.

McMillan, Margaret, Dani Rodrik, and Karen Horn Welch. 2002. "When Economic Reform Goes Wrong: Cashews in Mozambique." Draft (July).

Meagher, Patrick. 2002. "Anti-Corruption Agencies: A Review of Experience." Institutional Reform and Informal Sector Center, University of Maryland (August 2).

Megginson, William, and Jeffrey Netter. 2001. "From State to Market: A Survey of Empirical Studies on Privatization." *Journal of Economic Literature* (June): 321–89.

Megginson, William L., Robert C. Nash, and Matthias van Randenborgh. 1998. "The Privatization Dividend." *Journal of Finance* 49(2). Also summarized in FPD Note No. 68, World Bank.

Mehlum, Halvor, Karl-Ove Moene, and Ragnar Torvik. 2003. "Institutions and the Resource Curse." Draft, 29/2002. Oslo University, Department of Economics and Economics Working Paper Archive at Washington University in St. Louis.

Meier, Gerald, and Dudley Seers, eds. 1984. *Pioneers in Development*. New York and Oxford: Oxford University Press

Mellinger, Andrew D., Jeffrey D. Sachs, and John L. Gallup. 1999. "Climate, Water Navigability, and Economic Development." Working Paper No. 24 (September). Center for International Development, Washington, D.C.

Mendoza, E. 2001. "Credit, Prices, and Crashes: Business Cycles with a Sudden Stop." NBER Working Paper No. 8338. National Bureau of Economic Research, Cambridge, Mass.

Messick, Richard. 1999. "Judicial Reform and Economic Development: A Survey of the Issues." *World Bank Research Observer* 14(1): 117–36.

Michaely, Michael, Demetris Papageorgiou, and Armeane Choksi. 1991. *Liberalizing Foreign Trade: Lessons of Experience in the Developing World*. Cambridge, Mass.: Blackwell.

Michalopoulos, Constantine. 1999. "Trade Policy and Market Access Issues for Developing Countries: Implications for the New Millennium Round." Policy Research Working Paper 2214. World Bank, Washington, D.C.

Milanovic, Branko. 2004. "Why We All Do Care about Inequality (but Are Loath to Admit It)." Working Paper, Carnegie Endowment for International Peace, Washington, D.C.

Milesi-Ferretti, Gian-Maria, Roberto Perotti, and Marco Rostagno. 2002. "Electoral Systems and the Composition of Government Spending." *Quarterly Journal of Economics* 117: 609–57.

Minsky, H. 1992. "The Financial Instability Hypothesis, Capitalistic Processes and the Behavior of the Economy." In C. Kindleberger and J. Laffargue, eds., *Financial Crises: Theory, History and Policy*. Cambridge, U.K.: Cambridge University Press.

Mishkin, F., ed. 2001. *Prudential Supervision: What Works and What Doesn't*. Chicago: University of Chicago for the National Bureau of Economic Research.

Mishra, Banamber, and Matiur Rahman. 1998. "Exports, Foreign Aid, Exchange Rate, and Economic Growth: Empirical Evidence from 28 Low-Income LDCs." *Scandinavian Journal of Development Alternatives* 17: 21–31.

Moggridge, D. E. 1976. *John Maynard Keynes*. New York: Penguin.

Montiel, P. 2002. "Ecuador: Una Estrategia de Crecimiento para una Economía Dolarizada." *Cuestiones Económicas* 18(3): 133–225.

Montiel, P., and C. Reinhart. 1999. "Do Capital Controls and Macroeconomics Policies Influence the Volume and Composition of Capital Flows? Evidence from the 1990s." *Journal of International Money and Finance* 18(4) (August): 619–35.

Moog, Robert. 1997. *Whose Interests Are Supreme? Organizational Politics in the Civil Courts in India*. Ann Arbor, Mich.: Association for Asian Studies.

Moran, T. 1998. "Foreign Direct Investment and Development: The New Policy Agenda for Developing Countries and Economies in Transition." Institute for International Economics, Washington, D.C.

Moreira, Mauricio Mesquita, and Sheila Najberg. 2000. "Trade Liberalization in Brazil: Creating or Exporting Jobs?" *Journal of Development Studies* (36)3: 78.

Mukand, Sharun, and Dani Rodrik. 2002. "In Search of the Holy Grail: Policy Convergence, Experimentation, and Economic Performance." Draft, Harvard University.

Murphy, Kevin, Andrei Shleifer, and Robert Vishny. 1989. "Industrialization and the Big Push." *Journal of Political Economy* 97(5): 1003–26.

Murrell, Peter. 1992. "Evolution in Economics and in the Economic Reform of Centrally Planned Economies." In Christopher C. Clague and Gordon Rausser, eds., *The Emergence of Market Economies in Eastern Europe*. Cambridge, Mass.: Blackwell.

Mussa, M. 2002. *Argentina and the Fund: From Triumph to Tragedy*. Washington, D.C.: Institute for International Economics.

Myerson, Roger B. 1999. "Theoretical Comparisons of Electoral Systems." *European Economic Review* 43: 671–97.

Myrdal, Gunnar. 1972. *Asian Drama: An Inquiry into the Poverty of Nations*. New York: Random House.

Naim, Moises. 1995. "Latin America: The Morning After." *Foreign Affairs* (July/August).

———. 1999. "Fads and Fashion in Economic Reforms: Washington Consensus or Washington Confusion?" Working Draft of a paper prepared for the IMF Conference on Second Generation Reforms, Washington, D.C. (October 26). Online at http://www.imf.org/external/pubs/ft/seminar/1999/reforms/Naim.HTM.

Narayan, Deepa, Robert Chambers, Meera K. Shah, and Patti Petesch. 2000. *Voices of the Poor* (2 vols.). New York and Oxford: Oxford University Press.

Nash, John, and Wendy Takacs, eds. 1998. *Trade Policy Reform: Lessons and Implications*. Washington, D.C.: World Bank.

Nash, Manning. 1963. "Party Building in Upper Burma." *Asian Survey* 3 (April): 196–202. Reprinted in Scott (1972).

Nayak, P. Jayendra. 1999. "Regulation and Market Microstructure." In Hanson and Kathuria (1999): 266–304.

Ndegwa, Stephen N., and Brian Levy. 2003. "The Politics of Decentralization in Africa: A Comparative Analysis." In *Building State Capacity in Africa: New Approaches, Emerging Lessons*. Washington, D.C.: World Bank.

Nellis, John. 2002. "The World Bank, Privatization, and Enterprise Reform in Transition Economies: A Retrospective Analysis." Operations Evaluation Department Background Paper. World Bank, Washington, D.C.

———. 2003a. "Privatization in Africa: What Has Happened? What Is to Be Done?" CGD Working Paper No. 25 (February). Center for Global Development, Washington, D.C.

———. 2003b. "Privatization in Latin America." CGD Working Paper No. 31 (August). Center for Global Development, Washington, D.C.

Nellis, John, and Mary Shirley. 1991. "Public Enterprise Reform: The Lessons of Experience." Economic Development Institute Development Study. World Bank, Washington, D.C.

Nocum, Armand. 2004. "Lifestyle Checks to Resume." *Philippines Daily Inquirer*, May 13.

North, Douglass C. 1990. *Institutions, Institutional Change and Economic Performance.* New York: Cambridge University Press.

———. 1994. "Economic Performance through Time." *American Economic Review* 84(3): 359–68.

———. 2002. "Institutions and Credible Commitment." St. Louis, Mo.: Washington University.

North, Douglass, and Barry Weingast. 1989. "Constitutions and Commitment: The Evolution of Institutions Governing Public Choice in Seventeenth-Century England." *Journal of Economic History* 49(4): 803–32.

Obstfeld, M. 1994. "The Logic of Currency Crises." *Cahiers Economiques et Monetaires* 43:189–213.

Ocampo, Jose Antonio. 2004. "Latin America's Growth and Equity Frustrations during Structural Reforms." *Journal of Economic Perspectives* 18(2): 67–88.

Oliva, Maria-Angels. 2000. "Estimation of Trade Protection in Middle East and North African Countries." IMF Working Paper No. 00/27, February 1. International Monetary Fund, Washington, D.C. Online at http://www.imf.org/external/pubs/ft/wp/2000/wp0027.pdf.

Olson, Mancur. 1965. *The Logic of Collective Action: Public Goods and the Theory of Groups.* Cambridge, Mass.: Harvard University Press.

———. 1982. *The Rise and Decline of Nations.* New Haven, Conn.: Yale University Press.

———. 2000. *Power and Prosperity: Outgrowing Communist and Capitalist Dictatorships.* New York: Basic Books.

Organisation for Economic Co-operation and Development (OECD). 1996–2002. Indicators of Tariff and Non-Tariff Trade Barriers.

———. 1998. *The Role of the Legislature.* Paris: OECD.

Osborne, David, and Ted Gaebler. 1992. *Reinventing Government: How the Entrepreneurial Spirit Is Transforming the Public Sector.* Reading, Mass.: Addison-Wesley.

Palacios, Robert J., and Montserrat Pallares-Miralles. 2000. "International Patterns of Pension Provision." Social Protection Discussion Paper No. 9. World Bank, Washington, D.C.

Palley, Thomas I. 2003. "Lifting the Natural Resource Curse." *Foreign Service Journal* 80(12): 54–61.

Panagariya, Arvind. 2003. "Miracles and Debacles: Do Free-Trade Skeptics Have a Case?" Economics Working Paper Archive, Washington University in St. Louis, International Trade Series No. 0308013.

Paul, Samuel. 1995. *Strengthening Public Accountability: New Approaches and Mechanisms.* Bangalore, India: Public Affairs Centre.

———. 2003. "The Report Card Survey: A Ten Year Retrospective." Seminar presentation, World Bank, November.

Perry, G. 2003. "Can Fiscal Rules Help Reduce Macroeconomic Volatility?" Policy Research Working Paper Series No. 3080. World Bank, Washington, D.C.

Perry, G., and L. Servén. 2002. "The Anatomy of a Multiple Crisis: Why Was Argentina Special and What Can We Learn from It?" Draft. World Bank, Chief Economist's Office, Latin America and the Caribbean Region, Washington, D.C.

———. 2003. "The Anatomy of a Multiple Crisis: Why Was Argentina Special and What Can We Learn from It?" Working Paper No. 3081. World Bank, Washington, D.C.

Perry, Guillermo, Daniel Lederman, William Maloney, and Luis Servén. 2003. "Lessons from NAFTA for Latin America and the Caribbean." Latin America and the Caribbean Region, World Bank, Washington, D.C., April.

Persson, Torsten, and Guido Tabellini. 2000. *Political Economics: Explaining Public Policy.* Cambridge, Mass.: MIT Press.

———. 2004. "Constitutional Rules and Fiscal Policy Outcomes." *American Economic Review* 94(1): 25–45.

Persson, Torsten, Gerard Roland, and Guido Tabellini. 2003. "How Do Electoral Rules Shape Party Structures, Government Coalitions, and Economic Policies?" NBER Working Paper No. 10176. National Bureau of Economic Research, Cambridge, Mass.

Persson Torsten, Guido Tabellini, and Francesco Trebbi. 2000. "Electoral Rules and Corruption." CEPR Working Paper. Centre for Economic Policy Research, London.

———. 2003. "Electoral Rules and Corruption." *Journal of the European Economic Association* 1(4): 958–89.

Philp, Mark. 2003. "Why Systems Produce Corruption." Draft. University of Oxford.

Pistor, Katharina, Martin Raiser, and Stanislav Gelfer. 2000. "Law and Finance in Transition Economies." EBRD Working Paper 48. European Bank for Reconstruction and Development, London.

Platteau, Jean-Philippe. 2004. "Collective Action and the Commons: The Role of Inequality." In Baland, J. M., P. Bardhan, and S. Bowles, eds., *Inequality, Cooperation, and Environmental Sustainability*. Princeton, N.J.: Princeton University Press.

Pohl, Gerhard, Robert Anderson, and Simeon Djankov. 1997. "Privatization and Restructuring in Eastern and Central Europe—Evidence and Policy Options." Technical Paper No.368. World Bank, Washington, D.C.

Polidano, Charles. 1999. "The New Public Management in Developing Countries." Public Policy and Management Working Paper No. 13 (November). Institute for Development Policy and Management, University of Manchester, U.K.

Pollitt, Michael G. 2003. "Electricity Reform in Chile and Argentina: Lessons for Developing Countries." Paper presented at the Cambridge-MIT Institute Electric Power Autumn Research Seminar. Cambridge, Mass. November 7.

Porcalla, Delon. 2004. "BIR Exec in Life Style Check Suspended." *Philippines Star*, May 20.

Porto, Guido. 2003. "Using Survey Data to Assess the Distributional Effects of Trade Policy." Draft. World Bank, Washington, D.C.

Posner, Daniel. Forthcoming. "Measuring Ethnic Fractionalization in Africa." *American Journal of Political Science*.

Poterba, James M. 1996. "Budget Institutions and Fiscal Policy in the US States." NBER Working Paper 5449. National Bureau of Economic Research, Cambridge, Mass.

Powell, John Duncan. 1970. "Peasant Society and Clientelist Politics." *American Political Science Review* 64(2): 411–25.

Pradhan, Menno, Asep Suryahadi, Sudarno Sumarto, and Lant Pritchett. 2001. "Eating Like Which 'Joneses?' An Iterative Solution to the Choice of a Poverty Line 'Reference Group.'" *Review of Income and Wealth* 47(4) (December): 473–488.

Prado, C. 1972. *História e Desenvolvimento*. São Paulo: Editora Brasiliense.

Prasad, E., K. Rogoff, S. Wei, and M. Kose. 2003. "Effect of Financial Globalization on Developing Countries: Some Empirical Evidence." Draft. International Monetary Fund, Washington, D.C.

Prayas Energy Group. 2003. "Performance of Private Electricity Distribution Utilities in India: Need for In-Depth Review and Benchmarking." Occasional Report. Prune, India.

Pritchett, Lant. 1996. "Measuring Outward Orientation in LDCs: Can It Be Done?" *Journal of Development Economics* 49.

———. 1997. "Divergence, Big Time." *Journal of Economic Perspectives* 11(3) (Summer): 3–17.

———. 2000. "The Tyranny of Concepts: CUDIE (Cumulated, Depreciated, Investment Effort) Is Not Capital." *Journal of Economic Growth* 5(4): 361–84.

———. 2003a. "Reform Is Like a Box of Chocolates: Understanding Growth Disappointments and Surprises." Draft (September), Harvard University.

———. 2003b. "Who Is Not Poor: Proposing A Higher International Standard for Poverty." CGD Working Paper 33, November. Center for Global Development, Washington, D.C.

Pritchett, Lant, and Michael Woolcock. 2004. "Solutions When the Solution Is the Problem: Arraying the Disarray in Development." *World Development* 32(2): 191–212.

Przeworski, Adam, Michael E. Alvarez, Jose Antonio Cheibub, and Fernando Limongi. 2000. *Democracy and Development: Political Institutions and Well-Being in the World, 1950–1990*. New York: Cambridge University Press.

Pyramid Research. 2001. *Communications Markets in Mexico—Blurring Barriers and Escalating Competition*. Cambridge, Mass.: Pyramid Research.

Qian, Yingyi. 2000. "The Process of China's Market Transition 1978–98: The Evolutionary, Historical, and Comparative Perspective." Stanford University, Calif., April.

———. 2002. "How Reform Worked in China." Department of Economics, University of California, Berkeley, August.

Radelet, Steven, and Jeffrey Sachs. 1998. "The Onset of the East Asian Financial Crisis." Draft. Harvard Institute for International Development (March 30).

Radelet, Steven, Cristina Garcia, and Mumtaz Hussain. 2000. "Trade and Exports." Background paper examining the state of the Andean Region for the Andean Competitiveness Project, April.

Rajkumar, Andrew Sunil, and Vinaya Swaroop. 2002. "Public Spending and Outcomes: Does Governance Matter?" Policy Research Working Paper No. 2840 (May). World Bank, Washington, D.C.

Ramachandran, S. 1997. "The Veil of Vouchers." FPD Note No.108. World Bank, Washington, D.C.

Ramey, G., and V. Ramey. 1995. "Cross-Country Evidence on the Link between Volatility and Growth." *American Economic Review* 85(5): 1138–51.

Ravallion, Martin. 1994. "Measuring Social Welfare with and without Poverty Lines." *American Economic Review* (American Economic Association) 84(2) (May): 359–64.

———. 2001. "Growth, Inequality and Poverty: Looking beyond Averages." *World Development* 29(11): 1803–15.

———. 2003a. "Inequality Convergence." *Economics Letters* 80(3): 351–56.

———. 2003b. "The Debate on Globalization, Poverty, and Inequality: Why Measurement Matters." Development Research Group Working Paper 3038. World Bank, Washington, D.C.

———. 2004. "Pessimistic on Poverty?" *The Economist*, April 4.

Ravallion, Martin, and Michael Lokshin. 2004. "Gainers and Losers from Trade Reform in Morocco." Policy

Research Working Paper No. 3368. World Bank, Washington, D.C.

Razin, Assaf, Efraim Sadka, and Chi-wa Yuen. 1999. "Excessive FDI under Asymmetric Information." NBER Working Paper No. 7400. National Bureau of Economic Research, Cambridge, Mass.

Redding, S., and Venables, A. 2003. "Geography and Export Performance: External Market Access and Internal Supply Capacity." CEPR Discussion Paper No. 3807. Centre for Economic Policy Research, London.

Reinhart, Carmen, and Graciela L. Kaminsky. 1999. "The Twin Crises: The Causes of Banking and Balance-of-Payments Problems." *American Economic Review* 89(3).

Reinhart, Carmen, K. Rogoff, and M. Savastano. 2003. "Addicted to Dollars." NBER Working Paper 10015. National Bureau of Economic Research, Cambridge, Mass.

Reinikka, Ritva, and Jakob Svensson. 2003. "The Power of Information: Evidence from a Newspaper Campaign to Reduce Capture." Policy Research Working Paper 3239. Development Research Group, World Bank, Washington, D.C.

———. 2004. "Local Capture: Evidence from a Central Government Transfer Program in Uganda." *Quarterly Journal of Economics* 119(2).

Reserve Bank of India. 1998. *Report on Currency and Finance 1998/99.* Bombay: Reserve Bank of India.

Reynolds, Lloyd. 1983. "The Spread of Modern Economic Growth, 1850–1950." *Journal of Economic Literature* 21: 940–77.

Rigobon, Roberto, and Dani Rodrik. 2004. "Rule of Law, Democracy, Openness, and Income: Estimating the Interrelationships." NBER Working Paper No. 10750. National Bureau of Economic Research, Cambridge, Mass.

Robinson, James A. 2002. "States and Power in Africa by Jeffrey Herbst: A Review Essay." *Journal of Economic Literature* XL (June): 510–19.

Robinson, James A., Ragnar Torvik, and Thierry Verdier. 2002. "Political Foundations of the Resource Curse." CEPR Discussion Papers 3422, June.

Robinson, M. 2002. *The Microfinance Revolution,* Vol. 2: *Lessons from Indonesia.* Washington, D.C.: The World Bank.

Rodden, J., Gunnar Eskeland, and Jennie Litvack, eds. 2003. *Decentralization and Hard Budget Constraints.* Boston: MIT Press.

Rodríguez, Francisco, and Dani Rodrik. 2000. "Trade Policy and Economic Growth: A Skeptic's Guide to the Cross-National Evidence." Electronic Working Papers No. 9901, University of Maryland, Department of Economics. Published in *Macroeconomics Annual* 2000. Cambridge, Mass: MIT Press. Online at http://ksghome.harvard.edu/~.drodrik.academic.ksg /papers.html.

Rodrik, Dani. 1992. "The Limits of Trade Policy Reform in Developing Countries." *Journal of Economic Perspectives* (6)1.

———. 1997a. "TFPG Controversies, Institutions, and Economic Performance in East Asia." NBER Working Paper No. 5914. National Bureau of Economic Research, Cambridge, Mass.

———. 1997b. "Trade Policy and Economic Performance in Sub-Saharan Africa. Draft, Harvard University.

———. 1998. "Who Needs Capital-Account Convertibility?" In Stanley Fischer and others, *Should the IMF Pursue Capital-Account Convertibility?* Essays in International Finance No. 207. Princeton, N.J.: International Finance Section, Princeton University.

———. 1999a. "The New Global Economy and Developing Countries: Making Openness Work." Policy Essay No. 24. Overseas Development Council, Washington, D.C.

———. 1999b. "Where Did All the Growth Go? External Shocks, Social Conflict and Growth Collapses." *Journal of Economic Growth* 4(4): 385–412.

———. 2001a. "Development Strategies for the 21st Century." In Boris Pleskovic and Nicholas Stern, eds., *Annual World Bank Conference on Development Economics 2000,* 85–108. Washington, D.C.: World Bank.

———. 2001b. "Why Is There So Much Economic Insecurity in Latin America? " *CEPAL Review* 73: 7–30.

———. 2002a. "Trade Policy Reform as Institutional Reform." In B. M. Hoekman, P. English, and A. Mattoo. *Development, Trade, and the WTO: A Handbook.* Washington, D.C.: World Bank.

———. 2002b. "Feasible Globalizations." Discussion Paper No. 3524. Centre for Economic Policy Research, London.

———. 2003a. "Growth Strategies." CEPR Discussion Paper No. 4100. Centre for Economic Policy Research, London.

———, ed. 2003b. *In Search of Prosperity: Analytic Narratives on Economic Growth.* Princeton, N.J.: Princeton University Press.

———. 2003c. "Economic Reform without Rules of Thumb." Draft, Harvard University, October. Available online at http://ksghome.harvard.edu/~drodrik/ Stiglitzconferencenotes.pdf.

Rodrik, Dani, and Ricardo Hausmann. 2003. "Discovering El Salvador's Production Potential." Draft (September).

Rodrik, Dani, and Arvind Subramanian. 2003. "The Primacy of Institutions." *Finance and Development* 40(2): 31–34.

———. 2004. "From 'Hindu Growth' to Productivity Surge: The Mystery of the Indian Growth Transition." IMF Working Paper 04/77. International Monetary Fund, Washington, D.C.

Rodrik, D., and A. Velasco. 1999. "Short-Term Capital Flows." NBER Working Paper No. 7364. National Bureau of Economic Research, Cambridge, Mass.

Rodrik, Dani, Arvind Subramanian, and Francesco Trebbi. 2002. "Institutions Rule: The Primacy of Institutions over Integration and Geography in Economic Development." IMF Working Paper 02/189. National Bureau of Economic Research, Cambridge, Mass.

Rofman, Rafael. 2002. "The Pension System in Argentina: Learning the Lessons." Background Paper for Regional Study on Social Security Reform, Office of the Chief Economist, Latin America and the Caribbean Regional Office. World Bank, Washington, D.C.

Rogoff, Kenneth. 1985. "The Optimal Degree of Commitment to an Intermediate Monetary Target." *Quarterly Journal of Economics* 100: 1169–89.

Romer, Paul M. 1983. "Dynamic Competitive Equilibria with Externalities, Increasing Returns and Unbounded Growth." *Journal of Monetary Economics* 26: 47–75.

———. 1986. "Increasing Returns and Long-Run Growth." *Journal of Political Economy* 94: 1002–38.

Rose-Ackerman, Susan. 1978. *Corruption: A Study in Political Economy.* New York: Academic Press.

———. 2004. "Poor Governance and Corruption." Preliminary draft, Copenhagen Consensus Challenge Paper. Yale University.

Rosenbluth, Frances, and Michael F. Thies. 2001. "The Electoral Foundations of Japan's Banking Regulation." *Policy Studies Journal* 29(1): 23–37.

Rosenstein-Rodan, Paul. 1943. "Problems of Industrialization of Eastern and South-Eastern Europe." *Economic Journal.*

———. 1984. "Natura Facit Saltum: Analysis of the Disequilibrium Growth Process." In G. Meier and D. Seers, eds., *Pioneers in Development.* New York: Oxford University Press.

Rostow, Walt Whitman. 1952. *The Process of Economic Growth.* New York: Norton.

———. 1960. *The Stages of Economic Growth: A Non-Communist Manifesto.* New York: Cambridge University Press.

———. 1962. *The Process of Economic Growth,* 2nd ed. New York: Norton.

Sachs, Jeffrey D., and Andrew M. Warner. 1995a. "Economic Reform and the Process of Global Integration." *Brookings Papers on Economic Activity,* 1 (25th Anniversary Issue).

———. 1995b. "Natural Resource Abundance and Economic Growth. Paper No. 517a, Harvard Institute for International Development.

———. 1997. "Sources of Slow Growth in African Economies." *Journal of African Economies* 6(3): 335–76.

———. 2001. "The Curse of Natural Resources." *European Economic Review* 45(4): 827–38.

Saiegh, Sebastian, and Mariano Tommasi. 1999. "Why Is Argentina's Fiscal Federalism So Inefficient? Entering the Labyrinth." *Journal of Applied Economics* II(1): 169–209.

Sala-i-Martin, Xavier. 2003. "The Disturbing 'Rise' of Global Income Inequality." NBER Working Paper No. 8904. National Bureau of Economic Research, Cambridge, Mass.

Sala-i-Martin, Xavier, and Arvind Subramanian. 2003. "Addressing the Natural Resource Curse: An Illustration from Nigeria." IMF Working Paper 03/139. International Monetary Fund, Washington, D.C.

Sala-i-Martin, Xavier, Gernot Doppelhofer, and Ronald Miller. 2003. "Determinants of Long-Term Growth: A Bayesian Averaging of Classical Estimates (BACE) Approach." University of Cambridge Faculty of Economics and Politics, Columbia University Department of Economics, and Columbia University Department of Economics.

Sanguinetti, P., and M. Tommasi. 2003. "Intergovernmental Transfers and Fiscal Behavior: Insurance versus Aggregate Discipline." *Journal of International Economics* 62(1): 149–70.

Sarkar, S. 2000. "On the Investment-Uncertainty Relationship in a Real Options Model." *Journal of Economic Dynamics and Control* 24(2): 219–25.

Savastano, M. 1992. "The Pattern of Currency Substitution in Latin America: An Overview." *Revista de Análisis Económico* 7(1): 29–72.

———. 1996. "Dollarization in Latin America." In P. Mizen and E. Pentacost, *The Macroeconomics of International Currencies: Theory, Policy, and Evidence.* Cheltenham, U.K.: Edward Elgar.

Schady, Norbert R. 2000. "Political Economy of Expenditures by the Peruvian Social Fund (FONCODES), 1991–1995." *American Political Science Review* 94(2): 289–304.

Schiantarelli, F., I. Atiyas, G. Caprio, J. Hariss, and A. Weiss. 1994. "Credit Where It Is Due? A Review of the Macro and Micro Evidence on the Real Effects of Financial Reform." In G. Caprio, I. Atiyas, and J. A. Hanson, eds., *Financial Reform: Theory and Experience.* New York and London: Cambridge University Press.

Schick, Allen. 1998. "Why Most Developing Countries Should Not Try New Zealand's Reforms." *World Bank Research Observer* 13: 123–31.

———. 2003. "The Performing State: Reflection on an Idea Whose Time Has Come but Whose Implementation Has Not." Paper presented at the OECD Global Forum on Governance, London School of Economics, December 2–3.

Schmukler, S., and L. Servén. 2002. "Pricing Currency Risk under Currency Boards." *Journal of Development Economics* 69(2): 367–91.

Schroeder, Larry. 2002. "Mechanisms for Strengthening Local Accountability." Draft, World Bank, World Bank, Washington, D.C. Online at http://www1.worldbank.org/publicsector/decentralization/Feb2004Course/Background%20materials/Schroeder.doc.

Scott, James C. 1972. "Patron-Client Politics and Political Change in Southeast Asia." *American Political Science Review* 66(1): 91–113.

Seers, Dudley. 1962. "A Model of Comparative Rates of Growth in the World Economy." *Economic Journal*, March.

Selowsky, Marcelo, and Ricardo Martin. 1998. "Policy Performance and Output Growth in the Transition Economies." *American Economic Review* 87: 350–53.

Sen, Amartya. 1999. *Development as Freedom.* New York: Knopf.

Senhadji, Abdelhak S. 2000. "How Significant Are Departures from Certainty Equivalence? Some Analytical and Empirical Results." *Review of Economic Dynamics* 3(3): 597–617.

Servén, L. 2003. "Real Exchange Rate Uncertainty and Private Investment in LDCs." *Review of Economics and Statistics* 85(1): 212–18.

Servén, Luis, Rui Albuquerque, and Norman Loayza. 2003. "World Market Integration through the Lens of Foreign Direct Investors." Draft (February). World Bank, Washington, D.C.

Shah, A., and S. Thomas. 1999. "Developing the Indian Capital Market." In J. A. Hanson and S. Kathuria, eds., *India: A Financial Sector for the Twenty-First Century.* New York: Oxford University Press.

———. 2003. "Securities Market Efficiency." In J. Hanson, P. Honohan, and G. Majnoni, eds., *Globalization and National Financial Systems.* New York and Oxford: Oxford University Press for the World Bank.

Shatz, Howard, and Anthony Venables. 2000. "The Geography of International Investment." In Gordon L. Clark, Meric S. Gertier, and Maryann P. Feldman, eds., *The Oxford Handbook of Economic Geography.* Oxford: Oxford University Press.

Shaw, E. 1973. *Financial Deepening in Economic Development.* New York: Oxford University Press.

Shepherd, Geoffrey. 2003. "Understanding Public Organizations: An Aid to Reform in Developing Countries." Draft, World Bank, PREM Network, Public Sector Governance.

Sherif, K. 2003. *The Fiscal Cost of State-Owned Banks in Selected Economies of Central and Eastern Europe.* Draft. World Bank, Washington, D.C.

Sherif, K., M. Borish, and A. Gross. 2003. *State-Owned Banks in the Transition.* Europe and Central Asia Private Sector and Finance Sector Development Unit, World Bank, Washington, D.C.

Shirley, M., and C. Menard. 2002. "Cities Awash: Reforming Urban Water Systems in Developing Countries." In M. Shirley, ed., *Thirsting for Efficiency: The Economics and Politics of Urban Water System Reform.* Oxford: Elsevier.

Shleifer, Andrei, and Daniel Treisman. 2004. "A Normal Country." NBER Working Paper No. 10057. National Bureau of Economic Research, Cambridge, Mass.

Smoke. 2001. *Fiscal Decentralization in Developing Countries: A Review of Current Concepts and Practices.* Geneva: United Nations Research Institute for Social Development.

Solow, Robert M. 1956. "A Contribution to the Theory of Economic Growth." *Quarterly Journal of Economics* 70: 65–94.

———. 1957. "Technical Change and the Aggregate Production Function," *Review of Economics and Statistics* 39(3): 312–20.

———. 1971. "Growth Theory: An Exposition." New York and Oxford: Oxford University Press.

Standard and Poor's. 2003. *Emerging Markets Database.* New York: Standard and Poor's.

Stapenhurst, Rick. 2000. *The Media's Role in Curbing Corruption.* Working Paper, World Bank Institute, Washington, D.C.

Stasavage D. 2003. *Public Debt and the Birth of the Democratic State: France and Great Britain 1688–1789.* New York: Cambridge University Press.

Stein, E., E. Talvi, and A. Gristani. 1998. "Institutional Arrangements and Fiscal Performance: The Latin American Experience." NBER Working Paper No. 6358. National Bureau of Economic Research, Cambridge, Mass.

Stigler, George J. 1971. "The Theory of Economic Regulation." *Bell Journal of Economics and Management Science.* Reprinted in Stigler (1975).

———. 1975. *The Citizen and the State: Essays on Regulation.* Chicago: University of Chicago Press.

Stigler, George J., and Claire Friedland. 1962. "What Can Regulators Regulate? The Case of Electricity." *Journal of Law and Economics* 5: 1–16.

Stiglitz, Joseph. 2001. "From Miracle to Crisis to Recovery: Lessons from Four Decades of East Asian Experience." In Joseph E. Stiglitz and Shahid Yusuf, *Rethinking the East Asian Miracle.* Washington, D.C.: World Bank.

Stiglitz, Joseph, and Karla Hoff. 1990. "Rural Credit Markets: Puzzles and Policy Perspectives." *World Bank Economic Review* 5: 235–50.

Stiglitz, Joseph, and The Initiative for Policy Dialogue on behalf of The Commonwealth Secretariat. 2004. "An Agenda for the Development Round of Trade Negotiations in the Aftermath of Cancun."

Strauss, John, Kathleen Beegle, Agus Dwiyanto, Yulia Herawati, Daan Pattinasarany, Elan Satriawan, Bondan Sikoki, Sukamadi, and Firman Witoelar. 2004. "Indonesian Living Standards before and after the Financial Crisis: Evidence from the Indonesia Family Life Survey." Online at www.rand.org/nsrd/capp/pubs/indo.html.

Strömberg, David. 2001. "Radio's Impact on New Deal Spending." Draft, Princeton University, Princeton, N.J.

———. 2002. "Mass Media Competition, Political Competition, and Public Policy." *Review of Economic Stud-*

*ies.* Online at http://www.iies.su.se/~stromber/MediaComp.pdf.

Sturm, J, and J. de Haan. 2001. "Central Bank Independence and Inflation in Developing Countries." Working Paper No. 511. Center for Economic Studies and the Ifo Institute for Economic Research.

Subramanian, Arvind, and Devesh Roy. 2001. "Who Can Explain the Mauritian Miracle: Meade, Romer, Sachs, or Rodrik?" IMF Working Paper 01-116. International Monetary Fund, Washington, D.C. Online at http://www.imf.org/external/pubs/cat/longres.cfm?sk=15215.0.

Summers, Lawrence H. 1999. "Distinguished Lecture on Economics in Government: Reflections on Managing Global Integration." *Journal of Economic Perspectives* 13(2).

———. 2000. "International Financial Crises: Causes, Prevention, and Cures." In Papers and Proceedings of the One Hundred Twelfth Annual Meeting of the American Economic Association, *The American Economic Review* 90(2): 1–16.

Sundararajan, V., and T. Balino, eds. 1991. *Banking Crises: Cases and Issues.* Washington, D.C.: International Monetary Fund.

Suryahadi, Asep, Sudarno Sumarto, and Lant Pritchett. 2003. "Evolution of Poverty during the Crisis in Indonesia." *Asian Economic Journal* 17(3): 221–41.

Suryahadi, Asep, Anna Wetterberg, Sudarno Sumarto, and Lant Pritchett. 1999. "A National Snapshot of the Social Impact of Indonesia's Crisis." *Bulletin of Indonesian Economic Studies* 35(3): 145–52.

Swann, T. W. 1956. "Economic Growth and Capital Accumulation." *Economic Record* 32: 334–61.

Tabibian, Mohammad. 2003. "Manufacturing Sector's Long-Term Strategy and Development in Iran." Institute for Research on Planning and Development in Iran (February).

Taliercio, Robert, Jr. 2003. "Designing Performance: The Semi-Autonomous Revenue Authority Model in Africa and Latin America." Draft (August). World Bank, Washington, D.C.

———. 2004. "Administrative Reform as Credible Commitment: The Impact of Autonomy on Revenue Authority Performance in Latin America." *World Development* 32(2): 213–32.

Talvi, E. 1997. "Exchange Rate–Based Stabilization with Endogenous Fiscal Response." *Journal of Development Economics* 54(1): 59–75.

Talvi, E., and C. Vegh. 2000. "Tax Base Variability and Pro-Cyclical Fiscal Policy." NBER Working Paper No. 7499. National Bureau of Economic Research, Cambridge, Mass.

Tanzi, Vito, and Hamid Davoodi. 1998. "Corruption, Public Investment, and Growth." In H. Shibata and T. Ihori, eds., *The Welfare State, Public Investment, and Growth.* Tokyo: Springer-Verlag.

Temple, Jonathan. 1999. "The New Growth Evidence." *Journal of Economic Literature* 37(1): 112–56.

———. 2000. "Growth Regressions and What the Textbooks Don't Tell You." *Bulletin of Economic Research* 52(3): 181–205.

———. 2003. "Growing into Trouble: Indonesia after 1966." In Dani Rodrik, ed., *In Search of Prosperity: Analytic Narratives on Economic Growth.* Princeton, N.J.: Princeton University Press.

Temu, Andrew, and Jean M. Due. 1998. "The Success of Newly Privatized Companies: New Evidence from Tanzania." *Canadian Journal of Development Studies* 19(2): 315–41.

Tendler, Judith. 1997. *Good Government in the Tropics.* Baltimore: Johns Hopkins University Press.

Thomas, Duncan. 2004. "Financial Crises and Poverty: The Case of Indonesia." In Harrison (forthcoming).

Thomas, Vinod, and John Nash. 1991a. *Best Practices in Trade Policy Reform.* Oxford, New York, Toronto, and Melbourne: Oxford University Press for the World Bank.

———. 1991b. "Reform of Trade Policy: Recent Evidence from Theory and Practice." *World Bank Research Observer* 6(2): 219–40.

———. 1992. "Trade Policy Reform: Recent Evidence from Theory and Practice." In R. Adhikari, C. Kirkpatrick, and J. Weiss, eds., *Industrial and Trade Policy Reform in Developing Countries.* Contemporary Issues in Development Studies. Manchester, U.K.: Manchester University Press and New York: St. Martin's Press.

Timmer, Peter, and Ashley Timmer. 2004. "Reflections on Launching Three Books about Poverty, Inequality, and Economic Growth." *WIDER Angle,* No.1/2004. World Institute for Development Economics Research, Helsinki.

Tirole, Jean. 2002. *Financial Crises, and the International Monetary System.* Princeton, N.J.: Princeton University Press.

Tommasi, Mariano. 2002. "Federalism in Argentina and the Reforms of the 1990s." Stanford University Center for Research on Economic Development and Policy Reform, Palo Alto, Calif.

Topalova, Petia. 2005. "Trade Liberalization, Poverty and Inequality: Evidence from Indian Districts." In Harrison (forthcoming).

Transparency International. 2004. *The Global Corruption Report.* Berlin: Transparency International.

Tsikata, Yvonne. 2003. "Integrating into the Global Economy: Challenges, Experiences, and Policy Lessons from the Integrated Framework." Draft, World Bank, Washington, D.C.

United Nations Conference on Trade and Development (UNCTAD). 1987. *Handbook of Trade Control Measures of Developing Countries–Supplement.*

———. 1994. *Directory of Import Regimes.*

United Nations–WIDER. World Income Inequality Database. Online at http://www.wider.unu.edu/wiid/wiid.htm.

U.S. Census Bureau, International Programs Center. http://www.census.gov/ipc/www/pas.html.

U.S. General Accounting Office (GAO). 1993. *Foreign Assistance: Promoting Judicial Reform to Strengthen Democracies.* GAO/NSAID-93-149. Washington, D.C.: GAO.

van de Walle, Nicolas. 2001. *African Economies and the Politics of Permanent Crisis, 1979–99.* Cambridge, U.K.: Cambridge University Press.

Van Rijkeghem, Caroline, and Beatrice Weder. 2001. "Bureaucratic Corruption and the Rate of Temptation: Do Wages in the Civil Service Affect Corruption and by How Much?" *Journal of Development Economics* 65: 307–31.

Velasco, Andres, and Alejandro Neut. 2003. "Tough Policies, Incredible Policies?" NBER Working Paper No. 9932. National Bureau of Economic Research, Cambridge, Mass.

Virmani, Arvind. 2004. "India's Economic Growth: From Socialist Rate of Growth to Bharatiya Rate of Growth." ICRIER Working Paper No. 122. Indian Council for Research on International Economic Relations, New Delhi (January). Online at http://www.icrier.res.in/wp122.pdf.

Von Hagen, Juergen. 1992. "Budgeting Procedures and Fiscal Performance in the European Communities." European Economy—Economic Papers 96. Commission of the EC, Directorate-General for Economic and Financial Affairs (DG ECFIN).

Von Hagen, Juergen, and Ian Harden. 1996. "Budget Processes and Commitment to Fiscal Discipline." IMF Working Paper 96/78. International Monetary Fund, Washington, D.C.

von Hirschhausen, C., and B. Meinhart. 2001. "Infrastructure Policies and Liberalization in the East European Transition Countries—Would Less Have Been More?" *Internet Journal of the Centre for Energy, Petroleum and Mineral Law Policy—CEPMLP*, Vol. 9.

von Hirschhausen C., and P. Opitz. 2001. "Power Utility Re-Regulation in East European and CIS Transformation Countries: An Institutional Interpretation." Presented at the 2001 International Society for New Institutional Economics (ISNIE) Conference, September 13–15, Berkeley, Calif.

Wacziarg, Romain, and Karen Horn Welch. 2003. "Trade Liberalization and Growth: New Evidence." NBER Working Paper No. 10152. National Bureau of Economic Research, Cambridge, Mass.

Wade, Robert. 1985. "The Market for Public Office: Why the Indian State Is Not Better at Development." *World Development* 13 (April): 467–97.

Wade, Robert, and Ian Hardin. 1995. "National Budget Processes and Fiscal Performance." *European Economy: Reports and Studies* 3: 311–418.

Wagstaff, Adam. 2001. "Inequalities in Health in Developing Tide?" Draft, World Bank, Washington, D.C.

Walmsley, Terri Louise, and Alan L. Winters. 2003. "Relaxing the Restrictions on the Temporary Movement of Natural Persons: A Simulation Analysis." CEPR Discussion Paper No. 3719. Centre for Economic Policy Research, London.

Webb, Steven B. 2003. "Argentina: Hardening the Provincial Budget Constraint." In Jonathan Rodden, Gunnar Eskeland, and Jennie Litvack, eds., *Decentralization and Hard Budget Constraints.* Boston: MIT Press.

Wei, Shang-Jin. 1996. "Intra-National versus International Trade: How Stubborn Are Nations in Global Integration?" NBER Working Paper 5531. National Bureau of Economic Research, Cambridge, Mass.

———. 2000. "How Taxing Is Corruption on International Investors?" *Review of Economics and Statistics* 82(1) (February): 1–11.

Weingast, Barry. 1995. "The Economic Role of Political Institutions: Market-Preserving Federalism and Economic Development." *The Journal of Law, Economics and Organization* 11(1).

Weiss, Andy, and G. Nitkin. 1997. "Performance of Czech Companies by Ownership Structure." Unpublished World Bank seminar paper.

Wellenius, Bjorn. 1997. "Telecommunications Reform—How to Succeed." Public Policy for the Private Sector Note 130. World Bank, Washington, D.C.

Weyland, Kurt. 2003. "Good Governance and Development—A Skeptical View." Draft, University of Texas, Austin.

Wilder, Andrew. 1999. *The Pakistani Voter: Electoral Politics and Voting Behavior in the Punjab.* Karachi: Oxford University Press.

Wilkinson, Steven. 2000. "Consociational Theory and Ethnic Violence." *Asian Survey* XL(5): 767–91.

Williamson, John. 1990. "What Washington Means by Policy Reform." Chapter 2 in John Williamson, *Latin American Adjustment: How Much Has Happened?* Washington, D.C.: Institute for International Economics. Updated November 2000.

———. 1995. "The Management of Capital Inflows." *Pensamiento Ibero Americano,* January-June.

———. 2000. "What Should the Bank Think about the Washington Consensus?" Paper prepared as background to the World Bank's *World Development Report 2000,* July. Online at http://www.iie.com/publications/papers/ williamson0799.htm.

———. 2003. "From Reform Agenda to Damaged Brand Name: A Short History of the Washington Consensus and Suggestions for What to Do Next." *Finance and Development* 40(3): 10–13.

———. 2004a. "The Washington Consensus as Policy Prescription for Development." Paper prepared for lecture at the World Bank, January.

————. 2004b. "The Years of Emerging Market Crisis: A Review of Feldstein." *Journal of Economic Literature* XLII (September).

Williamson, John, and Roberto Zagha. 2002. "From Slow Growth to Slow Reform." Institute for International Economics, Washington, D.C. (July).

Williamson, Oliver E. 1975. *Markets and Hierarchies: Analysis and Antitrust Implications.* New York: Free Press.

————. 1985. *The Economic Institutions of Capitalism.* New York: Free Press.

Winters, Alan L., Neil McCulloch, and Andrew McKay. 2004. "Trade Liberalization and Poverty: The Evidence So Far." *Journal of Economic Literature* XLII (March): 72–115.

Wood, Adrian. 1988. "Global Trends in Real Exchange Rates: 1960–84." Discussion Paper No. 35. World Bank, Washington, D.C.

Woodhouse, Andrea Fitri. 2002. "The Dynamics of Rural Power in Indonesia: Fighting Corruption in a World Bank Community Development Project." Draft (June). World Bank, Washington, D.C.

World Bank. 1988–2004, various issues. *World Development Report.* Washington, D.C.: World Bank.

————. 1993–2004, various issues. *Global Economic Prospects.* Washington, D.C.: World Bank.

————. 1993. *The East Asian Miracle: Economic Growth and Public Policy.* New York and Oxford: Oxford University Press for the World Bank.

————. 1994a. *Averting the Old Age Crisis.* Washington, D.C.: World Bank.

————. 1994b. *India: Issues in Trade Reform.* Washington, D.C.: World Bank.

————. 1996. "Indonesia, Dimensions of Growth." Report No. 15383-IND. World Bank, Washington, D.C.

————. 1997a. "China Engaged: Integration with the Global Economy." China 2020 Series, September. World Bank, Washington, D.C.

————. 1997b. "Indonesia: Sustaining High Growth with Equity." Report No. 16433-IND. World Bank, Washington, D.C.

————. 1998a. "Argentina: Financial Sector Review." Report No. 17864-AR. World Bank, Washington, D.C.

————. 1998b. *Public Expenditure Management Handbook.* Washington, D.C.: World Bank.

————. 1999. "West Bank and Gaza: Strengthening Public Sector Management." World Bank, Washington, D.C.

————. 2000a. "Anti-Corruption in Transition, A Contribution to the Policy Debate." World Bank, Washington, D.C.

————. 2000b. "Bolivia: From Patronage to a Professional State: Institutional Governance Review." Poverty Reduction and Economic Management Network. World Bank, Washington, D.C.

————. 2000c. *East Asia, Recovery and Beyond.* Washington, D.C.: World Bank.

————. 2000d. *Progress toward the Unification of Europe.* Washington, D.C.: World Bank.

————. 2000e. "Securing Our Future in a Global Economy." Latin America and the Caribbean Region. World Bank, Washington, D.C.

————. 2000f. "Trade Blocs." Policy Research Report. World Bank, Washington, D.C.

————. 2000g. *Can Africa Claim the 21st Century?* Washington, D.C.: World Bank.

————. 2000h. "Sri Lanka: Recapturing Missed Opportunities." Poverty Reduction and Economic Management, South Asia Region. World Bank, Washington, D.C.

————. 2001–04, various issues. *Global Development Finance.* Washington, D.C.: World Bank.

————. 2001a. *Finance for Growth: Policy Choices in a Volatile World.* Washington, D.C.: World Bank.

————. 2001b. "From Natural Resources to Knowledge Economy: Trade and Job Quality." LAC Research Report. World Bank, Washington, D.C.

————. 2001c. *Aid and Reform in Africa.* Washington, D.C.: World Bank.

————. 2002a. "Anticorruption in Transition: A Contribution to the Policy Debate." World Bank, Washington, D.C.

————. 2002b. "Globalization, Growth and Poverty: Building an Inclusive World Economy." Policy Research Report. World Bank, Washington, D.C.

————. 2002c. "Transition: The First Ten Years: Analysis and Lessons for Eastern Europe and the former Soviet Union." World Bank, Washington, D.C.

————. 2003a. "Administrative Charges in Second Pillar Pensions in ECA: A Case Study Approach." World Bank, Washington, D.C.

————. 2003b. *Better Governance for Development in the Middle East and North Africa: Enhancing Inclusiveness and Accountability.* Washington, D.C.: World Bank.

————. 2003c. "Combating Corruption in Indonesia— Enhancing Accountability for Development." Report No. 27246-IND, Poverty Reduction and Economic Management Unit, East Asia and Pacific Region (November 12). World Bank, Washington, D.C.

————. 2003d. "Doing Business" Web site. Online at http://rru.worldbank.org/DoingBusiness/.

————. 2003e. *East Asia Integrates.* Washington, D.C.: World Bank.

————. 2003f. *Gender and Development in the Middle East and North Africa: Women in the Public Sphere.* Washington, D.C.: World Bank.

————. 2003g. *Jamaica Country Economic Memorandum.* Washington, D.C.: World Bank.

————. 2003h. *Malawi Country Economic Memorandum: Policies for Accelerating Growth.* Washington, D.C.: World Bank.

————. 2003i. *Malawi Integrated Framework Diagnostic Trade Integration Study.* Washington, D.C.: World Bank.

————. 2003j. *Trade, Investment, and Development in the Middle East and North Africa—Engaging with the World.* Washington, D.C.: World Bank.

————. 2003k. "Trade Policies in South Asia: An Overview, Volumes I and II" (Discussion Draft, May). World Bank, Washington, D.C.

————. 2003l. *Unlocking the Employment Potential in the Middle East and North Africa: Towards a New Social Contract.* Washington, D.C.: World Bank.

————. 2003m. *Zambia Country Economic Memorandum: Policies for Growth, Diversification, and Poverty Reduction.* Washington, D.C.: World Bank.

————. 2003n. *Zambia: The Challenge of Competitiveness and Diversification.* Washington, D.C.: World Bank.

————. 2004a. "Legislation on Freedom of Information: Trends and Standards." PREM Note 93. World Bank, Washington, D.C.

————. 2004b. *Corruption in Enterprise: State Interactions in Europe and Central Asia 1999-2002.* Washington, D.C.: World Bank.

————. 2004c. *Doing Business 2004: Understanding Regulation.* Washington, D.C.: World Bank.

————. 2004d. "Leveraging Trade for Development: The World Bank Research Agenda." Progress report to the Board of Directors. World Bank, Washington, D.C.

————. 2004e. *Reforming Infrastructure: Privatization, Regulation, and Competition.* Washington, D.C.: World Bank.

————. 2004f. *World Development Indicators* database. April. Washington, D.C.: World Bank.

————. 2005a. *At the Frontlines of Development.* Washington, D.C.: World Bank.

————. 2005b. *Development Challenges in the 1990s.* Washington, D.C.: World Bank.

————. 2005c, forthcoming. *Public Debt Trends and Decompositions in Emerging Market Economies between 1990 and 2003.* Washington, D.C.: World Bank.

*World Currency Yearbook* (for 1985, 1990–93). International Currency Analysis, Brooklyn, N.Y.

World Trade Organization (WTO). 1994–2003, various issues. *Trade Policy Review: Country Reports.*

World Trade Organization (WTO). 1998. "Jamaica Trade Policy Review." Geneva: WTO.

Wurfel, David. 1963. "The Philippines." *Comparative Studies in Political Finance: A Symposium, Journal of Politics* 25 (November): 757–73. Reprinted in Scott (1972).

Wyplosz, C. 2002. "Fiscal Discipline in Emerging Market Economies: How to Go about It?" Draft. Graduate Institute for International Studies, Geneva, and Centre for Economic and Policy Research, London.

Yaron, J., M. Benjamín, and G. Piprek. 1997. *Rural Finance: Issues, Design, and Best Practices.* Washington, D.C.: World Bank.

Yusuf, Shahid, and Simon J. Evenett. 2002. *Can East Asia Compete? Innovation for Global Markets.* New York and London: World Bank and Oxford University Press.

# Index